8 · 29 · 1981

THE
GUGGENHEIMS

AN AMERICAN EPIC

By John H. Davis

THE GUGGENHEIMS
VENICE
THE BOUVIERS

THE

GUGGENHEIMS

AN AMERICAN EPIC

by JOHN H. DAVIS

WILLIAM MORROW AND COMPANY, INC.
NEW YORK   1978

Library of Congress Cataloging in Publication Data

Davis, John Hagy (date)
  The Guggenheims.

  Bibliography: p.
  1. Guggenheim family. 2. Businessmen—United States—Biography. 3. Art patrons—United States—Biography. 4. Jews in the United States—Biography.
I. Title.
HC102.G8D38   338′.092′2 [B]   77-20069
ISBN 0-688-03273-7

BOOK DESIGN AND BINDING   CARL WEISS

First Edition

2   3   4   5   6   7   8   9   10

FOR

N.W.D.

CONTENTS

INTRODUCTION   *11*

PROLOGUE / A GUGGENHEIM WILL   *19*

I. MEYER AND BARBARA—1828–1905:
   FOUNDING AN AMERICAN DYNASTY

1 / OUT OF THE GHETTO   *37*

2 / THE HAVEN CITY   *45*

3 / ROASTED PIGEONS DO NOT FLY INTO ONE'S MOUTH   *49*

4 / BONANZA IN COLORADO   *58*

5 / THE CONQUEST OF MEXICO   *65*

6 / STRUGGLE FOR POWER   *73*

7 / THE GOOGS OF NEW YORK   *77*

8 / DEATH OF A PATRIARCH   *86*

II. LORDS OF THE EARTH—1905–1923:
    BUILDING THE GUGGENHEIM EMPIRE

1 / ON THEIR OWN   *95*

2 / GUGGENMORGANS AND MORGANHEIMS   *100*

3 / MINING THE GLOBE   *109*

4 / HARVEST OF WAR   *119*

5 / THE GREAT SCHISM   *127*

III. SEVEN BROTHERS AND TWO HUNDRED FIFTY MILLIONS—1918–1959: ON THE USES OF WEALTH

1 / A FORTUNE TO SPEND   *137*

2 / ISAAC: ON DAUGHTERING OUT   *142*

3 / DANIEL AND FLORENCE: A FIRST STEP INTO SPACE   *150*

4 / MURRY AND LEONIE: CHILEAN NITRATES AND THE CHILDREN OF NEW YORK   *171*

5 / SOLOMON'S SECOND SPRING   *198*

6 / KING SOLOMON'S MUSEUM   *223*

7 / BENJAMIN: ON DROPPING OUT, PART I   *232*

8 / SENATOR SIMON, OR DEMOCRACY IN AMERICA   *243*

9 / ALL SIMON'S SONS   *252*

10 / WILLIAM, OR GATENBY WILLIAMS: ON DROPPING OUT, PART II   *277*

IV. REBELS AND ANGELS—1923–1977: THE FOURTH GENERATION

1 / EMPIRE IN DECLINE   *289*

2 / COLONEL BOB   *291*

3 / AMBASSADOR HARRY: GUGGENADO AND MACHADOHEIM   *301*

4 / PEGGY: LIBERATED IN EUROPE   *308*

5 / PEGGY AND GUGGENHEIM JEUNE   *319*

6 / PEGGY IN NEW YORK: ERNST, POLLOCK, AND ART OF THIS CENTURY   *331*

7 / HAROLD LOEB: *THE WAY IT WAS*   *349*

8 / GLADYS GUGGENHEIM STRAUS: CARRYING ON   *365*

9 / THE QUIETER ONES: EDMOND AND WILLIAM, JR.   *371*

10 / KING SOLOMON'S DAUGHTERS   *377*

11 / BENJAMIN'S OTHER DAUGHTER   *406*

12 / PEGGY IN VENICE: THE LAST DOGARESSA   *411*

13 / HARRY THE MAGNIFICENT: THE LEGACIES   *437*

14 / HARRY THE MAGNIFICENT: THE GLORIFICATION   *448*

V. THE SURVIVORS—1945–1978:
THE FIFTH AND SIXTH GENERATIONS

1 / AFTER HARRY: A FAMILY IN FRAGMENTS 459

2 / PETER O. LAWSON-JOHNSTON: THE ANOINTED 466

3 / THE CALIFORNIA GUGGENHEIMS: BOB, JR. AND DANIEL M.: NEW BEGINNINGS 481

4 / ROGER W. STRAUS, JR., PUBLISHER 496

5 / IRIS LOVE: BONANZA ON KNIDOS 511

6 / WILLIAM GUGGENHEIM III: AMEN 526

GENEALOGICAL TABLES 541

NOTES AND SOURCES 545

BIBLIOGRAPHY 577

AUTHOR'S NOTE AND ACKNOWLEDGMENTS 589

INDEX 595

Illustrations are found following page 176 and page 382.

INTRODUCTION

IN THE LAST HUNDRED YEARS ONE PEOPLE HAS HAD A GREATER IN-
fluence on our civilization than any other: the Jews.

Almost half the human race now professes to live in accordance
with the political and economic theories of a Jewish thinker who died
in 1883, Karl Marx. Albert Einstein, another Jewish thinker, born
four years before Marx's death, revolutionized our concept of the
physical universe: Out of one of his theories came the most fateful
invention of the twentieth century: atomic fission. Still another Jewish
thinker, Sigmund Freud, born when Marx was thirty-eight, revolutionized our concept of human nature through his theories of the
subconscious: millions now seek emotional salvation through techniques of psychotherapy pioneered by him.

Among the countless Jews who have exercised a profound influence
on the thought and institutions of our times these three stand out as
giants. But there have been many more of enormous stature and influence in almost every area of human endeavor. Martin Buber in
theology. Henri Bergson and Ludwig Wittgenstein in philosophy.
Gustav Mahler and Arnold Schoenberg in music. Wassermann, Schick,
and Salk in medicine. Casimir Funk, the discoverer of vitamins, in
biochemistry. Pissarro, Modigliani, and Chagall in painting. Heine,
Proust, Kafka, and Maurois in literature. Leo Szilard, Niels Bohr, and
J. Robert Oppenheimer in physics. Benjamin Disraeli, Léon Blum,
and Leon Trotsky in politics. The Rothschilds in high finance. The
Guggenheims in mining and patronage of the arts and sciences. Since
the Nobel Prize was instituted in 1901, it has been awarded to over

fifty Jews. And the astonishing thing is that the Jews constitute less than one-half of 1 percent of the total world population. Furthermore, what is equally astonishing is that prior to the nineteenth century the Jews had produced almost no one of extraordinary intellectual and artistic distinction, save for the philosopher Benedict Spinoza, since the birth of Jesus of Nazareth.

Clearly what we have been witnessing for the past hundred years has been nothing less than an artistic and intellectual renaissance of a people comparable only to that which the Greeks experienced in the fifth century B.C. and the Italians experienced in the fifteenth and sixteenth centuries.

A renaissance does not happen to a people simply because that people is more gifted than another, though native gifts are, obviously, an important ingredient. Rather it usually happens as a response, or as a reaction, one might say, to a previous repression.

The extraordinary flowering of the arts and sciences—of poetry, physics, mathematics, philosophy, painting, sculpture, architecture— that occurred in Italy throughout the fifteenth and sixteenth centuries, and which then spread to northern Europe, and peaked there in the seventeenth century, was, among many things, a reaction to centuries of repression of artistic and intellectual freedom enforced by the Church of Rome. Emancipated from the centuries-old tyranny of the Church, the human spirit could at last soar and invent as never before since the days of Augustan Rome and Periclean Athens.

So, also, the Jewish renaissance of the nineteenth and twentieth centuries has been a reaction to centuries of repression in the ghettos of Europe enforced by the Christian majority and the Jewish rabbis. Gradually, during the decades following the French Revolution and the Napoleonic wars—a period of roughly seventy years, now often referred to as the Emancipation—the European Jews freed themselves from the restraints of the ghetto and in their new freedom and exultation exploded in a burst of genius and talent such as the world had seldom seen before.

But the Jewish renaissance was not only an expression of emancipation from the ghetto, it was also one of emancipation from *Jewishness*. For centuries Jews had been condemned to adhere to the closed, tribal, ritualistic religious and intellectual tradition of Judaism with its essentially backward gaze toward the glories and struggles of the Jewish people before the Diaspora. Now, however, they were suddenly not only free of the ghetto, they were free even to free themselves from the tradition that for so long had nurtured them in adversity.

Thus we find that nearly all the greatest Jews of the Jewish renaissance have repudiated Judaism. Preceded by Spinoza and Heine, both of whom renounced Judaism, Marx, Disraeli, Freud, Mahler, Proust, Einstein, Wittgenstein, and Schoenberg all repudiated the religion of their fathers. Indeed it was often the very process of repudiation that contributed to the freshness and originality of their thinking. Now, suddenly, after more than two thousand years in one dogmatic, past-obsessed tradition, and centuries of being forced to live in the closed world of the ghetto, they were free to think and act for themselves. What an exhilaration they must have felt.

With so much hitherto confined energy and talent suddenly released in Europe, it was only natural that rivalry, jealousy, and opposition would arise among the Christian majority that had had the humanitarian generosity to let the Jews out of the ghettos. Hence the outbreak of anti-Semitism that began to appear in the latter half of the nineteenth century, culminating in the Nazi holocaust of the following century. The Nazi persecution of the Jews would never have happened had the Jews not been let out of their ghettos. And hence, also, the creation of the state of Israel, which may be interpreted as both an expression of the Jewish renaissance and a sort of compensation, or reparation, to the Jews for the sufferings they had endured during the holocaust.

One chapter in this immense drama of Jewish emancipation and renaissance, probably the central drama of the modern era, is the story of the Guggenheim family in America.

In no country in the world have the Jews experienced greater freedom and opportunity, or attained greater achievements than in the United States of America. We have recited the names of some of the great figures of the Jewish renaissance of international scope (some of whom, like Einstein and Schoenberg, became American citizens). The list of eminent American Jews is almost equally impressive. The jurists Benjamin N. Cardozo, Felix Frankfurter, Louis D. Brandeis. The playwrights Lillian Hellman and Arthur Miller. The musicians Nathan Milstein, Isaac Stern, Bruno Walter, Yehudi Menuhin, Artur Rubinstein, Vladimir Horowitz, and Leonard Bernstein. Publishers Joseph Pulitzer and Adolph S. Ochs. Popular composers Jerome Kern and George Gershwin. Novelists Isaac Bashevis Singer, Bernard Malamud, and Saul Bellow. Financiers Jacob Schiff, the Lehman brothers, Solomon Loeb, and Felix Warburg. Industrialists and philanthropists Daniel, Solomon, and Simon Guggenheim.

In the story of the Guggenheims all the elements of the great Jewish drama of the nineteenth and twentieth centuries are present: the emancipation from a European ghetto in the mid-nineteenth century; the migration to a new land; the rapid attainment of vast wealth; the gradual shedding of Jewish traditions; the wonderful flowering of talent in the third and succeeding generations.

But the story of the Guggenheims is more than a chapter of the Jewish emancipation and renaissance, it is also a most significant chapter in the history of the United States. Few American families have realized the American Dream of rising from poverty and obscurity to wealth and influence to the extent the Guggenheims have. And certainly in the process of realizing that dream few families have made so many contributions to American civilization as have the Guggenheims. The fact that the Guggenheims, alone among American families of great wealth, and alone even among the educational institutions and governmental agencies of the American republic, had the vision to provide the first significant financial support of aviation and rocketry, to provide what amounted to the first official encouragement of the research that ultimately resulted in the Apollo XI mission to the moon, is reason enough for us to assign them a preeminent place of influence in our civilization. (Especially since it now appears that the establishment of colonies in space may be the only way the human race will be able to endure.) But, as we shall see, the influence of this lively, colorful family has extended to many other fields besides aeronautics. Through the five Guggenheim foundations active today there is scarcely an area of the arts and sciences in America that the family has not influenced profoundly. No other American family has had a greater influence on modern painting and sculpture than the Guggenheims. Few American families have exceeded the Guggenheims' influence on literature, scholarship, technology, and the sciences. So vast, in fact, has been the Guggenheims' impact on contemporary American civilization that it can be said that they have been certainly *the* most influential Jewish family in America, and one of the five or six most influential American families of the twentieth century.

"Leadership requires great aristocratic families with long traditions of administration and rule; old ancestral lines that guarantee for many generations the duration of the necessary will and the necessary instincts."

—FRIEDRICH NIETZSCHE

"Aristocracy is one of the goals of democracy."

—ERIC BENTLEY

"I would suggest that a society which affords some of its members extraordinary privilege and celebrates the fact, instead of apologizing for it and validating its less privileged members in their sense of grievance, will enjoy an unparalleled sense of human possibility."

—EDGAR Z. FRIEDENBERG

"When Christianity is once destroyed, one will become more appreciative of the Jews."

—FRIEDRICH NIETZSCHE

THE

GUGGENHEIMS

AN AMERICAN EPIC

PROLOGUE

A
GUGGENHEIM
WILL

ON THE MORNING OF MARCH 12, 1970, IN HIALEAH, FLORIDA, HARRY F. Guggenheim set his signature on his last will and testament. Two months later, in New York City, he altered the will with a first codicil. With these two documents he provided for the distribution after his death of his share in the largest fortune ever amassed by a Jewish family in America, and the largest family fortune ever made from mining and metallurgy in history.

Harry Guggenheim was eighty years old in May, 1970. His family had been in America 123 years. Harry had been the most influential male of his generation—the fourth since the Guggenheims had left their European ghetto—his cousin Peggy, the most influential woman. Not long before he executed his will Harry had arranged for Peggy's huge collection of modern art—then, as now, housed in her Venetian *palazzo*—to be willed to their late uncle Solomon's foundation, of which Harry was president, thus consolidating what would become, on Peggy's death, one of the largest private collections of modern art in the world, a collection that has been variously estimated as being worth from $150 million to $200 million.

The consolidation of the two collections into one foundation had been one of Harry's most satisfying achievements over the past few years. Another satisfying achievement, one that would gratify his heirs considerably, had been the sale, in 1970, of his Pulitzer Prize-winning Long Island newspaper, *Newsday,* to the Times Mirror Company, publishers of the *Los Angeles Times* and the New American Library, for $75 million. Harry had started the paper—primarily to give his third wife, the talented, restless Alicia Patterson, whom he made editor-in-chief, something to do—on a mere $750,000 in the early 1940s. The over one-hundredfold return on the original investment bested even his father's most celebrated business coup: Old Daniel Guggenheim had bought the Chuquicamata Copper Mine in Chile, the largest copper deposit in the world, for $25 million in 1910, after having declined to buy it for $25,000 ten years before, and had sold it in 1923, over Harry's protest, for $70 million.

(The Guggenheims had always been good at this sort of thing.

Today Peggy likes to point out that, though she had not collected art for investment purposes, she paid only $250,000 for her $30 million collection. And Roger Straus, the publisher, a Guggenheim on his mother's side, nephew to Harry and cousin to Peggy, takes pride in having bought twelve Herman Hesse titles for only $12,500 when the market for the German author was depressed, then sold six of them to Bantam Books for $1.2 million in 1970.)

The *Newsday* deal had not been Harry's only success of this kind in recent years. There had also been his career as a racehorse owner. Harry loved horses almost as much as he loved himself and had been extremely successful in breeding and training them. What began in 1934 as a one-horse outfit—the one horse, a yearling, costing $400 —ended as the country's leading money-earning stable, winning $757,000 in 1959.

Harry's art foundation, horse racing, and *Newsday* successes had sweetened somewhat an old age considerably embittered by various disappointments. Some of these disappointments were reflected in Harry's will, and especially in the codicil to his will. They had to do with people—relatives and associates—who had let Harry down, or who Harry thought had let him down.

Harry's disappointments were, however, occasioned not so much by other people's shortcomings as by ineluctable circumstances and the peculiar makeup of his character.

The ineluctable circumstances were his lack of sons in a family that had been, for some time, steadily "daughtering out." Harry himself had had three daughters from two of his three wives. His uncles Isaac, Solomon, and Benjamin had fathered a total of nine daughters and no sons. Four of the five males of Harry's generation had died young, one a suicide. Harry, as principal heir to the Guggenheim fortune and traditions, had needed sons, either blood or surrogate, and reliable ones, especially reliable ones in his own image, had not been easy to find.

The peculiar nature of Harry's mind and character was a partner to his principal disappointment. Like many men of his generation, Harry was dogmatic and authoritarian in his beliefs and attitudes. His vision of the world was limited by his being an heir to an immense mining fortune. His family had made its resplendent way in the world believing in hard work, family unity, aggressive personal initiative, conservative politics, the essential *rightness* of private exploitation of natural resources, and, above all, in Everlasting Material Progress with capitals E, M, and P. And these were the beliefs that guided Harry's life also. If a relative or business associate did not share them Harry might go along with him for a while, but would ultimately reject him. Egotist that he was, what he wanted most to carry on the Guggenheim ethos was simply a carbon copy of himself.

Lack of sons Harry was only too well aware of. The nature of his own mind and character was another matter. Again, like many men of his generation, he had time for everything but self-examination. More than likely he had only the vaguest notion, if that, of what his faults and limitations were.

Harry had been casting around for a male heir for some time. What he needed was a young man to whom he could entrust the bulk of his fortune, the future of Guggenheim Brothers and *Newsday,* and two of the Guggenheim foundations.

First, he had singled out a nephew, Oscar Straus, one of his sister Gladys' sons. Oscar was an able man of forty-five who had been having difficulties gaining promotion in the formerly Guggenheim-controlled American Smelting and Refining Company. (His father, Roger W. Straus, had been president of the company, but his chief antagonist had succeeded him.) On February 16, 1959, Harry had issued a memorandum to the partners of Guggenheim Brothers stating, among many things, that "the firm is not going forward, which means, unless cared for, it will go backwards," that, in his opinion, which turned out to be erroneous, "the firm should return to the first principles of the founders and seek new projects in the field of the exploitation of the products of nature useful to man," and that "I suggest that . . . the firm be under the impetus of a new and energetic young partner with commercial ability and general knowledge in this field in which he should devote full time. . . . I have in mind for this partnership," the memorandum continued, "my nephew, Oscar Straus. . . . I believe he has the qualifications suitable for this task together with the highest personal standards, that would make a congenial and valuable partner of the firm. His devotion to the family tradition is both in his training and generations of inheritance."

But Oscar Straus soon proved unable to rejuvenate the firm. The spirit of the times was against him. Harry, in trying to reorganize Guggenheim Brothers, had failed to realize that a natural resources company operating outside the United States in 1959 was a very risky proposition. No sooner do you develop a property than the locals try to snatch it away from you. Gone were the halcyon days when the Guggenheims could move into a backward country like Angola or Chile and·buy up all the best mines available. (Now, as one of Harry's second cousins, Bill Guggenheim, puts it, when you move into an underdeveloped country to take over a natural resource, the locals will allow you to stay there just long enough for you to do the spadework, then they throw you out.) Before long Harry began quarreling with his nephew over Oscar's apparent inability to develop "new projects in the field of the exploitation of the products of nature useful to man." Oscar was as opinionated, dogmatic, and intractable as Harry. It had been, in part, these character traits that had cost him promotion at American Smelting and Refining. After a while the two men could not even remain in the same room together. As a result, Oscar lost out on becoming Harry's principal heir, senior partner of Guggenheim Brothers, and a power in the two foundations Harry had jurisdiction over. Harry turned to another relative.

At this juncture in the history of the House of Guggenheim there were scores upon scores of females left, but not many males. And the few males bearing the name of Guggenheim were not very promising so far as Harry was concerned. One had dropped out of Yale and had given little indication of being able to grapple with the business world, and the other two had removed themselves permanently, and perhaps wisely, to the painless shores of southern California. Eliminating these from any consideration, Harry turned to his grandson, Dana Draper, son of his youngest daughter, Nancy.

To Dana, a young man in his twenties at the time Harry began to take an interest in him, Harry offered the world. If Dana worked hard and successfully he stood to become Harry's principal heir, the beneficiary of a multimillion-dollar trust fund, a partner in Guggenheim Brothers, part owner and publisher of *Newsday,* and the head of two Guggenheim foundations.

Prior to seizing upon Dana Draper, Harry had written his errant daughter Nancy, an amateur ballet dancer and acrobat who had been living for some time in California:

> I have always hoped that my children and grandchildren would carry on the best traditions of the family to the best of their abilities. Briefly, the best traditions have been developing some of the great natural resources of the world, i.e., creating wealth for the use of mankind, and, as a reward in our free enterprise system, amassing fortunes which have been bequeathed in very large part to imaginative foundations for the future benefit of mankind.

The idealistic terms in which Harry couched his hopes appealed to Dana Draper and the young man came east to claim his opportunity.

Dana Draper, twenty-five years old in 1965, the year he went to work full time for Harry, was a typical child of the 1960s. An exponent of the counterculture, he was just about everything his grandfather was not, and stood for just about everything his grandfather was against. A sensitive young man who wore his long, wavy blond hair to his shoulders, he habitually sported a kerchief around his neck instead of a tie, wore jeans and T-shirts instead of suits, and carried a satchel on a long shoulder strap. By contrast, the tall, swarthy, blue-eyed, barrel-chested Harry rarely wore anything but a dark business suit, starched collar, and regimental-striped tie, and when he did carry something, which was rarely, it was not even an attaché case, but a briefcase. Politically Dana gravitated toward the New Left. Harry had been an ultraconservative Republican all his life. Dana had artistic abilities and aspirations: He was interested in sculpture and photography. Harry might have taken pride in running an art museum, but having an artist *in the family* was another matter. Though he was quite willing to spend money on art it may be safely assumed he would not readily subsidize an artistic career for his grandson. Dana was also an environmental conservationist and Harry, of course, was committed to "exploiting the products of nature useful to man."

Clearly the stage was set for a classic confrontation of the generations. Harry had a difficult time acknowledging his grandson was his. Nevertheless he put him to work on *Newsday,* hopeful that he would develop into a newspaper publisher and would eventually shape up into a fresh new edition of Harry. The young man had already served something of a Guggenheim apprenticeship, doing short stints from time to time in the Solomon R. Guggenheim Museum, the Guggenheim nitrate fields in Chile, and Harry's Cain Hoy plantation in South Carolina.

It wasn't long, however, before grandfather and grandson began to clash. First of all, Harry did not like the way Dana dressed. If the boy only wouldn't come to the office in jeans, T-shirt, and satchel. Second, Dana took no interest in Guggenheim Brothers. He wanted to preserve nature, not exploit it. Third, the boy's politics were so far to the left as to appear to Harry downright "pinko." To Harry, the Eisenhower-and-Nixon Republican, leftist politics in the Guggenheim family was simply heresy. Fourth, the young man did not particularly take to *Newsday*. He was very sensitive about being the boss's grandson among a cadre of seasoned professionals. Why should *he* be groomed for the top job when there were a dozen people on the paper, including Harry's wife's nephew, Joe Patterson Albright, one of the major stockholders to boot, who had much more of a right to be boss than he did? Because he was a *Guggenheim* Harry would thunder back. For God's sake, boy, have more of a sense of who you *are*!

In the end it didn't work out. Harry began to see his own world challenged by the likes of young Draper and he reacted ruthlessly, violently. He told Dana he had to either shape up (to Harry's image) or get out. Dana chose to remain true to himself. He refused to divest himself of his jeans, kerchief, satchel, environmentalism, and liberal political philosophy, left the paper, and returned to California and his photography and sculpture. For this allegiance to self he forfeited a multimillion-dollar inheritance—Harry did not mention him in his will—and whatever positions he might have attained in the various Guggenheim enterprises and foundations. (Harry also threw him off the boards of his own foundation and the Guggenheim Museum.) Once Dana had left, Harry resumed his lifelong search for a son. A son, a son. His empire for a son.

For a while he toyed with the idea of making a "son" out of his nephew-in-law, Joe Albright, but finally decided to look outside the family. After a brief search he came up with Bill D. Moyers, Lyndon Johnson's former press secretary. The year was 1967.

Moyers was thirty-three years old at the time, bright, personable, and experienced. Gradually he took control of the paper, shaping it to his own beliefs and prejudices. Harry liked him at first. Besides giving him de facto control of *Newsday,* he left him a substantial legacy in his will: $100,000 plus a 20 percent interest in his worldwide mining companies, including Guggenheim Brothers.

But, inevitably, discord set in. Actually it was built into the relationship from the beginning. Moyers was a liberal Democrat. Harry, as we know, was a conservative Republican. On most domestic and foreign issues Harry was tough, Moyers a bleeding heart. The Vietnam War was on. Harry was a hawk, Moyers a dove. After Nixon became President Moyers criticized him relentlessly in editorial after editorial. Harry was willing to acknowledge some of Nixon's shortcomings, but he wanted more fairness shown to the President: The man couldn't be *all* bad. And so it went.

The final blowup, however, was not occasioned by Harry's and Moyers' differences of opinion, but by Moyers' interference in Harry's efforts to sell *Newsday*. Harry had been dickering with the Times Mirror Company over the sale of the paper, and Moyers was against the sale to that conservative organization. The liberal Moyers was sure that Times Mirror would not retain him as publisher. He therefore began sounding out *The New York Times*, Time-Life, and other publishers as potential buyers without telling Harry. Harry got wind of these negotiations and reacted by quickly consummating the sale of *Newsday* to Times Mirror, and, in so doing, liquidating Moyers, who resigned upon the sale. He then struck Moyers out of his will by codicil. Another son had been discarded.

Not long before these events took place, Harry had contracted cancer of the prostate. By then he had alienated so many people in and out of his family that there were few, beyond his daughter Joan, and her husband, and his nephew Roger Straus, who would spare the time to comfort him in what would be his final illness. But one who did spare the time was his second cousin, Peter O. Lawson-Johnston, a grandson of his late uncle Solomon. Harry had always liked Peter. Since 1956 Peter had worked in such Guggenheim-controlled companies as the Feldspar Corporation and Pacific Tin. Later he was taken in as a partner at Guggenheim Brothers. Peter was affable, hardworking, intelligent . . . and he wore conservative, Ivy League clothes. A handsome young man—slim, clean-cut, blue-eyed, with sandy hair and a firm chin—half Jewish by birth, an Episcopalian in practice, he was forty-two years old at the time cousin Harry contracted cancer.

Regularly Peter called on Harry at his Manhattan townhouse at 34 East Seventy-fourth Street. Occasionally he would even go out to see the old man at his lovely ninety-acre estate, Falaise, at Sands Point on Long Island. Every once in a while the two would run into each other at the offices of Guggenheim Brothers, a couple of blocks from Wall Street. Gradually the two cousins grew closer. They discussed, among many things, the *Newsday* sale. They discussed Bill Moyers. In time Harry realized he had finally found his son.

This realization was solemnized in the codicil with which Harry altered his will shortly after the sale of *Newsday*. In revoking the articles giving Moyers a bequest of $100,000 and 20 percent of the value of his worldwide mining interests, Harry substituted articles adding $100,000 to the already substantial trusts created for Peter and awarding Peter *all* his interest in Guggenheim Brothers and *all* his other mining interests.

Harry Guggenheim had written a most unequal will and then made it even more unequal by codicil. To his three daughters, Nancy Draper, Joan Van de Maele, and Diane Meek, he left only $250,000 apiece, plus an apartment in New York and a gatehouse on his Long Island estate to Joan. To Peter Lawson-Johnston and to the Harry Frank Guggenheim Foundation, of which Lawson-Johnston was made chairman of the board, he left thrusts amounting to some twenty-three million, six million for Peter and seventeen for the foundation.

(Not long after the will was probated, daughter Nancy Draper, who had had multiple marital disappointments and a mastectomy, and who was now stunned with financial disappointments as well, committed suicide.)

An unequal will. But then Harry Guggenheim, American Renaissance prince—mining magnate, financier, author, publisher, aviator, naval officer, racehorse owner, aviation pioneer, art patron, museum president, philanthropist, ambassador—had never believed in the concept of equality, social, economic, sexual, or extraterrestrial. Harry never pretended to be, and never made excuses for being, anything but an extraordinarily privileged rich man. The story is told that once, during the Depression, as he was pulling up to his office in downtown Manhattan in his chauffeur-driven, custom-built limousine, an unemployed loiterer stuck his head through the car window and, in an ugly tone of voice, cried, "Dirty capitalist!" "Flatterer, flatterer!" Harry cried back, as he got out of the car. No, egalitarianism had little space in Harry's character or credo.

The elaboration of the trusts took up thirty of the forty-eight pages of Harry's will. With infinite care the lawyers had attended to what America has been all about ever since the Founders decided to separate from the mother country to avoid taxes: the protection of capital. So carefully were the trusts for individuals and foundations worked out that the government stood to collect only $13 million out of a gross estate of approximately $50 million.

Among other provisions of the will: salaries to his servants for life; bequests of $100,000 each to his chief of staff, George Fountaine; his son-in-law Albert Van de Maele; Pembroke College, Cambridge; the North Shore Hospital on Long Island; the Sloan-Kettering Institute for Cancer Research in New York; $200,000 to his lawyer and friend, Leo Gottlieb; his 4,000-acre Daniel's Island off the South Carolina coast, to his foundation; his 15,000-acre Cain Hoy plantation, also in South Carolina, which included his stables and beloved horses, to become part of the residuary trust for Lawson-Johnston; his files, including the Lindbergh and Goddard correspondence, to the Library of Congress; all loans made to his daughters and their husbands excused; his Long Island estate, Falaise, with all its works of art, to Nassau County to be operated as a museum.

(Not long after Nassau County took possession of Harry's house, they allowed, for a consideration, the director of *The Godfather* to shoot some scenes on the property. One of these was the repulsive, startling scene of the Hollywood mogul waking up to find a severed, bleeding horse's head on his bed. *Harry*'s bed!)

But what about Israel, what about the Jews? Where were the legacies to the Jewish charities, to the struggling new Jewish nation, from this scion of America's richest and most influential Jewish family? To such questions Harry would have answered that he had his own special Jewish charities, generously provided for by his own foundation, and that his father Daniel's foundation had recently contributed a rehabilitation pavilion to the Rothschild-Hadassah Medical Center on Mt. Scopus, Jerusalem. This, in his opinion, took care of his family's obligations toward the Jews. Besides, his Uncle Sol, though a generous contributor to Jewish charities all his life, had always been skeptical about the advisability of creating, and then supporting, the state of Israel on the grounds that "Judaism is a religion, not a nationality," and that its creation might conceivably bring more misfortunes upon the Jews than blessings, and Harry usually maintained that position.

Yes, Harry knew what he was doing when he made out his will. He had been particularly explicit in giving a rationale for its inequality. In designating Peter Lawson-Johnston as his principal heir, the will stated that for Peter to carry on effectively as head of the family he must have "adequate financial resources." "While inherited wealth," the will read, "can sometimes lead to a parasitic life and be destructive to society and the legatee, it can also be the means of constructive work on behalf of humanity and the greatest ultimate happiness to the legatee.

"If I were to provide for all of my family equally, none of them, in my opinion, would be in a position to carry on the family tradition effectively."

Use of the phrase "family tradition" was important. For in his will Harry was not only disposing of a family fortune, he was disposing, as if that were possible, of his family's traditions as well. The will went on:

> In planning the distribution of my estate, one of my primary objectives has been to arrange matters in such a way that one of the members of the Guggenheim family would have the opportunity and would assume the responsibility of carrying on the Guggenheim family tradition in the constructive use of the funds available to him. The Guggenheim family has helped to develop the natural resources of the world, has pioneered in the development of the air age and rocket age, and has, in many other respects, through both its business activities and its philanthropies in education and art, benefited mankind in general in many parts of the world and especially in the United States and the Western Hemisphere.
>
> The initial requirements for one to carry on such a tradition are those of character, integrity, a capacity for leadership, innate ability, preferably a superior education, and an urge to work and a determination to succeed. . . . On the basis of long and careful observation of his potentialities, I believe that Peter O. Lawson-Johnston, a grandson of my uncle, Solomon R. Guggenheim, is fully qualified to carry on creditably the Guggenheim family tradition. I have given my trustees discretion to make distributions of principal to Peter to enable him to use his human and financial resources for the progress of man in the best traditions of the Guggenheim family.

And so Lawson-Johnston received his formal investiture as the Guggenheim standard-bearer after Harry's death.

The traditions he was called upon to maintain and promote were considerable, though, despite the high-sounding phrases of Harry's will, he was by no means in a position to "carry on" the whole of "the Guggenheim tradition." The $100 million John Simon Guggenheim Memorial Foundation, dispenser of the Guggenheim Fellowships, created as a reaction to personal tragedy by one of his grandfather's brothers, was beyond Lawson-Johnston's jurisdiction: Roger Straus was the only Guggenheim on the board. The $17 million Daniel and Florence Guggenheim Foundation, sponsor, among many things, of the Goldman Band concerts in New York City, the aforementioned hospital in Israel, and several advanced jet-propulsion laboratories, was also beyond his jurisdiction. That foundation, established by another of his grandfather's brothers, was headed by Gladys Guggenheim Straus and her son Oscar, and Peter did not sit on the board.

(It will be evident at this point that the Strauses did not accept Lawson-Johnston's investiture as sole knight-errant of the Guggenheim tradition with exceeding satisfaction. However, they have since learned to live with it and have come to hold Lawson-Johnston in considerable affection and respect.)

Nor did Peter have anything to do with several other areas of Guggenheim munificence. He had nothing to do with the $25 million Guggenheim Pavilion and endowment fund at Mount Sinai Hospital in New York, or with the new $12 million Guggenheim Pavilion at the Mayo Clinic, or with the Murry and Leonie Guggenheim Building at New York Hospital, these created from funds donated by another granduncle. Nor did he have anything to do with the schools of aeronautical engineering Daniel and Harry had established at New York University, the Massachusetts Institute of Technology, the California Institute of Technology, the Georgia Institute of Technology, the University of Washington, Stanford University, the University of Michigan, and Princeton. Nor did he have anything to do with the many charities his second cousin, M. Robert Guggenheim, Jr., administered on the West Coast.

What Peter did have in his charge, among the truly Medicean body of Guggenheim benefactions, was the Solomon R. Guggenheim Foundation, of which he had been elected president and trustee, and the Harry Frank Guggenheim Foundation, of which he was made chairman and director. The Solomon R. ran the museum on Eighty-ninth Street and Fifth Avenue, which Frank Lloyd Wright had designed and Harry had guided to completion (battling with Wright, Robert Moses, the city of New York, and Sol's German artistic advisor all the way) and was by now established into a reasonably comfortable routine. The Harry Frank was a daring, and strangely eccentric, venture into the unknown—essentially into the behavioral sciences and such mysteries as "man's competition for sustenance, sex, and domination," and would represent one of Peter's most puzzling and difficult challenges in the years to come.

So far as the businesses Peter inherited were concerned, they were little more than bits and pieces of the now crumbled Guggenheim empire. It was his job to pick up the pieces, if he could, and start anew.

Harry Guggenheim died of cancer at the Sloan-Kettering Memorial Hospital in New York nine months after he had sold *Newsday* and written the first codicil to his will. *The New York Times* honored him by printing his obituary on the front page. In an age of specialization, Harry had led a life closer to the Italian Renaissance ideal of universality than perhaps any other American of his generation. He had been both a man of action and a man of thought. He had been a man of immense inherited wealth and considerable personal achievement. He had served his country as naval aviator, aeronautical pioneer, and ambassador. He had served the arts as the guiding spirit and president of one of the most daringly conceived museums in the world. He had served his heirs by adding some $40 million to the family fortune. In providing the initial financial support for aviation and rocketry, he had even played a significant role in developing Saturn V, the rocket that sent Apollo XI to the moon.

The Guggenheim future now belonged to Harry's first cousin, M. Robert Guggenheim, Jr., and to Robert's son, Daniel, in southern California; to William Guggenheim III, a second cousin, in Florida; to the Strauses in New York; and, above all, to Peter O. Lawson-Johnston, as designated family chief and heir.

Along with the trust funds and presidencies of family foundations and businesses Peter also inherited the principal desk in the great walnut-paneled, leather-chaired Partners' Room at Guggenheim Brothers in the Equitable Building at 120 Broadway in downtown New York City.

High on the thirty-fifth floor, and dominating an imperial panorama of office towers, the Jersey meadows, the Hudson River, and New York Bay, the vast room and its relics are a veritable museum of the Guggenheim past.

Here, on one wall, is the framed drawing of Meyer and his seven sons, the original partners of the first family firm, M. Guggenheim's Sons, founded when all the brothers were still united. Here, scattered about the room, are the five desks, made out of the same heavy, dark German walnut as the walls, of the five original partners of Guggenheim Brothers, successor to M. Guggenheim's Sons, founded when the brothers were no longer united. Here, on a table, is a framed reliquary containing a "True Piece of the first hangar in the world—Kitty Hawk." Here, near one of the walls, is the great partners' meeting table with the huge gilt-framed portrait of Harry above it. Here, on a small table near Peter's desk, is another sacred relic, the framed National City Bank canceled check, dated March 1, 1923, for $70 million made out to Guggenheim Brothers and signed by an official of Anaconda Copper. Here, strewn over various tables, are the company reports from Angola, Malaysia, Brazil, Alaska, Chile . . .

Here, also, ranged along the walls, are the gilt-framed portraits of six of the original seven Guggenheim brothers, their square footage commensurate, it is said, with the importance of the Guggenheim represented. Here, in a middle-sized portrait, is poker-faced Isaac, the eldest but not the ablest, standing in the forest of his immense Long Island estate, Villa Carola, looking like a gentle, tired British lord. There, on another expanse of walnut, is the smallish, colored photograph of dapper, sad-eyed Senator Simon, donor of the Guggenheim Fellowships. Here, above one of the room's two marble fireplaces, is the large portrait of the great Daniel, mightiest of all the Guggenheims, foster father of U.S. aviation and rocketry, patron of Lindbergh and Goddard, Daniel looking sprightly and imperious in dark jacket, stiff collar, and purple cravat. There, above a paneled door, not far from Simon, is the small, oval portrait of dandified dropout Benjamin, Peggy's father, who drowned with the *Titanic* in 1912. Here too is the not-so-large portrait of sober-faced Murry Guggenheim, donor of clinics and pavilions to the children of New York, Mount Sinai Hospital, New York Hospital, and the Mayo Clinic. Here, over another fireplace, is the ample portrait of the fearless Solomon, whose grandson now presided over the room in which the brothers Guggenheim had ruled their empire for so many years. And there, next to Lawson-Johnston's desk, hangs the portrait of grave, white-whiskered Meyer, the Guggenheim founding father.

One hundred and twenty-eight years had passed since Meyer Guggenheim had left the ghetto village of Lengnau in German-speaking Switzerland. During their brief American adventure his descendants had been everything, done everything, that their ancestors in Lengnau, as Jews, had been prevented from being and doing for so many years. They had been industrialists, financiers, senators, yachtsmen, titled aristocrats, army officers, naval officers, racehorse owners, dog breeders, publishers, ambassadors, archaeologists, socialites, writers, art patrons, plantation owners, ranchers, aeronautical pioneers, and benefactors of foundations on a lavish scale. Their American experience had been so rich and varied as to seem fictional, unreal. No other Jewish family in America, and few Gentile ones for that matter, could match them in wealth and honors earned and in variousness and magnificence of lives lived.

Was there a key to this tremendous outpouring of energy and talent? From what conditions of privation and limitation did the Guggenheims spring, that, once unleashed in a free society, they were impelled to prosper and flower as princes, as kings?

The answer to these questions lies in early nineteenth-century Switzerland and specifically in the quiet little village of Lengnau, in the state of Baden, which Meyer Guggenheim left in 1847 to begin his family's astonishing adventure in the New World.

I

MEYER AND BARBARA

(1828-1905)

FOUNDING AN

AMERICAN DYNASTY

In the first generation thee must do well, in the second marry well, in the third breed well, then the fourth should take care of itself.

—Quaker formula on the way
to found a family

'Tis a happy thing
To be the father unto many sons.

—Shakespeare, Henry VI

THE GUGGENHEIMS

GENEALOGICAL CHART

(FOR PART I)

SIMON MEYER GUGGENHEIM (1792–1869)
m. (1) SCHÄFELI LEVINGER
m. (2) RACHEL WEIL MEYER

MEYER GUGGENHEIM (1828–1905)
(From Schäfeli Levinger)
m. BARBARA MEYER (1834–1900)
(Daughter of Rachel Weil Meyer
by her first husband)

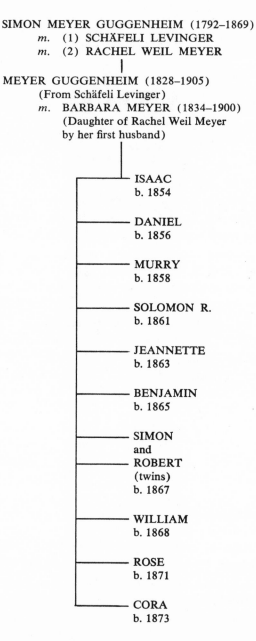

ISAAC
b. 1854

DANIEL
b. 1856

MURRY
b. 1858

SOLOMON R.
b. 1861

JEANNETTE
b. 1863

BENJAMIN
b. 1865

SIMON
and
ROBERT
(twins)
b. 1867

WILLIAM
b. 1868

ROSE
b. 1871

CORA
b. 1873

*For complete genealogical information consult
genealogical tables on pages 541–544.*

CHAPTER

1

OUT OF THE GHETTO

THE VALLEY OF THE RIVER SURB WINDS GENTLY THROUGH GREEN pastures and orchards of pear, apple, cherry, peach. In the spring the apple trees blossom into little white clouds; buttercups and dandelions appear in the bright green meadows; geraniums and daisies sprout in the window boxes of red-roofed farmhouses. Summer brings rich gardens of celery, endive, and cabbage to the low, rolling hillsides, and clumps of brown-and-white and Swiss brown cows to the pastures. In the fall, the vineyards turn red and gold, and the bare trees reveal the sparkling Surb tumbling through the little valley.

Here and there along the road following the river, stand wooden crosses bearing pallid, bleeding Christs: The canton of Aargau is predominantly Catholic. Now and then slim, onion-domed spires of churches peep from behind quiet hillsides. Forested uplands range the far distances, never rising high enough to become mountains, never distracting attention from the bright serenity of the valley below.

One of the two villages in the valley of the Surb is Lengnau, a community of some 1,700 souls. Crossing a narrow bridge leading from the main road, one arrives almost immediately in the *Dorfplatz* of the tiny village, dominated by the synagogue. The little white-washed housefronts surrounding the *Platz*, one of which belongs to the *Gasthaus*, display the *Fachwerk* typical of German-speaking Switzerland, a design of crisscrossing wooden beams resembling Tudor-style architecture. There are geraniums sprouting from these window boxes too. A fountain plays in the tree-lined *Platz*. There is rarely much going on. Every once in a while a farm boy drives a flock of sheep, or a few cows, up the *hauptstrasse* bordering the square. Or a motorbike comes to a blustery halt in front of the *Gasthaus*. Otherwise the village is still, save for the constant tumbling of the stream, the trickling of the fountain . . .

An idyllic setting. But this gentle Swiss land, this benign village, was once not very gentle or benevolent to people like the Guggenheims.

Simon Guggenheim, tailor, lived and worked in house No. 64, near the bridge over the Surb, from 1830 until his emigration to America in 1847. His ancestors had lived and worked in and around the same area for at least 150 years.

Like most of the houses in Lengnau, Simon Guggenheim's was a multiple dwelling and had two entranceways, one into a hall serving the first-floor apartments, the other into the hall and stair to the apartments above, one for the Christians living in the building, one for the Jews. For centuries in Lengnau the Christians had refused to enter and leave their houses across the same threshold as that used by their Jewish neighbors.

But this was but a token of the indignities Jews had had to endure in Switzerland ever since they had arrived there fleeing persecutions in Germany. The Swiss at this time were convinced that the Jews were solely responsible for murdering the Son of God and had to pay for their cosmic crime unto eternity.

During the sixteenth and seventeenth centuries, one Swiss community after another expelled the Jews from within its confines, blaming population pressures. By 1776 only one state of the Swiss Confederation, the earldom of Baden, remained open to them. But even in Baden they were not entirely welcome. Eventually they were restricted to only two communities within the state, Lengnau and Endigen. These two villages of the Surb valley then became ghettos for the whole of Switzerland.

Lengnau and Endigen were both farming communities, but Jews there were not permitted to engage in farming. In fact, they were not permitted to possess real estate other than their own homes. Households in the two villages were limited to 108, which meant that a Jew often had to wait for years before he could own his own house. Furthermore, a Jew's house had to have a straw roof rather than a tiled one, and could be bought only after it had been offered at auction three times and no Christian had taken it. Once bought, a Jewish home could not be enlarged, nor could its exterior be altered. The Jews of Lengnau and Endigen were not even regarded as citizens.

They were "Alien Protection Fellows," or "Tolerated Homeless Persons Not To Be Expelled." This euphemism meant that they were little more than serfs of the *Landvogt* of Baden. To retain their status of "Alien Protection Fellows" and the possession of their homes, they were required to purchase from the *Landvogt*, at intervals of sixteen years, a document known as the "Safe Conduct and Patronage Letter." This document was often so expensive as to cost a Jewish household half a year's earnings. Sometimes richer Jews were required to purchase the document more frequently than every sixteen years or risk expulsion. Thus the wealth of the Jews was kept under strict control. As soon as a Jew became rich, he had to turn over a good portion of his wealth to the *Landvogt*.

There were many other injustices. When a Jew traveled beyond the borders of Lengnau, as he was often compelled to do to earn a living, he had to pay a special "Jew toll." The army of the Swiss Confederation did not accept Jews; nevertheless, a Jew had to pay a special fee for the privilege of not serving in the army.

To add insult to insult, few occupations were open to the Surbtal Jews to earn a living. They could be moneylenders, peddlers, grocers, tailors, but little else. They could not be doctors or professors. They could deal in money but they were not allowed to mine or smelt the metals coins were made from. Most of them were peddlers, who left their homes Sunday afternoons and traveled throughout Baden and the other cantons during the week, accumulating guldens and paying them out in Jew tolls and special peddling taxes, and then returning home Friday evenings with what was left. Often they were beaten by Christians as they traveled through the villages peddling their wares. And sometimes when they returned to Lengnau after weeks of travel, they would find that Christian mobs had plundered and burned their homes. These last outrages did not go unpunished, however. They would so disturb the *Landvogt*, accustomed as he was to reap such handsome profits from renewing the "Safe Conduct and Patronage Letters" of "his Jews," that he would exact heavy fines from the guilty Christians and thereby reap a double profit.

Other indignities. The *Landvogt's* charter of 1760 to the Surbtal Jews required that the Jews "should not marry nor allow marriages between poor persons," and that "all Jewish brides coming into this country must bring a dowry of at least 500 guldens" (a portion of which would then be taxed). The same charter also stipulated that the Jews of Lengnau be denied the right to burial within the community (they had to maintain a cemetery outside the village limits), and that a Jew must sell any property he owned to a Christian any-time a firm offer was made.

For well over a century the Guggenheims of Lengnau suffered these injustices and indignities, accumulating resentment upon resentment, frustration upon frustration. But these resentments and frustrations may have been nothing compared to those they had experienced in Germany, before they came to Switzerland.

During the first millennium of the Christian era, when the Christian movement was still in its infancy, the Jews of Europe were not per-secuted to any significant extent. It was not until the Church orga-nized the vast proselytizing campaign that resulted first in the Cru-sades, next in the subjugation of all Europe, that the Jews began to suffer persecution. Christian soldiers returned from the Holy Land filled with hatred against the Jews who had killed their Christ. The expanding Church saw the Jews as a threat to its ever-increasing authority.

(Only for a brief period, in the thirteenth century, under the ex-traordinarily enlightened reign of Emperor Frederick II of Hohen-staufen, who, among his many benefactions, established a center of Hebrew studies at the University of Naples, did the Jews escape widespread persecution during the Middle Ages.)

It is assumed, but it has never been proved, and probably never will be, that the Guggenheims of Lengnau, and later of Philadelphia and New York, originally came from the village of Guggenheimb, now Jugenheim, in northwestern Bavaria, a hilly, densely forested area that has long been known as excellent country for hunting quail, deer, hare, and wild boar, and is the ancestral home of the Battenberg family, progenitors of Prince Philip, Duke of Edinburgh. The sup-position that America's greatest Jewish family originally came from this small south German town rests upon the undisputed fact that Jews in Germany were not given surnames during the Middle Ages and, in the Renaissance, when they were required to have them, they were forced to take the name of the town in which they lived. Firm proof, however, remains impossible since the records of the births, deaths, and marriages of Jews in Guggenheimb have long since been destroyed by zealous Christians.

Assuming, though, that the Guggenheims originally came from Guggenheimb, it may be further assumed that throughout their resi-dence there they had to endure periodic humiliations simply because they were Jews.

When Pope Eugenius III launched the Second Crusade in the

twelfth century, his missionaries' eloquence led thousands of Christian peasants and landless persons in Germany to attack Jews and burn down their synagogues.

When the Black Death invaded Germany in the mid-fourteenth century, many Christians blamed the pestilence on the Jews—they had "poisoned the wells," they had "bribed the devil"—and took revenge by torturing and murdering them.

Often a German potentate would literally pawn the Jews in his realm to raise funds:

> We, Ludwig of Bavaria, announce that we are selling to the noble Jean of Rappoldsheim, the imperial Jews of Ribeauville for 400 marks silver, for which sum the Jews are to belong to him and his heirs, to enjoy them in accordance with the rights attached to this privilege, until the day when we or our successors in the Empire have returned to the said noble or his heirs the said sum of 400 marks.

During the Thirty Years' War which ravaged Europe between 1618 and 1648—the great struggle between Protestantism and Catholicism that finally resulted in a Protestant industrial North and a Catholic agrarian South—the Jews were caught in the middle and were alternately wooed, plundered, consulted, tortured, and killed by both sides.

Most likely it was during the savagery of the Thirty Years' War— surely one of the bitterest and bloodiest wars in all history—that the Guggenheims of Guggenheimb emigrated to then-safer Switzerland. Where they first settled in Switzerland is not known. All that is known is that by 1696 they had ended up in the ghetto village of Lengnau in the gentle valley of the Surb.

For it is in the year 1696 that the name Guggenheim first appears in the official documents of Baden in the form of an entry referring to "der Jud Maran Guggenheimb von Lengnau."

Whether Maran Guggenheimb is a bona fide ancestor of the American Guggenheims is open to question. More than likely he was, for in 1702 a certain Jacob Guggenheim, authenticated ancestor of the American branch, was brought to court for illegally owning the house of Maran Guggenheimb and owning, as well, with his brother Samuel, a vineyard on Wettinger Hill, just outside the village. Later in 1702 a mob of Christians burned down Jacob Guggenheim's house.

Jacob Guggenheim, it appears, was a leader in the Jewish community of Lengnau. He was a *parnas*, or elder, of the Lengnau synagogue, and was considered a genuine *lambden*, or scholar, of Hebrew studies. When the Lengnau ghetto's charter expired in 1732, Jacob Guggenheim and one Raphael Pickert were selected by the approximately 250 Jewish families of the Surb valley to testify on their behalf before the Diet of the Swiss Confederation in Zurich. There was danger that, reacting to ever-mounting Christian pressure, the *Landvogt* might expel all the Jews from the two Surbtal communities.

Jacob Guggenheim had to resort to blatant flattery and submit to equally blatant blackmail to save himself and his fellow Jews from expulsion. Once before the Diet, he praised the *Landvogt* extravagantly and finally gave in to what the *Landvogt* wanted all along, a much higher price for "his Jews" to remain in the Lengnau ghetto.

Not long after these events, one of Jacob's sons, Joseph Guggenheim, was involved in a controversy which, for a while, was discussed all over Switzerland.

Jacob had sent Joseph to a Talmudic school in Metz, in Alsace, and while he was there he was invited to Zurich by one Johann Caspar Ulrich, a Protestant pastor who had met Jacob when he had spoken so eloquently before the Swiss Diet. Pastor Ulrich, a Christian of missionary zeal, attempted to convert Joseph Guggenheim to Christianity, and, after many vicissitudes, including two nervous breakdowns on the part of Joseph, succeeded, much to the outrage of Jacob and the entire Jewish community of Switzerland. For his heresy the Guggenheims of Lengnau subsequently struck him from the family's rolls. (Joseph, unknowingly, thus became the herald of things to come, the first of many Guggenheims, stretching to the present day, who renounced Judaism in favor of Christianity.)

Jacob was so enraged over his son's conversion that he was led into direct confrontation with Pastor Ulrich and the Christians of Switzerland. After endless debates, reported widely in the journals of the day, the *Landvogt* demanded that Jacob be compelled to purchase the privilege of remaining in Lengnau for 600 florins, a considerable sum in those times. Jacob paid the toll.

One of Jacob's sons was Isaac Guggenheim, who, by 1800, had become the richest Jew in Lengnau. Isaac, a pitiless moneylender all his life, known as "Old Icicle," was a patriarchal figure in the Lengnau ghetto. Solemn, taciturn, bearded, habitually wearing skullcap and caftan, he ruled unofficially over both the Jews of the village and the Guggenheim family. When he died in 1807 at the age of eighty-four, he left an estate valued at 25,000 florins. The estate, one of the largest left by any Jew in Lengnau, consisted of an immense trunk of coins and goods Old Icicle had accepted as collateral on loans. Among these were 830 gold and silver coins, 72 plates, a mortar, a frying pan, 2 kneading pans, a Sabbath lamp, a brass coffee pot, 19 sheets, 15 towels, 8 nightshirts, and a child's potty.

Isaac Guggenheim's oldest son and principal heir was Meyer, who married a German woman, a certain Fraulein Vogel from Gailengen, in 1775. Meyer and his wife had eight children, one of whom, Samuel, is commemorated in the Partners' Room at Guggenheim Brothers in New York for having rescued a child from a fire, and another of whom, Simon, at age fifty-five was to leave Lengnau with his son, Meyer, to begin the Guggenheims' grand adventure in America.

By the time Simon began working as a tailor in house No. 64 by the Surb, the fortune that his grandfather, Old Icicle, had accumulated had dwindled to very little and the Guggenheim family had to rely wholly on Simon's meager earnings to survive.

Thirty years later, in 1847, Simon's economic position was little better than it had been when he first began tailoring. His wife, Schäfeli Levinger, had died in 1836 and so he had had to raise his son, Meyer, and five daughters alone. Young Meyer, now twenty, worked as a peddler, traveling through Switzerland and Germany, but the daughters were a burden. They would not be permitted to marry in Lengnau unless they were provided with sufficient dowries.

Even fifty-five-year-old Simon himself was not allowed to marry in Lengnau. He had become attached to a forty-one-year-old widow, Rachel Weil Meyer, who had three sons and four daughters. But though she possessed some money, and Simon did own his own shop and furnishings, Simon was not able to convince the Christian authorities of Lengnau that they had enough money to marry.

Simon's frustrations were so great that he and Rachel were compelled to take desperate action. They decided to pool their limited resources and take themselves and their children to America. By that time word had come back to Lengnau from other emigrants that there were no ghettos in America and no proscriptive laws against Jews.

It was an enormous step for a fifty-five-year-old widower and a forty-one-year-old widow who had both spent over half their lives in a tiny Swiss village to take, but they took it. Simon sold his little house and shop by the Surb, and, pooling his resources with Rachel's, traveled with twelve of their children to Coblenz on the Rhine. From there they went by riverboat to Hamburg and from Hamburg they took a sailing ship to Philadelphia.

Once in America, the Guggenheims, like thousands of other European immigrants from oppressed classes, would take their unconscious revenge against the ruling class of their native land. Without individualizing their former oppressors in their minds, they would nevertheless show the *Landvogt* of Baden, the Diet of the Swiss Confederation, the stuffy, moralistic Christians of the valley of the Surb what kind of people they had prevented from marrying, from owning land, from freely choosing a profession, from accumulating capital, from living where they wanted to, from mining and smelting silver and gold. And what is more they would show them on a global scale. They would live in grander and more magnificent palaces than the *Landvogt*'s. They would own properties larger than the entire valley of the Surb. They would not have to plead for their lives before diets; they would serve in the Senate of their new country's confederation. They would not only mine and smelt metals used in coins, they would own and operate the largest and richest silver, copper, and gold mines in the world. And as they progressed in their adopted country they would acquire riches and honors and splendors so vast as to make the self-satisfied Christians of Lengnau look like beggars, slaves.

So tightly did the centuries of restriction, repression, and persecution of the Jews wind the spring of Guggenheim ambition that it would take many a generation before the spring would wind down, the momentum give out. And then, even in the family's twilight, there would still be bursts of energy, flashes of talent, such as few of the good Christian burghers of Baden had ever known, or imagined.

CHAPTER

2

THE HAVEN CITY

IT TOOK OVER TWO MONTHS FOR THE SHIP ON WHICH THE GUGGEN-
heims and the Meyers sailed from Hamburg to reach Philadelphia.
Years later Meyer Guggenheim would tell his children about the un-
believably crowded conditions below decks. There was little or no
privacy. At night the steerage passengers huddled against one another
in rat-infested holds. For sustenance there was only hardtack, dried
fruit, fish, and strictly rationed wine and water.

But, Meyer would add with a twinkle, these discomforts and priva-
tions scarcely bothered him, for it was during the voyage that he fell
in love with fifteen-year-old Barbara Meyer. For Meyer and Barbara
the long days passed quickly. They used all their ingenuity to find
ways of being together, away from the other passengers and away
from the prying eyes of their families. By the time they sailed up the
Delaware River they had decided to get married, once Meyer had
enough money.

First, however, it was Father Simon's and Mother Rachel's turn
to marry. The ceremony was performed shortly after arrival and then
the combined family—fourteen persons in all—settled down in a
rented house in a nameless laborers' district, probably little more
than a slum, outside Philadelphia.

The year was 1848. James K. Polk was President. Most of the recently expanded nation he presided over was still undeveloped and
unsettled. The continent's thick forests, brawling streams, wild, lonely
mountains were still unscarred and undefiled. The United States, victors in a two-year trumped-up war, had just swindled Mexico out of

largely untouched California, Nevada, Colorado, Arizona, Utah, and New Mexico. In the two years prior to the Mexican War the U.S. had annexed Texas and acquired the Oregon Territory. "Manifest Destiny" it was called. The Gold Rush was just beginning. The Indians had not yet been exterminated. Women could not yet vote. Blacks were still enslaved.

Few of the great American families, whose ranks the Guggenheims would join in the twentieth century, had yet attained wealth and influence by 1848. Patrick Kennedy, great-grandfather of John F. Kennedy, had arrived on Noddle's Island, Boston Harbor, only one year before and was still as poor, if not poorer, than he had been in famished Ireland. The forebears of Henry Ford had arrived fifteen years before, also from Ireland, and were still humble dirt farmers. John D. Rockefeller, son of a New York trader, was only nine years old. Only the Astors, Du Ponts, and Vanderbilts were already on their way to great riches.

The Philadelphia to which the Guggenheims came in 1848 was one of America's most attractive and tolerant cities. Founded by William Penn toward the end of the seventeenth century, as a "haven of refuge for persecuted people who chose to be guided by the inner light of conscience," part of the "Holy Experiment" of Pennsylvania, it had been the capital of the colonies during the revolutionary period, the capital of the United States from 1790 to 1800, and was now the financial center of the seventy-two-year-old nation, though it would soon yield this last distinction to New York.

The founders of Philadelphia had laid the city out on what was thought to be the plan of ancient Babylon. William Penn had declared that he wanted it to be a "greene countrie towne . . . always wholesome." When the Guggenheims arrived the city still lived up to its original conception. The red-brick-paved streets, bordered by trees, were laid out on a symmetrical grid. Most of the houses were of red brick with white, gray, green, or red shutters and had small gardens in back. The principal public buildings, like Independence Hall, were also of red brick and were usually surrounded by spacious parks.

Socially, Philadelphia was far from democratic in 1848. The city had a reputation for being tolerant to newcomers, but that was about all. Wealth and social standing were concentrated in a very small fraction of the city's 100,000 inhabitants, and were limited to Christians of northern European origins, excluding Ireland. There were about 2,500 Jews living in the city at the time, out of about 50,000 living in the entire country. There was no ghetto, but the Guggenheims, as Jews, however free they were to make money, could never hope to enter the closed world of Philadelphia society—still the most hermetic in America—no matter how much money they earned.

As soon as they were settled domestically, Simon and Meyer went to work as peddlers. Most housewives in Philadelphia in those days bought their household goods from door-to-door salesmen, rather than make the trip into the center of town to buy at the dry-goods store. Peddling seemed to Simon and Meyer the quickest and surest way to accumulate some money. Setting up shop as tailors would require capital, of which they had none, and acquiring a clientele would take too much time.

And so the fifty-six-year-old Simon began peddling on the streets of Philadelphia and the twenty-one-year-old Meyer began peddling in the more arduous, but more lucrative, Pennsylvania anthracite country.

Simon would come home every day, but Meyer would remain away all week, leaving every Sunday with his backpack full and not returning until the celebration of the Sabbath, which began with a family meal Friday evening. Father and son peddled a bit of everything: shoestrings, lace, stove and furniture polish, ribbon, pins, spices, needles.

Meyer's German stood him in good stead with the Pennsylvania Dutch. He soon built up a solid clientele of coal miners' wives and their local suppliers, and a few Pennsylvania farmers. He did not have to pay a Jew toll coming and going from Philadelphia and, though he must have met with endless indignities and discomforts, he prospered. Simon prospered too, but he had more competition than Meyer: There were swarms of foot peddlers on the streets of Philadelphia, most of whom were younger than he.

For some reason, probably because the iron coal-burning range had only recently superseded the kitchen fireplace, Meyer's best-selling item in his backpack became stove polish. Sales of stove polish were most satisfying, but it did not take long for Meyer to realize that while he made only one or two pennies out of each can sold, the manufacturer was making thousands of dollars out of the innumerable cans *he* sold. With the mixture of intrepidity and good judgment that was to guide him to commercial success after commercial success all his life, young Meyer decided to manufacture his most popular item as well as sell it. Forthwith he traveled to a German chemist in Bethlehem, who analyzed the formula of the polish Meyer was selling and instructed him how to make it. Not long afterward Meyer discovered a way of making stove polish that would not leave a residue of black lead on a housewife's hands, and, not long after that, Simon was staying home making the polish with a secondhand sausage-stuffing machine and Meyer was out selling it. Soon Meyer was making eight cents profit on a can rather than a penny. The Guggenheim stove polish business was established.

But Meyer, all through his life, was never willing to rest on the laurels of success in one line of business. No sooner did he succeed in one venture than he would attempt another.

And so as soon as he began making good money out of manufacturing and selling stove polish, he plunged into something else. This time it was selling essence of coffee.

Coffee in 1848 was a rich man's drink. People of modest means could not afford it. However, by using the cheapest coffee beans available, distilling an essence from them, then mixing that essence with certain flavoring agents such as chicory, a product could be obtained which, when mixed with hot water—like instant coffee today—would make a cheap coffee drink that was strong enough and had a tolerable taste.

One of Meyer's stepbrothers, Lehman Meyer, had been manufacturing coffee essence alongside Simon and his sausage-stuffing stove polish machine, but it was not selling as briskly as it should. Meyer added coffee essence to his stove polish line and the coffee essence sold very well indeed, for Meyer was a master salesman.

By 1852, four years after his arrival in the United States, Meyer Guggenheim had made enough money from stove polish and coffee essence, and was well-enough established in both businesses, to be able to marry his beloved Barbara.

The marriage was celebrated at Keneseth Israel Synagogue in downtown Philadelphia and then the couple left Simon and Rachel's ménage and went to live in a rented house by themselves. Meyer was twenty-four, Barbara was nineteen. Together they would found one of the greatest industrial dynasties of modern times.

3

ROASTED PIGEONS DO NOT FLY INTO ONE'S MOUTH

ONCE MEYER AND BARBARA HAD SETTLED DOWN TO MARRIED LIFE, Simon and Rachel gradually faded out of the Guggenheim picture. In time their other children married and produced children whose descendants' modest lives would stand out in sharp contrast to the splendor in which Meyer and Barbara's progeny would live. Simon died in 1869 at seventy-six, a worn-out but presumably contented man. He had accomplished his principal objective of giving his children and stepchildren a new start in a new world, and by 1869 there were eight grandsons to carry on the family name. When Rachel died is not known: The records are mute; she may even have returned to Switzerland.

During Simon's declining years Meyer gradually assumed the center of the Guggenheim stage and would hold it until his death in 1905.

"It is not observed in history that families improve with time," wrote George William Curtis, the American historian and essayist, in 1887. "It is rather discovered that the whole matter is like a comet, of which the brightest part is the head; and the tail, although long and luminous, is gradually shaded into obscurity."

It may well be that Meyer, incandescent head of the comet Guggenheim, was the ablest and most extraordinary Guggenheim of them all, never to be surpassed, at least in such virtues as imagination, daring, cleverness, perseverance, industry, courage, energy, faith. Some of his children and their descendants possessed extraordinary

qualities—qualities Meyer never had the time or education to acquire
—and were able to devote themselves to more rarefied and noble activities than merely making money, but they all started their lives with
substantial privileges and inheritances. Meyer had started with nothing but his native gifts.

Meyer Guggenheim was a caricature of the nineteenth-century Jew.
He was a small, reticent, suspicious loner with long, curly brown
hair, long rabbinical whiskers, and a beard. When he became prosperous, he always wore a long, black frock coat (perpetually flecked
with cigar ashes) and a floppy, wide-brimmed black hat. He was
single-mindedly devoted to making money. Contemporaries observed
that his love of money bordered on the pathological. It has been said
that no American multimillionaire started out quite so humbly as
Meyer Guggenheim (at first he was really little more than a beggar)
and no one, not even his near contemporary, John D. Rockefeller,
pursued wealth quite so obsessively.

Physically Meyer was not particularly prepossessing or impressive:
a short, slender build, slightly stooped from years of trudging through
Switzerland, Germany, and Pennsylvania with a heavy pack on his
back; a longish, triangular face, refined in its contours, and with
lively, slightly humorous brown eyes, but with a heavy, potato nose
(which was to reappear in nearly all his descendants), and very full
lips; a kindliness in his overall expression, especially as he grew older,
but also a coldness, at times a terrible coldness. Meyer Guggenheim
was capable of love—on occasion—and pleasure—he enjoyed music,
fresh shellfish, and cold white wine—but no one, *no one* would ever
put one over on him.

Other characteristics. He was, according to a son, "taciturn by
nature," "he wasted few words," and "kept his own counsel." Generally he shrank from wide public contact and had no appetite for
large groups of people, especially great crowds. Infinitely wary, wary
to the point of paranoia, he trusted the motives of no one outside his
family. He was always on the alert for an ulterior purpose on the
part of both friend and foe. The reverse side of every proposition
had to be examined carefully for its lurking peril. Every promise
carried a concealed menace.

It was a cardinal point of Meyer Guggenheim's creed—conditioned
by centuries of oppression and tyranny in Germany and Switzerland
—that safety and happiness in this world lay only in money. It was
a harsh, dog-eat-dog world and only money could protect you from
being devoured or swept away. Thus, acquiring money, more and

more money, became to him a kind of consecration to the exclusion of all other concerns. A vigilant opportunist, he remained ever on the alert for every chance that might come his way. "Roasted pigeons," he never tired of repeating, "do not fly into one's mouth." You must shoot the birds first, then roast them, before you can eat them. For Meyer it was no sacrilege to do business on the Sabbath. On the contrary, he would work hard every Saturday of his life. Some of his best pigeons flew his way on the Sabbath, when his rivals were at rest with their guns across their laps. Business was the very breath of his life, his very being. It was Meyer Guggenheim and his family against the world, with no quarter asked and no mercy expected from either side. "He kept books of small, neat figures," one of his sons was to write in 1934, "and knew that every change he had made had improved his financial status, had moved him a little nearer to his goal." Tenacious and daring in earning money, he was correspondingly cautious in spending it. Deep down he always remained a Swiss penny pincher. Every penny, so hard won, should be spent reluctantly, prudently. Except to earn more money. Investment was another matter. Spend only to earn, then and only then could one spend lavishly, recklessly.

And what of Barbara? From all accounts Barbara Meyer was the perfect complement to Meyer Guggenheim. In the early days she was the eager confidante and supporter of all his hopes. Later, after the children were born, "her every energy and thought was bent toward making agreeable the lives for which she was responsible." Joyously dedicated throughout her long life to her house, her husband, and her children, she took little interest in Meyer's business affairs, less interest in public affairs, and never sought to rival her husband or challenge him in anything. He was supreme in his role as head of the family and chief provider. She was supreme in her role as head of the household and loving wife and mother. Being "liberated" from the home and from household chores would have seemed like utter madness to her. There is no question that Meyer's phenomenal potency as a man—as a father, and as a provider—was immeasurably enhanced by his wife's full acceptance of her essentially passive maternal role.

Barbara Guggenheim was a pleasant-looking, but not beautiful, woman. The shape of her head and the cast of her features were heavy, Germanic. More than likely there was a strong dose of German blood in her veins, as there undoubtedly was also in Meyer's. She had a variation of the same potato nose as her husband. She was inclined toward plumpness. As a girl and young woman she had lovely, long auburn hair and unusually fair skin. Her brown-and-gray eyes were warm and benevolent.

If marriage was life's supreme business to Barbara, charity was life's next most important concern. All her life she denied herself personal indulgences and gave liberally to the poor. In the words of a son, "charity was as natural to Barbara Guggenheim as industry was to her husband. If he laid the foundation for the future world-wide Guggenheim business enterprises, as certainly did she sow the seeds that would one day grow into the equally widespread Guggenheim philanthropies."

As Meyer prospered, he and Barbara moved to a small house at 443 Green Lane in the suburb of Roxborough. Here Meyer opened a grocery store and in 1854 Barbara presented him with their first son, whom they named, prophetically, Isaac, after the wealthiest of Meyer's Swiss forebears. Three more sons followed in rapid succession, Daniel in 1856, Murry in 1858, and Solomon in 1861.

When the Civil War broke out, Meyer—still operating his grocery store and conducting his stove polish and coffee essence business—began speculating successfully in clothing items and foodstuffs—shoe pegs and mustard seeds, among other things—needed by the Army of the Potomac. Meyer himself never went to war. True to his creed, he made money from the war.

So successful, in fact, was he in making money from the war, that he was able to accumulate enough capital to become a major whole-sale merchant of spices, his next business.

Meanwhile, four more children were added to his responsibilities. Jeannette, his first girl, was born in 1863, Benjamin in 1865, and twin sons, Simon and Robert, in 1867. Meyer was only thirty-nine and Barbara thirty-four, and they already had seven sons and a daughter. But they were far from finished. After the twins were born, they moved to a better house on Franklin Street in Philadelphia, and promptly had three more children, William in 1868, Rose in 1871, and Cora in 1873. Twice more they moved, always to more fashionable addresses: first to North Seventeenth Street and finally to North Sixteenth Street.

By 1873, Meyer, at forty-five, was a prosperous wholesale spice merchant, with little reason to venture into something new. Nevertheless, in that year he went into still another business, the manufacture of lye. Housewives in those days made their own soap out of lye from wood ashes and fat derived from home butchering. Why not manufacture lye and thus produce another household necessity? There might be good money to be made in such a venture. Roasted pigeons do not fly into one's mouth, however, and so Meyer, with characteristic resourcefulness and ingenuity, quickly bought up certain patent rights that were going begging, bought a small factory, and soon was putting a new product on the market cheaply and in large quantities, under the name of the American Concentrated Lye Company.

Before long, however, the Pennsylvania Salt Company, which also sought to manufacture lye, brought suit against Meyer for what they claimed was patent infringement. After a sharp battle, the courts sustained Guggenheim. Frustrated, Pennsylvania Salt offered to buy Meyer out. For a while Meyer played hard to get. Then he sold his American Concentrated Lye for $150,000 and promptly retired from the lye business forever.

Soon more pigeons fit for roasting flew his way. He realized that railroads represented the most lucrative investment of the day. Someone gave him a tip on the Hannibal and St. Joseph Railway, a small line that hauled freight in and out of booming Kansas City, and which the financier Jay Gould was interested in. The company was in trouble, earnings were dropping, dividends were being passed, the stock had slumped to twenty dollars a share. Owners of the stock had begun to dump. Meyer bought as they dumped and came up with 2,000 shares.

Meanwhile Meyer's tip proved genuine. Jay Gould was trying to put together a great new rail system, to be known as the Missouri Pacific. The Hannibal and St. Joseph was a necessary link in this system. Gould and his associates began buying Hannibal stock. Meyer let the titans in New York buy and buy while he held. After a while, Jay Gould, impatient to gain full control, sent a lieutenant to Philadelphia to coax Meyer into selling his shares. Meyer held. The stock continued to go up. Finally Meyer sold for the top dollar, realizing a whopping profit of $300,000.

Now Meyer had about $450,000 in capital. The stage was set for his next business: importing laces and embroideries from Saxony and Switzerland.

It was a time when women of every age *had* to adorn their petticoats, pantalets, summer dresses with rows upon rows of dainty embroidery and cutwork—what came to be known as "Hamburg edgings." By the 1870s one of Barbara's uncles in Switzerland had established a small factory for embroidering by machine. The Jews of

Switzerland had been emancipated from the ghettos and all proscriptive laws by proclamation in 1863 and were rapidly seizing opportunities everywhere in Europe. Barbara's uncle had acquired the embroidery factory, had made a success out of it, and had sent Meyer
samples, suggesting that he import the product and sell it in the
United States.

Ever quick to spot a lucrative new opportunity, Meyer entered
into partnership with one Morris Pulaski and soon the firm of Guggenheim and Pulaski, importers of fine laces and embroideries, was
flourishing.

More than flourishing. It was a gold mine. Guggenheim and Pulaski
was the first to enter the field and it held its lead. The dainty Swiss
laces and embroideries poured into Philadelphia and the profits
poured into Guggenheim and Pulaski's accounts. So much money
did Meyer make from this business that he was able to take two giant
strides into the future: move across North Sixteenth Street and buy a
horse and surrey.

Meyer's last-born son, William, writing in 1934, related how important the move across North Sixteenth Street was.

> It was one of those curious thoroughfares, inexplicably developed in
> communities all over the world, where opposing pavements take on
> quite different character . . . Trees of equal age shaded both sides;
> but there all similarity ended. The modest houses on the east looked
> enviously across to the west where they were greeted with the façades
> of more pretentious homes. Aspidistras and palms adorned the windows
> on both sides of the street; but the foliage was richer and greener, the
> curtains finer, the draperies stiffer, in those bigger houses to the west.
> One had only to stroll once along this street to realize that its narrow
> cobbled ribbon was a gulf. The Guggenheims had established their
> residence on the humbler side.

Later on in his narrative William came to the move:

> Meantime occurred an important event in the history of the Guggen-
> heims: they moved across the street! To them the significance of cross-
> ing North Sixteenth Street eclipsed either the traversal of the Atlantic
> or the transfer of their activities from Roxborough to Philadelphia.

In considering the future driving ambitions and taste for splendor
and magnificence of Meyer's sons let it never be forgotten that, even
though they became the sons of a millionaire, they were all born
and reared on the wrong side of the Philadelphia tracks.

Meyer and Barbara had brought up their children with a good

balance of discipline and indulgence. First of all, father and mother represented successfully the roles and images of male and female to their sons. Meyer was always very much the male in the household. His word was law. Infractions of the law brought the whiplash and the hairbrush beating. Money was not dispensed easily. There were no regular allowances given. A service had to be performed before money was handed out, and then the amount given would be minuscule. Barbara, on the other hand, was all-forgiving, all giving, and all loving. Her children grew to adore her, and when she died some of them were shattered. The Meyer-Barbara upbringing proved to be singularly beneficial and productive. All their seven surviving sons and three daughters grew into sexually normal adulthood, married, and had children of their own.

So far as religion was concerned, Barbara saw to it that the children were brought up in Judaism—she herself was profoundly religious—but Meyer, who wasn't at all religious, was more concerned that his children receive the best education available and so rather than send them to the Hebrew schools, which were not considered particularly good in those days, he sent them to the better Catholic day schools where, of course, they were indoctrinated in another religious viewpoint. The Guggenheims' synagogue, the Keneseth Israel, in which the Ashkenazic ritual was observed, was considered the most lax of all the synagogues in Philadelphia, and so it is safe to say that the Guggenheim children did not receive much of a grounding in the religion of their forefathers.

Though they were to become wizards in business, none of the Guggenheim boys, except William, liked school or showed any particular aptitude for schoolwork. What irked the older boys most was that the Philadelphia high schools condemned them to "useless" classical studies, when they would have much preferred a "practical" education in business.

After a while Meyer, always a shrewd judge of character, realized that none of his sons, save the studious William, would ever become much of a scholar, and so he put the oldest, Isaac, to work with an uncle (one of Barbara's brothers); sent Daniel to Switzerland, where the ghettos had been abolished, to perfect his German and study the embroidery business; sent Solomon too to Switzerland, and specifically to the Institute Concordia in Zurich, where he too was to polish his German and study business; and sent Murry also to Switzerland, to St. Gall, the embroidery center, there to study embroidery manufacture firsthand.

This left the younger seven children at home, Jeannette, Benjamin, the twins—Simon and Robert—William, Rose, and Cora. From this time on a sharp division between the older and younger Guggenheim sons, which had, in a way, always existed, was accentuated. Isaac, Daniel, Solomon, and Murry, who were destined to mastermind the Guggenheim empire one day, were trained in Europe, and in European manners and customs, while Benjamin and William and Simon, who would not play such a conspicuous role in the business, remained in America. Robert, Simon's twin, died from a fall off a horse at age eleven. The girls were eventually sent to the Sacred Heart Convent in nearby Torresdale, and then to finishing schools in Paris, to prepare them for marriages into wealthy Jewish families.

In time the older boys came home from Switzerland, full of first-hand knowledge of embroidery and lace manufacture, with their German and their manners polished, and Morris Pulaski retired from the embroidery-importing business of Guggenheim and Pulaski. Meyer then formed the firm of M. Guggenheim's Sons in 1877 (later incorporated in 1882), giving each son an equal share in the partnership. At first, only the four oldest—Isaac, Daniel, Murry, and Solomon—were qualified to work in the business, and divide its profits, but Meyer assured each of his younger sons that there would be a place in the business for them too and that they would divide the profits equally with their older brothers. This arrangement annoyed Isaac, the oldest, who had been working in Guggenheim and Pulaski for several years already, and felt that on the basis of seniority he was entitled to a greater share of the profits. But Meyer was convinced that any inequalities in the partnership would only breed discontent among the brothers and overruled Isaac's objections. "True," Meyer said, "when the younger ones first come in they are more bother than they are worth. During this period the older ones must carry the load. But in time all that changes. The day arrives when the older ones wish to retire. Then the younger ones must carry the load. Besides, let us not forget the wives! If the wife of one partner hears that the partner-husband of another is making more money, trouble follows."

One day, to emphasize his point, so the story goes, Meyer gathered his seven sons around a long mahogany table in his office, and, after a brief pause, gave each a stick. He then told them to break the sticks and they did as he told them. Another pause, then he produced a bundle of seven sticks held together by a band, and asked each son to break the bundle. The bundle was passed around. None of the sons was able to break it.

"You see, my boys," Meyer said, "singly the sticks are easily broken, together they cannot be broken. So it is with you. Together you are invincible. Singly, each of you may be easily broken. Stay together, my sons, and the world will be yours. Break up and you will lose everything."

It was a lesson five of the brothers were to heed to extraordinary advantage. The two who did not heed it, or who were perhaps obstructed from heeding it by the others, were to have radically different destinies.

And so by the late 1870s M. Guggenheim's Sons, importers of fine laces and embroideries, was firmly founded, with four sons in the business and three more about to join. The business thrived, as did Meyer's other concerns, for he remained also an importer of spices, a dry-goods merchant, and a stove polish manufacturer. By 1879 Meyer Guggenheim, at fifty-one, thirty-two years after leaving the Lengnau ghetto, was a near-millionaire: He had, perhaps, around $800,000. The Guggenheim family was well established in its adopted country and again Meyer had every justification to simply sit back on his laurels and let the money pour in. But, as it turned out, the Guggenheims were only just beginning their extraordinary climb to dynasty and empire. None of them, however, was even remotely aware of this, for in that prosperous year of 1879 there was still nothing on the Guggenheim horizon that even barely hinted at the immense riches to come.

CHAPTER

4

BONANZA IN COLORADO

A SINGLE, SUDDEN DECISION, TAKEN IN NEARLY TOTAL IGNORANCE OF what its consequences might be, a decision, which, on its face value, was nothing short of wild speculation, was ultimately responsible for what the Guggenheims became and what they are today. Had this decision not been taken, the Guggenheims would, more than likely, have remained in Philadelphia as modestly prosperous lace and embroidery importers, and, like the descendants of Meyer and Barbara's sisters and brothers, would have remained in nearly total obscurity as well. Shakespeare's familiar lines are apt:

> There is a tide in the affairs of men,
> Which, taken at the flood, leads on to fortune;
> Omitted, all the voyage of their life
> Is bound in shallows and miseries.

Meyer Guggenheim probably did not know that the great full tide had come in his affairs when, in fact, it did come, but, knowingly or unknowingly, he took it at the flood, and, instead of shallows and miseries, he and his sons went on to victory upon victory.

The full tide came in the form of a mining speculation. In 1881 Meyer bought a one-third interest for $5,000 in two lead and silver mines, the "A.Y." and the "Minnie," in California Gulch on the outskirts of the booming mining town of Leadville, Colorado. He bought the interest from an old Quaker acquaintance, Charles D. Graham, a grocery-store owner and speculator in Western mineral lands, who had borrowed to buy his two-thirds interest and then couldn't pay half the note when it was due. The mines had been fair to middling producers, nothing extraordinary, and had so far been very expensive to operate. Leadville itself had been thriving for over a decade. By the time Meyer took his flyer with the A. Y. and the Minnie the town boasted 120 saloons, 150 gambling houses, 1 opera house, and 35 whorehouses. It even had a *Deutsch Zeitung,* which pleased Meyer no end. Famous writers and actors occasionally recited in the opera house, Oscar Wilde among them. He delighted his readers back home by reporting that in one saloon he spotted a sign reading "Please do not shoot the pianist, he is doing his best."

Meyer Guggenheim knew absolutely nothing about mining at the time he entered into his Leadville speculation. Friends, relatives, and associates, regarding mines as worthless get-rich-quick traps for the unwary, thought he had finally made a mistake.

A few weeks after he bought his interest, little Meyer, in his long frock coat, floppy hat, and muttonchops, was in California Gulch standing among a crowd of grimy miners peering down a seventy-foot shaft and listening to a stone dropped by the mine superintendent splash in the water below. The mines were flooded. To "unwater" them would cost around $25,000. Meyer's partners did not have the money. So Meyer bought out one partner, thereby obtaining control of the mines, and, with four oil-well pumps, each driven by a twenty-five-horsepower engine, began unwatering both the A. Y. and the Minnie. During the pumping he returned to Philadelphia.

After the unwatering Meyer received reports that miners were taking about fifty tons of ore a day out of the Minnie alone. This compared very favorably with the two hundred tons a month the two mines had been producing before they became flooded. But along with these reports there were also more requests for funds to effect repairs and further unwatering. Meyer sent the money, and waited hopefully for more favorable reports. There were more requests for money. Meyer paid. Before long he was growing very anxious about his investment. He had already sunk anywhere from $30,000 to $70,000 (reports vary) into the venture.

Then one warm August Friday in 1881 a telegram from Leadville arrived at Meyer's office on Front and Arch streets. Meyer was sure it was another request for funds from his superintendent. Instead the telegram announced:

RICH STRIKE FIFTEEN OUNCES SILVER
SIXTY PERCENT LEAD

It was a bonanza.

The A. Y. and the Minnie, named after the original pioneer owners, A. Y. Corman, and his wife, Minnie, who had sold their property for practically nothing, were indeed extraordinary mines. The ore in them, though highly refractory, was nevertheless found to have a higher silver content than any of their neighboring properties. In fact, they had the highest silver content of any mine in Leadville. This was due to the presence in very large quantities of pure native silver. The white metal seemed to run everywhere in the black depths of both mines. Sometimes it appeared in the form of great, twisting, silver wires. Frequently, it was spun into the shape of birds' nests. Sometimes long white wires of almost pure silver ran from nest to nest to nest, terminating in great white webs of spun metal.

Soon Meyer was earning $17,000 a month from his mines—about $100,500 a month in today's money—and he found himself a celebrity in Philadelphia. A reporter from the *Ledger* interviewed him:

"Is your mine for sale, Mr. Guggenheim?"

"No, sir, the mine it is not for sale," Meyer answered, in his thick *Schweizerdeutsch* accent. "I would not sell my share for half a million cash money. I have made a thorough investigation of the property and if what the geologists tell me is true, we could get three or four millions cash money out of the mines. I think it is better to work such a property myself than to form a company."

Meyer worked the mines himself, from his office in Philadelphia, assisted by 130 miners and supervisory personnel in Leadville, and by 1887 they had produced 9 million ounces of silver and 86,000 tons of lead. Two miners on a single twelve-hour shift could pull down enough ore from the stopes to pay all the mines' expenses for one day. The miners went on strike time and again, and time and again the strikes were broken, usually with the aid of armed state militia or hired thugs. Meyer never had much patience with striking workers. He himself had been a worker, the lowliest of workers, and he had never struck, only worked harder and harder.

By 1888 the A. Y. and the Minnie were earning Meyer about $750,000 a year. Before the mines were exhausted they would yield the Guggenheims over $15 million. And they were just the beginning of the family's mining ventures, the first tentative steps toward a worldwide empire of copper and silver and gold.

It did not take long, after the mines had become profitable, for Meyer to take his next giant step.

Quickly he realized, much to his annoyance, that the Holden Smelter at Denver, to which he sent his ore to be refined, was eating up most of his profits. The smelters were, of course, the middlemen of mining. Solution: build his own smelter; own both the raw material and the means to refine it. Accordingly Meyer sent his third-youngest son, Benjamin, to Colorado to investigate and negotiate. On Benjamin's recommendation, Meyer bought stock in the Denver smelter and together with Edward R. Holden formed a new company, which they called the Philadelphia Smelting and Refining Company. Forty-nine percent of the stock went to Holden and an associate. The remainder, with control, passed to Meyer Guggenheim. Forthwith, Meyer began building, at a cost of $500,000, a new smelter at Pueblo, Colorado. It was the first step toward the Guggenheims' control of the smelting industry in America.

Now Meyer did an extraordinary thing, which exemplified what in William's words was "his ruling passion—the advancement of his sons." He signed over his controlling share of the Philadelphia Smelting and Refining Company to the lace and embroidery importing firm of M. Guggenheim's Sons, stipulating, again in the words of William, "that the three younger brothers be admitted as equal partners in the new venture also." Once more complaints from the older brothers, who, according to William, "had begun to lose track of the fact that their places in the sun had been bought with Meyer's foresight and kindness rather than with their personal efforts." Once more Meyer remained adamant. Once more he told them that "they were like single sticks easily broken, but that bound together they could resist whatever force could be brought to bear on them." "It is my desire," he said, "and my resolution to see you so united as to assure your invincibility."

The older sons gave in, as they would always do, to Father Meyer. Benjamin and William, both in their early twenties, were then sent into field service in the new venture. Benjamin, the first Guggenheim to go to college, left Columbia University's School of Mines to become the A. Y. and Minnie's bookkeeper. William, upon graduating from the University of Pennsylvania, went to work in the assay and laboratory department of the mines and later at the family's new smelter at Pueblo. The older boys were, at first, too busy with the lace and embroidery business to hurl themselves immediately into mining and smelting. They remained behind, in Switzerland, Philadelphia, and New York, attending to various administrative matters.

Soon, however, it became apparent that the lace and embroidery business had to be gradually phased out so that Meyer and all his seven sons could concentrate wholly on mining and smelting. By then Isaac was married and had three daughters; Daniel was married and had a son, and both were working, along with the as yet unmarried Solomon, in the family's recently established New York office. Murry was still in Switzerland looking after the remnants of the embroidery business there. Simon was in Spain, acquiring some European polish and a knowledge of Spanish that would stand him in good stead when the Guggenheims invaded South America.

Meyer ordered Murry and Simon back to America and commanded all his sons to concern themselves with the new business.

What made the new concentrated deployment of M. Guggenheim's Sons so imperative was the inescapable and terrifying fact that the Guggenheims' smelter business was beginning to lose money and soon threatened to entirely wipe out Meyer's fortune. There were labor troubles. There were management troubles. The smelter workers, for instance, struck against the twelve-hour day, ore piled up in the yards, prices went down. William Guggenheim, fresh out of college, his head full of unworkable theories, was constantly quarreling with the smelter superintendents. Before long, losses from smelter operations were soaring as high as $500,000 in six months. When the Guggenheim boys assembled in New York they were aghast at what was happening. They could not believe that one of their father's enterprises could suddenly turn so sour, could threaten even to reduce them to paupers.

So alarmed did Meyer's older sons become that they began incriminating their father for going into the smelting business in the first place. What were they doing in this business they knew nothing about when they had had a perfectly sound, predictable lace and embroidery business already well established?

In response to this Meyer gathered his sons around him in M. Guggenheim's Sons' New York offices and told them to stand fast. William described the meeting:

> He was no longer young and the wealth which was being swept away was more the fruit of his labors than that of his sons. He sought to dissipate their fears and to instill in them the confidence with which he himself faced the future. He could not believe that his instinctive touch for success had failed him at last. This venture, like all others, must succeed. Very quietly he went about reassuring the doubters. The loss had been enormous: that there was no denying; but they must not be discouraged. He impressed upon them the fact that everything he pos-

sessed was back of them in this—even the A.Y. and Minnie mines would be sacrificed, if necessary, to carry on to a successful conclusion. They all knew what the mines meant to their father: to him they were the chief source not only of his income, but also of his interest in life. His offer to toss them into the scales in their support allayed the panic which had seized them and clinched the point. They began to plan again, determined that they would not be beaten in their ambitious undertaking.

Later Meyer told them that if they were content to remain just respectable lace importers, no one would ever hear of the name of Guggenheim. *He* wanted the name of Guggenheim to ring out over the whole country, over the whole world! He wanted each son, all seven, to become millionaires. They could never become millionaires selling laces all their lives. They had to go out and snatch new, ever more lucrative opportunities; they had to go out and take fortune by the throat. "Roasted pigeons do not fly into one's mouth."

Several months went by, then operations slowly began to take a turn for the better. The workers, coaxed by armed strikebreakers, agreed to remain on a twelve-hour day and went back to the furnaces. The surplus stocks of ore began to diminish. The price of silver stabilized.

It was at this time that Meyer's smelter partners, frightened at the terrible losses they had recently sustained, offered to dispose of their 49 percent interest in the Pueblo smelter to the Guggenheims. Meyer immediately furnished his sons with the money necessary to purchase this minority interest and the Philadelphia smelter at Pueblo became wholly owned by the firm of M. Guggenheim's Sons.

The Guggenheims in 1888 and 1889 then pulled up their stakes in Philadelphia and moved to New York. By this time New York had replaced Philadelphia as the financial capital of the nation and had rapidly become the nerve center of American big business. It was essential now that the Guggenheims be in the capital of American capitalism. Besides, society in Philadelphia *still* remained so exclusive that no newcomer, and certainly no Jew, could hope to get even close to it, no matter how wealthy he became. Socially, nothing had changed since Meyer arrived forty years before, nor would it ever change. Old Philadelphia families like the Biddles, the Cadwaladers, and the Ingersolls, priding themselves on being the *original* Americans, the ones who were there in the first capital from the beginning, formed a closed aristocracy. New York society was and always would be much more open. Not birth, but wealth and talent were what counted in Manhattan. Even a Jew could ascend into the social stratosphere there.

Consequently, in 1888 Meyer closed out the embroidery business, moved the last remnants of M. Guggenheim's Sons of Philadelphia to 30 Broad Street in downtown Manhattan, and the following year he and Barbara moved into a large brownstone with a garden in back on West Seventy-seventh Street opposite the American Museum of Natural History. Sons Isaac, Daniel, and Solomon already had brownstones of their own in Manhattan's West Fifties, just off Fifth Avenue. Among Daniel's near neighbors were the Astors, the Vanderbilts, and the Rockefellers.

The stage was now set for the first great test of the Guggenheim brothers' "invincibility." Meyer was getting old and would soon relinquish all responsibility for the family's mining and smelting operations to his seven sons.

CHAPTER

5

THE CONQUEST OF MEXICO

IT TOOK ONLY THREE YEARS AFTER THE COMPLETION OF THE FIRST smelter in Pueblo before the brothers Guggenheim had built up a powerful machine capable of undertaking most any mining enterprise. In the words of William, "each of the brothers was proficient in his own way and the division of labor among them followed the lines indicated by their various talents." Isaac, the oldest and most conservative, acted as treasurer, attending to bank loans and credits. Daniel, the most energetic and ambitious, became chief organizer and negotiator. "It was he who would later lead the firm out of the simple, but profitable, operating field into the more hazardous terrain of promotion and exploitation." Murry, with an inborn taste and aptitude for statistics, handled and sold the metals. Solomon, the "hearty good fellow of the family," became "the popular contact man." Benjamin had developed into an excellent operating superintendent. Simon, affable and easy-going at this as yet trouble-free point in his life, "devoted his attention to the purchase of ores and the maintenance of friendly relations with the miners." William, the kid of the family, had a technical metallurgical education from the University of Pennsylvania, and firsthand experience with the A. Y., the Minnie, and the Pueblo smelter.

Behind them all was Meyer, officially retired, but always there, guiding, counseling. And Barbara, inexhaustible source of encouragement, of compassion, of love.

Behind them, also, was luck, consistently one of the Guggenheims' closest allies. The ancient Romans had had the sense to make luck one of their chief gods. The vast temple to Fortune at Palestrina, just outside Rome, testifies to the enormous importance the Romans placed on luck. Who knows what votive offering the Guggenheims made to the deity after their Pueblo smelter veered so disastrously into the red? Whatever it was, it must have been gratifying, because precisely at the time when it appeared possible that the Guggenheims could go down in premature ruin, Congress, in the spring of 1890, passed the Sherman Silver Purchase Act and in so doing gave the Guggenheims a sudden, unexpected shot in the arm. By this act the Treasury agreed to buy 4 million ounces of silver each month. Soon the price of silver rose from 90 cents to $1.25 an ounce. And the net profits of the Pueblo smelter rose to $60,000 a month, or $500,-000 a year.

Before long it became the most profitable smelter in the West, "the A. Y. and Minnie of smelters," as William put it. With single-minded determination and unstinting energy Meyer and his boys squeezed every last penny out of both mines and smelter. They beat the railroads down on freight charges, threatening to stockpile ore and often carrying out the threat. By force of arms they evicted miners who squatted on their claims. Time and again they employed armed strikebreakers to force striking miners back to work. They fought, and won, all suits brought against them . . . by miners, workers, other mine owners, partners.

So encouraged were the Guggenheims by the successful Pueblo operation that they soon decided to take another giant step: plunge into mining and smelting in Mexico.

For some time the Guggenheims had been importing lead and silver ores from Mexico for their Pueblo smelter. The ores were metal rich and yet, thanks to peon labor, relatively cheap. But then the McKinley Tariff Act of 1890 was passed, and suddenly a heavy duty was slapped upon imported ores. The other American mine owners, the Guggenheims' competitors, had done their lobbying in Washington, and, among their fellow Christians, had found ample support. Bringing ore in from Mexico now would not be so cheap.

The Guggenheims' response to this sudden reversal of good fortune was characteristically quick and daring. Build smelters in Mexico with cheap Mexican labor and smelt Mexican ores there, not far from where they were hauled out of the Mexican earth. Profit margins could conceivably be enormous.

Accordingly, Dan and Murry made a rapid tour of Mexico, with

Meyer's blessing, but not with Barbara's (she feared bandits), and concluded that several mines should be leased or bought in the north, near Monterrey in Nuevo Leon, and a smelter built in Monterrey, and several more mines should be leased or bought in the south in Jalisco, near Aguascalientes, and a smelter built in Aguascalientes also.

The matter was discussed exhaustively at a meeting at M. Guggenheim's Sons, in their new offices at 2 Wall Street, and approved by old Meyer and all seven sons. Now all that was needed to get started was a concession from the Mexican government. It was decided that Dan should go down and obtain the concession, which would be the first of its kind, directly from the president of Mexico.

Mexico in 1890 was a desperately poor country that had been exploited for centuries by a thin upper crust of proprietors who were either Spanish-born or of Spanish descent and had consistently abused both the country's resources and its native Indian populations. It was still in a very real sense a conquered nation, even though more than 350 years had passed since Cortez and his 555 men and 16 horses had marched from Veracruz to Tenochtitlán and tricked Montezuma into surrendering his kingdom. The descendants of Cortez' soldiers and the Spanish colonists who followed them—a minute fraction of the total population—were still on top, and the Indians, vast in number and mostly destitute, still remained on the bottom. These Indians, once the proud creators of North America's only genuine native civilization, had lost everything, their leaders, their arts, their riches, their independence, their gods. By 1890 they had fallen into a chronic, sullen indolence. Those who had once been lords of the earth were now "cheap labor"—to be exploited by people like the Guggenheims.

But not only had Mexico been abused by her Spanish conquerors, she had also been abused by the Catholic Church, which came to own three-quarters of all her land, and, to add insult to injuries, had also been severely mistreated by her great neighbor to the north. In 1810 Mexico encompassed all of what is today Texas, New Mexico, Arizona, Utah, California, Nevada, and Colorado. In 1836 Texas declared and won its independence from the mother country. The remaining areas were lost to the United States at the conclusion of the U.S.-Mexican War in 1848, the same year Meyer Guggenheim had arrived in Philadelphia.

It was to this poor, unfortunate country, still oppressed by Spanish overlords and the Catholic Church, still seething with resentment against the United States, that Daniel Guggenheim went in 1890 as

a modern conquistador, bent upon subduing Mexico to the enlarge-
ment and glorification of the rising House of Guggenheim.

Porfirio Díaz was in power at the time. Part Spanish, part Mixtec
Indian, an Indian to the Indians, a Spaniard to the Spaniards, he
had taken an important part in the revolution that overthrew Emperor
Maximilian in 1867 and was now an absolute dictator. As head of
the progressive, supposedly "enlightened" *Científico* party, as opposed
to the old-line conservatives, Díaz believed that Mexico's salvation
lay in industrialization through foreign capital.

Daniel Guggenheim, at thirty-four, was a bright young man—short,
quick, intense, of medium build, dapper in dress, European in manner
—who believed with religious conviction in the essential virtue and
inevitableness of material progress, especially if such progress brought,
as a concomitant, progress to the House of Guggenheim as well. He
was also a born general, one in whom command was instinctive.
People usually did his bidding.

It was, in the end, a case of the right man meeting the right man
at the right time. What Díaz wanted, Guggenheim, and only Guggenheim, was prepared to provide. What Guggenheim wanted, Díaz, and
only Díaz, was empowered to give.

Not long after he arrived in Mexico City, Daniel Guggenheim
found himself surprisingly at home, more at home, in fact, he later
confessed to his family, than he had felt in his own country. Dan's
ten years in Europe had given him a social polish and assurance, an
appreciation of elegance that stood him in good stead in Mexico City's
aristocratic society, and benefited him much more than it had in the
rough-and-tumble, vaguely anti-Semitic society of New York. He
found himself instantly well liked by the upper-class Mexicans, who
did not consider him at all a gringo, and he took quickly to them.
Soon he was seeing everyone he had wanted to see.

He had his first meeting with Díaz in the sumptuous National
Palace on the Zócalo, in the heart of the Aztec city Cortez had conquered 369 years before. Other meetings followed and there were
dinners, banquets. By the time it was all over Dan had all he wanted
. . . and more. He had twisted the wily Díaz around his little finger.
Not only did he get the concessions for the two smelters at Monterrey
and Aguascalientes, he also received permission for the Guggenheims
to "undertake the exploration and exploitation of any mine they may
want to lease or buy in Mexico." And he got Díaz to agree to let the
machinery for all mines and smelters come in duty free. And to
exempt from state and municipal tax all capital that would be spent

in Monterrey and Aguascalientes. The agreement was signed December 12, 1890.

Upon Dan's triumphant return to New York the brothers met with Meyer and reorganized themselves into a more efficient unit. Isaac, now a quiet, ultraconservative family man of thirty-six, was assigned to look after the last remnants of the embroidery business and made treasurer of the new smelting business. Daniel, thirty-four, was unanimously chosen to oversee the entire mining and smelting business from New York and to plan future expansion. Murry, thirty-two, was made Western manager in charge of sales. Simon, twenty-three, just back from study in Spain, was made mining representative in Denver, chief buyer of ores and supplies, and chief contact man with Western miners. Benjamin, twenty-five, was put in full charge of the Pueblo smelter and William, at twenty-two, was made his assistant. It fell to Solomon, thirty, to get the Mexican venture underway. He would go forthwith to Monterrey to lease and purchase mines and build the new smelter. Then he would do the same thing at Aguascalientes.

Meyer, sixty-two at the time, could not have been more delighted with the way things had worked out. He was in total agreement with the new reorganization and in total sympathy with the new venture. Jubilantly he told his boys that *now they must have no other ambition than to control all mining and all smelting on the North American continent.*

When young Solomon Guggenheim arrived in Monterrey in 1891 to erect the town's first big smelter (there was already a small one in existence) he found a poor dusty adobe community of 25,000 inhabitants with unpaved streets, open sewers, and no hotel. It was a furnace by day and a lunar plain at night. When it rained the streets became streams of mud. During dry spells they were canyons of dust. The people, mostly Indians, lived a day-to-day existence, barely above subsistence level. Most of the time the men sat around in the plaza in their enormous, wide-brimmed hats, smoking and talking, while the women washed the family laundry in the rocky creek that spilled through the center of town. Eighty years later this sleepy community was to become Mexico's most important industrial city, boasting the country's largest steel mill and a population of over one million.

For Sol Guggenheim, Monterrey was his first great challenge, his first real opportunity to show his father and his brothers what he was made of. True, he had successfully shouldered important responsibilities before—it was he who had sold the family embroidery factories in Switzerland at St. Gall and Plauen—but these transactions were nothing compared to erecting a brand-new industry in wild and primitive Mexico.

At thirty, Sol was short, robust, active, with steady, determined eyes and a long, curled-up moustache. He had charm and manners, liked good wines and beautiful women, and was often taken by the Mexicans as a Latin, rather than a gringo, to his consistent advantage. Already he was known for his courage. Throughout his life, Sol was never afraid of anything or anybody. He used to beat up schoolboys in Zurich who teased him because he was a Jew. Years later, when Frank Lloyd Wright was planning Sol's museum in New York, Sol's daring and courage were the qualities Wright extolled most to intimates.

Before Solomon left New York the Guggenheims had organized the Compañía de La Gran Fundición Nacional Mexicana. Now, for this new company, Sol began purchasing and leasing plant sites, importing machinery, looking for ore. For days he rode over deserts, up mountains, sleeping in straw huts, eating tortillas and frijoles, combating dysentery, insects, rashes, bandits, wearing a loaded revolver in his belt. In time he purchased a site for the smelter, obtained the all-important water rights, and made the necessary railway agreements for freight and sidings. He also leased four mines, the "Cedral" for iron, the "Reforma" for lead, and the "Parena" and the "Encantada" for silver. Then he called for William to come down and supervise the actual construction of the smelter. Will said he would come if the brothers gave him the title of general manager for Mexico. They did. He came. Sol, his work done, his worth proved, returned to New York. For the next four years he would shuttle back and forth between the two countries building up the Mexican properties until they ran themselves.

William Guggenheim, the youngest, most scholarly, and most educated of the Guggenheim brothers, was a bright, mercurial, whimsical boy who looked much younger than his twenty-three years, and, in his own words, appeared "not at all semitic." He was very fond of girls. In Pueblo he had been called "Prince Billy" by the belles who hung out in the town's most popular saloon, Peppersauce Bottoms.

Once in Monterrey, Will found that the most eligible senoritas in town, full of rumors of his family's wealth, were all lying in wait for him. Will amused himself by naming the more conspicuous "plaza walkers," as he called them, after the most famous American trotting horses of the day. The most decorative, "a tall girl with elastic step and easy graceful swinging body" he called "Maude S." With customary nonchalance Will played the field as tactfully as he could, taking his pleasure and avoiding ensnarement.

All kinds of things happened that impeded the progress of the smelter but young Will overcame everything.

The heavy machinery had to come in by siding, but the Scottish engineer hired to lay the siding spent all his time at the Foreign Club drinking tequila. When Will would urge him to get to work on the siding, the Scot, who had apparently "gone native," would set down his tequila and mumble "*mañana.*" One evening Will took the engineer out, hoping, in buttering him up, to cajole him into getting to work, and the two began drinking Texas corn whiskey. Will was not much of a drinker. While the Scotsman drank on Will collapsed under the table and was carried home to his lodgings, where he remained for almost two days, "deathly sick." On the third day he got up, still feeling shaky, went out and immediately bumped into the Scot, who informed him blithely that he had completed the siding, that the corn whiskey had finally given him the necessary "inspiration."

Then there was the problem of the leaning smelter stack. After the stack had been built it began to lean, and remained leaning, at about the angle of the Tower of Pisa. Will asked the masons who had built it to go up inside and check. They refused even to go near the stack. So the intrepid Will entered the flue chamber and climbed up the inside ladder 150 feet, finally appearing at the top to the thunderous applause of the workers assembled below. He found that though the .stack was leaning, it was basically sound.

Then there was the case of the chief engineer, Van Yngling, who had aroused the jealousy of a Mexican by flirting with the Mexican's wife. Late one night the work camp awoke to horrible screams coming from Van Yngling's quarters. People went to their windows and saw "four men in sombreros and trailing sarapes disappear into the bushy undergrowth beyond." Van Yngling had been stabbed thirty-two times. After the murderers were caught, Sol Guggenheim inquired of the authorities when they would be brought to trial. "They will not be brought to trial," the police laughed. "Why not?" Sol asked. "They have been shot," was the reply.

It was all Will could do the next day to persuade the other American workers not to quit their jobs. But the eloquent Will—a master of oratory all his life—succeeded in persuading them, and the great work went on.

Then there were labor problems, of course, all of which were eventually solved by Will. For instance, the Mexican laborers, never much motivated by the work ethic, toiled for about a dollar a day. They realized that at that high wage they would only have to work a quarter as many days as they would for someone else and so that is what they did. Finally Will had to offer them free housing and low prices at a company store to keep them on the job full time. But there were stretches when even that didn't work and thugs had to be employed to herd the peons into the blazing smelters at gunpoint.

The Mexican miners, all Indians, were not easy to deal with either. They loathed work and loved tequila as much as the smelter workers. After a while the Guggenheims had to hire a private militia to keep the peons hauling ore out of the earth. Sometimes jealous local mine owners would send their militias into battle against the Guggenheims'.

But in the end, all was completed, the ore was mined and delivered, the great blast furnaces were blown in and the first plume of black smoke drifted over the Monterrey sky to the cheers of the assembled populace. In the first year of its operation the Guggenheim smelter at Monterrey paid off its entire capital investment. Old Meyer was pleased to note that whereas the Pueblo smelter's payroll was $19,200 a week, the Monterrey payroll was only $3,840.

On the basis of these encouraging results, Solomon went to Aguascalientes, where he bought the famed Tepezala copper mines, a herald of things to come, purchased a site for another smelter, and created a second company, the Gran Fundición Central Mexicana. Again Will was brought in to supervise the construction of the new smelter. Again there were problems—this time one of the engineers was shot by a Texas outlaw who was also gunning for Will—but again all went well in the end and two smelters went up, one for copper and one for lead.

By 1895 the Guggenheim smelters at Pueblo, Monterrey, and Aguascalientes were bringing in a net profit of over $1 million a year and the Guggenheim brothers had become the foremost industrial power in Mexico.

CHAPTER

6

STRUGGLE FOR POWER

DESPITE HIS SONS' SPECTACULAR SUCCESSES IN MEXICO, OLD MEYER Guggenheim was still far from satisfied. He had wanted each of his seven boys to become a multimillionaire and it was unlikely they would do so by dividing the profits of only three smelters. Furthermore, had he not told them that their ambition should be nothing less than the control of all mining and smelting in North America? They were still far from realizing that goal. Whenever he saw that grandiose ambition failing in a son, he would lecture him and, urging him to push forward, would inevitably start muttering about roasted pigeons not flying into one's mouth.

While the Guggenheims had been carving out their mining and smelting empire, other business interests had been carving out their mining and smelting empires as well. Toward the end of the century the inevitable clash between the Guggenheims and "the others" came. Meyer and his boys were quick to perceive that in this clash their great moment had arrived.

In 1889 the Guggenheims had formed the Guggenheim Exploration Company, or "Guggenex," an independent corporation whose purpose was to search for potentially profitable mines throughout the world, purchase them, develop them, and then invite public participation in them. Dan Guggenheim was made president. Before long people like King Edward VII of England were buying shares in Guggenex ventures.

At about the same time, Henry H. Rogers, an associate of William Rockefeller, and Adolph Lewisohn, an important copper producer, had formed the United Metals Selling Company, a trust formed to dominate the sale of metals in America. The success of this trust led to the formation of a still-larger trust, the American Smelting and Refining Company (later called ASARCO), a trust consisting of twenty-three different smelting concerns designed to give Rockefeller interests control of all mineral resources under the American soil. It was an era of combination. The powers in U.S. business, like J. P. Morgan and John D. Rockefeller, were against "wasteful" competition. Combination, "Morganization," as it was later called, was the solution. The Guggenheims were asked to join the new smelters' trust. They declined.

ASARCO was formed and the huge new company declared it was worth $65 million. H. H. Rogers was the company's mastermind. William Rockefeller was its chief backer. Both were determined to ruin the Guggenheims because they were trying to go it alone and because they were Jewish.

Now the Guggenheims were greatly challenged. They could compete favorably against individual mines and smelters. But could they compete successfully against this giant?

Daniel Guggenheim mulled the matter over. The more he thought about it, the more he realized that the formation of ASARCO was not so much a threat, but an opportunity, the much-longed-for opportunity for the Guggenheims to win complete control of mining and smelting in America.

Dan realized that the Guggenheims were simply too big now to be squeezed out. ASARCO had to come to terms with them. And Dan would make sure the terms would be tough. The war was on.

Dan, with Meyer solidly behind him, mobilized his brothers for the battle. And immediately there were two casualties. Ben and William defected. They were frankly frightened of such grandiose schemes, which would inevitably cause the Guggenheims to enter into partnership with outsiders. They wanted the Guggenheims' concerns to remain strictly a family business limited to family-owned properties. Meyer was deeply disturbed by the schism in the family ranks and again began talking interminably of sticks and bundles of sticks and roasted pigeons not flying into mouths. But the older brothers were not so disturbed. If Ben and Will wanted out, let them get out. That would mean less division of spoils later. And besides, Ben and Will were a couple of spoiled brats anyway, kids who had grown up when Meyer was already wealthy, kids who had been too young to remember living on the wrong side of the tracks, who had never had to be the hardheaded businessmen their older brothers always had to be.

And so now there were five Guggenheim boys against the world. As it turned out, they made an unbeatable team. As one member of the ASARCO trust later put it, "What one Guggenheim missed, another was sure to think of. As soon as you thought you were outsmarting one, another would be putting one over on *you!*"

Once again, that "tide in the affairs of men" had come to the Guggenheims. This time it had come not to Meyer, but to his boys, and specifically to Dan. And once again it was "taken at the flood."

Once again, too, luck played a vital role. In 1900 workers struck the ASARCO trust for two months. Dan quickly seized his chance. He convinced mine owners throughout the West and in Missouri and Kansas to sell their ore to the more stable and unstruck Guggenheims. He increased production, especially in Mexico. Soon the Guggenheims were flooding the world market with cheap lead and silver, driving down prices everywhere.

At the end of 1900 ASARCO profits were $3.5 million and Guggenheim profits were $3.6 million. One hundred thousand dollars more for the Guggenheims and they owned only *one-quarter* as many mines and smelters as the trust.

ASARCO shares fell. And Dan and a new associate, William Whitney, began buying up shares. Soon the Guggenheims owned a sizable chunk of ASARCO, enough, at least, to make themselves felt at stockholders' meetings, if necessary.

The Rockefeller interests, seriously worried now, made another attempt to buy out the Guggenheims. Dan said he would sell for $45 million, which was what the courts had capitalized the Guggenheim business as being worth on the basis of a net annual profit of $3.6 million.

But Dan stipulated that the trust would not receive the newly organized Guggenex, a firm with a vast potential, nor even all of the rich new Mexican properties. If the trust wanted these *they also had to take the brothers Guggenheim, the whole lot of them, and put them on the board.*

There followed months of courtroom battles, boardroom battles . . . When the smoke cleared the American Smelting and Refining Company and the Guggenheims were one. Daniel Guggenheim was chairman of the board and president. Solomon Guggenheim was treasurer. Isaac, Murry, and Simon were members of the board. William Whitney was on the board. Daniel was also chairman of the executive committee, which contained, as well, three other Guggenheims. And the Guggenheims and their allies owned 51 percent of the stock.

The Guggenheims were now firmly in control of mining and smelting in America and each of the brothers, including Ben and Will, who retained their shares in the old business, was, on paper at least, a multimillionaire.

Now, finally, Meyer could say that his life goals had been realized. Years later son William was to write of his father: "The determination that his children should have advantages which had not been available to him was the spur of his ambition, the driving force of all his efforts."

Yes, now and only now were his sons established in a business that would provide them and their heirs with substantial incomes for generations and generations and generations to come. Now and only now was he, Meyer Guggenheim, the refugee of a Jewish ghetto, assured that the name of Guggenheim was secure from all threats, that it would ring out over the world and endure down through the years as long as America itself would endure.

CHAPTER

7

THE GOOGS OF NEW YORK

WHILE THEIR SONS WERE SPORADICALLY PUTTING TOGETHER ONE OF the great industrial empires of modern times, Meyer and Barbara Guggenheim entered their last years together in the unfamiliar surroundings of New York's upper West Side.

Barbara had not wanted to move from Philadelphia, but Meyer had insisted on it, not for himself and Barbara, but for the boys. The boys had to have their parents nearby—for advice, encouragement, consolation—as they struggled to advance themselves in business.

Not that New York in the 1890s was an unattractive place, it was just unfamiliar. Barbara missed the red-brick-paved streets, the green parks and gardens, the old red brick houses of the city in which she had given birth to her eleven children. New York, however, was far from the immense, intimidating, man-dwarfing metropolis it is today. Its buildings were still constructed on a human scale and still harmonized with their natural setting. Herbert Satterlee, a son-in-law of J. P. Morgan, writing of the New York of the 1890s, observed that "New York was still a friendly, neighborly city and was a pleasant place in which to live."

What most appealed to Meyer about New York was, of course, the opportunities for making money. Opportunities to make money were almost limitless in New York in the 1890s. In the words of Oliver Wendell Holmes, the city had become "the tip of the tongue that laps up the cream of the commerce of a continent." Meyer dabbled in the stock market and lapped up shares of Tennessee Iron, American

Cotton Oil, American Tobacco, Texas and Pacific Railroad; the list was endless.

Opportunities for social advancement were also much greater than in staid old Philadelphia. Philadelphia society was one of maintenance, of status quo, whereas New York society had become one of attainment. Sidney Fisher, the Philadelphia diarist, expressed the fundamental difference in these terms:

> . . . Philadelphia, unpretending, elegant and friendly, containing many persons not rich, but few whose families have not held the same station for many generations, which circumstance has produced an air of refinement, dignity and simplicity of manner, wanting in New York. In New York wealth is the only thing that admits, and it will admit a shoe-black, poverty the only thing that excludes and it would exclude grace, wit, and worth.

To be sure, there were opportunities for some social advancement in nineteenth-century Philadelphia, but a Jew, for instance, could get only so far, and that was not nearly so far as he could get in New York. In New York a sort of Jewish aristocracy, some would prefer to label it a plutocracy, had already been formed by the 1890s. It was headed by a group of families, all of German origin, whose extraordinary ability to make money had thrust them to the pinnacle of the New York social order, to a place equal to, though separate from, the established Gentile elite. Among these families, who later came to be known as the "Crowd," were the Seligmans, the Strauses, the Goldmans, the Sachses, the Loebs, the Kuhns, the Schiffs, the Lewisohns, the Lehmans.

The Gentile elite, people like the Astors, the Vanderbilts, the Whitneys, the then-*nouveau* Rockefellers, tended to stiff-arm this emerging Jewish aristocracy, but so did the Jewish aristocracy tend to stiff-arm them.

One member of the Crowd took the trouble to describe the chief differences between the two upper classes in terms not particularly complimentary to the Gentiles, stating that the Vanderbilt-Astor people were characterized by "publicity, showiness, cruelty, and striving," whereas "ours was based only on family and a quiet enjoyment of the people we loved."

By this time the Jewish elite were still smarting from their first great slap in the face, indeed what was perhaps the first major instance of anti-Semitism in America: the celebrated Seligman-Hilton affair.

During the first century of the United States' existence the country

was expanding too rapidly and economic opportunities were too plentiful for anti-Semitism to take root. Anti-Semitism, a form of xeno-
phobia, usually appears under conditions of overcrowding, limited
opportunities, and intense competition.

But by the time of the United States' centennial, the eastern part
of the nation had become so populous and developed, and certain
Jewish and Gentile families had made so much money and had acquired such inflated opinions of themselves, that it was inevitable
they would someday come into close competition with one another
in their frantic stampede to "lap up" more and more of "the cream
of the commerce of a continent."

A year after the centennial celebration, America's most prominent
Jew, Joseph Seligman, whose niece would one day marry a Guggenheim, traveled with his family to Saratoga Springs in his private railway car for his annual summer vacation at the vast 834-room Grand
Union Hotel, then perhaps the most fashionable watering place in
the country. When he arrived at the front desk, accompanied by his
wife, children, retainers, and mountains of luggage, he was turned
away by the reception clerk, who had instructions to do so solely
because Seligman was a Jew. Seligman was infuriated. He had been
there the year before and, as the richest Jew in America, had socialized
as a financial equal with Astors, Vanderbilts, and Whitneys. He had
served his country well in the past. He had sold bonds in Europe to
finance the Union Army during the Civil War. Lincoln, who was his
friend, had offered him the post of Secretary of the Treasury and he
had declined. He had attended White House dinners at which guests
had found him jovial and amusing. His successes in Gentile society had
convinced him that prejudices against Jews had broken down and
that he could repeat in America the social triumphs of the Rothschilds
in Europe. The slap in the face at Saratoga was a severe blow to these
beliefs.

After returning to New York, Joe Seligman went promptly to court,
bringing suit against the Grand Union's owner, Judge Henry Hilton,
accusing him of violating Seligman's civil rights. Judge Hilton, in turn,
did nothing to soothe Seligman's injured feelings. On the contrary,
he released a letter to the press in which he stated:

> I know what has been done and I am fully prepared to abide by it.
> . . . As the law yet permits a man to use his property as he pleases, I
> propose exercising that blessed privilege, notwithstanding Moses and all
> his descendants may object. . . . Personally, I have no particular feel-
> ing on the subject, except probably that I don't like this class as a general

thing and don't care whether they like me or not. If they do not wish to trade with our house, I will be perfectly satisfied, nay gratified, as I believe we lose much more than we gain by their custom.

Soon the press of the entire nation took up the quarrel between the Jewish banker and the Christian hotel owner. Hilton barefacedly argued that it was "bad for business" to have Jewish residents at the hotel, since Christian "high society resented their presence." Henry Ward Beecher, the most influential Christian preacher of the day, took the Jews' side of the issue. But in the end Seligman received no satisfaction whatsoever from the courts and had to try to reconcile himself to the fact that he had only stirred up a hornet's nest of hatred and bigotry. Far from ceasing such practices, hotels stepped them up. Not long after Hilton's rebuke Austin Corbin, developer of the Long Island Railroad and the Manhattan Beach Company, forerunner of Coney Island, announced:

> We do not like the jews as a class. There are some well-behaved people among them, but as a rule they make themselves offensive to the kind of people who principally patronize our road and hotel, and I am satisfied we should be better off without than with their custom.

From then on hotel after hotel after hotel hung signs outside their gates admonishing prospective guests: WE CATER ONLY TO A GENTILE CLIENTELE.

This ugly affair represented the inauguration of blatant, outspoken anti-Semitism in America. The Gentiles, probably long nurturing resentments against the rise of Jewish population, wealth, and influence within their midst, finally joined the issue and from 1880 on Christian social and business circles became more shameless than ever in their exclusion of Jews, no matter how high their cultural or financial position.

By the time the Guggenheims had risen to prominence in New York, the Seligman-Hilton affair had been largely forgotten, but its social effects had remained and festered. There was Jewish society and Gentile society and though the twain did plenty of business together, they did not, as a rule, meet. The same applied among the *petite bourgeoisie* . . . and in between.

More than likely this state of affairs did not particularly concern Meyer Guggenheim. We know that Meyer and Barbara had few social ambitions for themselves, and could not have cared less whether they were invited to Mrs. Astor's balls or Mrs. Vanderbilt's white-gloved garden parties. Barbara was a simple, shy woman whose social life was wholly restricted to her relatives. Meyer himself never was the slightest bit interested in Society-with-a-capital-S, Jewish or Gentile.

Meyer was, as we have seen, interested only in money. Nevertheless, he and Barbara were very much interested in seeing their children marry well. "Why aim low?" Meyer would always ask. If his children were ambitious in business, they should also be ambitious in marriage.

But how could their children meet the scions of the great Jewish families of New York? Answer: at the synagogue. Not long after Meyer and Barbara arrived in New York they divested themselves of the orthodoxy of their forebears—Meyer was never very attached to Judaism anyway—and became Reformed Jews, members of the fashionable Temple Emanu-El on Fifth Avenue, the richest Jewish congregation in the world. It was here, in this citadel of Reformed Judaism, that they began to mingle with people like the Seligmans, the Schiffs, the Loebs, the Lewisohns, the Strauses.

Meyer and Barbara, however, did not cut very fashionable figures. Meyer never wore anything but a rumpled Prince Albert frock coat whose lapels, we have already noted, were perpetually white with cigar ashes, and was constantly chomping on a usually unlighted, wet cigar. He talked very little—had no small talk whatsoever—and when he did say something he revealed a pronounced tendency to utter his favorite little Swiss-German axioms, like Roasted Pigeons Do Not Fly Into One's Mouth. Barbara also spoke with a thick *Schweizerdeutsch* accent and never wore fashionable clothes.

But their sons and daughters were a different breed. True, they were not an especially handsome lot (with the exceptions of Ben and William)—they were all cursed, in varying degrees, with the Guggenheim-Meyers potato nose. Still they had acquired a gloss, a manner, lacking in their parents. Even though the Guggenheims were considered terribly *nouveau* by the other up-and-coming Jewish families, who referred to them contemptuously as "the Googs," the boys and girls were at least a cut above the cigar-chomping Meyer and that dumpy Swiss *hausfrau* of his.

It fell to the younger ones to make the most "social" marriages. Isaac and Dan were already married to nice, unpretentious, not-very-wealthy Jewish girls from Philadelphia: Carrie Sonneborn and Florence Shloss. In 1890 Dan and Florence had their second son, the future standard-bearer of the family, Harry. Murry had married a European girl, an Alsatian, Leonie Bernheim, while working in Switzerland. Simon married well enough, to Olga Hirsch, daughter of a rich New York realtor and diamond merchant. And so had Solomon, whose bride was Irene Rothschild, daughter of a prosperous New York businessman, not a relation to the great European family. But these marriages, socially speaking, were nothing compared to the marriages of Rose, Cora, and Ben. Rose Guggenheim, Meyer and Barbara's tenth child, returned from Madame Bettlesheimer's finishing school in Paris and promptly married Albert Loeb, nephew of Solomon Loeb, one of the founders of Kuhn Loeb & Company and the sponsor of the Loeb Classical Library. Cora married Louis F. Rothschild, founder-to-be of the investment banking house, L. F. Rothschild & Company, again not a relation to the European Rothschilds, but destined to approach them in wealth. And in 1895 Benjamin, aged thirty, married the socially impeccable—from the Jewish standpoint —Florette Seligman, daughter of the millionaire financier James Seligman, brother of Joseph of the Great Snub, and in so doing joined the Guggenheims to the aristocracy of New York Jewry.

By the time Dan engineered the family's great coup in gaining control of the American Smelting and Refining Company, the Guggenheims had finally made it into the inner sanctum of New York's wealthiest and most influential Jewish families. They had been accepted, with some reservations, by people like the Loebs, the Schiffs, the Kuhns, the Seligmans. They were "Googs" no longer, they had made it into the Crowd. Later Meyer's grandchildren would marry into other, even grander, Jewish families—the R. H. Macy's Strauses and the Gimbel's Gimbels—and would spread out into prominent Gentile families as well, including the British peerage.

But even though they became accepted members of New York's, and therefore the United States' Jewish elite, there was always something that set the Guggenheims slightly apart, aside from the fact that they became far richer than anyone else. For one thing, all the other families in the Crowd were German; the Guggenheims, though possibly German in the remote past, were Swiss. For another, all the other families were in either finance or merchandising. The Guggenheims—alone among the great Jewish families of America—were in heavy industry. The Guggenheims somehow sensed the differences, for, in contrast to the other princely Jewish families, they alone did not limit their social life to Jewish society. The sons' generation soon found they were quite accepted in Gentile society and came to count among their close friends people like William Whitney, Charles Lindbergh, Theodore Roosevelt, Averell Harriman. Dan's son Harry became, with relative ease, the first Jew to be admitted to the over-whelmingly WASP New York Jockey Club.

For Meyer and Barbara, however, social life in their closing years meant family and only family. Almost the only times they mingled with the Crowd were at Temple Emanu-El.

Every Friday evening the entire Guggenheim clan then present in New York would meet in the brownstone at 36 West Seventy-seventh Street for a great family dinner. The boys' wives, always in intense competition with one another, would dress up in their latest finery for the occasion, and the whole family, as many as seventeen, would sit down at a long table surrounded by ferns under an enormous, blazing crystal chandelier. If there were grandchildren present, Meyer would question them like a drill sergeant, exacting clear answers and enforcing a strict discipline. He was the grand patriarch, founder not only of a business empire, but a dynasty, and expected and received deference from everyone. These reunions did not have anything to do with religious observance. Meyer never approved of Orthodox Jewish religious observances, which, he claimed, set Jews too much apart. So far as he was concerned, anything that interfered with his and his children's becoming thoroughly assimilated into American life was to be avoided at all cost.

Meanwhile his boys had built vast and splendid palaces for themselves on a forlorn stretch of Jersey shore and Meyer would visit them during the summer months. Barbara, who had diabetes, was usually not well enough to join him.

Each of the boys had tried to outdo the other in splendor and magnificence. Daniel had built an ornate Italian *palazzo* at Elberon, a sort of Jewish Newport, though a good deal sadder and drearier than its soon-to-be-mournful Rhode Island counterpart. He named his new estate Firenze, after his wife and her favorite Italian city. Solomon, fresh from his triumphs in Mexico, had countered with a huge Victorian mansion called The Towers, after its Moorish onion domes and gables, also at Elberon. Simon put up a reproduction of a Southern Colonial mansion a la *Gone With the Wind*. And Murry, the quiet one, outdid them all with his marble reproduction, complete in every detail, of Le Petit Trianon at Versailles. Meyer would go from one establishment to another, pleased beyond words at these visible symbols of his sons' success. Yes, they had made up for those ghetto laws forbidding Jews to own property in Lengnau.

Years later, Peggy Guggenheim dismissed the whole Elberon enclave as a "dreary ghetto," which, in a sense, was what Newport was to become also.

By the turn of the century Barbara Guggenheim's health had begun to fail seriously, and she would have to retire early from those Friday-evening family gatherings that had become her chief joy in life.

On January 2, 1900, her youngest sons, Benjamin and William, temporarily forsaking the family business, sailed for a pleasure trip to Europe. Thanks to their pioneering work in Colorado and Mexico, both were multimillionaires, though only in their early thirties. Now they were going to live it up on the Continent. Forty-eight hours after their arrival in Paris they received a telegram saying that Barbara was deathly ill. Immediately they canceled all their plans and took the next ship back to New York. For a while after their return, Barbara lingered on, fighting her diabetes, in a time when there was no insulin. Then, on March 20, she died.

Her death had a shattering effect on everyone, particularly on her younger children. Rose suffered a nervous breakdown—nervous prostration it was called in those days—and remained confined to her bedroom for months. The carefree Benjamin temporarily became a recluse. The sensitive William, in his own words, "finding that consolation only intensified his anguish, kept to his room and refused to see anyone." Referring to himself in the third person, he lamented:

> He knew that she must die, and he had come face to face with death before, but not with such terribly intimacy. He realized for the first time man's ultimate helplessness. The time of mortals is limited; the termination of everyone's uncertain journey lies only with the will of God. In his bitter sorrow Will felt all foundations swept away and his soul lost.

It had been only a year before her death that Will had designed and had built the grandiose family mausoleum in Salem Fields, Jamaica, Long Island, at a cost of over $100,000, or about $635,000 today. The huge, octagonal structure, worthy of a Roman emperor and the largest in the cemetery, large enough to accommodate generations and generations and generations of Guggenheims, larger even than the neighboring Seligmans' mausoleum, was constructed of white marble in Italian neoclassical style—it has been called a free version of the Tower of the Winds in Athens—and it was to it that the Guggenheims brought their beloved Barbara on March 23, 1900. Only one member of the family had preceded her to the mausoleum, her firstborn daughter, Jeannette, who had died giving birth to a daughter in 1889.

Barbara Guggenheim had exemplified all those virtues of woman it is fashionable to minimize and deride today. She had never wanted to be anything more than a good wife and a good mother, and in these high roles she had excelled beyond anything her husband or her children demanded or expected. In the words, again, of William, the only Guggenheim son who ever bothered to write anything down, "her whole life, her whole affection, revolved about her family . . . riches did not spoil her, her graciousness and sweet unselfishness remained intact."

As a memorial to their mother, the brothers Guggenheim gave $350,000 ($50,000 each) to Mount Sinai Hospital in New York for a wing to be named after her. For his memorial, Meyer contributed $60,000 more to the $50,000 he had already given to the Jewish Hospital in Philadelphia. Will, acting apart from his other brothers, gave the United Hebrew Charities $50,000 toward a permanent endowment to be known as the Barbara Guggenheim Memorial Fund and pledged another $50,000 in matching funds for every $50,000 donated to the fund. The income was to aid poor Russian Jews, who, at the time, were beginning to pour into the United States in unprecedented numbers.

These charities, inspired by the life of Barbara Guggenheim, were the first of hundreds of individual bequests, amounting to millions upon millions of dollars, which the Guggenheims were to dispense in America and throughout the world. Barbara herself, as William pointed out, had inaugurated those charities as a young woman in Philadelphia, giving to the neighborhood poor, and, in so doing, had instilled the example and spirit of charity in her seven sons. In a very real sense, the five Guggenheim foundations flourishing today, more than 130 years after Meyer and Barbara left the Lengnau ghetto, are but one vast memorial to Barbara and her instinctive ideal and living example of what a woman should be.

CHAPTER

8

DEATH OF A PATRIARCH

AFTER BARBARA WAS LAID TO REST IN THE GREAT MAUSOLEUM at Salem Fields, Meyer returned to his brownstone on West Seventy-seventh Street, there to live out his last lonely years, visited occasionally by a son, a daughter, a grandchild, an old friend.

His principal consolations now were music, his trotting horses, the business successes of his sons.

Meyer, like most central Europeans, had always loved good music. In the early Philadelphia years he compelled each of his four oldest sons to learn a musical instrument—the cello, the violin, the piano, the flute—so that he might enjoy a little music in the evening. A miniature orchestra was thus formed and every morning at six practice began in the basement. The sounds, however, so disturbed the neighbors that after a while they sent the police in to break up the sessions. The boys were only too happy about this and the orchestra was eventually disbanded. Only Solomon, who played the cello, continued his musical studies.

In his retirement Meyer developed a particular liking for Wagner. Often he would go to Carnegie Hall to hear a Wagner overture, or to the new Metropolitan Opera House to hear *Tannhäuser, Die Meistersinger* or *Der Ring des Nibelungen.* Obviously Meyer knew little of Wagner's socialistic ideas. One wonders how he reacted to the Nibelheim scene in *Das Rheingold,* the scene in which Alberich, the dwarf mine owner—Meyer was also very short—drives his brutalized miners to dig more and more gold. No, this aspect of Wagner must have passed Meyer by. What probably appealed to Meyer

Guggenheim about Wagner was the composer's power and grandiosity, qualities which he, Meyer, was not devoid of. Strange bedfellows as they may seem, the old capitalist, who had struggled for years to erect a mining empire, was not far in spirit from the megalomaniacal composer, who had struggled an equal length of time to erect an artistic empire. And so little Meyer, sitting at the Met with a daughter or an in-law, would swiftly succumb to the splendors of the *Tannhäuser* overture, Siegfried's Rhine journey, the closing scenes from *Götterdämmerung,* recognizing these titanic strivings as his own.

Trotting horses were his other diversion. He kept a stable of them on West Seventy-seventh Street and almost every day he could be seen flying through Central Park in his barouche, cigar in mouth, muttonchops and Prince Albert coat trailing in the wind.

And, of course, there were always the diversions of the stock market. Meyer kept an office in his son-in-law Albert Loeb's Wall Street firm and there he would do a little trading and fondling of his stock certificates, which were kept in the firm's vault.

Satisfactions Meyer had in abundance during his closing years, chief of which was, of course, the growing wealth of his sons, but there were also many disappointments. One that caused him much bitterness was the disintegration of his sons' unity. When Will and Ben refused to join Guggenex and the American Smelting and Refining Company, and split from the older brothers and sailed off on their pleasure trip to Europe, the old man was sorely dismayed.

He was even more dismayed when, several months later, Will turned up married to one Grace Brown Herbert, a Gentile divorcée from California.

It is not known how or where Will met his bride. All that is known is that he married her in Hoboken on November 30, 1900, and promptly installed her in a suite at the Waldorf-Astoria, while he continued to live at home with his father, where he had established temporary quarters upon his return from Mexico. For a while he was afraid to tell Meyer. He knew the old man would be furious over the fact that Will's wife was a Gentile, a divorcée, and a *nobody.* Hadn't Meyer told his sons to aim high? But after a few weeks Will told Daniel and Daniel was just as furious as his father would have been.

Daniel took charge. He conferred with his lawyers. Then he commanded Will to go to Europe and Grace to go to North Dakota, where it was easy in those days to get a quick divorce. Dan assured Grace she could have all the money she needed after the divorce was final. Grace pleaded that she didn't want money, all she wanted was her darling Will. Finally the imperious Dan had his way, as usual. He shipped acquiescent Will off to Europe where Will promptly had an affair with a French baroness in Paris, and convinced Grace to get a Chicago divorce. The divorce was granted on March 20, 1901, and immediately thereafter the Guggenheims settled $150,000 on the divorcée, a princely sum in those days.

Old Meyer was severely shaken by the whole affair. He had been fond and proud of his youngest son, the only Guggenheim to earn a college degree, and to have him betray that opinion of him was bitter indeed. As for the divorce settlement . . . was this how his hard-earned money was going to be thrown away? Was this a portent of what was going to happen to the Guggenheim fortune?

It appeared so, for no sooner had the William Guggenheim-Grace Brown Herbert affair been settled than old Meyer himself was sued for $100,000 by a certain Hanna McNamara, a forty-five-year-old lady who claimed she had been Meyer's mistress for twenty-five years. In court she asserted that Meyer had promised to marry her after Barbara's death, then did not keep his promise. Meyer was outraged and publicly offered $10,000 to anyone who could produce convincing evidence he and Hanna were ever together. Friends and relatives went around snickering and for a while it appeared the Guggenheims would lose another $100,000 to a fortune hunter. In the end the judge threw out the case on the basis of insufficient evidence. (Later Meyer's granddaughter Peggy asserted that Hanna McNamara was definitely not his mistress; his cook was, and had been, even before Barbara's death.)

Much embittered by these underhanded assaults on his hard-won wealth, Meyer turned to causes that were dear to his Jewish heart. Alarmed when the tsarist Black Hundreds brought about the horrendous pogrom in the Kishinev ghetto early in 1903, Meyer prevailed on his business friends the Whitneys to get Grover Cleveland to speak at a Carnegie Hall protest rally. Over $100,000 was pledged at the rally to help the Kishinev Jews.

Then, in 1904, he began to fail. He had prostate trouble and other old men's ailments. He stayed at home. Doctors, friends, associates, relatives came and went. He had two operations, both in his own home: He was suspicious of hospitals. Now, while convalescing, he would reminisce about his life, about his native Lengnau, and the hard early years in Philadelphia. Yes, he had stepped on many toes, and on many heads, on his way to wealth. As had the good Christians

of the Surb valley stepped on the heads of his forefathers for generations. But he had made up for all that.

On Thanksgiving Day, 1904, Meyer underwent his final prostate
operation. All his life he had distrusted outsiders and he was not
about to develop a sudden faith in them now. He would *not* have his
operation in a hospital, a captive of all those Christians; he would
have it in his own home. This was agreed. When the surgeons suggested he take an anesthetic, he protested again, telling them there
were "two things you couldn't sell a Jew—anesthetics and life insurance," and lay back on the dining-room table to await the knife.
Agreed again. No anesthetic. As the surgeons cut in he called for a
cigar. One of his choicest was thrust in his mouth. Then, as they cut
deeper, he asked for music. The nurses put a record on the great
tubalike phonograph. Puffing on his cigar and listening to the music
—was it his favorite, Wagner?—Meyer suffered the painful operation
to the end, without losing consciousness.

His recovery was slow, however, and before long he had a bad
cold. The doctors ordered him to go to Palm Beach. He spent a few
days there at the Royal Poinciana Hotel, did not get any better, and
was then taken to a rented cottage on Lake Worth. There he died on
March 15, at seventy-eight.

The funeral at Temple Emanu-El was attended by all his children,
in-laws, and grandchildren, and by the elite of New York Jewry,
Jacob Schiff, the Kuhns, the Loebs, the Seligmans, the Strauses,
among others. Then he was buried beside Barbara in the mausoleum
at Salem Fields. There were the expected eulogies, the tributes. It
was proclaimed that he had not "built upon the prostrate forms of
others," but most people in Temple Emanu-El that day, who had
known Meyer well, and knew what the business world was all about,
knew that he could not have accomplished what he had accomplished
without injuring other men. Or, at least, without profiting from the
sufferings of others. Hadn't he made his first significant money from
the Civil War—which he had not volunteered to fight in? Wasn't it
the capital thus accumulated that enabled him to become first an
importer of spices, next a manufacturer of lye, then a speculator in
railroad shares, and finally an investor in lead and silver mines? And
had he ever shown the slightest sympathy for a mine owner or a
smelter owner he forced out of business? Or for an underpaid worker
who wanted more money, or for an overworked miner who wanted
to work fewer hours? Or for a destitute Mexican peon who was too
old or too tired to work Meyer's furnaces in 115-degree heat? No, it

is only by building on the "prostrate forms of others" that great fortunes are made. Balzac had written: "Behind every great fortune there is a crime." Perhaps, in fairness to Meyer, if Balzac had known of Meyer's career, he would have added: "But behind some great fortunes there is often sheer luck." It is reasonable to assume that without that lucky strike in Colorado, Meyer would have been importing embroideries and laces to the end of his days.

It has been observed that many men founded business empires, but not many founded business empires *and* family dynasties. Meyer founded both and in so doing is entitled to much respect. The Guggenheim epic is one of concerted family endeavor. Its only parallel in our time is the history of the Rothschilds in Europe.

Extraordinary as many of Meyer's qualities were, we must nevertheless guard against glorifying or romanticizing a type like Meyer Guggenheim. Successful as he was, his opportunistic, exploitive career was not a particularly noble form of achievement. Probably his greatest success was as a father and grandfather. His children and grandchildren, who would go on to loftier and more life-enhancing achievements than his, always spoke of him with love and respect and gratitude, and revered his memory.

Meyer's last will and testament revealed an estate of $2,256,280 in real estate and stocks and bonds held in New York State, plus the by-now nearly exhausted A. Y. and Minnie mines in Colorado, which he had been leasing for $60,000 a year. Most of his holdings in New York were in American Smelting and Refining preferred and common stock, railroad bonds, and stock in Tennessee Iron and American Tobacco. The greater part of his estate he left to his daughters, Rose Loeb and Cora Rothschild, and to Nettie Gerstle, a granddaughter by his deceased daughter, Jeannette. Eighty thousand dollars went to various Jewish charities. Nothing to speak of went to his sisters' families in Philadelphia, only a $10,000 bequest to a nephew, Leon Beyle. By then the poor relations had been largely forgotten and their tracks covered up. The A. Y. and the Minnie were left to all nine surviving children, to "share and share alike."

On the surface not an exceptionally large estate. Only $2,256,280 plus the two leased and much-depleted mines. But, in addition to what he left outright, Meyer also left seven multimillionaires, all of whom he had set up in business with substantial initial stakes. At the time of Meyer's death in 1905, his seven sons' holdings in Guggenex, M. Guggenheim's Sons, and American Smelting and Refining amounted, on paper, to no less than $75 million, or over

$9 million for each son. In terms of the dollar's purchasing power in 1905 relative to that of 1976, this would be roughly equivalent today to an aggregate of $476 million, and $68 million for each son.*

Those sons were quick to show their gratitude toward their dead father. Not long after Meyer died they donated enough money to assure the completion of a home for aged Jews that had been started, then abandoned, two years before in Lengnau.

The Schweizerisches Israelitisches Alterasyl stands on a hill overlooking Lengnau and the gentle valley of the river Surb. Today there are some fifty-six elderly Jews living there, mostly from Germany, Austria, and Switzerland, but also a few from Poland and Russia. Several are survivors of Nazi concentration camps. There is a small synagogue on the premises and most of the old people worship there every morning and evening. The building is not particularly impressive—typical institutional architecture, it could be a grade school or a small private clinic—but the overall effect, the flavor of the place, is powerful. We sense right away that this modest building has been a much-valued refuge for the helpless and the oppressed. We imagine what scenes took place there during the Nazi persecutions, when scores of aged Jews stumbled into the building only a few steps ahead of the SS.

Several portraits hang on the walls of the Alterasyl's main dining room. Some are of recent Swiss benefactors, including distant cousins of the American Guggenheims. The most conspicuous, however, are of Daniel Guggenheim, Murry Guggenheim, Solomon Guggenheim, and old Meyer.

Opposite Meyer's portrait a great window opens onto the Swiss countryside. Beyond the trees and shrubbery surrounding the building one glimpses bright green fields of lettuce and endive, rich orchards of apple and peach. Far to the right, over a succession of rolling, wooded hills, lies the Israelite cemetery, where Meyer's and Barbara's ancestors lie buried. Far below, the red-tiled roofs of Lengnau can be seen, clustered around the old synagogue, and beyond them the flashing of the river Surb.

The old ladies of the Alterasyl are well acquainted with the Guggenheims, or, at least, they think they are. "Oh, an American Guggenheim came here a year or so ago," one of them will pipe up.

---

* All dollar amounts for the years 1848 to 1974 have been converted in terms of their purchasing power in 1976 dollars calculated on the basis of the Consumer Price Index, Table 122, Handbook of Labor Statistics, U.S. Department of Labor, Government Printing Office, Washington, D.C.

"We were trying to decide then where Meyer Guggenheim's house was." "*That* was Meyer Guggenheim's house, see that rooftop on the right, near the river?" another *alte Dame* will chirp, pointing out the window. "No," another will exclaim, "I'm told it's that other one, near the bridge." "No, it's the third one over from the synagogue." Arguments. Discussions. The *alten Damen* enjoy the dispute. It gives them something to do. They soon branch out into a new argument. "Oh, what does it matter? He left here three hundred years ago!" "No, it was two hundred fifty, I read it somewhere." "You're wrong, it was only one hundred fifty, and I can tell you *he was glad to leave*." A nurse comes by and breaks it up: "Oh, *liebe Damen,* let Meyer Guggenheim's soul rest in peace."

II

LORDS OF THE EARTH

(1905-1923)

BUILDING THE
GUGGENHEIM EMPIRE

The Americans are a mighty race devoted to the pursuit of wealth with a perseverance and contempt for life which might be called heroic if such a term could be applied to any but virtuous efforts.

—Alexis de Tocqueville

Behind every great fortune there is a crime.

—Honoré Balzac

When kings build, then the carters have work to do.

—Johann von Schiller

GUGGENHEIM MINING AND SMELTING EMPIRE IN 1910

(FOR PART II)

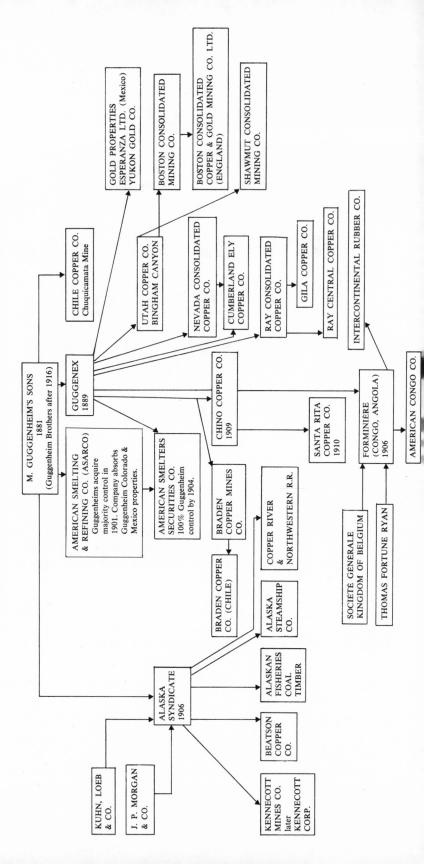

CHAPTER

1

ON THEIR OWN

BACK TO THE OFFICE. BACK TO THE MINES AND SMELTERS. ON TO Utah, Nevada, New Mexico, the Yukon, Alaska, Mexico again, the Congo, Bolivia, Chile. On to more and more copper, the first gold, more and more silver and lead, the first diamonds, the first tin, more copper, more silver, more gold.

A few days after Meyer's funeral the Guggenheim boys went back to their desks and business as usual or, rather, business with a vengeance.

Dan, as chairman and president of American Smelting and Refining, had two desks to go back to, one at ASARCO headquarters, and one upstairs in the same building, 165 Broadway, in the Partners' Room of M. Guggenheim's Sons. The two offices were connected by a secret stairway that opened on both ends to camouflaged doors of wall paneling hung with paintings. (Dan did not always want his left hand, ASARCO, to know what his right hand, the Family, was up to.) Isaac, Solomon, Murry, and Simon occupied the other desks at M. Guggenheim's Sons. There were no places in the room for the two defectors, Ben and Will.

From this dark-wood, leather-chaired stronghold in downtown New York, the Guggenheim boys ruled their ever-expanding empire.

Meyer's greatest asset, besides his own drive and brains, had been his sons. They had been his chief instrument of power. Given his paranoid nature, his business partners had to be blood relatives, people in whom he could place absolute trust, or else he could not work with them. His faithful and ever-fertile Barbara had given him no fewer than seven partners. Without them he could never have realized his grandiose ambition of dominating mining and smelting in North America.

Carefully, patiently, Meyer had groomed his boys, nurturing their abilities, tailoring their education to their inclinations, bringing them along to a sense of their high responsibilities and destinies. Proudest had he been of Daniel, Solomon, and Murry, especially Dan. These three, he knew, would never let him down. Not quite so proud had he been of Isaac. Isaac lacked a certain spunk, a certain push. Perhaps, as the eldest, too much had been expected of him. Perhaps Meyer, struggling so hard in the tough early years, had given him the hairbrush too hastily and too often. Or perhaps Isaac had been subdued too forcefully by his little upstart brother Dan, knocked, as it were, out of his rightful place as future head of the family by Dan. Whatever the case had been, Isaac, to be sure, was always there, plugging away, but he had never made much of an impact on the business, and he had always selfishly opposed the entry of the young ones into the firm, an attitude Meyer had always scorned. As for the young ones—Simon, Ben, and Will—born and brought up to easier and softer ways when Meyer had already made good money, Meyer had had high hopes for them also. When college-educated Ben and Will dropped out of the firm he could scarcely believe it, never mind accept it. But Simon was a solid, capable young man. He could always be counted on. Someday Meyer knew he would join ranks as an equal with Dan, Sol, and Murry and work hard and well for the House of Guggenheim.

And now they were on their own. Meyer was dead. No longer could the seven Guggenheim boys count on the old capitalist's advice, experience, his unflagging moral support.

Dan was quick to fill the void. Immediately upon his father's death, he assumed full and unqualified leadership of the family and its business interests. Dan, as we have seen, had already assumed the burden of family leadership even before Meyer's death—it had been he, primarily, who had forced Will to divorce his bride of a few weeks—but now he took over as absolute monarch, deferring to no one. As chairman of the board and president of ASARCO, chief operating officer of M. Guggenheim's Sons, and undisputed leader of the family, his word in matters Guggenheim was uncontested, as good as Guggengold or the tablets of Moses.

Daniel Guggenheim, destined to become one of the greatest industrial leaders of all time—his policies were to mean economic life or death to entire nations—was very short, barely over five feet, very quick and agile, very bold and adventurous, and was possessed of a truly demonic energy. His early portraits reveal an expression of such intensity—mouth set firm, eyes blazing—as to give the impression that he was always on the verge of exploding. This potential explosiveness he habitually kept under rigid control, and so, in his middle age, he suffered much from hypertension and stomach ulcers.

To call Daniel Guggenheim "Napoleonic" would appear to be laboring a cliché, but Napoleonic is precisely what he was. He was no taller than Napoleon; had Napoleon's squat, barrel-chested build; like Napoleon, his father also came from a backwater; and he was, like the Corsican, a relentless and indefatigable conqueror and empire builder, who, becoming drunker and drunker and drunker with success after success after success, finally made an enormous blunder, which almost nullified his early conquests.

Dante had written, "Rarely to the branches does human worth mount up." We have already cited William Curtis' remark that families "do not improve with time." Daniel Guggenheim's life and career contradict both dicta. He had, in the words of a contemporary, "a positive genius for big, world-wide, constructive business." He was actually superior to his father in almost every role . . . but father.

Dan, in an interview granted to the *Wall Street Journal,* asserted that "tenacity" was man's chief virtue in business. "Tenacity" was, according to him, much more important than "intelligence." By his definition "tenacity" meant, above all, a single-minded purposiveness, ruthlessly and unwaveringly pursued. In his case, this signified a veritable mania for profits, an unswerving devotion to the great god of Earnings Per Share, the Almighty Figure Below the Bottom Line.

Not long after Daniel Guggenheim took control of ASARCO he went out on a limb, not the first, and certainly not the last, he would go out on—the Guggenheims were forever going out on limbs—and hired for Guggenex a celebrated mining engineer by the name of John Hays Hammond at the then-highest salary ever paid an employee of a corporation in world history: $250,000 a year, plus a 25 percent interest in all mining properties Hammond discovered and the Guggenheims later acquired.

The year was 1903. When there were no income taxes and the dollar could purchase much more than it can today, $250,000 a year would be roughly equivalent to $1.6 million a year today, perhaps more. The 25 percent interest in properties discovered could, in terms of relative purchasing power, amount to anywhere from $12 million to $32 million a year for Hammond today. Journalists were quick to point out at the time that Hammond earned in two and a half hours what a pick miner at the A. Y. and the Minnie earned in one year.

In awarding this staggering salary and commission arrangement to Hammond, Dan Guggenheim had established a policy from which the Guggenheims would never waver: Always pay the highest salaries for the best possible talent.

Hammond's job was to comb the planet in search of rich ore bodies. By the time the Guggenheims got to him he had compiled a glittering record. He had, among his many achievements, rediscovered and reopened the fabled King Solomon's mines in Rhodesia, which he had estimated had produced over $100 million worth of gold before the industrial era, and he had been instrumental in helping Cecil Rhodes gain control of South Africa's diamonds.

Hammond was a swashbuckling character who was just as at home camping in a remote desert wilderness, accompanied by a handful of armed native guides and a pack of purposely famished watchdogs, as he was in his ten-room gilded suite at the Waldorf-Astoria, surrounded by liveried servants uncorking bottles of champagne for his girl friends and business associates. Usually he was roaming the untouched wastes of four continents on horse- and camelback. When he was in the United States he habitually traveled in his own private railway car, accompanied by a secretary, two valets, a wine steward, and a French chef.

It took only a little over a year for Dan's investment in Hammond to pay off. In his first year with Guggenex Hammond made $5 million for the Guggenheims and $1,250,000 in salary and commissions for himself.

With Hammond out scouring the earth for new, undeveloped mineral deposits, the Guggenheim boys sat at their desks in lower Manhattan, did their homework, met once a day around the great mahogany table of the Sticks and Bundle of Sticks story, made the important decisions (which had to be unanimous), and let the money flow in from every corner of the globe.

By 1907, two years after Meyer's death, the Guggenheim boys had reorganized and redeployed once more, and were poised on the verge of their period of greatest expansion. Dan, a peppy fifty-one, was in full control of American Smelting and Refining, Guggenheim Brothers, Guggenex, and the family; Isaac, the arch-conservative, now fifty-three, but looking and acting much older, had been relegated to what was essentially a bookkeeper's job, treasurer of American Smelting; Murry, a shy, rather dour man of forty-nine, and Solomon, an ebullient high-liver of forty-six, were, with Dan, but not with Isaac, members of the executive committee of American Smelting and Refining, and, with Dan again, composed the triumvirate that ran Guggenheim Brothers and Guggenex. Simon, forty, had just purchased himself a seat in the United States Senate—it was convenient to have a member of the family looking after things in Washington —and Ben, forty-two, and Will, thirty-nine, were still out of it, trying to represent something significant on their own, but not succeeding.

Ahead lay tons of gold nuggets in the Yukon River, a mountain of copper near Kennecott Creek in Alaska, a copper canyon in Bingham, Utah, mountains of tin in Bolivia, more silver and gold in Mexico, acres of diamonds in the Congo and Angola, the immense Chuquicamata copper lode in Chile.

CHAPTER

2

GUGGENMORGANS
AND MORGANHEIMS

PROSPECTORS WINDING THEIR WAY ALONG ALASKA'S KENNECOTT
Creek had first beheld the lode as a gleaming patch of green on a
treeless mountain. There, rising out of the naked Wrangell Range,
was this one, emerald-crested peak, like a mirage, the Arctic equiva-
lent of a palmless oasis in the desert. Rumors had it that the mountain
was almost solid copper.

When Dan Guggenheim got wind of this tantalizing verdigris summit he sent Guggenex' top assayer, Pope Yeatman, up to examine
the property. It took months for Yeatman to make his way through
the roadless, uncharted wilderness. After he examined the mysterious
slope, which had not one trace of vegetation on its greenish surface,
he reported that the samples of ore he had taken assayed 70 to 75
percent pure copper, and that there were millions and millions of
tons of it available. It was, in his estimation, one of the largest and
purest deposits of copper in existence. He was not wrong. The great
"Bonanza Lode" above Kennecott Creek proved to be the richest
copper deposit in the world.

To mine this treasure in that high, frozen waste, transport the ore
over two hundred miles to the sea, and then ship it to the Guggenheims' smelter at Tacoma, Washington, would, however, cost more
than even the Guggenheims could afford, or borrow. Alaska was the
last American frontier in 1907. There were no roads, no railways,
no communications of any kind to facilitate such a titanic venture.

There was only one way the Guggenheims could get control of
Kennecott copper and that was to team up with one of the reigning

titans of high finance and thereby combine Guggenheim capital, daring, and mining expertise with vast economic resources. And who else was there commensurate with such a task as developing Alaska's copper mountain than the great J. P. Morgan, the most powerful financier in American history.

John Pierpont Morgan was most decidedly not a man in the conventional American grain. He prided himself on being an imperial aristocrat, a man of lordly manner and fastidious tastes. He dressed his huge bulk very formally—stiff collar, stickpin, morning coat, pepper-and-salt trousers—and had a special fondness for rare first editions and Italian Renaissance prints. He had little respect for, or love of, the common people, the democratic way of life, the "rights" of the average American citizen. In fact, he had little but contempt for his fellow Americans. He believed in the survival of the fittest. He believed he was one of the fittest. He had *proved* he was one of the fittest, if not *the* fittest.

Daniel Guggenheim, who, at the time, was not nearly as important a businessman as J. P. Morgan, let it be known that he wanted a connection with Morgan, that he felt he and Morgan, and only he and Morgan, had it within their power and ability to attempt such a massive undertaking as the exploitation of Alaska's mineral wealth.

At the rumor of this desire there came forth one Arnold "Arctic" Bratnober, a noted mining engineer who already had twenty years under his fur hat exploring the Far North, some of it already with the Guggenheims.

Bratnober suggested to Dan Guggenheim that he pay a call on the great Morgan and suggested to Morgan that he receive Dan Guggenheim. Morgan had already let it be known that he had no love for the Jews—the "Waldorf Crowd," he called them—but the money potential in this enterprise succeeded in tempering his anti-Semitism. He agreed to discuss Alaska with Dan.

Later, in an interview in the *Wall Street Journal*, Bratnober recalled the momentous meeting:

> As we went up the steps [to the Morgan Bank] Daniel said to me: "Brat, suppose you are mistaken, or suppose Mr. Morgan has forgotten—there's a whole lot of supposes that keep me from just believing that he has really, as you say, decided in his own mind to come along with us."
>
> Darned if Dan Guggenheim—the bravest business venturer I've known—didn't seem to be really trembling. Of course the stake was stupendous. I snapped at him: "Say, Mister, if you really want to be a cold-footer,

why the devil don't you come up to Nome where we can really do our freezing. Right here, now, is our Sunshine Minute. Snap out of the icicles."

"I was only joking, Brat," Dan said, and maybe he was anyhow. I couldn't push the conversation any farther, for right there at the inside doorway coming forward was J. Pierpont Morgan himself, and with a mighty cordial greeting. No, it was not the first time the two had met. But it was the first time ever that there had been any possible approach to a business conversation, looking toward any mutual understanding.

We sat in [Bratnober went on] at Mr. Morgan's desk an hour and it was straight talk every second. The two men were in every particular different. Mr. Morgan's words were few, mostly questions, some of them pretty curt. He was there to listen—and how Dan Guggenheim did keep him at his listening. I have heard speeches in every country in the world —a lot that have been fetching—but never one that had the pull in it that Daniel's did. If you have seen one of those new fangled blazing things they call an electric welder, you can have some idea of that burning speech. I had no notion that anybody began to know Alaska as I knew it, but there I was learning better. It was as if a bursting-open furnace door flared full in Mr. Morgan's face as Mr. Guggenheim suddenly stopped short with . . .

"Is there something else, sir, that . . ."

"Yes," said Morgan, "I want you to see Mr. Charles Steele, my lawyer partner. He's perfect at translating facts and figures into law-proof shape. He will like your ardor: you will like his comprehension, and"—we were rising at the hint his own rising gave—*"I am ready for action."*

And so, before long, the deal was set. The great "Alaska Syndicate" was formed, composed of the Guggenheims, J. P. Morgan, and a hastily recruited third partner, Jacob Schiff. The Guggenheims contributed a little over a third of the capital and all the administrative and engineering know-how. Morgan and Schiff and a few of their friends put up the rest of the money. The terms of the final agreement granted the Guggenheims the lion's share of the profits. The syndicate's first project would be the mining of Kennecott Mountain.

The difficulties of the undertaking were of staggering dimensions. First, a two hundred-mile, $25 million railroad had to be constructed over vast river deltas, over moving glaciers, through deep, unexplored canyons, from the sea to Kennecott Mountain. Then a multimillion-dollar breakwater had to be thrown across the exposed bay at the marine terminus of the railroad, and a harbor built to accommodate large freighters. Then a steamship line had to be bought or formed to transport the copper ore to the Guggenheim smelter at Tacoma.

To fuel the mining camp, the railroad, the harbor, the steamships, accessible coal mines had to be found, bought, and developed. To construct camps and warehouses, make railroad pilings and scaffolding, build mining sheds, huge forests had to be bought or leased and cut down. And all this had to be done in one of the bleakest wildernesses on the face of the earth.

But the Guggenheims had met with plenty of difficulties before, had taken enormous risks before, as had J. P. Morgan and Jacob Schiff, and they were not about to be cowed by the present one. The ultimate prize was too great. Dan Guggenheim's ambition had become nothing less than to control all the natural resources of Alaska.

Accordingly, the Alaska syndicate, which soon came to be known as the "Guggenheim Trust," bought Kennecott Mountain and several hundred thousand acres of adjoining territory in the Wrangell chain, bought two hundred miles of railroad right-of-way to the sea, bought seacoast land at Katalla Bay, Valdez, and Cordova, bought the Northwestern Steamship Company, bought Northwestern Commercial, a service company, bought every Alaskan coal mine they could get their hands on, bought endless forests, and, perceiving that ships could transport fish as well as copper, bought, as a sideline, Northwestern Fisheries, the most important fishing and canning industry in the Western United States, Canada, and Alaska, for good measure.

When the Guggenheims arrived in Alaska, the Russians had left it only forty years before: They had been there for over a century.

The first Russian colonists in Alaska, "with God far above, and the Tsar far away," had built Orthodox churches and founded towns which still bear their Russian names: Baranov, Shumagin, Wrangell, Sitka. The first Russian governor of the colony, a Siberian merchant appointed by the tsar, one Aleksandr Baranov, established his capital in the lively little frontier town of Sitka. From there he presided over an enormous wilderness populated by Aleutians, Eskimos, and four Indian tribes—the Tsimshiani, Tlingiti, Athapaskani, and Haida—descendants of peoples who, like the ancestors of the American Indians, had once lived along the banks of the great Siberian rivers. It had been the Aleutians who had given Alaska its original name, *Alakshak,* "Great Land."

Ignorant of Alaska's mineral resources, and somehow lacking in the initiative to search for them, the Alaskan Russians, a happy-go-lucky lot it appears, who gave brilliant balls in the "Tsarist Court" of Sitka at which vast quantities of vodka were consumed, confined their commercial activities exclusively to fishing and the fur trade. After more than a hundred years of Russian rule the Great Land had produced very little revenue for the tsar.

And so the tsar felt he had pulled off one of the most profitable business coups in history when he sold his North American province to the United States in 1867 for $7.2 million, even though this amounted to less than two cents an acre. As for the Americans, most of them at the time agreed with the tsar, regarding the purchase as a ridiculous extravagance: "Seward's Folly," after Secretary of State William H. Seward, who vigorously promoted the purchase; and "the insane ambition to possess a huge block of ice," as one senator put it.

For a couple of decades or so it appeared that the tsar and the senator were right. But, now, forty years later, the Guggenheims and J. P. Morgan were about to finally cash in.

Not long after the Guggenheim-Morgan syndicate moved into Alaska, cartoonists in the United States created two monsters, polar bear figures with Jewish noses and enormous gloved hands, which they called Guggenmorgan and Morganheim, and depicted them gobbling up Alaska.

The cartoonists were not far from the truth. Before long, the Guggenmorgans and the Morganheims were buying up everything in Alaska they could get their hands on: copper mines, iron mines, coal mines, fish canneries, forests. At the rate they were going it would not be long before they literally owned the territory.

Soon the cartoonists' protests would be joined by the first great American environmentalists, Theodore Roosevelt and his evangelistic chief forester, Gifford Pinchot, and the Guggenheims and J. P. Morgan would finally meet their match.

Meanwhile the great work proceeded. After $1.5 million worth of false starts at Katalla and Valdez, the Guggenheims' gangs of railway laborers and supplies of heavy machinery were unloaded at Cordova, where the great $25 million Copper River and Northwestern Railroad to Kennecott was to begin. Men by the thousands poured into Cordova from depression-plagued San Francisco, Tacoma, and Seattle. They slept on the wooden floors of saloons and bunkhouses and worked for three dollars a day, paying fifty cents for a meal, and a dollar a night for a bunk. The year was 1907.

After the Guggenheims got their roadbed over the hills surrounding Cordova, they were immediately confronted with the great marshy Copper River delta. In the winter it was full of snow, ice, slush, and frozen mud. In the spring and summer there were frequent floods and the mud fanned out for miles and miles.

By late summer the mud had become so deep that tens of thousands of wooden piles had to be driven down into the mud and millions of cubic yards of glacial moraine had to be spread across the delta to allow the roadbed to traverse it. No sooner had this Herculean task been performed than the vast twin glaciers, Miles and Childs, had to be confronted. One presented an immense, solid wall of ice four miles wide and three hundred feet high. The other was two and a half miles wide and three hundred feet high. A 1,150-foot-long bridge, costing $1.5 million, had to be built between the two glaciers. In the winter of 1908 gangs of Guggenheim-Morgan laborers, working in sixty-below-zero weather, their faces and hands lashed by fifty-mile-an-hour winds coming down from the Chugach Mountains, drove thousands upon thousands of huge wooden piles through seven feet of ice and forty feet of moraine as temporary supports for the bridge spans. By spring two spans had been swung out onto permanent supports. The piers for these spans were sunk over sixty feet into the frozen riverbed and were made of solid concrete eighty-six feet around and sheathed with heavy steel rails to stand up against the glacial icebergs that would batter them in the Copper River's raging current.

In the winter of 1909 the crews worked in shifts from sunrise to midnight trying to complete the third and last span, racing with the imminent spring thaw. Unfortunately, the dreaded thaw came earlier than expected and Copper River threw up a seven-foot crust of ice, heaving it against the wooden scaffolding that held up the third span. By sunset of the first day of the thaw, the scaffolding had been moved fifteen inches out of place. All night the men worked with steam lines melting the ice around the piles, while other crews rigged tackle that moved the 450 feet of scaffolding back into position. An hour and a half after the span had been moved from the scaffolding and attached to the permanent concrete and steel piers, the ice broke up altogether. Great blocks were hurled against the scaffolding, causing it to crumple into the river. Soon the pile drivers, too, were swept away by the rampaging current. But the vast glacier bridge was by now in place, secured to the permanent piers in the nick of time. On with the work . . .

Now the roadbed had to be blasted through the narrow Abercrombie Canyon. The Arctic wind blew down the canyon at forty-five to seventy-five miles an hour. The men had to work half-hour spells and then race to shacks to catch their breath and warm their hands and feet. Seventeen-ton dynamite charges were used to blast out the walls of the cramped V-shaped canyon to lay the roadbed. No sooner were the rails laid in the canyon than great drifts of snow repeatedly blocked the way. One trainload of 160 men ran into a colossal drift and the rotary snowplow stalled. Within a few minutes the train was buried and remained snowbound for twenty-one days. Later the snow turned to ice and the rails were covered with a sheath of ice six inches to two feet deep. The rotary snowplow was derailed 1,050 times in fifty miles.

Finally, in early summer, the Guggenheim gangs emerged from the canyon and advanced up the Copper River, driving piles down into the mud, filling in the marshes with moraine, gaining the Chitina River in midsummer, then the Nizina, and finally reaching Kennecott Creek by fall. The last spike in the railway, driven in early 1911, was made from Kennecott copper. By then the great Copper Mountain was already being mined.

From the shores of Kennecott Creek the railway workers and miners could look straight up some four thousand feet to the naked, bright-green summit of the Bonanza Lode. The miners and their horses climbed the rocky, frozen face of Kennecott by a zigzag trail. Cables were dragged up by man, horse, and mule, and within five or six months an aerial tramway, four miles long, connected the summit of the mountain with the valley and the railroad below.

Wooden sheds were constructed over the face of the mountain, and working from these sheds, the miners blasted tunnels into the frozen rock and earth.

And so, in this remote Arctic Nibelheim, the copper ore was mined in wind, rain, hail, snow, and ice, torn out of the frozen mountain, heaped into steel buckets, and shot down the four-mile tramway to the waiting gondola cars in the valley. The work was arduous beyond all imagining and many a miner fell dead upon his pick.

But no sooner was the final copper spike driven into the railbed than the first trainload of ore was ready. That first trainload bore ore assaying 75 percent copper, compared with the 2 to 3 percent ore in the great porphyry copper mines of Utah and Nevada. Each gondola car carried $12,000 to $15,000 worth of copper. The first cargo to leave Cordova for the smelter at Tacoma was valued at $500,000.

Kennecott's copper soon became the cheapest in the world. With the development work about one-third completed by the end of 1911, the Alaska syndicate counted a net profit of $1,658,000 from the first mining of Bonanza Lode ore. By the end of 1912 Kennecott had paid dividends of $3 million to Morgan, Schiff, and the Guggenheims. But that was just the beginning, a faint glimmer of things to come. World War I was not far off and the Bonanza Lode and its adjacent mines, supplying the Allies with most of their high-grade copper, would rain such tons of money down upon the Guggenheims as to cause them actual embarrassment. By 1918 the Guggenheims had extracted over ten times as much money from Kennecott alone as the Russians had received for all of Alaska fifty years before.

Spurred on by their success, Guggenmorgan began buying up more potential Alaskan wealth, more coal mines, more iron mines, forests upon forests without end. Soon it appeared that the unthinkable was happening and the cartoonists had not been exaggerating. If someone, something did not stop them, the Guggenmorgans and Morganheims would someday own *all* the wealth of Alaska.

Alaska in the early years of the twentieth century had become the last frontier of the American Dream, the last place where an American could feel truly free, the last place where a man could go with just his own wits and carve out an honest, abundant, independent, self-reliant life for himself. Thus the press, the few environmentalists active at the time, and a significant portion of the American people began to vigorously oppose the Guggenmorganization of Alaska.

The *Wall Street Journal* called the syndicate's activities "the second purchase of Alaska." Other papers observed that it was Alaska's fate to remain always a colony. First a colony of Russia, then a colony of Guggenmorgan.

No one was more vociferous on behalf of conserving Alaska for the Americans rather than the Guggenmorgans than the idealistic Gifford Pinchot, who had been chief of the Forest Service division of the Department of Agriculture under Presidents McKinley, Theodore Roosevelt, and Taft. Since 1908 he had also been head of the National Conservation Commission.

Gifford Pinchot believed with all his heart and mind that the riches that lay under and upon the American earth belonged to all the American people and should not be owned or controlled by a handful of "industrial spoilers" as he termed them. The railroad to Kennecott and the mining of Kennecott was already a *fait accompli*, so he could not do much about that. But what he could do something about, he thought, was a Guggenheim-Morgan plan to buy 950,000 acres of virgin forest and a 60-million-ton coal deposit, the latter worth approximately $25 million.

There followed a prolonged battle in the corridors of government and the courts of law. Secretary of the Interior Ballinger contended that only an organization with the size, expertise, and financial resources of the Guggenheim-Morgan syndicate, only Big Business, had the capability to exploit the natural resources of such a vast and inaccessible territory as Alaska. Pinchot countered time and again with his noble argument that the wealth of Alaska belonged to all the American people and should be exploited only by U.S. governmental agencies and small, independent operators. The debate drew the attention of the entire national press. The monsters Guggenmorgan and Morganheim appeared in more and more cartoons. The battles dragged on. . . .

Fortunately for the Guggenheims, the family had an ace in the hole. Simon, second youngest of the seven brothers, was, by the time of the controversy, a United States senator. Simon did not accomplish very much during his six years in Washington, but he did manage to squelch the conservationist Pinchot forces. In the end, the Ballinger people, aided and abetted by Senator Simon Guggenheim, won the day, making a few token concessions to the conservationists along the way, and Guggenmorgan and Morganheim remained lords of Alaska, as secure in their possession of the Great Land as the *Landvogt* of Baden had been in his possession of the Jews of Lengnau only sixty-five years before.

CHAPTER

3

MINING THE GLOBE

WHILE THE GUGGENMORGANS WERE PUSHING INTO ALASKA, THE
Guggenheims were simultaneously pushing into just about everywhere
else. There were four brothers propelling the ever-expanding empire
from New York and one moving an occasional mountain in Washington. The two on the sidelines, Ben and Will, would, in addition to
cashing in their ever-increasing dividends, also contribute their own
two cents of advice from time to time. The mere conquest of Alaska
was not nearly enough to occupy five, and sometimes seven, Guggenheim brains. There were so many other tantalizing opportunities to be
taken at the flood. There were rivers of gold in the Yukon, more copper in Utah, Nevada, and Chile. There was tin in Bolivia and Malaya.
There was more gold, silver, and lead in Mexico; there were acres
and acres of diamonds waiting to be plucked from the Belgian Congo
and Angola.

The Guggenheim business strategy, devised by Dan and rubber-
stamped by the others, was essentially threefold:

One, and this would always be a cardinal principle of the Guggenheims, *you always go in for big development when the business barometer is low.* (They had gone into Alaska at the time of the worst crash
since the Civil War.)

Two, and using Wagnerian symbolism this might be called the
Nibelheim philosophy, *you always use the cheap labor and raw materials of undeveloped countries to depress your own country's industries, to force its wages and prices down until they are so cheap*

you can afford to buy them up and sew them into your own mo-nopoly.

Three, in the metals industry *there was no use competing unless you owned everything from mine mouth to finished product. You had to own the mine and processing plant, and also control the marketing of the metal.*

This triple strategy worked so well wherever and whenever it was put into practice that it did not take the Guggenheims long to realize that it could be applied to control not merely the mineral wealth of North America, but also that of the entire world.

Consequently, that is precisely what the family set out to do. Old Meyer had been content for his sons to gain control of all mining and smelting on the North American continent. Son Dan went a few steps further: gain control, also, of all mining and smelting on the rest of the planet.

Herein lay one of the great American paradoxes. The American people, through their elected representatives, solemnly professed to the world in speech after speech that America sought no man's terri-tory, that America had no imperialistic aims. Yet all the while, through the efforts of men like the Guggenheims, America was stead-ily building up the greatest commercial empire on the face of the earth. America covets no land, but Sherwin-Williams paints "cover the earth"; we are shown the ads with the thick paint oozing down over South America and Africa. America seeks no man's territory, but the Coca-Colonization of the world must also extend to Easter Island, the Seychelles, Tasmania. It may not be the will of the American people, but it most certainly is the will of the officers and boards of directors of Sherwin-Williams and Coca-Cola.

Thus the American empire, the most extensive and powerful com-mercial and military empire in world history, was willed not by the American people or their elected representatives—many of whom would even deny the empire's existence—but by a handful of strong-minded, talented, industrious, acquisitive people like the Guggen-heims.

It would be tedious to dwell on every rock in the vast Guggenheim industrial monument. We can but mention in passing a few of the stones and concentrate, for a bit more space, on some of the grander boulders . . . and brighter gems.

We have not yet mentioned the building of the Perth Amboy re-finery in 1894, supervised by Ben and manned by cheap imported labor, "Hunkies" and "Japs," as they were called, which is still belching smoke over the Jersey meadows, smoke that can be seen on a clear day, at this writing, from the offices of Guggenheim Brothers on the thirty-fifth floor at 120 Broadway in New York City.

We have not yet mentioned the new lead refinery in Salt Lake City, which still belches *its* fumes over the Great Salt Lake.

We have only briefly mentioned the Tacoma smelter, whose task it would be to refine Kennecott bonanza ore (for arranging the purchase of this smelter Bernard Baruch collected a fee of $1 million).

Nor have we mentioned all the new mines and smelters established in Mexico, at places like San Luis Potosi and Veracruz. Neither have we mentioned the fabulous Esperanza, the richest gold mine in all Mexico, the mine dreamed of but never found by Cortez and his conquistadores, which the Guggenheims acquired around the time of Meyer's death, and which gave them a thousandfold return on their investment.

John Hays Hammond busied himself with finding mines for the Guggenheims in Mexico. He tried, unsuccessfully, to buy the extremely rich Palmilla gold and silver mine in Chihuahua. The property on which the mine was located had been inherited by one Pedro Alverado from his peon father, who had been ignorant of his land's potentialities. It turned out to be a bonanza. According to Hammond:

> Alverado spent his first million in building a Mexican palace in the small village near his mine and equipping it with Parisian furnishings. One bathroom would have made his house unique in the village and certainly would have served his needs. In his desire to impress the world at large, he had twelve bathrooms installed. The possession of a piano was a sure sign of opulence, so he ordered not one, but fifteen. . . . Later he offered to pay off the national debt of Mexico and was ignored. So he changed his allegiance and made out a new will providing for the payment of the national debt of the United States. After he had been swindled, as he thought, by the exorbitant charges of the American plumbers who were installing the twelve bathrooms, he cut the United States out of his will.

The greedy plumbers, it appears, also caused Alverado to cut the Guggenheims out of his plans as well. No matter how much money the brothers offered him for the Palmilla he always refused to sell.

On to other mines, other stones.

While the Guggenmorgans were attacking the Bonanza Lode overlooking Kennecott Creek, another combination, the Guggenryans, were conducting an operation in the Congo and Angola which was, and would continue to be, equally lucrative. The story, in brief, is this:

Leopold II, King of the Belgians, wanted to organize a company to develop the natural resources of the Congo, known in those days— the early twentieth century—as Leopold of Belgium's personal slave camp.

Leopold, terribly busy keeping his mistresses happy, summoned the great American capitalist, Thomas Fortune Ryan, to take charge of realizing his ambitions.

Thomas Fortune Ryan was a big (over six feet), red-faced, beefy American capitalist of Irish descent who had made millions from various speculations (tobacco, Equitable Life, rubber, among others) and who lived in a vast Fifth Avenue palace containing, among other extravagances, a palm court with a fountain and a private Catholic chapel. When Leopold proposed to him that he help develop the natural resources of the Congo, the discussion eventually turned to metals, and Ryan, being more of an expert in commodities, suggested that the Guggenheims handle this sphere of activity. The King, well aware of who the Guggenheims were, was in complete agreement.

Upon his return to America, Thomas Fortune Ryan summoned Dan Guggenheim to his Fifth Avenue mansion, and, so the story goes, upon entering the palm court, Dan momentarily lost his composure, thinking he was in Ryan's chapel. Guggenheim did not know whether to genuflect, cross himself, or fall flat on his face. And so he stood still and bowed his head as if he were attending a service in Temple Emanu-El. The huge, leonine Ryan, sensing Dan's sudden lack of assurance, took the diminutive metals magnate by the arm and, leading him to the more recognizable library, started right in talking turkey. Ryan liked Guggenheim immediately and later complimented him publicly, saying: "Dan's a big man. He bores with a big auger."

The result of all this was the formation of the Société Internationale Forestière et Minière du Congo, often referred to as "Forminière." King Leopold retained 25 percent interest in the company for himself, 25 percent was kept by the Kingdom of Belgium, and the remaining 50 percent was split fifty-fifty between Ryan and the Guggenheims.

The final agreement granted the Guggenheims and Ryan exclusive rights to prospect for minerals in an area roughly forty-five times as large as Belgium, with the proviso that the mines found and developed could be worked by Ryans and Guggenheims for ninety-nine years.

Subsequently Guggenryans formed two companies: the American Congo Company, which would exploit minerals, and the Intercontinental Rubber Company, which would exploit commodities. Dan and his brothers were in charge of the first, Ryan the second.

There were, as usual, severe labor problems. The local laborers, like the Mexicans of Monterrey and Aguascalientes, did not particularly enjoy working, especially in mines, no matter how much money was offered them. The Belgians had tried to force them to work at gunpoint, and under threat of confinement to concentration camps, and although this "worked," it brought too much public scorn down upon their heads for the Guggenryans to attempt similar measures. Eventually the Guggenryans built entire native villages for their workers, surrounded them with farms stocked with thousands of cattle, and created company stores with low, low prices. With these fringe benefits the native laborers accepted wages of a dollar or two a month plus free salt, calico, and cheap trinkets.

In time the Guggenryans found and exploited some gold and, eventually, millions upon millions upon millions of dollars worth of diamonds. The diamond fields spilled over into Portuguese Angola and the Guggenryans easily obtained a concession there also.

The Guggenryans no longer mine diamonds in the Congo, but they still take them out of Angola, despite the recent civil war. The Solomon R. Guggenheim Museum on Eighty-ninth Street and Fifth Avenue in New York owns 12,342 shares of Diamang, the Angolan diamond company. After the outbreak of the civil war the stock fell from $110 a share to $10, for a net loss to the museum of $1,234,200.

The Guggenheim boys always liked to have lots of different metals from lots of different places cooking in their furnaces at the same time. If one mix did not boil into profits, another would. And so while the great Alaskan and Congo gambles were being risked, for richer or for poorer, the boys mounted still another gigantic operation, this time in the Klondike, to dredge the gold-bearing sands of the Yukon River's fabled Bonanza Creek. Gold worth $100 million had already been sifted and sucked out of these sands and Hammond the Omniscient estimated there was at least another $100 million left to be taken.

Consequently, it was not long after Hammond's appraisal that the Guggenheims began moving hundreds of laborers and tons and tons of heavy equipment into yet another vast, empty wilderness. Dan and Sol personally made the long trip north to inspect the operation. In time, several colossal river dredges—the largest ever constructed up to that day—were erected from matériel that had traveled in hundreds of wooden crates for five thousand miles; a two-thousand-kilowatt-power hydroelectric plant was built, and living quarters, warehouses, laboratories, sheds, and offices were put up along sixty-two miles of Yukon River flume, ditch, and pipeline. For a while the venture paid off. By 1916 the Yukon Gold Company had disbursed $7,583,000 in dividends to the Guggenheims and other stockholders, but finally labor and development costs became so high that they cut profits to nil and the operation had to be shut down. The dredges were then towed to Malaya and set to bringing up tin instead of gold. They are still dredging, in what is known today as Malaysia, under the banner of Guggenheim-controlled, New York Stock Exchange-listed Pacific Tin.

The Yukon Gold Company was the first Guggenheim *partial* success. Until then, everything had been Midas-touch, inexhaustible bonanza. From now on there would also be some failures.

Nipissing was the first Guggenheim business failure, the first metal that not only did not warm in, but never even reached, the oven. Nipissing was a vein of almost 100 percent pure silver near Hudson Bay. After hearing reliable reports about it, the Guggenheim brothers founded a company in 1906, sold shares to around two hundred investors, sank $10 million into the venture themselves, and then, for the first time, sent John Hays Hammond up *post-factum* to personally inspect the property. Hammond traveled part of the way in his private railway car, accompanied by his valet, wine steward, and chef, and the rest of the way on horseback and sled. Observing the glittering strip of almost pure-white silver, he smiled to himself, his guides, porters, and dogs, and returned to the Partners' Room at M. Guggenheim's Sons still smiling. Soon word got around Wall Street that Hammond was smiling. Nipissing shot from $3.24 to $25.00 to $34.73 a share.

By this time in the story of the House of Guggenheim, if it became known that the Guggenheims and Hammond were after a property, shares in the property would skyrocket overnight.

Not long after the great boom in Nipissing shares, some of Hammond's subordinates went up to inspect the vein and found that, rich as it was, it petered out at twenty feet. As soon as he could get word of this to the Guggenheims, the family dumped its shares; the bottom fell out of the Nipissing market; Hammond the Great, the Infallible, "retired" amid much uncomplimentary publicity; and eldest Guggenheim brother Isaac, who had never been much of a whiz, suffered a nervous breakdown and had to be removed to a clinic in his ancestral Switzerland.

As might be expected, a public uproar ensued. Unsettled by the hostile reaction, the Guggenheims reimbursed some 150 investors over $1,450,000 for their losses in Nipissing, in addition to absorbing a multimillion-dollar loss on their own account.

But, luckily, or rather, strategically, other metals were always cooking in the Guggenheim furnaces. For example there was Bingham Canyon copper in Utah.

The Guggenheims developed what became the biggest copper operation in the world at Bingham Canyon. It was a new kind of undertaking for them because Utah copper was in porphyries, not veins, and had to be mined by the open-pit method. Hammond had estimated that there were five to ten million tons of 2 percent copper porphyries covering the sides of Bingham Canyon and that it could be mined very profitably indeed. Subsequently, in addition to conducting mining operations, the Guggenheims built the vast Magma copper mill, which became the largest mill in America, with 575 flotation tanks to separate the copper from the other materials in the porphyries and which still pours forth clouds of gas and fumes over Great Salt Lake. And they also built railroads and labor camps.

When the operation was fully underway, in 1910, John D. Rockefeller, Jr. visited it, and as he beheld the great steam shovels at work on the twenty-four terraces that lined the porphyry mountain from canyon bottom to the very top, he exclaimed: "It's the greatest industrial sight in the whole world."

A half century before, Brigham Young and his Latter-Day Saints had scorned the copper canyon, as Young had scorned all mining for that matter. "The true use of gold," he told his Mormons, "is for making culinary dishes." During the California Gold Rush, when some of his followers asked him for permission to go to the gold mines, he said: "If you want to go to the gold mines, go, go and be damned!"

To work Bingham Canyon's copper the Guggenheims imported cheap foreign labor, for the most part illiterate, bewildered Japanese, Hungarian, and Greek miners, who knew no English. Simon, in Washington, made sure they were hustled rapidly past the immigration authorities. Dan Jackling, the Guggenheims' manager-superintendent, ran the Bingham mine as a virtual slave camp, backed up by the Utah state militia.

"Give me your tired, your poor, your huddled masses yearning to breathe free," Emma Lazarus had written for the inscription at the base of the Statue of Liberty, presented by France as a gift to the United States in 1876. But at Bingham Canyon it was more like: "Give me your tired, your poor, your huddled masses yearning to breathe free . . . so we can exploit them as cheap labor."

The huddled masses at Bingham Canyon, however, soon caught on to what was being done to them and promptly expressed their fervent desire to be free of the slave status the Guggenheims and their minions had arranged. They managed, among other things, to elude the Utah state militia long enough to parade through the streets of Salt Lake City crying out: "Must we go to Russia for freedom?" They kept up a state of guerrilla warfare against their overseers within the mine. Later, in 1912, six thousand of these "Japs" and "Hunkies," armed with rifles and nitroglycerin, seized the mine and fought a virtual war with the Utah state militia and the Guggenheims' security forces. There were many casualties.

By this time mining and smelting in America had become man-killers. In addition to low pay, the workers had to endure crushed limbs, respiratory diseases, and chronic back problems. In the year of the revolt of the "Japs" and "Hunkies," one man in four at American Smelting and Refining suffered a disabling disease. The rebellion, however, put the Guggenheims on notice and eventually reforms were instituted. Meanwhile the profits from Bingham Canyon copper exceeded even Hammond's wild prognostications. Dividends in 1910 alone were $4,648,000. Even those who had paid the highest price for shares in Utah copper stock before 1910 made from 500 to 1,000 percent on their investment. By 1912 the Guggenheims' share in the mine was worth over $30 million. By 1935 over 225 million cubic yards of ore and waste had been moved from Bingham Canyon, or roughly the same amount of yardage displaced in building the Panama Canal, and the mine had yielded some $200 million in dividends.

But Bingham Canyon copper and Kennecott copper were not enough copper for the Guggenheims. The family had realized that the increasing use of electric cables would make copper one of the most sought-after metals in the world. The Guggenheims never did anything halfway. Not with Dan in charge. If they could, they would corner all the copper in the world. And so, in 1907, the year of a severe stock-market crash (remember, always go in for big development when the business barometer is low), they had bought a substantial interest in the Braden mine in Chile, and then in 1910, they had made their grandest gamble of all by buying the great Chuquicamata copper mine, 9,500 feet up in the Chilean Andes, for $25 million.

Once more we must indulge in superlatives. Chuquicamata, mined first by the Incas in the fifteenth century, proved to be the greatest copper mine on the planet, greater and richer even than Kennecott or Bingham Canyon.

The Guggenheims knew, of course, that they had gotten hold of a rich property when they bought it, but they had no real idea of the staggering dimensions of the copper deposit until they began mining it. As it turned out, no less than 300 million tons of high-grade porphyry ore lay close to the surface on Chuquicamata Mountain.

Again the extraordinary Guggenheim luck had held. Thirty years after striking the A. Y. and the Minnie bonanza, they had struck another, and this was the biggest bonanza of all.

Again the difficulties in exploiting the property were overwhelming. Chile was a poor, undeveloped country with no roads or rails in the interior, no electricity, except in the largest coastal cities, and very little water. Chuquicamata was forty-five miles from the nearest water supply, and fifty-five miles from the nearest source of electric power. It was one of the driest and most desolate places in South America, a vast waste of sand and rocks, avoided even by birds.

Once more, the Guggenheims were fully equal to the challenge. Bringing to Chile the first large-scale industrial development in that country's history, they built a modern port and a $3.5 million electric-power plant at Tocopilla, ninety miles from Chuquicamata. They built cables to get the power to the mine. They built a fifty-five-mile, mountain-hopping aqueduct to bring in water. They built a road from the mine to the sea and they built an entire town at the base of Chuquicamata Mountain. Literally inventing a new technology—a vastly improved reduction process (the brothers were always in the vanguard, whether it was in technology or art)—the Guggenheims eventually overcame all difficulties, as they had in Colorado, Mexico, Alaska, the Congo, Angola, and Utah, and made Chuquicamata into the most productive and profitable copper mine on earth.

By the first rumblings of World War I, the Guggenheims were in control of 75 to 80 percent of the world's silver, copper, and lead, and could literally dictate the prices of all three of these essential metals.

With the limitless demands of total war imminent, the family now stood on the threshold of riches so vast as to seem inconceivable, even to the overheated imagination and ambition of a Meyer Guggenheim. It would not be long now before the Guggenheims would assume their thrones alongside those other reigning American princes—the Rockefellers, Mellons, Vanderbilts, and Fords—as one of the five wealthiest families in the United States.

CHAPTER

4

HARVEST OF WAR

DANIEL GUGGENHEIM HAD KNOWN WAR WAS BREWING AND HAD positioned himself well to collect maximum rewards from the upheaval for the House of Guggenheim.

When hostilities actually broke out, he found himself taking the baths at Carlsbad, his favorite German spa. Hurriedly he returned to the United States and announced breathlessly to the press: "For the first time the world's marts lie at our feet uncontested. Our European competitors are hopelessly crippled for the time being and it is up to us to reap the benefits."

If the rest of America, always slow to understand the implications of war, was not ready to reap the benefits, at least Dan was. Kennecott had already swung into full production. The vast open pits of Bingham Canyon were, amid intermittent guerrilla warfare between miners and state troopers, also in full production. The smaller mines in Nevada, New Mexico, and Chile were churning away. And now, with constant prodding, Dan was readying Chuquicamata for its role as the greatest producer of them all.

Many businessmen had thought the Guggenheims were preparing their own suicide, developing so many copper properties. Too many eggs in one basket. A worldwide decline in demand for copper could wipe them out overnight. But Dan knew better. As early as 1912 he had confided to friends and associates that he thought the world was soon going to blow up and that the belligerents would need all the electric cable, and hence all the copper, they could get.

Dan also knew that World War I would result in the economic

ascendancy of the United States over Europe. He therefore wasted no time in convincing the government (he was on friendly terms with both Taft and Wilson) to get off the large corporations' backs and allow them to take full advantage of their crippled competitors.

By now Daniel Guggenheim was listened to in all the halls of power of the Western world. His business policies could affect the destinies of entire nations, such as Chile, and it was said he could make or break a government with a telegram.

Napoleon had once declared that the three most important things in war were money, money, and money. The Guggenheims were ready with money also. The firm of M. Guggenheim's Sons was one of the first corporations in America to subscribe to J. P. Morgan's $500 million Anglo-French war loan of 1915. The Germans had no idea what an enemy they had in Guggenmorgan. And Dan's wife, Florence, went out and personally sold $4 million worth of war bonds.

By the time of the loan, the first big new orders for Guggenheim copper began coming in from Britain and France. The Guggenheims were not caught napping. On March 1, 1915, mighty Chuquicamata finally moved into full production. Braden Copper, the family's smaller operation at Rancagua, Chile, was already producing. In Alaska, the fabulous Bonanza Lode of Kennecott was producing, in record volume, the purest copper the world had ever seen. Soon the Guggenheims were shipping hundreds of millions of dollars' worth of copper to England and France.

Meanwhile development costs in Alaska—that $25 million railway, among other items—proved so burdensome that the Guggenheims had to incorporate Kennecott Mountain and offer shares in the "Wondrous Lode" to the public, for the first time. Millions more were thus raised to mine Bonanza. So great became the war demand for Kennecott copper that Cordova, Alaska soon became the world's biggest copper port. Before long a million dollars' worth of copper a week was being shipped out of Cordova. The Tacoma smelter, furnaces blazing twenty-four hours a day, was overwhelmed. The year Kennecott went public its net profits were $22,460,000, or $5.10 a share. In that same year Bingham Canyon earned a net profit of $39,738,000, or $12 a share.

The unprecedented wartime demand for Guggenheim copper resulted, among other things, in the need for a reorganization of M. Guggenheim's Sons. Accordingly, on March 7, 1916, the old firm and Guggenex were dissolved and a new partnership formed which called itself "Guggenheim Brothers." The partners were Daniel, Solomon, Murry, Simon, and Isaac, plus an injection of fresh new blood —Dan's young son Harry, aged twenty-six, and Murry's boy, Edmond, twenty-eight, and one outsider, William C. Potter, a former vice-president of Morgan Guaranty who had collaborated with the Guggenheims in Alaska. The organization of Guggenheim-controlled American Smelting and Refining remained substantially the same.

Meanwhile the Guggenheims were growing a bit edgy over the fact that though the war was on in Europe, America was merely helping out, not actually fighting in the conflict. Edgy, for although the Guggenheim brothers were steeped in German culture, spoke German, vacationed in Germany, and always felt more at home in Frankfurt or Zurich than in Boston or Chicago, a German victory in the war would hurt them severely, perhaps even bring them to financial ruin.

On April 16, 1917, President Wilson and the Congress declared war on the Central Powers and the Guggenheims heaved a huge sigh of relief. With America in the war the Allies, and all the Guggenheim financial war babies, would be safe.

Isaac the Timid, Isaac of the nervous breakdown over Nipissing, made so bold as to exult to the press:

> I will say that the longer the war continues in Europe, the better it will be for us. In a short time the trouble abroad will make the United States the money center of the world and we are certain to become a creditor, rather than a debtor, nation.

Isaac had wisely refrained from mentioning the Guggenheims in his prognostications. But, of course, he was also well aware that as long as the war continued in Europe, the better it would be not only for the United States, but also for the House of Guggenheim.

And so it turned out to be. Now it was that the great full harvest was finally reaped by the family. Now it was that all the struggles of the past seventy years finally received their reward. During the years 1915 to 1918 the Guggenheim mines and smelters worked night and day at top capacity. In 1916 alone American Smelting and Refining sold $234 million worth of metal to Britain and France. By the end of the war Guggenheim coppers—not to mention Guggenheim leads and silvers—had paid more than $210 million in dividends, or $52 million a year.

At the height of the war the Guggenheims found themselves much criticized in the press and in the halls of Congress for being profiteers. This criticism was applied, by extension, to the Jewish people, since the Guggenheims had become, by then, perhaps America's most prominent Jewish family.

There was also widespread suspicion that the German-Jewish plutocracy—so devoted to German culture—secretly favored Germany in the war and was also helping the Bolsheviks undermine the tsar.

As a consequence of these criticisms and suspicions, a wave of anti-Semitism broke over America that threatened to erase many of the social gains Jews had made since the turn of the century. It had been only recently, for example, that the Jewish banker and patron of the arts Otto Kahn had found himself accepted everywhere. Now he and the other wealthy German-Jewish families suddenly found themselves excluded from society, and it became more difficult than ever for a Jew to get into the right bank, the right university, the right club.

The Guggenheims, never much concerned about Society-with-a-capital-S, were nevertheless worried about being pilloried as profiteers. *They* considered themselves Patriots-with-a-capital-P and wanted to be considered as such by the public. After all, were they not supplying the United States and its allies with essential war matériel, without which the war could not be prosecuted successfully? Were they not subscribing to huge war loans to sustain the Allies and also selling war bonds to the public? And were not their sons going off to war, Harry as a naval aviator, one of the first of the breed, and his brother Robert and cousin Edmond as army officers?

Nevertheless the press, Congress, the people, and finally President Wilson himself demanded that they lower their prices. At this the Guggenheims were quick to argue that the law of supply and demand held even in war. In the end, it was only when a furious Wilson threatened nationalization of the metals industries that the Guggenheims agreed to peg the price of copper at 23.5 cents a pound, when the price could easily have risen to over 30 cents. The prewar level had been 12 to 14 cents a pound.

In addition to their troubles with the government, the Guggenheims also suffered labor problems. In 1916 Kennecott paid dividends of $15,320,000 while its miners' salaries remained under $1 million. What a mine the Wondrous Lode was! The lowest-cost copper mine in the world, it was able to produce a pound of copper for only 5.1 cents. When, finally, the famished, frozen miners struck, the Guggenheims refused to negotiate with the union and evicted the miners from their bunkhouses. In thirty-below-zero weather the men then moved down Copper River to the first piece of non-Guggenheim territory they could find and established strike headquarters and shelter. The Guggenheims immediately circulated rumors that the Germans had instigated the strike and convinced the U.S. Government to bring in armed strikebreakers. After some weeks a settlement was reached. Wages were raised 25 cents a day and new, warmer bunkhouses were built. The Kennecott strike was, however, but a trifling episode of labor unrest. There was labor unrest everywhere throughout the United States during the war. Things got to such a boil that President Wilson was compelled to call a meeting between the lords of capital and the lords of labor in the council room of the American Federation of Labor building in Washington, May 15, 1917. Representing capital: John D. Rockefeller, Jr. and Daniel Guggenheim. Representing labor: Samuel Gompers, president of the AFL.

Both Guggenheim and Rockefeller had reputations of being tough with labor. When the "Hunkies" at the Guggenheims' Perth Amboy refinery struck in 1912, Dan had brought in the notoriously vicious Wadell-Mahon strikebreakers and four strikers were shot. And when the miners at the Rockefeller-owned Colorado Fuel and Iron Company struck and set up a tent camp of their own at Ludlow, Colorado, apart from the company's facilities, Rockefeller's armed guards fired into the tents, resulting in the deaths of nineteen women and children.

Gompers knew he was sitting down with a couple of the toughest capitalists alive, and, as might be expected, he had little sympathy for them, but he did not let his feelings interfere with his statesmanship. He called upon capital to unite with the cause of labor in winning the war and "spreading democracy to Central Europe."

Dan Guggenheim was so inspired by Gompers' speech that, jumping to his feet, he gushed:

This is a great revelation to me. Yes, it is a revelation and has inspired me. I have felt for some years that my work was near its end; that I might be allowed to take things a little easier. You see, I have worked for forty-five years and I was thinking of turning over my work to my two sons and my son-in-law. But recently I arranged things so they could all go to the front when the call came, and I could go back into harness and do the work they were going to do for me. When the call came from President Wilson and President Gompers, perhaps I felt I had enough on my shoulders. But I came here and I want to say that I am prepared to do anything I can do—just so long as I am able to carry it out. . . . You're on the right track. You're doing the right thing. [Turning to Gompers, Dan added] I am prepared to offer my services, Mr. President.

My services are at your disposal and at the disposal of your entire organization.

At this Gompers leapt to his feet and shouted: "I congratulate Mr. Guggenheim. He has simply taken a new lease on life."

After which the two men, both Jews, one Swiss-German, American-born, the other Dutch, born in a London tenement, each in a radically different camp, embraced.

Later Daniel condescended to declare:

> I favor labor unions, because unionism sometimes helps the workers in disputes with capital, and capital sometimes gets very arbitrary. Capital is becoming more humane. . . . Only when the federal and state governments take up the matter of the unemployed and the care of the unfit will conditions improve. This may sound like socialism, but these are my views. . . . I don't think there can be too much legislation along humanitarian lines. Surely no man who has been successful can be happy when he realizes the condition of the workers. We must see that the worker not only gets sufficient wages, but also that he gets some of the comforts and luxuries of life. I believe in the democratization of industry.

And so, for a while, there was peace. Still, despite Dan's humanitarian eloquence, the Guggenheims kept a tight rein on their labor force throughout the world and most strikes after the great Gompers-Guggenheim Embrace were either forcibly broken or settled on Guggenheim terms. In support of the Guggenheim position, which certainly was no harsher than that of the other great American capitalists, Solomon Guggenheim piously stated to the press: "I believe that the wage earner is more extravagant in proportion to his earnings than the millionaire."

In the end the facts had to be faced. During the great period of Guggenheim business expansion, as in the great period of Vanderbilt, Morgan, Harriman, Rockefeller business expansion, things were run on the basis of huge dividends and starvation wages. What is more, the Guggenheims, despite Dan's verbal acceptance of unionism, remained steadfastly against the open shop. "Yellow-dog" contracts were the order of the day. With the Guggenheims, however, at least it can be said that nothing they did, or provoked, was ever on a small scale. Many historians are agreed that among the Guggenheims' many achievements, their harsh labor policies in the Western and Mexican mines and smelters were one of the causes of both the formation of the International Workers of the World (IWW) and the interminable Mexican Revolution of 1910–1930.

When the smoke of World War I drifted away from the battlefields, council chambers, mines, smelters, and factories, the Guggenheims, though scarred by many battles—military, economic, political— emerged vastly, inconceivably rich.

How rich? It is difficult to say. It is not easy to assign precise worth to mines, which deplete in value much more rapidly than other assets. Averaging out a composite of several historians' and economists' estimates, and judging, as carefully as possible, the evidence at hand, we can put the family's net worth at the end of the war as something in the neighborhood of from $250 million to $300 million, or from $850 million to $1 billion in today's money, which was enough to rank them, financially, second only to the Rothschilds among Jewish families.

This enormous economic advancement, of course, left the family extremely vulnerable.

Though the Guggenheims considered themselves patriots who had supplied the Allies with vital raw materials without which they might not have been able to win the war, others considered them merciless Shylocks, exacting every pound of flesh for their metals.

Foremost among these accusers was Henry Ford, an admitted anti-Semite. Not long after the war ended, Ford—whose immortal utterance was "History is bunk"—published the spurious, scurrilous "Protocols of the Elders of Zion" for the first time in America in his privately owned paper, the *Dearborn Independent*. The "Protocols" was essentially an inaccurate survey of Jewish history, which assigned the Jews the diabolical ambition of wanting to rule the world.

In more or less the same breath—at least in the same publication —Ford asserted that men like himself, who made factories, really owned them, but the exploiters of mines and other natural resources, like the Guggenheims, were profiteering from property that really belonged to all. In Ford's own words: "Why should such men as the Guggenheims be paid for ore in the ground in the state of nature?"

The Guggenheims took this slur in stride, as they had taken countless others, ever since they were hounded out of Guggenheimb, Germany, and Lengnau, Switzerland, and forced to emigrate to Philadelphia.

So far as they were concerned, they had done a lion's share in "making the world safe for democracy," and were entitled to their rewards.

That they had done a lion's share in furthering the war effort no one would have disputed. What people began to dispute after the war was not so much the value of the contributions of the protagonists and their minions, but what the war had been all about in the first place. With so many democracies faltering, despotisms rising, and millionaires thriving, had it been a war to make "the world safe for democracy" or just one to make the world safer for people like the Guggenheims?

CHAPTER

5

THE GREAT SCHISM

MEYER GUGGENHEIM HAD ALWAYS URGED HIS SEVEN SONS "TO BE as one." "Together," he had told them, time and again, enacting the fable of the sticks and the bundle of sticks, "you will be invincible. Singly, each of you may be easily broken. The world is a dangerous place," he would go on, "full of snares and treacheries. Stay together, my sons, and the world will be yours. Break up, and you will lose everything."

It took many years for the Guggenheims to understand fully the implications of this paternal admonition. When they finally did understand, it was too late. The sticks had come apart, some were easily broken, and they could not be bundled together again.

The first defection in the ranks—Will and Ben dropping out of active partnership in M. Guggenheim's Sons in 1901—did not hurt the family too much at the time. But it was to have serious consequences in the future.

It will be remembered that Ben and Will dropped out ostensibly because they objected to the family going into partnership with outsiders. But, although there are no records to prove it, there is ample circumstantial and hearsay evidence that it was really the older "practical-minded" brothers who pushed the neophyte, college-educated Ben and Will out of active participation (Ben and Will still retained some financial interest in the partnership) so they would not interfere with the older brothers' concepts of management and, more importantly, would not share in the profits of future ventures.

In any case, the Guggenheims did not experience any immediate diminution of profits or adverse publicity from the departure of Ben and Will from the firm.

It was not until Will married the Gentile divorcée, Grace Herbert, and Dan forced them to divorce, settling $150,000 on the divorcée, that the Guggenheim image began to suffer in the press. And from the standpoint of sticks and bundles of sticks, who knows whether it had been Will's separation from the firm that had caused him to marry the unacceptable Grace Herbert, or whether he would have perpetrated the unthinkable marriage even if he had been an active partner on the day of his engagement?

No, it was not until Will brought his furious $10 million suit against his brothers over Chile Copper in 1916 that the crest of the House of Guggenheim suffered its first serious tarnishing and the public was to behold the brothers as adversaries for the first time.

It happened thus:

William Guggenheim had "retired" as an active partner in M. Guggenheim's Sons after ten years of duty, much of it pioneering in Mexico, at age thirty-one, on an income of $250,000 a year, to devote himself, in his own words, "to philanthropy and good works."

Under the terms of the partnership agreement of 1893 he still shared in the profits of all ventures undertaken by the firm before his retirement and would be given an opportunity to participate financially in all future ventures, if he so wished.

Time and again he and brother Ben signed documents waiving their right to participate in this venture or that one. One of the waivers pertained to the formation of the Chile Copper Company to exploit Chuquicamata Mountain. Ben and Will signed it January 4, 1912.

Three and a half months later, carefree, fun-loving Ben drowned with the *Titanic* on her maiden voyage, leaving three daughters, Hazel, Benita, and Peggy, and was thus forever removed from participating in future business ventures.

Four years after that mishap, Chuquicamata swung into production and was hailed by the press as the largest and richest copper mine in the world. The incredible Guggenheims, headlined the *Wall Street Journal*, had struck their *fifth* bonanza.

By this time, 1916, Will's income had dwindled to something less than $250,000 a year. Astonished by the fabulous wealth of Chuquicamata, he went to brother Dan and asked to be let in on the deal. He would repudiate his waiver. Dan refused.

Stung to the quick, and goaded by reports of Chuquicamata's staggering potential, Will went to his lawyers and brought suit against his five older brothers for $10 million. He charged fraudulent concealment. When he was first informed about Chuquicamata, the mine was passed off as small change and so he and Ben had willingly waived their rights to participate in its exploitation. But, he claimed, the brothers knew all along how rich the mine was. They simply concealed the extent of its wealth from Ben and Will in order to collect a greater share of the profits for themselves.

And so, all of a sudden, here were the Guggenheim brothers in court with all the press watching.

On one side of the courtroom sat the five stocky figures of Isaac, Daniel, Murry, Solomon, and Simon. On the other side sat the refined, slender Will, seething with hatred, his second wife at his side. Between them was arrayed the most expensive legal talent in New York.

The newspapers of the day repeatedly observed that William looked "like an artist" in his "blue flannel trousers and high soft collar," as he stood facing his brothers, "who looked like typical American businessmen."

The action hinged entirely on the waivers Will and Ben had signed on January 4, 1912, permitting the older brothers to form the Chile Copper Company to exploit Chuquicamata and divide the profits among themselves.

The five older brothers' lawyers pointed out that Will had repeatedly signed waivers renouncing participation in new ventures, and, of course, he *had* signed the Chile Copper waiver after having been fully apprised of the facts.

Will's attorneys exhibited the partnership agreement of 1893, which forbade any of the brothers to enter any mining deal individually. Will's retirement in 1901, they maintained, had been only temporary. In 1911 he had been accepted back in active partnership for a brief period—and this was true—as a member of the board of the International Steam Pump Company, one of brother Ben's less successful ventures. And they produced witnesses testifying that Will had not been accurately informed of the future worth of Chuquicamata.

The first week of the trial caused the faces of the "Copper Kings" to be splashed all over the newspapers of Europe and the United States. The second week of the trial promised to reveal to the world the financial secrets of the hitherto mysterious M. Guggenheim's Sons and the recently formed Guggenheim Brothers.

Their faces adorning the papers did not particularly disturb Dan, Murry, Sol, Isaac, and Simon, but having the financial data of the intensely private M. Guggenheim's Sons and Guggenheim Brothers aired was more than they could bear. Will had played his trump card. The brothers decided to settle out of court.

It was rumored at the time that Will collected $5 million, although neither side would reveal the figure to the press. To this day it is impossible to ascertain for sure how much Will got. All that is known beyond doubt is that several years after the settlement, Simon, who was closer to Will than the other brothers, set up a million-dollar trust fund, which could not be borrowed against, for Will and his wife. Guggenheims today speculate that spendthrift Will quickly ran through the $5 million settlement, went back to the brothers for more, and received the ironclad trust to keep him quiet and, it was hoped, solvent, forever.

Will's suit disposed of, the brothers went back to business as usual, which, at the time, as we have noted, was principally supplying the Allies with copper during World War I. While some more bad publicity came the Guggenheims' way during this period—their denunciation as war profiteers—none of it had anything to do with the unity or disunity of the brothers.

It was not until 1922 that the Guggenheims suffered their next major indignity. Again, it did not have anything to do with the unity or disunity of the brothers, but was nevertheless a prelude to the schism to come.

The reader must now recall that the Guggenheims ran two organizations. One was the family-owned Guggenheim Brothers, a sort of holding company, and the other was the giant, New York Stock Exchange-listed American Smelting and Refining Company.

A curious relationship existed between the two business concerns. Daniel was chairman and president of American Smelting and Refining, and also chief operating partner of Guggenheim Brothers. A secret stairway, still in existence, connected Dan's office in American Smelting with the Partners' Room of Guggenheim Brothers, one floor above. The door to this stairway opened onto a length of wood paneling, hung with paintings, in the Guggenheim Partners' Room. Evidently Dan scurried back and forth between his two offices, using only this stairway, and not the principal means of access serviced by elevators.

This fact attains some significance only when we consider that in

1922 the board of directors of American Smelting and Refining accused the Guggenheims of quietly and surreptitiously milking the company, and at a stockholders' meeting had the family voted out of control. The charge was that Guggenheim Brothers had milked American Smelting and Refining by letting it carry expenses and take huge risks in the discovery and exploitation of natural resources, then to skim off the cream of those discoveries for themselves.

To be sure, several Guggenheims remained on the board, but they and their allies were no longer a majority. Not long after this unpleasantness, Daniel Guggenheim "retired" from his eminences in the company, and brother Simon became president of American Smelting and Refining, assisted by Dan's son-in-law, Roger W. Straus.

The matter was much publicized in the press, where it was noted that though the Guggenheims still played an important role in American Smelting, all they actually *controlled* any longer was Guggenheim Brothers.

Guggenheim Brothers was, however, still a very powerful outfit. The partners owned, among lesser properties, tens of thousands of shares of Kennecott Copper Corporation, Utah Copper Corporation (Bingham Canyon), Diamang (diamonds in Angola), almost all of huge, seemingly inexhaustible Chuquicamata, and a huge block of American Smelting and Refining.

In 1923 the Guggenheim partnership was composed of Daniel, Murry, Solomon, Simon, and William C. Potter, representing the old guard, and Harry and Edmond, representing the new generation. Isaac had died the year before at sixty-eight.

By 1923 the older brothers, smarting from their loss of control of American Smelting and Refining, had begun to think about taking their profits, while they were still able, and retiring or, at least, semi-retiring, and turning over most of the work to the young bloods, Harry and Edmond.

It was precisely at this time that Anaconda Copper Corporation came forward with an offer to buy 2 million of Chile Copper's 3.8 million shares for $70 million cash.

Receiving $70 million clear, while still keeping 1.8 million shares, was most tantalizing, especially to the older Guggenheims. Dan, Sol, Murry, and Simon had been through the wars and wanted to retire someday on a little more than paper. Accordingly, Dan circulated a memorandum among the partners expressing favorable interest in Anaconda's proposal and calling for a meeting to consider it.

The meeting took place around the long mahogany table in the Partners' Room on the thirty-fifth floor of the Equitable Building, the same table around which Meyer had assembled his seven boys some forty years before and talked of sticks and bundles of sticks. It turned out to be the most violent, momentous partners' meeting in Guggenheim Brothers' history.

The two sides were soon drawn. On the side of selling: the oldsters, Dan, Murry, Simon, and William C. Potter. On the side of holding on: the youngsters, Dan's son Harry, and Murry's son, Edmond. Sol, who sympathized with the young, and was usually reluctant to sell anything, tended toward holding on as the discussion began.

The meeting lasted hours and hours. Dan, heading the old guard, argued passionately for not holding out for the top dollar, for taking a healthy profit and running. Did the younger ones have any conception of what a *risk* their fathers had taken, developing a mine 9,500 feet up in the Chilean Andes, with no readily available water or power, no roads, no trained labor force? That they were now able to collect $70 million in cash for this gigantic gamble was too good to be true, certainly too good to turn down.

But to the young bloods, selling the richest copper mine on earth, for *any* price, was sheer folly, was madness. Steadfastly they opposed it, backed up by Sol. If Chuquicamata was sold, they remonstrated, why should they remain partners of Guggenheim Brothers? What would there be left?

Discussions, arguments . . . the Partners' Room of Guggenheim Brothers that day shook with the conflict between young and old. Little Dan pounding on the table, getting up, storming around the room, his son Harry, tall and blue-eyed, trying to shout his father down. Stolid Murry seconding Dan. Edmond seconding Harry. Small, dark Simon repeating over and over again: "There's no choice but to sell, there's no choice but to sell." The dapper, good-natured Sol trying to pacify both sides.

In the end the old had their way. Dan, Murry, Simon, and William C. Potter drew Sol over to their side and voted down the young five to two. A two-thirds majority was all that was needed according to the articles of partnership.

Thus was the vast and rich-beyond-all-imagining Chuquicamata sold by the Guggenheims to Anaconda Copper on March 1, 1923. (Anaconda then ran it most profitably until it was nationalized by Salvador Allende in 1970. Under the subsequent military dictatorship the company did not get back the mine but did receive some compensation.)

And thus did Harry and Edmond, a few days later, carry out their partners' meeting threat and resign from Guggenheim Brothers. Their fathers and uncles had had their way, but in so doing they had lost the business allegiance of their sons.

Losing that allegiance spelled the death of Guggenheim Brothers, but no one in the family realized it at the time.

The sale of Chuquicamata was the largest private sale of a mining property in world history to date, and this was enough to content Dan, Murry, Simon, William C. Potter, and, somewhat reluctantly, Sol. Converted into today's figures, the Guggenheims had realized a net profit of some $160 million on the transaction. Now they were conceded to be the owners of the largest fortune ever amassed by a Jewish family in America and the press observed they had probably made more money in less time than any family in United States history, except their archenemies, the Fords.

At the time of the Great Sale Dan was sixty-seven, Murry was sixty-five, Sol sixty-two, Simon fifty-six. Each was worth around $50 million. Harry, thirty-three, and Edmond, thirty-five, were living off funds given to them by their fathers.

Not long after the controversial sale Dan suddenly bounced back from "retirement" and from the ignominy into which he had been relegated by his son and his nephew, and he declared that Chuquicamata profits would not be salted away but would be ventured into still another field, nitrates. You could not keep Dan down for long.

"Chilean nitrates," he exulted, "will make us rich beyond the dreams of avarice!"

Dan was wrong. When the family strayed from metals and went into chemicals they suddenly lost their Midas touch: The nitrates did not turn into gold.

The Guggenheim family was now divided. The bundle held only four sticks, Dan, Murry, Sol, and Simon. Isaac and Ben were dead. Will was totally alienated, and had been for some time. Sol was not nearly as enchanted by big business as he had been before: He would soon branch out into art. And Harry and Edmond, temporarily fed up with their elders, were going their own separate ways.

From now on the Guggenheim family would never again "be as one." Though they would go on to ever more splendid achievements, there would be rivalries, envies, divorces, breakdowns, feuds, permanent alienations, suicides.

From now on the Guggenheims, acting more as individuals than as a family, would devote themselves more to spending than to making.

They had a great deal of money to spend and, with the exception of a few inevitable playboys, they would spend it even more grandly and courageously, and certainly more nobly, than they had made it.

III

SEVEN BROTHERS AND TWO HUNDRED FIFTY MILLIONS

(1918-1959)

ON THE USES OF WEALTH

Who gives in health gives gold; in sickness, silver; after death, lead.

—Hebrew Proverb

And if thy brother should become impoverished, and be without means, thou shalt uphold him and have him live beside thee . . .

—Leviticus 25:36

Money is like muck, not good unless spread.

—Francis Bacon

Exegi monumentum aere perennius.
"I have built me a monument more enduring than bronze."

—Horace

THE GUGGENHEIMS

GENEALOGICAL CHART

(FOR PART III)

MEYER GUGGENHEIM (1828–1905)
m. BARBARA MEYER (1834–1900)

ISAAC (1854–1922)
m. CARRIE SONNEBORN
- BEULAH (b. 1877)
- EDYTH (b. 1880)
- HELENE (b. 1886)

DANIEL (1856–1930)
m. FLORENCE SHLOSS
- M. ROBERT (b. 1885)
- HARRY FRANK (b. 1890)
- GLADYS (b. 1895)

MURRY (1858–1939)
m. LEONIE BERNHEIM
- EDMOND (b. 1888)
- LUCILLE (b. 1894)

SOLOMON R. (1861–1949)
m. IRENE ROTHSCHILD
- ELEANOR (b. 1896)
- GERTRUDE (b. 1898)
- BARBARA (b. 1904)

JEANNETTE (1863–1889)
m. ALBERT GERSTLE
- NETTIE (b. 1889)

BENJAMIN (1865–1912)
m. FLORETTE SELIGMAN
- BENITA (b. 1895)
- MARGUERITE (PEGGY) (b. 1898)
- HAZEL (b. 1903)

ROBERT (1867–1876) — **SIMON** (1867–1941)
m. OLGA HIRSCH
- JOHN SIMON (1905–1922)
- GEORGE DENVER (1907–1939)

WILLIAM (1868–1941)
m. (1) GRACE B. HERBERT
m. (2) AIMEE L. STEINBERGER
- WILLIAM JR. (b. 1907)

ROSE (1871–1945)
m. ALBERT LOEB
- HAROLD (b. 1891)
- EDWIN (b. 1894)
- WILLARD (b. 1896)

CORA (1873–1956)
m. LOUIS F. ROTHSCHILD
- LOUIS F. JR. (b. 1900)
- MURIEL B. (b. 1903)
- GWENDOLYN (b. 1906)

*For complete genealogical information consult
genealogical tables on pages 541–544.*

CHAPTER

1

A FORTUNE TO SPEND

THE PLUMP, MIDDLE-AGED LADY WALKS INTO THE CORSET SHOP AND asks for "one of those Guggenheim foundations." The slender young woman, newborn infant in her arms, walks into the foundation office and is greeted with: "Frankly, Miss Ellis, the Guggenheim Foundation had been led to expect a book of poems."

The cartoons, which appeared in the mid-1930s, were in agreeable contrast, so far as the Guggenheims were concerned, to those that had appeared before and during World War I depicting the family as vultures tearing at the carcass of Mexico and polar bear monsters about to gobble up all of Alaska. They reflected the great change that had occurred in the Guggenheim style and ethos since the family had acquired its place in the capitalistic sun. Now the Guggenheims were no longer heartless exploiters of man and nature, but respected benefactors of humanity, or, as in the case of Ben and Will, harmless spendthrifts whom one could criticize but not dislike.

The great metamorphosis, a gradual process, had begun during the years immediately following World War I, and especially after the sale of Chile Copper to Anaconda, and coincided with the Guggenheims' most concerted period of monument buying and building.

No sooner had the Guggenheims reaped their immense harvest from World War I, and ascended into the heaven of the American superrich, than they began to move from the Jersey Shore to the North Shore of Long Island, from Elberon, the Jewish Newport, to more fashionable Sands Point, near Port Washington, preserve of people like the Goulds, Whitneys, Pratts, Astors, Woolworths . . . and the setting for Fitzgerald's *The Great Gatsby*.

William, who was to adopt the Fitzgeraldian pseudonym Gatenby Williams, was the first to move, followed by Isaac, Daniel, Solomon, and, much later, Simon.

As the war was drawing to a close Will bought a fifty-acre estate on the Sound—a large white Colonial house with farm—and promptly began throwing huge Gatsby-like lawn parties there under striped tents. Isaac then bested him by building, in 1918–19, a vast, ornate, $2 million, forty-room Italian Renaissance palace on a hill overlooking Hempstead Harbor, adjoining the Woolworth property. He surrounded his palace with marble fountains and statues, carefully manicured Italian gardens, a nine-hole golf course, and a hundred more acres of pine and oak woods. He called it Villa Carola. Later, Solomon, who liked to summer in Britain, renting a different castle each year, would buy the place from Isaac's estate for $610,000 cash and rename it Trillora Court. In the meantime, Daniel outdid everyone, including his WASP neighbors, by purchasing the kingly, unfinished Castlegould from the financier Howard Gould. A colossal stone edifice in a mixture of Jacobean and Gothic styles, the main house—there were several houses on the property—contained seventy rooms, was surrounded by a moat, approached by a drawbridge, and was situated on 350 acres of farm and woodlands bordering the Harriman estate and, like Villa Carola, overlooking Hempstead Harbor.

Ensconced in these monuments to their power and authority, amid the bastions of some of the most formidable names in the American WASP aristocracy, with rivers of money steadily pouring into their accounts from all over the globe, the Guggenheims could finally lean back and enjoy the exalted status they had won among American capitalists.

But no sooner did they begin to lean back and spend and enjoy for a change than they began to recognize a certain moral hollowness in their lives, a moral hollowness that, to be sure, was not only at the center of their lives, but at the center of the entire American business culture as well.

They had made a lot of money—and honestly, by the canons of their day—but what did it all amount to in the end but six more or less average men glutted with money and possessions—far more than they could ever need, unless it was to feed some deep-down, fearful insecurity—leading rather flat, bourgeois lives?

They had made a lot of money, but what were they, in the end, but a clan of shrewd, practical, predatory men, consuming a great deal but ultimately producing nothing of lasting value, doing nothing but what all the rest were doing, only on a grander scale?

They had made a lot of money, but they had made much of it at the expense of the planet, often to the ruination of vast areas. Piles of debris and broken rocks, and heaps of slag, are all that remain of former Guggenheim operations in Colorado. In Bingham Canyon, Utah, where the Guggenheims created the world's first open-pit copper mine, there is now a vast devastation, the earth so gouged and lacerated as to seem the scene of some cosmic disaster. Kennecott: an entire mountain destroyed in Alaska. Chuquicamata: an entire mountain destroyed in Chile. Rivers everywhere contaminated with the detritus of Guggenheim mines and smelters. Yes, the Guggenheims had made a lot of money, but what respect had they had in their relentless pursuit of wealth for the rights of mountains and rivers and the rights of men and women to enjoy them?

They had made a great deal of money, but what had they done for beauty, justice, truth; what had they done to add to the joys, or to alleviate the sufferings, of their fellow man?

Not very much. In fact, a good case could have been made—and was, by many journalists and biographers—that much of the Guggenheims' colossal fortune had been made at the cost of grievous human suffering. Furthermore, had their exploitive undertakings enhanced the earth and its life, or had they had the opposite effect and changed "the soft airs and green mosses of verdant valleys" into smoke, slag, and filth?

These questions may not have occurred to the Guggenheims as they basked in the sun of their phenomenal financial success, but they were most certainly brought to their attention by the press of their day. The family was only too well aware that to the public at large they were still monstrous Guggenmorgans trying to bearhug Alaska and/or equally monstrous vultures picking at the corpses of Mexico and Chile.

To be sure, and fair, they had already been charitable to a certain extent. Mother Barbara, it will be recalled, had sought to instill a spirit of charity in her children from the very beginning, and they had responded first by erecting memorials to Barbara's and Meyer's lives, and then by donating large sums in their memory to Mount Sinai Hospital in New York, the Schweizerisches Israelitisches Alterasyl in their ancestral Lengnau, and other charities. But these were relatively insignificant compared to what their resources could accomplish if put to good use, and they knew it.

Clearly it was time now to do something else with their money rather than just make it earn more money. Having gouged the earth of its resources for over forty years, wasn't it time now to begin plowing some of the wealth back?

Yes it was, and once again it was the four consuls of the Guggenheim empire—Dan, Sol, Murry, and Simon—who showed the way, Isaac and William proving to be as fainthearted in spending, unless, as in William's case, spending on women, as they had been in earning. Ben, having gone down with the *Titanic*, never got a chance to show what constructive use he would have made of *his* money. (By the time of his drowning he had given every indication of following the example of brother Will.)

It has been said that what makes the Guggenheim fortune different from all other American fortunes is the speed with which it was put together and the daring with which it was spent. Thus, just as they had been pioneers in business, always plunging into the unknown, constantly discovering and developing new natural resources with the most up-to-date technology, so Dan, Sol, Murry, and Simon, each in his own way, would become pioneers also in philanthropy (in a time when income and estate taxes were far from confiscatory), each finding, to his surprise, a second career for himself, one fully as exhilarating as the first, the four of them setting forth on such uncharted seas as aviation, rocketry, support of individual scientific and artistic creation, and nonobjective art, seas on which no other American millionaires had yet sailed.

Such, in fact, became the Guggenheim brothers' zeal and gusto in paying the money back, each trying to outdo the other as they had done in building their summer homes, that by 1975, fifty years after they had begun unburdening themselves of their wealth, the foundations that Dan and Harry had created were each worth four or five times as much as any of their descendants; the foundation Murry had created was worth six or seven times as much as any of his descendants; and the ones Solomon and Simon had founded were worth fifteen to twenty times as much as all of their descendants combined.

In the end, it was in giving, rather than in making, that the Guggenheims were to redeem their image and reputation and earn an honored place in the history of their country.

So famous and influential, in fact, became the Guggenheims'

laboratories, university institutes, museums, hospitals, and foundations that by 1975 their early business career had become almost totally obliterated from the public memory, and even those thousands of people who benefited from Guggenheim munificence had little or no idea where the money originally came from.

CHAPTER

2

ISAAC: ON DAUGHTERING OUT

OF THE SEVEN GUGGENHEIM BROTHERS, THE ONE WHO MOST EM-
phatically did not lead the way in giving was Isaac.

Isaac Guggenheim, as Meyer's firstborn son, and first hope for
the continuance of his business and his family, was expected to head
the family, head the family business, and perpetuate the family name.
He accomplished none of these. His life was, in a sense, a triple
failure, if only because hopes for him had been so high, a long,
quietly unfolding drama of insecurities never conquered, of expectations never fulfilled. As a consequence, though he became very
wealthy, riding on his more adventurous brothers' coattails, Isaac
never felt secure enough in himself to accomplish anything very
significant with his money. Not even remotely approaching his four
middle brothers in giving, he spent a major part of his fortune bol-
stering his own insufficient ego by building, furnishing, and maintaining his palatial $2 million Sands Point estate, and subsidizing a
worthless grandson, whom he vainly hoped would carry on the family business, and, above all, the family name.

If, as the psychologists like to point out, every family has its
victors, survivors, and victims, Isaac most certainly must be classified
as something between a survivor and a victim, though, admittedly,
not so much a victim as his youngest brothers, Ben and Will.

First Isaac was victimized by his father, then by his brother Dan,
then by his wife, then by nature, then by the WASPs of Sands Point,
and, finally, after his death, by his grandson.

Victimized by his father. Born and brought up when Meyer was still far from being a rich man, Isaac had to bear the burden of his father's high expectations, and therefore suffer periodically from Meyer's frequent disappointments over the way he was not measuring up. As a child Isaac got to know the whip, the belt, and the hairbrush more frequently than his younger brothers. The slightest transgression, the slightest hint that he might not be living up to his role as future standard-bearer of the family, the slightest indication that he might think that roasted pigeons *would* fly into his mouth, and he would be across Meyer's knee with his pants down getting what was coming to him.

Nevertheless, despite the frequent punishments he had to endure for his transgressions and, above all, for his shortcomings, Isaac was still led to believe for much of his youth that he would someday take his rightful place as head of the family. Until Meyer realized what sort of stuff Dan was made of . . .

Then, for Isaac it was downhill all the way. As soon as Dan came of age, he quickly displaced his older brother as family leader and held that position, undisputed, until his death.

But Dan was only one usurper Isaac had to contend with. After Dan came five others. Murry, Sol, and Simon also proved to be stiff competition. And then, when Isaac had grown into manhood, his mother, whom he adored, had to give all her attention to the last two upstarts, Benjamin and William. Not to mention the three girls.

It was all too much for poor Isaac. His insecurities inevitably got the best of him. Thus did he vigorously oppose the younger brothers' entry into the family business on equal terms with the older ones, much to his father's annoyance. And thus did he oppose his brothers' wanting to get control of American Smelting and Refining because he feared partnership with outsiders.

Victimized, albeit unintentionally, by both his father and his brother Dan, Isaac became very quiet and aloof, very conservative in his tastes, beliefs, and behavior, unable to make friends easily, unable to bear with grace the strain of business risk.

Unlike his next-older brothers, who always looked to the future—metals—he had habitually looked to the past—laces and embroideries—and it was with great reluctance that he closed out the latter business and assumed his duties as treasurer of the new one, a position whose responsibilities he then took perhaps too seriously. Lacking the courage of the others, he would always get jittery when his brothers would go out on a limb, as they frequently did, and would want to crawl back toward the trunk. When Nipissing silver on Hudson Bay proved to be a bust, and the Guggenheims were compelled to reimburse investors to the tune of $1,450,000, his brothers just wrote the whole thing off and turned their attention elsewhere, but Isaac suffered a nervous breakdown and had to be confined to a clinic in Switzerland.

After he recovered he took to feeding his insecurities and in his late middle age became quite plump. Tall, heavy, with bulging cheeks and a handlebar moustache, he could easily have been taken for a prosperous, somewhat sad-eyed restaurateur.

Bernard Baruch, reminiscing about the brothers Guggenheim, with whom he had transacted much lucrative business, described Isaac as "taller than the others, and perhaps the best looking, but their inferior as a businessman . . . He was a good man, Isaac, but overly conservative, and I doubt if he would have gone very far on his own."

As it happened, the strong one in the Isaac Guggenheim branch of the family turned out to be Isaac's wife. Carrie Sonneborn, daughter of a prosperous Philadelphia merchant, was a dynamic little red-headed woman with loads of excess energy and a sharp tongue. She was geared to a faster tempo than Isaac, was also more thick-skinned, and, soon after their marriage, she began bossing him around. As the years went by she put on a lot of weight, and with the authority of this extra bulk, she bossed him even more. So much did she come to boss him that Isaac was compelled to take frequent "business trips" to maintain his equilibrium and self-esteem. But, unhappy as he was, he never left her. Nor, unlike some of his brothers, did he console himself by dallying with other women. Puritanical to the core, and perhaps a bit masochistic, he took his victimization in marriage on the chin, just as he had taken his victimization in the parental nest.

If only Carrie, or God, or nature had given him a son, there would have been some compensation. Isaac desperately wanted to produce a male heir, a strong, capable son to carry on the Guggenheim name and someday take control of the Guggenheim empire. His father had expected this; he, too, had expected it, but once again, he was destined to be victimized, this time by nature. Try as they would, he and Carrie were unable to produce other than three daughters. Healthy, vigorous daughters, but still only daughters. Their names were Beulah, Edyth, and Helene. Isaac loved them, but he could never get over the disappointment that at least one of them was not a boy. That he, eldest son of the House of Guggenheim, heir to the world's largest private mining fortune, did not himself have a male heir was nothing less than a cosmic injustice.

Fortunately, his three daughters married well and he was able to project his dynastic ambitions onto his sons-in-law, and finally onto one of his grandchildren. Beulah married a New York businessman by the name of William I. Spiegelberg, and glory be to Jehovah, had a *son*, William I. Spiegelberg, Jr. Edyth married the wealthy banker turned naval officer, Louis M. Josephthal, founder of Josephthal & Company, investment bankers, who eventually became Admiral Josephthal, and Helene, after marrying and divorcing Edmund Haas, married Lord Melvill Ward of Great Britain.

When William I. Spiegelberg, Jr. grew into young manhood, Isaac, with pathetic insistence, convinced him—and his parents—to change his name to Isaac Guggenheim II. It took some convincing. At first, Spiegelberg senior opposed the idea and was seconded by his son. But Isaac held the trump card: money, inheritance. If Spiegelberg junior would change his name to Isaac Guggenheim II he would receive a major legacy from Isaac's estate, about $5 million. Otherwise, little or nothing. This was enough to tip the scales, and, after the necessary documents were drawn up and the young man was shown the will, William I. Spiegelberg, Jr. accepted his bribe and duly changed his name to Isaac Guggenheim II.

With that all-important piece of dynastic business settled, Isaac turned his remaining energies to what would be his most enduring achievement, the construction, immediately after the war, of his princely $2 million, 205-acre Villa Carola, at Sands Point, a villa that would cost at least $6.7 million to build today, probably more.

Yes, now he would build a monument that would fittingly proclaim the power and glory of the House of Guggenheim to the world. After securing his majestic hilltop site, he summoned the foremost architects and interior decorators of the day and drew up plans. It was decided to reproduce, with a few variants, a great Italian country villa in high Renaissance style. The outer walls would be of terracotta, the roof of red tile, and there would be an observation tower and a porte cochere. Inside, on the main floor, long vaulted galleries, supported by marble columns with finely carved capitals, would enclose a paved court with fountain. The large drawing rooms, reception rooms, the music room, the billiard room, Isaac's study, the high Gothic library, would open off the galleries. The walls and ceilings of most of these rooms would be paneled in Indian teak and hung with rare antique damask. A large organ would be installed behind finely carved wooden spindles in the main living room. The dining room, which would face southwest, would be decorated and furnished in the style of Louis XVI. Upstairs there would be ten bedrooms, also paneled in teak, with adjoining baths, a breakfast room, three sitting rooms, several storerooms, a pantry, and the servants' quarters. The house would contain forty rooms in all and would be surrounded by geometrical Italian gardens with sculpted hedges, marble statues of the Renaissance and early baroque periods, fountains, and thick groves of pine and ' ak. The property would be entirely surrounded by stone walls and high iron fences, and would contain also two gatehouses, a beach house, and a private yacht landing, stables for as many as twenty horses, two garages, two greenhouses, twc barns, and other outbuildings to be used as servants' and groundkeepers' quarters.

While work on the place was underway, Isaac made discreet inquiries about applying for membership in the exclusive, overwhelmingly WASP Sands Point Bath and Golf Club, where he hoped to play golf, a sport he enjoyed very much. To his profound shock and dismay, he was informed he would be turned down because he was a Jew.

Victimized now by his WASP neighbors—the Woolworths and the Astors owned property adjoining his and were members of the club— Isaac's grandiose plans for Villa Carola and the splendid life he was going to lead there suddenly lost their promise.

Isaac's spunk, however, was not yet all used up. After catching his breath, he reacted to the unspeakable slight by canceling much of his landscaping plans and creating his *own* private nine-hole golf course on the property. Not only that, he also hired the best golf-course designer in the country to lay out the course, ordering him to duplicate what he considered were the finest holes in the United States.

In two years the main house was ready for occupancy; several hundred thousand dollars had been spent on paintings and furnishings, the gardens were laid out, the statues and fountains set in their places, and most of the secondary buildings were completed. A year later the golf course was ready.

In these lordly surroundings Isaac Guggenheim passed the last years of his life. He and Carrie gave small, quietly sumptuous dinner parties in the gold-paneled, red-damask Louis XVI dining room. Often, in the evening, they would invite a few friends in and listen to some of the finest organists of the day play Bach, Handel, and Frescobaldi. The daughters and their families would come out on weekends and during the hot summer months, and then the great marble galleries would ring to a sudden new life. Isaac liked to garden and would often personally attend to the more than one hundred potted plants surrounding his villa. During the winter he went about in heavy Scottish tweeds closely overseeing the cultivation of fresh fruits and vegetables in the greenhouses; he delighted in serving his *own* Brussels sprouts, lima beans, strawberries, and greengage plums at his 410 Park Avenue apartment when there was snow on the ground. During the summer he and Carrie and the girls would take daylong trips on the Sound in the family yacht. And, whenever he got a chance, Isaac would play golf on his magnificent course, often with brothers Solomon, Murry, and Dan. During the last two years of his life, no fewer than 18 servants and 104 grounds keepers toiled for him and his not-too-large family at Villa Carola.

But Isaac was not destined to enjoy his estate for long. He died on a visit to England in the fall of 1922, at sixty-eight, only three years after his monument was completed, leaving $18 million in securities plus Villa Carola to his heirs.

After $2.5 million in estate taxes were paid, $2 million went to each of his daughters, Beulah Spiegelberg, Edyth Josephthal, and Helene, Lady Ward. Trust funds of $100,000 each were established for his three granddaughters. Another $100,000 went to the Sydenham Hospital and the Federation of Jewish Charities. And Isaac Guggenheim II (né Spiegelberg) received two-thirds of Isaac's holdings in Guggenheim Brothers-controlled Caracoles Tin Corporation, or about $5 million on paper. The "rest and residue," about $4 million, went to the rambunctious Carrie, who would outlive her husband by eight years.

Isaac Guggenheim II was expected to go into Guggenheim Brothers and, as one of the major stockholders in Caracoles Tin, was also expected to take a leading managerial role in that company. But as it turned out, he took no interest in Guggenheim Brothers, Caracoles Tin, or even in bearing the name of Guggenheim. Five years after Isaac senior died, he sold his shares of Caracoles Tin for about $4 million, changed his name back to William I. Spiegelberg, Jr., and was banished from the heart, mind, and rolls of the Guggenheim family forever.

It took years after this double cross, after this last victimization, for the line of Isaac Guggenheim to redeem itself. Finally, generations later, a great granddaughter of Isaac's by the name of Iris Love came along who, with her grandmother Edyth's encouragement and financial aid, blossomed into one of America's most daring and accomplished archaeologists, the discoverer of the Temple of Aphrodite on Knidos, among many other ancient remains, and the identifier of the hitherto unidentified head of Aphrodite in the British Museum.

Not long after the settlement of Isaac's estate, many of Villa Carola's paintings and furnishings, which had cost around $250,000, were sold at auction for $75,000 and brother Solomon bought the villa and its grounds and golf course from the estate, again at auction, at the bargain price of $610,000 cash. Solomon and his family then lived in it, during the period in which Solomon began collecting modern art and planning his museum, until his death in 1949.

After Solomon's death a group of real estate developers were about to buy Villa Carola, then known as Trillora Court, and carve it up into a housing development of one-acre plots, when Thomas Watson, Jr., president of IBM, discovered the property and promptly bought it for his company.

Villa Carola now serves as both IBM's Management Training Center and as a country club for the company's New York State employees. (The center's manager, however, is quick to point out that any employee is eligible to use the club, and there are 160,000 employees in America and 130,000 abroad.)

The Management Training Center gives courses to specially selected ("selected for success") executives in "interpersonal relationships," "life planning," "management style," foreign affairs, and advanced computer programming.

A fitting end to Villa Carola and Isaac's dream of erecting a lasting monument to the House of Guggenheim? Yes, in a way, for a convincing case could be made that Guggenheim Brothers, with its pioneering worldwide operations, was one of the American empire's first multinational companies, and IBM a logical descendant. And why shouldn't 290,000 of the new privileged, rather than a mere handful of the former breed, now have access to the golf course, the tennis courts, the beach house, the yacht landing?

Still, there is something curiously incongruous about the scenes that now take place daily at Villa Carola. We shall not dwell on the groups of gray-suited, on-the-way-up executives one sees strolling down the 1,500-yard, elm-lined "contemplation walk," or speak about the snack bars that now adorn the golf links, but pause briefly to behold the specially selected young IBM employee sitting amidst Venetian mirrors, Savonarola chairs, an organ hiding behind delicately carved spindles, and tapping away on a time-shared IBM computer terminal. Tap, tap, tap. Click, click, click. Tap, tap, tap. Click, click, click. Well, if not Isaac, the others—especially Dan and Sol—would have liked it. Yes, Dan and Sol would have been most pleased.

3

DANIEL AND FLORENCE:
A FIRST STEP INTO SPACE

WHEN SATURN V SLOWLY LIFTED OFF ITS LAUNCHING PAD AND streaked into the heavens, on its way to disgorging the space capsule that landed the first human being on the moon, few people were aware that some two hundred patents to Saturn's rocket system once belonged, in part, to a foundation created by Daniel Guggenheim in 1924. Such was the torrent of words the immediate $30 billion event called forth, that the origins of the event were almost entirely ignored.

Many of these patents had been infringed by the United States government during the acceleration of its guided missile and space programs throughout the 1940s. In 1951 Mrs. Esther C. Goddard, widow of the rocket pioneer Robert H. Goddard, and the Daniel and Florence Guggenheim Foundation, which had financed Goddard, filed a joint claim for government infringement of Goddard's work. Ten years later, the complex litigation ended with an award of $1 million to Mrs. Goddard and the Guggenheim Foundation, the largest government settlement in the history of U.S. patents.

The long suit clearly established the crucial importance of Goddard's work to the space effort, and vindicated, once and for all, Daniel Guggenheim's faith in the future of rocketry. Thirty-two years before the settlement of the patent-infringement suit, Dan had risked his reputation and his money by financing the unknown, and frequently ridiculed, rocket pioneer at a time when no one else in America, least of all in the government, was farsighted and bold enough to back him.

It was typical of Dan to spend his money chiefly on advanced technological research. Not for him, as it would be for two of his brothers, the subsidization of such elusive pursuits as nonobjective painting and avant-garde verse. No, Dan had spent a lifetime discarding obsolete technological processes and searching for, and applying, new ones. The new reduction processes he had employed at Bingham Canyon and Chuquicamata had revolutionized the copper industry. But never, in his most feverish bursts of enthusiasm, did he imagine that the money he had put into rockets in 1929 would someday result, for better or worse, in landing a man on the moon.

One of Wall Street's favorite quips during the heyday of the Guggenheims was to describe the brothers as resembling the numeral one million, a one followed by six zeros.

The characterization was, of course, unfair for the hydraheaded intelligence that was the brothers Guggenheim, unfair, decidedly, to the shrewd, genial Solomon, and, to a lesser degree, unfair also to the steady, financially acute Murry, and to the latently inspired Simon, but it did do justice to the last three zeros—Isaac, Ben, and Will—at least so far as the later development of the business was concerned, and most certainly it did justice to the one, the indomitable, the inexhaustible "Mr. Dan."

Would the Guggenheim boys have vanquished Rockefeller forces on two occasions, including wrenching control of American Smelting and Refining away from the smelters' trust, won the anti-Semitic J. P. Morgan over to their cause, taken such staggering risks as laying down a $25 million railroad over moving glaciers to mine a frozen mountain of copper in Alaska, or investing $25 million in mining another copper mountain 9,500 feet up in the Chilean Andes, without Daniel? Unlikely. Isaac, Ben, and Will had consistently opposed Daniel's expansionist policies, and Solomon, Murry, and Simon were never prime movers; they habitually followed the paths opened up by Dan. No, it was always Dan who led the way; it was always Dan who was willing to give the impossible a try; Dan who went to obtain the concessions from the President of Mexico; Dan who took on the Rockefeller dragon twice, and defeated it twice; Dan who got J. P. Morgan interested in developing Alaska; Dan who made the Congo and Angola deals with Thomas Fortune Ryan; Dan who decided to expand into Bolivia and Chile.

"Mr. Dan," as he was known in lower Manhattan, and in the worlds of mining and smelting, was one of those fortunate men who are able to live up to all their era expects of them. During the heroic years of Dan's career—1890–1923—the ideal American male had to be a businessman—professional men, artists, academics were not very highly regarded—who was hardworking, individualistic, resourceful, "progressive" (in business, not politics), expansionist, "moral" (sexually), and acquisitive. He was not expected to be much of a team player. He was supposed to hurl himself into the fray, no-holds-barred, and get what he could get, not exclusively for himself, of course, but for himself and his family. Dan fitted the ideal in every way. He was an indefatigable worker; often he worked sixteen hours a day. He was very independent, very autocratic, always insisting on having his own way, and almost always getting it. He was dynamic and "forward-looking": Ruthlessly he would discard obsolete methods and employees. He was conservative politically, but adventurous in business. He believed in Progress-with-a-capital-P, believed it was divinely ordained and everlasting, and would have most certainly been outraged if someone were to suggest the word was really a euphemism for greed. He was a fine, upstanding family man. He was puritanical: He did not waste his time, energy, or money on mistresses. He was not frivolous: He had no interest in entering Society-with-a-capital-S. He was 1,000 percent committed to the faith of United States industrial imperialism. He believed with Calvin Coolidge that "the business of America is business." He wished to own as much of the world's goods as he possibly could. He was very bourgeois, very single-minded, and often a bit tedious. When asked by *Forbes* magazine what the secret of his business success was, he responded: "A combination of tenacity and tact." Then, elucidating on tenacity, which he seemed to equate with aggressiveness, he said: "You see, roasted pigeons do not fly into one's mouth."

He was immensely respected by his peers, who often praised his leadership ability, fair dealing, and large-mindedness. Bernard Baruch described him as "one of the three small men I've known—the others were Samuel Gompers and Henry Davidson—who sat taller than most men stand. I see Dan yet, a little fellow sitting in a big chair and dominating the entire room from it. Physically small, you understand, but big in spirit. He was no double-dealer. He had piercing eyes, strong features, and wonderful teeth, a wonderful smile."

Short physically (after the Nipissing fiasco he was called "The Little Nipper"), he was also very down-to-earth intellectually, was always impatient with abstractions and generalities. Facts were what interested him, above all facts that led to substantial figures below the bottom line.

Leaving school, which he detested, at seventeen to go to work as a trainee in the family embroidery mill at St. Gall, near Zurich, he was educated principally in the factory and the office, and in German ways of thinking and doing business. From his seventeenth to his twenty-seventh year he lived, trained, and worked in German-speaking Switzerland and in Germany itself, absorbing such traditionally Germanic traits as industriousness, dogmatism, and rigorous personal discipline, characteristics that would stay with him all his life. In many respects his culture was more Germanic than American or Jewish, a statement that could be made also about the Guggenheim family as a whole. He spoke German fluently, felt very much at home in Frankfurt, Hamburg, and Zurich, admired German science and industry, loved German wines, adored German music, especially Beethoven and Wagner, and his favorite vacation retreats were the German spas Carlsbad and Baden-Baden.

One trait he possessed, which is not ordinarily associated with Germans, especially Swiss-Germans, was generosity. No, more than generosity—magnanimity. Two episodes illustrate this, the brightest side of his personality . . .

When Dan heard about the San Francisco earthquake he immediately sent $50,000 to the mayor with the telegraphed instructions: NO RED TAPE GIVE IT TO THE PEOPLE AT ONCE. Not long thereafter, two carts, hauled by drays from a bank in Sausalito, went to the city and distributed the cash to the neediest victims.

Several years later, while driving his car in lower Manhattan, Dan knocked down and seriously injured the son of a poor Italian immigrant. Immediately he leapt out of the car, confronted an angry, menacing crowd, took the boy in his arms, got back into his car, and, telling a policeman to follow, rushed to a hospital. He then waited at the hospital until the boy's parents were found, commiserated with them, paid all the hospital and medical bills, then, after the child recovered completely, still continued to help out the family financially.

A man of unusually generous sentiments and actions, there was, however, one thing he was most emphatically not generous about, and that was communism. Dan soon recognized in bolshevism a force that would prevent the very existence of people like himself and after its triumph in Russia he combated the ideology wherever he thought he detected it.

In an article for *The New York Times* he wrote:

> The radicals in the labor movement are demanding what is virtually the control of industry. The demand is in essence an attempt for a class autocracy of labor which is nothing less than Bolshevism.

I have been told by unimpeachable authority that when the Bol-
sheviki took control of certain mines in Siberia, the workmen ordered
the former foremen, superintendents, engineers and managers, into the
mines as laborers, and they then took over the management of the
mines. The leader elected to become manager was to write out a lot of
figures on pieces of paper and then tear them up and smoke cigarets.
The result of such management was just about what could be expected
and the mines were abandoned.

As for Dan's own labor policies, they were always based on his
overriding concern for production and profits. "Labor," he once
wrote, "can only get what it produces. If it wants more, it must produce more." And: "Profits are the life blood of business, and greater
profits can be made only through more efficient, increased production."

In the last analysis Dan's social and economic philosophy envisioned
a state of affairs not unlike that of the great landed estates of the Middle Ages. The modern industrialists, like himself, were the feudal overlords, and the clerks and workers were, or at least should be, in his
schemata, the faithful, obedient, well-fed, uncomplaining yeomanry.
Any disruption of this divine order was heresy and should be repressed
accordingly.

These dogmatic beliefs, united with an exceptionally bold and dynamic temperament, guided Dan to the making of a vast fortune, and
with that fortune, in his later years, he made several very important
contributions to Western civilization.

But before he began making these contributions he first took care,
as brother Isaac had, to establish himself and his immediate family
in the imperial style he felt he deserved.

In his vast Castlegould, which he renamed Hempstead House,
Daniel Guggenheim lived like the emperor he was, surrounded by a
Rembrandt, two Rubenses, a Van Dyck, herds of cattle, flocks of
sheep, stables of horses, a golf course, peacocks and pheasants, servants, farmers, and grounds keepers by the score.

The great stone house with its central tower, its turreted walls and
battlements was situated on a promontory of Sands Point overlooking
Long Island Sound, not very far from Villa Carola, and along that
stretch of shoreline where F. Scott Fitzgerald envisioned much of the
action of his *Great Gatsby*.

Howard Gould had built the castle in 1901, importing twenty-eight
Italian stonecutters, masons, and sculptors to carve its windows, por-
tals, cornices, battlements, columns, capitals, towers, gargoyles. For
Dan, who bought not only the castle, its outbuildings and their 350

acres, but almost all the contents of the house as well, Castle-gould represented an extraordinary bargain. Since Dan possessed the same last initial as Gould, he did not have to go to the trouble and expense of having G's cast for the huge wrought-iron, spear-crested fence that enclosed the entire property, or for its four iron gates, nor did he have to have G's sewn on the linens, or engraved on the silver-ware, or on the gold service, or baked into the crockery, or carved into the woodwork above the fireplaces, or engraved or carved on any number of other fixtures, such as doors and bedsteads, or in any number of other places throughout the property, such as the stables, barns, greenhouses, beach house, casino. To his delight, there were hundreds of G's all over the estate. He particularly admired the great iron G, painted gold against a black shield, that adorned the main gate. Yes, it was as if the Guggenheims were predestined to inhabit the former bastion of the Goulds.

Dan loved the place. It was the appropriate monument, already packaged, to his grandiose ambitions and worldwide achievements. The great entrance hall, with its high-vaulted Gothic ceiling in gray stone and immense silver pipe organ, was worthy of any monarch in Europe. As was the enormous palm court with fountain on the ground floor, which Dan filled with over 150 rare plants and orchids. As were the precious sixteenth-century Flemish tapestries, the paintings—Rembrandt's "Portrait of an Old Woman," Van Dyck's "Portrait of a Nobleman," two huge canvases by Rubens. As were the guesthouses, the amusement houses, the huge stone barns, stables, and storehouses. Yes, worthy of any monarch in Europe, worthy, a dozen times over, of the *Landvogt* of Baden.

As soon as he took possession of the estate, Dan set about creating a self-sufficient, self-contained feudal domain for himself and his family, complete with every luxury and convenience the mind could imagine. In so doing he fulfilled one of the most cherished dreams of the early-twentieth-century American heart: the attainment of the trappings of the European aristocracy.

He built a nine-hole golf course with clubhouse (he did not even bother to try to join the local country club). He built tennis courts. He built a bowling alley. He built a beach house in rustic clapboard in which he installed a swimming pool. He built another stone barn, which he decorated with stuffed moose heads and in which his son set a brilliantly painted Sicilian cart depicting the triumphs of another monarch, Charles V, King of Spain, Italy, and the Netherlands, and Emperor of the New World. He spruced up the casino, the piggery,

the hennery, the pheasant and peacock houses, and built an amusement house which he called Tally-Ho. And on his 350 acres he raised
thoroughbred horses, ran a dairy, slaughtered his own cattle, hung
his own beef, cured his own hams, sausage, and bacon, raised his own
fruits and vegetables, canned his own preserves, killed and ate his
own hens and pheasants. Seventeen servants and two hundred farmers
and grounds keepers helped him in these efforts. And there were also
in residence a golf pro, a tennis pro, and a riding master.

As grand patriarch of the House of Guggenheim, Dan loved nothing so much as to gather his entire immediate family around him at
Hempstead House and enjoy watching them run around the grounds,
bowl, ride, swim, play tennis and golf. By the mid-1920s that family
consisted of his wife, Florence, three married children—M. Robert,
Harry Frank, and Gladys—and eight grandchildren—four boys and
four girls. M. Robert, by that time, had given every indication that
he would turn out to be the spectacular playboy he became; Harry had
proved both his mettle and his versatility by playing a vital role in
readying Chuquicamata for production, earning two degrees from
Cambridge, and winning his wings as a naval aviator; and the reliable,
capable Gladys had shown her good judgment by marrying Roger Williams Straus, son of Oscar Straus of the R. H. Macy Strauses, U.S.
ambassador to Turkey under three presidents, and member of Theodore
Roosevelt's Cabinet, and the first Jew in American history to occupy
a cabinet post. Reminiscing about his youth at Hempstead House,
Gladys Straus' younger son, Roger W. Straus, Jr., the publisher, recalls the castle, the golf course, the stables, the tennis courts, the
bowling alley, the indoor pool, the beach, and sighs: "Yeah, it's been
downhill ever since."

Recognizing that Harry, not Robert, would be the one who would
carry on the leadership of the House of Guggenheim after his death,
Daniel, in 1923, gave Harry and his wife 90 of his 350 acres, plus
$250,000 to build and furnish their own house. The result was the
magnificent reproduction Norman château Falaise, perched on a cliff
overlooking the Sound, and destined to play a central role in the
Guggenheim drama to come.

With that bit of dynastic business taken care of, Dan turned his at-
tentions, for the first time in his life, toward giving away some of his
fortune.

For years he and his wife, Florence, had been contributing sums of
money, some large, some small, to certain charities that were close to
their hearts, particularly Florence's heart. In 1924 they decided to

institutionalize this giving by establishing the Daniel and Florence Guggenheim Foundation for "the promotion, through charitable and benevolent activities, of the well-being of man throughout the world." There were five signers to the original deed of gift: Mr. and Mrs. Dan and their three children.

Some years before the establishment of the foundation Dan had outlined his philosophy of money in a letter to Harry:

> . . . Money, to me, for the luxury that it will give me has very little value. But money is power, and the power is the thing to use, not to abuse. With money, or with power, you can accomplish a great deal in the world for yourself and the world. For yourself, because of the satisfaction you will obtain from accomplishing for the world.

When one considers the pharaonic luxury in which Daniel and Florence Guggenheim lived, both at Hempstead House and in their ten-room suite in the St. Regis Hotel in New York, with all the services and servants of the hotel at their beck and call, one cannot help but wink at the first part of Daniel's statement. But knowing the relish with which he spent his fortune, we must accept the second part unquestioningly.

The first grants of the new foundation went mostly to organizations in which Florence was interested. These included the free Goldman Band concerts in New York's Central Park, the American Women's Association (Florence was a member of the board and a fighter for women's rights all her life), such Jewish associations as the Jewish Theological Seminary, the Hebrew Orphan Asylum, and the United Jewish Campaign (Florence took much more interest in Jewish affairs than Dan did), the New York Botanical Gardens, the Symphony Society of New York, the Catholic Writers' Guild.

In time the Daniel and Florence Guggenheim Foundation took over total support of the popular Goldman Band concerts, which became Florence's favorite benefaction. A gracious lady with an authoritative, aristocratic bearing, taller than Dan, she attended every opening night until her death in 1945. Today the concerts are held principally in the Guggenheim bandshell in Damrosch Park, Lincoln Center.

By 1975 the foundation had made over four hundred grants to ninety-eight organizations in the United States and abroad, including hospitals and medical institutes in Chile, the Congo, and Israel.

But Dan's bold stroke in giving turned out not so much to be the

Daniel and Florence—with its rather conventional agenda of bequests
—but his creation, in 1926, of the Daniel Guggenheim Fund for the
Promotion of Aeronautics.

It has been said that there is nothing so timid as a large sum of
money. Confronted with the task of spending their fortunes, most
American millionaires before Daniel Guggenheim tended to play it
safe by fertilizing such readily acceptable fields as education, public
libraries, medicine, public health. Dan, however, decided to gamble
with very risky cards and subsidize an activity in which there was very
little public or governmental interest, one which was considered, at
best, little more than a manifestation of technological exhibitionism.

It was his son Harry who first led Dan into the unexplored territory
of aeronautics. For Dan it soon became every bit as exciting as prospecting for copper in Alaska.

Harry had become intoxicated by the possibilities of aviation as a
naval pilot in World War I. When he returned to the United States
after the war he was appalled to find American aviation far behind
that of Europe, languishing for lack of enthusiasm and money. The
government seemed to be totally ignorant of its potential, and a surprisingly conservative American public balked completely at the idea
of a commercial airline. Such was the state of U.S. aviation at the
time that Eddie Rickenbacker, leading U.S. ace in World War I, went
into the automobile industry rather than aviation after he returned
from the war.

The faith with which young Harry Guggenheim, in his early thirties,
approached aviation sounds pathetically naïve to us today, with what
we know of the airplane's unique capacity for destruction. He wrote:

> Airplanes are the harbingers of peace, the instrumentality that will
> bring about a lasting sympathy among the nations. . . . What is the
> greatest single contribution the airplane has to make toward human
> progress? . . . It is annihilation of space . . . and therefore closer
> communion between various communities. . . . The airplane will bind
> nations together through increased understanding.

Later, in one of his frequent bursts of enthusiasm reminiscent of
the days of the J. P. Morgan deal or the Samuel Gompers Embrace,
Daniel echoed his son, in a somewhat lower key, by declaring, immediately after watching a test flight, "We must realize that the air
age is already here. Once realized, our provincialism will fall away
from us. Universal flying will make us all neighbors."

Burning with an evangelistic passion to do something important to promote aviation, young Harry Guggenheim conceived the idea of creating a school of aeronautics at New York University, which would be the first of its kind. Toward this end, he decided to write a circular letter on the subject and send it to a few of the wealthiest bankers and industrialists in America, asking them to support the project.

Harry was staying with his father at Hempstead House at the time, while the finishing touches were being applied to Falaise, and after he had written the letter he showed it to Dan, asking him for his comments. Dan looked at the letter as if he were inspecting a sample of ore, said he would like to sleep on it, and went to bed. He would discuss the matter with Harry at breakfast in the morning.

During that night at Hempstead House modern American aviation, and eventually modern American astronautics, were incubated and born.

Daniel arose in the morning, joined his son in the walnut-paneled, stained-glass-windowed Elizabethan breakfast room, and over scrambled eggs, bacon, toast, and coffee, served by a liveried, white-gloved houseboy, told Harry not to bother to send the letter out, that he would put up the money himself, all that was needed.

The year was 1925. The Daniel and Florence Guggenheim Foundation was already in its second year. As we have seen, it was dedicated largely to Florence's favorite organizations. Now something had come along that could grip Dan personally. And also perhaps make up in a way for that terrible break in the ranks—Harry and Edmond resigning from Guggenheim Brothers over the sale of Chile Copper—the company that owned and operated Chuquicamata—two years before.

On June 15, 1925, Daniel's gift of $500,000 to New York University was announced and America's first school of aeronautics was born. At the ground-breaking ceremonies that October Dan told the four hundred notables present:

> As I am an old man whose active days are past, I shall dedicate the rest of my life to aviation, the greatest road to opportunity which lies before the science and the commerce of the civilized countries of the earth today. I shall do this as part of my duty to my country, whose ample opportunities have ever been at my hand and whose bountiful blessings I have had the good fortune to enjoy.

Encouraged by the favorable reception to his gift—the press lauded it from coast to coast—Dan then took an even bolder step and proposed to the U.S. government the establishment of a $2.5 million fund for the promotion of aeronautics.

Calvin Coolidge was President at the time and when Harry approached him with the idea, seeking official government sanction and moral support, Coolidge was at first not particularly impressed.

To Harry's impassioned praise of the airplane and its ability to get people from one place to another faster than any other means of transportation, Coolidge the philosopher responded: "What's the use of getting there quicker if you haven't got something better to say when you've arrived?"

But in the end the President gave his blessing, if somewhat half-heartedly, and on January 16, 1926, the Daniel Guggenheim Fund for the Promotion of Aeronautics was established with an initial grant of $500,000. Later, $2 million more was added, and, still later, another $475,000. The purpose of the fund was "to provide for aviation at a critical period of its infancy immediate, practical, and substantial assistance in its commercial, industrial, and scientific aspects."

In celebration of this event the papers ran a cartoon entitled "Nursie Guggenheim," which showed Dan holding a $2.5 million bottle to the mouth of an infant called American Aviation and saying: "He certainly is hungry."

Among the many opportunities the fund opened up, it gave the hitherto footloose and unemployed Harry something to do. At thirty-six he became president of the fund and hurled himself into its business with almost religious dedication. This was what he believed in. This was what he wanted to do in life.

Such was the devotional awe Harry brought to aviation that he went out of his way to obtain a sliver of the first airplane hangar in the world, at Kitty Hawk, North Carolina, which he then placed, with sincere piety, in a sort of reliquary in the Partners' Room of Guggenheim Brothers.

Harry wasted no time in getting down to work. He opened an office on Madison Avenue, hired Ivy Lee, the public relations wizard who had done such a superb job enhancing the Rockefeller image, and by the end of 1926 the fund was financing and publicizing its first projects.

Few people connected with the fund were fully aware at the time of the immense significance of what they were doing. But Harry knew. He knew full well, as his correspondence during the period attests, that his family was nothing less than Queen Isabella financing the Columbuses of the twentieth century.

One of Harry's first projects was to popularize flying by sponsoring tours of famous aviators. After Comdr. Richard E. Byrd made his spectacular, round-trip flight over the North Pole on the *Josephine*

Ford, piloted by Floyd Bennett, Harry sent Bennett out in his plane on a tour of forty U.S. cities. Later, after Lindbergh, whom Harry had encouraged, made his historic transoceanic flight, Harry financed Lindbergh's subsequent tour of forty-eight states and twenty-three state capitals in his *Spirit of St. Louis.* Harry also put Falaise at Lindbergh's disposal so that he could write *We,* the log of his flight, in peace, away from the lionizers who continually pounced on him.

While these tours were going on, admirably publicized in all the newspapers of the nation by Ivy Lee, the fund set up the Full Flight Laboratory for the Study of Fog-Flying, with Lt. James H. (Jimmy) Doolittle in charge. On the morning of September 24, 1929, after a year of intensive work, Jimmy Doolittle, seated in a completely covered cockpit and guided entirely by instruments perfected in his laboratory, took off from Mitchel Field, flew away from the field, turned around, recrossed it, turned again, and came back, landing a short distance from his starting point. Instrument flying had been born and Dan and Harry were most pleased.

Subsequently the Fund financed the perfecting and manufacture of the first gyroscopic compass for aircraft; a $100,000 prize for the manufacture of the safest aircraft; a model weather-reporting service; the first American commercial airline—Western Air Express—operating between Los Angeles and San Francisco; and schools of aeronautical engineering at MIT, Georgia Tech, California Institute of Technology, the University of Washington, Stanford, Harvard, Syracuse, and the University of Michigan. It also financed the Hungarian aerospace engineer Theodor von Kármán, inventor of the wind tunnel, smooth flight, designer of the DC-3, and first recipient of the National Medal of Science.

On February 1, 1930, in the seventy-fourth and last year of Daniel Guggenheim's life, the fund was liquidated, having accomplished its goals. American aviation was at last on a firm footing; the public attitude had changed from apathetic indifference to enthusiastic support; and Harry could rejoice that he and his father had been largely responsible for these achievements.

The Guggenheims' efforts on behalf of aviation were far from over, however. While the Daniel Guggenheim Fund for the Promotion of Aeronautics was being phased out, the Daniel and Florence Guggenheim Foundation took the boldest step of all and made a grant to an obscure physics professor in Massachusetts who was experimenting with rockets he hoped would one day land a man on the moon.

The professor, Robert H. Goddard of Clark University, was a frail, solitary, withdrawn, prematurely bald genius who, since youth, had dreamed of ushering man into an era of journeys beyond the earth.

Born into an old Yankee family whose original American ancestor had emigrated with the Puritans from England to Massachusetts in 1666, Goddard had suffered throughout grade school from frequent colds, attacks of pleurisy and bronchitis, and extreme shyness. Later he developed tuberculosis and remained tubercular all his life. He was given a stern, puritanical upbringing, in the old New England tradition; was taught since childhood to disdain sensual pleasures and concentrate wholly on duty. It appears that he did not take much of an interest in the sensual side of women until he was in his mid-thirties. Then, all of a sudden, he became interested in salesgirls, waitresses, clerks, Western Union typists. One day, according to a diary entry, he met a telegraph operator in a cafeteria. He asked her to go out with him. She declined. The next day he saw her with a much younger man. Later he asked a waitress out and she told him she did not go out with "elderly" men. By then, though a comparatively young man, he was somewhat stoop-shouldered and completely bald. He did not marry until he was over forty and it took him years to get up the courage to propose. He often confessed to intimates, and his diary, that he never felt very comfortable in society and, given the fragile state of his health, we can assume he never felt very comfortable on earth either.

Duty, duty. Duty for young Goddard soon took the form of dreams, and later concrete plans, to enable man to escape the earth. These dreams he did not limit to mere interplanetary travel. No, since he was quite sure there was no life on the moon or the planets of our solar system, he became interested, above all, in reaching the nearest stars, to find out whether they had life-sustaining planets around them, and, not stopping there, in *intergalactic* travel as well.

However, since the stars and galaxies were light-years away, it would take decades, generations, entire lifetimes, and more to reach them, even at the fastest possible speeds. How to get around this difficulty? Answer: freeze human protoplasm; in this way human life could be prolonged for space journeys of over a thousand years!

> If there were some substance like formaline [he wrote] which would permeate every tissue, and kill all bacterial life except the spores; and besides, the body were placed in a sealed glass containing nitrogen, and, perhaps, the temperature remained constant, and a little above freezing, there seems no reason why the body might not remain in this passive condition indefinitely, since decay is absolutely arrested from the mo-

ment the passivity is assumed, although the same amount of moisture is present, as when the body is active. . . .

Young Goddard would let nothing, not even death, stand in the way of his plans to get as far away as possible from the earth and the human condition.

Came time for action. First he proved, for the first time, with an ingenious experiment employing a vacuum-sealed tunnel, that rockets could propel themselves in a vacuum, and hence, in outer space. Then, in July, 1929, he hauled a strange-looking contraption called "Nell" to his Aunt Effie's cabbage patch in Auburn, Massachusetts, and, amid roaring flames, sent the world's first liquid-fueled rocket into the air. The event was quickly followed by the arrival of police cars, fire trucks, ambulances. Aunt Effie's neighbors had complained of the tremendous explosion. One of them, an old lady, said that "waves" from Goddard's rocket "had pierced the apex of her heart." A Boston newspaper headlined: MOON ROCKET MISSES TARGET BY 238,799 MILES. After the smoke cleared, Goddard announced to the press: "If we had a million dollars, we *could* send a rocket to the moon, but where would we get a million dollars?"

Where indeed? Certainly not from the likes of such conservative millionaires as the Rockefellers, Mellons, Du Ponts, Carnegies. (Goddard had already been turned down by the Du Ponts, who, he claimed, were interested only in stealing his ideas, and had met with an equally cold shoulder from the Carnegies.) But when Lindbergh got wind of Goddard's experiment and comment he knew just where to go for the money.

Daniel Guggenheim received Lindbergh in his library at Hempstead House. There, before a fire in the great high-ceilinged, wood-paneled room with its Gothic, leaded windows and shelves upon shelves of books, Lindbergh told the aging capitalist about Goddard's experiments and his future plans and needs.

After the presentation Dan asked Lindbergh, in his usual blunt manner—the same manner he had used for years in interrogating prospectors, explorers, engineers about ore properties—"You believe these rockets have a real future?"

"Probably," Lindbergh replied. "Of course one is never certain."

"But you think so . . . and this professor of yours, he really seems capable?"

"As far as I can tell he knows more about rockets than any man in this country."

"How much does he need?"

"For a four-year project, he would need twenty-five thousand dollars a year."

"Do you think it's worth my investing a hundred thousand?"

"Well, of course, it's taking a chance. . . . But if we're ever going beyond airplanes and propellers we probably have to go to rockets. . . . Yes, I think it's worth it."

Dan trusted Lindbergh implicitly and made up his mind on the spot. He would give $50,000 "seed money," as he called it, for the first two years and $50,000 for the next two if Lindbergh and Harry and their advisory committee, reviewing Goddard's work, still agreed. Lindbergh immediately telephoned the news to Goddard. It was the first significant financial support the professor had received and he was so overjoyed he took his wife out for a Chinese dinner. Rarely did the frugal Goddards dine in restaurants.

Shortly thereafter the Daniel Guggenheim Fund for the Measurement and Investigation of High Altitudes was formed, with funds advanced from the Daniel and Florence Guggenheim Foundation, and Goddard moved to Roswell, New Mexico, where more favorable conditions for firing rockets existed than in his Aunt Effie's cabbage patch.

At Roswell, Goddard rented a pueblo-style ranch house with what he called a "nice little field"—about 16,000 acres—attached. Here, on this, America's first rocket proving ground, he conducted his experiments, with support from the Daniel and Florence Guggenheim Foundation, for the next eleven years. Out of these experiments came both the bazooka and the multistage rocket.

Not long after Dan made his momentous decision to finance Goddard, the stock market crashed and J. P. Morgan, Jr. asked the Guggenheims to contribute to a $250 million pool to help shore up the market. Guggenheim Brothers, led now by Murry, for Dan and Sol had both retired, was the only nonbanking institution invited to participate in the pool, which was quite an honor, and it made its contribution, confident the market would soon turn around. When it failed to do so, a collective shudder passed through the family, for, as usual, they were way out on a limb.

The Crash was bad enough—as it turned out the Guggenheims suffered heavy paper losses in their major holdings, Braden, Kennecott, and Anaconda—but what hurt them most in 1929 was the discovery that same year, by a German scientist, of a way to make synthetic nitrate cheaply.

It will be recalled that after the Guggenheims sold their controlling interest in Chile Copper to Anaconda in 1923, against Harry's and Edmond's objections, they then went into the nitrate business.

Dan concluded a $373 million deal with the Chilean government to control all the private nitrate output of the country. Nitrate, a prime source for fertilizers, was also an essential ingredient for munitions, and given the congenital belligerency of men and nations, Dan thought it would have a limitless future. Before long, Guggenheim Brothers owned 98 percent of the nitrate in Chile and controlled 85 percent of the world's production.

For a while it looked as if the Guggenheims had cornered still another vital natural resource, but after the discovery of the synthetic process, their monopoly was broken and the world was soon flooded with cheap nitrate. Consequently the Guggenheims lost much of their market . . . and their investment. And Harry, noting incredulously that Dan had finally lost his Midas touch, had a chance to tell his father "I told you so."

By the middle of 1930 Daniel Guggenheim, who had been suffering intermittently from heart disease and ulcers for the past few years, had become aware that he was not going to live forever and that, though he was still a very wealthy man, he was definitely not going to become, as he once phrased it, "rich beyond the dreams of avarice." The stock market had not bounced back, as he had thought it would, and he had to face the bleak truth that Chilean nitrate was the first natural resource the Guggenheims had touched that did not immediately alchemize into gold. The realization was not good for either his ulcers or his heart.

About the only piece of good news Dan received at the time of the Crash was the appointment of his son Harry, by President Hoover, to be United States ambassador to Cuba. Dan had made a healthy contribution to his friend Hoover's campaign and he was gratified to see the investment had paid off. It also made up, in a way, for the rift with Harry over Chile Copper and the subsequent nitrate fiasco. To celebrate the appointment Dan gave a sumptuous, gold-plate dinner for fifty at Hempstead House, after which the handsome young ambassador was sent on his way to Havana.

As the clouds of economic depression and the failure of the nitrate gamble began more and more to darken the great halls of Hempstead House, Daniel Guggenheim suffered a further decline in his health and, in an effort to ameliorate his condition, left in August, 1930, to take the cure at Carlsbad, returning to Hempstead House in September.

By the middle of September he was feeling feeble and depressed. Normally very active, always bustling around, he would now spend the entire day sitting by the fire reading, with his great German shepherd, Bismarck, at his feet. As he grew weaker, he was compelled to leave the library and take to bed. The end came suddenly, at eleven o'clock in the morning of September 28. Dan was talking with his doctor, Florence, and Harry in his bedroom when a heart attack came and he just lay back in his chair, smiled, and died. It was all over in a matter of minutes.

A few days before he died he was discussing Goddard with his daughter, Gladys Straus, and said: "I'm not going to live to see it, but you'll live to see the mail shot over to Europe."

The remark was typical of Dan's childlike faith in the wonders of technology. What that faith could not envision was that before Goddard's rockets shot the mail to Europe they would be thrusting German V–2's to the destruction of London, for the Germans used Goddard's published patents to build their rockets.

All his life Dan was incapable of seeing that a mere mechanical contrivance like an airplane or a rocket could magnify not only the powers of good but also of evil.

It remained for succeeding generations of Guggenheims to ask themselves whether the Guggenheim air and space patronage had promoted life, beauty, truth, and justice more than it had helped unleash undreamed-of powers of destruction. As the third, fourth, and fifth generations pondered the total destruction from the air of Dresden, Hiroshima, Nagasaki, and Berlin, the destruction of much of London, and the defoliation from the air of South Vietnam, a number could not help concluding that Dan's sublime faith in aeronautics might have been unjustified. And yet, hadn't that faith been responsible for subduing the horrendous tyrannies of Nazi Germany and Imperial Japan?

And, assuming we shall not be able to solve the three greatest problems facing mankind—nuclear arms proliferation, overpopulation, and pollution—might not space travel and ultimately colonization of artificial satellites be the only way humanity will be able to escape the destruction of the earth?

But then, who knew what terrible tyranny the space rocket and its potential offspring, the manned artificial satellite, armed with invulnerable nuclear weapons, might impose on man some day?

* * *

In 1930, however, the airplane and the rocket were still in their innocence and no one, least of all the journalists, expected that anything but unlimited benefits would come from them. And so the newspapers not only hailed Daniel Guggenheim as "the Foster Father of U.S. Aviation," but they also extolled him as one who had "ushered in a new age of progress for mankind."

The reputation of Daniel Guggenheim had come a long way since the days when he and his brothers were repeatedly depicted as monstrous exploiters of what should have been the common wealth of all men. Thanks to Dan's philanthropy, the polar bears Guggenmorgan and Morganheim had metamorphosed into two splendid birds, Guggenlindbergh and Goddardheim.

The New York Times printed Dan's obituary on the front page, main left-hand column, also hailing him as the foster father of American aviation. That Dan was also the foster father of the U.S. multinationals, and one of the founding fathers of the American empire, was entirely overlooked, except by Chile. The Chilean papers praised him for bringing the first large-scale industry to Latin America and did not mention his patronage of aviation and rocketry.

As soon as Dan's death was announced in the papers, hosannas poured into Hempstead House and out of the columns of the press from all over America. Dr. Carl T. Compton, president of MIT, called Dan "the outstanding patron of aviation in America." Bernard Baruch extolled him as "a noble, simple, sweet, magnificent soul." Adolph Ochs, publisher of *The New York Times*, wrote Florence: "I well know the deep affection and admiration you had for each other, your accord in all things, you were ideally mated." And Francis H. Brownell, chairman of the board of American Smelting and Refining, wrote:

> Whenever word went 'round that "Mr. Dan" had decided this or wished that, there was no questioning, but only complete obedience to the dictates of a mind which was recognized by all to be so superior as to be followed implicitly, and all the more readily as he was so universally loved as well as admired.

Among the pallbearers at the packed funeral in Temple Emanu-El were Dwight W. Morrow, Bernard Baruch, John Hays Hammond, Elihu Root, Jr., and Charles Lindbergh. President Hoover, struggling with the deepening Depression, had given up going to millionaires' funerals and cabled his condolences and regrets.

*   *   *

The acquisitive society celebrates the acquisitive man. Not long after the front-page obituary came the exhaustive, sometimes full-page, reportages on Daniel's will.

Mr. Dan's net worth during the last decade of his life had oscillated between $20 million and $50 million, depending on market conditions, but when he died, eleven months after the Crash, his estate was almost insolvent. He had given away around $10 million during his lifetime . . . to members of his family and to his foundations. Now stocks were way down and the Chilean nitrate venture, in which Dan had invested several millions of his own capital, was all but dead. It took almost ten years for the estate "to come back," and when it did, it came back to something in the neighborhood of $25 million, which would be around $86 million in terms of relative purchasing power today.

Dan's major bequests were $2 million outright to trustworthy son Harry; $2 million outright to trustworthy daughter Gladys; $2 million, in trust, to spendthrift son M. Robert; $1.5 million to the Daniel and Florence Guggenheim Foundation; and $475,000 to the Daniel Guggenheim Fund for the Promotion of Aeronautics. Among the minor bequests: $250,000 to his sister Cora Rothschild, who had missed out on a substantial inheritance from her father; $250,000 to Nettie Knox, a niece; $200,000 in cash to his wife, Florence. Estate taxes eventually took around $4 million (the estate was not finally settled until 1940). And the "rest and residue," some $6,950,000 worth of property, including Hempstead House and all its paintings and furnishings, went to Florence.

Two months after Dan died, a black Ford truck, called "the Hearse," hauled a liquid-oxygen-propelled rocket called "Nell" onto the launching pad of America's first rocket-testing center at Roswell, New Mexico. Nell was the most advanced rocket the world had ever seen and it had been assembled thanks entirely to Guggenheim money. Now it went up, thanks to Guggenheim money, to the then-unheard-of altitude of 2,000 feet, achieving a maximum speed of five hundred miles per hour, the greatest speed of a man-made contrivance up to that time. After the test, the rocket's inventor, Robert H. Goddard, wrote an exuberant report to Ambassador Harry F. Guggenheim in Cuba, informing him of the success of the launch.

Florence Shloss Guggenheim continued to live in the cathedrallike immensity of Hempstead House for a decade after Dan's death, reigning over her family and over the Daniel and Florence Guggenheim Foundation as a sort of dowager empress. Then she built for herself a smaller house, Mille Fleurs—only twenty-five rooms—in Provençal style, not far from Hempstead House, "to simplify her life," and in which she lived until her death in 1945.

In 1940 Florence put Hempstead House at the disposal of British war orphans, then, in June, 1942, she deeded the place to the Institute of Aeronautical Sciences. Later, the U.S. Navy purchased the estate from the Institute for the bargain price of $332,000 (it had cost over $3 million to build) and used it for its Special Devices Division. Some of the special devices that were discussed and/or studied and planned were the hydrogen bomb and the guided missile. During the early 1950s German rocket scientists, including Dr. Wernher Von Braun, were brought over and housed at Special Devices. From their efforts and those of the second generation of American rocket pioneers (Goddard died in 1945) emerged the nuclear-armed intercontinental ballistic missile. Dorothea Straus, Daniel's grandson's wife, described the house at this time in one of her books:

> The castle was circled by barbed wire and posted with guards. The Gothic windows revealed no sign of life, but I knew that beyond the thick stone walls supernatural ideas were being hatched as in a Witch's Sabbath. This was a nursery of fledgling atomic monsters conceived and given birth to by the enemy for our use in war.

The great house and its acreage now belong to Nassau County, and are used occasionally by the county for receptions and exhibitions.

Of Daniel and Florence's three children, M. Robert became one of America's most charming wastrels; Gladys, the public-spirited wife of the president of American Smelting and Refining and the president herself of the Daniel and Florence Guggenheim Foundation; and Harry, the versatile Guggenheim standard-bearer from 1930 to 1971, furtherer of his father's businesses and philanthropies, and foster father, even more than Dan, of U.S. aviation and the country's grand adventure into space.

By mid-century, Harry, using funds from his father's foundation, had established the Daniel and Florence Guggenheim Aeronautical Laboratories and Jet Propulsion Centers at Princeton and Caltech, the latter known as GALCIT, and had endowed Robert H. Goddard professorships at both institutions. By then virtually all of America's senior aerospace engineers were graduates of Guggenheim-sponsored schools.

Foremost among those schools now is the partially Guggenheim-funded Jet Propulsion Laboratory at Caltech in Pasadena, an out-growth of GALCIT, known throughout the world of aeronautics as JPL. JPL's contributions to America's space program have been numerous and crucial. Explorer I, America's first unmanned satellite, utilized JPL-devised solid-fuel upper stages and JPL instrumentation. By the late 1950s and early 1960s, JPL had supervised the develop-ment of the Ranger, Pioneer, Surveyor, and other space probe projects. In 1976 a JPL Viking unmanned spacecraft softlanded on Mars. It was at this time that JPL gained worldwide attention by its develop-ment and management of the NASA Deep Space Network (DSN). And in 1977 the JPL-designed unmanned spacecraft Voyager I and Voyager II, containing a message for possible extraterrestrial intel-ligences, were launched on missions that will take them past Jupiter and Saturn and ultimately out of the solar system on man's second probe—Pioneer 10 and 11 were the first—into outer space.

CHAPTER

4

MURRY AND LEONIE: CHILEAN NITRATES AND THE CHILDREN OF NEW YORK

MURRY GUGGENHEIM, THIRD OF THE SONS OF MEYER AND BARBARA, usually played it safe. In business he had the unenviable function of being the no-man of an incredibly dynamic organization, the brake on the impetuous engine Dan. Rarely, if ever, would he initiate an idea or project of his own. Sentimentally he was equally unadventurous. Unlike his four younger brothers, all of whom enjoyed a richly diversified love life, he knew and loved only one woman during his entire lifetime, and that was his Alsatian-born wife, Leonie. So attached was he to the tall, statuesque Leonie Bernheim, whom he had courted as a young man along the shores of Lake Lugano, that, in the words of a nephew, "he never gave another woman so much as a passing glance." Socially he was also very conservative. He did not make friends easily and did not nurse the slightest wish to be part of society, Jewish or Gentile (one is tempted to say that he probably would not have cut a very dashing figure in either society, had he chosen to join). Ninety-eight percent of the time he preferred only the society of his wife. As might be expected, when it came to spending money, whether his own—which amounted to a considerable fortune—or his firm's, he was something of a tightwad. Though his benefactions were munificent, he did not part with his money easily, and gave only after his brothers set the example . . . and estate taxes went up.

Murry's forte was dealing with numbers. He had a mathematical mind, liked statistics, was the sort of man who did a lot of paper work in his head. He was one of the country's foremost experts on copper sales, having a special sense for that fine, ephemeral moment when copper should be either bought or sold. In addition to being chairman of the finance committee of American Smelting and Refining and a partner of Guggenheim Brothers, he was both a director of, and agent for, Kennecott Copper, of which he was, of course, a major stockholder.

Bernard Baruch described Murry as "extraordinary—definitely so —but quiet, very quiet." Others were not so complimentary. One of his former partners described him as "a dour personality, a pessimist." Brother William did not have much to say about him in his autobiography except that he had "a natural taste for statistics" and "handled and sold metals." Son Edmond recalled that "Dan had daring, but many a difficulty was avoided because of a word of caution in the nick of time from my father . . . the finest car on earth needs a brake." Outwardly the straight man par excellence, Murry had a number of curious idiosyncrasies. He was fixed and precise about everything except his name, which he signed at various times Murry, Murray, Morris, and Morry. (Was this third son, sandwiched in between the mighty Daniel and the genial Solomon, a bit unsure of exactly who he was?) Hardheaded, tough-minded in business, he had a soft spot for beauty, loved flowers, and helped support the New York Botanical Gardens. Former associates recall him sitting in the boardroom with his derby hat on, a bouquet of flowers on the table in front of him. During the discussions he would raise the flowers to his moustached, potato-nosed face, close his eyes . . . and then usually say no, or "not yet," to whatever proposal was being made.

Given his rather cramped personality, it was unlikely that Murry would spend his money daringly, and he didn't. What he eventually spent it on was eminently praiseworthy, but, unlike Dan's blind leap into space, also eminently safe and acceptable: He established a free dental clinic for the poor children of New York.

First, however, and in this he did resemble his older brothers, first, before philanthropy, he took care to establish his children as impregnably as possible.

In keeping with his less-than-exuberant nature, Murry did not bother to create a Villa Carola or buy a Castlegould for the greater glory of the House of Guggenheim. True, he had once erected a copy of the Petit Trianon on the Jersey shore, chiefly out of competition with brothers Isaac, Dan, and Sol, who had put up their Italian palaces and Victorian phantasmagorias there, but after he sold it at a decent profit, he ceased entertaining vast building projects. About the only significant luxury he permitted himself was his $100,000 yacht, *Leonie*, which he kept at St. Petersburg, Florida. No, it was not in Murry's character to spend hard-earned money recklessly on ostentation. It was in Murry's character, instead, to *conserve* money. And conserving money meant, among other things, not letting the government get what he had.

And so, instead of great houses, he decided to beat Public Enemy Number One and set up handsome trust funds for each of his two children, Edmond and Lucille, before he died.

Thus in 1917, while the Great War was pouring unprecedented profits into the Guggenheims' accounts, Murry established two $6 million trust funds for his beloved son, Edmond, and his beloved daughter, Lucille.

The two trusts, Murry took care to stipulate, were revokable. They were not absolute gifts, for at any time the settlor could regain title to their principal sums.

This made Edmond and Lucille a little nervous. Each was earning anywhere from $300,000 to $350,000 a year from his/her trust and neither took kindly to the idea that at a moment's notice their father could legally take their income away from them. Therefore, in 1925, they both brought pressure to bear on Murry to make the trusts absolute by revoking his power to cancel them.

Meanwhile, in 1924, Congress included in its revenue act of that year a provision calling for a tax on all gifts valued at $50,000 or more.

Murry, cognizant of this, called his lawyers and asked if revoking his power to cancel his children's trusts would subject his children to the recently enacted gift tax. The lawyers said it would not. So Murry made the trusts absolute.

Not long after he made them absolute, the federal government demanded and, after a long legal battle that went all the way to the Supreme Court, collected a gift tax from Murry Guggenheim of $3,449,000, the largest gift tax ever paid by a single individual up to that time.

A year later, in 1926, Congress took the gift tax off the books and kept it off until 1932. Thus Murry had been compelled to pay a gift tax that he could have avoided by waiting until 1926 to make the trusts absolute.

After paying up, Murry, though still a very rich man, thought of himself as destitute. According to his lawyer, Leo Gottlieb, "he did not buy a single suit for over a year."

Between taxes and legal fees, Murry had to part with some $5 million all told. In the end, the two gifts had cost him a total of $18 million. For Murry the tightwad this was a bit too much, and so, in addition to not buying a new suit for a year, he took his legal business away from the firm of Gottlieb and Cleary forever.

Edmond and Lucille, of course, felt little pain over their father's defeat by the Internal Revenue Service. They now owned their trusts outright and very nice trusts they were. So sagely did Murry invest them that even in the depths of the Depression Edmond's trust earned him $332,000 per annum and Lucille's $327,000. These incomes made Edmond and Lucille the wealthiest members of the third generation during the 1930s.

Murry had pinned high hopes on Edmond—a tall, muscular man who would have been quite handsome had it not been for the inevitable potato nose—expecting him to take a leading role in managing the Guggenheim empire, and was sorely disappointed when he dropped out of Guggenheim Brothers in 1923, in protest over the sale of Chile Copper, which he had helped develop. Since Edmond was earning over $300,000 a year from his trust, he saw little point in continuing to work for what he thought was a much-depleted Guggenheim Brothers and giving most of his income from the partnership to the government.

Besides, Edmond liked sports too much to be happy spending eight hours a day sitting at a desk in gloomy Guggenheim Brothers. He had been a star second baseman on the Yale baseball team. And he was a good amateur boxer and an excellent golfer. Accordingly, upon his resignation from the firm in 1923, at the age of thirty-five, he "retired" on his bountiful income to devote the rest of his life to golf. At this second occupation he was most successful. In 1929 he won the President's Trophy in the twenty-fifth annual autumn golf tournament at Pinehurst, North Carolina.

Edmond married three times. His first wife, Marron Price, was a high-spirited girl who bore him his only child, a daughter, Natalie, and became a passionate devotee of the airplane. In 1934 she set out to do "the loop" around South America with the handsome, dashing pilot Russell Thaw. That was enough for Edmond and he divorced her, much to Murry's annoyance, for Guggenheims did not divorce. His second marriage, to Jeanne Russell, also ended in divorce in 1952.

Three years later he tried again, this time with Marion Kaufmann, with whom he remained until his death. The third Mrs. Edmond Guggenheim now lives quietly in Scottsdale, Arizona, and Westbury, Long Island.

Daughter Natalie was even less fortunate in marriage than her father. First, she eloped with one Tom Gorman, son of a Manhasset, Long Island, railroad baggage master. The marriage enraged both Murry and Edmond, and they forced Natalie to have it annulled immediately. She then went on to marry an acceptable young man of Park Avenue parentage by the name of Robert Michael Studin, whom she eventually divorced. Later she married Frederick Talbert of San Francisco, who died. She is now Mrs. B. B. Short of Honolulu and the possessor of her father's 1917 trust, plus many more millions.

Murry's only daughter, Lucille, fared no better in marriage. First she married with great pomp and divorced with much publicity, Fred A. Gimbel of the department-store Gimbels. Then she married and divorced Jack E. Bonar, the father of her only child, Jean. Later she became Mrs. Peter P. Summerer. She died an extremely wealthy lady of seventy-eight.

It took a while for Murry to recover sufficiently from the gift-tax debacle to feel he could spend some more money. Finally, after his brothers' philanthropic examples, especially Dan's, had goaded him, and the new estate tax laws had goaded him even more, he decided to establish his own foundation in 1929, with an initial gift of $2 million, or $11 million less than what he had given his two children.

The general aims of the Murry and Leonie Guggenheim Foundation, purposely kept flexible, were "the promotion, through charitable and benevolent activities, of the well-being of man throughout the world," and its specific aim was "charitable and benevolent assistance to the children of greater New York through the practical application of dentistry and oral hygiene."

This latter aim took the form of the establishment of the Murry and Leonie Guggenheim Dental Clinic at 422–28 East Seventy-second Street between York and First avenues in New York.

It has been said that "your teeth can ruin your life." There is a direct connection between one's teeth and one's central nervous system. Bad teeth can destroy a person not only physically but also emotionally. Quite aware of this, for he himself had had dental problems, Murry had discovered that tens of thousands of New York children were growing up without even the most elemental dental care. Such, in fact, was the backward state of U.S. public-health services at the time that one-half of all schoolchildren in New York who reached the age of eight were victims of untreated cavities. Some 600,000 of these were from homes whose financial status made private treatment impossible. Dental care, Murry concluded from his investigations, was "the most generally slighted aspect of U.S. pediatric medicine."

The Murry and Leonie Guggenheim Dental Clinic was designed to remedy this deplorable lack in public-health services. It was the first of its kind in New York and became the largest of its kind in the United States. At its inception the clinic was staffed by sixty-seven employees and twenty-five dentists and maintained seventy-eight chairs. Soon around three hundred poor New York schoolchildren a day were showing up for free treatment.

To *The New York Times*, Murry's clinic was every bit as daring as Dan's subsidization of moon rockets. "The Guggenheims," one of its writers sang, perhaps not unjustifiably, "are initiating something so farsighted in its humaneness that to those who have studied the history of the child in human progress, it has some of the quality of a dream."

Murry was the president of his own foundation, and as he put more and more money into it, the clinic began to absorb more and more of his attention, energy, and time. This is not to say, however, that he neglected the affairs of Guggenheim Brothers. On the contrary, after Dan's death in 1930 he had to work harder than ever at Guggenheim Brothers for, as we have seen, it was to Murry the No-man that the full burden of the great nitrate gamble fell.

Thus it was that throughout the Great Depression Murry Guggenheim spent the hours between eight-thirty and five-thirty every day grappling with nitrates at 120 Broadway, then from six to eight P.M. grappling with poor children's teeth at East Seventy-second Street. While son Edmond, enjoying his trust fund, played golf, and daughter Lucille, reveling in hers, pursued her various marital adventures.

Daniel Guggenheim, author of the Guggenheims' momentous switchover from metals to chemicals, never lost faith in nitrates, even when the bottom began to drop out of the market with the creation of the first synthetic nitrate by the Germans.

Simon Meyer Guggenheim, born in Lengnau, Switzerland, 1792, died in Philadelphia, 1869.

NASSAU COUNTY MUSEUM

Meyer Guggenheim, born in Lengnau, 1828, died in New York, 1905.

COURTESY MRS. HAROLD A. LOEB

Barbara Meyer Guggenheim, born in Lengnau, 1834, died in New York, 1900.

COURTESY MRS. HAROLD A. LOEB

Meyer and Barbara Guggenheim surrounded by their family in 1889. The men (left to right): William (standing), Simon, Isaac, Meyer, Solomon, Murry, Daniel, Benjamin.

The women (left to right): Cora (front row), Carrie (Mrs. Isaac), Leonie (Mrs. Murry, standing), Barbara, Jeannette (front row), Florence (Mrs. Daniel), and Rose.

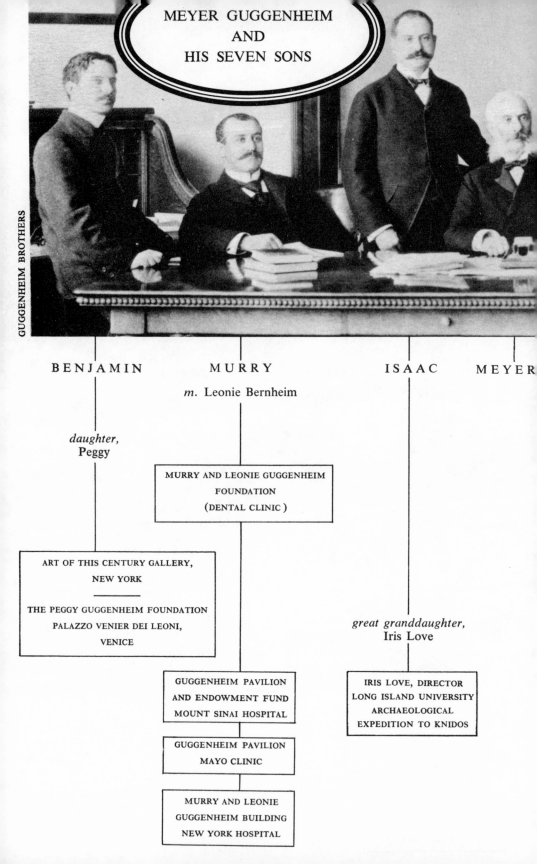

MEYER GUGGENHEIM
AND
HIS SEVEN SONS

GUGGENHEIM BROTHERS

BENJAMIN   MURRY   ISAAC   MEYER

m. Leonie Bernheim

daughter,
Peggy

MURRY AND LEONIE GUGGENHEIM
FOUNDATION
(DENTAL CLINIC)

ART OF THIS CENTURY GALLERY,
NEW YORK
————
THE PEGGY GUGGENHEIM FOUNDATION
PALAZZO VENIER DEI LEONI,
VENICE

great granddaughter,
Iris Love

GUGGENHEIM PAVILION
AND ENDOWMENT FUND
MOUNT SINAI HOSPITAL

IRIS LOVE, DIRECTOR
LONG ISLAND UNIVERSITY
ARCHAEOLOGICAL
EXPEDITION TO KNIDOS

GUGGENHEIM PAVILION
MAYO CLINIC

MURRY AND LEONIE
GUGGENHEIM BUILDING
NEW YORK HOSPITAL

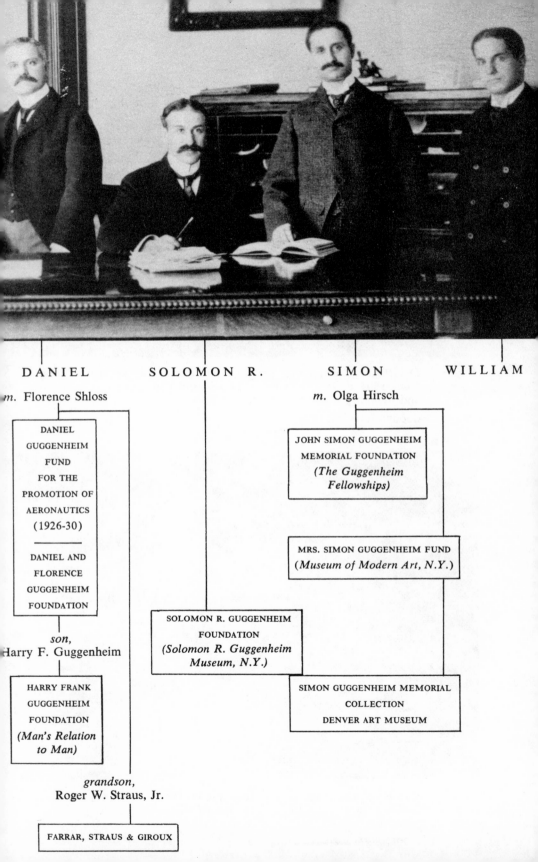

DANIEL   SOLOMON R.   SIMON   WILLIAM

m. Florence Shloss

DANIEL
GUGGENHEIM
FUND
FOR THE
PROMOTION OF
AERONAUTICS
(1926-30)
———
DANIEL AND
FLORENCE
GUGGENHEIM
FOUNDATION

m. Olga Hirsch

JOHN SIMON GUGGENHEIM
MEMORIAL FOUNDATION
*(The Guggenheim
Fellowships)*

MRS. SIMON GUGGENHEIM FUND
(Museum of Modern Art, N.Y.)

son,
Harry F. Guggenheim

SOLOMON R. GUGGENHEIM
FOUNDATION
*(Solomon R. Guggenheim
Museum, N.Y.)*

HARRY FRANK
GUGGENHEIM
FOUNDATION
*(Man's Relation
to Man)*

SIMON GUGGENHEIM MEMORIAL
COLLECTION
DENVER ART MUSEUM

grandson,
Roger W. Straus, Jr.

FARRAR, STRAUS & GIROUX

Daniel Guggenheim (1856–1930). Head of the Guggenheim family from 1905 to 1930. Chairman and president of American Smelting and Refining, 1901–1919. Foster father of U.S. aviation and rocketry.

Florence Shloss Guggenheim (1863–1944), Daniel's wife. Co-founder, and eventually president, of the Daniel and Florence Guggenheim Foundation.

Hempstead House, formerly Castlegould, Daniel Guggenheim's residence at Sands Point, Long Island, from 1917 to 1930. It was here that the first significant financing of U.S. aviation and rocketry was decided upon and then implemented, thus ushering in the Space Age.

Castlegould stables, one of the fourteen structures on Daniel Guggenheim's Sands Point estate. In 1929 there were over two hundred grooms, servants, and grounds keepers working on the estate.

Isaac Guggenheim (1854–1922). Builder of Villa Carola, Sands Point, now IBM Management Training Center.

Murry Guggenheim (1858–1939). Founder of the Murry and Leonie Guggenheim Foundation and children's free dental clinic.

Benjamin Guggenheim (1865–1912). Went down with the *Titanic* in 1912.

William Guggenheim (1868–1941).

*"Another Triumph in the Far North
The great American Trust has discovered Alaska."*

REPRINTED WITH PERMISSION FROM *The Minneapolis Tribune*

"How Absurd! He Wants His Own Country."

Guggenheim—"He and his brothers are commercial kings by grace of some able, some daring, and some lawless achievements; he is a senator of the United States by grace of his millions . . . and for no other reason in the world."

LIBRARY, STATE HISTORICAL SOCIETY OF COLORADO

"Have you one of those Guggenheim foundations that I've heard so much about?"

COPYRIGHT, 1938, REGISTER AND TRIBUNE SYNDICATE (COURTESY ELEANOR CASTLE STEWART)

"Frankly, Miss Ellis, the Guggenheim Foundation had been led to expect a book of poems."

DRAWING BY GARDNER REA; © 1937, 1965 *The New Yorker* MAGAZINE, INC.

Senator Simon Guggenheim (1867–1941), at the time he founded the John Simon Guggenheim Memorial Foundation (the Guggenheim fellowships) in memory of his firstborn son.

CULVER SERVICE
COURTESY *Fortune* MAGAZINE

John Simon Guggenheim (1905–1922). Son of Simon, died of mastoiditis and pneumonia at seventeen.

NASSAU COUNTY MUSEUM

George Denver Guggenheim (1907–1939). Son of Simon, committed suicide in the Paramount Hotel, New York City, at thirty-two.

WIDE WORLD PHOTOS

Harry F. Guggenheim, son of Daniel and Florence, with Robert H. Goddard, rocket pioneer, and Charles A. Lindbergh, at Dr. Goddard's Roswell Field, New Mexico, rocket launching site, 1935. It was here that the Space Age was born.

GUGGENHEIM BROTHERS

The Baroness Hilla
Rebay von Ehrenwiesen
(1890–1967).

**BLACKSTONE STUDIOS
THE HILLA VON REBAY
FOUNDATION**

Solomon R. Guggenheim (1861–1949) and the Baroness Hilla Rebay.

THE REBAY FAMILY ARCHIVES

(Left to right): Mrs. Solomon R. Guggenheim (Irene), Wassily Kandinsky, the Baroness Hilla Rebay, and Solomon R. Guggenheim at the Bauhaus, Germany, 1929.

GUGGENHEIM BROTHERS

Solomon R. Guggenheim with Frank Lloyd Wright.

Frank Lloyd Wright, the Baroness Hilla Rebay, and Solomon R. Guggenheim examining a model of the Guggenheim Museum.

William Guggenheim (1868–1941) presenting busts of Hamilton, Lincoln, and Franklin to the Republican National Committee, November, 1939. Left to right: Alexander Hamilton, a great great grandson of the first secretary of the treasury; William Guggenheim; and Lt. Comdr. Franklin Bache Huntington, great great great grandson of Benjamin Franklin.

WIDE WORLD PHOTOS

William Guggenheim with two of the former show girls to whom he left his estate.

WIDE WORLD PHOTOS

Many people, however, felt that the Guggenheims, in selling Chile Copper to Anaconda, departing from metals, and hurling themselves into the nitrate business, were doing nothing but laying the foundation for their own dissolution.

These doubts did not unduly disturb the irrepressible, ever-optimistic Daniel. During the last year and a half of his life, he was forever telling the press that the natural nitrate industry would revive and even surpass the synthetic because of "improvement in production methods." Dan always thought technology could solve anything. Time proved him to be wrong.

Believing departed brother Dan's prognostications (having followed them successfully all his life)—and encouraged by the fact that many farmers still favored natural nitrate fertilizers to synthetic—Murry, in 1931, led his brothers Solomon and Simon into the formation of a vast trust to monopolize all the nitrate in Chile. The name of the trust was the Compañía de Salitre de Chile—Cosach for short—and it soon became the largest corporation in all South America and the Guggenheims' biggest gamble, surpassing even Kennecott and Chuquicamata. Cosach's board of directors was composed of four Chilean government officials, five bankers, a German nitrate expert, a representative of the independent Chilean producers, and Cappelen Smith, a metallurgist in the employ of Guggenheim Brothers. To finance the venture, the Chilean bankers floated a $40 million bond, the Guggenheims put up $10 million cash, and a consortium of U.S. banks invested $9 million.

(At this point it must be mentioned that, thanks to sizable loans from Lehman Brothers and L. F. Rothschild & Company, the Guggenheims already controlled the Anglo-Chilean Nitrate Company and the Lautaro Nitrate Company, and were engaged in a desperate effort to make natural nitrate profitably marketable by developing an inexpensive process for treating raw nitrate of soda. Their total investment in these enterprises, including money owed, was something in the neighborhood of $80 million.)

Before long Cosach needed more money, and by the fall of 1933, thanks to more loans (the family's credit was still good) the Guggenheims had a total of $48 million invested in the trust.

At this juncture, the Guggenheim process for treating nitrate of soda cheaply and making the natural product profitable was finally perfected and right away it threatened to throw thousands of Chilean laborers out of work.

Cosach now realized it would get nowhere without the Guggenheim-controlled nitrate companies and the Guggenheim nitrate process, and so it struck a deal with Murry, which, on the surface, looked like the greatest coup in Guggenheim business history.

Cosach had capitalized itself at an exaggerated $375 million. For a 50 percent interest in the Guggenheim-controlled companies, it offered 8 million shares of Cosach stock, and for the Guggenheim nitrate process it offered a cool $30 million.

Murry, Solomon, and Simon accepted the offer. The Guggenheims had spent only $100,000 in perfecting the process, and 8 million shares of Cosach looked something like $175 million.

Not long after the deal was signed, Murry found himself criticized throughout Chile, first for demanding so much stock for the Guggenheim nitrate companies, and, second, for threatening to throw so many Chileans out of work with the new process. All of a sudden, Murry the Quiet became Murry the Malefactor of Great Wealth. It was a role he was not accustomed to, one which he resented bitterly in the light of his recent benefactions.

For a while Cosach looked like the most lucrative deal the Guggenheims had ever made: $30 million for a $100,000 process and $175 million for an initial investment of $128 million. But then, in 1934, the Depression suddenly came to the Chilean nitrate industry—the synthetic product was competing with the natural better than ever and world demand had not improved—and the Guggenheims' 8 million shares of Cosach were suddenly not worth the paper they were written on.

Soon world demand for natural nitrate began to dry up entirely and Chile's greatest industry virtually closed down.

Thousands were already unemployed due to application of the Guggenheim labor-saving process, now thousands more were thrown out of work.

It wasn't long before revolution broke out. The new Chilean government revoked Cosach's charter and in one stroke its shares became worthless.

By 1936 the Guggenheims had lost over $60 million of their investment, their largest single loss by far on any business venture. In contrast to this debacle Anaconda Copper was doing very well. Of its 1936 net earnings of $16 million, one-fourth came from formerly Guggenheim-owned Chile Copper Corporation.

The collapse of the Guggenheim nitrate venture in Chile dealt the family an almost mortal blow. Almost, but not quite. For the Guggenheims were still the principal owners of Kennecott Copper, a $335 million corporation in 1937, and American Smelting and Refining, a $161 million corporation in the same year. They also owned healthy chunks of stock in Anaconda, United States Rubber, and Diamang, the Angolan diamond operation.

Nevertheless, by 1939, the year of Murry's death, the family was nowhere near as rich, in terms of both financial influence and purchasing power, as it had been in the 1920s. Ironically, it had been Dan's daring that had both built the family fortune and paved the way for its dissolution. If only Murry's original no to nitrates had been heeded. But, ironically again, it was Murry's yes, when he had all the power to himself, that led to the eventual near-ruin.

As it turned out, it took World War II to bring the Guggenheims back, financially, to something close to where they had been after World War I. Nitrates, we have noted, were a prime raw material for munitions. When World War II broke out, the demand for nitrate was so great that the synthetic product proved insufficient to meet it (most of the synthetic nitrate plants were in Germany) and natural nitrate suddenly took a new lease on life. The Guggenheims still held sizable interests in Anglo-Chilean and Lautaro nitrate. Cosach was hastily revived, in a somewhat different format. Before long, Chile and the Guggenheims could not even meet the increased demand. As for copper, demand for Kennecott's and Anaconda's metal far exceeded supply. As for other metals—zinc, tin, silver, lead—American Smelting and Refining's furnaces once again blazed at white heat twenty-four hours a day to meet the new wartime needs.

Thus, once again, the Guggenheims were a mirror of the United States economy as a whole. If it had not been for Hitler's war, the American economy might never have risen out of the long depression of the 1930s. If it had not been for Hitler's war, the Guggenheims might never have survived the great nitrate disaster of the 1930s and become the formidable cultural force they became in the postwar years.

Murry Guggenheim died in 1939 at eighty-one. During his last, much-embittered years, the Murry and Leonie Guggenheim Dental Clinic had become the ruling passion of his life. It was a most soothing compensation for the nitrate mess. Murry used to like to go to the clinic and see the Board of Education buses unload the children— mostly blacks, Hispanics, Italians, and Lower East Side Russian Jews —after school. He would stand there in the entrance hall, his derby hat on, a fragrant flower in his buttonhole, and watch the children on their way to the dental chairs, and he would feel the satisfaction that nitrate had denied him. By the year of his death, 30,200 poor children had received free dental treatment thanks to his generosity. His only regret at this time was that, owing to severe losses sustained in Chile, he was unable to donate nearly as much money to his clinic as he wanted. Thus did the depression in Chilean nitrate affect the teeth of the poor children of New York.

Because of the terrible losses the Guggenheims had sustained in Chile, Murry's estate at the time of his death was much depleted. But thanks again to Hitler's war, it came back eventually to something in the neighborhood of $30 million. Of this, $5 million went to the dental clinic; Edmond got a bequest of $400,000; sister Cora Rothschild collected $100,000; and the "rest and residue" was divided into two trusts for Leonie. The first trust specified that upon Leonie's death the principal would go to Edmond, and upon his death, to his daughter, Natalie. The other specified that upon Leonie's death the principal would go to Lucille's daughter, Jean Bonar. Thus Lucille herself was left out of the will. She had by then annoyed Murry so much with her marriages and divorces that he had decided her 1917 trust was all she was ever doing to get.

Murry's long, full-column obituary in *The New York Times* hailed him as a patron of music (he had helped finance the Goldman Band concerts with brother Dan) and, of course, as the founder of a children's free dental clinic. It also mentioned that he had donated the central display greenhouse to the New York Botanical Gardens in Bronx Park, and with his brother-in-law Jacques Bernheim had erected a dormitory for three hundred students at the Cité Universitaire in Paris, a benefice for which Murry had been made an officer of the Legion of Honor. Nothing was said of his mortal struggles with Chilean nitrate.

After Murry's death Edmond took over the presidency of the Murry and Leonie Guggenheim Foundation and its dental clinic, helped by his mother, Leonie, and daughter, Natalie, both of whom sat on the board. He then ran the clinic very ably for the next thirty years, finding the work almost as exhilarating as golf, and much more satisfying than mining and smelting nonferrous metals. By 1962, 39,388 children a year were coming to the clinic for free treatment, sometimes a thousand a day. By 1969 the foundation's assets stood at $40 million . . . and Edmond, now eighty, had begun to tire of the responsibility of administering them.

Murry Guggenheim had written in his will:

> It is my hope and wish that events of the distant future, which no
> man can foresee, will not result that the Foundation will feel obliged
> to exercise the power to give my corporate trustee the initiation of a
> final disposition through other charitable channels, of the principal of
> the trust created.

And yet events of the distant future did conspire to do exactly that.
These events were Edmond's old age and the advent of welfare and
Medicare, which, in a sense, preempted the work of the clinic.

Thus, in the last years of his life, did Edmond Guggenheim preside
over "the disposition through other charitable channels, of the principal of [his father's] trust." First, he closed the clinic on Seventy-
second Street and donated the building and much of its equipment to
New York Hospital. Then he gave $22 million toward a new building
and endowment fund for Mount Sinai Hospital, and $12 million for
a new pavilion at the Mayo Clinic. The sum given to Mount Sinai
was the largest ever given to that hospital by one man.

The rest of Murry's wealth ultimately ended up in the purses of
three women: his daughter, Lucille, her daughter, Jean Bonar, and
Edmond's daughter, Natalie, each of whom came to control sizable
fortunes.

And so the ultimate beneficiaries of Murry's share in the great
pioneering struggles in Colorado, Mexico, Utah, the Yukon, Alaska,
and Chile, were, besides the clinics and hospitals, three multimarried
women who had taken no part whatsoever in these struggles and knew
very little about them. The same could be said of Isaac's share, since
his wealth also passed largely to women. None of these third- or
fourth-generation heiresses, it should be pointed out, established a
foundation of her own.

As it turned out, the fate of Isaac's and Murry's wealth was a
herald of things to come, for by the mid-1970s most of the Guggenheim fortune not in the foundations was in the hands of women, safely
invested in high-yield, low-growth securities.

Since Edmond had no sons, the Guggenheim name in Murry's line
died with him. It lives on now only on large bronze plaques and in
cold institutional lettering, reading the Murry and Leonie Guggenheim Building, New York Hospital; the Murry and Leonie Guggenheim Pavilion, Mount Sinai Hospital; the Murry and Leonie
Guggenheim Pavilion, Mayo Clinic.

CHAPTER

5

SOLOMON'S SECOND SPRING

BEHOLD SOLOMON R. GUGGENHEIM IN ALL HIS GLORY.

Here he is, the most stylish of the brothers, immaculately turned out in a Savile Row gray pinstriped suit, vest, high white starched collar, gray silk tie, and pearl stickpin, sitting in the living room of his huge eight-room suite at the Plaza, the principal suite, opening onto the balconies and flags above the main entrance, the rooms filled with precious Old Masters, the entire staff of the hotel at his push-button beck and call. Here he is spending a week or two in January at his lovely 1828 Greek Revival "winter place" on the East Battery in Charleston, South Carolina. Here he is playing golf on the private course of his 205-acre estate at Sands Point, Trillora Court, formerly brother Isaac's Villa Carola, driving the ball past mossy baroque statues and fountains, formal Italian gardens, stands of pine, oak, and birch. Here he is in the early fall shooting grouse in Scotland at his lodge and preserve on the Glenkinde Moor. Here he is a month or so later, hunting again, this time geese, ducks, and sage chickens, at his vast 8,000-acre cattle ranch and game preserve near the Snake River at Island Park, Idaho. Here he is shooting deer and ducks at his 1,200-acre plantation, Big Survey, in the moss-hung woods of Yemasee, South Carolina. Here he is on his 305-foot ocean-going yacht, the *Trillora*, a former World War I destroyer, the fastest yacht in the world, capable of whisking him to his office in lower Manhattan from Sands Point in only forty minutes. Here he is with his handsome wife, Irene, his three daughters, one of whom is married to a British earl, being entertained at his son-in-law's four-hundred-year-old ancestral estate in Ulster. Here he is at his desk in the vast wood-paneled Partners' Room at Guggenheim Brothers, surrounded by gilt-framed portraits of his brothers, his father, his grandfather, himself, discussing with brothers Murry and Simon a $50 million nitrate deal in Chile, the latest financial reports from their diamond mines in the Congo and Angola, their tin mines in Bolivia and Malaya, their rubber plantations in the Congo, their huge holdings in Kennecott and Anaconda Copper.

Here he is, one of the great princes of the American empire, blessed with everything his countrymen ever dreamed of possessing, here he is, at sixty-five, only one generation removed from a European ghetto, holding the world in his hands . . . and he is bored.

Something is missing. He has everything. And nothing. He is semi-retired from business—the pioneering, the buccaneering are over—now all he has to do is hold on to what he has, and that is not a terribly exciting occupation. His wife, Irene, is a fine woman, a good wife and mother, but also a dull woman: It has been a long time since she has stimulated him, either physically or intellectually; the marriage is comfortable but stale. In the last analysis, what does he have to look forward to but increasing enfeeblement, failing powers, old age? Oh yes, there are his daughters and grandsons . . . their lives are important to him, but he has the rest of his own life to live. His fortune. Ah, how much of his fortune would he give for youth? What good are riches to an old man if they suffocate him, if they do not bring him more health, more vigor, more stimulation, more *life*?

Enter a thirty-six-year-old, blue-eyed, red-headed German baroness and painter. Enter like a hurricane, sweeping away, in one great cleansing wind, all fatigue, all despair, all world-weariness. Enter, take possession, and, in return, give the aging king energy, hope, enthusiasm; give the old buccaneer a second spring.

Solomon Guggenheim first met the baroness Hilla Rebay von Ehrenwiesen in New York in 1927. She had come from Paris, where she had been exhibiting her works, with a letter of introduction from Irene's sister, Gertrude de Paats. Solomon was immediately impressed by her and asked her to do his portrait. She declined because she did not like realistic portraiture anymore; she had put that mode behind her and was now painting only nonobjective works. Whereupon Sol, who enjoyed needling, joking, piqued her by saying, "No, it's probably because you don't know how to do a portrait anymore." Whereupon she rose to the bait, they discussed the fee, he gave her much more than she asked—$9,000—and she executed the portrait, making him look much younger than his sixty-five years. The painting was later destroyed by Solomon's heirs.

While she painted him (weekends at Trillora Court) they discussed art. Solomon, who possessed the most refined sense of style of all the Guggenheim brothers, loved great painting, but he did not know much about it. Irene knew more and her taste ran to Old Masters. So Sol had bought Old Masters, some works of the late medieval and early Italian Renaissance periods, some fifteenth-century Flemish panels, some paintings of the Barbizon School, a Joos van Cleve, some Audubon prints and Oriental illuminations . . . and some Watteaus, as many Watteaus as he could get his hands on.

The baroness did not hesitate a second to tell him that what he had been collecting was all wrong for a man of his vision and means. Why, a man of his immense wealth and pioneering spirit should be helping *contemporary* artists, the artists of the future.

Her emphasis on pioneering struck its mark. As the weeks went by, and her portrait of the Grand Old Man neared completion, she unfolded her self-styled "revolutionary" ideas about nonobjective art with the passion of an evangelist, and, in the end, won Solomon over. Yes, by Jehovah, if he had pioneered in mining and metallurgy all his life, why should he not be a pioneer, also, in art?

It was not long before Hilla introduced him to the abstractions of the Polish-born Rudolf Bauer, the Russian-born Wassily Kandinsky, and the Hungarian-born Laszlo Moholy-Nagy, all of whom were living outside the countries of their birth. Solomon was vastly impressed by an abstract watercolor by Bauer and later he dated his conversion to nonobjective art from first beholding that work. (Time was to prove that he had been far more expert in judging ore bodies.) One thing led to another and, in 1929, Solomon found himself in Germany, with Irene and the baroness, visiting "the father of abstract art," Wassily Kandinsky, who was teaching at the Bauhaus in Dessau. At the meeting, which was to have momentous consequences for all presént, as it was for all modern art, Solomon took Kandinsky by the hand and, delivering a little formal speech, said: "Mr. Kandinsky, you and I have something in common. You have made a revolution in art, I and my brothers, by sponsoring the development of new methods of mining, have made a revolution in that industry." He then purchased Kandinsky's "Composition 8" and two other paintings, thus beginning a collection of Kandinskys, now housed in the Solomon R. Guggenheim Museum, which became the largest in the world.

The baroness now virtually took charge of Solomon's life, and his money, and, rushing him here and there, brought him into face-to-face contact with all the up-and-coming nonobjective painters of the day, introducing him into exhilarating new worlds he had never even approached before, and encouraging him always to buy, buy, buy. In the process, she collected healthy commissions from the painters, the first trickle of money of what was to become a very substantial fortune earned off Mr. Sol. Years later, Sol's youngest daughter, Barbara, who had no use for the baroness, would say: "Well, she came over here to find a rich American, *and she found one!*"

It would be unfair, however, to characterize Hilla Rebay as a mercenary. True, she needed money, like everyone else, and spotted in Solomon a bottomless pit of it, but it is even more true that she was an utterly, even fanatically, devoted soldier of art. Art was her life, her religion. She had little thought for anything else. Everyone who came in contact with her was overwhelmed by her zeal. She was an apostle of nonobjective painting. Many people were convinced she was unbalanced. Often her writings appeared utterly impenetrable. Whatever the condition of her mind and spirit, it took a person of her manic, impetuous temperament to galvanize and give direction to Solomon Guggenheim's fortune. Before Sol met Hilla, he did not know what to do with his money, or with the rest of his life. Thirty-two years after he met her his money had collected the most extensive private collection of modern art in existence and had erected the most daring art museum in the world.

Hilla Rebay possessed a certain genius, there was no doubt about it. She had an inexhaustible zest for life and art, a sort of volcanic enthusiasm, and very few inhibitions. She was extremely talkative, and spoke her mind, with no concessions to diplomacy, in a thick German accent, making dozens of charming mistakes. When she was talking about something that interested her very much she would often get extremely excited and her words would come out in waves, torrents. When she did not know the correct English word she would supply German and French words without bothering to make any explanations. In conversation she was capable of abrupt metamorphoses of mood. She might be expatiating with wild enthusiasm on some painter, her eyes shining, a look of ecstasy on her face, then she might suddenly remember some past injury or insult and would shift to a mood of violent rage. Now her words would slash about the room, her eyes would bulge, her face redden, and the past offender would be buried under an ocean of abuse. Like many German women, she was either at one's feet or at one's throat. While she admired you she would do anything for you, but cross her, just once, and she would try to annihilate you. Naturally gregarious and exuberant, when she met someone for the first time, especially someone rich or famous, she would light up and her greeting would gush and boom. When she entered a room full of people, she would soon dominate the gathering, drawing everyone to herself. She thought of herself in grandiose terms. It was her mission, and hers alone, to bring nonobjective art to the attention of the world.

Physically, Hilla looked like a lady wrestler—short, stout, bulky— but she had a sensitive, extremely expressive face. Everyone noted the depth and life in her eyes, and she had a big, happy smile. Her clothes were grand opera. She always wore a big silk scarf around her neck and liked outlandish hats with ostrich feathers. Her lawyer has described her at-home dress as "half-bedroom, half-living room." She might greet you at the door in a bathrobe, hat, and high-heeled shoes.

Intellectually, she was dogmatic, authoritarian, and somewhat bigoted. She held certain fixed prejudices and beliefs and would not waver from them, or suffer opposition to them. Though her closest friends and associates were Jews, she frequently uttered anti-Semitic statements. She liked to dominate conversation and she liked to give orders. Few people could resist her, least of all Solomon Guggenheim. When she wanted something from Sol she got it. In the end she got hundreds of paintings, millions of dollars, and a museum. She was a female Wagner and Solomon was her King Ludwig. The comparison is not so far-fetched. Both she and Wagner needed rich patrons and found them. Both dreamed of erecting temples to art, albeit different arts, and erected them.

Born in Strasbourg, Alsace, in 1890, the daughter of Prussian Baron Franz Joseph Rebay von Ehrenwiesen, a general in the German army, she studied art, against her father's wishes, at Düsseldorf and Paris, and exhibited her work in Paris, Munich, Bern, Zurich, and Berlin before coming to America. Among her most important shows were with the "Secession" group in Munich and at the Der Sturm Gallery in Berlin. At the latter she met the first great abstractionists, Delaunay, Gleizes, Léger, Chagall, Kandinsky, and Bauer.

Although she was a professional painter, with something of a career already launched, once she met Solomon Guggenheim, and gained his confidence and attention, she gradually came to realize that her mission in life was no longer simply to paint (though she did continue painting . . . not terribly well) but to promote nonobjective art, and herself, with Solomon's money.

It had not taken Hilla long, after first getting to know Sol, to observe how free-spending he was with his fortune. Solomon Guggenheim had no false humility or shame about being very rich. He enjoyed being rich, enjoyed throwing his money around, and never pretended to be anything but a very privileged, very wealthy capitalist. He made no excuses, for instance, for such extravagances as giving thousand-dollar tips to the Plaza doorman to allow him to keep his Pierce Arrow perpetually parked near the main entrance to the hotel. Once, on a trip with his family from Southampton to Cherbourg, his daughter Eleanor, who had been lingering with a boyfriend, was late for the sailing and missed the ship. When she finally arrived at the pier, Eleanor telegraphed her father on the ship, announcing her presence on the dock, and Sol promptly gave the captain $10,000 to turn the vessel around (in the middle of the English Channel) to pick her up, much to the annoyance of the other passengers, most of whom were trying to make train connections from Cherbourg to Paris. Then there was also the story of how Sol had had an entire lake in New Jersey dragged to find a pair of ten-dollar eyeglasses lost by a niece. Yes, the baroness soon saw that Solomon was no tightwad. Now it was up to her to give his spending some meaning and direction.

Fortunately for her goal, Solomon Guggenheim, at sixty-six, fell madly in love with her. She was so different from the people he normally came in contact with, so different from the staid Irene. All his life, with the exception of the Mexican adventure, he had had to deal with relatively sober, rational businessmen, people who kept their emotions under strict control. Now he had this wild, instinctive, half animal–half angel on his hands, a person who reacted, passionately, to everything, and it refreshed him no end.

Soon he was writing her letters, addressing her "Dearest Hillachen," and signing them "with much love, Sol." Soon they were taking excursions together on his yacht. Soon she was visiting him, alone, at Big Survey, deep in the privacy of the Yemasee, South Carolina, pinewoods.

Whether they had sex together remains an open, and perhaps irrelevant, question. Hilla, responding angrily to the inevitable gossip, insisted that they didn't. But, knowing Solomon's lifelong penchant for the well-turned leg, the ample bosom, the . . . one is inclined to assume they did. That Sol enjoyed many affairs during his married life was no secret. He did not tell his wife for some time that he had bought his yacht because he liked to entertain his girl friends on it. One of his favorite mistresses, the one he enjoyed directly before Hilla, was the governess of his daughter Eleanor's children. Sol's niece Gladys Straus recalls today that his girl friends were the most beautiful women she had ever seen. Frequently Sol would expatiate to his nephews Harry Guggenheim and Harold Loeb on the care and feeding of mistresses. "Never make love to a woman before breakfast," he advised them. "You might have a better offer before lunch." And, he would emphasize, when it comes time to part, it is always extremely important to be generous, very generous. "You've got to always cushion the shock."

Whatever the case—sex or no sex—a very tender love developed in Solomon's breast for Hilla. His letters to her, hundreds of which are on file in the Hilla Rebay Foundation's archives, attest that he became genuinely devoted to her, that he held her in high esteem and warm affection. To back up that esteem and affection with something concrete he rented an apartment in New York for her, gave her a monthly stipend, both lent and gave her scores of valuable paintings, and eventually built her a magnificent estate in Connecticut and left her a million dollars in his will.

Certainly Hilla's philosophy of nonobjective art could not have appealed much to a mind as orderly and logical as Solomon Guggenheim's, so it must have been her other qualities that won him over.

Hilla's philosophy, which she expounded in a continuous flow of articles, blurbs, broadsides, letters, written in her own special brand of Teutonic English, eventually became something of a joke in the New York art world. Mrs. Aline B. Saarinen, the *Times'* associate art editor, labeled it "mystic doubletalk."

In her essay "New Age," Hilla wrote:

> Paintings of earthly make-believe never represented truth on which the universal law is based. Their materialistic pretense brought no progress. The creative Non-objective painting, however, develops the spiritual evolution of man. Based on refinement and balance, its beautification of lawfully ordered space brings an ever-increasing enjoyment to those who live with it, because its secret is the rhythmic element which allows so many approaches as it has themes. Its designs of contrasting lines, points, and forms, and its themes of colour, can be seen from many angles. The further the onlooker advances, the more visionarily he perceives the rhythmic element which holds it together and a

spiritual third dimension which is alive to those visionarily trained eyesights.

In the relentless exposition of her philosophy of nonobjectivism, Hilla took many occasions to praise her patron.

Mr. Guggenheim [she wrote], whose life work consists in revealing and opening up the hidden wealth of the earth, is a leader in the mining industry. Sometimes, in spite of discouragements, he continues his vocation to lead with the same intuitive foresight that attracted him to other fields: namely, the ethereal spirit of art as a counterbalance to earth.

Then, in a letter to Sol, she put the topping on the cake:

As Jesus, the great redeemer of mankind, who visioned life's reality, as not objective, but non-objective, that is, spiritual, called Christian, became the most famous man on earth, your courage and belief in the artistic form of spiritual expression of the non-objective electrically rhythmic evidence in art proves equally as great.

Armed with her "philosophy," her innate dogmatism, her energy, and Sol's money, the baroness Hilla stormed into the art world of the 1930s with Sol in tow and bought up every promising nonobjectivist in sight. By 1939 she had coaxed Solomon into buying fifty Kandinskys, fifteen Gleizeses, six Légers, five Moholy-Nagys, three Chagalls, four Delaunays, two Feiningers, and every work, scores and scores of them, that ever came off the easel of Rudolf Bauer.

At first the paintings were hung in Sol's Plaza suite (the Old Masters became confined to Irene's room, while the new masters were hung everywhere else), but soon the walls outside Irene's domain got overcrowded and it became necessary to rent space for them in some offices at Carnegie Hall. As the collection grew and grew, Sol pondered its future, and in 1937 institutionalized it by creating the Solomon R. Guggenheim Foundation "for the promotion and encouragement of art and education in art." Finally, in 1939, spacious quarters were rented at 24 East Fifty-fourth Street, the entire collection was gathered there, and, on June 1, it opened as "The Solomon R. Guggenheim Collection of Non-Objective Painting" with Baroness Hilla Rebay von Ehrenwiesen in charge.

It was at about this time that Sol's entire collection of Old Masters was sold at auction for $341,000.

Irene, as might be expected, was most displeased. As she had been displeased all along by Sol's mad infatuation with the baroness and his equally mad venture into nonobjective art. Oh, how she was annoyed that day at the Plaza when Hilla barefacedly seized her antique silver teapot and poured tea for her—Irene's—guests at the head of *her* table, while she, Irene, had to stand dumbly by. Once Solomon tried to explain it all to her. He had been a pioneer in Mexico, prospecting for mines. He had been a pioneer in Alaska, in Chile, always prospecting for promising ore bodies. Now he was a pioneer and prospector in art. He was prospecting for new artists, promising mines of art. Sometimes a mine becomes exhausted and you have to look for something else. Irene took the whole thing personally. So she and her Old Masters were exhausted. And Hilla and her nonobjectivists were still to be explored. Well, I'll tell you, Solomon, whom she habitually referred to in her correspondence as her "worser half," you'll never find mines as rich as Watteau and me. As she silently took Hilla and Moholy-Nagy on the chin. Poor Irene. Here Sol was, enjoying his second and third springs, and she was having to witness it all as a spectator, and witness it alone, without her Old Masters to comfort her. But he was always kind and generous to her and this was a consolation in the winter of her life, without the slightest chance for a change of season. Years later, Gladys Straus defended her uncle by saying: "Sol was getting old and tired and without purpose in life. Aunt Irene was so stodgy. Hilla gave Uncle Sol a whole new existence, and it was so *good* for him. All of us saw how much he perked up after Hilla came on the scene."

Good for him in more ways than one. For not only did Hilla give Solomon back his youth, but she also gave him something almost as important, something that had eluded him so far, and that was fame.

Solomon Guggenheim had been a capable businessman, but not a great one, and, as we know, he had been consistently overshadowed by brother Dan all his business life. When *The New York Times*, or *Forbes* magazine, or *Barron's* wanted a statement on the economy from the Guggenheims, as they frequently did, it was almost always Dan's statement that was published. Then, when Dan began subsidizing aviation and rocketry, he got more attention in the press. But now, with the Solomon R. Guggenheim art foundation and museum of nonobjective painting firmly established, and the baroness holding exhibitions of the Solomon R. Guggenheim collection in Sol's native city, Philadelphia (1937); his winter city, Charleston, South Carolina (1938); and his daughter Barbara's adopted city, Baltimore (1939), the name Solomon Guggenheim was suddenly in lights. The press celebrated him for his pioneering in modern art, for giving the American public its first exposure to contemporary European non-objective painting. It was in art, finally, that Sol won the fame that had passed him by in business.

But it was not long before Solomon's newfound fame began to backfire, as fame often does, thanks chiefly to the misplaced enthusiasms and mystic double-talking of the originator of his fame, the irrepressible Hilla, and to the increasing presence in his collection of Hilla's favorite painter, and favorite lover, Rudolf Bauer.

When he created his art foundation Solomon stated that he had done it "to the end that this country may become one of the great art centers of the world and may be accelerated in the process of developing its own great art works as the older nations have done."

This noble, if somewhat chauvinistic, intention was, unfortunately, not fully realized. The arbiters of the New York art world had difficulty taking the baroness, her catalogues, and her favorite painter, seriously. When she would state blithely in a catalogue that "the three principal nonobjective objects—the circle, concentrated continuity in itself, the square, a more spiritual form in relation to space, and the triangle, perhaps less spiritual—were all perfected absolute forms of purity and beauty" the critics would get their backs up.

The New York Times critic, Edward Alden Jewell, wrote that her catalogue of the Moholy-Nagy show was "a dead loss." Another critic described one of Hilla's most cherished Bauers as a "cross between a college pennant, a billiard table, London Bridge (falling down) and thirteen microbes, under a microscope."

In 1942, when the art dealer Edith G. Halpert complained that "the Solomon R. Guggenheim Foundation does not concern itself with American artists," the baroness wrote an angry letter to her protesting that she was exhibiting Moholy-Nagy "who had transferred his residence to the United States in 1937," and she was using an "American instrument," which she called "Mr. Dockum," for "projecting slides of paintings on a screen."

Then there were occasional mishaps. Hilla liked to continuously pipe recorded music into the galleries, mostly Bach. Occasionally the phonograph, which was located in the basement and run by Hilla, would get stuck while Hilla was away, and visitors had to try to concentrate on London Bridge (falling down) and thirteen microbes, under a microscope, exhibited, as were all the other paintings, at knee level, to a constantly repeated chord in E flat. For a while, during the first year of the museum's operation, the roof leaked and overdressed ladies on rainy days found themselves sloshing around, and ocassionally slipping into, puddles before the Rebays, the Kandinskys, the Bauers.

The Rebays and the Bauers. Aline Saarinen, noting that Hilla had placed many of her own paintings on display, together with scores of Bauers, wrote that the museum's exhibits were

> dominated in a somewhat immodest fashion, with paintings by the museum's own director . . . and by those of her once close friend, Rudolf Bauer. Though hers are spirited and his obviously competent, it is the consensus of most qualified critics that the work of neither would receive emphasis in any other museum.

The Rebays and the Bauers were indeed a problem, especially the Bauers. Hilla not only admired, no, worshiped, Bauer's work, she was also for a while desperately in love with him.

Rudolf Bauer was a wild-eyed, wildly emotional, unscrupulous Polish Jew who painted geometrical abstractions and "cosmic" pictures somewhat in the manner of Kandinsky's "circle" paintings. Hilla first met him when they were both exhibiting at Der Sturm in Berlin, and she immediately fell for both him and his paintings. Bauer was in severe financial straits at the time, and Hilla vowed that she would dedicate her life to ameliorating his condition.

Hilla regarded herself not only as an artist of the first rank, but also as a great patron of the arts. In one of her many letters to Solomon she claimed to be the "first to recognize the value of van Gogh, Rousseau, Gauguin, Cézanne, Lembruck, almost unknown in 1910, 1911 when I bought their works." An article on her in *Palm Beach Life*, January, 1963, emphasized this self-awarded role:

> Hilla Rebay determined as a youngster that if she ever crossed the path of a genius she would personally see to it that he would not suffer the fate of a Rembrandt reduced to a poorhouse and Mozart buried in a pauper's grave. She would see to it that he should live in comfort and ease. . . . She made this vow in the person of Rudolf Bauer, the painter whose fortunes were undermined by the ascent of Hitler to power in Germany. It was she who won his release from a German prison. It was she who brought him to America, although broken in health. It is said that she even insisted Bauer be given the two Duesenbergs he deserved.

Hilla believed Bauer to be a once-in-a-thousand-years genius, like Wagner, and stated in her essay "New Age":

> Bauer planned to create a new temple of art in Germany, a sort of

Bayreuth, to which people would travel with the intention to enjoy the best in spiritual art, music, painting, poetry, philosophy, and abstract expression.

In her inimitable prose, Hilla, in "New Age," defended her oft-misunderstood idol:

> It took two hundred years of human incapacity until the deaf average became able and eager to hear Bach's majestic messages as often as today. So what could a Bauer expect of average, who for so long were unable to feel joy in great music, which concerned only the primitive ear, an organ so far behind in faculty to the complicated eye as information agent, clever and even message-sender.

Years later, Wassily Kandinsky's wife stated that Hilla's twofold concept of the Guggenheim Museum was first, as a realization of Bauer's dream of a new Bayreuth and second, as a showplace for Bauer's work.

Bauer and Kandinsky knew each other in the Der Sturm days. At first they were good friends, but, gradually, owing to Bauer's outrageous behavior in Kandinsky's regard, Kandinsky came to detest him.

In the first place, Bauer blatantly plagiarized Kandinsky and tried to pass his Kandinskyesque style off as wholly his own. Second, when, through Hilla, Bauer heard that the fabulously wealthy Solomon R. Guggenheim was interested in buying Kandinskys, Bauer went to Kandinsky and bought some of his paintings cheaply, pleading that he was "just a poor artist" who admired Kandinsky's work and wanted to study it. Then he turned around and sold the paintings to Solomon at an enormous profit. Third, after Bauer had thoroughly insinuated himself into the heart and mind of Hilla, and the mind and collection of Solomon Guggenheim, he tried to see to it that Solomon stopped buying Kandinskys and bought only Bauers.

After a while, Sol, on Hilla's suggestion, was buying all of Bauer's production. By 1939 Solomon had no fewer than fifty-eight Bauers in his collection, and in 1942 Max Ernst, who by then was living with Sol's niece Peggy, was prompted to dub the museum of nonobjective art "the Bauer House."

With the proceeds from these sales and the resales of cheaply bought Kandinskys, Bauer built himself a magnificent villa in Berlin's West End and put over the entrance the inscription "Home of the Spiritual in Art," another plagiarism, for Kandinsky had written a book in 1912 entitled *Concerning the Spiritual in Art*. The exuberant, spendthrift Bauer then filled the House That Sol Built with extravagant furniture—great gilded baroque chairs with red velvet seats, elaborately carved grandfather clocks that did not run, huge blue-and-white porcelain Bavarian *Kachelofens*—placed two colossal double beds in his bedroom, employed a maid and a chef, and kept a huge black Labrador to scare people because, according to Madame Kandinsky, "he was a sadist"; crammed his walls with his own paintings, mounted on purple velvet and framed in richly carved gilt; and sent a note to Kandinsky: "Henceforth you must exhibit all your paintings in my house." When Kandinsky retorted that he would rather hang in museums where all the people could see his work, particularly young people, Bauer snapped back: "To hell with the young people, they can't afford paintings."

Came Hitler and the war and Bauer promptly got in trouble with the Nazis. He began speculating illegally in marks and dollars. Irritated by the Nazis' attitude toward the Jews, he hung an American flag out his window as a military parade passed by in review. Soon he was in a concentration camp doing forced labor, awaiting the gas chamber.

Whereupon Hilla the Loyal went into action. By now—1941—Hilla's brother, Baron Franz Hugo Rebay von Ehrenwiesen, was an officer in the Nazi Ministry of the Interior. Hilla got in touch with him and told him that she and Solomon Guggenheim wanted to get Bauer out of the camp and to America "at any price."

Franz Hugo responded that the price might be his head, but he would try. He did not sympathize much with Hitler anyway, especially the Führer's attitude toward the Jews. Letters, hand-carried messages, packets containing American dollars passed across the Atlantic. Franz Hugo did put his head on the block (later he himself was thrown in a concentration camp), Solomon put part of his bankroll on the block, some Jew-killer high in the SS pocketed his very substantial payoff—if you could sell a Jew for good money why bother to gas him?—and miraculously, Rudolf Bauer landed in Hilla's arms some months later.

(With Sol's inexhaustible resources, Hilla also claimed to have sponsored the flight of Marc Chagall from Nazi-occupied Paris and the escape from the Nazis also of Klee and Léger.)

There were, of course, some difficulties to be overcome before Bauer was able to settle down. He had brought quite a few pornographic paintings with him which U.S. Customs would not let through; he had been detained at Ellis Island; and there had been a fight over the questionable paintings, which Bauer lost before he was released.

Once Bauer got past customs, however, Hilla persuaded Solomon to buy him a "nice house" on the New Jersey shore "to make up for the one he lost to the Nazis." Since Bauer had suffered so much at the concentration camp, she also convinced Sol to buy him "the two Duesenbergs he deserved." And she persuaded him also to give the genius a monthly income in return for his production, which would be enough for him to retain a live-in housekeeper.

So here was Rudolf Bauer, now installed in a big house near Elberon, not far from where Sol had built his Victorian mansion, The Towers, with a handsome income and a beautiful live-in housekeeper catering to his every need.

Hilla was beside herself with joy. Every weekend, when her duties at the museum were over, she would rush out to New Jersey to see her beloved Rudolf, anxious to inspect his production, and perhaps bring some of it back triumphantly to Sol, anxious also to fold herself into his wounded arms.

She would leave no stone unturned to comfort her genius lover. Once, at the end of a long, laudatory letter to Sol, extolling him as a prince of art—"you have all your life been so constructive, so visionary, so wise and considerate of others, so hopeful"—she asked him to send $5,000 to Bauer right away "to make him feel good."

Things went along swimmingly for a while, then, for some mysterious reason, Bauer's "production" began to dry up and, worst of all, he no longer seemed terribly enthusiastic about Hilla's visits.

The reason for this surprising turn of events—after so many risks had been taken and money spent to save the artist from the gas chamber—was that Bauer had fallen in love with his lissome upstate-New York live-in housekeeper. Not only had he fallen in love with her, but he then committed the unthinkable and married her.

German women, we have observed, are either at your feet or at your throat. When Hilla was asked to accept the unacceptable she went to war. She wrote Solomon a letter referring to her former lover as "this foul fool who runs to everyone because he can't judge, even to his worst enemies, like your niece Peggy Guggenheim, who pokes fun at him without him even knowing it," and asking him to cut off Bauer's monthly stipend, which he did. She also persuaded him never again to purchase another Bauer. And she wrote Rudolf a letter calling his upstate-New York live-in housekeeper-wife a tramp, a whore.

Mrs. Bauer then counterattacked with a suit against Hilla for libel and defamation of character. Hilla asked Sol for legal aid. Wary of bad publicity and gossip, he passed his own lawyers by and selected an obscure New Jersey attorney to handle the matter. After an expenditure of $11,000 Hilla won her case.

Of course the whole episode exhilarated the eighty-one-year-old Solomon no end. Yes, the days of adventure and struggle were not over.

Not over by far. Immediately after his wife's defeat, Bauer himself went into action against Hilla, to gain revenge. He denounced Hilla, a German alien, to the FBI for spying for the Nazis, and before long Hilla was in prison.

The sequence of events was as follows:

Hilla had, in the meantime, been established by the magnanimous Solomon in a lovely fourteen-acre estate at Greens Farms (near Westport), Connecticut, which he had paid for entirely and which she had named Franton Court. The main house had eighteen rooms and twenty-eight Bauers.

After Bauer informed on Hilla, FBI agents sneaked into her Greens Farms property, climbed into her linden trees, and, armed with binoculars and telescopes, kept her under twenty-four-hour surveillance.

Hilla was a bird watcher; she kept notes on the birds she observed at Franton Court, and she told Solomon in a letter that she believed "some enormous cranes" had nested in her linden trees. (She was a trifle nearsighted.)

It was the time of the great submarine scare. Not long before, a German submarine had been sighted, and positively identified, in *Long Island Sound*! Hilla had some curious habits. At night she used to go from room to room in Franton Court turning lights on, looking around the room, spilling a tear or emitting a growl over a Bauer, then turning the lights off. The FBI agents perched in her trees took this on-and-off light switching as signals to Nazi submarines. One night, after Hilla had switched a dozen lights on and off, they moved in with guns drawn and bloodhounds slavering, and took the dirty Nazi submarine signaler.

In the process of taking her, they discovered in a loft over her garage 1,400 pounds of sugar, 500 pounds of coffee, and three huge cases of tea, the principal supplements to her vegetarian diet, the foods she absolutely could not do without, and the next day the papers labeled the curator of the Solomon R. Guggenheim Museum of Nonobjective Art a hoarder.

Hilla was then taken to Boston and was incarcerated, without trial, in a federal prison as an enemy alien.

Enemy alien! Why, she protested, going into sputtering, stuttering fits, she had applied for American citizenship, was director of an American museum of modern art, and was a sworn enemy of Hitler and his henchmen. *Mein Gott!* she exclaimed, exploding with indignation, members of her family in Germany had risked their lives to get Jewish artists out of Hitler's clutches.

Solomon Guggenheim loved Hilla Rebay and, loyal to her to the last, he went to bat for her. He wrote a strong letter to Attorney General Francis Biddle:

> Baroness Rebay is a distinguished artist in her own right, and is probably the chief exponent of non-objective painting. Whether or not one may like it, or believe it, it is unquestionably a tremendous influence for culture, and is the subject for study of numerous artists and institutions throughout this country and the rest of the civilized world. Proof of this is indicated in the quantity of letters we receive daily from museums, educational institutions, and people in general from all parts of the world. Baroness Rebay has been, and is, devoting her life to the furtherance of creative painting. Nothing else is of interest to her. No one else has so complete an appreciation of it, or is able to transmit such appreciation to others.
>
> As a result of the helpfulness of Baroness Rebay to me in the purchase of paintings, and of my consequent realization of her artistic knowledge and talent, as well as her high integrity, I became interested in non-objective painting, and came to believe it would prove to be the art of the future. In 1937, backing my belief with a substantial fund, I caused to be organized the Solomon R. Guggenheim Foundation. . . . Since she was so well suited for the position, I persuaded Baroness Rebay to become Curator of the collection.
>
> If Baroness Rebay should not be permitted to return to her work with the Foundation, it would probably survive, since it has already achieved a permanent place among the art institutions of the world. But there is no question that the loss of Baroness Rebay would be a severe blow to it. . . . It is my conviction that Baroness Rebay is not only harmless to any interests of the United States, but is a force for good here. . . . To prevent her from proceeding with her work would result in a great public loss, and no public gain.

Finally, not receiving much satisfaction from the Attorney General, he went all the way to the top, to President Franklin D. Roosevelt, and pleaded his case. Solomon Guggenheim was a conservative Republican, but he made it known to Roosevelt that he and his family and his millions really looked rather kindly on him and his Administration. Not long after the visit Hilla was released.

Hilla came out of the whole thing temporarily disillusioned, but still very much intact, still full of idealism and ambition, and ever more full of devotion and gratitude to Sol. Yes, Sol had never let her down, and she knew now he would never, never let her down. After a pause at Franton Court to catch her breath, she was ready with her next project, the most grandiose of all.

As for Bauer, the gods eventually had their revenge. His upstate-New York wife left him and, shortly thereafter, he went insane and had to be committed to an asylum.

Thirty years later, Thomas Messer, director of the Solomon R. Guggenheim Museum under Sol's grandson's presidency, summed up Bauer saying: "Rebay vastly overrated Bauer because she was in love with him, then Bauer became vastly underrated."

One person who never overrated Bauer was *The New York Times'* Aline Saarinen. After one Bauer-dominated show she had had enough and suggested in an article that "The Museum of Non-objective Painting turn over its collection and its funds, including those set aside for the erection of its permanent home, to one of New York's established museums specializing in modern art."

Hilla was angered, but not daunted, by these remarks. Solomon was hurt and offended by them. Now his patronage of nonobjective painting was earning him more bad publicity than good, more ridicule than praise. The subsequent newspaper reports of his director's arrest and incarceration for being a Nazi collaborator and the discovery of her hoard of sugar, coffee, and tea did not make matters any better, especially for a member of one of New York's leading Jewish families.

In very tactful, diplomatic letters Solomon suggested that Hilla resign. He would continue to support her and protect her, and use her as his "artistic advisor," but she must leave her post at the museum.

Hilla, however, had absolutely no intention of resigning. Far from it, she wanted Sol to build a larger, permanent museum for his collection, wanted him to commission the world's greatest architect to build it and, once it was built, wanted him to put her in complete charge.

In a letter of March 10, 1945, Hilla had cried, in reply to one of Sol's hints she resign:

> My interests have never bothered you as much as yours have bothered me who gave up even sleep and food and rest and enjoyment

and friends and travels and visiting and health and home life, my own Art, my music, my books and sports and many other interests just to build up the Foundation.

That was too much for Sol. He kept her on. With their differences temporarily reconciled, they then set their minds to planning what was to become the most controversial art museum in the world.

The Grand Idea. Whose was it? Members of the Guggenheim family today will resolutely tell you that it was Irene's idea to get Frank Lloyd Wright to build his extraordinary memorial to Solomon.

However, given Irene's antipathy toward nonobjective art and her jealousy of the baroness, it seems unlikely. Besides, there is a wealth of indirect evidence suggesting the museum was wholly the baroness's idea.

First of all, it is a matter of record that Hilla and Bauer always had it in mind to erect a temple of art, along the lines of Wagner's Festspielhaus in Bayreuth.

Second, Hilla did invent, and put into operation, a circular staircase to exhibit nonobjective paintings at the World's Fair of 1939 in New York.

Then there is all the written and oral testimony. According to *Palm Beach Life*, January, 1963: "It was the Baroness Rebay who selected Wright to design the building." Albert Thiele, partner in Guggenheim Brothers and close friend of Solomon's, has stated: "It was Hilla who recommended Wright to Solomon." In an announcement to the board of trustees of the Solomon R. Guggenheim Foundation, Sol's nephew Harry Guggenheim, who, in the meantime, had become president of the foundation and museum, wrote:

> To the plans of this museum Miss Rebay gave the first design, indicating a building with no entrance to be seen, with no staircases, but a slowly ascending ramp to show paintings without a break of thought or feeling due to staircases. She has worked with Mr. Wright on the essentials of this museum for the last eight years.

Hilla's lawyer, Francis P. Schiarolli, now senior partner of Connecticut's prestigious law firm, Cummings and Lockwood, states categorically: "It was Hilla who got Wright to design the museum. She worked closely with Wright on the design and she brought over her nephew, Roland Rebay, also an architect, from Germany to work alongside Wright on the model." Solomon's lawyer, Chauncey Newlin, of White and Case, has stated: "Hilla Rebay had the idea of a monument to S.R. She was convinced Wright should be the architect."

And Thomas Messer, present director of the museum, states: "The creative initiative of S.R.'s life came from Miss Rebay. She was an art missionary, a fanatic, and what she suggested to Mr. Guggenheim, he did."

By the time—early 1940s—Solomon Guggenheim first got in touch with Frank Lloyd Wright about building a permanent museum for his collection, Wright enjoyed a reputation as "the greatest architect in the world." He himself, never one to underestimate his abilities, would go a bit further and intimate he was the greatest architect of all time.

When a young engineering student in the Midwest (there were no architectural schools in existence at the time), he had been much struck by the decline of architecture in the Western world and came to "detest the pilaster, the column, the entablature, the cornice, all the architectural paraphernalia of the defunct Renaissance."

When he went to work for the great skyscraper builder Louis Sullivan, in Chicago, Wright was further depressed by the eclecticism of his fellow American architects. All they seemed to be able to do was put up mongrel copies of Italian Renaissance, English Colonial, French Gothic, Classical Greek.

Worse yet, he sensed that the majority of architects were selling out to mere commerce and expediency.

Everywhere [he wrote in his *Testament* of 1957] these inventions of science by ignorant misuse of a new technique were wiping out the artist. He was himself now becoming a slave. The new chattel. I saw in these new "masters" no great motive above the excess of necessity-for-profit; all likely themselves by way of their own assembly lines to become machines. The kind of slavery that now loomed was even more monstrous and more devastating to our culture now dedicated to senseless excess, so it seemed to me, than ever before. Slavery more deadly to human felicity than any yet devised. . . . The pole-and-wire men in the name of social necessity had already forged a mortgage on the landscape of our beautiful American countryside, while all our buildings, public and private, even churches, were senseless commitments to some kind of expediency instead of the new significance of freedom we so much needed.

In other writings Wright emphasized his belief in "the sovereignty of the individual" and his exalted idea of the architect "as the savior of the culture of modern society." And time and again he pitted himself in his writing against "this world of abortive boxes endeavoring to look tall."

At their first meeting Solomon Guggenheim and Frank Lloyd Wright hit it off beautifully. Each developed a profound respect for the other that was to stand them in good stead during the endless troubles ahead.

Solomon was getting a breath of fresh mountain air at Peckett's Hotel in Franconia Notch, New Hampshire, when Wright brought him the first plans. According to Wright, "When the Grand Old Man saw the first sketches I made he went over them several times without saying a word or looking up. When he did look up there were tears in his eyes. 'Mr. Wright,' he said, 'I knew you would do it, this is it.' "

Solomon formally accepted the plans by letter in 1944. The building was not to be erected until sixteen years later.

Meanwhile there were questions of style and site. The baroness had her say on style in her own inimitable fashion in a letter to Wright of September 5, 1946:

> . . . Great paintings are not a materialistic reference to God's creation of infinitely changing illusions called "earthly matter" but . . . direct expressive tokens of the Creator's mind itself. [Care must be taken, therefore,] to see that the Museum building does not swallow all the attention. Painters do not count, architects do not count, the building counts as a frame, but only as a candlestick to light. . . . God does not want your brain (as His is far superior); he wants your love.

On the question of site, New York Parks Commissioner Robert Moses had some firm ideas, which he did not hesitate to express publicly. He favored an eighty-acre hilltop site at Spuyten Duyvil on the far western edge of the Bronx, overlooking the Hudson River. The museum would be placed on the hilltop, a truly spectacular setting, and the foundation would keep up both the building and the eighty wooded acres surrounding it.

After some consideration, Sol vetoed this idea on the grounds that the site was too inaccessible for most New Yorkers and, in 1944, selected and bought an empty lot at Fifth Avenue and Eighty-ninth Street (subsequently adding two adjoining lots), which was to become the permanent site of the museum.

The site selected, Frank Lloyd Wright then produced the scale model of the museum. It was unveiled at a luncheon at the Plaza and a photograph was taken of Wright, Hilla, and Solomon beaming upon the revolutionary construction. It was a scene out of the Italian

Renaissance: Julius II examining Michelangelo's model of Saint Peter's, with Vittoria Colonna looking on.

Not long after selecting the site and approving the scale model, Solomon suddenly got cold feet about the entire project. "We've got to wait until building costs go down," he wrote Hilla, "before we can start construction."

A little while later he wrote Wright the same thing and enclosed a check for a thousand dollars as a retainer, and "evidence of good will."

Two years passed and Solomon still had cold feet. On July 5, 1949, he wrote Wright: "My great fear is that unless we in this country are more careful, the politicians will bring the United States to the same pass as Germany and France. While I have provided liberally for both the museum building and its endowment, it could be that, when the time comes for materialization of our plans, the money in this country will have much less value than today."

Solomon had so far given $3 million to his foundation and museum and he had earmarked another $5 million for them in his will. As Solomon's health began to fail—he had cancer of the prostate—Hilla did not want to take any chances and asked him point-blank how much he had left the museum and her in his will. He told her, and while she was satisfied with her legacy, she was not at all content with what he had left the foundation and museum. At her insistence, he upped the figure to $8 million.

Three months after changing his will, on November 3, 1949, Solomon died at Trillora Court at the age of eighty-eight.

He had written his final declaration of faith in his foundation and museum six months before, in April:

Pioneering always attracted my attention as an advance, through contribution, to the increase of mankind's material and cultural wealth. Once I was convinced of the worthiness of the goal, difficulties could not deter me. The first time I saw a non-objective painting in Europe, I was enchanted by its appeal and I saw in this Art a medium for the American painter to exceed the past, since the rhythmic element is a typical appealing faculty of the American.

In spite of much misunderstanding and almost discouraging advice, I created a large collection of such paintings and I have never regretted my intuitive decision nor my great faith in this Art, as it grew on me, and I wished others to share my joy.

At the outset I was warned, by my co-worker Hilla Rebay, that I could not live long enough to see the coming recognition of such an outstanding artistic advance. However, our combined efforts have already given me today the greatest satisfaction since the results of our unerring pursuit of this development are now being internationally acclaimed. Letters, articles and visitors from all over the world, and experts from such countries as France, Spain, Italy, Switzerland, Holland, Belgium, Norway, England, Sweden, Denmark and Germany are giving us daily evidence of an overwhelming success, as well as of the desperate need in this world for a new way to educate children.

This Art can bring to them, from the very outset, a solid build-up of their rhythmic sense, on which their lives should be based and, through its ordering influence, a development of their creative powers, with which a long, successful, self-contained life can be accomplished. The guidance of each child to higher realities of aesthetics, a relationship beyond materialistic needs, is the only solid way to peace for mankind, since a complete re-organization through a different line of education is needed. All heretofore search for intellectual objective recognition has been proven a failure through destructive events. This can be avoided if the natural aesthetic sense for rhythmic order, wisdom and self-control is strengthened in our youth. I can see no better way to this goal than to bring children into contact with these creative paintings and their permanent, silent and powerful influence.

I have lived to see on record thousands of reports to this effect, given us freely by the American public, which prove the recognition given to this Art today by educators and teachers. But equally designers, industrialists, physicians, students, even prison authorities, join the institutions of learning in proclaiming its great influence to advancement. It has been proven that America today is considered not only as a leading music center but also as the new center of Art, since it became evident that Paris is now imitating us and following in our footsteps in the recognition of non-objectivity, which eventually will have the greatest effect on leading the brotherhood of mankind to a more rhythmic creative life and so to peace.

Solomon Guggenheim's passing was much mourned by his family, his associates, and his friends. He had been the most amiable and well-liked of the seven sons of Meyer and Barbara, as well as the most versatile. A much-beloved father and grandfather, his daughters and grandsons speak of him today in warmly affectionate terms. Among his most devoted friends were Averell Harriman, who was his neighbor both on Long Island and in Idaho, Dwight Morrow, Thomas Cochran—a Morgan partner—and Albert Thiele, for years his chief assistant at Guggenheim Brothers, all of whom delivered eulogies upon his death.

Albert Thiele, now in his late eighties and living in a large house on the dunes in East Hampton, Long Island, emphasizes four of Solomon's most outstanding qualities: optimism, integrity, magnanimity, and loyalty.

Optimism. When things looked black Sol always said times would change for the better. He was always a buyer, rarely a seller—had sided at first with the young against the sale of Chile Copper—and he firmly believed, as he stated once in a letter to Hilla, "most men are trustworthy."

Integrity. No one with whom Solomon did business—and they ranged all over the globe—ever had reason to doubt his honesty or goodwill. His word could always be trusted. He never went back on a promise. What he said, he meant. Such was the correctness of his behavior throughout the long Chilean nitrate mess that in 1945 the Chilean government conferred its highest civil decoration on him.

Magnanimity. He was the most spontaneously giving, of his self and his money, of all the brothers. His children, nieces, nephews, his business associates always got a warm, affectionate greeting from Sol. And he supported with unstinting generosity his wife, his three daughters, his sons-in-law (none of whom had any money, including the earl), his six grandsons, Hilla, his foundation and museum, and some fifty-odd personal servants and employees.

Loyalty. This was the quality Hilla, above all, could testify to. Sol's wife was against her. His daughters were against her. His nephew Harry couldn't stand her. None of his business associates could take her. Frequently she had exposed him to ridicule and abuse. But he stuck by her to the end, defending her over and over and over again, and even leaving her, at the expense of his legitimate heirs, a substantial legacy in his will.

Another quality, which Thiele did not mention, but which nearly every other person who had come into contact with Solomon did mention, was courage. It took a great deal of courage to build the Guggenheim empire, and Solomon had supplied a good measure of it. Then he had supplied an equal measure of it in plunging into the unexplored, possibly infernal, regions of modern art.

The long, two-column obituary in *The New York Times* mentioned everything but the central influence in Sol's life. It mentioned that he held 162,000 shares of Kennecott Copper Corporation in 1940, which brought him $562,922 in dividends in that year alone. It said that he had been the "weather vane" of Guggenheim Brothers, the one who "studied the utterances of public men, election returns, trends of public opinion," and made "prophecies of the future." It mentioned that he had been the treasurer for twenty-six years of the New York Public School Athletic League. But when it came to his interest in nonobjective art, to which relatively little space was given, it made no mention whatsoever of the baroness Hilla Rebay von Ehrenwiesen. Irene had seen to that. It was she who had sent the obituary to the *Times*.

There were many tributes, but the greatest tribute of all came several years later, from Frank Lloyd Wright. "Solomon Guggenheim," said Wright, "was the only American millionaire I ever met who died facing the future. All the others cuddled up to the past."

The will was an elaborate document, sixty pages in length, which must have made a lot of people very happy indeed.

The ranch and Island Park Land and Cattle Company in Idaho, and the Elgebar Company (El for Eleanor, Ge for Gertrude, Bar for Barbara) and Big Survey plantation in South Carolina went to daughters Eleanor and Barbara (Gertrude had died).

Trillora Court and the house on the East Battery in Charleston were to be put at Irene's disposal for the rest of her life, then willed to Eleanor and Barbara.

Each child of sister Rose Loeb received $50,000, and $50,000 went to each child of sister Cora Rothschild.

The Schweizerisches Israelitisches Alterasyl in Lengnau received $5,000 in memory of Meyer and Barbara.

Fourteen hundred shares of Kennecott Copper went to Albert Thiele.

Two trusts, amounting to approximately $10 million each, went to the families of Sol's two surviving daughters in a very complicated arrangement that awarded the actual monies to Eleanor's and Barbara's children with the stipulations that a certain percentage of income would go to Irene and, upon her death, to Eleanor and Barbara, before the grandchildren came into full possession of their money. By this arrangement only one estate tax was paid over a span of three generations.

All Sol's paintings not yet in the Museum of Non-objective Art went to his foundation, with the exception of a few Old Masters that he had kept in Irene's bedroom and sitting room at the Plaza, and which went to Irene.

Eight million dollars—two for the construction of the new museum, and six for permanent endowment—went to the Solomon R. Guggenheim Foundation.

And 6,000 shares of Kennecott Copper, 1,500 U.S. Rubber preferred, 5,000 U.S. Rubber common, 1,400 Standard Oil of New Jersey, 5,000 Anaconda Copper, and 400 Barber Oil, with a market value at time of death of approximately a million dollars, went to Baroness Hilla Rebay von Ehrenwiesen.

No, Sol had not forgotten his advisor, curator, and donor of the last quarter of his life. Years later Sol's lawyer, Chauncey Newlin, of White and Case, commented on Sol's legacy to Hilla: "S.R. was, very indebted to the baroness. . . . She gave him an importance and reputation. But for her there would be no Guggenheim Museum and his name would have passed into anonymity."

CHAPTER

6

KING SOLOMON'S MUSEUM

HARRY GUGGENHEIM, SOL'S NEPHEW, SUCCEEDED TO THE PRESI-
dency of the Solomon R. Guggenheim Foundation upon Sol's death,
and immediately collided with the museum director, the baroness
Rebay.

Thus it was left to two natural enemies to realize Solomon's plans
for a permanent museum.

Harry and Hilla were light-years apart temperamentally and intellectually. Harry was a capable executive, and a man of considerable
energy, but he knew precious little about art, least of all nonobjective
art, and did not have much sympathy for the artistic temperament.
Being dogmatic and somewhat dictatorial himself, it was only natural
he would clash with his exceedingly dogmatic and dictatorial museum director.

The Hilla-Harry battle was waged over a period of fifteen years.
Fortunately for posterity, it is all preserved in the Hilla von Rebay
Foundation archives in New York. Some samples:

HARRY: . . . a constant repetition of your views about the policies and
administration of the Museum which are in direct opposition
to those of the President of the Foundation, all of the officers
of the Foundation, and all of the other trustees of the Foundation . . . your views are often expressed in insulting and
scurrilous terms.

HILLA: . . . If I ever was insulting, it certainly was a return engagement, and there is no question, what is more gentleman or
lady-like; to attack a lady without checking for correctness the

information given by a proven liar, schemer and others of the same kind, or defending by letters in privacy a great cause, though, sad to say, aggressive of necessity . . .

HARRY: . . . It seems abundantly clear that you are not happy with your present relationship with the Foundation and how its affairs are being conducted. I am sorry this is so, but I see no prospect of conditions changing . . .

. . . we all wish very much to save you any unhappiness . . . and it seems to me that the way to do this would be for you to discontinue your duties and responsibilities as a trustee of the Foundation . . .

HILLA: [telegram] . . . I was not called in nine months to any full trustee meeting. Will be interesting to know how minutes explained my absence and *for history* how Hilla Rebay was treated.

HARRY: . . . we are discontinuing your $575 monthly payment for secretarial and other expenses . . . we are withdrawing and discontinuing all emeritus titles, including yours of Director Emeritus . . .

HILLA: [at end of rope] . . . I was almost unprotectedly exposed when the foundation was forced onto me and with enemies of the foundation's work encouraged secretly in our own ranks until my lungs and heart condition in the summer of 1951 were so choking due over work, so as to be hopelessly ill and considered by five surgeons and specialists to have only two to four weeks to live and now I marvel at how I was able to overcome death due to Tibetan training. But I am still not rid of the burdens of the responsibility due to international renown and obligation to my late great co-worker, S.R.G.

At the height of the battle Hilla let loose her most violently anti-Semitic invective against Harry, calling him every insulting name a Jew has ever been called, and not sparing the other trustees either, especially Albert Thiele, whom she referred to contemptuously as a "rug merchant."

The upshot of it all was that Hilla first lost her job as museum director, then her position on the board, and finally all her emeritus titles.

In retaliation Hilla kept some four hundred paintings, sculptures, and other works of art Solomon had lent her, including some of his finest Kandinskys, at Franton Court, which was in direct violation of a written agreement Sol had made with her before his death. According to the agreement, in return for the approximately one million dollars' worth of securities he left her in his will she was to give back all the paintings he had lent her during their twenty-three years of association.

Harry appointed James Johnson Sweeney, a curator at the Museum of Modern Art, to succeed Hilla as director, and under him the Guggenheim Museum took on a new authority and professionalism. In addition to relegating the Rebays and the Bauers to the cellar, Sweeney added some 250 new paintings to the collection, including some superb Picassos and Cézannes.

Meanwhile the Great Project for the Frank Lloyd Wright-designed museum was getting nowhere. First of all, Sol's estate was not settled until 1952, and thus it was not until then that the money for the museum was transferred from the estate to the foundation. Secondly, the application for a building permit, made immediately after the transfer of funds, was quickly turned down by New York's Department of Building and Housing on grounds that Wright's plans transgressed the metropolitan building code in no fewer than thirty-two ways.

On hearing this latter bit of news Frank Lloyd Wright went into a rage. To Harry he exploded: "Architecture, may it please the court, is the welding of imagination and common sense into a restraint upon specialists, codes, and fools." And he urged him to do something about the New York City government's specialists, codes, and fools. Harry told him to go back to work.

Wright did go back to work. At the Frank Lloyd Wright architectural schools at Taliesin in Wisconsin, and Taliesin West in Arizona, the master's assistants worked overtime to revise the plans.

Permit hearings then dragged on for four years. It almost seemed as if the New York City bureaucrats really *wanted* to obstruct the work of the genius.

Wright, at the time, was not too complimentary about New York. "It is fit only for cockroaches," he declared, "indeed is inhabited only by cockroaches, and is well on its way to becoming so crowded that soon the cockroaches will have to walk on the tops of the taxicabs." His formula for improving New York? "Bomb it."

Finally, on March 13, 1956, the New York City bureaucrats came through with the permit. But then, just as all problems seemed to have been solved, Wright and Sweeney began to squabble.

Wright wanted to create an architectural masterpiece that would publicize, down through the ages, the names of Frank Lloyd Wright, architect, and Solomon R. Guggenheim, donor. All museum-man

Sweeney was interested in was a satisfactory space in which to display paintings . . . and also store paintings . . . and administer museum affairs.

Sweeney did not like Wright's curved walls and cantilevered ramp. He did not believe these architectural innovations, however daring they might be, would show paintings off to their best advantage. Wright retaliated by stating that only this way could you display a large collection of paintings "without any intervening interruptions," such as doors, elevators, pillars, staircases, hallways, and so on, and that it was certainly more restful for the body and the feet to view them this way, "with gravity doing part of the work." In the end Wright won his point with the trustees, and Sweeney was presented with a virtual *fait accompli*: The ramp and sloping walls would remain in the design.

Sweeney wanted lots of space in the building for carpentry, photography, storage, restoration. Wright contended that all these functions could be accommodated by another, more conventional, building located nearby.

Sweeney wanted artificial lighting, so the paintings could be seen easily anytime, day or night. Wright, who always strived to be "true and close to nature," wanted natural light, which, to Sweeney, was "totally unrealistic." "What about cloudy days?" Sweeney cried. Sweeney got his artificial light.

Sweeney wanted the exhibit walls to be white. Wright thought that would make them look like "the toilets of the Racquet Club" and suggested they be tan instead. They were eventually painted white . . . after Wright's death.

Sweeney wanted the museum to be "a teaching instrument." Wright wanted it to be a showcase, and, above all, a showplace. Sweeney was interested in function, Wright was interested in aesthetic appearance.

(Many years later an embittered Sweeney stated that Wright had first designed the construction for another purpose—"a jam factory or something"—then, when the realization of that purpose fell through, he presented the same design for the museum "so he wouldn't have to go to the trouble of constructing a new model." This contention has never been proved.)

As the building neared completion, Wright began to tell Sweeney exactly how he should hang the paintings. This infuriated Sweeney and he got the trustees to agree to hold a competition. Sweeney hung two bays; Wright hung two bays. The trustees chose Sweeney's method.

Not long after that Frank Lloyd Wright took seriously ill at Taliesin West, and on April 9, 1959, died in a hospital in Phoenix.

Sweeney was now on his own and was quite delighted: *Mors tua, vita mea.* But the Great Peace did not last very long. A year after the museum's opening, Sweeney and Harry—who had patiently mediated the long Wright-Sweeney quarrel—got into a furious argument over the fundamental purpose of the museum. Sweeney steadfastly maintained that museums were "teaching instruments," "aids to art appreciation," and asserted that Harry and the board were "much more interested in pleasing and entertaining the public." "Museums," said Sweeney, "should never try to attract the public by pleasing, but rather by educating." Harry and the board listened to these arguments, firmly disagreed with them (Harry wanted to publicize the name of Guggenheim and therefore wanted as many people as possible to visit the museum), and Sweeney was compelled to resign.

Upon submitting his resignation in the summer of 1960 Sweeney said he was leaving because "of differences between the ideals held by the Board of Trustees with reference to the aim and use of a museum, and my own ideals which I feel I have a responsibility to follow."

The gala opening, which had been preceded by a preview and a reception, was held on October 21, 1959. There were the usual speeches. Arthur S. Flemming, U.S. secretary of Health, Education, and Welfare, delivered a message from President Eisenhower. Henry Cabot Lodge, U.S. ambassador to the United Nations, also spoke, as did Robert Wagner, mayor of New York, and New York City's parks commissioner, Robert Moses, whose wife was distantly related to Frank Lloyd Wright. Moses, in his speech, refused to comment on the building since he was "an ex officio trustee with janitorial privileges at the Metropolitan Museum of Art." He went on to say: "We need not debate how much of Cousin Frank was genius and how much was, let us say, showmanship. Genius even in small proportions is very rare indeed and we should always greet it with a cheer."

Among the other notables present were Bernard M. Baruch, Mrs. Wassily Kandinsky, and Harry F. Guggenheim.

Absent were the three people ultimately responsible for the building, the donor, the architect, and the inspirer.

Mrs. Wright was present, however, and she told reporters that had her husband lived he would have preferred to stay away rather than have to look at the alterations of the interior effected against his will by director Sweeney.

As for Hilla . . . she viewed the proceedings from Franton Court with utter contempt. Later, when the foundation asked her to give back at least some of the paintings Solomon had lent her, she retorted, "Why should I take down the precious paintings from the walls of my house and give them to a pigsty?"

The Solomon R. Guggenheim Memorial Museum—so named by Harry, who rejected the name Museum of Non-Objective Art—soon became, and has since remained, one of the most controversial buildings ever constructed in the United States. It has been likened variously to a snail, a turnip, a cement mixer, a child's sand castle, a nuclear power plant, an inverted cup and saucer, a bird house for vultures on Mars.

After the opening, comments on the building poured forth from all over the United States and the World.

Sol's niece Peggy Guggenheim did not like it very much. "The museum resembles a huge garage," she wrote. "It is built on a site that is inadequate for its size and looks very cramped, suffering from its nearness to adjacent buildings. It should have been placed on a hill in [Central] Park . . . the rising ramp, Wright's famous invention, coils like an evil serpent. The walls bend backwards and a cement platform keeps one at a respectful distance from the pictures. Nothing could be more difficult than viewing them from this angle."

Emily Genauer, art critic for the *New York Herald Tribune,* called the museum "the most beautiful building in America." London's *Art News and Review* said: "It was fascinating in broad daylight, while at night a surrealist element is introduced by the rivers of light that flow between the curved darkness of the spiralling ramps." Belgrade's *Politika* enthused that it "conquers the soul by its aspect and pride." Philip C. Johnson, one of the two architects of the Seagram Building, and director of the department of architecture and design at the Museum of Modern Art, called the interior "one of the greatest rooms created in the twentieth century." Moscow's *Izvestia* was all sneers: "The art of the fat ones . . . soiled with lines and blotches that do not express anything."

Whatever its merits and demerits—and there are certainly plenty of both—it is an incontestable fact that the Solomon R. Guggenheim Collection and Museum have had an enormous impact, for better and for worse, on the artistic taste of mid-twentieth-century Americans, perhaps more than any other single institution of their kind. On the for-better side they exposed American artists and the American public to the seminal abstract works of such twentieth-century masters as Kandinsky (170 paintings in the collection), Klee (140), Léger, Mondrian, Moholy-Nagy, for the first time on a significantly large scale, and in so doing helped create a welcome revolution in taste from the eclecticism that preceded them.

On the for-worse side they have fostered, especially in recent years, tendencies that can only be termed negative, destructive, nonart, antiart, antilife. Leaving the good, the true, the just, the beautiful, the disciplined, the balanced, the healthy behind in the limbo of the passé, the Guggenheim Museum now gives us works like Kenneth Noland's "April Tune" (1964), which consists of a huge boring blank space of uniform color bounded by thin stripes along its upper and lower edges, an almost entirely blank canvas. Suffice it to say that neither the baroness Rebay, for all her misplaced enthusiasms, nor Solomon R. Guggenheim, for all his lack of artistic training, would have countenanced the inclusion of such an affront to art and life in their museum . . . although Rebay could almost have written the blurb in the catalogue (published by the foundation in 1970):

> In the most recent of [Noland's] horizontal band paintings, of which "April Tune" is an example, a large area of color is framed above and below by relatively thin stripes. Although this area is in fact a rectangle, the framing bands insist that it be read not as an area but simply as a wider band of color.

By the time the Guggenheim Museum began adding such questionable artworks as "April Tune" to its collection, Baroness Hilla Rebay von Ehrenwiesen was mercifully dead.

Throughout the 1960s she had waged a constant battle with the trustees of Sol's foundation and museum to retain at Franton Court some two hundred paintings Sol had lent her (but which she claimed he had given her), a battle which saw her removal as "director emeritus" of the foundation and her final, irrevocable alienation from both the Guggenheim Museum and the Guggenheim family.

Hilla did not have much of a case to retain possession of the paintings because Sol had written her a letter before he died telling her that in return for the substantial legacy he left her she was to give the paintings back to the museum, and this was stipulated also in Sol's will.

Nevertheless, from her stronghold at Franton Court, armed with Sol's legacy and the top legal talent in Connecticut, she battled on, chiefly out of principle, the principle being that she had been cruelly wronged, that the museum was all her idea, and she should have been its permanent director. The case was eventually settled after Hilla's death in September, 1967, with the sale, by Hilla's executors, of a large part of her collection, including the best Kandinskys, to the Solomon R. Guggenheim Foundation, for a million dollars, a bargain for the museum.

By the end of her seventy years Hilla Rebay had become a very wealthy woman. The million dollars in gilt-edged securities Sol had left her in 1949 had ridden the bull market of the 1960s so well that by 1969 it was worth over $5 million.

On an income of $250,000 a year, Hilla lived out her last days as a sort of High Priestess of Art, visited by artists and art scholars from all over the world, enjoying her renown, her visitors' sympathy over the cruel way the Solomon R. Guggenheim Foundation had treated her, her vast collection of abstract paintings, the fourteen-acre nature preserve and bird sanctuary Solomon had given her.

Not long before her death Hilla established her own art institution, the Hilla von Rebay Foundation, "to promote non-objective art and scholarship," with headquarters at Franton Court. It was to this foundation, whose main purpose was to help struggling young artists, that she then left a large part of her estate, specifically two million dollars' worth of paintings; Franton Court, with its fourteen acres of gardens, nature preserve, and bird sanctuary; and a million dollars in cash and securities. The rest of the estate went to taxes, various friends and employees, and, in great part, to her brother in Germany, Franz Hugo, who, it will be remembered, as a Nazi official had helped her smuggle so many artists out of Europe during Hitler's war, and to her nephew, Roland, an architect, who had studied with Wright, and worked with him on the musuem, and to her niece, Maria Teresa. Thus did a portion of the Guggenheim fortune end up in the small Bavarian village of Wessling-am-See. Roland Rebay has since built dozens of Frank Lloyd Wrightesque houses in southern Bavaria.

The Solomon R. Guggenheim Memorial Foundation and Museum is now under the presidency of one of Solomon's grandsons, Peter O. Lawson-Johnston, who is also head of what is left of Guggenheim Brothers, and it is upon his shoulders, and those of his museum director, Thomas Messer, that the future of the museum now rests.

Whatever that future might be—glorious, neutral, destructive—the building will remain, barring a bombing or a razing, as the ultimate monument to the Guggenheim family and to the genius of Frank Lloyd Wright. Such, in fact, has become the fame of the building already that it was the one architectural construction by Wright selected to appear on the U.S. postage stamp commemorating the life-work of America's greatest architect.

The ultimate monument to the Guggenheims. There it stands, a lone testament of creative initiative and original inspiration, an apparition of tomorrow, amid Fifth Avenue's endless parade of staid nineteenth-century imitations, its blocks and blocks and blocks of overblown pseudo-Renaissance, pseudo-Gothic, pseudo-Romanesque, pseudo-Jacobean, pseudo-Georgian, pseudo-Classical, pseudo-Venetian, its blocks and blocks and blocks of early, middle, and late Metro-Goldwyn-Mayer, and quality steel-and-brick East Bronx slum.

There the Guggenheim Museum stands proclaiming that once a headstrong, recklessly devoted woman had an idea; an energetic, individualistic American family had the money and the courage to accept and finance the idea; and one great American artist had the genius to transform the idea and the money into an enduring work of art.

Thus did the Guggenheims, 111 years after their arrival in America, accomplish the miracle of alchemizing gems and metals into art. From the mountains of Alaska, Utah, Mexico, Bolivia, and Chile, the river-beds of the Yukon and Malaya, the plains of the Congo and Angola, they had gouged out the native riches of the earth in such vast quantities that they could be measured only in thousands of tons and millions of cubic yards, then metamorphosed them into works more durable than copper and lead, more valuable than silver and gold.

CHAPTER

7

BENJAMIN: ON
DROPPING OUT, PART I

THE PORTRAIT OF BENJAMIN GUGGENHEIM IN THE PARTNERS' ROOM of Guggenheim Brothers is the smallest in the room. It displays a handsome, if somewhat soft, young face in a high Edwardian collar and rests in a simple oval frame, without a trace of gilt, above a door leading to the hall of the minerals. The meager square footage of the portrait places the subject far below Isaac, Daniel, Murry, Solomon, and Simon in importance, but not entirely in last place. William is not even represented on the walls.

Though clearly in sixth place among the brothers, Ben held a number of firsts in the family that entitle him to his own special claim to attention. He was the first of the seven brothers to go to college, the first to go into mining, the first to drop out of the family business, the first to lead a life more oriented toward pleasure than work, the first to collect paintings, the first to produce a child with outstanding abilities, the first to become an expatriate.

Meyer Guggenheim possessed no formal education to speak of, was always conscious of the lack, and so was most anxious that his younger sons make up for his deprivation by receiving a college education. Accordingly, Ben was packed off to Columbia in 1882, becoming the first Guggenheim to enter an institution of higher learning.

Ben did not take to college. He found most of his courses—emphasis on metallurgy—unexciting, soon became restless, and dropped out after his second year. Meyer, sorely disappointed, then offered him a job in the New York offices of M. Guggenheim's Sons, but

Ben found laces and embroideries dull, the offices gloomy, and the Wall Street area "depressing."

There was only one thing to do with him and that was send him off to the mines in Leadville, Colorado. Since the other brothers were still principally involved with laces and embroideries, Ben thus became the first Guggenheim to work directly in mining.

As it turned out, Ben found the Cloud City very much to his liking. He was assigned as a bookkeeper to the A. Y. mine, a fairly big job— ten acres of land, three shafts, and one hundred men. He would sit in a shack near shaft number three, with a revolver strapped to his belt, keep track of the mine's income and expenses, make out and handle the payroll. At night he would go down to Tiger Alley in "The Row" and dance with prostitutes at fifty cents a dance, or play three-card monte with miners and mule skinners at Crazy Jim's, or drink corn whiskey at the Comique Saloon at twenty cents a glass.

In due course, Ben advanced to the position of manager of the family smelter at Pueblo (which he had also helped build), an important responsibility, and a key step in the formation of the Guggenheim empire. In this capacity he acquitted himself rather well, proving to be a shrewd judge of character (he hired an excellent superintendent), and a respected leader of men. He also proved to be a fine connoisseur of Rocky Mountain females, becoming, with brother Will, a favorite with the most sumptuous belles at Peppersauce Bottoms.

He did not, however, prove to be as good a judge of ore bodies. In 1900 he was offered a piece of Bingham Canyon. On asking how high the copper content ran, he quickly lost interest when told it was only 2 percent. It remained for Dan to buy the mine—then the largest in the world—for thirty times the money some years later.

Eventually Ben was brought back from Colorado and put in charge of the new Guggenheim metals refinery at Perth Amboy, New Jersey, which also put him within easy striking range of New York. Handsome and rich, with a seemingly limitless future before him, young Ben Guggenheim had no trouble cutting a swath through the wealthiest and most beautiful Jewish girls in Manhattan.

After a season or two of playing the field, he settled on the financially promising, but by no means beautiful, Florette Seligman, daughter of James Seligman, brother of the great Joseph, of J. W. Seligman & Company, then America's richest Jewish bankers.

The Seligmans were ambivalent about the marriage, which was celebrated in 1895. They considered "the Googs" upstarts without polish and tradition—why Joseph Seligman had dined with Abraham

Lincoln!—but were pleased with the idea of the money the great mining and smelting family represented. When the engagement was announced, the American Seligmans wired the European Seligmans: "FLORETTE ENGAGED GUGGENHEIM SMELTER." The telegram arrived garbled: "FLORETTE ENGAGED GUGGENHEIM SMELT HER."

Six years after the marriage, in 1901, at the culmination of Dan's great campaign to wrest control of American Smelting and Refining from William Rockefeller, Ben, distrustful of Dan's grandiose plans for expansion, upset about going into partnership with outsiders, piqued by what he felt was Dan's conscious effort to deny the younger brothers significant responsibility in future ventures, and desirous of tasting the pleasures of Europe, resigned as an active partner in M. Guggenheim's Sons, and, at the age of thirty-six, retired on an income from his mining investments of approximately $250,000 a year.

It was a fateful decision, for in dropping out so early in the game Ben and his heirs were to miss out completely on the grand era of Guggenheim business expansion—miss out on Kennecott, Bingham Canyon, the Congo, Angola, Bolivia, and Chile Copper—and Florette, and daughters Benita, Peggy, and Hazel were to suffer the financial consequences.

After a trip to Europe to celebrate his new freedom from his brothers, Ben established himself and his family in a lavish, five-story townhouse on the corner of Seventy-second Street and Fifth Avenue in New York. For neighbors there were people like the James Stillmans, the William Rockefellers, and President Grant's widow.

Benjamin's new place was of a splendor and magnificence—here and there a trifle overdone—typically Guggenheim.

On entering the great house one passed through two glass doors, with a vestibule in between, to arrive in a marble entrance hall with fountain. On one wall was a huge, stuffed American golden eagle with wings spread and chains dangling from its talons that Ben himself had shot, illegally, in the Adirondacks. A marble stairway led to the great representational rooms on the next floor: the vast dining room hung with seventeenth-century Flemish tapestries; the conservatory filled with rare plants; a reception room hung with a huge tapestry showing Alexander the Great in triumph; the opulent Louis XVI parlor with huge gilt-framed, floor-to-ceiling mirrors and authentic Louis XVI furniture, and tapestries that had once adorned one of the royal Bourbon residences in the Loire. In the midst of this last salon stood a gilded concert grand piano, and on the parquet floor there rested an incongruous, and much discussed, bearskin rug whose red tongue and yellow teeth often fell out. Florette wanted the beast removed, but Ben, who claimed he had killed it out West, wouldn't hear of it. On the third floor there was a library with red velvet-hung walls, large glass bookcases containing unread leatherbound editions of the classics, portraits of Meyer and Barbara, and a tiger-skin rug that Ben made no claim to have shot. On this floor, also, there were galleries hung with costly paintings, among them several fine Corots, Watteaus, and Henners. Ben and Florette each had their own separate bedrooms, dressing rooms, and parlors, also hung with museum-quality paintings. The fourth floor was entirely reserved for the children, and the fifth, with its low ceilings and small narrow windows, was for the servants.

In this house Ben and Florette raised three daughters, Benita (named after Ben), Marguerite (known as Peggy), and Barbara Hazel (known as Hazel), to add to the Guggenheims' ever-burgeoning store of females. In this house, also, Florette held interminably long and insufferably dull (according to Peggy) tea and bridge parties for the ladies of New York's German-Jewish *haute bourgeoisie*, and Ben installed a slim, red-headed trained nurse, in a room of her own, to massage his chronically neuralgic head, and administer to those other needs which Florette was either unwilling, not expert enough, or not asked to fulfill.

In regard to Ben's penchant for the trained nurse, and others like her who followed, Harold Loeb, a nephew, once observed: "Of all the Guggenheims, Ben was the most extravagant in his amorous divagations, even introducing them into his own house . . . women were drawn to him, partly because of his warm smile, but principally, I suspect, because he really liked women, they sensed he did, and women like to be liked."

Since Ben's marriage to Florette was essentially a marriage of two family fortunes and never pretended to be otherwise, we can easily excuse Ben's "divagations." Besides, Florette, it appears, possessed several unappealing traits. One of these was—odd for a rich girl— an excessive attachment to money. She loved to receive money, but she was very stingy about spending it. She habitually underpaid her eleven servants and undertipped waiters and hotel porters. In France the porters got wise and marked her bags with X's, so at the next hotel the luggage would mysteriously not arrive in her room. She judged her daughters' suitors wholly in terms of their financial resources. A young caller might be acceptable in every way—family, profession, salary—but if he had no money, no *capital*—salary, no matter how high, meant little to her—if he had no capital to speak of, he was labeled "N.G.," No Good, and asked not to call again. The good life for a woman, was, to Florette, living off substantial *unearned* income, and living meant mostly long bridge parties in her Louis XVI parlor, with equally long intermissions for gossip and tea.

Florette, however, was almost normal in comparison to some of the other Seligmans, a family some members of which had slipped quickly into decadence in only three generations, thanks probably to Florette's mother. This strange lady—a torment to James Seligman all his life—had the habit of going around to shopkeepers in her neighborhood and asking, day in and day out: "When do you think my husband last slept with me? Answer me, when do you think it last was?" Her sister was an aspiring soprano, and would sing scales standing at bus stops and walking along Fifth Avenue. This sister's husband, after fighting with her for over thirty years, finally tried to kill her and one of their sons by striking them over their heads with a golf club. When they refused to die he ran to the Central Park reservoir and drowned himself by plunging into the water with heavy weights tied to his feet. Then there was Florette's perennially unemployed brother, who ate almost nothing but charcoal and, as a result, had coal-black teeth and a black tongue. For drink he guzzled whiskey before his charcoal breakfast and sucked ice during the day, carrying his ice in a zinc-lined pocket. An incurable gambler, he threatened time and again to commit suicide unless Florette's father made up his losses. He finally shot himself after losing a sum James Seligman had given him that was supposed to last him the rest of his life. Ben's daughters and grandchildren were destined to suffer periodically from their genetic legacy.

Ben's reaction to Florette and her relatives was to philander and travel. Often he did both at the same time. Ben had taken a liking to Paris, where he had also taken an apartment and established a business, and it was there that he had his most notorious affairs. One of them was with a certain Marquise de Cerruti, whom Peggy has described as "neither pretty nor young . . . but she had the same agreeable quality (maybe sensuous) of the trained nurse." Florette was not so kind. She habitually referred to her as "the monkey" and noted frequently that she possessed "black teeth."

Ben, in his early forties, had blossomed into a very good-looking man, full of pep and fun. Daughter Hazel today describes him as "small-boned, blond-skinned, gray-haired, with light-colored eyes

. . . all the other Guggenheim brothers were dark and did not look nearly as Aryan as my father."

In his expensive English-tailored suits, high collars, foulard ties with stickpin, boutonnieres, spats, patent-leather shoes, he was a curious sort of hybrid, an American-Jewish Edwardian swell.

It is a credit to Ben's honesty, though not to his good sense, that he did not hide his amours from his family. Florette and the three girls were perfectly well aware who the Marquise de Cerruti was, as they had been fully aware of who the trained nurse was, and the role both played in Ben's life.

Peggy, twelve at the time, remembers bumping into *la marquise* all over Paris, at Rumpelmayer's, while Peggy was gorging herself on ice cream, at Lanvin's with her mother, while they were trying on dresses, in the Bois, where the whole family would take a Sunday stroll.

One Sunday morning, Ben, Florette, and the three girls were strolling in the Bois, on the Avenue des Acacias, when they accidentally bumped into the marquise dressed in a suit made entirely of baby lamb. As soon as the marquise passed by, Florette scolded Ben vehemently for being so extravagant. To keep her quiet Ben gave her enough money to have an identical suit made for herself. Being a practical person, Florette the Businesswoman promptly put the money into stocks and bonds.

After Marquise de Cerruti came a "young blond singer." For a while Florette seriously contemplated divorcing Ben, but the other Guggenheims, descending on her en masse as was their custom in times of crisis, talked her out of it, claiming it would be "so bad for the business," and hence for *her* bank account also. Florette was therefore compelled to accept her husband's philandering. According to Peggy, she became a terribly unhappy woman.

Benjamin Guggenheim had the typical playboy's syndrome. His older brothers did not grow up as a rich man's sons, but he did. He therefore was never aware of the intense struggles his father had had to go through to earn his fortune. All was so easy. Furthermore, being a late child, he was spoiled by everyone, especially mother Barbara, whose inexhaustible love and compassion was, at this stage, not always counterbalanced by Meyer's severity, as it had been with the other children. Early Ben became used to a life of self-gratification. When, in 1901, he was faced with the choice of leaving the Guggenheim firm with a share of the profits in accordance with the amount of work he had so far put into the business, or remaining and working as hard as the other brothers, he chose the easier path. Though he would have less money, he would enjoy more freedom and more self-gratification.

This is not to say, however, that Ben spent all his time merely playing around. He also cultivated business interests of his own. In Paris, which he came to prefer to New York, he had established the International Steam Pump Company, an organization which, among its diverse activities, made the elevators for the Eiffel Tower. Nevertheless, his playing around must have interfered seriously with his business, since it wasn't long after its founding that International Steam Pump began to falter and Ben found himself pouring more and more of his capital into what proved to be a bottomless hole.

In the spring of 1912, Benjamin, who had been away from his wife and children for eight months, presumably looking after the affairs of International Steam Pump in Paris, decided to return to New York to celebrate daughter Hazel's ninth birthday. Accordingly, he booked passage on a steamer from Le Havre to New York. Because of a wildcat stokers' strike he had to change ships at the last minute, and so took a place, or rather three places, the other two for his gentleman's gentleman, Victor Giglio, and the young blond singer, on the White Star Line's *Titanic* instead.

It was the *Titanic*'s maiden voyage and the White Star Line had billed it as the safest ship afloat. The list of distinguished passengers included Isidor Straus, co-owner of R. H. Macy's and uncle of Gladys Guggenheim's husband, Roger, Bruce Ismay, president of the White Star Line, and John Jacob Astor 4th.

The captain of the vessel was determined to set a world record for a transatlantic crossing. With engines at full speed ahead, he tore across the North Atlantic shipping lane heedless of the gigantic icebergs that drifted down that time of year from the thawing Arctic.

On the night of April 14, one of these silent monsters, showing an insignificant, unthreatening head, barely visible through the fog, tore open the *Titanic*'s bottom with its immense underwater bulk and, a few minutes later, the vessel had shipped so much water and had listed so heavily to starboard, that it was quite clear to the captain and everyone else it would sink.

It was during the next frantic minutes that playboy Ben Guggenheim showed the other side of his character—the traits he had often

displayed during his brief mining career in Colorado and Mexico—
and became, literally overnight, a hero to his family.

Events followed one another that night with a terrible urgency.
Soon it was apparent that there were not enough life jackets for all
and that there were not enough places in the lifeboats for more than
600 of the 2,100 passengers aboard.

Benjamin Guggenheim and his gentleman's gentleman were sleeping when the *Titanic* struck the jagged underwater bulk of the iceberg.
Shortly after the almost noiseless collision, Ben's room steward, John
Johnson, awakened Ben and Giglio, told them what had happened,
and urged them to get dressed.

He then handed them life preservers and they strapped them on.
Ben complained his hurt his back and he took it off. When Johnson
suggested it was time to go, Ben said he wanted to collect a few more
precious belongings and would meet him on deck.

By then Ben and Giglio had decided how they were going to meet
their fate. They both discarded their life jackets, combed their hair,
put on some cologne, dressed in their evening clothes, went up on
deck, gave their life jackets to two women and told Johnson they
were going down with the ship "like gentlemen."

A short while later, Johnson spotted Ben walking briskly along the
deck helping women into lifeboats. "Women and children first!"
"Women and children first!" he was shouting, while other men hurled
women aside in their frantic rush to gain places in the lifeboats for
themselves.

Finally an officer ordered Johnson to man an oar and Ben went
up to him and gave him a message for Florette: "Tell her I played
the game straight to the end and that no woman was left on board
because Ben Guggenheim was a coward."

A few minutes later the waves began crashing over the decks and
within an hour of the collision 1,517 people were drowning in the
twenty-seven-degree waters as the *Titanic* sank beneath them.

All the Guggenheims knew Ben was on the *Titanic*.

Florette, Benita, Peggy, and Hazel were going home from James
Seligman's birthday party, crossing from the West Seventies to East
Seventy-second Street, when they passed a newspaper boy shouting
"Extra! Extra!" According to Hazel, "My beautiful sister Benita, who
must have had a sort of ESP, begged my mother to stop and buy the
extra, saying 'Something terrible must have happened to Poppa's
boat.' . . . My mother assured her nothing could happen to the

Titanic as it was foolproof. This occurred eight hours before the *Titanic* hit the iceberg."

After word of the sinking did reach New York, Daniel Guggenheim wired the *Carpathia*, which had picked up many survivors, and asked if Benjamin Guggenheim was aboard. No, was the answer. This news was then relayed to Ben's daughters, but not yet to Florette.

Refusing to believe Ben had gone down with the ship, a contingent of incredulous Guggenheims, Dan's son M. Robert, Rose's son Harold, and Murry's son, Edmond, went down to meet the *Carpathia*'s survivors in the last-ditch hope that Ben would be among them. Alas, he was not, but all was not lost, for a young blond, introduced by an officer as "Mrs. Benjamin Guggenheim," did come down the gangplank announcing that Ben had given up his life to save hers.

Later this news was confirmed, in a modified form, by steward John Johnson at Daniel Guggenheim's suite in the St. Regis. Florette was present, and when Johnson gave her Ben's message, he went no further, never mentioning the young blond singer.

In Ben's defense, if he needs any, no "Mrs. Benjamin Guggenheim" ever turned up on the official passenger list of the *Titanic* and the young blond singer, if she ever really existed, was never heard from again.

Ben Guggenheim's death at forty-seven was a catastrophe for his little family. Peggy and Hazel suddenly became very religious and, for the first time, began going to services at Temple Emanu-El regularly. Both have subsequently confessed that they never fully recovered from the disaster and have been searching for a father ever since. Hazel, at seventy-three, still has nightmares about the *Titanic*. Peggy, at seventy-six, says she thinks of her father's horrible death every day of her life.

Catastrophe in more ways than one. It was found immediately after Ben's death that his business affairs were in almost total disarray. Not only had he forfeited what would have been a colossal fortune had he remained in the family business, but he had also lost most of the money he had invested in International Steam Pump. The relatively small amount left was tied up in high-growth, low-yield stocks that were so depressed they could not be sold.

The last news was kept from the money-conscious Florette and so she continued to live in the same sumptuous manner as always. Meanwhile the brothers went to work to salvage what could be salvaged. Even Will, who had invested in International Steam Pump, was pressed into service, the situation was so desperate.

Without telling Florette where the money was coming from, Daniel, Murry, Solomon, and Simon advanced her funds from their own accounts to meet her considerable current expenses. When Florette heard about this, however, her Seligman pride flared up. Seligmans did not take handouts from anyone. She told the Guggenheim brothers to stop giving her money and drastically cut down on her scale of living. She left the big house on Seventy-second Street and moved herself and her daughters into a small apartment. She let most of her servants go. She sold many paintings, tapestries, and jewels. She began dipping into her own personal funds.

During this difficult time Peggy developed "a complex about no longer being a real Guggenheim." "I felt like a poor relation," she wrote later, "and suffered great humiliation thinking how inferior I was to the rest of the family."

Four years after Ben's drowning, the situation was saved by the death of Florette's father, James Seligman, who left Florette a small fortune, around $2 million. Florette immediately reimbursed Daniel, Murry, Solomon, and Simon for the funds they had advanced her.

It took seven years for Ben's six brothers and their lawyers to finally settle his tangled, debt-ridden estate. Solomon and William bore the brunt of the work. When the papers were finally cleared off the desks there remained only $1,850,000 for distribution to Ben's heirs. Benita, Peggy, and Hazel each received $450,000 in trust, and $500,000 went to Florette. It was estimated by Sol and Will that Ben had lost something in the neighborhood of $8 million.

Their comparatively meager inheritances (remember, Dan's children were to get $2 million apiece, and Murry's well over $8 million apiece) and their missing out on such future Guggenheim bonanzas as Chile Copper, made Peggy, Hazel, and Benita among the poorest Guggenheims of their generation. Florette, however, alleviated their financial distress somewhat by leaving each of them $500,000, in trust, so, in the end, each daughter had $950,000 at her disposal. What Peggy then did with her money was nothing less than miraculous. Showing herself to be a *real* Guggenheim after all, she parlayed around $250,000 in income from her inheritance (she could not touch the principal) into a $30 million collection of modern art.

And then, later, driving home the point—by God, she was going to show the world who a *real* Guggenheim was—she created her own foundation, the Peggy Guggenheim Foundation, and willed to it her entire collection, plus her galleries in Venice.

Benjamin Guggenheim had done nothing much with his money by

the time he went down with the *Titanic* in 1912, except lose most of it. But then none of his brothers had done anything particularly significant with his money by 1912 either. Had Ben lived into the late 1920s, he might well have done something constructive with his fortune also (let us give him the benefit of the doubt). It was thus left to Peggy, destined to become the most celebrated member of the fourth generation, to make up for what the *Titanic* disaster prevented.

CHAPTER

8

SENATOR SIMON, OR DEMOCRACY IN AMERICA

THE SILVER PUNCH BOWLS IN DENVER'S BROWN PALACE WERE AS big as washtubs the night of January 15, 1907, and the great silver trays held thousands of cigars. The men, in high starched collars, swallowtail coats, and pepper-and-salt trousers, went about with glasses full among the potted palms, slapping each other on the back, while the women, in long, tightly corseted gowns and ostrich-feather boas stood in clumps admiring and condemning one another's jewels, hairdos, clothes. At the height of the festivities, as still more great silver tubs of punch were lifted in, along with still more trays of cigars, the grand piano sounded a few chords and the candidate's triumphant campaign managers led the multitude in song to the tune of "The Good Old Summertime."

> The good old Guggenheim
> The good old Guggenheim,
> He'll make the Prince of Senators,
>   Simon Guggenheim
> Just watch his smoke, there's lots of it,
> And that's a very good sign,
> It means he's always doing things,
> Is Simon Guggenheim.

When Alexis de Tocqueville visited the United States Congress, some seventy-five years before Simon Guggenheim was elected to the Senate, he noted that "when one enters the House of Representatives . . . one is struck by the vulgar demeanor of that great assembly," whereas in the Senate "there is scarcely a man to be seen there whose name does not recall some recent claim to fame . . . Every word uttered in this assembly would add luster to the greatest parliamentary debates in Europe."

"What is the reason for this bizarre contrast?" he asked. "Why are the elite of the nation in one room and not in the other? Why does the former assembly attract such vulgar elements, whereas the latter has a monopoly of talents and enlightenment?"

De Tocqueville answers his own question in his *Democracy in America*: "I can see only one fact to explain it: the election which produces the House of Representatives is direct, whereas the Senate is subject to election in two stages . . . first the citizens of the state elect their state legislators, then those legislators, acting as an electoral body, elect a man to the Senate."

What de Tocqueville neglected to add, though his remarks imply it, is that it is much easier for a famous and wealthy man to bribe a few dozen state legislators than the populace of an entire state. Thus the political hacks—the demagogues, flatterers, charlatans—get elected to the House, while the distinguished millionaires, or those who command the financial support of the distinguished millionaires, get elected to the Senate.

Hence the Senate's reputation as "the most exclusive millionaire's club in America," a reputation that has endured, with full justification, despite the constitutional amendment providing for the direct election of senators, down to the present day.

All of this and more was amply understood by the sixth son of Meyer Guggenheim, the shrewd, quick, witty, and exceptionally broad-minded Simon, United States senator from 1907 to 1913, and, by a tragic turn of fate, one of the most farsighted benefactors of the arts and sciences in American history.

To the Guggenheims' credit, it must be emphasized that, unlike many of their WASP confreres, they never held any fuzzy illusions about America and its political and economic system.

Coming as they did from the servitude and confinement of a Jewish ghetto, they knew, first of all, that in contrast to the words of the Declaration of Independence, all men are created enslaved and unequal, and that it is the task of each man to escape his native bondage and inequality through the use of his wits, energy, and courage. Second, they knew that freedom in America meant essentially the freedom to make money, and that it is the American's most cherished dream to become as rich—that is, as unequal—as possible. And third, they knew that in America there really was only one political party, even though its members might be found in both the Democratic and Republican parties, and that was the Owners' Party . . . and that, as a consequence, the legislatures did not represent the populace at large, but the wealthy few who could afford to pay for congressional campaigns.

Simon Guggenheim's campaign for the U.S. Senate was so barefacedly corrupt (if we accept the premise that elections are supposed to represent the will of the people) that there is something almost refreshing about it. He did not try to fool anybody. "I have preserved a list showing the names of every person to whom I have paid a dollar, and what it was paid for," he was quoted by the Denver *Post* as saying in a speech. "If I am not nominated I will publish the list. And I want you to understand that if you nominate another man, I will spend $300,000 to defeat him."

Why bother? we are tempted to ask. Why did Simon Guggenheim bother to go to all the trouble and expense of running for the U.S. Senate when he already had all the money and prestige he needed?

The answer is that Simon, though he had the money, did not have all the prestige he needed, and he wanted that additional prestige desperately. As one of the younger brothers, he had had to struggle all his life to appear worthy in the eyes of his older brothers, to make sure they did not consider him in the same breath as the frivolous Ben and the spendthrift Will. It was an uphill fight and he eventually realized he could not win it simply by being his older brothers' viceroy in the West. Scouting for and buying ores, and overseeing the operations of the Western and Mexican mines and smelters was not enough. Simon needed something more, something his older brothers did not have, and that was election to public office.

Given his strong position in Colorado—the Guggenheims literally ruled the wealth of the mountain states—and the influence of money in U.S. politics, winning high public office was, for Simon, not an unrealistic ambition. Especially since the greatest political issue of the day was silver and Colorado was a silver state and Simon Guggenheim's family owned the choicest silver mines in Colorado.

The silver issue boiled down to a matter of inflation versus deflation, cheap currency versus hard currency, easy credit versus tight credit. In 1873 the U.S. government, trying to contract the money supply as a deflationary measure, refused to coin any more silver, thus threatening the "Silver Princes" of the Western states and their miners and minions with possible ruin. The gold standard had temporarily won the day. But then in 1878, and again in 1890, the government was forced to expand the money supply and went back to coining silver, thus threatening the gold standard, and causing outcries from all sustainers of deflation and tight credit.

It was no surprise to anyone when Simon Guggenheim, Silver Prince, took his political stand as a silver Republican, an advocate of unlimited coinage of silver.

First he tried for lieutenant governor of Colorado, but was forced to withdraw because, at twenty-nine, he was underage. Then he tried for governor and was forced to withdraw again, this time by his older brothers, because his "silverism" was making too much trouble for them in the hard-money, gold-standard climate of Wall Street.

It was at this time that the Moses of silverism, William Jennings Bryan, a Democrat, made his ringing peroration on behalf of silver:

> If they dare to come out in the open field and defend the gold standard as a good thing, we will fight them to the uttermost. Having behind us the producing masses of the nation and the world, supported by the commercial interests, the laboring interests, and the toilers everywhere, we will answer their demand for a gold standard by saying to them: You shall not press down upon the brow of labor this crown of thorns, you shall not crucify mankind upon a cross of gold.

The popularity of Bryan, especially among the working people and the residents of the state of Colorado, encouraged Simon to pursue his political ambitions despite his having been thwarted in two attempts to run for office, and he began laying plans to capture a seat in the U.S. Senate.

Meanwhile events in New York suddenly brought the Guggenheims a surge of popularity in the Western states. The family refused to join the hated, Rockefeller-financed smelters' trust, which enforced, among other disagreeable things, the twelve-hour workday, and, to embarrass the trust, the Guggenheims embraced the eight-hour day, to the joy of every miner in the West.

Sensing from this approval that his moment had come, Simon, who had just married the vivacious, talented Olga Hirsch, began purchasing his Senate seat in earnest.

Not long before his marriage he had given five hundred new suits of clothing to the poor boys of Denver. On his wedding day he had gone a step further and presented free turkey dinners to one thousand poor Denver boys. Now he financed lavish parties for the employees of the Denver *Post*; he donated buildings to the University of Colorado, the Colorado School of Mines, and the State Agricultural College. And, most important of all, he began promising and distributing largesse to the members of the Colorado state legislature, the body, in the days of indirect election of senators, which he hoped would elect him.

Simon's method was simple. He would personally finance any state legislator's campaign for reelection in return for his vote, and once he, Simon, was elected, would help his electors and their families in any way he could. One bewildered state senator, a farmer by the name of Morton Alexander, was naïve enough not to fully understand how this worked at first, and, upon asking Guggenheim's campaign manager, "What about the people?" was told, "To hell with the people." Then, when he protested he had almost no financial resources of his own to sustain another political campaign without broad popular backing, Alexander was told, "Don't worry, the Guggenheims will take care of everything."

Later Alexander balked at supporting Guggenheim and was surprised one day to return to his farm to find his fence torn down and his lawn trampled.

More tractable legislators were to find themselves sudden owners of stock in Guggenheim-controlled companies, all of which were booming at the time.

These fortunate men finally elected Simon Guggenheim United States senator from Colorado by a vote of sixty-eight to twenty-seven.

Many were outraged by the election.

Colorado State Senator Tully Scott demanded that a coin be struck in honor of the election showing "Simon Guggenheim with foot firmly placed upon the neck of a prostrate miner with pick in hand and with appropriate background of smokeless mills and abandoned mines, the whole relieved by a broad border of dollar marks."

Another state senator contemptuously referred to Simon as "nothing but a walking bank account."

The *Miners' Magazine* went a bit further. His benefactions, it said, make "fawning sycophants forget the lawless methods by which this Caesar has become a monarch in our industrial realm and makes them forget that his gold is but the minted product that came from the misery of overworked human beings . . . Simon could not be convicted of murder, yet every smelter of his has populated cemeteries with the remains of men who have gone down to premature graves because Simon and his brethren place more value upon profit than upon human flesh."

Bitterest of all the outcries took the form of an anonymous letter printed in the Denver *Post*. Let Simon beware, it ranted, not ever to return to Denver again. Not ever to try to enter any of Denver's best clubs or highest social circles. He would never get into the Denver Club or the Denver Athletic Club in a million years. Let him not forget that he is a Jew. And let him not forget that everyone in Colorado knows he is "a voluptuary and sensualist," that everyone knows he is a "Napoleon Bonaparte without a brain."

Simon himself quietly defended his purchase of his Senate seat, stating, with his usual candor: "The money I have contributed has helped to elect these men and naturally they feel under obligation to vote for me. It is done all over the United States today. I do not consider that it is wrong and neither do I think that it can in any sense be called bribery." Later he said: "I wish to state clearly that I am going to Washington to represent all the people; that I am free and untrammeled and under obligation to no interest, company, railroad, or corporation."

Not long after the election, American Smelting and Refining, now controlled entirely by the Guggenheims, went back to the twelve-hour workday in Colorado, a double cross that earned the Guggenheims the undying enmity of the Western miners.

And so Simon Guggenheim took his place in the United States Senate, along with eighteen other multimillionaires, including Nelson W. Aldrich of Rhode Island, father-in-law of John D. Rockefeller, Jr., Henry Du Pont of Delaware, Henry Cabot Lodge of Massachusetts, and, two years later, Elihu Root of New York. These eighteen millionaire senators were the ones who headed the committees dealing with federal finance, taxation, and tariffs. Now, with Simon in their ranks—and his family's fortune was larger than any of theirs—they had a powerful new ally. Ninety-six times did Simon vote for the ultraconservative schedules of the Payne-Aldrich tariff. His speeches on such subjects were usually very blunt and very brief. "It is of importance," he once declared, in one of his shortest addresses, "to keep out the cheap Spanish lead and also the Australian lead."

Not long after they settled in Washington, Simon and Olga Guggenheim established a reputation for themselves as a host and hostess on a grand scale. No other politician in Washington, including the

President, commanded such vast resources for entertaining. When the Silver Prince threw a big party it was always *the* social event of the season.

Simon at the time was a short, dark, stocky figure with a black moustache, a prominent chin, and, of course, the almost inevitable Guggenheim potato nose. The most Semitic of all the brothers in appearance, he was also one of the most sensual in his tastes and habits. He liked gourmet food, fine imported wines, Havana cigars, and beautiful women. In Spain—where the farsighted Meyer had sent him for two years to learn the language spoken south of the Rio Grande—he had grown used to a southern European manner of living. He took time over the pleasures of the table and saw nothing wrong in maintaining an *amante*. People found him quiet, elegant, and courteous, yet at the same time a bit of a rough diamond. He smoked too many cigars and had too vigilant an eye for the ladies. The "old" families of the Denver Club had never accepted him and, though he entertained so lavishly in Washington, certain WASP strongholds never tendered him invitations. His tall, long-necked, stately wife, Olga, was an accomplished linguist, a perceptive connoisseur of the arts, a superb hostess, a good amateur musician, and, fortunately for Simon, was southern European enough in outlook herself to be able to tolerate his many mistresses, some of whom rivaled even brother Solomon's in their glory. She gave two sons to Simon— John Simon and George Denver.

As many had predicted, Senator Simon Guggenheim did not contribute very much to his nation during his lone term in the Senate. He rarely made a speech, and when he did, it was usually very brief. He did not sponsor any significant legislation. Perhaps his most sustained effort was to lead an unsuccessful filibuster against the bill that established the Department of Labor. (It was not for nothing that he was known as "the most conservative man in the Senate.") But he did manage to capture plenty of federal construction projects for his state, take care of the financial needs of the Colorado state legislators, attend to the problems of his Colorado constituents, and keep employment at high levels in Colorado's mines and smelters.

And, of course, he never failed to safeguard the worldwide interests of the House of Guggenheim, to his older brothers' everlasting thanks. During his incumbency the U.S. government purchased plenty of silver, allowed copper and lead prices to soar, slapped high tariffs on all foreign metals, and, after a bit of an environmental skirmish, let Guggenmorgan and Morganheim get away with unrestricted exploitation of the natural resources of Alaska.

A poem published in the *Washington Times* in March, 1910, summed up pretty well the way Simon and his brothers were regarded at the time.

THE GOBBLING GUGGENHEIMS

The Guggenheims will get you if you
    don't watch out;
They're gobbling all the coal lands of
    the West and North and South.
It simply is appalling when you think
    what they're about.
They'll surely gobble everything inside
    the earth and out.

They've gone into Alaska and optioned
    all the coal;
They've searched the mountains over
    and gobbled all the gold.
The water rights they do not own are
    very few, I'm told;
In fact this clan of Guggenheims is
    growing all too bold.

In Denver, Colorado, they own the
    whole blamed town.
The copper mines they cabbaged and
    nailed securely down.
The state was bought by Simon, and
    he did the job up brown.
For he wears the senate toga now and
    owns our Washington.

It really looks a good deal like they'd
    gobble all in sight.
On top the earth or under it, so fearful
    is their might.
They'll gobble all there is to get and
    turn you inside out.
The Guggenheims will get you if you
    don't watch out.

One of the most applauded acts of Simon's career in the Senate was his vote for the constitutional amendment providing for the direct election of U.S. senators, an amendment that was a direct outcome of his own election as senator. (He was, in fact, the last senator to be elected indirectly.) Privately he confided to friends that the amendment would make little difference in the composition of the Senate. It might even result in more millionaire senators, he opined, because it would cost even more money to conduct a political campaign among the entire population of a state than among a few dozen state legislators.

Simon, of course, was right. Seventy years after he had decided to put his money into a Senate seat rather than into a Villa Carola or a Hempstead House, seventy years later, in the year of the United States Bicentennial, the United States Senate was still the most exclusive millionaires' club in America, with some 30 percent of its membership possessing assets in excess of one million dollars. And, just as it was in Simon's day, it is these millionaire senators who continue to occupy the most important places on the committees of finance and taxation.

Simon Guggenheim did not run for reelection in 1912 and resigned his Senate seat on March 1, 1913. By then he had accomplished his purpose. His older brothers had finally accepted him. To honor their distinguished younger brother, Daniel, Murry, and Solomon created the new positions of chairman of the board of American Smelting and Refining, chairman of the board of American Smelters Securities, and chairman of the board of Guggenheim Exploration Company, and appointed Simon to all three positions. Thus Simon could now go back to the far more serious business of making money. And with an added feather in his cap. Henceforth he would be referred to exclusively as "the Senator," a title that would remain with him until his death.

Heaped with so many honors, titles, and appointments, it appeared to everyone that Simon Guggenheim, at forty-seven, had reached the culmination of his life and career. However, a far different, and infinitely more noble, climax awaited him eleven years later, one that would all but obliterate his careers as a senator and a businessman and earn him a lasting place in the history of his country.

CHAPTER

9

ALL SIMON'S SONS

. . . to promote the advancement and diffusion of
knowledge and understanding, and the appreciation
of beauty, by aiding without distinction on
account of race, color, or creed, scholars,
scientists and artists of either sex in the
prosecution of their labors.
    —FROM THE STATEMENT OF PURPOSE, CHARTER,
        JOHN SIMON GUGGENHEIM MEMORIAL FOUNDATION

ONE SPRING DAY IN 1922 JOHN SIMON GUGGENHEIM, SEVENTEEN-
year-old son of Senator Simon Guggenheim, died suddenly of pneumonia and mastoiditis at Phillips Exeter Academy in New Hampshire.
He had done well at Exeter, showing promise as a scholar, and had
been admitted to Harvard for the following year.

Seventeen years later, George Denver Guggenheim, thirty-two-
year-old son of Senator Simon Guggenheim, and heir to one of
America's greatest fortunes, went one November morning to the
Abercrombie & Fitch sporting-goods store in New York, purchased
a big-game hunting rifle, took a room in the Paramount Hotel, and,
several hours later, placed the gun barrel to his head, pulled the
trigger, and blew his brains out. He had been under surveillance by
a male nurse for some time.

Olga Guggenheim had waited almost ten years to give birth to her
first child. During this time, as each year brought fresh disappointment, she had consulted the most eminent gynecologists in America.
When the boys finally were born—in 1905 and 1907—she and Simon

had been exultant. Simon had wanted sons desperately. He had seen his brothers Isaac, Solomon, and Ben produce nine daughters among them. He did not think much of one of Dan's two sons, and did not consider Murry's son, Edmond, especially brilliant. Who was going to lead the House of Guggenheim in the years to come? When John Simon was born in 1905 Simon was so jubilant he celebrated the event by giving $80,000 to the Colorado School of Mines.

Subsequently he made it quite clear to his two boys that he expected them to measure up. The day would come, he never tired of repeating, when they would be called upon to help lead the greatest mining and smelting empire in the world.

John did measure up, in his own fashion. Though he did not give much indication of becoming an industrial leader—he was much too sensitive—he was an excellent student and had shown he was capable of hard work.

George Denver was a very different type. Erratic, rebellious, and very high-strung, he had often incurred his father's wrath by showing far too strong an inclination toward play rather than toward work. At Harvard, where he was a member of the class of 1929, he was well liked, but he was an indifferent, aimless student. A fellow classmate described him as "all dressed up and no place to go."

After George Denver graduated from Harvard, Simon took him into Guggenheim Exploration Company as a trainee, then assigned him to the nitrate fields in Chile.

It did not take long for the dapper, pleasure-loving George, used to the amenities of Cambridge and New York, to tire of the rigors of the desolate, parched, oven-hot nitrate deserts of Chile. Before long he complained of illness and was back in New York, fooling around. No, he told his father, who was now president of American Smelting and Refining, having succeeded Dan, no, he was *not* going back to the gloomy offices of Guggenheim Exploration.

Simon came down hard on him. When Simon was tough, he could be very, very tough. He reminded his son that the Guggenheim family was short on males in his generation and that since John Simon had died, he, George Denver, was all there was left to carry on Simon's line. He reminded him also that he had already given him a million-dollar trust fund, and had left him $10 million in his will, so he would have the necessary resources to fulfill his responsibilities and uphold his name as a son of the House of Guggenheim. And he reminded him for the one-hundredth time that he was expected to take his rightful place in *the family business*.

It was an old litany for George Denver. A tiresome litany. But there was not much he could do but give in. Reluctantly he went back to work for Dad. Though George accomplished very little, Simon nevertheless made him a member of the executive committee of American Smelting and Refining—*that* looked nice on the masthead—and a director of a subsidiary, the General Cable Corporation.

But George's real interests lay elsewhere. His million-dollar trust fund enabled him to lead a gay life in Manhattan and he began keeping very late hours, making the rounds of New York's night spots and speakeasies. He was frequently seen in the company of equivocal people: call girls, bootleggers, and especially homosexuals. He turned to drink and dabbled in drugs. Before long his personality—never too stable—began to disintegrate and he became manic-depressive. Physicians were consulted and he was given insulin shock treatment, which made him worse. He became acutely paranoid, suspicious of everybody. After several suicide attempts, a male nurse was assigned to keep him under constant guard. Somehow he escaped the nurse that cool November morning in 1939 when he managed to make his deadly purchase at Abercrombie & Fitch and check into the Paramount Hotel under the name of Herbert Hildebrand of 143 Sutter Street, San Francisco.

It was the assistant manager of the hotel who discovered the body. Guggenheim had not informed the hotel when he was checking out and, after repeated calls had failed to rouse him, the assistant manager entered the room with a passkey . . . to find the fully clothed body of George Denver on the floor with a .300 magnum big-game rifle under him, the original store wrappings not far away.

In George's pockets were his calling cards, his driver's license, and $325 cash. Although his driver's license listed his address as his parents' apartment at 630 Park Avenue, it was discovered that he really lived at 146 Central Park West, and that he shared the apartment with a man.

The deaths of their two sons were cruel shocks to Simon and Olga and could well have ruined their lives. It is a tribute to both of them that they were able to transform the double tragedy into one of the most inspired benefactions in American history.

There had been little or nothing in Simon Guggenheim's career even to hint that he would one day create something as noble as the John Simon Guggenheim Memorial Foundation.

As a young man, Simon had rebelled against his father's wishes that he go to college, pleading that he "had no head for book learning." Throughout his career in Colorado and Washington he never evinced any serious interests other than politics and mining. When his nephew Harold Loeb, an accomplished writer and friend of F. Scott Fitzgerald and Ernest Hemingway, appealed to him for help in financing his literary review, *Broom*—now regarded as the finest literary review of the immediate post-World War I era—Simon turned him down, saying, "Our feeling is that *Broom* is essentially a magazine for a rich man with a hobby . . . I am sorry you are not in an enterprise that would show a profit at an earlier date." And in 1910 the senior United States senator from Virginia, Thomas S. Martin, wrote a constituent who had asked him to appeal to Senator Simon Guggenheim for aid to a Virginia college: "Mr. Guggenheim does not, so far as I have been able to observe, take any broad view of educational or other public interests . . . I do not think it will be possible to get any generosity for the cause of education from the Guggenheims."

To what, then, may we ascribe Simon's conversion from self-serving politician and hard-boiled industrialist to one of the most farsighted benefactors of the arts and sciences in modern times (in an era when income and estate taxes were by no means confiscatory)?

Unquestionably to the death of his elder son and, to a lesser but also significant degree, to the tragic deterioration of his younger son . . . and to the influence of his advisors.

For the dynastic-minded Simon, the destruction of his sons was a catastrophe of enormous magnitude. What was his immense wealth for if it was not for his sons? What were his labors at Guggenheim Brothers and American Smelting and Refining for if not to provide vehicles for the advancement of his sons?

But these considerations were, in a way, peripheral. Simon had yearned for his boy, he had waited almost ten years for him, and he loved him very much.

After John's death, Simon, in his acute sense of loss, began to withdraw into himself and ask questions of himself and his Creator he had never paused to ask before. He also turned his attention and his hopes to George Denver, and realized, to his additional sorrow, and to George's frustration, that the poor boy, already nervous and high-strung and of indeterminate sexual leanings, could not be counted on.

Gradually Simon evolved the idea of creating a memorial to his lost older son and began consulting with his closest friends and associates as to what form that memorial should take.

One of these associates was Carroll Atwood Wilson, general counsel for both American Smelting and Refining and Guggenheim Brothers. Wilson, a tall, engaging man, with a broad, humanistic culture, had been a Rhodes scholar and was, in his off-hours, a devoted student of American literature. It is not known for sure, and it probably will never be known for sure, but it appears reasonably certain that the original idea for the John Simon Guggenheim Memorial Foundation came, in part at least, from Carroll Wilson, just as the original idea for the Solomon R. Guggenheim Foundation and its museum came from Hilla Rebay. Since John Simon had been a promising scholar, what could be a more appropriate memorial to him than a foundation to assist scholars, scientists, and artists? And what could be a better model for such a foundation than the trust that other mining magnate, Cecil John Rhodes, had established in Great Britain for English-speaking peoples, from which Carroll Wilson had benefited?

Whatever the case, what *is* known for sure is that Carroll Wilson suggested to Simon that he consult with two other Rhodes scholars to formulate definitive plans for the new foundation. These were Frank Aydelotte, secretary to the Rhodes Scholarship Trust for the United States, president of Swarthmore College, future director of the Institute for Advanced Study at Princeton, and Henry Allen Moe, a man of many facets—mathematician, naval officer, lawyer, and journalist.

After several months of gestation, Wilson, Aydelotte, Moe, and the Senator agreed on a format for the foundation, and on March 16, 1925, the day of the foundation's incorporation, Simon endowed it with an initial gift of $3 million worth of securities, an amount destined to multiply forty times.

What Wilson, Aydelotte, Moe, and the Senator devised was unique in American philanthropy. Fellows were to be selected by juries of experts in their fields. Then they were to be given money for whatever they wanted to do, even if it was doing nothing. A Fellow could paint, write, compose, or experiment, or he could simply travel, read, or contemplate. Or, as Peter Lyon once put it, he could "just go abroad and moon through European galleries and spend Guggenheim's good American dollars in European cafés." (Though it was hoped that such types as these last would not get past the screening.) And he did not have to hand in any work or reports when his term as a Fellow was over.

In his letter of gift Simon wrote:

. . . The name of John Simon Guggenheim embodied in the title is that of a dearly beloved son who was cut off by death on April 26, 1922, just as he had completed his preparation for college. In this great sorrow, there came to Mrs. Guggenheim and myself a desire in some sense to continue the influence of the young life of eager aspiration . . .

Further on Simon wrote that he looked forward "to an endless succession of scholars, scientists, and artists" devoting themselves to "the advancement and diffusion of knowledge and understanding and the appreciation of beauty" with the foundation adding continuously thereby "to the educational, literary, artistic, and scientific power of this country." Toward the realization of this end he wished that "systematic arrangements be made to assure these opportunities under the freest possible conditions."

He went on to specify that the initial deed of gift be absolute, that the foundation was to enjoy the powers of an absolute owner.

In his concluding paragraph the Senator expressed hope "that this Foundation will advance human achievement by aiding students to push forward the boundaries of understanding, and will enrich human life by aiding them in the cultivation of beauty and taste."

Was there in all United States philanthropy a succession of statements of intent more noble and inspiring than these? Had there, in fact, been uttered in America ideals as splendid as these—ideals not just tossed to the winds, but backed up by securities like Kennecott Copper, Anaconda Copper, and American Smelting and Refining—since the days of the Founding Fathers?

To whom may we ascribe these spacious and refreshing conceptions? Were they Guggenheim's or Wilson's or Aydelotte's or Moe's? No one today at the foundation seems to know for sure, so let us give the Senator the benefit of the doubt, aware that suffering brings wisdom, and, at the same time, credit Carroll Wilson with being prime catalyst.

The John Simon Guggenheim Memorial Foundation is, in the words of its present secretary-general, Gordon Ray, "the one institution in the United States with an exclusive and permanent commitment to the principle of assistance to superior scholars, scientists, and artists." As such it plays a unique and vitally important role in the higher American civilization.

By the end of 1976, 39 Guggenheim Fellows had received the Nobel Prize and 90 had received the Pulitzer Prize. Of the 80 National Book Awards given through 1976, 44 have gone to Guggenheim Fellows. And of the 1,066 members of the National Academy of Arts and Sciences, 349 have held Guggenheim Fellowships. In the light of these figures, it is easy to understand why a Guggenheim Fellowship has come to be regarded as not merely a financial assist, but virtually a form of intellectual knighthood in the United States.

Aaron Copland was one of the first year's selections. He was then known only to his teachers. Stephen Vincent Benét was among the second year's selections. His fellowship enabled him to write *John Brown's Body*. Norbert Wiener, mathematician and father of cybernetics, was also among the second year's selections, as was Linus Pauling, future Nobel laureate, and at the time both were virtually unknown. Thomas Wolfe, James T. Farrell, and Edmund Wilson were also among the early selections. Later James A. Van Allen, Harvey E. White, Vladimir Nabokov, W. H. Auden, Gian Carlo Menotti, Hart Crane, Robert Penn Warren, John Kenneth Galbraith, and Alfred Kazin won fellowships. Robert Penn Warren wrote *All the King's Men* on a Guggenheim. W. H. Auden wrote *The Age of Anxiety*. John Kenneth Galbraith wrote *The Affluent Society*. Paul A. Samuelson, Nobel in economics, held a Guggenheim. James D. Watson, Nobel in medicine and physiology, wrote *The Double Helix,* an account of his discovery of the structure of DNA. Henry Kissinger, another Nobel Prize-winner, wrote one of his first books on a Guggenheim.

And Guggenheims gave vital assistance to Pulitzer Prize-winners Conrad Aiken, Samuel Barber, John Berryman, Elliott Carter, Leon Edel, Paul Horgan, Allan Nevins, Katherine Anne Porter, Arthur M. Schlesinger, Jr., Virgil Thomson, Peter Viereck, Marianne Moore, Eudora Welty.

It is difficult to imagine what might have been the state of America's cultural life over the past fifty years had the John Simon Guggenheim Memorial Foundation not existed. Certainly the United States government did precious little during the period to foster individual scientific and artistic creation, other than to grant foundations tax-exempt status (except for the Fulbright program, which was modeled after the Guggenheim Foundation and which is now being allowed to expire). And the other foundations were, on the whole, more generous to institutions than to individuals.

When all is said and done it must be admitted that the American government, the big corporations, and most of the private foundations had fallen scandalously short in their duty toward exceptionally gifted creative individuals, and if it were not for the extraordinarily open-hearted and broad-minded Guggenheim the country would have missed an irreplaceable enrichment. As Peter Lyon put it, the Guggenheim became "an unexampled investment in America's futures."

Furthermore, if the purpose of man, as most of the greatest religious and philosophical thinkers have told us, is emphatically not the random, futilitarian activity so characteristic of our business culture today, but self-realization and self-perfection, and if man's place and role in the universe are to be part of the continuously unfolding process of the otherwise inert universe becoming conscious of itself, then it is only institutions such as the John Simon Guggenheim Foundation that truly promote man's purpose on earth.

Thanks, in part, to the Guggenheim Foundation, many exceptionally talented Americans were given a chance to develop their gifts. They and their families have been lavish in praise of their Maecenas.

Stephen Vincent Benét's wife wrote of her husband: "When he applied for the Guggenheim Fellowship in December, 1925, he was twenty-seven years old. He had a wife, and a child under two. Another child was to be born in early fall. He lived entirely by his writing and he wanted very much to take time to write a long poem. To say the Fellowship meant a great deal to us under those particular circumstances is to deal in understatement."

After Benét delivered the manuscript of *John Brown's Body* he took a vacation. When he returned he found that his long poem had been selected by the Book-of-the-Month Club. Later, it would be awarded a Pulitzer Prize. Delighted beyond words, he went to the foundation's headquarters in New York to thank the secretary-general, Henry Allen Moe.

"Let's not be silly," Moe told him, "it is I who must thank *you*. Hereafter, if anyone objects to granting a fellowship to a poet, I have only to point to you."

Gian Carlo Menotti, Pulitzer Prize-winning composer and director of the Festival of Two Worlds at Spoleto, has been lavish in his praise of the Guggenheim, which enabled him to write his opera, *The Consul*. In his article "A Plea for the Creative Artist," he wrote that the John Simon Memorial "has become the father of America's outcasts," observing that the United States has never shown much interest in the well-being of its creative artists and also of its scientists seeking to explore new frontiers of knowledge (rather than applying knowledge already won). Observing also that American parents often look aghast at a child who wishes to embark on an artistic career and that a wealthy American father will rarely give financial assistance to a son who wishes to become a poet, a painter, a composer, Menotti went on to say that "In a certain sense the Guggenheim . . . is playing the part of the ideal father to these American outcasts. Without them, I really do not know what many young American artists would do."

Katherine Anne Porter, the novelist, won her Guggenheim in 1931. Years later she gave out this statement:

> I wrote Mr. Moe full of contrition that I hadn't turned out a book the year of my fellowship. And Mr. Moe wrote me that nobody had expected me to. That the grant was not just for the work of that year, but was meant to help me go on for all my life. . . . In the most absolute sense that Guggenheim Fellowship has helped nourish my life as a writer to this day.

Alfred Kazin, the literary critic, three-time holder of a Guggenheim —in 1940, 1947, 1948—states:

> My first Guggenheim made it possible for me to work uninterruptedly for a year on my first book, *On Native Grounds: An Interpretation of Modern Prose Literature*. I can't easily express how much this fellowship meant to me. . . . That first fellowship was everything to me. It felt like the most wonderful gift. And did more than anything else to launch the first book that made everything after it possible. I know how much other writers owe the Guggenheim: my own debt is inexpressible.

In still another statement, Kazin wrote: "On the whole, I would say that the Guggenheim Foundation has by its support of the individual and by its concern with talent, done more for American thought, learning, and art than any other foundation in the United States."

Willárd F. Libby, winner of the Albert Einstein Award in 1959, and the Nobel Prize in chemistry in 1960, has echoed Kazin, writing:

> The Guggenheim Foundation is the best qualified selector of unknowns of ability the whole philanthropic field has seen. Its record is without parallel. The Guggenheim fellowship is valuable beyond all proportion to the money it carries.

In a particularly moving tribute to the Guggenheim, Kay Boyle, who married Peggy Guggenheim's first husband, Laurence Vail, wrote:

The man who works through the grace and dedication of his mind, seeking the means to give substance to his thought, is forever in need of confirmation of the value of his search. There is so much uncertainty, pain, hope, and the contrary of hope, in the lonely inquiry he is making that the reserve of courage is likely to go dry, the search be abandoned, and what is lost to letters, to art, to science, and philosophy can never be known.

The Guggenheim Foundation and its Fellowships stand, primarily, as confirmation. The belief implied in the granting of a Fellowship is an essential portion of the gift that is made. . . . When I became a Fellow, now many years ago, it was to me a confirmation of my belief that the imponderable presence of poetry was vital to men. That a committee of enlightened individuals had responded to a tentatively expressed belief has done much to sustain me as a writer.

From the hazardous field of serious musical composition, certainly the most difficult artistic career to pursue in America, Aaron Copland writes:

I can hardly exaggerate the value of the award that I received during what I believe was the first year of the Foundation's existence—1925. I was at that time a young composer recently back from studies in Paris, and badly in need of the kind of freedom the Fellowship afforded. . . . Needless to add, I consider the role played by the Foundation to have been absolutely indispensable in the development of the present-day school of American composers.

John Kenneth Galbraith, former U.S. ambassador to India, is equally effusive:

I did most of the work on *The Affluent Society* while blessed with a Guggenheim. I don't think I could have managed it otherwise . . . in any case, it would have been a struggle. So blessed was the help that I repaid the grant out of royalties, but as assistance to Harvard graduate students. So there was even a multiplying effect of sorts.

Linus Pauling, recipient of two Nobels, one in chemistry and one in peace, presently chairman and director of the Linus Pauling Institute of Science and Medicine, at Menlo Park, California, is most explicit about how much his Guggenheim meant to him:

I feel that the Guggenheim Fellowship was of great importance to me. My wife and I were able to spend the time between March 1926 and September 1927 in Europe, with the support of the Guggenheim Fellowship. This opportunity brought me into contact not only with Professors Arnold Sommerfeld, Niels Bohr, and Erwin Schrödinger, but also with many of the younger theoretical physicists, including Heisenberg, Pauli, Heitler, and London. It gave me confidence in my own method of attacking the problems of chemistry and physics in which I was interested, and much of my later work has been based upon the knowledge and experience that I gained during these nineteen months . . .

. . . The period in Europe during 1926 and 1927 was of great importance to my career. The Guggenheim Fellowship made this stay in Europe possible. If the Guggenheim Fellowship had not been awarded to me, in the second year of the operation of the Foundation, there is the possibility that I would not have been able to go to Europe, although there is also the possibility that I would have received a Rockefeller Fellowship, perhaps a year later than the period of the Guggenheim Fellowship. From my observation of the recipients of Rockefeller Fellowships and Guggenheim Fellowships, I may say that the Guggenheim Fellowship, which permitted me complete freedom in determining the nature of my activities, probably was much better, with respect to the development of my career, than the Rockefeller Fellowship would have been.

". . . Complete freedom in determining the nature of my activities . . ." This characteristic, of course, is what distinguishes the Guggenheim from all other foundations and has been the one policy most responsible for its extraordinary success.

Much of the credit for assuring this unprecedented freedom to the Guggenheim Fellows—if not all the credit—belongs to the foundation's secretary-general from 1938 to 1954, Henry Allen Moe, who also served later as a trustee and as president.

Guggenheim Fellows are unanimous in their praise of Dr. Moe. Linus Pauling is only one of many who consider him to have been the greatest of all foundation directors. During his term as secretary-general he presided over a renaissance in art and learning comparable to that which flourished in some of the courts of central Italy during the fifteenth and sixteenth centuries. Hardworking, highly intelligent, sensitive, yet tough, Moe gave of himself unsparingly in his passionate and relentless quest for excellence.

Henry Allen Moe possessed a profound, inalterable belief in the supreme importance of the creative individual. Some of his published remarks on this subject give more of the measure of the man than any secondhand characterization:

It seems to be the accepted doctrine, [he wrote in 1955] that no man is indispensable. Perhaps this is true if the objective is . . . mere sur-

vival; but, clearly, the doctrine has no basis in truth if the objective is
something more. . . . All of the great breakthroughs, to what we call
progress, have been made by men who were, indeed, indispensable . . .
we are determined to continue our search for indispensable men . . .
when we find them we shall continue to let them know that they, not
we, are indispensable, and that our conduct toward them will be warm
and friendly, helpful and understanding. We understand that if they
knew what they would create, it could not be creative: we understand
that what they need is room for the exercise of their trained imagina-
tions. We aim, quite simply, to provide that room.

Sometimes the creative individuals Moe admired so much gave him
a lot of trouble. It is also a measure of the man's greatness that he
never let his difficulties with aberrant Fellows shake his faith in their
ultimate worth, or his own judgment in awarding them a fellowship.

One of the most difficult of the indispensables was a literary genius
of the first rank, the poet Hart Crane.

Crane was awarded a fellowship for the year 1931–32 with enthusiastic recommendations from Louis Untermeyer, Allen Tate, and Edmund Wilson. It was a year when money, for anything, was not easy
to come by. Crane was elated and went to Mexico where he felt his
grant would go further.

There was, of course, something eminently fitting about Hart Crane,
poet, going to Mexico and returning some Guggenheim money—
albeit a pittance—to the country the Guggenheims had exploited for
so long.

Crane's Guggenheim year in Mexico turned out to be sporadically
productive, but, in the main, it was tragically self-destructive, a long
succession of affairs (with both sexes), drunks, fights, nights in jail,
court fines, flights of inspiration, troughs of depression, hangovers,
culminating in the disruption of a U.S. embassy reception in Mexico
City and finally in suicide.

Full of joy and confidence, and looking forward to what promised
to be one of the most productive years of his life, Crane took a house
in the country not far from Mexico City.

No sooner did he settle down to work, however, than he began
to experience acute loneliness, a psychic state that had plagued him
all his life. Loneliness for Crane usually led to drinking and so he
began to frequent the local taverns well into the night. Drinking, in
turn, led to fights with barmen and taxi drivers, whom he would

forget to pay. And these fights would land him repeatedly in jail. U.S. consuls had to be called to bail him out.

It finally took a woman to break this vicious circle and help vindicate Henry Allen Moe's faith in Hart Crane. She was Peggy Cowley, and she had gone to Mexico to get a divorce from the critic Malcolm Cowley. Crane was a homosexual, but with Peggy he experienced heterosexual love for the first time. The experience elated him. Proudly he swaggered into his neighborhood bar where everyone knew him to be homosexual, and announced: "Boys . . . Boys, I did it, I did it!" Soon he was desperately in love with Peggy and his head was swarming with poetry.

Later Peggy reminisced: "He was in love and wanted me with him every moment. . . . His energy seemed inexhaustible. He was keyed to the highest pitch. It was his first experience in loving a woman. He had found something beyond sensuality; he felt purified of the sense of guilt which he had always had as a homosexual. . . . Most of his sex life before had involved persons whom he picked up when drunk and the satisfaction of sex was the end of the acquaintance."

Crane's love for Peggy Cowley renewed the promise of his Guggenheim year. He began composing "The Broken Tower" and later embarked on "Havana Rose." Joyously he wrote Henry Allen Moe: ". . . Indeed my enthusiasm has been a little too intense so far. Now that I have a place entirely to myself I expect to make better progress with my creative projects than has ever been possible before. I don't think I have ever had quite such ideal surroundings."

Lesley Simpson, a friend of Crane's, remembers Hart's first conception of "The Broken Tower."

> I was with Hart Crane in Taxco, Mexico, the morning of January 27th this year, when he first conceived the idea of "The Broken Tower." The night before, being troubled with insomnia, he had risen before daybreak and walked down to the village square. . . . Hart met the old Indian bell-ringer who was on his way down to the church. He and Hart were old friends, and he brought Hart up into the tower with him to help ring the bells. As Hart was swinging the clapper of the great bell, half drunk with its mighty music, the swift tropical dawn broke over the mountains. The sublimity of the scene and the thunder of the bells woke in Hart one of those gusts of joy of which only he was capable. He came striding up the hill afterwards in a sort of frenzy, refused his breakfast, and paced up and down the porch impatiently waiting for me to finish my coffee. Then he seized my arm and bore me off to the plaza, where we sat in the shadow of the church, Hart the while pouring out a magnificent cascade of words . . .

But these bursts of creative inspiration were inevitably followed by a fresh relapse into drinking. One binge began at his house, progressed to a bar in Mexico City, and ended at a reception at the American Embassy where Hart became so objectionable that he had to be carried bodily off the grounds. Later he was arrested and thrown in jail for what was reported by the police as "a street disturbance."

When Henry Allen Moe was informed of these episodes by the representative of the Guggenheim program in Mexico, he wrote back: "Mr. Crane can write perfectly grand verse, but I don't think he can do it when he is drunk. I hope he does sober up. If he doesn't, he will find his Guggenheim fellowship terminated." Later Moe wrote directly to Crane telling him he was "jeopardizing his fellowship."

Crane did not sober up. But somehow he remained fairly productive, writing surprisingly well when he was drunk, and so Moe did not take his fellowship away from him.

When the fellowship was over, however, and Crane found himself without a cent to his name, he became overwhelmed by money fears (he had debts to pay off in the States) and began drinking very heavily again. He began to experience terrible anxiety about returning to the United States, where he felt people were hostile to him and his poetry was not appreciated. Since he had not heard from the magazine to which he had sent "The Broken Tower," he felt his poem had been a failure. Gradually he resolved upon suicide. He made one abortive attempt to kill himself by drinking Mercurochrome. Finally he ended it once and for all by leaping off the ship to New York. His body was sighted, life preservers were thrown him, but he made no attempt to reach them. "The Broken Tower" was eventually published to great critical acclaim. Moe quietly placed the poem on his shelf of works accomplished by his Fellows. Hart Crane's Guggenheim year had been a success.

Henry Allen Moe had not made an error when he selected Hart Crane for a Guggenheim. However, he was by no means infallible and did reject some candidates who were absolutely first-rate.

One of them was one of the greatest composers of the twentieth century, Arnold Schoenberg, who was at the end of his financial rope when he applied.

Others were the precocious young novelists Truman Capote and Gore Vidal, who were both turned down in 1945. That year one of the writing fellowships coveted by Capote and Vidal went to future Watergate conspirator E. Howard Hunt.

Another was America's most gifted and original writer during the period 1935–55, Henry Miller.

We can perhaps excuse Moe for turning down Schoenberg. He was sixty when he applied and there was a twenty-five-year-old musical genius by the name of Samuel Barber applying at the same time. Beauty before age: The grant for music that year went to Samuel Barber. And we can even excuse him for turning down Vidal and Capote. Both were barely in their twenties at the time, not too young for composers, but certainly very young to be considered full-fledged novelists.

Henry Miller, however, was another story. Miller had already published his astonishingly original *Tropic of Cancer* and *Tropic of Capricorn*. He was known and acclaimed, though admittedly by a relatively small band of cognoscenti. He had been living in Paris for ten years and wanted to return to America and do a book about his native land. Lacking the necessary funds, he applied for a Guggenheim. His references were excellent. His work was controversial, but no one could deny its literary worth. The foundation turned him down.

Miller wrote his book anyway, at great personal sacrifice. It was *The Air-Conditioned Nightmare* and was published by New Directions in 1945. In *The Air-Conditioned Nightmare* Miller obtained his revenge against the Guggenheim foundation.

In one episode he described a meeting in a federal penitentiary with an Irish priest who showed him some stained-glass windows done by one of the convicts "as if it were a huge joke." "Idiot," exclaimed Miller in his book, "even in prison they try and ruin the artist. The only thing in the whole penitentiary which interested me was those stained-glass windows. It was the one manifestation of the human spirit free of cruelty, ignorance and perversion. And they had taken this free spirit . . . and were trying to transform him into an educated jackass. Progress and enlightenment! Making a good convict into a potential Guggenheim prize winner! Pfui!"

But this was nothing compared to his closing remarks. In one of the most subtly devastating attacks against the prevailing cultural establishment in modern American literature, Miller ended his *Air-Conditioned Nightmare* with a short statement about his having been rejected by the Guggenheim and the news that "when the rejections came, I found in my envelope a mimeographed copy citing the names of those to whom awards had been made and for what purpose." He then listed some of the awards "for the reader's delectation":

Dr. Ernst Cleveland Abbe, Associate Professor of Botany, University of Minnesota: Studies of the bearing of historical, climatic, and geological factors on the vegetation of a heavily glaciated region in the eastern sub-arctic.

Dr. Roy Franklin Barton, Teacher of Mathematics, St. Andrew's High School, Sagada, P.I.: the recording, translating and annotating of the Hudhud, a series of epics chanted as work songs and at death wakes by the Ifugaros, a pagan, terrace-building people of the Philippine Islands.

Dr. Adrianne Sherwood Foster, Associate Professor of Botany, University of California: a comparative cytohistological study of the meristems of buds and tropical ferns, gymnosperms and woody angiosperms.

Dr. Dorothy Mary Spencer, Lecturer in Anthropology, University of Pennsylvania: Studies of the Mundari-speaking people in the Chota Nagpur Plateau, Bihar, India.

Clearly Miller had a point, which is still valid today. He did not make the point, he implied it. Ezra Pound made the point when he wrote: "Education that does not bear on life and the most vital and immediate problems of the day is not education, but merely suffocation and sabotage."

Yes, by the time Henry Miller applied for his fellowship, the John Simon Guggenheim Memorial Foundation had begun to go to seed a bit, to seed in a spreading wasteland of irrelevant, academic, pedantic suffocation and sabotage.

Why was Henry Miller turned down for a Guggenheim? Roger W. Straus, Jr., the publisher, son of Gladys Guggenheim and a trustee of the John Simon Guggenheim Memorial Foundation, has provided a perplexing answer. "Of course he was turned down," he thunders, "just as he would be turned down again if he applied today . . . because he's a *goddamned anti-Semite,* that's why, just read the *Tropics.*"

Whether Henry Miller really is anti-Semitic is a question only Miller himself could answer. Certainly there are unflattering references to the Jews in the *Tropics,* but there are also unflattering references to the Lithuanians, the Italians, the Poles, the American people as a whole.

Early in *Tropic of Cancer* Miller writes:

In fact almost all Montparnasse is Jewish, or half Jewish, which is worse. Henry Jordan Oswald turned out to be a Jew also. Louis Nichols is a Jew. Even Van Norden and Cherie are Jewish. Frances Blake is a Jew, or a Jewess. Titus is a Jew. The Jews are snowing me under. . . .

Of them all the loveliest Jew is Tania, and for her sake I would become a Jew. Why not? I already speak like a Jew. And I am as ugly as a Jew. Besides, who hates the Jews more than a Jew?

Probably the most insulting reference to the Jews in the *Tropics* is in *Capricorn*.

Writing about "the Jews from Delancey Street" who invaded his neighborhood in Brooklyn when he was a boy, Miller takes off:

This brought about the disintegration of our little world, of the little street called Fillmore Place, which like the name itself was a street of value, of dignity, of light, of surprises. The Jews came, as I say, and like moths they began to eat into the fabric of our lives until there was nothing left but this mothlike presence which they brought with them everywhere. Soon the street began to smell bad, soon the real people moved away, soon the houses began to deteriorate and even the stoops fell away, like the paint. Soon the street looked like a dirty mouth with all the prominent teeth missing, with ugly charred stumps gaping here and there, the lips rotting, the palate gone. Soon the garbage was knee deep in the gutter and the fire escapes filled with bloated bedding, with cockroaches, with dried blood. Soon the kosher sign appeared on the shop windows and there was poultry everywhere, and lox and sour pickles and enormous loaves of bread. And with the change, the English language also disappeared; one heard nothing but Yiddish, nothing but this sputtering, choking, hissing tongue in which God and rotten vegetables sound alike and mean alike.

Admittedly not a very flattering description. But what he has to say about the WASPs elsewhere in the book and throughout *The Air-Conditioned Nightmare* is no less insulting. And hadn't Simon Guggenheim established his foundation to "promote understanding . . . by aiding without distinction on account of race, color, or creed, scholars, scientists, and artists . . ."? Should Henry Miller's "creed" —if we went to label his opinions and prejudices that—be held against him in applying for a Guggenheim fellowship? Shouldn't artistic excellence be the sole criterion for selection?

The fact remains that, aside from the alleged anti-Semitism of Henry Miller, the John Simon Guggenheim Memorial Foundation, which started out so magnificently in its support of creative artists, slowly abandoned the creative artist during the 1950s and 1960s, and concentrated more and more of its resources on supporting projects of senior professors from the major universities.

According to research published by Bernard Peach in the *South Atlantic Quarterly*:

. . . from their peak of over 50 percent in 1933, however, the proportion of awards to creative artists and non-academics has steadily decreased. Awards for 1961 show 11 percent going to creative artists and 7 percent to non-academics. It is not surprising, therefore, that the Foundation has received criticism which reverses that of the early thirties. The sharpest comes from a fellow, winner of a Pulitzer Prize, who says: "I do not like its emphatic shift from the humanities and the creative arts to its current wholesale aid to Ph. Demons in science and sociology; doctor this and doctor that; and I happen to know of any number of first-rate writers, painters, and composers who have applied to it in vain. The Guggenheim, which has always professed to be giving aid to the arts, has largely ceased to do so."

This was written in the early 1960s. According to Dr. Gordon Ray, the foundation's present secretary-general, there has been, during the period 1965 to 1977, a shift in emphasis toward the arts and humanities. Let us hope it will continue. To neglect the highest activities of the human spirit in favor of the sort of regurgitory scholarship, the "suffocation and sabotage," prevalent today in the universities is indeed scandalous.

Turning back to the halcyon days of the John Simon Guggenheim Foundation, what of the donor? And the donor's wife?

They thrived. Simon Guggenheim threw himself into the work of his foundation, in the office of chairman of the board, with gusto. After 1929 the mining and smelting business went a bit sour, as we know. But the 1930s was a rich and exciting period for the arts and sciences. And so Simon easily and joyfully made the transition from developer of natural resources to developer of human resources, from discoverer of ore bodies to discoverer of human talents.

For Simon the prime activity of his foundation was not very different from the prime activity of his family's mining business. It was, in a word, grubstaking; it was taking chances on a prospect. "He used to say," Henry Allen Moe has recalled, "when you are grubstaking, you take chances. You act on the best evidence you've got, but still you've got to take chances, because nothing is certain in the end."

Simon loved to take chances. A mountain of copper in Alaska, a mountain of copper in the Chilean Andes? Take a chance. And now an untried twenty-five-year-old composer from Tennessee? A young poet and novelist from North Carolina? Take a chance.

Not long after its creation, the John Simon Guggenheim Memorial

Foundation became the guiding passion of its donor's life. With the family nitrate business beginning to go to pieces in Chile, and son George Denver beginning to go to pieces in New York, it was the one enterprise with promise in Simon's charge.

Before long, Simon initiated a program of Latin-American exchange fellowships with an additional gift of one million dollars.

In his second Letter of Gift he wrote:

> My brothers and I have long been engaged in commerce with many of the republics to the south of the United States, and we know that there are no longer any important factors of economic isolation separating us. But a similar commerce of things of the mind, of spiritual values, is yet to be accomplished. . . .
>
> It is our conviction that this may best be accomplished by aiding scholars and artists of other lands. Such aid should be afforded under the freest possible conditions to men and women devoted to science and liberal studies, great teachers, creators of beauty, and generally to those devoted to pursuits that dignify, ennoble, and delight mankind.

Thus was Simon able to give back some of the money he and his brothers had gouged out of the Central and South American earth. The first grants went to citizens of Mexico, Argentina, Chile, and Cuba, countries in which the Guggenheims had substantial business interests. Later Puerto Rico, Brazil, Peru, and Uruguay were added. By 1950, fellowships were being awarded to scholars and artists of all the Latin-American countries.

As the foundation developed, and the first successes became evident —Stephen Vincent Benét's Pulitzer; Harold L. Davis' Pulitzer (for *Honey in the Horn*); Arthur Compton's Nobel for physics—Simon was simultaneously plagued by the relentless deterioration of his son, George Denver. The young man lived sometimes at home, sometimes at an apartment he kept on Central Park West. Frequently he got into trouble with the police, and with his boyfriends, who saw in him the ideal target for blackmail. Vainly did Simon try to interest him in the family business, and in his new foundation. George Denver had no use for any of it. A constant torment to himself and his parents, he grew more and more paranoid, more and more self-destructive.

The worsening condition of his son took a toll on Simon, tough as he was. For every success in business—and during the Depression years there were not many—or with the foundation—and here there were many—he was confronted, when he returned home from the office, by a fresh new failure of his son. In the morning Henry

Allen Moe might come into Simon's office to tell him that Arthur Compton, Guggenheim Fellow of 1926, had just won a Nobel for physics, and in the afternoon the doctor might phone to inform him that George had made another attempt to kill himself and had to be given another insulin shock treatment. As a result of this daily unhappiness, Simon, in his sixties, began to acquire a sad, wounded look around his eyes, and he would confess to a few intimates that his son's tragedy was poisoning his life. He had been able to build a monument to his first son. What could he do for his second?

To console themselves, Simon and Olga turned to other interests. They traveled widely. Simon cultivated mistresses. Olga cultivated the fine arts.

One of Simon's grandnephews remembers that Simon "was always surrounded by beautiful women." His niece, Gladys Straus, recalls that he had a French mistress of rare beauty. Barefacedly he would book passage for his current mistress on the same transatlantic liner he and Olga were taking to Europe. Sometimes she even would be seated at their table and Olga would not know who she *really* was. After dinner Olga would comment on the curious coincidence that the woman seated next to Simon had exactly the same jewels as she.

Meanwhile Olga, who not only had money of her own but had received a substantial trust from her husband, established a multimillion-dollar fund to enable New York's Museum of Modern Art to acquire "works of the highest excellence." "One gambler in the family is quite enough," she would say, as, instead of grubstaking a speculative prospect, she would stick to the tried and true. Her fund was, in the words of Alfred H. Barr, Jr., director of the museum's collections, to be devoted to "only such works she felt would have permanent value, and were, therefore, indispensable to the museum."

The result was a magnificent collection, one of the finest ever assembled by a single donor in New York. After twenty years of careful buying, the Mrs. Simon Guggenheim Fund's collection at the Museum of Modern Art numbered forty-four important works. Among them were eight Picassos, five Matisses, four Légers, a Braque, a Chagall, a Gauguin, a Hopper, a Miró, two Modiglianis, Rousseau's *Sleeping Gypsy,* Peter Blume's *The Eternal City* (painted on a Guggenheim fellowship), and sculpture by Brancusi, Maillol, and Rodin.

Olga Guggenheim also enriched the Denver Art Museum by adding many paintings, sculptures, and other works of art to those she and Simon had already given this institution. In 1952 she initiated the Simon Guggenheim Memorial Collection with the gift of an entire early-seventeenth-century English Tudor room. She continued to add to the collection each year until her death in 1970, when the museum received from her estate twenty-five paintings, including a Rubens and a Tintoretto.

Olga Guggenheim was a convert to Episcopalianism, and she and Simon, who never was much attached to Judaism, became members of fashionable St. Thomas Episcopal Church at Fifth Avenue and Fifty-third Street. Here the Guggenheims mingled with an essentially upper-class WASP society, and it was from these people, rather than from the German-Jewish Crowd, that Olga and Simon drew their closest friends.

In 1952 Olga was honored by the National Institute of Arts and Letters, which gave her their annual award for distinguished service to the arts.

At the award-giving ceremonies it was mentioned that Olga kept a tenth-rate tapestry, a perfectly atrocious piece of kitsch, hung on the wall of the entrance to her lavish 1040 Fifth Avenue apartment (the same building in which Gladys Guggenheim Straus and Mrs. Aristotle Onassis now live) to "remind her continuously of her mistakes."

Simon Guggenheim died of pneumonia in 1941, at seventy-three, and was rewarded by a page-long, double-column obituary in *The New York Times*. By then his foundation possessed assets of $8 million. In his will Simon had made his foundation the residuary legatee of his estate, which was valued at approximately $50 million, the largest of the seven brothers', and so the John Simon came into another $20 million after Simon's death. Ten million of this had been destined for son George Denver, who had shot himself two years before. (There would have been more for the foundation, but we know by now what Chilean nitrates did to the Guggenheims' fortune.) In succeeding years, as Simon's mistresses began to die off, the foundation was further enriched by the trust funds he had established for them. Then, when Olga died in 1970, at ninety-three, without immediate heirs, she left the bulk of her estate, some $40 million, to the foundation. These combined funds, some $70 million, were then so well invested by the treasurer, Ernest H. Lundell, Jr., that the foundation's net worth by 1972 was something in the neighborhood of $120 million. It is presently around $100 million due to the drop in the stock market. From earnings from this sum the foundation is able to distribute approximately $4.5 million worth of fellowships each year.

After Simon's death, Olga Guggenheim functioned as president of the John Simon Guggenheim Memorial Foundation for many years and was president emeritus at the time of her death in 1970.

During this twenty-nine-year period the foundation survived two crises that could have easily destroyed it. Both originated in the U.S. Congress.

The first was precipitated in 1951 by Representative Cox, Democrat from Georgia. Alarmed because Alger Hiss had once served as president of the Carnegie Endowment, Cox introduced a resolution calling for a full-scale investigation of the foundations. He was especially concerned about the John Simon, which he charged was spreading "radicalism throughout the country to an extent not excelled by any other foundation." Why it even had been discovered that Aaron Copland, one of the first Guggenheim Fellows, had written for the *New Worker* and the *New Masses*!

As it developed, the most noteworthy things to come out of the Cox probe, which, in the end, did not accomplish very much, were Henry Allen Moe's wonderful statements in defense of the John Simon Guggenheim Memorial Foundation.

In response to one question about the John Simon's "philosophy," he said,

> I hold fast to what Mr. Justice Jackson of the U.S. Supreme Court wrote: "If there is any fixed star in our constitutional constellation, it is that no official, high or petty, can prescribe what shall be orthodox in politics, nationalism, religion, or other matters of opinion." I believe that if this Foundation . . . should attempt to prescribe "what shall be orthodox in politics, nationalism, religion," natural science, social science, art, or in any other manifestations of the mind or spirit, it had better not be in existence.

In response to the Cox committee's question "In your opinion could the functions of foundations be effectively performed by government?" Moe answered:

> In my sharp opinion the question as stated is an improper question in our free country. It is no proper question that suggests, even in the form of question, that government might do what private goodness—religious goodness, indeed—wishes to do and, by and large, does well.

It violates the spirit of philanthropy—the desire to do good with one's money—which has been one of the most powerful motivating forces of good men throughout all recorded history. It violates the essentially religious motives of donors.

And I shall add, as the final part of my answer to Question G-2, that you may ask anybody who has a basis for judgment, whether or not I, as this Foundation's principal executive officer, can get, or cannot get, more of social value per dollar of Guggenheim Foundation money, with less overhead, than any government agency could possibly do.

The next congressional attack on the foundations erupted in 1969, during the presidency of Richard Nixon. In that year the Committee on Ways and Means of the Ninety-first Congress included among its "tentative decisions" on tax reform the statement that "private foundations are to be denied the right to make grants directly to private individuals." If this decision had become more than tentative, it would, of course, have destroyed the purpose of the John Simon Guggenheim Memorial Foundation once and for all.

What was the motivation behind this apparently senseless attack? According to Gordon N. Ray, it stemmed from McGeorge Bundy's alleged abuse of the Ford Foundation, of which he is president, in giving Ford grants to former members of Robert Kennedy's staff after Kennedy was murdered.

In his "Report of the President" for 1967 and 1968 Dr. Ray, referring to previous congressional attacks on foundations, had this to say on the subject:

> The Congress's harsh treatment of foundations seem to reflect a widespread mood of disillusionment with all institutions designed to foster intellectual and creative leadership. It is being asked with mounting asperity whether universities, research institutions, foundations, and the like are really making the contribution towards the advancement, indeed even the stability, of society that the special status accorded them is intended to ensure. Another manifestation of this distrust has been an abrupt drop in federal fellowship funds available for advanced workers in science and scholarship. So the Fulbright program is being allowed to expire; the National Science Foundation offers hardly more than half as many senior fellowships as in earlier years; and the National Endowment for the Humanities has had to interrupt its awards to established scholars, at least for one year.

For a while faces at the John Simon were very glum. But then, when the Tax Reform Act of 1969 was finally passed, everyone heaved a sigh of relief, for though the act did prohibit "nonobjective grants to individuals," it exempted from this prohibition "private foundations which engage in extensive programs involving grants to individuals chosen as a result of open competitions," where "expertise and fairness replace whims and personal relationships." Thus no more grants to politicians' hangers-on, foundation donors' nephews, foundation presidents' favorites, but grants to the sort of people to whom the John Simon had always given money.

By 1976, fifty-two years after its birth, the John Simon Guggenheim had every reason to be most proud of its vast accomplishment. By then almost 10,000 scholars, artists, and scientists from North and South America had received vital assistance from the foundation; the foundation's assets had soared over $100 million, and its place in the cultural life of the Western hemisphere had become nothing less than monumental.

The magnificent conception with which Simon Guggenheim, Carroll Wilson, Frank Aydelotte, and Henry Allen Moe were seized exemplifies the very best of American civilization in the twentieth century. Brand Blanshard, Sterling Professor of Philosophy at Yale University, put it thus:

> The Foundation is the Socratic midwife of American scholarship. It has helped bring to the birth all sorts of insights, theories, and systems, scientific hypotheses and works of art. I cannot think how anyone could have made a more imaginative or decisive contribution to American scholarship than Senator Guggenheim did in his magnificent letter of gift. He was moved to make the gift because he had lost a son. He gained some thousands of sons and daughters who will always think of his name with thanks and honor.

". . . to promote the advancement and diffusion of knowledge and understanding, and the appreciation of beauty by aiding without distinction on account of race, color, or creed, scholars, scientists, and artists of either sex in the prosecution of their labors."

Was there in all United States philanthropy a statement of intent more noble and inspiring?

The other Guggenheim brothers had done some splendid things with their money. But compared to Simon's foundation, Dan's aeronautics, Murry's dental clinic, Solomon's art museum seem parochial. For Simon, as Peter Lyon once put it, "took all of art and knowledge as his province."

The John Simon Guggenheim Memorial Foundation remains to this day the Guggenheims' most glorious achievement. As long as the American republic endures, and the American empire—upon which the John Simon depends for its resources—endures, there should be no end to Guggenheim sons and daughters.

"An endless succession of scholars, scientists, artists . . ." "He is a Guggenheim . . . She is a Guggenheim," people will say, pointing out this writer, this painter. "He was a Guggenheim, you know . . . You know, she was a Guggenheim," they will say, referring to this Pulitzer, that Nobel. Guggenheims by the hundreds of thousands there will be. Lord, what a family Simon and Olga spawned! But how many times did Simon Guggenheim pause in the midst of his enormous responsibilities and close his eyes and cry out to himself and his God: "My sons, my sons, oh, my sons, my sons, my sons"?

CHAPTER

10

WILLIAM, OR
GATENBY WILLIAMS:
ON DROPPING OUT, PART II

THERE MAY NOT HAVE BEEN A PORTRAIT OF WILLIAM GUGGENHEIM in the Partners' Room at Guggenheim Brothers, but Will made up for that by writing his own illustrated autobiography, under the pseudonym Gatenby Williams, publishing the book himself, under the imprint of the Lone Voice Publishing Company, and mailing inscribed copies to each of his surviving brothers. Whether Solomon, Murry, or Simon then placed a copy in the Partners' Room to make up for their previous omission is anybody's guess.

The portrait that emerges from Gatenby Williams' book is that of a cheerful, intelligent, somewhat spoiled, idealistic prig, who was a bit removed from reality and not overly pleased with his Jewish ancestry.

Early in his book Will noted that all the Guggenheim brothers except Benjamin and himself were dark and that anyone seeing his "light complexion and the cast of his features would not have surmised his semitic ancestry." Most observers, in fact, agreed that Will was the handsomest of the Guggenheim boys and noted that his face did have a decidedly Germanic, even Anglo-Saxon, rather than Jewish, cast. He was also fortunate to have escaped, to some degree, the Guggenheim potato nose, though no Guggenheim could entirely avoid bearing a trace of that protuberance.

Will took his un-Semitic appearance seriously and consciously strove to be as un-Jewish as possible. In his middle years he ceased going to Temple Emanu-El, ceased observing the Jewish holy days, and frequented, for the most part, Gentile society. He even gave himself a WASPian pen name. One wonders where in the devil he got Gatenby from. Had living in a Scott Fitzgerald setting been too much for his perfervid imagination?

Will's life was a three-way dropout, but one would never surmise that from his autobiography. First, he dropped out of the family business, then he dropped out of the family, then he dropped out of his own religion and race. But the only hint of this triple defection in his book is a remark that "Will was always the exception."

Will was just different from the others, that's all there was to it.

He was scholarly and contemplative, whereas his brothers had "no head for book learning." He got higher marks than any of his brothers at school, almost always stood at the top of his class. He was the only brother to graduate from college. By his own autobiographical admission, he was "more sensitive to the innerness of things." "Few pause for beauty in the quest for gold," he wrote. Frequently in his book he refers to his "fundamentally artistic temperament."

Daniel and the others were lucky to have been able to fulfill the ideal for the American male in their time, to have been able to be exactly what their society expected, and wanted, them to be: tough, aggressive, hard-driving businessmen, men who were able to wrench a lion's share of the world's wealth from out of the bare guts of the earth, then multiply that share many times over. William found himself in a much less advantageous position. He was not the dynamic-young-businessman type. He was more inclined to a life of reflection. The drama of his existence was one of finding a means of self-realization in a society in which his personality type was not appreciated.

It was, in a sense, the old story of the plight of the artistic personality in America. The American ethos in William Guggenheim's day was, in the last analysis, not democratic but Darwinian, not egalitarian but competitive and exploitive, may the toughest, the strongest man win. In such a society the man whose impulse is to praise, understand, celebrate, portray—the artist—is bound to suffer. William Guggenheim was not an artist, but he possessed an artistic temperament. His impulse was not to exploit, but to create, to understand. In his writings he went on record as being against exploitation. In a chapter in his autobiography entitled "Credo," he wrote: "A program for the conservation of natural resources should be rigorously adhered to that we may avoid impoverishment of nature's bounteous gifts. Exploitation is worthy only of the severest condemnation."

We may easily imagine the reactions of Dan, Murry, Solomon, and Simon to such a statement. They, who had been the first Americans to exploit the mineral wealth of Alaska, gutting an entire mountain, the first Americans to employ strip mining in the West (at Bingham Canyon), the first Americans to exploit the mineral wealth of Mexico, Bolivia, and Chile, with absolutely no regard for the "impoverishment of nature's bounteous gifts." They would, of course, have publicly approved such a statement, if it temporarily served their purposes, but privately they would have nodded their heads and smiled, and said to themselves: "Poor little Will."

Will was always at odds with his brothers, was utterly overwhelmed by them. Given his sensitive temperament, to have had five aggressive older brothers always ganging up on him, must have been, to say the least, a trial.

First Isaac had objected to Will's being brought into the firm on an equal basis with the others. Then Daniel, playing the role of meddlesome mother-in-law, had forced him to divorce his first wife. Then Isaac, Dan, Sol, Murry, and Simon had concealed the true value of Chile Copper from him, so as not to share the profits with him, and he had been forced to haul them all into court.

Was there any wonder why Will "retired" from M. Guggenheim's Sons in 1901, at age thirty-three, to enjoy his income of $250,000 a year, and devote himself to the things that were closest to his heart: literature, philosophy, the theater, and women?

Especially women. Early in his autobiography Will described an episode from his childhood involving a woman, which, he thought, was quite significant:

> Miss May, a delicate young woman, developed a great fondness for her star pupil. She found pretexts for keeping him after his schoolmates had been dismissed for the day. Then she would seat him upon the desk, where he watched gravely while she corrected papers. Occasionally she would lean over and kiss him. This, too, was part of his education; gave him his first intimation of the charm he was capable of exerting on people.

Years later, on his whirlwind tour of Europe with Ben, immediately after resigning from M. Guggenheim's Sons, he spent some time in Monte Carlo, where:

> The women were stunningly gowned, many of them extremely at-

tractive, and their charm and modishness were not lost on him. "Philanthropy" may have been more than one interpretation and during his sojourn in Europe he never hesitated to explore its variety.

Guggenheim took readily to life in Europe:

Will wandered about France, making his headquarters also at the capital. Such opportunities for leisure and relaxation were for him unprecedented; he enjoyed himself thoroughly, shaking off the accumulated fatigue of his years in the West and Mexico, and his health improved rapidly.

Wherever Will stayed word soon got around that a very rich American was in residence. This subjected him to repeated attacks from mercenaries:

During these diversions in Paris and environs, the spectacular affair of a beautiful Italian prima donna, whose photograph was plastered all over the city, busied everybody's tongue. A rich and handsome Russian prince had been her lover for a year or more, in which time he had parted with the trifling sum of a million francs. His noble family, however, determined to pull in the purse strings, refused to meet any further expenses, and forced him to return home. With her cash income thus abruptly cut off, the singer resumed her interrupted career as an operatic star. She moved into an apartment in the same hotel and on the same floor where Will was residing. He frequently heard her voice floating through the hall when she was practicing. One morning a knock sounded at his door. Answering, he was presented with a mysterious envelope. He opened it and to his complete amazement found within a bill made out to him for a $500.00 piano which had to be delivered to the soprano. He murmured an automatic *Merci* and closed the door. This was indeed a curious method of introduction. Surely she needed a piano; she did possess an exquisite voice. Yet . . .

He dropped the bill in the waste-basket.

In later years whenever he heard the renowned prima donna's name, and it was often mentioned, he would smile inwardly and think, perhaps with regret, what an episode he might have had with her if only he had paid for that instrument.

As it turned out, Will was destined to have his fill of episodes with women, especially with his first wife.

Grace Herbert Guggenheim had collected a $150,000 divorce settlement from the Guggenheims and had promptly married a young Frenchman, Jules Roger Wahl, who proceeded to get rid of the $150,000 as if it were nothing but a case of Chablis. Broke and disgusted, Grace managed to get the marriage annulled.

Meanwhile Will had married Aimee Lillian Steinberger, a friend of his sisters Cora and Rose. The two settled down to wedded life in a $700,000 Italianate townhouse at 833 Fifth Avenue, assisted by twenty-one servants and two chauffeurs, and three years later they had a son, William, Jr.

By this time Grace was flat on her back in one room reading lurid, tempting accounts of Benjamin Guggenheim's marital troubles (Florette was threatening a costly divorce because of the young blond singer) and she decided to strike again.

She wrote Will a letter:

I would take the time to read this if I were you. The enclosed speaks for itself, further explanation is not necessary. . . . As your brother [Ben] that feared notoriety a few years ago seems to have gotten his share a few days ago from the accounts in the various papers, I too may go and tell my story as I can get money enough from a certain newspaper. . . . You will no doubt remember my marrying you was all your doing and thank God I have letters to that effect. You ought to be ashamed of yourself, a man with your money to allow me to want for money enough to support myself. In the past I have kept quiet. Now the world shall know it all.

Soon the papers reported that Grace would be disposed to settle for $250,000. If Will would not fork over, she would attempt to annul her divorce, obtained in the state of Illinois, on the grounds that since neither partner was a resident of Illinois, the divorce was obtained by fraud.

This latter threat alarmed the entire Guggenheim family because if Will's divorce was found illegal, he and his wife, Aimee, would be living in bigamy and their son—one of the precious few males of the third generation—would be illegitimate.

Dan put Guggenheim Brothers' top legal talent on the case, and, after a long battle, which caused Will's name to appear in headlines in all the major newspapers, was victorious. The divorce decree was upheld.

During the proceedings the Guggenheim lawyers, referring to Grace's action, said, among other things: "Her motive is foul and her object blackmail. Her conduct is void of conscience, and is immoral and shocking."

Though the judges upheld the divorce decree, they emphatically did not approve of the way it was obtained: "The decree of divorce . . . was obtained as the direct result of frauds and the procuring of said decree was an outrage against the laws of the state of Illinois and a fraud upon the Circuit Court in Cook County."

This was, of course, another way of saying that Guggenheim money could accomplish almost anything, even the purchase of illegal divorces.

William made no mention of his first marriage in his autobiography (nor did he mention his suit against his brothers) but he did have a few priggish things to say about his second. Referring to the period just before he met Aimee, he wrote: "Being but thirty-five years old and a man of great wealth and individual charm, he was much sought after and he enjoyed his share of society."

Then, these prenuptial remarks:

> Shortly before the wedding, Will decided to purchase a townhouse of his own and a country place. With his usual thoughtfulness he consulted the wishes of his prospective bride and the two of them with high hope and eager excitement frequently investigated together. After a critical and extensive search throughout Manhattan and the suburbs, 833 Fifth Ave. was selected for their city residence and a choice estate at Sands Point, Long Island, on the Sound, for the country one.

From troubles with Grace Herbert to troubles with Aimee.

Aimee Guggenheim was a very domineering woman who had kept her innate bossiness under wraps until William junior was born. After that major dynastic event—the name of Guggenheim would live on! —Aimee began pushing Will senior around. She had the bulk, as well as the personality, to do it. Aimee was a big lady, taller and heavier than her husband, and made herself look even taller and bigger by habitually wearing great bird-of-paradise feather hats and ostrich-feather boas.

Aimee did not get along with the other Guggenheim brothers— they were, after all, impossible in-laws—and let her husband know it. She would frequently observe that Will was the only brother with a college degree and the others—a bunch of ignoramuses, in her opinion—had no respect for Will's culture. She complained also that the other brothers bullied and even cheated Will, which was true. It was she who was a prime instigator behind Will's $10 million suit against his brothers over Chile Copper. Gradually Aimee succeeded in alienating Will from the other Guggenheims. She wanted him all to herself. So *she* could bully him instead of the brothers. By the time Will junior was nineteen, Will senior could not take his wife's bossiness any longer and they separated. Will then bought himself a four-story mansion at 3 Riverside Drive where he lived the remainder of his life.

That remainder was devoted to a curious mixture of philanthropic, intellectual, artistic, and amorous pursuits.

Will named the principal rooms in his new house after the principal metals upon which his fortune was based: the *Salon d'Or,* the *Chambre de Cuivre,* the *Chambre d'Argent,* the *Bureau de Plomb.*

In the *Chambre de Cuivre,* which he used as his studio, he devoted himself to his philanthropic, intellectual, and artistic pursuits. The *Salon d'Or* was reserved for Love.

Alas, the philanthropy that emanated from the *Chambre de Cuivre* was of rather base metal—or shall we call it low-grade ore?—compared to that of his brothers, whose vast foundations Will lived to see gain world renown. William was rich—he had perhaps $5 million plus a million-dollar trust fund established for him by Simon—but by dropping out of Guggenheim Brothers at such an early date he forfeited, as had brother Ben, what would have been an enormous fortune. His largest bequests, therefore, were small change if stacked up against the major donations of Dan, Solomon, Murry, and Simon. They were $50,000 to United Hebrew Charities, in memory of his mother, and $50,000 to Mount Sinai Hospital in memory of his mother and father. His other "philanthropic activities" consisted of modest contributions to various charities and making up the deficits of various organizations to which he belonged.

These organizations were the Pennsylvania Society, of which he was treasurer from 1909 to 1926 (autobiography: "Will always managed to have a steadily increasing surplus on hand"); the University of Pennsylvania Club, of which he was also a deficit-making-up treasurer; the American Defense Society (during World War I); the International Benjamin Franklin Society, of which he was a deficit-making-up member; and the American Philosophical Society, to which he was elected in 1930.

Membership in these organizations gave Will a chance to make speeches—something he loved to do—and throw lavish dinners, something he also loved to do.

He gave a huge banquet for Italo Balbo, the Italian aviator, and was rewarded with the title "Commendatore dell' Ordine della Corona d'Italia," which he later renounced because of Italy's declaration of war against Britain and France in 1940.

He gave another huge dinner for "hundreds of distinguished guests" to honor Rear Admiral Robert E. Peary, the polar explorer, and was rewarded with laudatory newspaper articles he hoped would neutralize the bad publicity he had received as a result of the "mining" activities of Grace Herbert. And in his capacity of chief deficit-making-up member of the International Benjamin Franklin Society, he contributed dubiously to the campaign of Alfred M. Landon against Franklin D. Roosevelt by presenting Landon with a bust of Benjamin Franklin, and stating, "No individual or political body could spend more than they had and remain solvent. You well typify his patriotism, thrift, and economic sanity. May Franklin's spirit ever inspire you."

Other *Chambre de Cuivre* activities included writing articles like "Is Jesus Here Today?" "Bolshevism and Its Cure," "The Crucial Need for Sound Money"; song lyrics like "Jubilee" and "Crumbs of Love," and a long love poem, "My Orchid." Then, of course, there was Will's Lone Voice Publishing Company and *William Guggenheim* by Gatenby Williams. Another major work, also to be published by Lone Voice, was planned but never written. It was to be entitled *Lover At Large* and promised to be something of a less-than-literary cross of Boccaccio, Casanova, and Frank Harris.

Lover at large. Prince Billy had begun his amorous career in the mining camps of the Wild West and Mexico. After many vicissitudes, including two attempts at legitimate union, he picked up where he had left off years before at Peppersauce Bottoms and the plazas of Monterrey and Aguascalientes, this time in the more luxurious setting of the *Salon d'Or* at 3 Riverside Drive in New York City.

Will loved the theater and in his later years he became one of its most generous angels. One of the fringe benefits of this form of philanthropy that he liked best was being able to entertain showgirls in the *Salon d'Or,* rationalizing it as business.

The plays Will financed were not always commercially successful and after a while he began to suffer heavy losses. These, combined with the large presents he was compelled to give his "protégées," substantially reduced his capital. When the Depression came, and wouldn't go away, and some of his major holdings, like Kennecott, Anaconda, and American Smelting, began to pass dividends, Will found himself having to tighten his belt. He eliminated two manservants and a secretary from his staff, keeping only his gentleman's gentleman and three maids. He sold his estate at Sands Point.

In the midst of these troubles, however, an event occurred that brought Will great joy. His son, William, Jr., married into the old New York aristocracy—she was a Beekman—and in 1939 the couple produced a son whom they named William Guggenheim III.

As we know, Isaac, Solomon, and Benjamin had daughtered out. And Simon's two sons had both died childless. That left precious few males bearing the name Guggenheim in the fourth and fifth generations. The birth of Will's grandson was therefore vigorously applauded by the whole family and for a while divisions were healed. The family now had a male heir who could carry on the Guggenheim name. Will's honor as a man was vindicated at last.

In his autobiography Will summed himself up in his late sixties:

> William Guggenheim, aside from his silvery hair and a somewhat rounder waist-line, looks nearly the same as he did thirty years ago. . . . He is wise enough to keep fit by leading a sane and regular existence. . . . He rests upon his laurels. . . . His career is sharply divided by two amazing contrasts: one of harsh hazardous struggle in the rugged West and undeveloped Mexico; the other of a creative, cosmopolitan club-man in the very heart of ease and civilization. . . . It is true he has never had to fight the hideous discouragements of poverty; but it is also true that wealth has not clouded his perceptions.

Not long after penning this self-appreciation, Will's perceptions did begin to cloud a bit and he ceased living a sane existence. By the time he entered his seventieth year, he had, in fact, gone completely gaga.

What was left of his fortune was being steadily drained away by a succession of showgirl protégées. If the miracle of miracles could be accomplished in the *Salon d'Or*, the girl could have all she wanted.

By the time of Will's final illness there were four miracle workers left. They were two long-stemmed showgirls and two beauty-contest winners, Miss America of 1929, and Miss Connecticut of 1930. Assiduously did they attend the bedside, in turn, of their dying angel.

Not long after Will finally succumbed, on June 27, 1941, the Associated Press flashed photos of Will with two of his protégées to all subscribing papers, with the caption:

> GUGGENHEIM WITH TWO GIRLS NAMED IN WILL. William Guggenheim, of the famous copper family, who died last month at 72, is shown here with two of the former showgirls to whom he left his estate. . . . The will was filed yesterday, but there was no assurance that the estate's estimated $1,000,000 value would stand up.

The estate's estimated million-dollar value did not stand up. At least for the protégées. Aimee Guggenheim saw to that. She challenged the will in court and received the share to which she was entitled by New York State law, and saw to it that her son got his rightful share also. After these shares and all debts and taxes had been paid, all there was left for the four girls was $1,305.04 apiece. During Aimee's suit it came out that since Will's retirement from M. Guggenheim's Sons in 1901, the seventh son of Meyer Guggenheim had run through some $8 million.

Fortunately for Will junior and Will III, there remained the iron-clad, not-to-be-borrowed-against, automatically-passed-down-to-descendants trust fund of a million dollars established by Simon for Will and his heirs after the Chile Copper case. This passed forthwith to Will junior and is currently being enjoyed by Will III.

The Guggenheims were, of course, appalled by the publicity surrounding the settlement of William's estate. Brothers Solomon and Simon were still alive, and so were sisters Cora and Rose, and then there were dozens in the next generation with name and reputation at stake. Yes, Will had always been the exception. Lovable, but . . . look what he did with all that hard-earned money, all that copper, gold, silver, and lead that had been torn out of Colorado, Utah, Mexico, Alaska, and Chile at such high risk by such bone-crushing labor . . .

Ah yes, but look what Will alone among the brothers did for the family in posterity. Look what he did for history. The autobiography by Gatenby Williams! None of the other brothers ever bothered to keep any records or write anything down. They were always too busy making money to take the time to record what they were doing, either in business or in philanthropy. And they had almost no sense of history.

But Will did take the time. If it were not for *William Guggenheim* by Gatenby Williams much of the early history of the Guggenheims in Philadelphia, the early pioneering in Colorado and Mexico would have been irretrievably lost.

William Guggenheim, alone among the seven brothers, knew where the Guggenheims stood in history and he wrote it down at the end of his autobiography:

> The House of Guggenheim—Meyer, Barbara, and their children— has been unique in American annals, having faintly an old-world, indeed one might almost say a feudal flavor about it. . . . It is improbable that the tale will ever be paralleled.

Bravo, Will. It matters not so very much what one does with one's life, so long as one finally has a glimmer, so long as one finally, if even faintly, *understands*.

IV

REBELS AND ANGELS

(1923-1977)

THE FOURTH

GENERATION

Wealth to us is not mere material for vainglory, but an opportunity for achievement.

—*Pericles*

. . . it is not avarice which is a vice, but extravagance, its opposite.

—*Arthur Schopenhauer*

The measure of an action is the sentiment from which it proceeds. The greatest action may easily be one of the most private circumstance.

—*Emerson*

There is no nobleman in Europe more exclusive in his pleasures or more jealous of the slightest advantages assured by a privileged position than the wealthy American.

—*Alexis de Tocqueville*

Stay away from the arts—they're Jews.

—*Richard M. Nixon*

THE GUGGENHEIMS

GENEALOGICAL CHART

(FOR PART IV)

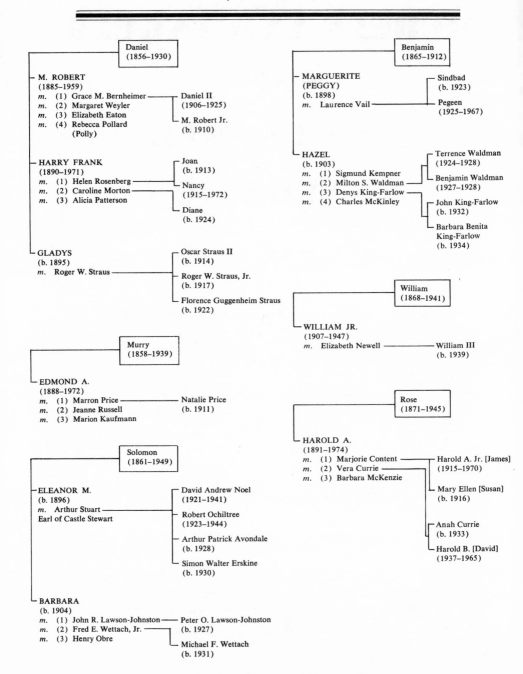

Daniel
(1856–1930)

— M. ROBERT
(1885–1959)
m. (1) Grace M. Bernheimer —— Daniel II
m. (2) Margaret Weyler   (1906–1925)
m. (3) Elizabeth Eaton   — M. Robert Jr.
m. (4) Rebecca Pollard   (b. 1910)
       (Polly)

— HARRY FRANK   — Joan
(1890–1971)   (b. 1913)
m. (1) Helen Rosenberg —— Nancy
m. (2) Caroline Morton   (1915–1972)
m. (3) Alicia Patterson   — Diane
                                (b. 1924)

— GLADYS   — Oscar Straus II
(b. 1895)   (b. 1914)
m. Roger W. Straus ——   — Roger W. Straus, Jr.
                                (b. 1917)
                             — Florence Guggenheim Straus
                                (b. 1922)

Benjamin
(1865–1912)

— MARGUERITE   — Sindbad
(PEGGY)   (b. 1923)
(b. 1898)
m. Laurence Vail ——   — Pegeen
                                (1925–1967)

— HAZEL   — Terrence Waldman
(b. 1903)   (1924–1928)
m. (1) Sigmund Kempner   — Benjamin Waldman
m. (2) Milton S. Waldman ——   (1927–1928)
m. (3) Denys King-Farlow   — John King-Farlow
m. (4) Charles McKinley   (b. 1932)
                             — Barbara Benita
                                King-Farlow
                                (b. 1934)

William
(1868–1941)

— WILLIAM JR.
(1907–1947)
m. Elizabeth Newell ——— William III
                           (b. 1939)

Murry
(1858–1939)

— EDMOND A.
(1888–1972)
m. (1) Marron Price ——— Natalie Price
m. (2) Jeanne Russell   (b. 1911)
m. (3) Marion Kaufmann

Rose
(1871–1945)

— HAROLD A.
(1891–1974)
m. (1) Marjorie Content ——— Harold A. Jr. [James]
m. (2) Vera Currie   (1915–1970)
m. (3) Barbara McKenzie   — Mary Ellen [Susan]
                                (b. 1916)

                             — Anah Currie
                                (b. 1933)
                             — Harold B. [David]
                                (1937–1965)

Solomon
(1861–1949)

— ELEANOR M.   — David Andrew Noel
(b. 1896)   (1921–1941)
m. Arthur Stuart ——   — Robert Ochiltree
Earl of Castle Stewart   (1923–1944)
                             — Arthur Patrick Avondale
                                (b. 1928)
                             — Simon Walter Erskine
                                (b. 1930)

— BARBARA
(b. 1904)
m. (1) John R. Lawson-Johnston —— Peter O. Lawson-Johnston
m. (2) Fred E. Wettach, Jr. ——   (b. 1927)
m. (3) Henry Obre   — Michael F. Wettach
                                (b. 1931)

For complete genealogical information consult
genealogical tables on pages 541–544.

CHAPTER

1

EMPIRE IN DECLINE

THE RISE OF THE HOUSE OF GUGGENHEIM WAS ATTRIBUTABLE, IN great part, to extraordinary good luck. Luck of truly astonishing dimensions. If ever a family illustrated the maxim that luck goes to the lucky, it was the Guggenheims.

The richest silver lode in Colorado, acquired for only $5,000. The births of no fewer than eight sons. The great bonanza in Alaska. The bonanza in Utah. The bonanza in Chile. All the bonanzas in between.

As long as the bonanzas and the sons kept coming, the Guggenheims could only walk on clouds, soar among the stars. But when their luck turned sour, when the hoped-for bonanza became a certified bust, when the hoped-for sons became daughter after daughter after daughter, the family went into reverse. The decline began.

Mines are wasting assets, and wealth based wholly on mining becomes quickly exhausted unless new mines are constantly being discovered and developed.

From the standpoint of perpetuating family business dynasties, sons can also be wasting assets. If they do not produce more sons the line and its potential also become quickly exhausted. For a family with a large business, a son with sons is a bonanza, a son with only daughters is all too often a bust.

The wealth of the House of Guggenheim in the 1930s came, as we know, principally from stock in five natural resources industries: Kennecott Copper, Anaconda Copper, Diamang (the Angolan diamonds concern), Chilean nitrates, and American Smelting and Refining. Of these, Chilean nitrates we know was a disaster, and Kennecott, Anaconda, and Diamang were not only wasting assets, but two of them were highly vulnerable to political upheavals in none-too-stable Angola and Chile. Only American Smelting and Refining, with its exceptional capacity for exploration and development, possessed much potential for growth.

The wealth of the Guggenheims was also derived from the labors of seven sons. But of these seven sons, we know that Isaac, Solomon, and Benjamin had only daughters and Simon's two boys died young. That left in the fourth generation only four males: Dan's two sons, M. Robert and Harry Frank, Murry's Edmond, and William's William, Jr. Of these M. Robert was never very promising, Edmond was promising only in sports, and William, Jr. was sickly (he would die at thirty-nine). That left only Harry to carry on and it will be recalled that he dropped out of Guggenheim Brothers in 1923 upon the sale of Chile Copper to Anaconda.

The Guggenheim situation, then, by the mid-1930s, was not very promising. The great Chilean nitrate gamble had not panned out. Kennecott, Anaconda, and American Smelting were more or less just holding their own. And sometimes not even that: American Smelting was even passing dividends now and then. Furthermore, none of the few fourth-generation Guggenheim males was involved in the family business. M. Robert was devoting his energies to dogs, yachts, and women. Edmond was spending most of his time playing golf. Harry was floundering around trying to find himself. William, Jr. was taking trips to European spas for his fragile health. The only Guggenheim male with his name on a Guggenheim company masthead was Simon's suicidal George Denver, who, as he struggled with his ever-deepening despair, somehow managed to serve as a member of the executive committee of American Smelting and Refining.

By 1939 only the Guggenheim foundations were flourishing. While the businesses were immobile or dying, and the grandsons were not doing much of anything, the Murry and Leonie Dental Clinic was filling more and more poor children's teeth, the Daniel and Florence was finding more and more projects to subsidize, Solomon was adding more and more paintings to his museum of nonobjective art, and the John Simon was extending its grants to more and more scientists, scholars, and artists. This was a herald of things to come. The day would arrive when there would be no Guggenheim family or business to speak of any more, and the name of Guggenheim would evoke only a museum, a palace on the Grand Canal, a hospital on East Seventy-second Street, a pavilion at the Mayo Clinic, a band concert in Central Park, a fortunate young man who received a grant to write poetry in Costa Rica for a year.

CHAPTER

2

COLONEL BOB

> Every wealthy family supports at least one gentleman in leisure. I have elected to assume that position in mine.

WITH THESE WORDS, PRONOUNCED IN EARLY MANHOOD, M. ROBERT Guggenheim, elder son of Daniel and Florence and heir apparent to the Guggenheim dynasty, expressed the philosophy that would guide the conduct of his life.

Most personal philosophies are never lived up to. It is at least somewhat to M. Robert's credit that he lived up to his. In glaring contrast to his hardworking father and uncles, M. Robert dedicated his life, single-mindedly, to his own amusement, becoming one of the most spectacular wastrels in American history.

Ah, the tales that are told of M. Robert. Taking time out from his short-lived job at the Tacoma smelter to break the transcontinental speed record racing a car from Seattle to New York. Running up staggering restaurant and nightclub bills against Guggenheim Brothers. Becoming a Catholic to marry his second of four wives, then divorcing her shortly thereafter. Owning five seagoing yachts in succession, each with the same name, *Firenze*. Pinching the behinds of all the old bags at Washington cocktail parties (termed by *Confidential* magazine "the American pincers movement"). Devoting his remaining energies to raising prize Schipperkes and Bedlington terriers. Invading the décolletage of aristocratic ladies at official dinners while serving as U.S. ambassador to Portugal. Entertaining his mistresses at smart Washington restaurants in full view of his fourth wife.

Why the son of Daniel should have turned out this way is best left to the psychoanalytical diggers to explain. The evidence they would have to go by is not very abundant, but what little there is at least contains a few revealing hints.

It is not easy to be the firstborn son of a famous and important father. Much is expected of you, and often you feel overwhelmed by the importance of your father. What can *you* do, with your meager gifts, to attract attention? Especially if you have a younger brother of ability, as M. Robert had in Harry?

Well, for one thing, you can be mischievous; you can be a hellion. This will attract plenty of attention, and might even land you a special place in the heart of your mother, since mothers usually prefer wild sons to little lambs.

Thus was M. Robert—always so overshadowed by his father and brother—compelled to a childhood of unremitting mischief. Sister Gladys recalls that he was always getting into trouble. At Hempstead House he would let animals out of their pens. He would flip silverware in the air at table. He would invade the servants' rooms. He would tease the cats and dogs, and his sister Gladys. He would play practical jokes on Father's houseguests.

Of course, all of this brought the hard fist of fatherly disapproval down on his head repeatedly, but mother Florence, stimulated in some curious way by Robert's naughty antics, still preferred him to her younger son, Harry. When Dan was not around she would indulge him shamelessly. If there was a last piece of dessert to be given out, it would be slipped to Robert, not Harry.

This combination of condemnation and approval bred in young Robert, as might be expected, a dislike of his father and an inordinate love of his mother. The dislike of his father he expressed in not even trying to do a good job in his father's business. The love of his mother he expressed in naming all his houses, stables, kennels, yachts "Firenze," and in phoning her every Sunday of his life at 1:00 P.M., no matter where he was—in one of his Firenzes, house or yacht, or in a Paris bordello.

Whatever Dan made M. Robert do, M. Robert did halfheartedly, or not at all. Dan made him go to the Columbia School of Mines, and, though he graduated, he did not do at all well in his studies. It was only because he was a Guggenheim that he managed to scrape by. Dan put him to work in Guggenheim Brothers and he worked so lackadaisically it was embarrassing. In desperation Dan had to ship him off to the smelter in Tacoma where M. Robert promptly took advantage of his distance from parental surveillance to make that race across the entire United States. When report of this escapade eventually reached Dan, he decided he wanted his son out of the business. Setting up a million-dollar trust fund for him, so he would not be compelled to make a fool out of himself in another job, he accepted his son's gleeful resignation.

All was not lost, however, during this abortive period. For M. Robert did make his contribution to the family by marrying Grace Bernheimer of New York and producing two sons, in a family that desperately needed sons, Daniel II in 1906 and M. Robert, Jr. in 1910. But no sooner was this dynastic feat accomplished than M. Robert's roving eyes and affections killed his marriage and he was forced to give his wife a substantial alimony and award her the custody of his sons.

His two boys then grew up outside the Guggenheim orbit and ethos, and so the dynasty, for all practical purposes, lost its logical fifth-generation heirs. Later, in 1925, young Daniel II died of a heart attack at eighteen during a track meet at Exeter, becoming the fourth Guggenheim male of his generation to die before producing any offspring.

Meanwhile M. Robert had gone to war as a lieutenant in the 69th Regiment. Going overseas, he became, in the words of his commanding officer, "the best goddamned general's aide in the United States Army." The accolade referred mostly to Robert's abilities as a party giver. It was at one of these parties that he got to know Lt. Dwight Eisenhower, a man who was to have a crucial influence on Robert's later life.

In a very real sense, Bob Guggenheim discovered himself in the army. It was something wholly his, something that had nothing to do with the family. And people who knew him at the time recall today that he definitely had a "command presence." After the war he remained in the reserves and eventually achieved the rank of colonel. From then on he was known as "the Colonel." In 1925 he was graduated from the Army War College, and from 1932 to 1935 he served on the staff of the War Department.

With his million-dollar trust fund churning out dividends and interest for him, there was not much need for Bob to do anything after World War I but look for another wife. He found her in one Margaret Weyher, a Catholic from Scranton, Pennsylvania. To marry her, Bob renounced Judaism and became a Catholic. As soon as this conversion was announced, reporters descended on father Daniel at his suite in the St. Regis for comment, and the old tycoon told them: "I'm delighted. My son has always been a very bad Jew. I hope they'll make a good Catholic out of him." M. Robert and Margaret then settled down to raising horses and dogs on Robert's Firenze Farms near August Belmont's estate at Babylon, Long Island. The marriage lasted only three years.

The divorce occurred in 1928 and Bob wasted no time in finding a replacement. This time it was a spirited horsewoman, and somewhat less-spirited Lutheran, Elizabeth Eaton, who was only too delighted to become the mistress of Firenze Farms with its stable of twenty hunters and jumpers.

The new marriage was given a sudden shot in the finances in the year 1930 with the death of Dan, who, as we know, left M. Robert $2 million in trust. This bonus guaranteed M. Robert an annual unearned income of $180,000, not bad for the beginning of the Depression, and enabled him to buy what became his prize possession, the passion of his life, his 180-foot Krupp-built yacht, which he named, as he had named all his stables, kennels, houses, prize dogs and horses, and four previous yachts, the *Firenze*.

If his father had put his surplus into aeronautics and rocketry, and his uncles had put theirs into clinics, art museums, and a foundation to award grants to "free individuals," M. Robert put what extra money he had into his yacht.

The *Firenze* had originally been built for Norman Woolworth, the five-and-dime heir. Its cabins had wood-paneled walls and were furnished like the rooms of a luxurious private house, with antique French and Italian furniture. There was a wood-burning fireplace in the living room. The dining room had places for twelve. M. Robert and Elizabeth loved to entertain on "the boat," as they called it. Surviving guests today remember the wonderful Poitiers paté, the Scottish grouse, the fresh honeydews, the solid-gold service, places at table set with five forks and six spoons, the white-gloved waiters standing behind each chair. The *Firenze* had a twenty-eight-man crew, of whom twelve were trained to double as servants at table, and carried a thirty-five-foot sloop. Three times the M. Robert Guggenheims traversed the Atlantic and back on the *Firenze*. After mother Florence died, leaving a sizable portion of her estate to her favorite son, Robert used the *Firenze* so much that upkeep of the yacht cost him $250,000 a year.

Besides the yacht, Bob and Elizabeth had other toys and pastimes with which to amuse themselves. There were the prize dogs, the jumping horses, the racing cars, the hunting, the high society. Elizabeth Eaton Guggenheim had a lot of spunk. Once she jumped 230 fences in a single day. She also liked to drive fast cars. In the winter she and Bob liked to be near the military, and once, while racing a car through Washington at an outrageous speed, she crashed into another car and left the scene of the accident. After the crash, she was summoned to testify why she did not stop to help the injured driver of the other car. "I did not know whether he was a gentleman," she replied.

All this frivolity was, of course, not lost on the leftist press. So this is what happens to the money distilled from the backbreaking toil of underpaid miners in Alaska, Utah, Mexico, Chile, the Congo, Angola. It goes into the pockets of a man with no sense of social responsibility, no intellectual interests, no concern with the business that is the source of his wealth, no interest in the philanthropies made possible by that wealth. All that copper, lead, zinc, gold, and silver torn at such human cost out of the earth. For what? To provide M. Robert Guggenheim with an oceangoing yacht on which he could serve champagne and caviar to his favorite mistresses. Such was the thrust of many a socialist broadside in the 1930s and 1940s. M. Robert Guggenheim had let himself become the prime target of the enemies of the system that had produced him.

None of this "pinko" criticism, as he termed it, bothered M. Robert however. Secure in his vast wealth and his scores of flatterers and hangers-on, he persevered in his implacable pursuit of pleasure. When boredom with Elizabeth Eaton—brought on by the excitement of his other girl friends—reached the point of exasperation, he divorced her and promptly took a fourth wife, who was married at the time he began courting her. She was Mrs. William Bird van Lennep, née Rebecca de Loatch Pollard, a doll-like blond from Virginia, whose father had been one of the pioneers in the development of Virginia Beach and whose mother was a member of the Colonial Dames. Few women can resist oceangoing yachts, vast estates, multimillion-dollar fortunes, and so it was not difficult for Robert to persuade "Polly" to divorce William Bird van Lennep and marry him. The wedding ceremony took place on board the *Firenze* in Miami, and the long, oceangoing honeymoon included stops at all the Central American countries, including Cuba, a hurricane that almost sank the happy couple, and a trip to California and back.

From 1938 to 1941 Bob and Polly Guggenheim lived exclusively on the *Firenze*, traveling all over the world, finally coming to rest in the Potomac in 1942. They then settled in Washington in a thirty-six-room Norman manor in Rock Creek Park which they called Firenze House, and in which Polly lived until 1976.

In addition to Firenze House, Colonel Bob also maintained an 1,800-acre plantation near Charleston, South Carolina, called Poco Sabo, a lovely old place, trees dripping with Spanish moss, an ancient Colonial house, a 10,000-acre hunting preserve nearby on which Bob killed a thousand birds a year hunting on tack ponies that stop as soon as the dogs point. Former guests at Poco Sabo remember lavish six-course, three-wines dinners, attended by antebellum characters, which would begin at eleven, "after three hours of drinking," and last through the consumption of as many as sixty birds shot that afternoon.

It was now, in the mid-1940s, that the final, ultimately disastrous, phase of M. Robert Guggenheim's career began. In the vastness of Firenze House—which included a grand ballroom, a paneled library with engravings said to be by Christopher Wren, a dining room that could seat thirty, a four-table billiard and pool room, and a bowling alley—Bob and Polly Guggenheim entertained and entertained and entertained. Among their closest friends, and most frequent guests, were Dwight Eisenhower, Speaker of the House Joe Martin, Gen. Curtis LeMay, and Hubert Humphrey.

By this time, Robert could count on an income from his investments of around $800,000 a year. Since $250,000 went for the yacht, he had around $550,000 left, minus taxes, with which to amuse himself, Polly, and his friends.

By the time Eisenhower was elected President, Colonel Bob Guggenheim was a certified member of that unofficial circle in Washington that runs everything, including the country, known as the Club.

Bob and Polly had worked hard to get Ike elected. Polly raised more money for him than any other woman in Washington, and Bob contributed a healthy $100,000 to his campaign.

As a reward for helping him into the White House, Eisenhower offered Robert an appointment as United States ambassador to Portugal and Robert accepted. The year was 1953.

It was, all things considered, an incredibly irresponsible appointment, as so many of Eisenhower's diplomatic appointments were. Guggenheim had a well-known reputation for offending people at parties. Polly says today she was always having to go around "pouring salve" on people's hurt feelings. Robert had never worked steadily at anything in his life. He had never run an organization or even an office. He had never held a diplomatic position. The only qualification he possessed to become U.S. ambassador to Portugal was his money. Together with Simon's Senate seat and Harry's ambassadorship to Cuba, Bob's ambassadorship was the third public office the Guggenheims had purchased.

M. Robert was delighted with the appointment. It would dissipate some of the criticism that constantly attended him. He had not accomplished much in life? Well, now he would accomplish something.

He would also contribute something sorely needed to his self-esteem. Too late in life he realized that he had made an enormous mistake in not sticking with the family business. He would have been much richer and more respected had he taken his rightful place in Guggenheim Brothers, or stayed with American Smelting and Refining. Now his ambassadorship would make up, in part, for his defection. It would be the salvation of his prestige.

But alas, try as he may, Ambassador M. Robert Guggenheim still remained Colonel Bob, the amiable, bumbling show-off and woman chaser.

Right away, as soon as he got to Portugal, he started off on the wrong foot. In his maiden speech in Lisbon he told a stunned audience, which included the president of Portugal, that, of course, he would have preferred the Court of St. James's, but Portugal was not such a bad second choice.

This remark, however, was soon drowned in the endless rounds of cocktail parties and dinners Ambassador and Mrs. Guggenheim gave at the embassy and at their official residence. Bob and Polly entertained with style and gusto, always serving the finest of everything. The Portuguese were only too happy to drink their champagne and eat their caviar. Soon they reconciled themselves to Bob's booming voice, his backslapping, his practical jokes, his gaffes, even his American pincers movements.

But then the inevitable happened. People in the embassy, noting his often childish behavior, had been predicting it would come sooner or later.

A splendid state dinner in the palace of the Portuguese president. The *crème de la crème* of the Portuguese aristocracy present. Tiaras and jewels. Sashes and decorations. Rare wines. The presidential cuisine.

At a certain point in the festivities, United States Ambassador to

Portugal M. Robert Guggenheim suddenly reverts to the mischievous little boy of Hempstead House, places two teaspoons end-to-end on one another, and flips one in the air . . .

. . . It falls into the cleavage of one of the noble ladies.

Silence at table.

Then, instead of letting the noble lady fish the spoon out herself, the Ambassador leaps to his feet and reaches into the cleavage himself, fumbling between her breasts for the utensil.

What happened next has not been recorded. All that is known is that a day or so later M. Robert Guggenheim was declared persona non grata in Portugal and was asked by the president of Portugal to leave the country.

The White House subsequently accepted the Colonel's resignation on August 10, 1954. In his letter of resignation, according to *The New York Times*, Colonel Guggenheim wrote to Eisenhower that he was "resigning for personal reasons and because of the factor of health."

And so Bob and Polly, divested of their ambassadorial stature, packed their bags and slipped back to Washington. It did not take long before word of what *really* happened began to make its way among members of the Club, Washington society, and the Guggenheim family. Yes, Bob had done it again. It was as if his whole life had been nothing but a series of rehearsals for this one tremendous faux pas.

Bob Guggenheim's reaction to the Great Disgrace was to simply go gaga, like his uncle William.

Now he would appear in top Washington restaurants with his mistresses, literally flaunting them for all to see, whereas before he had kept them under wraps. "Dad, O.K., but not in public," his son, Robert junior, would exclaim. And Robert senior would say: "Hell, I'm proud of it!"

Sometimes, while out with his wife, he would make sure in advance that his favorite girl friend would be at the table next to him, just so he could admire and wink at her from time to time.

Having no other opportunities in life to make conquests but women, and being in constant need of boosting his ego, M. Robert eventually fell into a kind of sexual frenzy. One woman after another. Each reaffirming his waning faith in his masculinity.

Toward the end, any creature who could perform the sort of miracles Uncle Will's protégées performed for him in the *Chambre d'Or* became the most important person in Bob's life. When death came in 1959, it was while M. Robert, at age seventy-four, was boarding a taxicab in Georgetown after visiting one of his favorites. It had been a strenuous session, much too much for his aged heart.

Three years later the federal government initiated an action to collect from the Colonel's estate $169,548 in gift taxes which it claimed M. Robert should have paid on $800,000 in gifts—"cash, jewelry, and a comparatively modest house in Georgetown"—presented to "an unidentified friend."

Later still, Bob's widow, Polly, who remarried, becoming Mrs. John H. Logan, characterized her husband as "loving it all." "He enjoyed what he had, enjoyed enjoying it, and loved entertaining his friends."

Can anything more be said about Colonel Bob? Is it really true that he had no ambitions beyond his own self-gratification? Taking a closer look, and something of a psychological gamble, do we not perceive that he may very well have fulfilled an ambition he never consciously stated to himself, or to anyone else, an ambition held, also unconsciously, by many members of his religion and race? And that was to be fully and unconditionally accepted into the Gentile upper class. His family had made it into the Jewish upper class long ago: There remained that heaven-on-earth of American Gentile social status to be scaled and attained.

Did M. Robert attain it? Yes, as thoroughly as any Jew has attained it, before or since. Step by step. Choosing the overwhelmingly WASP military as his preferred milieu. Renouncing Judaism in favor of Catholicism. Marrying three Gentile girls, the last a member of the Colonial Dames. Going around with people like Dwight Eisenhower and Omar Bradley. Getting into all the right clubs and getting invited to all the right parties in WASPian Washington. Allowing his son, M. Robert, Jr., to be brought up an Episcopalian. Had M. Robert had an ambition after all? It seems so. And, in keeping with the triviality of his life, what a trivial ambition it was . . . to pass for a WASP.

Bob Guggenheim went unto his forebears without leaving so much as a trace of a foundation or a *Gut Werk*. However, two monuments to his self-indulgent life remain: Firenze House in Washington, and his yacht, the *Firenze*.

Polly Logan remained the mistress of Firenze House until 1976, at which time the great mansion, one of the ten largest private residences in Washington, was sold to the near-bankrupt Italian government, to be used as their new embassy, for $4,500,000. Up until the time the Italians took it over there were still quite a few mementoes of the Colonel around. There was, for example, a prize Schipperke, a sprightly little black fellow, who guarded the immense house with the same quick strut his cousins use on the barges of Rotterdam. And there were one or two framed photographs here and there of the Guggenheims and the Eisenhowers smiling at one another. Most of the old photographs, however, and there were hundreds of them— M. Robert in his ambassadorial robes, M. Robert on his yacht, M. Robert hunting on a tack pony—lay in dusty heaps in the basement, near the now-unused bowling alley. "It's diplomacy," Polly would explain to visitors. "You see, I don't want to offend Mr. Logan."

As for the other *Firenze*, the yacht, it is now a Miami Beach restaurant-nightclub moored to the Fifty-ninth Street causeway and is called, in blazing neon, The South Seas. According to Polly, it has been restored to exactly the way it was when she and the Colonel cruised on it together. The wood-burning fireplace still burns wood. The dining room—now a "VIP" room—still has a table set for twelve. Polly visited it a while ago, on a trip to Miami, and describes it as "a beautiful old woman wearing her tiara." "You know," she says, "it looks kind of gaudy nice."

CHAPTER

3

AMBASSADOR HARRY: GUGGENADO AND MACHADOHEIM

Inherited wealth should be used for the progress of man. . . . People who make a business of pleasure are seldom happy.

WITH THESE WORDS HARRY FRANK GUGGENHEIM, YOUNGER SON OF Daniel and Florence, expressed the philosophy that would guide the conduct of *his* life.

Noble words. Words difficult to live up to. Words far more difficult to live up to than brother Robert's philosophy, if we can dignify Bob's brand of escapism with that term. And yet, all things considered, Harry came as close as humanly possible to living up to his high credo.

The Guggenheims were extremely fortunate to have produced a man like Harry in the fourth American generation. It was their only real piece of luck in their postbonanza days. Of the multitudinous offspring from seven sons and three daughters, Harry was the only one with the ability and sense of responsibility to consolidate the Guggenheims' past and present achievements and lead the family on to new achievements in the future.

Yes, Harry Guggenheim was quite a man. A chip off two of the old blocks, plus several new qualities and dimensions.

The dogged energy and determination of his grandfather and his father. His grandfather's and his father's Midas touch (at least until Dan touched Chilean nitrates). Old Meyer's guts and luck. Dan's guts and vision. And then the qualities and activities Meyer and Dan never had the education or time to cultivate or pursue. Harry the Aviator. Harry the Fighter Pilot. Harry the Diplomat. Harry the Public Servant. Harry the Author. Harry the Philanthropist, founder of his own foundation. Harry the Art Museum President. Harry the Cattle Raiser. Harry the Timber Plantation Owner. Harry the Mining Magnate. Harry the Aeronautical and Space Pioneer. Harry the Horseman, winner of the Kentucky Derby. Harry the Newspaper Publisher. How many Americans of his generation were so versatile, so many-sided? Harry the Renaissance Prince. Harry *Il Magnifico*.

Harry the Diplomat.

While M. Robert, flush with his $2 million trust fund, was embarking on his career of making "a business out of pleasure," brother Harry, true to his belief that "inherited wealth should be used for the progress of man," was off on a knight-errant effort, as U.S. ambassador to Cuba, to straighten out all Cuba's economic, social, and political ills.

Harry was fresh from his triumphs as president of the Daniel Guggenheim Fund for the Promotion of Aeronautics, when, in the fall of 1929, he took over as ambassador in Havana. President Hoover had originally offered him the job of assistant secretary of the Navy for aeronautics, but Harry had turned it down because he considered aeronautics a mere means to an end, a means of improving communications among peoples. What he really wanted was a diplomatic post, preferably in Latin America, where he could actually engage in improving relations among peoples.

Harry had worked hard for Hoover's election. When Hoover won, Harry cabled him:

YOUR VICTORY CONSTITUTES THE GREATEST VINDICATION OF DEMOC-RACY IN THE HISTORY OF THE WORLD. . . . ITS RESULT WILL MARK A NEW EPOCH IN HUMAN PROGRESS.

For this hyperbole, Harry's proven ability, and a generous campaign donation from father Dan, Hoover gave Harry Cuba. It was the only political appointment Hoover made to a diplomatic post in all Latin America.

It was also the most important diplomatic post in Latin America at the time. For Cuba was in the midst of a protracted crisis the outcome of which was to have profound consequences for the United States, and the world, thirty years later.

In fairness to Hoover's judgment, however, it must be admitted that Harry Guggenheim did possess many qualifications for the job, besides his money.

For one, he made a good appearance. Tall, muscular, blue-eyed, athletic, and somewhat Latin in expression and complexion, he possessed a rugged masculine charm that promised to stand him in good stead with the Cuban people. As a graduate of Cambridge (he left Yale because he ran into anti-Semitism there), he had received a superior education. He had also proved himself to be a capable executive as president of his father's Fund for the Promotion of Aeronautics. Furthermore, he was a born aristocrat, a product of three generations of hardy blood, rigorous training, great wealth, and exposure to good taste, and the Cubans felt honored by the appointment of a member of such a distinguished American family to their country.

Most important of all, his experience working for Guggenheim Brothers in Chile had given him a solid grounding in Spanish (he spoke the language fluently) and a better-than-average understanding of the problems of Latin-American countries.

That he possessed one all-important disqualification of course never crossed Hoover's mind. That disqualification was the bald fact of who Harry Guggenheim was and what he represented: a multimillionaire conservative Republican who owed his wealth primarily to his father's and uncles' exploitation of cheap labor and untapped natural resources in Latin-American countries, notably Mexico, Bolivia, and Chile. Whose side would Harry be liable to take in a dispute between the status quo, no matter how corrupt, and the rebellious opposition? For by now the Guggenheims incarnated the status quo. The grim underdog days of the ghetto had been forgotten, buried, erased from memory.

The Cuba to which Harry Guggenheim went in November, 1929, barely a few weeks after the Crash, was in a state of acute crisis, ripe for revolution.

The country was entirely in the hands of foreign capital. All the principal mines were American-owned. The sugar industry—and Cuba had a one-crop economy—was 70 percent owned by Americans. The street railway system in Havana was wholly American. Most of the major banks were owned by Americans and the major insurance companies belonged to Canadians.

Presiding over this vast slave camp of foreign capital was a brutal, graft-ridden gangsterism headed by a cruel dictator who worked hand in glove with Wall Street and the Chase National Bank.

His name was Gerardo Machado, and his son-in-law was head of the Chase branch in Havana. Shortly before Harry arrived in Cuba Machado had put down a minor revolution, killing hundreds, suppressing the liberties of the Cuban people, and instituting a police state.

Then, not long after "order" had been restored, and almost precisely at the time Harry took over as ambassador, the bottom fell out of the sugar market, as a result of the worldwide economic depression; there was a ruinous glut of Cuban sugar, tens of thousands of Cubans were thrown out of work, and a new wave of violence swept over the country.

Cuba was bound to the United States by a permanent treaty, concluded after the Spanish-American War. An amendment to this treaty—the Platt Amendment—forbade Cuba to enter into any agreement with a foreign power which would "impair or tend to impair the independence of Cuba," and gave the U.S. the right to intervene in Cuban affairs, militarily, if necessary, for the preservation of "life, property and individual liberty."

Thanks to the Platt Amendment, the American ambassador to Cuba held virtual life and death power over the Cuban government, and so Harry Guggenheim found himself with more real power at his command than any other American diplomat in South America.

No sooner had he settled into his residence at Vedado than Harry threw himself into the fray. This was the sort of activity he had been thirsting for. Boldly he confided to his personal, paid-from-his-own-pocket advisor, Dr. Philip C. Jessup, that by God he would straighten out the affairs of Cuba, even if he had to do it alone. His ultimate aim was to follow in the footsteps of America's ambassador to Mexico, Dwight Morrow, and virtually run the country.

Harry's first confrontation with Machado convinced him the dictator was every bit as ruthless, unscrupulous, and untrustworthy as Harry had been told he was, but still something in Harry's makeup prevented him from opposing him.

Among other things, Harry was receiving daily, at the embassy, letters from American businessmen such as this from a Chase official:

> It is only due to our close contact and friendship with Gerardo Machado and the Secretary of the Treasury that we are receiving interest payments at so early a date, as the payments mean a real sacrifice on the part of the government.

As it was, there was hardly an American businessman in Cuba

who did not swear by the Machado government. After all, most of them owed their privileges, profits, and concessions to the dictator. Machado was a businessman's dream. His policies, calculated to enrich himself above all, were much more favorable to U.S. businessmen than they were to the Cuban people. And what was Harry Guggenheim, former mining executive, and heir to the world's largest private mining fortune, but an American businessman?

Poor Harry. He Knew The Good But Could Do It Not. He knew who and what Machado was, knew he was a disaster for the Cuban people, knew reforms were badly needed, knew that American Platt Amendment intervention against Machado was fully justified, but was incapable of bringing himself to advocate it. He had acquired certain attitudes and prejudices during his years as a Guggenheim Brothers executive in Mexico and Chile which he simply could not overcome. He could not, no, he could not, manage much sympathy for rebels who threaten law and order.

And so he put his personal paid advisors, and his embassy advisors, to work studying every aspect of Cuba's manifold problems, sweated long hours over them himself, and finally came up with: "Political panaceas are not the final solution to Cuba's problems because politics do not constitute the basis of the difficulty. The fundamental cause of Cuba's problem is economic."

That let him off the hook so far as Machado was concerned.

Later he declared that he firmly believed the direction and inspiration of the opposition were with "political elements who were motivated by their own political gain, not the nation's welfare." He was therefore opposed to the rebel movement against Machado, the Union Nacionalistas, and refused to give them the slightest hint of support.

Instead he came out solidly for the dictator: "There is little doubt that, judged by standards of human progress, President Machado has given Cuba a better administration than any other president."

As the economic situation worsened, the price of Cuban sugar dropped to an all-time low, thousands and thousands of Cubans were reduced to a less-than-subsistence economy (while bankers, landowners, and U.S. business puppets continued to live prodigally in Havana), and violence increased until a state of virtual guerrilla warfare broke out in both the cities and the countryside.

In the midst of this crisis Harry announced that the "leaders of the opposition movement were taking advantage of a bad economic situation to further their own political gain" and advised Machado against any restoration of individual liberties: "Complete freedom of speech and press offers very definite dangers."

As the situation worsened, and scores were killed in intermittent fighting, Harry Guggenheim steadfastly stuck to the belief that the opposition wanted to keep the country in a constant state of alarm for selfish political purposes, and thus he would not lend them his or his government's support.

The violence increased in 1932. There were bombings, kidnappings, murders. Harry's life was threatened many times and he was compelled to double his bodyguard. At this juncture he could only urge Machado "not to murder too many of his political enemies."

Now what was left of the free press of Cuba was characterizing Harry as persona non grata—"You are nothing but a broker in dirty diplomacy"—was asserting that a sustained popular uprising against Machado was impossible because of Guggenheim, and was linking Harry's name to the despised dictator he supported by portraying two cartoon monsters in the papers—half Harry, half tyrant—called Guggenado and Machadoheim. Guggenmorgan and Morganheim, slightly metamorphosed, had risen from the dead.

Fall of 1932. More bombings. More murders. Terror on the streets of Havana. Hundreds more killed. As things got worse and worse, Harry finally came to the conclusion that something was radically wrong with America's Cuban policy. Cabling the State Department for U.S. intervention, he was met with dumb inaction. During his last months on the island Harry saw many die who had unsuccessfully asked for his protection and American intervention. Threats on the Ambassador's own life became so frequent that his friend Charles Lindbergh sent him a .38-caliber revolver with a quick-draw holster to be worn under his armpit. In his accompanying letter Lindbergh advised that the weapon not be used against "birds or other harmless animals."

By the end of 1932 it was evident that the Hoover-Guggenheim policy in Cuba had failed. A brutal dictatorship, lacking in popular support, suppressive of individual liberties, and sustained by irresponsible financial practices and American businessmen, legitimate and illegitimate, held absolute power over life and death on the island.

Such had become the state of affairs that the Cuban Patriotic League was moved to proclaim: "The precedent has been established that the U.S. will uphold Cuban governments in power, regardless of their legality."

This thought was later echoed in the *New York Herald Tribune*:

Events have so thoroughly vindicated this policy of non-intervention that it probably is established for all future time as the American Policy in Cuba.

It was with this idea resounding in his head that Harry Guggenheim made his way back to his home on Long Island.

A few months before, Herbert Hoover had written Harry:

It appears as if we may get through our particular term without any great disturbance in your territory, for which I am undyingly grateful.

Less than thirty years later, after as many years of American-supported tyrannies, Cuba was lost to America, and to the entire free world, under the president who appointed M. Robert Guggenheim United States ambassador to Portugal.

CHAPTER

4

PEGGY:
LIBERATED IN EUROPE

SHE WAS YOUNG, SHE WAS ATTRACTIVE, SHE WAS INTELLIGENT, SHE was financially independent, and she was free, at last, in Europe.

It had taken her Guggenheim uncles seven years to untangle her father's chaotic estate. Finally, in 1919, in her twenty-first year, she came into the first of her many inheritances: a $450,000 trust fund from Daddy, $22,500 a year for life, assuming the trustees remained competent, more if they were more than competent. The beginning of her fortune. After Peggy collected her birthright her mother—who would one day leave her an additional $450,000—was most upset. She could no longer control her. First liberation.

Clear out of her mother's apartment. Take a trip. Go across the United States. Niagara Falls to Chicago. Yellowstone Park. California. Hollywood. The Canadian Rockies. Mexico. Fall in love. Get engaged. Get disengaged.

Fix up her face. That damnable Guggenheim potato nose. That clown's nose. Everything about her face all right but the nose. On to Cincinnati, to the famous plastic surgeon who could give you a new nose.

Choosing the plaster model of the nose she prefers. A nose "tip-tilted like a flower." In the middle of the operation, performed under local anesthetic, the surgeon asks her to choose again: He is unable to tip-tilt that potato into a flower. She says stop and leave things as they are. After the abortive operation the nose remains painfully swollen and she refrains from going to New York where it might be seen. Hiding in the Midwest, waiting for the swelling to go down.

The nose becomes something of a weather vane. Every time it is about to rain it swells again, a built-in barometer. Resignation: A Guggenheim cannot rid him/her self of his/her potato nose. Riches are not everything. There are also noses. Sometimes you cannot be liberated from them.

An heiress, but what to do? Cousin Harold Loeb, Aunt Rose's son, has a little radical bookshop, The Sunwise Turn, near Grand Central Station. She likes Harold because he too is somewhat of a rebel; becomes a clerk in his store. Her Guggenheim aunts come by and purchase books "by the yard." They bring the dimensions of their empty bookcases and order in bulk, without knowing what they are buying, to fill up the spaces.

Those Guggenheim aunts! Carrie. Florence. Leonie. Irene. Olga. Rose. Cora. Each with who-knew-how-many millions. That New York Swiss-German and German-German Jewish *haute bourgeoisie*. The Suffocators. Peggy snubs them. Lets them buy books by the yard, but refuses to go to their luncheons, teas, and bridge parties. Second liberation.

After a while Cousin Harold's bookstore becomes a bore. She goes to Europe, where she is to remain first for twenty-one years, then, after a brief interlude in New York, for the rest of her life. At the age of twenty-three she loses her virginity—third liberation—to the man who will become her first husband. There, for a while, the liberating process ceases.

The man to whom young Peggy Guggenheim gave up her virginity was Laurence Vail, twenty-nine, a painter who had not yet found himself, and a writer who had not yet found himself, but who knew all the painters and writers who had found themselves, one of those types who know everybody but themselves, who lived in Paris and was known there as "The King of Bohemia." His mother, in Peggy's words, was "an aristocratic New England lady," and his father was a neurasthenic painter, perennially in and out of institutions, who was half Breton-French, half American. Laurence lived off a one-hundred-dollar-a-month allowance given him by his mother, who was financially independent, earning about $10,000 a year from a trust fund.

Peggy was fascinated by Laurence Vail.

> He appeared to me like someone out of another world, [she wrote in her autobiography] he was the first man I knew who never wore a hat. His beautiful streaky golden hair streamed all over as the wind caught

it. I was shocked by his freedom, but fascinated at the same time. He had lived all his life in France and he had a French accent and rolled his r's. He was like a wild creature. He never seemed to care what people thought. I felt when I walked down the street with him that he might suddenly fly away—he had so little connection with ordinary behavior.

Before long, she decided, in her usual headstrong way, that she was going to lose her virginity to *him*. After all, at twenty-three, it was about time she lost it to *somebody*. "I had a collection of photographs of frescoes I had seen at Pompeii. They depicted people making love in various positions, and, of course, I was very curious and wanted to try them all out myself. It soon occurred to me that I could make use of Laurence for this purpose."

She found her moment one day when he came to visit her at the Plaza-Athenée Hotel in Paris, where she was staying with her mother. Since Mother was out, she was able to "arrange herself" so that Laurence would want to make love to her. "When he pulled me towards him, I acquiesced so quickly that he was surprised by my lack of resistance." However, there was always the chance that mother Guggenheim might return at any moment, so she suggested they go to his hotel instead: "I think Laurence had a pretty tough time because I demanded everything I had seen depicted in the Pompeian frescoes."

It wasn't long before Peggy wanted Laurence Vail for keeps, and so when he nervously and impetuously proposed to her one day on the top of the Eiffel Tower (for which father Ben had built the elevators) she said yes at once. This surprised him, and he immediately took back his proposal. But Peggy wouldn't stand for any backtracking. She wanted him, and, in the end, she got him. The wedding took place in 1922 at the *mairie* of the Seizième Arrondissement and the reception at the Plaza-Athenée.

Mother Florette Guggenheim, and nearly all the other Guggenheims, especially the aunts and uncles, were most displeased. Laurence Vail was, to them, a quadruple mistake. He was a Gentile, a bohemian, unemployed, and he did not have a cent to his name. According to Peggy, the only reason why Mother G. finally gave in and assented to the marriage was because Laurence flirted with her, and, deprived widow that she was, she liked it. Florette had a habit of repeating everything she said three times. Once, when Peggy and Laurence were dining with her at the Ritz, Laurence tickled Florette's leg under the table and she said, as *sotto voce* as she could: "Shush, Peggy will see, Peggy will see, Peggy will see."

No sooner was Peggy married, however, than she felt "extremely let down." "Now that I had achieved what I thought was so desirable, I no longer valued it so much."

The couple went to Italy for their long honeymoon. In Rome Peggy looked up her favorite cousin, Harold Loeb, who had sold The Sunwise Turn and was now publishing a literary review called *Broom* in the Italian capital. Since Peggy wanted to retain her independence, she looked up all her former beaux in Rome, and Laurence, in retaliation, looked up some of his former girl friends. "I still felt distinctly let down by marriage," she confided in her autobiography, "and somehow thought it ought to be more exciting."

After Rome they went to Capri, where they stayed several months, then, after a tour through Italy, returned a second time.

Capri is a treacherous place. Its beauty, for all its sublimity, can be deadly evil, for it masks and, in a sense, blinds one to the incessant intrigue that unfolds behind the exuberant bougainvillea, within the blazing white walls of the villas, above the high foaming cliffs, in the serpents' pit of the *piazzetta*. Intrigue largely having to do with sex and money. Women after richer men than they already have. Men after sexier women than *they* already have. Men after men. Women after women. Men after men and women. Women after women and men.

When Peggy and Laurence arrived in Capri in 1922 the island was still a unique blend of primitive-rural and ultrasophisticated, with no middle class, or hordes of tourists, in between. Barefoot peasant women going about with huge bundles on their heads, and types like the Marchesa Casati, who went about in long silk dresses with a full-grown leopard at her side. Writers Compton Mackenzie and Norman Douglas were in residence, and there was a beautiful young descendant of Marie Antoinette's lover, one Fersen, who lived with an equally beautiful Caprese goatherd. Every evening the whole island congregated in the piazza, as they still do today, and people began jockeying for partners. After a while, Laurence's sister Odile joined her brother and Peggy immediately became very jealous of their relationship: "They gave one the feeling that they were made for incest. . . . When Laurence and Odile stalked together in the Piazza at the hour when everyone collected, I was made to feel nonexistent."

As it turned out, Peggy was unhappy on Capri, and it was Laurence who made her so. For one thing, he felt terribly inferior to the Guggenheims. He, with his one-hundred-dollar-a-month allowance from his mother, and Peggy with her $450,000 trust fund, with more to come from *her* mother and others. He, with his poor neurasthenic father, and Peggy with her six multimillionaire uncles who controlled her trust fund. He with his father who had no power over anything, including himself. And those Guggenheim uncles, rulers of a worldwide business empire, who could tell his wife what she could or could not do with her money, and who had gone on record as thoroughly disapproving of her marriage to the penniless bohemian, Laurence Vail.

One day, when Laurence and Peggy went to see the ruins of the emperor Tiberius' villa, which dominates, from a cliff top, the southernmost part of the island, Laurence told Peggy about how the Roman emperor used to have his enemies hurled down from the cliff and dashed on the rocks below, and how that was exactly what he wanted to do with her uncles. Whereupon Peggy burst into tears.

Sometime later, on their second trip to Capri, Laurence became jealous of one of sister Odile's new lovers, a married Italian, and attacked him in his club, where he was playing cards. A free-for-all followed, and Laurence ended up in jail. It took three weeks, and a large chunk of Guggenheim money, to bail him out.

Meanwhile, in 1923, Peggy had her first child by Vail, a boy to whom they gave the impossible name Sindbad, apparently Vail's idea.

It was at about this time, immediately before and immediately after the birth of Sindbad, that Peggy and Laurence began fighting more than usual. Laurence had a violent and uncontrollable temper and he liked to create scenes. Something of an exhibitionist, he especially liked to foment a ruckus in public. Some crippling sense of inadequacy was constantly gnawing at the root of his being. According to Peggy, he enjoyed "breaking up everything in the house . . . He particularly liked throwing my shoes out of the window, breaking crockery and smashing mirrors and attacking chandeliers. Fights went on for hours, sometimes days, once even for two weeks. . . . When our fights would work up to a grand finale, he would rub jam in my hair. What I hated most was being knocked down in the streets, or having things thrown in restaurants. Once he held me down under water in the bathtub until I felt I was going to drown."

What was causing these continual displays of impotence on Laurence Vail's part? Probably money. He was, after all, living wholly off Peggy. Peggy described the situation pretty clearly herself in her autobiography:

> Because of my money I enjoyed a certain superiority over Laurence and I used it in a dreadful way, by telling him it was mine and he could not have it to dispose of freely. To revenge himself he tried to increase my sense of inferiority. He told me that I was fortunate to be accepted in Bohemia and that, since all I had to offer was my money, I should lend it to the brilliant people I met and whom I was allowed to frequent.

It was only a matter of time before the marriage would break up and Peggy would experience her fourth liberation.

But before the inevitable, they managed to patch things up sufficiently to be able to take a few long trips. Peggy insisted on avoiding the northern countries as much as possible. "I really feel happy only in southern towns, or at least in Latin ones." Among the many places they visited, besides Italy, were Egypt and Palestine, with Peggy, of course, paying the bills.

As a Jewess—Peggy's own term—she felt both shame at herself and terrible disillusionment in Palestine, which was then under British mandate and which, in her words, "had just been given back to the Jews."

> For the first time in my life, [she wrote] I felt ashamed to have married outside my faith. The Jews of Jerusalem looked upon me askance. Palestine was a young country in those days, in spite of its extreme age. It did not seem to be working any too well. The only thing that really impressed me was the Wailing Wall. It mortified me to belong to my people. The nauseating sight of my compatriots publicly groaning and moaning and going into physical contortions was more than I could bear, and I was glad to leave the Jews again.

After Jerusalem it was back to Paris, and rounds and rounds of "fantastic Bohemian parties" which Peggy's stuffy mother did not approve of at all. "She was greatly disappointed I did not marry a Jewish millionaire," Peggy wrote, and she could not understand why her daughter did not like the conventional soirées she held for her American lady friends at the Ritz.

More parties. Endless hours spent talking, drinking, arguing, fighting at the Café du Dôme, La Coupole, the Sélect, the Dingo, the Deux Magots, the Boeuf sur le Toit. Trips to the Tyrol and to Venice, then pregnancy again and temporary residence in the Beau Rivage Hotel at Ouchy on Lake Léman to have the child. Laurence wanted a girl and got one this time. She was named Pegeen, and she was destined to lead a tragic life.

After Pegeen was born, Peggy and Laurence and their little family moved to a small village in the country, Pramousquier, not far from St. Raphael on the Côte d'Azur, making frequent trips into Paris in one of their three cars—the Lorraine Dietrich, the Hispano, or the Citroën. Laurence liked to drive very fast and he usually drank while he drove, rarely forgetting to bring along a plentiful supply of wine. Prior to the move to Pramousquier, he had had to serve another brief prison term for a row he had instigated in Paris. Still another sentence, six months—for throwing four bottles at someone in a restaurant—had been recently suspended with the proviso that if he did not maintain good conduct he would be automatically sentenced to imprisonment for a year.

More bohemian parties, this time in the cottage at Pramousquier, with guests from Paris and the Côte d'Azur. More scenes by Laurence whenever he suspected a guest was paying undue attention to his wife. Pramousquier was very primitive: no telephone, no supplies, no milk for the children, no iceboxes, no amusements, and, more often than not, no electric light. For a while, Peggy, the Rich American Sophisticate, enjoyed playing the Simple Rustic in the French countryside. For variety she and Laurence could always tear into Paris and do something crazy—like visit a brothel, get into a brawl at the Dôme—leaving the children behind with their peasant nurse.

It was, all things considered, a stupid, futile life. By comparison, the hated Guggenheim uncles in New York, to whose shrewdness, daring, and financial acumen Peggy and Laurence owed their wealth, were, for all their supposedly "dull bourgeois lives" (Peggy's words), paragons of purposefulness and sanity. Laurence Vail was particularly ridiculous. Under the protective umbrella of being an Artist—self-styled, for he had produced nothing of worth—he thought he could get away with the most extravagant, absurd, egotistical behavior. He even thought he could get away once with tearing off in the Hispano without Peggy, but on Peggy's money, to St. Tropez for a few days, and nights, "to dance in the bistros."

Some time before he took this risk, Peggy consulted a fortune-teller in Paris who told her she would meet a man in the South of France who would be her next husband.

The fortune-teller was right. The man was John Holms, an Englishman, married, a writer manqué, of whom Edwin Muir said: "Holms gave me a greater feeling of genius than any other man I have met, and I think he must have been one of the most remarkable men of his time, or indeed any time."

While Laurence was away on one of his jaunts to St. Tropez, Peggy invited Holms and his wife, whom she had met a few weeks before, to her house at Pramousquier. There were also other guests in the house. One night they all went swimming together naked. Somehow, in the words of Peggy's autobiography, "John and I found ourselves alone on the beach and we made love."

That did it. Things were not quite the same when Laurence the Egotist came back. He still thought he was Cock of the Walk, but he had been dethroned. Holms had been "better" than he was.

There ensued a sucession of scenes between Peggy and Laurence, Laurence and Holms, Peggy and Mrs. (Dorothy) Holms, Peggy and Laurence and John and Dorothy, that ended in a near-mortal battle between Laurence and John on the floor of John's house after Peggy had "gone over to kiss him."

The divorce agreement—concluded after seven years of marriage—made Peggy the guardian of Pegeen and Laurence the guardian of Sindbad. It was further stipulated that Peggy was to have Sindbad live with her for sixty days a year. No stipulation was made for Pegeen to live with Laurence. Peggy had to pay both lawyers. Hers cost $10,000 and Laurence's $5,000. In addition she had to give Laurence a monthly allowance, since he had no means of support.

With this nasty business settled, Peggy went to live with John Holms.

In her autobiography, Peggy was philosophical about the whole thing. Although the marriage had been "stormy," to say the least, she admitted she gained three very important things from it: one, her two children; two, a lasting friendship with Laurence Vail (they became much better friends after the divorce than they had been during the marriage), and, three, "total liberation from my early Jewish bourgeois upbringing."

This latter liberation, of course, also meant liberation from the suffocating tyranny of the Guggenheim family and their world. Those aunts. Those uncles. Those millions.

Yet, we shall see there was a profound contradiction at the center of Peggy Guggenheim's sense of liberation from her family. Though almost the entire first half of her adult life was nothing but a long, drawn-out rebellion against her New York *haut bourgeois* upbringing and the Guggenheims, during the second half of her life she became the proudest and most self-consciously *Guggenheim* Guggenheim of them all, as well as by far the most famous Guggenheim of her generation.

Once Peggy was liberated from the frantic Laurence Vail, she virtually enslaved herself to John Holms. It was a typical rebound situation. Confronted with the tremendous void of having Laurence no more, she could not face life alone and so collapsed into the arms of the only other man around for whom she felt some sympathy and affection, and collapsed so completely that she all but lost her identity in his. During the first two years of their relationship, she and Holms did almost nothing but make love and travel, sometimes bringing little Pegeen along, more often leaving her with her nurse. Slowly Peggy fell completely under his spell.

Holms was a tall, slim man with broad shoulders, a big chest, narrow hips, and he wore a scraggly black moustache and a goatee on his sallow, old-before-his-time face. He was very intelligent, in an impractical, abstract sort of way, and possessed an enormous fund of general knowledge. He wanted desperately to be a writer, but lacked the willpower to ever get anything down on paper. His trouble was alcoholism.

It took Peggy a while to discover what John's problem was. Although he drank a good deal, being with him was such an exciting experience that she tended to overlook, or ignore, his weaknesses. "I never led such a wonderful life before," she wrote in her autobiography. "John opened up a whole new world I had never dreamed of." Then, reiterating, unconsciously, the poor-little-rich-girl lament, the nobody-loves-me-for-myself-but-only-for-my-money litany, she wrote: "He loved me [not so much because of my money but] because to him I was a real woman." Later on in her book she threw still more praise at Holms: "I began to learn from him everything that I know today. . . . He was the only person I had ever met who could give me a satisfactory reply to any question."

This sensual and intellectual idyll did not last long, however. Two things were constantly poisoning it: Holms' alcoholism and the absence of Sindbad, whom Peggy "adored."

Not being able to write, because alcohol had the effect of paralyzing his will, John Holms became more and more unhappy, which caused him to drink more and more. "I was shocked," Peggy wrote, "by his paralysis of willpower. . . . In the end, he could hardly force himself to do the simplest things. . . . The amazing effort which it was to him to *will* anything was indescribable. . . . Sometimes he spent the whole day in bed with a hangover and got up only for the evening."

This was poison enough for any relationship, but there was also the problem of Sindbad. The little boy was living with his father, and Peggy missed him terribly. Often Laurence Vail refused to let Peggy see the boy and frequently he violated the divorce agreement and would not give him over to Peggy for the allotted sixty days, even though Peggy was supporting Laurence and the boy entirely out of her own pocket.

Then Peggy also had to endure the discovery that Laurence had had a little daughter by an unknown mother. This made her feel bad because she had once had to have a "curettage" performed, while she was married to, and pregnant by, Vail, by a Russian doctor called Popoff in a French convent. Apparently Dr. Popoff had been the accoucheur of the Grand Duchess of Prussia and now devoted his talents almost exclusively to "curettages." In the middle of the operation he would exclaim to his nun nurses: *Tiens, tiens, cette femme est enceinte."*

To further complicate this expatriates' soap opera, mother Florette returned to Paris and let Peggy know exactly what she thought of the domestic mess she had gotten herself into. She was most pleased Peggy had divorced Laurence Vail, since she had always considered him "N.G." But she would not forgive her daughter for relinquishing Sindbad and she thought Holms was dreadful because he had no money and did not work. So far as Florette Guggenheim was concerned, her daughter's life was nothing less than a disaster.

Fortunately for Peggy, though she did not realize it at the time, Holms died in 1934, at only thirty-seven, from minor injuries sustained in an auto accident. The doctors said he should have recovered, but alcohol had destroyed most of his internal organs as well as his resistance to infection. In the months immediately before his death he had frequently complained, while drinking: "I'm so bored, so bored, so bored."

After his death Peggy felt very guilty, as if she could have done something to prevent it. She remembered how humiliated Holms had felt when, at the end of each month, she sat down at her desk and paid all the bills. She remembered how unpleasant she had been to him at times because she felt he was keeping her from being with Sindbad. Overwhelmed with misery, she soon fell into the arms of another man, a friend of John's with whom she had already made love, unbeknown to John. His name was Douglas Garman, called "Sherman" in her autobiography.

The affair with Garman started off, and remained, for Peggy, a sweet-and-sour mélange of love's delight and crippling guilt. Sherman composed poems for her with lines such as: "Finding again what treasure lies in secret hushed between your thighs," and "For the wild gift between your thighs drove out the terror from my eyes."

But, though all of this was kind of fun, Peggy nevertheless felt "it was all very painful because of my unhappiness about John." "I had been completely dependent on him," she wrote. "I was incapable of thinking for myself. He had always decided everything and as he was so brilliant, it was much simpler to accept his judgments than make my own. . . . Apart from this, I had a bad conscience about being untrue to him only seven weeks after his death."

Douglas Garman, alias Sherman, was an Englishman five years younger than Peggy, a doctor's son who was interested in Marxism, and who was very poor. After the relationship had really become a relationship he made Peggy buy a cottage near South Harting. "Soon after this step," Peggy wrote, "I decided to commit suicide, I was still so unhappy about John. I therefore put the house in Sherman's name, as I intended to die."

Sherman was only too happy about the acquisition of this new asset, but he was far from happy about how he was getting along with Peggy. Peggy wrote: "I was all the time comparing Sherman with John and even went as far as to tell Sherman that he had bored John."

After a while, Sherman, who for a year had been reading Karl Marx to the exclusion of everything else, joined the Communist Party. "All the money I gave him," Peggy wrote, "which formerly went to paying for the building he had done on the house and on other things, now went to the Communist Party. . . . I had no objection to that at all. I merely got bored listening to the latest orders from Moscow, which I was supposed to obey." After a while Peggy herself enrolled in the party "just to please Sherman."

But life with "Sherman," in the end, did not work. One weekend Peggy and he had a row about communism, and, in Peggy's words, "I got so bitchy that he hit me. I slipped and fell. There was blood everywhere." Soon it was all finished between Peggy and Douglas Garman and Peggy was forced to admit to a friend: "I think my life is over."

As it turned out, Peggy was right. The sort of aimless, out-of-one-bed-into-another-bed life she had been leading *was* over. Now, a new, far more liberating life awaited her, one she never expected, but which was to become her salvation.

CHAPTER

5

PEGGY AND GUGGENHEIM JEUNE

SHE WAS THIRTY-NINE YEARS OLD, AND ALL SHE REALLY HAD TO
her credit was an unhappy marriage, two unhappy children, and half
a dozen momentarily exhilarating, but ultimately foolish, love affairs
with penniless, footloose men. Plus the trust fund, of course. That
credit she would never lose, thanks to the generosity of her unlucky
father, and thanks especially to the financial wisdom of her uncles—
Daniel, Murry, Solomon, Simon, William—those uncles against whom
the fourth generation of Guggenheims rebelled so ostentatiously, but
who, in the end, were responsible for laying the material bases for
their entire lives.

One wonders in reading Peggy Guggenheim's memoirs, art catalogue blurbs, and letters, and in listening to her conversation, whether
she ever had the remotest appreciation of the struggles it had taken
to earn her fortune. Did she realize it came from the most crippling
labor of all? Did she realize it came from just-off-the-boat "Hunkies"
and "Japs" who slaved in the open pits of Bingham Canyon; that it
came from frozen down-and-outers who had chosen the Guggenheim
mines in Alaska as their last hope; that it came from Mexican, Bo-
livian, Chilean, Congolese, Angolan peons working below ground
twelve hours a day for as little as eight cents an hour? Did she realize
it came from those stuffy bourgeois uncles who, for all their immense
wealth, were nevertheless there at their desks in the Partners' Room
at Guggenheim Brothers almost every day of their lives promptly at
nine and did not leave those desks until five-thirty?

Who knows? Perhaps by her thirty-ninth year she did. For it was in that year of her life that Peggy finally decided to do something more with that money earned by half-blinded, bent-before-their-time South American peons and strained, out-on-the-limb nine-to-five New York businessmen, than throw it away on impotent painters, paralyzed, alcoholic nonwriters, and British upper-middle-class communists.

What to do after fifteen years in and out of various, ultimately worthless beds? A friend, Peggy Waldman, suggested she either go into publishing, like Cousin Harold, or open an art gallery.

Since starting a publishing house would be too expensive, she decided on the art gallery. It would be the first gallery devoted exclusively to contemporary art in London.

Even that was an expensive proposition however. But precisely at the time she was debating the art gallery idea, mother Florette died, leaving her another $450,000 in trust. That gave Peggy $900,000 altogether. The stuffy, bourgeois uncles, whom Laurence Vail wanted hurled down Tiberius' cliffs (and who were ultimately responsible for sustaining his entire life, through the allowance Peggy gave him), invested their niece's money at roughly 5.5 percent, giving her an unearned income of nearly $50,000 a year, not bad at all in prewar Europe.

So now she *did* have enough money to open her own art gallery. After a brief search, she rented a second-floor gallery on Cork Street in London and engaged an old friend, Wyn Henderson, as secretary. It was Wyn who named the gallery "Guggenheim Jeune."

Opening an art gallery was not *such* a great departure from Peggy's former life because, after all, she had always liked, and had been interested in, painting and, of course, painters.

Her first exposure to great painting had been in her father's townhouse on Fifth Avenue. There she was continually surrounded by what her sister Hazel calls "museum-quality" paintings, so already as as a child she had become accustomed to living with important works of art.

Then, on her trip to Europe with Mother immediately after she had come into her first inheritance, she had dragged her mother and an assortment of friends, some of whom dropped out because they could not keep up with her, to "where every painting in Europe could be found." She also read "everything Berenson ever wrote." So far her taste leaned toward the traditional, but then she saw an abstraction by Georgia O'Keeffe and was immediately "converted" to modern art. Later Laurence Vail, painter, introduced her to most of the best-known painters of Paris, among them the man who was destined to play a decisive role in the development of her artistic taste, Marcel Duchamp.

Peggy wanted to devote her first show to Brancusi, but Brancusi was away from Paris at the time and so Duchamp suggested Cocteau instead. After Duchamp introduced her to Cocteau, it was settled: The opening show of Guggenheim Jeune would be his. Duchamp hung the show and it caused quite a stir in London and put Guggenheim Jeune on the artistic map. Before, during, and after the show Duchamp was Peggy's chief artistic mentor, teaching her "everything he knew about abstract and surrealist art." Later Peggy gave exhibitions to Wassily Kandinsky and the young surrealist, Yves Tanguy, and held shows of sculpture by Antoine Pevsner, Henry Moore, Alexander Calder, Constantin Brancusi, and Jean Arp, all of whom were relatively unknown at the time. She also held a collage show displaying works of Ernst, Picasso, Braque, and Miró.

Meanwhile, she had to fall in love again. This time it was with "a fascinating Irishman with green eyes, a thin face, nose like an eagle," who was a friend of James Joyce. In fact, he had even been in love with Joyce's daughter. He was another "mad drunk." He was another penniless one. He was another writer who could not bring himself to write. Peggy called him Oblomov, after Goncharov's hero who did not even have the willpower to get out of bed. To complete his misery, ever since his birth "he had retained a terrible memory of life in his mother's womb." Sometimes this memory "smothered him" and he was unable to speak. His name was Samuel Beckett.

Beckett, who later snapped out of his paralysis of will to write several contemporary masterpieces and win a Nobel Prize, was destined to play a vital role in Peggy's life, not so much as a lover as an advisor. It was he who convinced her to buy the work of contemporary artists, insisting she had a moral duty to interest herself in the art of her day.

Peggy and Beckett went to Joyce's fifty-second birthday party together. They gave Joyce a blackthorn walking-stick and some Swiss wine, Joyce's favorite drink. At the party Joyce offered a hundred francs to anyone who could guess the title of his next novel, which would soon be published. Peggy was sure Beckett would win the bet, since he had had the inside track as Joyce's daughter's former fiancé, but after the guesses were made the winner was not announced since Joyce wanted to keep the title of his book, which turned out to be *Finnegans Wake*, secret until publication day. The party ended with a drunk Joyce doing an Irish jig and a Beckett too drunk to satisfy Peggy's physical needs later on.

Since Beckett, when Peggy asked him what he was going to do about their life, invariably replied "Nothing," and since "he never seemed to make up his mind whether or not he was going to have me," Peggy finally had to give him up.

That was all to the good, because he had distracted her from her painting and her gallery and she was beginning to really find herself in this activity.

So back to the gallery and a show for Kandinsky. It had been Marcel Duchamp again who had introduced her to the great Russian abstractionist, who would be so avidly bought by her uncle Solomon.

At the time Kandinsky was most upset because Solomon, on the advice of Hilla Rebay, was buying Bauers instead of Kandinskys. With a great show of emotion, Kandinsky urged Peggy to convince her uncle to buy some of his early paintings "to complete Solomon Guggenheim's Kandinsky collection." Peggy immediately wrote her uncle Sol and received a "friendly answer saying that he had turned the letter over to the Baroness Rebay" and that she herself would reply.

After a while, Peggy did receive the reply:

Dear Mrs. Guggenheim "jeune,"

Your request to sell us a Kandinsky picture was given to me, to answer.

First of all, we do not ever buy from any dealer, as long as great artists offer their work for sale themselves and secondly will be your gallery the last one for our foundation to use, if ever the need to get an historically important picture, should force us to use a sales gallery.

It is extremely distasteful at this moment, when the name of Guggenheim stands for an ideal in art, to see it used for commerce so as to give the wrong impression, as if this great philanthropic work was intended to be a useful boost to some small shop. Non-objective art, you will soon find out, does not come by the dozen, to make a shop of this art profitable. Commerce with real art cannot exist for that reason. You will soon find you are propagating mediocrity, if not thrash [sic]. If you are interested in non-objective art you can well afford to buy it and start a collection. This way you can get into useful contact with artists, and you can leave a fine collection to your country if you know how to chose [sic]. If you don't, you will soon find yourself in trouble also in commerce.

Due to the foresight of an important man since many years collecting and protecting real art, through my work and experience, the name of Guggenheim became known for great art and it is very poor taste indeed to make use of it, of our work and fame, to cheapen it to a profit.

Yours Very Truly
HILLA REBAY

P.S. Now our newest publication will not be sent to England for some time to come.

Peggy was not exactly broken by the postscript. She was already well acquainted with Hilla's mystic double-talk and she could easily get along without it.

She told Kandinsky about the letter and all he could do was throw up his hands and admit defeat. Bauer was in. Kandinsky was out. Hilla was in charge.

Peggy's next big show after the Kandinsky was given during the second year of Guggenheim Jeune and it was for the promising young surrealist Yves Tanguy.

Tanguy was a thirty-year-old Breton sailor, a man with no formal education to speak of, and no artistic education other than a desultory private initiation into painting by André Breton.

Tanguy had once been insane and had been in an asylum. He was a curious physical specimen. A surprised, energetic face, with the mouth and eyes of an extraterrestrial creature, a being out of science fiction, his mouth a perpetually upturned crescent, his eyes always startled, his hair always standing straight up on end. Something of a social misfit (to say the least), he had been expelled from the French merchant marine. It was then that he began to take up painting, having been inspired to do so by a work of di Chirico. He became yet another one of that legion of artists in the 1930s whose work was little more than a public unburdening of their own psychoses.

"Since," in Peggy's words, "Surrealism was beginning to become known in England at the time . . . his show was a great success, and we sold a lot of paintings. . . . As a result, Tanguy suddenly found himself rich for the first time in his life and began to throw money around like mad. In cafés he used to make little balls of one pound notes and flicker them about to adjacent tables. Sometimes he even burnt them."

Peggy picked up a few Tanguys relatively cheaply, just as she had bought several Duchamps, Cocteaus, and Kandinskys, also at bargain prices. Often when she gave an artist a show, she would receive a painting free. It was in this rather inconspicuous way that one of the great private collections of modern art began.

Peggy might have been buckling down to work, at last, but she was nonetheless never one to let an interesting love affair float by when one happened to swim toward her net.

Now it was the turn of Yves Tanguy. Tanguy was married, but an inconvenience like that never hampered Peggy Guggenheim very much. After one of the many parties held during the time Tanguy's show was on in London, he and Peggy spent the night together in Peggy's flat. "After that," Peggy wrote in her autobiography, "it was difficult to see Tanguy alone because of his wife. Wyn [Henderson] came to our rescue and invited Mrs. Tanguy to lunch and kept her occupied all one afternoon."

Some weeks later Peggy and Tanguy "eloped" and went off to Peggy's house in the country to live together, at least for a while. This confused little Sindbad, who was staying with his mother at the time, because the child was used to seeing Tanguy with Mrs. Tanguy. While Tanguy was with Peggy, Sindbad kept asking for Tanguy's wife over and over again.

In the midst of this affair, Beckett returned, appearing suddenly at Peggy's country house. When he saw a photo on the mantelpiece of Peggy and Tanguy looking happy together he threw a fit. Although he could never quite summon the willpower to "have" her, to use her expression, he was nevertheless extremely jealous—like most impotents—of the other men in her life.

To avoid Beckett, Peggy returned to Paris and then began to have a terrible time with Mrs. Tanguy, who had become suspicious of her husband's relationship with Peggy. When Mr. and Mrs. Tanguy had "rows," sometimes Mrs. would disappear "for days."

The complexity and absurdity of this situation was unwittingly emphasized by Peggy in her autobiography: "Every morning Tanguy came to my house to fetch me. We spent the whole day together, then he went home to his wife. I was living in Beckett's apartment. He [Beckett] had gone to Brittany with his mistress in my car. I was still terribly in love with him. Tanguy once said to me: 'You don't come to Paris to see me, you come to see Beckett.' "

It was at this time that Lawrence Vail told Peggy she should marry Tanguy and Peggy answered back that she needed a father, not a son.

What happened to Peggy's children, psychologically, during this period is not revealed in her autobiography. Again, we shall leave it to the psychologists to interpret. The bare facts are: Sindbad continually saw his father with a different woman, and his mother with a different man; Pegeen continually saw the same.

Meanwhile, in the midst of all this juggling, these perpetually shifting musical chairs, Peggy found the time to fall for a well-known British collector of surrealists whom she called in her autobiography "Donald Wrenclose." Peggy described him as "extremely attractive, quite good-looking, had great success with woman, and was always having affairs . . ." She went on,

> He had one eccentricity . . . when he slept with women he tied up their wrists with anything that was handy. Once he used my belt, but another time in his house he brought out a pair of ivory bracelets from the Sudan. They were attached with a chain and Wrenclose had a key to lock them. It was extremely uncomfortable to spend the night this way, but if you spent it with Wrenclose it was the only way. . . . Once we slept under my favorite painting of Delveau's, the "Women with the Lamps." I was so thrilled, I felt as if I were one of the women.

Alas, in the end, everything palls, especially the wildest loves. After a while, Wrenclose-of-the-tied-wrists palled. Beckett-Oblomov palled. Tanguy palled. And Peggy, now facing life, the abyss, with *nobody*, fell for a married English sculptor by the name of Llewellyn, and "slept" with him right away.

Not long after this liaison was established, Peggy began to feel she was pregnant.

"Every time I thought I was, I decided I wasn't, and vice versa.

"One afternoon Llewellyn asked me to his house in Hampstead to see his wife's work. The minute I entered the room and saw her I knew we were both pregnant. Shortly after this, she had a miscarriage. The irony of the situation was that they wanted a child. I offered one to Llewellyn, but he refused it on the grounds that he could make a lot more."

So Peggy had to have another abortion. The doctor she consulted said she was much too old to have a child, "especially after not having had one for fourteen years." The matter was taken care of in an English nursing home, and it ended a long, and frequently silly, chapter in Peggy's life. From now on, it was more or less to hell with men, or at least with casual affairs, one after the other, and concentrate on something else.

That concentration took the form of what Peggy called "serious collecting."

It was about time. After setting up Guggenheim Jeune, she had given people the impression she had decided to do something constructive with her life and her money. But then she had let herself and others down by resuming her old in-and-out-of-various-unworthy-beds ways. When all was said and done, she really was not so different from her cousin, wastrel Colonel Bob. Both were in and out of lots of different beds. Both played. Bob played with dogs and yachts. Peggy played with art. One must respect the hierarchies in life. It is much worse to play around with art than it is to play around with dogs and yachts.

When you play at something rather than work hard at it, however, the iron laws of economics usually have their way. Thus it was that by the end of 1939, Guggenheim Jeune, a year and a half after its founding, had become a losing business and Peggy was having to pay for her playing by making up a deficit for the year of some six hundred pounds, or $2550.

Since there was no indication that the next year's results would be any different, and definite indication that they might be worse, there was nothing much she could do but close the gallery, which she did resignedly, knowing that at least she had made a brave try at introducing modern art to Britain.

What next? With no lovers and no gallery, Peggy was now at a double loss. No, a triple loss, because she was undergoing the Llewellyn abortion at the time.

It was a dark moment, but precisely when she felt she felt she was touching bottom, a knight in blazing armor came to her bedside in the nursing home where she was recovering from the Llewellyn thing. His name was Herbert Read, an old friend, destined one day to become Sir Herbert Read, Knight of the Garter.

Read was, in Peggy's words, "a distinguished-looking gentleman," older than herself, and he was just about the only man of prominence in Britain trying to promote modern art at the time. He had been a curator in several museums and now was editor of a review of the arts.

Peggy, who had been looking for a father ever since her real father went down with the *Titanic*, took to Herbert Read with a daughterly affection. Behind his back—for he was sensitive about his age—she referred to him as "Papa." When she got out of the nursing home she sat at his feet and listened to his endless, and most erudite, disquisitions on art. By her own admission, she learned more from him in a few months than she had learned from all the artists and pseudo-artists she had known up to that time, with the exception of Marcel Duchamp.

During these instructive sessions, which, to Peggy's relief, involved no sex—she had not yet fully recovered physically from the aborted fruit of her last sexual escapade—she and Read evolved the idea of opening a modern art museum in or near London, which would be the first of its kind in Britain.

Before long, Peggy made Read give up his job as a magazine editor and gave him a five-year contract as director of the new museum. Soon they persuaded Sir Kenneth Clark to rent them his country place for premises.

In the midst of these negotiations, Read got nervous about going in with Peggy on such a monumental venture and so he wrote one of the few friends he trusted, T. S. Eliot, for a reference on his prospective boss. Eliot was only too happy to endorse Peggy: "I have never heard Mrs. Guggenheim spoken of in any but the highest terms."

If Read was nervous about Peggy, Peggy was nervous about money. True, she was earning around $50,000 a year from her two trusts (and in 1939, $50,000 would buy what $205,800 buys today), but she had firm commitments of $10,000 a year to old friends and artists she had been helping to support for years, and supporting her ex-husband and children was costing her a minimum of $15,000 a year, so even though she was a Guggenheim—a name almost synonymous with Rockefeller for wealth in those days—she only had around $25,000 a year, less taxes, for herself, which was hardly enough to start a museum on.

But there still were plenty of rich Guggenheims around, so she appealed to the most promising, her art-loving uncle Sol, through his wife, her aunt Irene. By then Irene had been ignominiously supplanted in matters artistic by the baroness Rebay, and so Irene replied, with some sour grapes, that "the Baroness Rebay would have to be consulted and then maybe you will get a Bauer."

Peggy appealed to other sources, but 1939—with the Depression still on, and war impending—was not much of a year for raising money for anything, and she finally had to give up the museum idea. To pacify the much-disappointed Herbert Read, she gave him one half of his contracted five-year salary. After this matter was settled, Read continued to advise her in matters artistic and the two became lifelong friends.

With Guggenheim Jeune closed, the museum scheme fallen through, and war breaking out, Peggy conceived a new idea: to found a colony in southern France for painters to stay and work for the duration of the war. Tirelessly, she went about looking for a suitable place, inspecting dozens of old castles and palaces throughout the Midi. She did not find one, and finally gave up the idea altogether because she realized a castle full of painters would be more lethal than the war that raged beyond its walls.

Back to Paris, which was expecting a German invasion at any minute. Not much time to lose. Now was the time to add to her collection some things she could not afford before. Artists were selling their works for whatever they could get. She bought a Brancusi bird for only $1,000, a wonderful Léger also for $1,000 the day Hitler invaded Norway. Other artists were only too willing to unload. She acquired an Arp, a Giacometti, later some Max Ernsts, for almost nothing. Her war babies. Yes, no matter how much she rebelled against the family, Peggy certainly *was* a Guggenheim. Guggenheims always know what to do when a war is threatening, or on. The immortal words of Mr. Dan: "Always go in for big development when the business barometer is low."

It was during this frightening profitable period that Peggy ran into her future husband, Max Ernst, whom she had met briefly before. Meeting him again with the Germans about to invade France and carry them both off to concentration camps was an exhilarating experience for Peggy. "Ernst had a terrific reputation for his beauty, his charm, and his success with women," she wrote in her autobiography. "He had white hair, big blue eyes, and a handsome beak-like nose, that resembled a bird's." It was not long before she was—yes, she was far from cured—"madly in love with him."

Soon, however, things became too dangerous for love or art or anything but getting out alive.

Rumors of what Hitler had in store for the Jews in France were seeping through the country. Ernst had already escaped from one detention camp in southern France (he had been interned by the French as an enemy alien) and was not much thrilled by the prospect of being thrown into another. Peggy's friends warned her that, as one of the best-known Jews in Paris, she risked the concentration camp also.

Although she was, of course, concerned about her own safety, and that of her children, Peggy seemed more concerned at the time about her collection than anything else. Frantically she went to the Louvre and asked them to take her paintings and hide them in the secret place in the countryside where they were storing their other treasures.

To her immense surprise and disgust the Louvre sniffed its nose at the Peggy Guggenheim collection. In Peggy's words: "The Louvre decided my pictures were not worth saving and refused me space."

What they considered not worth saving were a Kandinsky, several Klees and Picabias, a cubist Braque, a Gris, a Léger, a Gleizes, a Marcoussis, a Delaunay, a Severini and two other futurists, a Mondrian, and several surrealist works by Miró, Max Ernst, di Chirico, Tanguy, Dali, Magritte, and Brauner. Her sculptures—by Brancusi, Lipchitz, Giacometti, and Moore—were not even considered.

In desperation Peggy got a friend to store the collection in a barn near Vichy. By then it was already apparent that southern France would collaborate with, rather than fall to, the Germans.

Peggy herself got out of Paris only two days before the German tanks arrived, bringing her two children with her. During the preceding week over two million Parisians had fled the city in cars, bicycles, buses, trains, on foot.

Soon it appeared certain that her paintings were far from safe in the barn near Vichy and she had them removed to a small provincial museum in Grenoble.

But after the fall of Paris, and the humiliation of the "peace treaty," it was doubtful if they were safe even in Grenoble.

There was no time to lose. Word was reaching southern France that the Nazis would be there any minute and no Jew or his/her property would be safe from concentration camp and confiscation.

At the last minute Peggy found there was a way she could ship her paintings from Marseilles to New York as "household objects," without inspection, and got them off this way in the nick of time.

Max Ernst, also terrified of the Nazis, managed to sneak himself and his paintings out by night from the farmhouse he was hiding in in the Ardèche.

Peggy, on hearing that Ernst had reached Marseilles with most of his works intact, immediately took upon herself the responsibility of helping to finance his escape to America. She did the same for André Breton and his family.

In exchange for her financing his escape, Ernst let Peggy choose "a great many pictures from every period." She bought them all for only $2,000 and it was that $2,000 that enabled him and his remaining paintings to reach the United States. After that lucrative transaction—these paintings were to be worth hundreds of thousands one day—she and Max celebrated his fiftieth birthday at the *vieux port*, "drinking wine he had brought from the Ardèche, and eating oysters."

"I felt extremely attracted to Ernst," she confided to her auto-biography, "and soon discovered I was madly in love with him: from then on my only thought was to save him from Europe and get him to New York. . . . When we arrived in New York on July 14th, 1941, it was fourteen years since I had set foot in America."

6

PEGGY IN NEW YORK: ERNST, POLLOCK, AND ART OF THIS CENTURY

THE HOUSE WAS A 1940S VERSION OF FATHER BEN'S FIVE-STORY, pre-*Titanic* Fifth Avenue mansion. A remodeled brownstone on the East River at Fifty-first Street, near Beekman Place. It had, in addition to the usual appurtenances, a huge living room that, according to Peggy, might have been "a baronial hall in Hungary," and a "chapel two stories high," which overlooked the river from a terrace. Pegeen had a whole floor to herself (Sindbad was with Laurence Vail in a house Peggy had rented for them in Connecticut). Max had a "beautiful studio" all to himself. And Peggy had so many rooms to herself, she was able to hang her entire collection in them.

It was in and around this New York brownstone, and in the gallery Peggy later opened on West Fifty-seventh Street, that the American, and to a certain extent, the European art world of the early 1940s revolved. This was the vital center. It was here, in these two places, that Max Ernst was launched in America, that the New York abstract expressionists got their first big chance, that Jackson Pollock was discovered, financed, bought, beatified, and canonized.

To expatriate Peggy Guggenheim's immense surprise, America was not such a bad place after all . . . especially if you had the money to rent a four-story townhouse near Beekman Place overlooking the breezy East River.

But aside from that fortuitous circumstance—the result, principally, of her Guggenheim uncles' shrewd investment policies (they did not involve her in Chilean nitrates, but kept her in good solid metals: silver, copper, tin, lead, gold)—America was most certainly the safest and most agreeable place to be in the entire Western world—outside of the great Latin-American backwater—during World War II. Not only was one safe from the bombings, the strafings, the tanks, the concentration camps, the food shortages, the sadistic bullying by the Nazi conquerors, but one was living the most powerful moment of a people and a nation. For it was during the years 1940 to 1945 that America rose to, and met successfully, the most formidable challenge in its history, a global, multiple-front, two-ocean war that threatened the survival of free institutions everywhere. It was a period during which labor, management, capital, and government cooperated to achieve the most prodigious feats of industrial production of all time. It was a period when blacks, half-breeds, and whites, and all their so-called "ethnic" subdivisions, temporarily suspended their relentless hostilities and worked together toward a common goal. It was a time when men were men, women were women, children were children, and the sexes and the generations were relatively at peace. It was also a time of energetic, innovative, and prophetic artistic and scientific creativity. During the early 1940s there were giants upon the American earth in almost every area of human endeavor: Franklin D. Roosevelt, Douglas MacArthur, George C. Marshall, T. S. Eliot, Albert Einstein, Robert Oppenheimer, George Santayana, Dmitri Mitropoulos, Vannevar Bush, Ezra Pound, William Faulkner, Chester Nimitz, Ernest J. King, Omar Bradley, Bruno Walter, Louis B. Mayer, Alfred P. Sloan, Henry Kaiser, John L. Lewis, Frank Lloyd Wright, Ernest Hemingway, Eugene O'Neill, Jackson Pollock, George Patton. Never before or since, with the possible exception of the period immediately preceding the War for Independence, and the first decade of the United States' existence, has there been such a concentration of talent and energy in America as there was during World War II. The early 1940s was certainly not the summit of American civilization, but it was the summit of American power, the political, economic, and military culmination of the land's 335-year occupation by Europeans and Africans.

All of this, of course, Peggy, Pegeen, and Max were quite unaware of as they settled into their spacious townhouse on Manhattan's East River. They were only aware that—to their surprise and delight—New York and, by extension, America, was a most satisfactory and even stimulating place to be while Hitler's armies were overrunning their beloved Europe.

Before settling down at Beekman Place, Peggy and Max had taken a trip across the United States (to show the country to Max) and had also done the rounds of New York.

The immense monotonies of the American continent had not aroused much enthusiasm in them, though they both liked San Francisco, and they had been glad to return to New York.

One of the many things they did in New York was visit Uncle Sol's museum. This was the baroness's Fifty-fourth Street establishment, not yet the Frank Lloyd Wright structure on Fifth Avenue and. Eighty-ninth Street. "It really was a joke," Peggy observed. "There were about one hundred paintings by Bauer in enormous silver frames which overshadowed the Kandinskys. . . . From the walls boomed forth music by Bach—a rather weird contrast. The museum is a beautiful little building completely wasted in this atrocious manner. Max called it the Bauer House. The Museum of Modern Art he called the Barr House; and Gallatin's collection in the New York University building was the Bore House."

They also went to Uncle Sol's suite in the Plaza Hotel, where, in contrast to what they had beheld in the Bauer House, they approved of almost everything: "The most beautiful Picassos, Seurats, Braques, Klees, Kandinskys, Gleizeses, Delaunays, Chagalls . . . I told my aunt Irene to burn all the Bauers and move these paintings to the museum. She said, 'Shush! Don't let your uncle hear that!' "

By now Peggy was "delirious" over the handsome, infinitely talented Max Ernst. The man had captured her affections totally, and, once he knew he had her hooked by the gills, he proceeded to torture her without mercy. It was yet another one of Peggy's seemingly endless succession of sadomasochistic relationships. She had the power—the house, the money, the connections; he had the genius. He was dependent on her for his very life (the escape from Europe) as well as for his livelihood. She was dependent on him only for his love. And he resented her material power over him.

To state that Max Ernst was a very complex personality is tantamount to stating, as if it were a revelation, that the universe is a very complex physical structure. The man was an artist of the first rank, but his personality was impossible, a mess of childish obsessions and contradictions which only the production of ten thousand all but indecipherable eruptions of his subconscious, represented as paintings, could possibly straighten out, if then.

Peggy herself was well aware of some of Max's deficiencies. In her autobiography she wrote: "Max, like all other babies, always wanted to be the center of attention. He tried to bring all conversations around to himself, no matter what they were about. . . . He loved beautiful clothes, and was jealous when I bought new dresses. . . . In his paintings he always portrayed himself in marvelous renaissance costumes . . .”

Max Ernst was one of seven sons of a strict, hardworking German teacher of the deaf and dumb. Born and raised in Cologne, he was, as a child, very imaginative and high-strung and in nearly constant rebellion against parental authority. Though he had displayed artistic gifts as a child, his father had tried to make him into a lawyer. But Max, by his own admission, “carefully avoided all forms of study that would degenerate into gainful employment.” Contrary to his father’s wishes, he took up painting and worked at it with an oedipal vengeance.

Once Max had mastered the fundamental techniques, and was developing something of a style of his own, he immediately identified with the avant-garde, becoming a leading figure in both the dada and surrealist movements. It had been Tristan Tzara who, in his “Dada Manifesto,” had set down the everlasting canon for dada: “Any work of art that can be understood is the product of a journalist.” The movement began with an infantile attack, in words and paint, on the past, on historic culture, as if everything that had been drawn, painted, or sculpted before the second decade of the twentieth century was utterly irrelevant. For impetuous young Max the past was his proper bourgeois teacher-of-deaf-and-dumb-children father. Kill it. Eliminate it altogether from sight. But then, once you eliminate the past, the bulk of human experience on this planet, what do you have left? What do you put down on canvas?

You don’t put down reality because all reality is inexorably linked with the past. So you put down dreams. You put down the *surreal*. After reading Freud, and beholding for the first time di Chirico’s “metaphysical vistas,” young Max knew just how he was going to express his dadaism. He was going to express it in the dreamlike imagery of surrealism. He was going to express it by executing paintings that bore absolutely no resemblance to anything ever seen, felt, or touched, in the past or present, on this earth before. That stolid, patient, teacher-of-the-deaf-and-dumb father of his had had to place actual lead pipes in the hands of his pupils to teach them what lead pipes were. Well, Max would put nothing in the hands of his audience they could possibly grasp, never mind name. It was more than *“épatez la bourgeoisie”*; it was confuse and baffle them completely.

By the 1930s Max Ernst had already become one of the two or three leading exponents of dadaism and surrealism in Europe. Eventually he would become the foremost surrealist in the world.

"Artists," Ezra Pound once observed, "are the antennae of the race, the voltmeters and steam-gauges of a nation's intellectual life."

Lewis Mumford said the same thing, in a bit more lumbering style, when he wrote: ". . . For it is first of all in the graphic and plastic arts, in literature, and in music, that distant tremors of the psyche are faintly recorded, as on a seismograph, often a whole century before they become visible and tangible."

Well, be it to Max Ernst's everlasting credit, that despite his mockery of the past, his silliness, his infantile rejection of all authority, he nevertheless did realize, as early as the late 1920s, that Germany and Europe were headed for disaster. His "Hordes," his "Europe After the Rain, I," his "Petrified City," his "Entire City," painted between 1927 and 1935, gave notice through their combination of emptiness, brutality, and monstrosity, of what was in store for his native Germany. By the mid-1930s Ernst had become an avowed enemy of Germany's Mad Angel of Destruction and Max was high on his enemy's list of Those To Be Eliminated.

Though Max was able to escape the war he had predicted for Europe, he was unable for some time to escape the war he had not predicted for Peggy's East River brownstone.

That war broke out as soon as the combatants took possession of the house. It was such an obviously bellicose situation, it is a wonder the quiveringly sensitive antennae of Ernst did not feel the storm clouds loading up with thunder in advance. Or maybe he did. We shall see that some of those seemingly indecipherable paintings of his might well have been forecasts of the War of East Fifty-first Street.

The weaponry. On Peggy's side: money (her unearned income, before taxes, oscillated during the early 1940s from $50,000 to $85,000 a year, depending on how much the government let her war babies—oh, that *copper!*—get away with); prestige: by now the Guggenheim name was synonymous in New York with money, power, class, and big art patronage. On Ernst's side: artistic genius of the first rank, a ferocious wit, an overheated, sometimes diabolical imagination, a secondary talent for irony, torture, revenge.

The circumstances. Peggy was a woman who desperately needed a man in her life. Why? Was it the early, sudden, *Titanic* deprivation of her father? She thinks so. As soon as one man set, not always in a warm glow, another *had* to rise up, in blazing radiance, over her horizon. She could not do without him, whoever he might be, whether he was Laurence Vail, or John Holms, or Marcel Duchamp, or Yves Tanguy, or Samuel Beckett, or Herbert Read, or the upper-middle-class communist, or Wrenclose-of-the-Chains, or the great Max Ernst. But it was always one man at a time, seldom two at once. Max, on the other hand, was a man who liked, or perhaps needed to have several women in love with him at the same time. His first marriage, to former schoolmate Louise Straus, which had given him his only child, Jimmy, had broken up because of this preference. Before his relationship with Peggy he had been juggling two mistresses at once, the painters Leonor Fini and Leonore Carrington. Also, as a rule, Max further complicated his love life by showing a decided preference for stupid, young, bitchy, vulgar girls over older (thirties, forties) women of intelligence, sophistication, and taste. So far as money was concerned, he simply did not have any. As soon as he sold a painting, he spent the proceeds. He could not possibly have lived the way he was living without Peggy. Without Peggy he would have been wearing suits bought in 1937 and living in one furnished room on East Eighth Street near Avenue B. No, much worse, perhaps. He might have been wearing striped overalls and living in Block VI, Buchenwald.

Peggy had received the warning signals even before she and Max left Europe. In her autobiography she wrote:

. . . as his painting was completely unconscious and came from some deep hidden source, nothing he ever did surprised me. At one time, when he was alone in France after Leonore had left, he painted her portrait over and over in all the landscapes he was soon to discover in America. I was jealous that he never painted me. In fact, it was a cause of great unhappiness to me and proof he did not love me.

Then, soon after the installation in the New York brownstone, the signals reappeared:

One day when I went into his studio I had a great shock. There on his easel was a little painting I had never seen before. In it was portrayed a strange figure with the head of a horse, which was Max's own head, and the body of a man dressed in shining armor. Facing this strange creature, and with her hand between his legs, was a portrait of me. Not of me as Max had ever known me, but of me as my face appeared as a child of eight. I have photographs of myself at this age and the likeness is unquestionable. I burst into tears the minute I recognized it and rushed to tell Max that he had at last painted my portrait. He was rather surprised, as he had never seen the photos.

This was only one-third of the painting, however. In the rest of it was "a figure which Max admitted to be Pegeen's back, and on the left-hand side was a terrifying sort of monster. It portrayed a woman in a red dress with her stomach exposed. This was undoubtedly my stomach, but the figure had two heads which resembled nobody. They were animal heads and one looked like a skeleton. Sidney Janis [an art dealer] claimed I was this monster, which he considered very strong." Because Peggy's hand was placed on Max's genitals, and because it was also portrayed between two spears, Peggy named the picture the "Mystic Marriage" and asked for it as a present, telling Max that "now he need never marry me, as this sufficed."

As it turned out, Max gave Peggy two presents, the painting *and* the marriage. The latter gift was bestowed, in 1941, impulsively, in a small town in Virginia against the advice of Sindbad, who told his mother Max was as vain as she was and "the whole thing wouldn't work." The merry couple had set off in a car with the vague intention of getting married, and had gone from state to state to state trying to meet the marriage qualifications. Turned down in New York, New Jersey, Delaware, and Maryland—a divorced alien German Catholic, during wartime, and a rich divorced New York Jewess, both without official residency in any state, were a bit much for local bureaucrats—they were finally able to meet the test in Virginia, thanks to cousin Harold Loeb, who was living there at the time and gave them "residency" in his house.

Marriage vows exchanged, it was right back again to war in the brownstone. Max refused to pay household expenses because Peggy was still supporting Laurence Vail, whom he detested. Thus, Peggy, much to her annoyance, was forced totally to support two men. As if this were not enough, Max refused to make love to her. A marriage *in bianco*, as the Italians say. Why, why, why? He wouldn't say. But he was not above disappearing occasionally with a cute little thing who caught his ever-vigilant eye. Once, when Peggy asked Max to inscribe some books of reproductions of his paintings, he merely wrote: "For Peggy Guggenheim From Max Ernst." This upset her because she remembered the loving words he had used in inscribing a book to Leonor Fini. "He always made me feel that he would have liked me much better if I had been young and vulgar. He admitted he liked stupid, vulgar girls."

So here was Peggy paying good Guggenheim money for a sexless marriage, and here was Max accepting the money and spending it on a bunch of little tramps.

Was there any wonder the "fights were awful and often lasted forty-eight hours, during which time we would not speak to each other?" These fights, Peggy admitted, "were about nothing of importance"—only he living totally off her and giving her no sex. "We fought if Max took my scissors without asking my permission. This annoyed me because they were the scissors John Holms had used to cut his beard. We fought if Max would not let me drive the car because he preferred to drive himself. We fought when he got bored because I had the flu and took too long to convalesce. We fought about the lay-out of my catalogue, after we had both worked peacefully on it together for hours. We fought most of all about his buying too many totem poles. It was all ridiculous and childish. The quarrels upset him terribly. He could not work, and wandered around New York for days. . . . The worst of it all was that we fought in public. We fought anywhere we happened to be."

As the marriage wore on, or rather wore out, things got worse and worse and worse. Leonore Carrington, Max's old flame, phoned repeatedly and Max would often take her to lunch. Normally he would wear old paint-spattered clothes around the house, but when he went out with Leonore he would dress up like a rooster. Sometimes he would spend the whole day with her, wandering around New York, something he never did with Peggy. "Max was so insane about Leonore," wrote Peggy, "that he really could not hide it. Once I made him bring her back to lunch and asked Djuna Barnes [the writer] to come and meet her. Djuna said it was the only time that Max seemed human, or showed any emotion. Normally he was as cold as a snake."

But Max was rarely content with just one extramarital affair. Soon "he became infatuated with a very wild and crazy young girl who was either perpetually drunk or under the effects of Benzedrine. She was very funny, quite pretty and full of life, but she was terribly American, and at the time he seemed to be nearly off his head. One could always tell if Max was excited about a woman: his eyes would nearly pop out of his head with desire, like Harpo Marx's."

Sometimes, to take revenge against these repeated humiliations, Peggy would go out on the town at night by herself for an anonymous evening "in search of adventure." New York is, of course, the ideal city for this sort of sport. You can go out to a place where nobody knows you and nobody you meet will ever see you again, and, using an assumed name, you can meet up with just about anything, from another sophisticated adventurer like yourself, to just another drunk stockbroker, to your murderer. One night, when Max never came back home, Peggy got high, rushed out of her brownstone and went to a bar on Third Avenue, where, posing as a "governess," she got mixed up with a table of men who took her money "for safekeeping," then took her to Chinatown to eat (on her money), then took her "home" to a dead-end street near the East River. Somehow Peggy got out alive, but without her money.

More scenes. More sorrows. The high bohemian soap opera of East Fifty-first Street careened toward its final smash-up. Peggy told Max that since she felt he did not desire her, he could have anyone else he wanted. But she found it impossible to "maintain this self-sacrificing attitude." One weekend in Southampton Max went off with the type he liked best, a "vulgar little bitch" also called Peggy, and it so completely spoiled Peggy G's weekend that she "would not talk to Max for days."

Whenever things became utterly impossible to bear, when her nerves were coming apart and she couldn't sleep without taking three or four pills, Peggy went to her ex-husband, Laurence Vail, who remained her best male friend and always managed to console her, if only by his mere presence. She did not make love with Vail anymore, but that somehow helped the relationship. It prevented them from being jealous of one another and fostered a spirit of compassion and understanding. (Later Peggy would confess that she always found husbands "much more satisfactory after marriage than during.") But with Max, for whom Peggy felt a wild sexual attraction, never requited, she was rarely compassionate or understanding. Sometimes she, Vail, and Max would find themselves together and Peggy would always complain about Max to Laurence in Max's presence, which, of course, made matters much worse.

Then, was Peggy Mrs. Max Ernst or Miss Peggy Guggenheim? She insisted on being called Peggy Guggenheim. Sometimes Max was ridiculed in public by being introduced as Mr. Peggy Guggenheim. No one ever called Peggy Mrs. Max Ernst.

It was now only a matter of weeks before Mr. and Mrs. Peggy Guggenheim would come asunder. Pegeen the Peacemaker tried over and over again to reconcile her mother and her stepfather, but it was to no avail. In the end, it took an art exhibit, entirely devised by Peggy, to precipitate the final break-up, which break-up, it must be emphasized, she never wanted because she sincerely loved Max Ernst.

Peggy had opened her avant-garde Art of This Century gallery on West Fifty-seventh Street, and—good women's liberationist that she was—had decided to hold a show there for thirty-one women painters. This proved to be her undoing.

For among the thirty-one painters was a lovely young married woman who was destined to turn Max inside out. Peggy had foolishly given Max the Womanizer the job of "going around to all the women, choosing their paintings, and carrying them off in the car to the gallery." As Peggy later wrote, "he adored this, as he loved women, and some of them were very attractive. . . . There was one called Dorothea Tinning. . . . She was pretentious, boring, stupid, vulgar, and dressed in the worst possible taste, but was quite talented and imitated Max's painting, which flattered him immensely. . . . She was so much on the make and pushed so hard, it was embarrassing."

One night Peggy opened a special delivery letter from Miss Tanning (her real name) addressed to Max. Enclosed was a piece of blue silk, which Dorothea claimed was her hair. It made Peggy "wild with jealousy." "After reading the letter I hit Max's face several times as hard as I could."

Now nasty event follows nasty event in rapid succession. Alexander Calder invites Mr. and Mrs. Peggy Guggenheim to a *bal musette* in a bistro on First Avenue, and Mr. Guggenheim insists on bringing Dorothea Tanning instead of his wife. The next day Peggy and Max go to a cocktail party and Miss Tanning arrives "unexpectedly" and goes right up to Max as if he were *hers*. Soon Max is living with Miss Tanning. But then, "a few days later, her husband came back from the navy on furlough and she and Max had to flee." "When Max came home I was nearly off my head and I told him I would commit suicide if he did not come back to me. . . . He then asked me if I would let him take Miss Tanning to Arizona, and come back to me afterwards. I nearly had a fit."

For a while Peggy could not sleep at night without massive doses of drugs. Max continued to paint every day in his studio in Peggy's house, then would dress up and go out with Dorothea Tanning. When Max would take Peggy out he would tell her all about the "gay life he led" with Miss Tanning. Once Peggy went to an opening at Julien Levy's gallery where she saw Miss Tanning "with her hair dyed turquoise . . . Inserted in her blouse, which was specially cut for this purpose, were little photographs of Max. . . . This really was too much for me. I was so disgusted that I decided I had had enough of the whole affair . . . and decided to put an end to it."

The end came upon the unexpected arrival of a new man in Peggy's life, an independently wealthy (her first of this genre) British writer by the name of Kenneth McPherson. After a "wild evening" with Kenneth, Peggy phoned Max at Dorothea Tanning's "asking him to find himself a studio and not come to the house anymore." That was it. Suddenly the War of East Fifty-first Street was over, and there was peace.

Years later, Max's son, Jimmy, received word that he had won a Guggenheim Fellowship. "What's that?" asked Max. After Jimmy explained, Max said pensively, "Oh, really? I had a Guggenheim once, but that was no Fellowship."

After their respective divorces, Max married Dorothea Tanning and remained married to her until his death in 1976 at the age of eighty-six.

Under the steadying and, at the same time, enriching influence of Dorothea, Max Ernst went on to one of the most creative periods of his life, one which culminated in the vast retrospective exhibition of his works held at the Solomon R. Guggenheim Museum in 1975, under the auspices of Solomon's grandson, Peter O. Lawson-Johnston.

For Peggy, the end of the war with Max meant not so much beginning with Kenneth McPherson, who turned out to be predominantly homosexual and eventually fell in love with one of Peggy's male houseguests, but going back to the gallery. Yes, it had been a long and bitter fight. But she had never let the battle deflect her from what she now believed was her primary mission in life, to bring the best in contemporary painting and sculpture to the attention of, if not the world, at least *le Monde,* the dimensions of which she knew so well. Though she was repeatedly discouraged, outraged, humiliated by Max's conduct (much of it, she admitted, brought on by her conduct toward him), she still persevered in her work, and that, after all, was the important thing, wasn't it?

Yes, it certainly was. No, it wasn't: She loved Max more than her work. Yes, it was; her work was much more important than just Max. No, it wasn't. Yes, it was . . . but . . . yet . . . if . . . it was hard for her to resolve the thing in her heart. After all, she was a woman. What means more to a woman, a real woman, her work, or her man? Her man, of course, but if you can't have him, work will just have to suffice. Peggy was ahead of the times.

On with the work.

The work was Art of This Century, a top floor on West Fifty-seventh Street between Fifth and Sixth avenues (only three blocks from the Bauer House), which Peggy's ambition and money, and a few people of extraordinary talent, had transformed into the most original art gallery on earth. The most formidable of the talents was the architect Frederick Kiesler. It was he who created a gallery which, in a matter of weeks, became the most discussed theater, for that is what it really was, of painting and sculpture in the Western world. The only condition Peggy imposed on him was that "the pictures should be unframed." Otherwise Kiesler could do what he liked.

What Kiesler liked was curved walls made of South American gumwood; paintings, unframed, as per instructions, mounted on movable baseball bats; spotlights on each painting, which went on and off in unison at planned intervals; two walls consisting of "an ultramarine canvas curtain like a circus tent"; a floor painted turquoise; some paintings hung on strings from the ceiling, at right angles to the walls, "looking as if they were floating in space"; a revolving wheel to show seven works of Klee without the viewer having to budge from one spot; another wheel, which could be turned by the viewer to behold the entire opus of Marcel Duchamp; little triangular shelves of wood supporting the sculptures "which seemed to float in the air." By comparison, Uncle Sol and "Aunt" Hilla's place, three blocks down, with its pretensions to being the most avant of the avant-garde, was the Vatican Museum.

What an opening it had been! *Tout le Monde*—that international village Peggy had lived in for over twenty years—was no longer in Nazi-occupied Paris, but was in New York, and *tout le Monde* came. A few of the Great Unwashed were also invited. Some came. Some did not. Hilla Rebay, though invited (to please Uncle Sol), did not come, but other Guggenheims showed up: Uncle Sol, Aunt Irene, Aunt Olga, Cousin Harry, Cousin Harold, Cousin Gladys. Peggy wore a white dress especially made for the occasion, and wore one Tanguy earring and one made by Calder, in order to show her "impartiality between Surrealist and Abstract Art." The press came in force and gave the show what Peggy termed "overwhelming" publicity. In a matter of forty-eight hours Art of This Century had easily replaced Uncle Sol's establishment as the capital of the New York avant-garde.

After the ill-fated show for thirty female painters, plus Dorothea Tanning—the show that Peggy says convinced her to renounce feminist altruism forever—Peggy organized a "spring salon" for young American artists. It was kind of a contest to pick out the most promising young talent in America at the time. The judges were a mix of tried-and-true museum types—Alfred Barr, James Johnson Sweeney, James Thrall Soby; one Real Live Artist—Piet Mondrian; and two patrons—Peggy Guggenheim and her gallery assistant, Howard Putzel.

It was from this "salon," or show, or horse race, or whatever you want to call it, that three of the great luminaries of American art of this century emerged: Jackson Pollock, Robert Motherwell, and William Baziotes, each of whom received nearly unanimous praise from the jury.

Soon after this event, Art of This Century became *the* center for all avant-garde American painters and sculptors in New York, almost a club. These eager young people, luckily but a sable-hair's breadth too old to be dragged into the European and Pacific slaughters, had been profoundly influenced by such European abstract and surrealist painters as Max Ernst, Marcel Duchamp, and André Breton, all of whom, with help from Peggy Guggenheim, had taken refuge from the European slaughter in New York. Under this influence these young Americans unwittingly started an entirely new school of painting, which Robert Coates, art critic of *The New Yorker*, called, and thus baptized for all time, "abstract expressionism." It was, most certainly, a typically American art. Immediate. Discordant. Unharmonious. Experimental. Often sensational. "Stripped," as Max Ernst once put it, "of all the dreadful baggage of history."

What happened next to Art of This Century, after Pollock, Motherwell, and Baziotes, was something of an anticlimax. For the record, Peggy discovered and gave first one-man shows to Hans Hofmann, Clyfford Still, Mark Rothko, and Adolph Gottlieb. And she also held one-man shows for such old-timers as di Chirico, Arp, Giacometti, Morris Hirschfield, and, not forgetting her own, Laurence Vail and daughter Pegeen, who had decided to follow more in her father's footsteps than her mother's and become not just a collector but a painter in her own right.

But what was all this compared to *the* great discovery of the spring salon? In Peggy's words: "it soon became evident that Pollock was the best painter," and by this she meant not just the best painter in the salon but the best in the United States.

Which comes first, the patron or the painter? In the case of Peggy and Pollock it is anyone's guess. It was, in the end, just one of those happy, infrequent coincidences.

Pollock was an unknown, poor, down-and-out carpenter who worked in her uncle Sol's museum on East Fifty-fourth Street, and painted on the side. Some of his stuff was shown to the boss's niece and her assistant, Howard Putzel, before the first spring salon. They liked it and put some of it in the salon. Then a few key people in *le Monde* praised it. All of a sudden the unknown was noticed.

No, far more than just noticed. After his first one-man show at Peggy's place Pollock was virtually canonized. Alfred Barr purchased one of his works—"The She Wolf"—for the Museum of Modern Art; Motherwell wrote a most enthusiastic piece on him for *Partisan Review*; Sweeney wrote a most complimentary piece on him for the official catalogue of Peggy's collection. Then, after Pollock's next show at Art of This Century, Clement Greenberg in *The Nation* sang: "Jackson Pollock's second one-man show establishes him, in my opinion, as the strongest painter of his generation, and perhaps the greatest one to appear since Miró."

As for Peggy, she was soon entirely swept up and away by Pollock. In her autobiography she wrote: "From 1943 to 1947, when I decided to return to Europe, I dedicated myself wholly to Pollock. . . . I welcomed a new protégé, as I had lost Max."

Dedicating herself wholly to Pollock meant first signing a contract with him awarding the young man a salary of $150 a month against sales. If $2,700 gross sales of paintings was not realized in a year, she was to get a certain number of canvases "free" to make up the difference.

And so Pollock gave up his carpenter's job at Uncle Sol's museum and went to work full time as a painter, turning over each completed canvas to Art of This Century. He and his wife, the painter Lee Krassner, lived and worked in a walk-up on East Eighth Street. There were not many sales, so Peggy, as per her contract, picked up a lot of early Pollocks for practically nothing.

Well, not for nothing really. Pollock was a strange, violent man and dealing with him was never easy. Once he and Peggy "tried to make love," and "when it didn't work," he got so mad he went into a rage and "threw his drawers out the window." Often he would insult his patron, then burst into tears.

Born on a sheep ranch in Cody, Wyoming, Pollock was used to open space and felt, in Peggy's words, "like a trapped animal" in New York. Once he had spent six months under psychiatric care in a mental institution. He was also a confirmed alcoholic. Periodically he would go on wild, self-destructive binges that would leave him impotent and exhausted. The artist may have been a genius, but the man was a mess. The artist made things that had never been made before. The man was many things men had been before. The artist was original. The man was not. The man was violent, exasperating, crude, brutal, boorish, and weak, characteristics only too common among American men of his social class. No wonder his art was so typically American: immediate, unhistorical, violent, sensational, strident, rough, brutal, and often silly. Someone once described Pollock's work as expressing "urban life in America: the lonely jungle of immediate sensations." And that description fits very well. This is not to deny the artist his genius. Pollock's best canvases erupt with an energy rarely, if ever, before seen in paint. Sweeney put it about as well as anyone: "Pollock's talent is volcanic. It has fire. It is unpredictable. It is undisciplined. Lavish. Explosive. Untidy."

"Unpredictable. Undisciplined. Untidy." So also in life.

Not long after Peggy awarded Pollock his $150-a-month contract, she commissioned him to paint a vast mural for the entrance hall to her East River brownstone. The work was to be twenty-three feet wide and six feet high. Marcel Duchamp suggested that it be put on a canvas, otherwise it would have to be abandoned when Peggy left her house, and the suggestion was accepted by both painter and patron. Pollock, delighted with his first big commission, then found a huge canvas and demolished a wall in his Eighth Street apartment in order to hang it up. Once it was in place, he stood before it, uninspired for days on end, unable to begin, getting more and more depressed. After a while he sent his wife away to the country, hoping some new ideas would come to him in her absence. When she came back she found him still standing in front of the vast blank space frowning and stomping his feet like a bull. Then, suddenly one day, months after he first received the commission, he attacked the canvas and finished it in only six hours, producing a now-acknowledged masterpiece of its genre, a flaming, pulsating dance of abstract figures in blue and white and yellow, over which he had dripped black housepaint directly from the can.

Once the enormous Thing, which he called simply "Mural 1943" was put in its destined place, Pollock, in Peggy's words, "got so drunk that he undressed and walked quite naked into a party Jean Connolly, who was living with me, was giving in the sitting room. Then he peed in the fireplace."

This was the unpredictable, untidy, undisciplined Jackson's first public pissing in a fireplace. Other similar untidinesses would follow. Several years later he peed in the fireplace of fellow artist Jan Muller's studio. Later, one winter in East Hampton, while taking a walk with some friends, he stopped and urinated in the snow, playing his stream back and forth in a 180-degree arc, and remarking, "I can piss on the whole world."

Pissing on the whole world. Spilling black housepaint direct from the can. Spilling it over all art that came before him, over all history that came before him. Pissing in fireplaces, smashing cars, picking fights in bars, insulting friends, getting drunk: These were some of the experiences or states of the soul that Jackson Pollock transferred into paint. The same experiences that were to lead him to his final experience: killing himself and a young girl who was with him in a drunken automobile accident near Springs, on eastern Long Island, in 1956, in his forty-fourth year.

Pollock's influence on the generation of painters who followed him was not very healthy, but it certainly was enormous.

"My painting does not come from the easel," he had written in 1947. "I hardly ever stretch my canvas before painting. I prefer to tack the unstretched canvas to the hard wall or the floor. . . . On the floor I am more at ease. I feel nearer, more a part of the painting, since this way I can walk around it . . . and literally be *in* the painting . . .

"I continue to get further away from the usual painters' tools such as easel, palette, brushes, etc. I prefer sticks, trowels, knives and dripping fluid paint, or a heavy impasto with sand, broken glass and other foreign matter added."

How many second-, third-, and fourth-rate Pollocks have we seen make hashes from these preferences?

For all his untidiness, unpredictability, brutality, alcoholic self-destructiveness, Peggy Guggenheim stuck by Jackson Pollock to the end . . . and beyond. He was, all alternatives considered, her most enduring discovery. Snubbed by her uncle Sol and "aunt" Hilla, turned down for a Guggenheim fellowship (as were all the other abstract expressionists), Pollock never really had any other patron in New York but Peggy Guggenheim. She and only she believed in him from the very beginning and remained faithful to him, often in the face of much opposition, to the very end.

A last show for Pollock at Art of This Century, and Peggy was ready to return to Europe. One by one they were all drifting back: Max Ernst and Dorothea Tanning, André Breton, Marcel Duchamp, Laurence Vail, and Pegeen Vail, now Mrs. Jean Helion. "Much as I loved Art of This Century," Peggy wrote, "I loved Europe more than America, and when the war ended I could not wait to go back. . . . I was also exhausted by all the work in the gallery, where I had become sort of a slave . . ."

Before leaving she lent Jackson and Lee Pollock money to buy a house in Springs, near East Hampton. While she was phasing out Art of This Century, not one gallery in New York would take over her contract with Pollock, despite the reputation Jackson had acquired under her aegis. And so, in accordance with her contract with the painter, all unsold Pollocks (she kept her gallery open on a reduced scale) were shipped to her in Venice where she had gone to live. In New York she had never sold a Pollock for more than one thousand dollars. In postwar Venice she could not get half a lira for one. So she unloaded her surplus "one by one, to various museums," giving Lee Krassner "one painting a year 'free.'" In her *Confessions of an Art Addict*, Peggy was to lament that she now had "only two of his best production left." "And so now Lee is a millionaire, and I think what a fool I was."

By the time Peggy returned to Europe she had played a major role, without really knowing it, in spawning the so-called New York School, the abstract expressionists of the 1940s, 1950s, and early 1960s. It is still far too early to evaluate that school in the perspective of art history. However, if artists are, in Ezra Pound's phrase, "the antennae of the race," then we can at least say that the antennae of the likes of Motherwell, Rothko, Gottlieb, Baziotes, and Pollock were most sensitive to their immediate environment in the late 1940s. Thirty years later all the symptoms of sickness they had sensed and expressed in paint became reality in New York.

Just before returning to her favored Europe, Peggy Guggenheim wrote and had published (by Dial Press) her autobiography under the title *Out of This Century*. She was the fourth Guggenheim, after Uncle Will, Cousin Harry, and Cousin Harold Loeb, to break into print.

The book, a most candid work, sparing no one, least of all herself and her first husband, Laurence Vail, who helped edit it, scandalized the other Guggenheims so much they dubbed it "Out of Her Mind" and immediately sent hordes of messengers and clerks out to the major

New York bookstores with orders to buy up every available copy. Thus, in no time, the book was entirely sold out. A second printing appeared. Again the Guggenheim minions descended on the book-stores of Manhattan. In the end the only people who got a look at the book were Peggy's friends, who, we know, were *tout le Monde*; people who bought it in Yonkers, the Bronx, Kansas City, and Tulsa; the gentle ladies who borrow from their local library; and the critics, who almost unanimously condemned the work on the moralistic grounds that it was disgraceful for Peggy to have been so unhypo-critical about herself, her friends, associates, and members of *her own family* as to write the truth about them, a judgment echoed by many of the people described in the book, especially Dorothea Tanning, who claimed the book held her up to scorn for revealing that she had abandoned an American naval officer during wartime while he was fighting for the good old U.S.A., to marry that foreigner Max Ernst.

Fourteen years later Peggy brought out a slightly expurgated and updated edition entitled *Confessions of an Art Addict*, published by Macmillan, which proved acceptable to the family, who let the title stand and kept the clerks and messengers at their desks at Guggen-heim Brothers and American Smelting and Refining doing what they should be doing, tending to the figures below the bottom line.

Actually they could not have done otherwise, the family, no matter how they might have felt about the new book, because by 1960 Peggy had turned the tables and had become the best-known Guggenheim of them all.

CHAPTER

7

HAROLD LOEB:
The Way It Was

Robert Cohn was once middleweight boxing champion of Princeton. Do not think that I am very much impressed by that as a boxing title, but it meant a lot to Cohn.

He cared nothing for boxing, in fact he disliked it, but he learned it painfully and thoroughly to counteract the feeling of inferiority and shyness he had felt on being treated as a Jew at Princeton. . . .

I never met any one of his class who remembered him. They did not even remember that he was middleweight boxing champion. . . .

Robert Cohn was a member, through his father, of one of the richest Jewish families in New York, and through his mother of one of the oldest. . . .

He wrote a novel, and it was not really such a bad novel as the critics later called it, although it was a very poor novel. . . .

He had a hard, Jewish, stubborn streak. . . .

I saw Cohn coming across the square.
  "Here he comes."
  "Well, let him not get superior and Jewish."

[Bill]: "Haven't you got some more Jewish friends you could bring along?"
[Jake]: "You've got some fine ones yourself."
[Bill]: "Oh yes. I've got some darbs. But not alongside of this Robert Cohn. The funny thing is he's nice, too. I like him. But he's just so awful."

"That Cohn gets me," Bill said. "He's got this Jewish superiority so strong that he thinks the only emotion he'll get out of the fight will be being bored."

[Mike]: "No, listen, Jake. Brett's gone off with men. But they weren't ever Jews, and they didn't come and hang about afterward."

"Does Cohn look bored?" I asked.
"That kike."

"I'm not one of you literary chaps." Mike stood shakily and leaned against the table. "I'm not clever. But I do know when I'm not wanted. Why don't you see when you're not wanted, Cohn? Go away. Go away, for God's sake. Take that sad Jewish face away. Don't you think I'm right?"

[Brett]: "Oh, darling, don't be difficult. What do you think it's meant to have that damned Jew about, and Mike the way he's acted?"

[Mike]: "I gave Brett what for, you know. I said if she would go about with Jews and bull-fighters and such people, she must expect trouble.

"You know," Mike went on, "Brett was rather good. I gave her a fearful hiding about Jews and bull-fighters, and all those sort of people. . . ."

[Mike]: "She had a Jew named Cohn, but he turned out badly."

The writer of this peevish, often adolescent, characterization was Ernest Hemingway in his first novel, *The Sun Also Rises,* and the butt of his peevishness, "Robert Cohn," was a Guggenheim— Harold Loeb, Rose Guggenheim's son, first cousin to Harry and Peggy, writer, social and economic thinker, inventor of the expression "technocracy."

By a curious destiny the life of the most famous American novelist of the twentieth century became closely intertwined with that of a son of America's most influential Jewish family of the twentieth century. It was a bad relationship and it haunted both men right down to their deaths.

Harold Loeb was the first professional writer and thinker the Guggenheim family produced and the first male in the family to make a radical break from the Guggenheim ethos and style.

The Guggenheim ethos, like that of the family's adopted country, was Darwinian, in some respects Nietzschean. "Heroic Materialism," "Heroic Vitalism," "Survival of the Fittest," "Will to Power" are expressions that come as close as any to describing the Guggenheim aura and ideology.

Harold Loeb, however, was a contemplative, a man more concerned with knowing and being than doing. During his long, varied, and productive life he never sought to accumulate riches or material power, he sought only to understand.

He felt different from his Guggenheim cousins from the very beginning. Reminiscing about his childhood in his autobiographical *The Way It Was,* he wrote: "Such an environment, in which no material desire need go unsatisfied, and with nearly a dozen grownups who seemed to exist solely to cater to a child's whims, often gives him a certain assurance—the rich man's assurance—and a feel of superiority. My cousins Harry and Edmond were not without it. Yet it passed me by completely . . ."

Later, while in college at Princeton, young Harold took a firm ideological stand against the Guggenheims and everything they stood for.

One of Harold's closest friends at Princeton was another member of the Crowd, Roger W. Straus, son of Oscar Straus, former cabinet member and U.S. ambassador to Turkey, and husband-to-be of Gladys Guggenheim, Dan's daughter.

The Ballinger-Pinchot environmental controversy over the use and abuse of America's natural resources was very much in the news at the time and both Roger and Harold were ardent supporters of Pinchot, the conservationist.

One afternoon while Roger and Harold were strolling along the road from Princeton to Lawrenceville, Roger was "talking about Pinchot's valiant crusade against the despoilers" when suddenly he stopped and stood looking at Harold. "Did you know," he asked, with great intensity, "that the Guggenheims are trying to steal Alaska?"

Harold did not know.

> Conditioned to hear the worst about the family, I merely shrugged my shoulders. After a sidelong glance to see how I was reacting, Roger continued walking and talking. He told me that my uncles were building a railroad to bring coal and ore out of their Kennecott mine. And at the same time they were trying to gobble up all the other Alaskan resources: mines, forest, fisheries . . . Pinchot was against it, Roger was against it, I decided I was against it too.

(Some years later Harold Loeb—now married, and the father of two young children—accepted a job at the Selby smelter in Tacoma, which was refining Alaskan copper ore, from his uncle Simon, former senator from Colorado, and then president of the Guggenheim-founded American Smelting and Refining Company; and still later Roger Straus—now married to a Guggenheim, and the father of three children—succeeded his uncle-in-law as president of American Smelting and Refining. The ideals of youth have a way of bending before adult necessities.)

Yes, it was not easy for Harold to be a Guggenheim. Since his mother was one of the poorest members of the family (Meyer had left her only $500,000), and his father was only comfortably well-off, not really rich, he had to grow into manhood seeing all his first cousins—Harry, Robert, Edmond, Gladys, Lucille, Barbara, Eleanor, among the many—become multimillionaires through inheritance, while he had to rely on his wits, occasional scraps from his father and mother's table while they were alive, a relatively meager inheritance after their deaths, to make ends meet.

It was, in a sense, far easier for Harold to be a Loeb. The Loebs were a talented, cultivated, if unspectacular, clan. Harold's grandfather, Marcus Loeb, was the brother of Solomon Loeb, one of the founders of Kuhn, Loeb & Company, investment bankers, and the father of James Loeb, sponsor of the Loeb Classical Library. The Loebs, a family that originated in the Rhineland, were intelligent; they had taste; and, unlike Harold's Guggenheim uncles, they were interested in more than mere moneymaking. (Harold described his Guggenheim uncles, before they had established their great foundations, as "seven copper magnates whose standard of living never seemed to catch up with their rising incomes.")

Easier to be a Loeb. As it turned out, Harold's flirtation with the Selby plant of American Smelting and Refining did not last more than two years. After an interlude in the army he bought a partnership in the Sunwise Turn bookshop on Thirty-eighth Street near Fifth Avenue "in order to familiarize myself with writers and writing." But his reason for not returning to the Guggenheim business went deeper than merely wishing such familiarization. "I wanted to make a complete break with my world," he wrote in *The Way It Was*. "I did not want to go back to business and devote my life to making money. I wanted to throw in my lot with such writers, painters, sculptors, poets, dancers, harpists, and crackpots as Mary Mowbray Clarke [an art historian who held sort of a salon in New York] had gathered about her."

But first, before he could become a full-fledged dropout, he had to clear the matter with his uncle Simon, who expected him back on the firing line at American Smelting and Refining.

He listened attentively as I told him about the bookshop, leaning back in his swivel chair and emitting from time to time an affirmative monosyllable which, somewhat surprisingly, he pronounced "Ya." [That was the Germanic syllable Meyer always emitted.] I spoke of my love of books, my abhorrence of smelters. I tried to convey my appreciation of his kindness. "You," I said, "you of the older generation have made it possible for us to do what we want to do."

"Ya," said Uncle Simon.

"It isn't that I'm lazy. One of my troubles at Selby was that I couldn't always find enough to do. It may be a defect of my character, but sometimes I felt I was not earning my pay."

"Ya," said the president of the American Smelting and Refining Company.

"Someday," I said, "I want to write. The bookshop is a step toward it. Would you mind if I did not go back to Selby?"

"No," said the ex-senator from Colorado, and dismissed me without making me feel ungrateful. Yet he must have wondered about my decision. He, his father and brothers had dedicated their lives to raising their family to financial heights, but I, one of the potential beneficiaries, chose to step down and play on a side street with a small bookshop. Doubtless he thought that a soft upbringing had weakened the moral fiber of his sister's child.

Harold ran The Sunwise Turn, employing his cousin Peggy Guggenheim as a clerk for two years, then sold his partnership in the store and with the proceeds started an international magazine of the arts called *Broom*, with offices in Rome. In its brief (1921–24) but extremely influential existence, *Broom* published the early work of such writers as Malcolm Cowley, Matthew Josephson, Ilya Ehrenburg, Hart Crane, Marianne Moore, Gertrude Stein, Sherwood Anderson, Conrad Aiken, John Dos Passos, William Carlos Williams, e. e. cummings, Louis Aragon, Amy Lowell, Wallace Stevens, Edgar Lee Masters, and Virginia Woolf, long before most of them were known to the American public.

Broom was also a pioneer in introducing School of Paris artists to Americans by reproducing works of Pablo Picasso, Henri Matisse, Fernand Léger, Paul Klee, George Grosz, and Wassily Kandinsky, also largely unknown at the time.

But the magazine soon ran into financial troubles and Loeb was compelled to turn to the Guggenheim uncles against whom he had once so self-consciously rebelled. At the eleventh hour, when the magazine was threatened with bankruptcy, Murry Guggenheim came through with $8,650, which assured *Broom* of at least one more year's existence.

Later, when the magazine was in even graver financial troubles Harold appealed to Uncle Simon. It was a risky move, considering that Simon had given Harold a high-paying job and unlimited opportunity, and Harold had turned it all down. In response to Harold's appeal for funds Simon write:

Dear Harold,

The day before you sailed I telephoned your mother and found that you were sailing the next day for Europe. I have since discussed with all your uncles the question of the endowment fund you wished for *Broom*, and I am reluctantly obliged to inform you we decided we would not care to make you any advances whatsoever. Our feeling is that *Broom* is essentially a magazine for a rich man with a hobby. I had some friends in the publishing business investigate the future prospects of *Broom*, and we are convinced that it would take a great many years before it could be put on a profitable basis, and even then the profit would not be a very large one, which you also explained to me.

Therefore, after taking all the circumstances into consideration, we have come to the conclusion we would not be helping you by financing you. I am sorry you are not in an enterprise that would show a profit at an earlier date, one more apt to be a financial success and one commensurate with your ability.

Trusting you had a pleasant trip across, believe me to be, as always, your affectionate uncle,

S. GUGGENHEIM

Harold wrote back:

From what little I know of your early career, it seems to me that you have more than once chosen the daring and visionary to the safety-first alternative, and that for you the visionary was often more commensurate with your ability than the enterprise "that would show a profit at an earlier date." And why not for me? Affectionately, Harold.

Harold did not receive a reply.

Years later Harold was to observe ironically that Uncle Simon set up "a foundation to assist aspiring writers, painters, scientists, over their difficult years" and that Uncle Solomon set up a foundation and museum that "featured Kandinsky, Klee, Grosz, and other artists who had first been published in America by *Broom*."

After *Broom* folded, Harold went to Paris, met Hemingway, and settled down to writing his first novel, *Doodab*.

How Harold Loeb came to write—a curiously self-conscious process, apparently not stemming from any vital inner compulsion, as is usually the case with most writers—is set down very clearly in *The Way It Was*:

> I suspect the real reason I did not go back [to America] was that I wanted to continue living and working with writers. Despite their vanity, their humbleness, their compensatory egoism, their volatility, their meanness, and their ridiculous generosity, they were in my opinion the only people fit to associate with. You could actually listen to them talk.
>
> For writers lived with an inner censor whose duty was to scrutinize thought and expression. Was it true or was it false? Was it singular or was it platitudinous? Was it original or was it repetitious? Was it of interest? Was it moving?
>
> This interminable questioning, the very essence of preparing your thought for presentation, affected their speech. A writer could not leave his worktable, workroom, bed, or tub, where every word was scrutinized, and become, of a sudden a careless word stringer. Consequently writers usually were worth listening to. Even the taciturn and slightly tongue-tied came out with thoughts that illuminated—at long intervals perhaps—but you did not have to listen to froth in between. And the bubbling, seething writers like Tom Wolfe threw bushels of ideas and images into the air and kept them floating there like stars from Roman candles. It was to be expected then that writers were the most satisfactory people to associate with.
>
> So I wanted to become a writer.

And so, very self-consciously, Harold became a writer, producing three not particularly well-received novels in a row, *Doodab, Professors Like Vodka,* and *Tumbling Mustard,* all published by Horace Liveright. A writer . . . and a rebel. By turning his back on the so-called American Dream of making the biggest pile of money one could possibly make, he had rebelled against everything his grandfather Meyer had stood for. Yet, at the same time, by a curious set of circumstances, his rebellion had something in common with Meyer's.

Meyer and his father had rebelled against the restraints of the Lengnau ghetto. But by the time grandson Harold had come of age the Guggenheims had created another ghetto in America, a ghetto of bourgeois respectability and great wealth, which, in many ways, was just as confining as the ghetto they had left behind in Europe. (Had not Meyer's father left Lengnau because the authorities there would not let him marry the woman he loved? Then, sixty years later, had not Dan forced brother William to divorce the woman he loved because she was not respectable, rich, and Jewish?)

Admittedly, Harold's rebellion was cushioned to a certain extent by some of grandfather Meyer's money (mother Rose gave her son a small monthly allowance and donated chunks of capital to him from time to time). Still, for a Guggenheim to be writing novels and palling around with the likes of F. Scott Fitzgerald and Ernest Hemingway in the high bohemia expatriate Paris of the roaring mid-1920s was indeed a rebellion of sorts, one had to admit.

It was also an ideological rebellion, as well as one of style, conduct, activity. While he published and edited *Broom,* Harold wrote two essays for his review—"Foreign Exchange" and "The Mysticism of Money"—which pretty well set forth his daring (for his time) philosophy.

A few excerpts will convey how unconventional his thought was, considering the milieu in which he was brought up:

From "Foreign Exchange":

> Another settlement of pilgrims [the expatriate artists] is finding its voice, for, like the Mayflower excursionists, they have crossed the ocean to escape economic oppression and spiritual coercion.
>
> The nation of their birth pays the highest rates known to man for certain special qualities. Bankers and promoters are so exuberantly rewarded that great industries are founded with the sole purpose of helping them disburse their annual accretion.
>
> But the talents of some men cannot or will not serve. Unfortunately the artist-pioneer usually belongs to this class. Thus we find men of the greatest importance to the cultural progress of America faced with the dilemma of deadening hackwork or flight.
>
> America, sweet land of liberty, has, by a curious inversion, become despotic. Originally the theory of democracy, of control by the majority, was planned to protect the rights of individuals, to act as a check against the encroachment of tyrannies of all kinds.
>
> The result of the extension of majority rule has been one curtailment of liberty after another. . . . In New York State, for instance, the license to teach is refused to any one who advocates "a form of government other than the government of the United States or of this State." As *The New Republic* points out, this would have prevented Woodrow Wilson from teaching, as he once recommended a Cabinet Government for the United States.

The legal restraints of this character dally far behind the social pressures. Breathing space can be found in a few scattered oases, but many find emigration to Paris more congenial.

From "The Mysticism of Money":

"The prerequisite of all living things and of their lives is: that there should be a large amount of faith, that it should be possible to pass definite judgments on things, and that there should be no doubt at all concerning values. Thus it is necessary that something should be assumed to be true, not that it is true" [Nietzsche]. This need has been satisfied in the past by what is termed religion. It is filled today in America by the *Mysticism of Money.*

Money, because that which was originally but a medium of exchange and a valuable metal, has become the measuring staff of all values and the goal and reward of all efforts conventionally accepted as proper.

Mystic because the validity of the money standard and the intrinsic merit of money making are accepted on faith, extra-intellectually. One does not question them; the rash interlocutor who seeks to know why the banker continues to augment his unspendable wealth is catalogued as slightly touched.

The result is that money and business—the making of money—have assumed a sacrosanct character.

Curiosity on making an acquaintance has shifted from interest in who were his forbears, or to what sect does he belong, to how much money does he earn, and how does he make a living.

Capitalism originated in Europe, perhaps in ancient Rome, but the American Colonies, which waged one of the first modern business wars, "no taxation without representation," have carried this form of civilization to its logical extreme as they were not hindered by vestiges of an older order. The differentiation between business in America and business elsewhere is that in America it is an end, a good in itself; its pursuit, the virtuous life. In Europe it is a means. . . . The fundamental rule of conduct for the devout is *Competitive Ostentation* [Harold, as a Guggenheim, knew what this was all about]. . . . They sometimes distribute lavishly to charities—with great élan and publicity it is true, for the motive-impulse is *Competitive Ostentation* rather than the good of the beneficiary. . . .

The deity of the Mysticism of Money is the most cruel of recent religions. He enforces a system of slavery, but unlike most ancient systems, the slaves are only cared for when their work is needed. When their services can be dispensed with, they are left to starve and perish as best they may.

It was the highly educated author of these lines, which perhaps

only a disaffected Guggenheim could have written, who met and be-
friended the relatively uneducated and unpublished Ernest Hemingway in the Paris of 1924.

Loeb and Hemingway liked each other . . . at first. They played
tennis together. They boxed. They sat around cafés together. They
talked about writing. They had the same circle of friends. They were
both athletes as well as aspiring authors. (Loeb, like Hemingway,
was tall, lean, and muscular; leaner, though, than Hemingway.) They
decided to go together to the fiesta in Pamplona.

And yet in *The Sun Also Rises*, a fictionalization of the goings-on
at Pamplona, Hemingway chose to betray their friendship with a de-
ceitful, backhanded attack that, in Loeb's words, "hit like an uppercut."

Why?

"What led my friend," asked Loeb, "to transform me into an in-
sensitive, patronizing, uncontrolled drag?"

The reasons were complex, but Harold eventually got to the bottom
of them and aired his interpretations in a number of magazine articles,
interviews, and also in *The Way It Was*, interpretations that have
since been corroborated in much Hemingway biography.

The crux of the situation lay in the fact that Harold Loeb, the
rich-kid Princetonian Jew, successfully out-Hemingwayed Hemingway, and Hemingway, the small-town, uneducated, chest-thumping
supermale egotist, couldn't take it. To get back at Loeb for being
everything he, Hemingway, wanted to be, but wasn't, he smeared his
friend in his first novel. But, of course, the reasons for desiring this
revenge, which turned out to be a genuine *schadenfreude*, went
deeper, and involved fundamental flaws in Hemingway's personality.

What was Harold Loeb that Hemingway wasn't?

For one, Harold came from a much richer family, from *two* much
richer families, in fact.

Second, as a Princeton graduate he had had a superior formal
education (Hemingway never went to college).

Third, he was a better athlete, regularly beating Hemingway at
both tennis and boxing.

Fourth, he was, at the time, a much more successful writer. Hemingway had published nothing yet but newspaper articles and a few
short stories in obscure little reviews. Loeb had edited a major literary
review, published numerous essays, and had recently published his
first novel, *Doodab*, the novel Hemingway referred to in *The Sun Also
Rises* as "a very poor novel." Furthermore, Loeb was trying (unsuc-

cessfully) to get Hemingway's first major literary efforts, *The Torrents of Spring* and *In Our Time,* published in New York.

Fifth, Loeb was usually more successful with women than Hemingway, at least with one very special woman, Lady Duff Twysden, the Lady Brett Ashley of *The Sun Also Rises,* with whom Loeb had had an affair, to the outrage of Hemingway, who had wanted to have one with her himself and so far hadn't succeeded.

Sixth, and this had really killed Hemingway, Loeb proved to be a much more courageous and nimble amateur bullfighter at the fiesta in Pamplona. At the "amateurs" Hemingway refrained from getting too close to the bulls, while Loeb, in one of several encounters, seized one of the bulls by the horns and with feet in the air allowed himself to be borne, like an acrobat, across the arena and deposited on the sands, feet first, with his horn-rimmed glasses intact on his nose, to the cheers of the assembled multitude.

And what was particularly galling about it all to the anti-Semitic Hemingway was that Loeb was a *Jew!*

But in *The Way It Was* Harold got back at Hemingway:

> Hem turned to ask me how I liked my first bullfight.
>
> "It was wonderful," I said, "though I'm not too keen on the theme. We all have to die, but I don't like to be reminded of it twice a day."
>
> "Balls," Ernest said.
>
> I asked Bill [Bill Smith, Hemingway's companion at Pamplona], "Were you as scared as I was before the barrier?"
>
> "Scareder than a snared rabbit," said Bill, "but once inside . . ."
>
> "Me, too," I said, "felt fine once I got inside. Wish I hadn't used my sweater." Then, in a lower voice, "Why do you think Hem kept so far from 'les Animaux'?"
>
> "He's not milked many cows," Bill said.

Though terribly wounded by Hemingway's offensive characterization, Harold Loeb let the matter lie for many years. Then, in *A Moveable Feast,* written shortly before his death, Hemingway, in Loeb's words, "chose to denigrate several of those who had assisted him generously when he needed help most [Ford Madox Ford, Scott Fitzgerald, Gertrude Stein, Loeb]." As a result, Loeb's old outrage flared up; he began an article in protest, then dropped the idea. But then, in 1966, A. E. Hotchner wrote his *Papa Hemingway* and the *Saturday Evening Post* ran a serialization of the book in which, Loeb noted, the real names of "the individuals Hemingway travestied in *The Sun Also Rises* were given." "Consequently," Loeb wrote, "I felt released from the reticence, or whatever the emotion was, which made me hesitate to rehash once again our old confusions."

As it turned out, Harold Loeb did a good job on Hemingway, returning the uppercut of *The Sun Also Rises* with some devastating rights to the jaw, and lefts to the middle, of his own.

For one thing, he pointed out that Hemingway, in his twenties, was not as poor as he made himself out to be (having to kill pigeons in the Tuilleries to feed his good wife and little baby), or as poor as one of his biographers, A. E. Hotchner, made him out to be, for, in addition to what he was making as a reporter for the Toronto *Star* and as an editor for Ford Madox Ford's *Transatlantic Review*, he benefited to no small extent from income off his wife, Hadley's, trust fund; in fact he was living mostly off his wife's money.

For another, he pointed out that Hemingway had a vicious, uncontrollable temper: "It was told that friends had had to hold him back from knocking down an old man, an American architect, who had inadvertently brushed the café table at which Hem was sitting. Also Hem had beaten up Paul Fisher for no apparent reason. He said he just felt like it."

So far as the events in Pamplona were concerned, Loeb, in *The Way It Was*, first demolished Hemingway's laborious contention that Robert Cohn was not wanted at the fiesta by introducing letters showing that his presence at Pamplona was all Hemingway's idea, and that Duff Twysden–Brett Ashley also approved of it entirely.

But, to dig deeper, what was the ultimate cause of Hemingway's "unnecessary nastiness"? . . . After reflecting on the matter for over forty years, Loeb came to certain firm conclusions. For one:

> In my opinion Hem never got over his disappointment at not going to college. And he wanted to be a champion of everything. So we may reasonably suppose, despite his disclaimer, that he himself would have liked to be champion of Princeton. Hem had mixed feelings for the Ivy League and the Rich. My guess is that it was his combination of envy, suspicion, and admiration for these categories that complicated his relations with Scott Fitzgerald and perhaps myself.

A. E. Hotchner, in *Papa Hemingway*, reported Hemingway had told him that the day after *The Sun Also Rises* was published, "I got word that Harold Loeb, who was the Robert Cohn of the book, had announced that he would kill me on sight." After Hotchner's book came out Loeb quickly denied he had ever voiced such an intention and hastened to offer an explanation of Hemingway's delusion: "Hemingway's belief that I threatened to kill him probably was due, I would guess, to something more deeply felt than my annoyance at his book."

A brief digression, then Loeb came forth with *his* uppercut.

There is a long history of similar delusions going back to his boyhood and culminating in his last illness. These delusions must have had their source in Hemingway's earliest experiences. At the dawn of memory, Hemingway went through an ordeal from which he may have never recovered. His mother, by a not unusual quirk or fancy, treated him as the twin of his slightly older sister. Marcelline wrote about it in her book. "Mother," she reports, "often told me she had always wanted twins, and that though I was a little over a year older than Ernest she was determined to have us be as much like twins as possible. When we were little Ernest and I were dressed alike in various outfits, in Oak Park in gingham dresses and in little fluffy lace-tucked dresses with picture hats. . . . Mother was doing her best to make us feel like twins, by having everything alike." Marcelline included in her book a photograph of Ernest in a girl's dress and hat.

Though Hem, in the years I knew him, did no more than mention Marcelline and his other sisters, and never spoke of having been dressed in girl's clothes, it is my belief that this experience accounts in part for several of his more important characteristics. One day he must have waked up to what was happening to him. Possibly a playmate called him a sissy. Thenceforth he overstressed his masculinity and hardihood. Later he was obsessed by fear of homosexuality and homosexuals and the fear of homosexuality is often linked by psychiatrists with paranoia.

So the chest-thumping, heavyweight-boxing, rhinoceros-killing, bullfighting, deepsea-fishing, supermale had gone around as a child in "fluffy lace-tucked dresses with picture hats"!

For Loeb subsequent oddities in Hemingway's personality and conduct were fully explainable. As a child, Hemingway, who had had to endure ridicule as a sissy, chose to be called by the nickname "the Old Brute." Perfectly understandable. Once, when he was sailing and was accidentally knocked off the boat by the boom, he accused his friend the steersman (and owner) of deliberately trying to kill him. Years later Edmund Wilson reported that, in Loeb's words, "Hem told him in all seriousness that on his recent trip through the southern states in a car with his young son he had at one point suddenly become aware that he had entered Mississippi. Realizing he was in

Faulkner country, he let the boy go to bed at the hotel where they spent the night. Then he had sat up till morning with his gun on the table in front of him."

"It seems to me," Loeb began his conclusion, "that Hemingway during his life tended to imagine offenses where none were intended, a not unusual characteristic, but one which, in his case, grew and intensified until it destroyed his equilibrium."

Then, the final, knockout blow: "By the time Hemingway and I met in the 1920s he was, I am now convinced, already too sick for friendship, and capable of its betrayal. . . . Nothing in our relationship justified the distortion of the real friend that I was into the Robert Cohn of *The Sun Also Rises*."

It is much to Harold Loeb's credit that in all his writings about Hemingway, Robert Cohn, and *The Sun Also Rises,* he never accused Hemingway of anti-Semitism. And yet anti-Semitic Ernest Hemingway, the white Anglo-Saxon Protestant from the Middle West, most certainly was. Was there really any intrinsic need, apart from expressing his dislike of the Jews, for Hemingway to have written about Cohn–Loeb: " 'Well, let him not get superior and Jewish.' "; " 'Haven't you got some more Jewish friends you could bring along?' 'You've got some fine ones yourself.' 'Oh, yes, I've got some darbs.' "; " 'He's got this Jewish superiority so strong . . .' "; " 'No, listen, Jake. Brett's gone off with men. But they weren't ever Jews . . .' "; " 'Does Cohn look bored?' I asked. 'That kike.' "; " 'I said if she would go about with Jews and bull-fighters and such people, she must expect trouble.' "; " 'She had a Jew named Cohn, but he turned out badly.' "?

One of the wonders of it all has been the critics' obliviousness to the fundamentally spiteful, anti-Semitic character of *The Sun Also Rises*. "An absorbing, beautifully and tenderly absurd, heart-breaking narrative," wrote *The New York Times* in its initial review, without ever alluding to the pettiness and nastiness of the characterization of Cohn. Entirely missed by the critics was the ominous fact that Hemingway's first novel included a spiteful, peevish, anti-Semitic smear, a revenge upon a friend who was guilty only of occasionally making Hemingway feel inferior.

It was, of course, not the first time a Guggenheim had had to endure an anti-Semitic attack. There had been many, of varying degrees of viciousness, since Meyer and his father had escaped from their European ghetto, hoping that they had permanently left Jew-baiting behind. The brothers had been caricatured mercilessly as brutish-looking Shylocks during their conquests of Mexico and Alaska. Simon had taken his share of abuse while a U.S. senator from Colorado. Isaac had been denied admittance to the Sands Point Country Club because he was a Jew. And now one of Meyer's grandsons had been travestied before the whole world in a work of American literature.

But, in one way or another, Guggenheims usually got back at their baiters. Isaac, it will be remembered, got back at the Sands Point Country Club by building his *own* much better golf course on his Long Island estate. And Harold got back, after a fashion, with his magazine articles and book. After a fashion because, to his annoyance, *The Way It Was* did not make as big a splash as he hoped it would. In the "Class Notes" for his forty-seventh Princeton reunion, Harold revealed his disappointment:

> You ask for news of me. What there is, is anti-climacteric. My book (*The Way It Was*) came out belatedly after years of work. For a while there was high excitement. Each morning, newspapers and magazines were scanned to see how the work was being received. Runs of despair followed periods of elation. You know you have made a contribution, but you are not secure in this belief and so seek confirmation. . . .
>
> . . . The high point was a midsummer Sunday with a photographer from *Time* snapping me in the garden with a spade, upon a rock beside the river, beneath the dogwood, while a nice young research girl was phoning me, it seemed like every fifteen minutes, to check a statement, phrase, or deduction.
>
> Then the review came out. It was a good review. But Lady Chatterley's ancient lover had chosen that very week to be suppressed. So out came my photos and the lead position. Again the day to be borne aloft on leathern shields was postponed. Soon afterwards the phone calls ceased, the letters began to scatter . . .

It was not such an easy thing for a Jew to demolish an American WASP folk hero before he died.

After this brief flurry of excitement Harold devoted the remainder of his life to bringing up his two sons and two daughters, marrying for the third and fourth times, looking after the investments he had inherited from his Guggenheim mother (who, in the meantime, had inherited substantial legacies from several of her guilty brothers), revising the articles on Zionism he had written for *The New Republic* during the 1930s ("only Zionism promises the perpetuation of the Jews as a people"), and elaborating the economic theories he had formulated during the 1930s, 1940s, and 1950s in his *National Sur-*

vey of Potential Product Capacity, Chart of Plenty, Full Production Without War, and *Life in a Technocracy.*

One last time did this most intelligent of the grandsons of Meyer Guggenheim return to his scarring relationship with Hemingway, writing an article entitled "Hemingway's Bitterness" for the *Connecticut Review* in October, 1967, six years after Hemingway's suicide, an article in which he elaborated all the reasons why he believed Hemingway had so cruelly betrayed his friendship.

Harold Loeb never quite got over what Hemingway did to him, rehashing the indignity to the end of his days. He died in 1974, at eighty-three, ending far more staunchly and peacefully than either of his other two so-called "lost generation" writer friends, Fitzgerald and Hemingway; survived by his fourth wife, Barbara McKenzie, two daughters (both sons had died), and nine grandchildren; hoping fervently that the name and achievements of Harold Loeb would prevail over Hemingway's repellent portrait of Robert Cohn.

CHAPTER

8

GLADYS GUGGENHEIM STRAUS: CARRYING ON

AFTER SENATOR SIMON GUGGENHEIM'S DEATH IN 1941 THE NAME of Guggenheim disappeared entirely from the list of directors and officers of American Smelting and Refining, the corporation the family had captured in 1901 and had built into one of the industrial giants of the world. Seven males there had been in the original Guggenheim partnership, yet not one single son of these felt inclined to remain in the family's principal business creation. Edmond, Harry, M. Robert, Harold Loeb—all put in an apprenticeship of sorts, then quit after a few years. And it will be remembered that Simon's younger son, George Denver Guggenheim, who managed to get on the company's executive committee, ended his association with ASARCO by firing a bullet into his head in 1939.

However, all was by no means lost so far as the family and ASARCO were concerned, because the Guggenheims did retain one very powerful member behind the scenes in the corporation, and that was Dan's daughter, Gladys, whose husband, Roger W. Straus, succeeded Simon as president and chief executive officer of the company.

Gladys Guggenheim Straus was the proverbial chip off the old block, the real successor to her father and to the Guggenheim quadrumvirate, the one member of her generation who, even more than Harry, seriously dedicated herself to continuing the Guggenheim business interests and philanthropic traditions, the one grandchild of Meyer and Barbara who truly carried on.

Daniel and Florence Guggenheim had been most pleased with their only daughter, Gladys. Even as a young girl she had revealed to them that she was everything her older brother, M. Robert, was not, and many things her younger brother, Harry, was not either. She was responsible, practical, hardworking, cheerful, attractive, energetic, faithful, even-tempered, charitable, and consistent. And wonder of wonders, among her generation, she even went to temple every Sabbath and holy day of her life. Here was a young lady who already was a loving, dutiful daughter, and gave every indication of becoming both a helpful, loving wife and a devoted mother.

It was an enormous satisfaction, therefore, for Dan and Florence that their beloved Gladys decided to marry Roger Williams Straus.

Gladys, a lively, good-looking young girl of eighteen, was just out of Rosemary Hall and was bound for Bryn Mawr. Roger, a handsome twenty-two, was just out of Princeton, and was bound perhaps for diplomacy but really for nowhere in particular. The two fell so much in love that Gladys gave up the idea of Bryn Mawr and Roger gave up whatever idea he had of entering the State Department. Daniel Guggenheim acted as a catalyst for the union. He let young Roger know that if he married the boss's daughter he had a future in American Smelting and Refining. Who knew? If he did reasonably well he could go all the way to the top. Not that Roger needed this assurance to persuade him to marry Gladys—the two would have married under any conditions—but it helped.

The family Gladys had decided to marry into was one of the most distinguished in New York. Roger's uncles Isidor and Nathan were the co-owners of R. H. Macy & Company, which was on its way to becoming the largest department store in the world. They, in turn, were the sons of the German-Jewish immigrant—from Otterberg, in the Rhenish Palatinate—Lazarus Straus, who had come to the United States in 1852, four years after the arrival of Meyer Guggenheim. Isidor, who went down with his wife and Ben Guggenheim on the *Titanic,* and Nathan had already made substantial fortunes. Roger's father, Oscar, was well off, too (he had also been a co-owner of Macy's), but his interests ran more toward government than business, so he was not quite so rich as his brothers. A Bull Moose Republican, he had been a close friend of Theodore Roosevelt, had served in his Cabinet as secretary of commerce and labor, and had served first as minister, then as United States ambassador to Turkey, under Presidents Cleveland, McKinley, and Taft. He had also been a devoted student of English literature and had written a much-respected biography of the founder of Rhode Island and champion of religious freedom, Roger Williams, after whom he named his son. Later he wrote a biography of Thomas Paine and a volume of memoirs, *Under Four Administrations.* Strauses had married into other very prominent German-Jewish families, the Kuhns of Kuhn, Loeb & Company, and the Lehmans of Lehman Brothers. Strauses had money, connections, culture, and political influence. Could there have been a more perfect match for a Guggenheim daughter than a Straus? Especially when the Straus in question was tall, handsome, healthy, charming, intelligent, and capable? And the union was not merely a bourgeois alliance, but a genuine love match as well?

The wedding, held in January, 1914, of the son of the most influential Jew in the U.S. government and the daughter of the most influential Jew in the American business world attracted a most distinguished array of guests and much attention from the press. The ceremony was held in the grand ballroom of the St. Regis Hotel and was attended by almost all the Strauses, Guggenheims, Lehmans, Kuhns, Seligmans, and Loebs, plus people like Mrs. Theodore Roosevelt and Mr. and Mrs. Andrew Carnegie. And there were also felicitations from such titans of international Jewry as Baron Édouard Rothschild of France. The bride and groom marched down the ballroom to their destiny past gilded standards garlanded with flowers and took their vows under a canopy of white roses and smilax sustained by eight columns of silver. Let no one forget the metal that paved the first fifteen years of the Guggenheims' journey toward this glittering moment.

After the wedding, resentful Western miners grumbled to the press that it cost a Guggenheim as much money to marry off his daughter as it cost to pay a miner for half his life's toil. To which the Guggenheims responded—to themselves—that the miner would not have had any toil or pay at all if it hadn't been for the initiative of the Guggenheims.

So now the Guggenheims were related by marriage not only to the Seligmans and the Loebs and the L. F. Rothschilds, but also to the Gimbels (Murry's daughter) and the R. H. Macy's Strauses. Two worldwide mining and metallurgical companies, three major investment banking concerns, and two great New York department stores were now safely in the family. In a mere twenty-five years the upstart "Googs" had secured a seemingly impregnable place for themselves in the German-Jewish aristocracy of New York.

And so, after The Jewish Wedding of the Year, Roger W. Straus became chief lieutenant of his father-in-law, Daniel Guggenheim, at American Smelting and Refining, and later chief lieutenant of his uncle-in-law, Senator Simon Guggenheim, and, finally, president and chief executive officer of the corporation, a position he held until his retirement at age sixty-five.

Roger also founded and was first president of the National Conference of Christians and Jews and became president and guiding spirit of the John Simon Guggenheim Memorial Foundation upon Senator Simon's death.

And while Roger was gradually ascending to his eminences at ASARCO and the John Simon, Gladys was exercising her own influence at ASARCO through him, happy that she was able, albeit in an indirect way, to carry on in her adored father's footsteps. What is more, she was also functioning as vice-president (later president) of the great benefaction established by her parents, the Daniel and Florence Guggenheim Foundation.

But power behind the scenes at ASARCO and power within the scene at the Daniel and Florence were only two of Gladys Guggenheim Straus's manifold activities. She also became vice-president of the board of trustees of Mount Sinai Hospital (to which the Guggenheims had contributed more money than any other private donor —some $25 million), president of the National Women's Republican Club, and the only female member on the eleven-member emergency food commission set up during World War II by Governor Thomas E. Dewey who, by the way, offered her husband Roger his choice of either a cabinet post or the Court of St. James's if he were elected to the presidency of the United States. Gladys also found time to be a vice-president and assistant editor of *Gourmet* magazine and the author of two cookbooks.

The benefactions over which Gladys Guggenheim Straus has presided, first as a trustee, then as vice-president of the board, then as president of the board of the Daniel and Florence Guggenheim Foundation, are so vast and varied and meritorious volumes could be written about them, and have been.

The criminal justice programs at Yale and Princeton "seeking ways to aid in bringing about improved function on the part of police, courts, and correctional institutions in the interest of more equitable justice and a better-integrated system of dealing with crime and those accused of crime." The New Horizons Boys' Ranch at Bly, Oregon, which provides "schooling, medical and psychological care and job training for boys aged ten to seventeen who have been in trouble at home or at school and are considered to be in danger of drifting into juvenile crime." The Institute on Man and Science at Rensselaerville, New York, "a seminar, research, and educational center where critical social problems of the evolving technological world are studied in depth." The Guggenheim Space Theater at the Hayden Planetarium of the American Museum of Natural History in New York, which is attended by about 500,000 people annually. The National Air and Space Museum of the Smithsonian Institution in Washington. The Mount Sinai Hospital Medical Center in New York. The Daniel and Florence Guggenheim Temporal Bone Dissection Laboratory, New York Eye and Ear Infirmary. Clark University for Dr. Robert H. Goddard's research in rocketry, the research that ultimately produced Saturn V. The Guggenheim Jet Propulsion Centers at Princeton and the California Institute of Technology whose "contributions to the sciences of flight culminated in the Apollo program of lunar exploration." The International Academy of Astronautics. The Guggenheim Memorial concerts, held by the Goldman Band in the Daniel and Florence Guggenheim Memorial Bandshell, Damrosch Park, Lincoln Center, which have recently enjoyed their sixtieth consecutive season. The American Women's Association. The American Jewish Committee. Montefiore Hospital. The Jewish hospitals of Cincinnati and Philadelphia. The United Jewish Appeal. The Daniel Guggenheim School of Aeronautics, New York University. The Federation for the Support of Jewish Philanthropic Societies. The Daniel and Florence Guggenheim Institute of Flight Structures at Columbia University. The Guggenheim Center for Aviation Health and Safety at Harvard University. The University of Chile. Chilean disaster relief. Temple Emanu-El. The Guggenheim Rehabilitation Pavilion, Rothschild-Hadassah Hospital, Mt. Scopus, Jerusalem.

And there were eventually also Straus benefactions to look after. The million-dollar-endowed Roger W. Straus chair in history at Princeton University, among others.

And there were also children to look after: Roger W. Straus, Jr., destined to become president of the highly respected New York publishing firm of Farrar, Straus & Giroux; Oscar S. Straus II, who became associated with American Smelting and Refining and Guggenheim Brothers; and Florence Guggenheim Straus, who married Max Hart, grandson of the founder of Hart Schaffner & Marx, and today a vice-president of that company.

Among the fifteen granddaughters of Meyer and Barbara, could there have been two more contrasting personalities than Peggy Guggenheim and Gladys Guggenheim Straus?

One the grande dame of international high bohemia, the other, one of the grande dames of the New York German-Jewish *haute bourgeoisie*. One the rebel against the New York German-Jewish *haute bourgeoisie*, the other the epitome of it. One who lost count of her lovers after she notched her one-thousandth, the other who knew no man but her husband and remained faithfully married to him for over fifty years. One who felt repugnance toward her fellow Jews at the Wailing Wall of Jerusalem and has not been to temple in years, the other a benefactor of institutions in Israel and a pillar of Temple Emanu-El in New York. One a woman of unconventional ideals, opinions, and beliefs, the other with the generally accepted, and characteristically undefined, ideas of her class, which is pretty near the summit of the American social order.

While her husband was alive, Gladys and her family divided their time between a New York townhouse and the magnificent Straus estate at Purchase, New York, which had once belonged to Ambassador Oscar and now belongs to Roger, Jr. Gladys now maintains an estate in Greenwich, Connecticut, and a spacious apartment on Fifth Avenue in New York, where she keeps the Rembrandt she inherited from her father.

Gladys Guggenheim Straus today is a gracious, attractive, alert old lady of quiet, solid achievement. Here is a Guggenheim daughter who, in the great tradition of noblesse oblige, has spent her life paying back the fortunes she inherited from her father, mother, and husband. Paying them back in hard work and devotion to her husband, his business, their friends, their children, and the multitudinous charities—over sixty of them—of her parents' foundation.

Looking back over the history of her family, she muses with daughterly pride and affection on her grandfather Meyer's extraordinary authority (she remembers him presiding like a monarch over family gatherings), on the energy, kindness, and generosity of her father, Daniel (the only brother of the seven who, in her opinion, possessed genuine ability), and with sisterly disapproval on the outrageous behavior of her older brother, Robert ("he was always getting into trouble, even as a child"), and on what she considers to be the testamentary injustice of her younger brother, Harry, leaving almost all his money to his foundation and his second cousin and almost nothing to his daughters. Her warmest sentiments she reserves for her younger son, Roger W. Straus, Jr. "He's the apple of my eye," she says, smiling like a young girl.

CHAPTER

9

THE QUIETER ONES:
EDMOND AND WILLIAM, JR.

SPECTACULAR, THEY WERE, THE FOURTH GENERATION OF GUGGEN-
heims. Ambassador Harry, America's knight-errant in Latin America.
Captain Harry, the fighter pilot in two world wars. Horseman Harry,
winner of the Kentucky Derby. Art patron Harry, guiding the construction of the most daring museum in the world. Colonel Bob, Ambassador Bob, Playboy Bob, Bob of the Firenze and the American Pincers
Movements. Peggy the grand patroness of the avant-garde, supporting, bedding down, even marrying the foremost artistic geniuses of
the century. Dogaressa Peggy assembling her great collection and
establishing her palace and museum on Venice's Grand Canal. Harold
Loeb creating an avant-garde literary review, writing three novels,
inventing new economic theories, battling Ernest Hemingway. Gladys
marrying an R. H. Macy's Straus, running one of the Guggenheim foundations, and seeing her husband rise to the presidency of
the worldwide corporation her father and uncles had created. Eleanor
marrying a British lord. Yes, these were a flamboyant bunch, people
with flair, these were Guggenheims who did extraordinary things, who
did not shun the limelight, who often gloried in the limelight.

But there were also Guggenheims of this generation of modest
achievement, or practically no achievement at all, Guggenheims who
loathed the limelight, who led as inconspicuous lives as possible, the
quieter ones, like Murry's son, Edmond, and William's son, William, Jr.

It will be remembered that Edmond was one of the richest Guggenheims of his generation, far, far richer, for example, than Peggy, or

Harry, or Robert—thanks to that whopping $6.5 million trust fund his father had set up for him in 1923 when Edmond was only thirty-five.

The wisdom of setting up that fund for one who was expected to lead the Guggenheim businesses triumphantly into the future, in a family short on males, could be a subject of useful debate, considering the fact that after Edmond received his first dividends and interest he quit Guggenheim Brothers and never worked very hard at anything again.

But give Edmond the benefit of the doubt. One must follow one's vocation, not conform to some abstract conception of what one must be, a conception devised by one's family, one's teachers, or one's friends. Edmond was a natural athlete, a tall muscular man, agile, beautifully coordinated, a star ballplayer at Yale, a first-rate tennis player, yachtsman, swimmer, and golfer. Better that he devote the rest of his life to the activities he liked best, and was best at, to golf, tennis, yachting, and swimming. Besides, business had never given him very profound satisfactions during his brief working life. He and Harry had spent the better part of their youth developing the richest copper property on earth, Chuquicamata Mountain in Chile, working in 100-degree desert heat, living in a crude barracks in a virtual wilderness a hundred miles from the nearest village, only to see his father and uncles sell it to Anaconda for $70 million, over his and Harry's objections. In the business world one could never be sure about retaining the fruit of one's labors.

And so Edmond became, after his retirement from Guggenheim Brothers, a top-flight amateur golfer, an avid tennis player, yachtsman, and swimmer. He also became president of the Murry and Leonie Guggenheim Foundation and ably ran its free dental clinic for poor New York schoolchildren after his father's death.

But even running that clinic eventually proved too much for him and, as we have seen, he felt compelled, against his father's testamentary wishes, to liquidate his father's foundation and distribute its assets to other medical institutions: $22 million to Mount Sinai Hospital, $12 million to the Mayo Clinic, and $1 million each to six other health facilities.

In 1952 Edmond married his third and last wife, a widow, Marian Kaufmann, and remained married to her until his death in 1972 at the age of eighty-four. It was, as Mrs. Edmond Guggenheim says today, "a marriage made in heaven. God gave us many happy years together." During the winter the two lived quietly in New York and in Florida or Arizona, and during the summer they lived quietly at Edmond's magnificent estate at Saranac Lake, in upper New York State. Like his quiet father, Edmond avoided Society-with-a-capital-S and went out of his way to shun all publicity or notoriety.

Unlike his father, uncles, and cousins Harry and Peggy, Edmond did not choose to have the institutions he helped named after him. When the board of directors of the Saranac Lake General Hospital voted to name the hospital—to which Edmond had given the largest single sum of money it had ever received—the "Edmond A. Guggenheim Hospital," he objected, saying that "the people of Saranac Lake contributed what they could. I am sure their contributions meant more to them than my contribution meant to me. I therefore insist it be called the Saranac Lake General Hospital."

When Edmond died he left his vast estate (he was the largest single noninstitutional stockholder of Kennecott Copper) to his third wife, Marian, and to his daughter by his first wife, Natalie, now Mrs. B. B. Short of Hawaii, and to the Roman Catholic Church, the Episcopal Church, the Jewish Federation, the Red Cross, the Salvation Army, and the Saranac Lake General Hospital. His lovely 150-acre summer home on Saranac Lake was left to the Roman Catholic Church to be used as a school for training young priests. Marian Guggenheim had told Edmond she did not want to live there without him.

Much praise was bestowed in the papers and in the minutes of meetings of several boards of directors on this unspectacular son of the House of Guggenheim when he died, but none could approach his widow's tribute, and so we shall give her the last word:

> He was the *most* of everything. The *most brilliant*. The *most handsome*. The *most generous*. I could go on ad infinitum. He was filled with joie de vivre and gave joy and happiness to the many who were fortunate in knowing him. He was a great athlete and won many trophies for golf, boating, and tennis. He was made Honorary Doctor of Law, Doctor of Humane Letters. He was extremely philanthropic, and a beautiful human being. What more need I say?

Even quieter than Edmond was William's (Gatenby Williams) son, William, Jr., the first Guggenheim to transform himself into a WASP, or rather a WJP.

Will junior spent his boyhood in his father's huge Italianate townhouse at 883 Fifth Avenue, catered to by no fewer than twenty-one servants and two chauffeurs (who drove him around in Daddy and

Mommy's two Rolls-Royces), and at Will senior's 150-acre estate at Sands Point, near the palaces of Isaac, Solomon, Murry, and Daniel. It was a Little Lord Fauntleroy existence, one not likely to produce a very dynamic character, and, in fact, the boy proved to be, from an early age, very shy and retiring.

After William, Sr.'s divorce from his second wife, Aimee, the boy went to live with his mother in a relatively modest New York apartment, and the embittered Aimee, who resented the Guggenheims' power and their interference in her and her husband's lives, consciously began to alienate her beloved son from the Guggenheim family, a process at which she proved most successful.

After having been educated, principally, by private tutors, and by his gentleman's gentleman, who accompanied him on several trips to Europe, looking after his tickets and luggage, and schooling him in the ways of hotel porters, maître d's, and other bandits, William, Jr. took a job as a Wall Street customer's man, and, thanks to some of his father's friends and exploiters, acquired quite a few well-heeled customers for his firm.

It was around this time—1937—that Will junior met and married a member of the old American WASP aristocracy, the slim, long-necked, Gibson Girl-type beauty, Elizabeth Newell. Elizabeth's paternal grandfather was a gentleman of Colonial British stock who had founded Quaker Oats, and her mother was a Beekman, a direct descendant of Wilhelmus Beekman (after whom Beekman Place was named), one of the original Dutch settlers of Manhattan Island, and one of the first burgomasters of Nieuw Amsterdam. Mr. and Mrs. Newell were in the New York Social Register and Mrs. Newell was an active member of the Daughters of the American Revolution.

William Guggenheim, Jr. was the first Guggenheim to unite with such an old and distinguished WASP family, one descended from the founders of the country, and it seems to have gone to his head. After his marriage, he renounced Judaism for Episcopalianism and became a pillar of the Episcopal Church of the Heavenly Rest at Fifth Avenue and Ninetieth Street. Then, as if to solidify this entry into one of the great strongholds of New York WASP society, after his son, William III, was born he had the boy promptly enrolled in the Sons of the American Revolution for which organization he was eligible thanks to his mother's Colonial ancestry. Gradually William, Jr. shed his Jewish friends (and his Guggenheim relatives) and, in the words of his wife, who is still alive and living on Fifth Avenue, frequented "only good Gentile society."

William, Sr. was very generous to his son financially, giving him a most ample allowance, and was overjoyed when Will junior produced William III, who could carry on his name and inherit his wealth. Senior had desperately wanted a grandson. Among other reasons, he wanted very much to vindicate his honor as a man in the eyes of his diffident, daughtered-out older brothers. Upon the birth of William III, Will senior bequeathed his million-dollar trust fund to Will junior, and Aimee Guggenheim announced to the world: "Whatever that boy wants, he's got it."

On the surface Will junior's life may have seemed as bright as a freshly refined bar of Guggenheim copper, but sadly enough he had been born with an enlarged heart and a leaking valve, had been declared 4F by the Army, and was not expected to live to an advanced age by his physicians.

It was wealth but not health and so it wasn't long after his marriage that Will junior was compelled to retire from hectic Wall Street and dedicate himself to more peaceful pursuits, such as the care and loving of his wife and son, and the other things that lay close to his ailing heart: his home, his photography, his animals, his music, his reading.

An intelligent, sensitive, gentle, cultivated man, he is remembered by his widow as a person of quiet affection and distinction, infinitely removed in temperament from his buccaneer uncles, who were responsible for setting up and overseeing the million-dollar-plus trust fund he received upon his father's death in 1941.

During World War II Will junior volunteered as an aircraft spotter and it was this activity that ultimately caused his premature death. He was assigned to spot from the high central tower of his uncle Daniel Guggenheim's palatial Hempstead House at Sands Point, which had been turned over by Dan's widow to the U.S. Navy. It was climbing those seventy-four stairs to the top of the tower every day that finally burst his heart and killed him, after a long agony in Mount Sinai Hospital, in 1947, at only thirty-nine years of age, only six years after his father's demise following strenuous exertions in the *Chambre d'Or* of his Riverside Drive townhouse.

The irony of the life of this Quiet One, in relation to the Guggenheim family as a whole, is that this Episcopalian, WASPian, Daughters-of-the-American-Revolution, Sons-of-the-American-Revolution, Social-Registered, alienated-from-the-Guggenheims branch of the Guggenheim family has turned out to be the only branch that has consistently produced male heirs, generation after generation. William III, a young man of thirty-seven who lives in Florida, has two young sons, William IV, age four, and Christopher Mark, age one. If the Guggenheim name is to continue in more than institutional lettering it will be wholly up to these two children because the rest of the family has completely daughtered out.

And so thanks to the quietest, most self-effacing, most infirm, most unspectacular, most un-Guggenheim Guggenheim of them all, *the name lives on.*

CHAPTER

10

KING SOLOMON'S DAUGHTERS

ON MAY 12, 1937, SOLOMON R. GUGGENHEIM'S ELDEST DAUGHTER, Eleanor May, Countess Castle Stewart, attended the coronation of the last British Emperor, King George VI, in Westminster Abbey, as the wife of a peer of the realm. As such she was entitled to a place at the ceremonies among the great lords and ladies of Britain, at a time when Britain still ruled half the world, and was later personally received by the new King and Queen.

For her coronation robes Eleanor wore a long red velvet cape trimmed with fur over a red velvet gown, and a tiara of diamonds, rubies, and emeralds her father had had made for her.

That Lady Castle Stewart occupied a privileged chair at the coronation of George VI was of no great import either to the British royal family, or to the British people. All the same, it was of no small significance to the Guggenheim family. By the time of George's accession to the British throne the Guggenheims had realized practically all the most cherished ambitions open to Americans. They had fulfilled not just one "American dream," the standard rags-to-riches one, but a dozen of them. They had become, as we know, multimillionaires, presidents, and directors of major New York Stock Exchange-listed corporations, U.S. ambassadors, a U.S. senator, founders of major philanthropic foundations, authors, aviation and space pioneers, world-famous patrons of the arts. There had remained, however, one last, and most cherished American ambition to be attained: accession into the European titled aristocracy.

The Founding Fathers of the United States of America, reacting against the aristocratic age in which they and their fathers had grown up, with its elaborate hierarchy of inherited privileges, had taken special pains to incorporate into the Constitution of the United States the negative provision that no titles of nobility could be conferred upon an American citizen and that any titled European emigrating to the United States would be required to renounce his or her title before being accorded full citizenship. Today, in fact, a titled nobleman emigrating to the United States must formally renounce his title before the U.S. immigration authorities in order to become eligible for U.S. citizenship.

This is, of course, precisely why Americans have always been so impressed by titles of nobility, and so avid to obtain them. (When Miss Grace Kelly of Philadelphia became Princess Grace of Monaco, one would have thought, from the gushings in the press, that the American millennium had finally arrived: a nice, clean-cut American girl becomes a real live *princess!*)

But, aside from the traditional American ambivalence in regard to titles—no titles allowed, yet I fall flat on my face before one—it so happened that by the mid-twentieth century certain American names had emerged above the smoke of subduing a continent, exterminating its inhabitants, and establishing the greatest military and commercial empire in world history—names such as Du Pont, Ford, Vanderbilt, Whitney, Morgan, Rockefeller, Mellon, Guggenheim. These names resounded in national, and also in world, consciousness with the same force and authority as the titles emperor, king, prince, duke had once resounded in the consciousness of the nations of the Old World. So that even though titles in the Imperial Republic were outlawed, they still existed, in a sense, in the mere names of certain influential families. Who, for example, could claim, in America's Bicentennial year, that the newly elected young governors of West Virginia and Maryland, John D. Rockefeller IV and Pierre Du Pont IV, bore names any less princely than those borne by the Hapsburgs, the Medici, the Bourbons, when those mighty families were in power? Or that Cornelia Vanderbilt Whitney bore a name any less "noble" than Isabella d'Este, or that Miss Peggy Guggenheim of Venice, Italy, possessed a name any less ducal than such *discendenti di dogi e dogaresse* as the countess Marcello, the countess Foscari, the countess Grimani?

Yes, it was a source of deep, visceral satisfaction for Solomon R. Guggenheim, son of a former Philadelphia street peddler, grandson of a poor Jewish *Schweizerdeutsch* tailor who had suffered at the hands of the noble *Landvogt* of Baden, to have one of his daughters marry the son of the Earl of Castle Stewart, a direct descendant of the royal house of Scotland, heir to a five-hundred-year-old title and an ancestral estate in Ulster, even though the young nobleman in question was as poor as the proverbial church mouse. His daughter, his immigrant peddler father's granddaughter, was now no less a lady than the countess Castle Stewart! Seventy-two years after the Guggenheims had escaped the oppression of the European nobility by emigrating to America, a Guggenheim had ascended into that very nobility. Was not this the ultimate American dream? Was not this what America was really all about?

But Eleanor was not Solomon's only daughter. There were also Gertrude and Barbara. Three daughters and no sons. Like brothers Isaac and Benjamin, Sol had, alas, daughtered out. However, so far as Guggenheim dynastic considerations were concerned, all was by no means lost with the line Sol had fathered. For it was Sol's grandson, Peter Lawson-Johnston, Barbara's son, who, twenty-two years after Sol's death, became the standard-bearer of the Guggenheim family in the 1970s.

Solomon R. Guggenheim, by all accounts, was devoted to his three daughters, even to the extent of naming one of his corporations after them, the Elgebar Corporation, a South Carolina timber operation. He also left each one of them $10 million, clear of taxes, in his will . . . in 1949 dollars. Today Eleanor and Barbara, whose legacies have multiplied handsomely, will both tell you, confidently, with no strain of self-justification in their voices, that even though their father had desperately wanted a son, "he loved us very much, and, in the end, was very happy to have us."

Three cheerful, sprightly, bright young girls, the daughters of Solomon and Irene Guggenheim. Eleanor, the oldest, now in her eighties, a short, energetic, affable, quick-witted girl, by no means beautiful, but attractive in her energy, the force of her personality, the alacrity of her mind. Gertrude, the middle sister, almost a dwarf, well under five feet tall and slightly hunchbacked, yet good-humored and kind, and full of goodwill. And then Barbara, the baby of the family, short, quick, bright, spunky, full of beans.

Three girls growing up in as privileged—to use one of the favorite expressions of social resentment—an environment as is available, or possible, in the United States of America.

Schooled by French and German governesses and private tutors who traveled with the family from one S.R.G. residence to another, and at private boarding schools in America, Britain, and Germany. Brought up in spacious New York apartments and huge country estates. Their childhood in Solomon's fifteen-room apartment at 743 Fifth Avenue, directly opposite the Vanderbilt palace, and in his great thirty-room Victorian mansion at Elberon, New Jersey. Later, the huge, balconied, beflagged Plaza suite (where Barbara remembers having to turn off all the lights as she progressed through the rooms, though the Plaza paid the bill: "We were brought up to be thrifty"); the 1,200-acre Island Park ranch in Idaho; the Big Survey plantation in South Carolina; Sol's lovely antebellum house on the Battery in Charleston; his rented summer houses and castles in England and Scotland. Still later, when Eleanor and Barbara were married, visits to the opulent Trillora Court at Sands Point; trips on Long Island Sound, the Atlantic, the Caribbean, on the 375-foot, 35-knot *Trillora*.

But all this luxury and variety, all these great estates, these ranches and yachts, these governesses, servants, tutors, apparently did not spoil the sisters Guggenheim. Sol, though something of a libertarian himself (Eleanor's governess doubled as his mistress), was a strict Victorian father, and he kept his girls in line. They had to account, in writing, on a ledger, for every penny of the small allowances he gave them. (Barbara remembers her father giving his valet fifty cents a week "to be put on the expense account for the allowance he gave me.") They had to do well in their studies, or else no allowance would be forthcoming. They were required by Solomon of the Iron Constitution to get regular exercise in the outdoors. Occasionally they even had to work. During the First World War Eleanor worked as a "farmerette" in Connecticut, using only the names Eleanor May, because "Guggenheim was so conspicuous, and I wanted to be accepted for myself." And they were indoctrinated into a most scrupulous honesty. Over and over again Sol would tell them, "We Jews have to be more honest than anyone else, because everyone always thinks the worst of us."

After the *jeunesse dorée*, a *jeunesse* whose gilt was admittedly tempered by a generous measure of probity, discipline, and strict education—shall we say it was more of a *jeunesse cuivré*?—came time for the girls to marry.

Eleanor was the first to go. Solomon loved to summer in England, his favorite European country, and during the summer of 1920 he met the Earl of Castle Stewart, who promptly arranged to introduce his son, Arthur, to Eleanor. The two met on July 1, took to each other at once, were engaged July 22, and married December 16. They were a curious-looking couple. Arthur was very tall (six feet, five inches) and lean and Eleanor was short and compact. But, as it turned out, they were ideally mated. The marriage produced four sons and lasted over forty years.

Arthur Stuart never expected to succeed to the peerage, for he had two older brothers. But then—*mors tua, vita mea*—both brothers were killed in World War I and Arthur became, upon his father's death, the seventh earl of Castle Stewart and the viscount Stuart (the family was heir to two distinctly separate titles bearing two variations of the same name).

Though Sol was impressed by Castle Stewart's title, Eleanor claims she wasn't. She loved Arthur for his person, not his title. Arthur had not been the first British nobleman she had met. One summer before she met Arthur, she had met another young lord.

"What do you do?" asked Eleanor, like a good American.

"I don't do anything. I'm a peer of the realm," came the reply.

"In America we call that a bum," said Eleanor, and never had anything more to do with him.

After the war Arthur became a teacher of English literature and classical studies at Rugby, but, in Eleanor's words, Arthur was "not too keen on teaching" and wanted very much to do something else.

But what else? The Stuarts, earls of Castle Stewart, may have been direct descendants of the Royal House of Scotland (from King Robert I; Mary Stuart, Queen of Scots, was also a distant relative), but all they possessed by the early 1920s was the ancestral seat, Stuart Hall, in Stuartstown, County Tyrone, Ulster, an ancient structure containing, among its many accretions, a chapel of the Church of England, and it went without saying that the estate was much more of a drain on, than a contributor to, the family's dwindling finances. Though a prospective peer of the realm, Arthur Stuart did not have a particularly brilliant future awaiting him. Teaching at Rugby. Could he maintain Stuart Hall on that? Neither Arthur nor Eleanor was very much thrilled with the prospect of keeping up appearances on a Rugby master's salary for the rest of their lives.

The day, however, was saved in 1922 by the ever-generous Solomon R. Guggenheim, who, fat with the profits of World War I, presented his daughter and son-in-law with what Eleanor refers to today as "a wonderful little cheque."

With this check, the amount of which Eleanor will not reveal, the

Castle Stewarts bought an 800-acre estate in Sussex, England, called Old Lodge, from Lady Delaware, whose husband was a direct descendant of the Lord Delaware who founded the American state bearing his name.

There was quite a bit of money left over from "the wonderful little cheque" after Old Lodge had been purchased and this was reinvested in good, solid, copper-edged American securities.

And so Arthur was able to leave Rugby and become master of Old Lodge. He remained a gentleman farmer for most of the rest of his life—raising Guernseys and selling their milk—except for a brief interlude in Parliament (1929–33) as a Tory MP, one of the few lords who sat in the House of Commons. Meanwhile Eleanor gave up her American citizenship and became a British subject. She never converted to her husband's Church of England, however, because "as a Jewess, I could never accept the divinity of Christ."

It was a happy, fruitful marriage, the union between Arthur Stuart and Eleanor Guggenheim. The two got along very well together and, thanks to Sol's generosity, were able to do more or less what they liked. Arthur interested himself in golf, shooting, forestation, and farming. Eleanor became deeply involved in British women's affairs, becoming president of the Federation of Women's Institutes of Sussex. The couple had four healthy sons, David, Robert, Arthur, and Simon. By the time of George VI's coronation in 1937, Lord and Lady Castle Stewart had led a rich and satisfying life together, and there was nothing on their horizon that even remotely hinted at the tragedies to come.

Solomon's generosity to his daughters was not limited to Eleanor. He also helped his middle daughter, Gertrude, to the extent of supporting her, in reasonably high style, for her entire life.

Because Gertrude was extremely small and slightly hunchbacked, it was not easy for her to find a husband who wasn't a blatant fortune hunter. After it appeared certain she would never marry, she moved permanently to England (she had gone to school there) to be near Eleanor, whom she loved very much. Solomon then bought her a large estate, Windy Ridge, at Coleman's Hatch, Sussex, near Eleanor's Old Lodge, in which Gertrude remained to the end of her days.

It was not easy for Miss Gertrude Guggenheim to bear the name she bore and be a dwarf and a hunchback. With her name and the money behind her she could have had the world at her feet had she

The Hon. Col. M. Robert Guggenheim (front, center), United States Ambassador to Portugal, on his way to present his credentials to the President of the Republic of Portugal.

WIDE WORLD PHOTOS

The Hon. Harry F. Guggenheim, United States Ambassador to Cuba (in aviator's uniform), with General Gerardo Machado, President of the Republic of Cuba (front, with hat), and William D. Pawley, aviation executive (center) in Havana.

GUGGENHEIM BROTHERS

Peggy Guggenheim in
1924.

MAN RAY

Peggy Guggenheim with Max Ernst in New York, 1942.

HUSTON-PIX
COURTESY OF *Time* MAGAZINE

Harold A. Loeb (1891–1974) at Tucson, Arizona, 1958.

Harry F. Guggenheim and his sister, Gladys Guggenheim Straus, attend the opening of the Robert H. Goddard Rocket Exhibit at New York's American Museum of Natural History, April, 1948, sponsored by the Daniel and Florence Guggenheim Foundation. (Left to right): Lt. Gen. James H. Doolittle, Dr. Albert E. Parr, director of the Museum, Mrs. Robert H. Goddard, widow of Dr. Goddard, Mr. Guggenheim, Mrs. Straus, and Charles A. Lindbergh. WIDE WORLD PHOTOS

Gladys Guggenheim Straus and Alicia Patterson Guggenheim at Harry Guggenheim's plantation, Cain Hoy.

GUGGENHEIM BROTHERS

Mrs. Henry Obre (Barbara Guggenheim) in the dining room at Andor Farm, in Monkton, Maryland, where she entertains at hunt breakfasts.

COURTESY MRS. HENRY OBRE

Eleanor Guggenheim, Lady Castle Stewart, at coronation of King George VI.

BASSANO, LONDON
COURTESY ELEANOR CASTLE STEWART

Peggy Guggenheim in her gondola, Venice.
ROLOFF BENY

Sindbad Vail, Peggy Guggenheim's son, and his second wife, Peggy, in Venice.

COURTESY PEGGY GUGGENHEIM

Hazel Guggenheim McKinley.

DENVER PUBLIC
LIBRARY

Karole (standing) and
Julia Vail, Sindbad and
Peggy Vail's daughters.

COURTESY SINDBAD VAIL

Pegeen Guggenheim (Vail) (1925–1967), on her mother's marble chair, in the garden at the Palazzo Venier dei Leoni, Venice.

COURTESY PEGGY GUGGENHEIM

Peggy Guggenheim with one of her grandsons, Nicolas Helion (Pegeen's son), and an unidentified friend, Palazzo Venier dei Leoni, Venice.

COURTESY PEGGY GUGGENHEIM

Peggy Guggenheim on her marble chair, in the garden at the Palazzo Venier dei Leoni, Venice.

ROLOFF BENY

HARRY THE MAGNIFICENT

Ambassador Harry making a speech at the Maine Monument, Havana, in 1931.

GUGGENHEIM BROTHERS

Harry in the winner's circle, with his Dark Star, winner of the 1953 Kentucky Derby.

GUGGENHEIM BROTHERS

Captain Harry ready to take off for an air strike from the *USS Nehenta Bay*, near Okinawa, June, 1945.

GUGGENHEIM BROTHERS

Harry with James H. Doolittle and Charles A. Lindbergh on the terrace of the swimming pool at Falaise. They are discussing plans for the Harry Frank Guggenheim Foundation.

GUGGENHEIM BROTHERS

Harry F. Guggenheim (1890–1971) at the time he was publisher and editor-in-chief of *Newsday* and president of the Guggenheim Museum and three Guggenheim foundations.

Peter O. Lawson-Johnston, Harry Guggenheim's principal heir, and his wife Dorothy ("Didi") at their estate in Princeton, 1976.

COURTESY PETER O. LAWSON-JOHNSTON

Peter O. Lawson-Johnston, president of the Guggenheim Museum, with Max Ernst at the opening of the Ernst retrospective, 1975.

PHOTO BY STEPHANIE RANCOU
COURTESY PETER O. LAWSON-JOHNSTON

The California Guggenheims. On the left: Daniel M. Guggenheim and his wife, Susan. On the right: M. Robert Guggenheim, Jr. and his wife, Shirlee. Newport Beach, California, 1976.

COURTESY M. ROBERT GUGGENHEIM, JR.

Farrar, Straus & Giroux author Carlos Fuentes, Dorothea Straus, and Roger W. Straus, Jr.

©JILL KREMENTZ

Iris Love on Knidos, 1970, at the time she discovered the Temple of Aphrodite.

PHOTO BY RUTH VAN SLYCK COURTESY LONG ISLAND UNIVERSITY

Iris Love on Knidos, 1976.

PHOTO BY MICHAEL CHESSER COURTESY IRIS LOVE

William Guggenheim
III and his wife, Judy,
at their Florida
home, 1976.

COURTESY WILLIAM
GUGGENHEIM III

William Douglas
Guggenheim
("Willy"), firstborn
son of Mr. and Mrs.
William Guggenheim
III, 1976.

COURTESY WILLIAM
GUGGENHEIM III

not been deformed. But, after a tormented girlhood, she managed to adjust to her condition and, with the financial help of her father and the love and moral support of her sister, she established certain charities in Sussex which earned her much admiration and respect in her adopted corner of Britain. For one, she turned one of the houses on her estate into a convalescent home for children . . . very young children, because older children were taller than she. Later she took war orphans into her own home, housing and supporting as many as twenty at a time. And she built a cottage on her property to be used as a holiday retreat for poor clergy. She died in her sixties of cancer and is affectionately remembered today in Sussex as a kind, lovable person who devoted her life to alleviating the sufferings of her fellowman. "Miss Guggenheim," they will tell you today at Coleman's Hatch, "was a great little lady."

And then there was Barbara, the youngest daughter, a small, quick-witted, good-humored girl who turned out to be not nearly so fortunate in love and marriage as her oldest sister.

After Eleanor had married *so well*, so *British*-well, Barbara was consumed with the idea of getting away from her chaperone and finding a good British husband for herself too, and so she rushed into marriage with John Robert Lawson-Johnston, a graduate of Eton, something of a playboy, grandson of the founder of Bovril (the beef soup concentrate), and, at the time he married Barbara, a member of the British diplomatic service.

Father Solomon did not think his son-in-law would ever make much money in the diplomatic service so he made him quit and go to Columbia to learn business administration and mining as preparation for eventually joining Guggenheim Brothers.

But after a son, Peter, was born, Lawson-Johnston began to lose interest in Barbara and the glorious future that had been planned for him at Guggenheim Brothers, and started to spend far too much time, for Barbara's or Solomon's liking, going to parties and nightclubs in Manhattan. And so Barbara, urged on by her father, divorced him, giving him a comfortable settlement. Young Peter then did not see his father again for twenty-one years.

Not long after breaking up with Lawson-Johnston, Barbara married again, this time Fred Wettach, a champion horseman from Elberon whom she had known since she was four years old. Wettach was a world-class champion jumper; Barbara also loved horses and rode. The two settled down to an active outdoor life on a farm in Maryland

(Solomon came through with another "wonderful little cheque"), raising horses and riding in horse shows, and had a son, Michael.

But the marriage to Wettach was not destined to last, and before long Barbara divorced again and married again. Her third husband was Henry Obre, also a gentleman farmer and horseman, and she remained married to him for thirty-eight years.

After Barbara came into her $10 million inheritance, Mr. Obre developed a crippling complex about his wife's money (he himself was poor) and fell easily into rotten peevish moods when he would be uncivil to Barbara even in public. He died at the Island Park ranch in Idaho, which Barbara had inherited, a man who never had the satisfaction of making a name for himself, or a fortune for himself, on his own.

Mrs. Barbara Obre now lives in a two-hundred-fifty-year-old white clapboard house in Monkton, Maryland, from which she runs her five-hundred-acre Andor Farm, one of the loveliest farms in the state. Her son, Michael Wettach, who once worked for Sammy Davis, Jr. and has never married, lives nearby at Merryland, considered the second best horse-breeding farm in Maryland after Alfred Vanderbilt's Sagamore, which is not far away. Another farming neighbor is Richard C. Du Pont, who also raises horses. Merryland has room for one hundred horses and the stables are usually filled up. There is a track on the property and the jockeys and trainers begin working out the horses in the early-morning mists at six o'clock. Michael himself is a jockey—a "gentleman jockey"—and he is usually out on the track at the crack of dawn with the other riders. Guests at Merryland are invariably awakened by the rutta-tut-tut of hooves on turf before, it seems, the sun has risen above the surrounding hills. Both mother and son ride with the local Elkridge-Harford Hunt and Barbara is famous for her hunt breakfasts, which usually consist of beefsteak and kidney stew, eggs Benedict, spoon bread, hot curried fruit, and Charleston Cup or Plantation Toddy, besides hot coffee and tea.

Before devoting himself exclusively to horses Michael Wettach enjoyed a fling in show business. As an assistant to Jule Styne he takes most of the credit for giving Jayne Mansfield her part in the stage production of *Will Success Spoil Rock Hunter?* with Walter Matthau. As an assistant stage manager to Sammy Davis, Jr., he reports the following episode, taken from Davis' autobiography, *Yes, I Can,* published by Michael's cousin Roger W. Straus, Jr. Sammy talking: " 'Michael, incidentally, is that blazer and those slacks the only clothes you own? I mean I understand about being broke but you're working steady—you must have at least one suit. After all, we are going to be celebrating.'

"He smiled, embarrassed. 'I'll wear a suit.'

"He left the table a few minutes later and George looked at me.

" 'Don't you know who Michael is?'

" 'What do you mean don't I know who he is? Who should he be?'

" 'His mother's a Guggenheim.'

" 'Then what's he doing working as our assistant stage manager?'

" 'He likes the theater.'

"When he came back I put down my fork. 'Michael, do you mean you've got money coming out of your ears and you've had the audacity to go sneakin' around here looking like Monday night on 125th Street—and stop blushing 'cause it won't help you. What is it with guys like you and Johnny Ryan? You with the dollar ninety-eight khaki pants and him Charley Undernourished with frayed collars? The two of you look like: "Send These Kids to Camp." Well, the party's over. Tonight we are starting a new game called "Give the check to the assistant stage manager." ' "

Barbara and Michael do not disguise the fact, obvious to anyone who visits Merryland and Andor Farm, that their life is horses, horses, and more horses. Since Barbara spends over $2,000 a month on feed alone, she considers herself "horse poor." "Seriously," she will tell you, "all my money goes to the horses and toward keeping up Merryland and Andor Farm. . . . There is almost nothing left over." Sometimes, though, a horse pays off. Barbara's Nightly Manner has won over $300,000. Her Oxford Flight was a two-stake winner. But she and Michael still have come nowhere near Cousin Harry's feat of winning the Kentucky Derby, which remains their ultimate goal. Horses, horses, and more horses, yet Barbara and Michael are also Guggenheims, so there is also art. Both mother and son continue to sit on the board of the Solomon R. Guggenheim Museum, whose chairman and president is none other than Barbara's firstborn son, and Michael's half brother, Peter Lawson-Johnston.

Barbara Obre, a most unpretentious, affable, and energetic woman of seventy-two, is today only too willing to admit the errors of her youth—after Eleanor married that British lord, she was under *such* a compulsion to marry equally, or at least almost, as well. However, she makes no bones about being immensely proud of the product of one of those errors, her son Peter. "He has taken hold," she will tell you, "of two Guggenheim foundations and all the Guggenheim businesses, and has infused them with new life. I know my father would have been so pleased." Then she will add: "By the way, the museum was *not* the B's idea [B for baroness, and bitch], but *Mother's!*"

While Barbara oversees the horse breeding on her and her son's nearly one thousand acres in Maryland, her sister Eleanor oversees the raising of beef cattle 3,500 miles away on *her* nearly one thousand acres in Sussex.

Since the coronation of George VI Eleanor has suffered, along with her adopted England, her share of tragedy. Her firstborn son, David, was killed during World War II, in North Africa, at only twenty years of age, and her second-born, Robert, was killed in Italy at twenty-one. That made four Castle Stewart males killed in two world wars. Then, in 1961, her husband, Arthur, a sufferer from chronic arthritis of the neck—he was in constant, unremitting pain—had a nervous breakdown over his illness and committed suicide.

Fortunately, her two younger sons have survived and are thriving. Arthur Patrick Avondale Stuart, eighth earl of Castle Stewart, is a gentleman farmer in Somerset, and has two children, Andrew Charles Richard, heir to the earldom, and Lady Bridget Stuart. And Simon Walter Erskine teaches school at Haberdashers Aske college preparatory, writes on educational psychology, and has three sons of his own, Thomas, Corin Edmund, and Tristram. Simon and his family live on Gertrude Guggenheim's former estate, Windy Ridge, not far from Old Lodge.

Eleanor herself has kept more than busy through the years as an officer and benefactor of the National Federation of Women's Institutes, which she describes as her "greatest passion," as senior billeting officer for Sussex during World War II (responsible for more than two hundred evacuees), as a school manager, a nursing assistant, and anonymous helper of friends in need. "No, I have *not* established any Guggenheim foundations like my cousin Peggy has," she will tell you. "I prefer private giving to institutional charity, and, insofar as is possible, I prefer anonymous giving because, frankly I don't like to be thanked!" What has given her more satisfaction than anything has been helping to put many of her less affluent friends' children through school and college. "I try to do it without their knowing about it," she says. "The child thinks it is his own parent who is financing his or her education."

Lady Castle Stewart is a woman of emphatic beliefs. Not only does she know exactly where she stands in regard to charity, but she also knows exactly where she stands in regard to the business of making money, especially making Guggenheim money.

It makes me so mad to read these articles condemning people like the Guggenheims for making their money by exploiting so-called cheap labor in underdeveloped countries. . . . Why, before my family went into Mexico there was no heavy industry at all there. We built the first big smelters in Mexico. All right, the workers received only fifty cents a day. *But before that they received nothing a day. They were starving.* The same applies to Chile. We brought the first industrial development to that country also. Why instead of blaming us, they should *thank* us for what we did. We helped raise them out of dire poverty, out of sub-human living conditions. . . . And also, are we not entitled to our rewards for having had the courage and intelligence to be the first to go into desolate places like Mexico, Alaska, and Chile with large-scale industrial development? Think of the risks we took. Oh, it makes me so sick. Do you know how much daring, how much boldness, it took to go into those places then? Why when my father was in Mexico scouting mines he slept with a loaded revolver under his pillow.

It is evident, from the vehemence of Lady Castle Stewart's defense, that she realizes full well that she enjoys the ease and magnificence of Old Lodge today mainly because her father and his brothers exploited cheap labor in Colorado in 1887 and in various underdeveloped countries for thirty or forty years thereafter.

And indeed she has something to defend and justify in Old Lodge and the life she has led there for over fifty years.

The place has a regal beauty about it, a rare quality of poetic magnificence that is rapidly vanishing from the planet. The stately mile-long driveway is lined on either side with great stands of pine, birch, and beech. Here and there one spies a mossy stone cottage through the trees: There are nine on the estate, not counting the main house. Bright green meadows, green even in winter, stretch out from either side of the tree-lined drive, climbing toward brownish-red hills of gorse and heather. There are no other dwellings in sight. In the middle distance stretch Lord Delaware's fields and some of neighboring Lord Gage's lands. (Lord Gage is a direct descendant of the British general who fought in the American Revolution.) In the far distance stretches the dark belt of Ashdowne Forest. Old Lodge itself lies at the end of the long driveway, a dark, rambling, mossy structure in Tudor style, surrounded by various cottages and outbuildings: the cook and butler's house, the squash court, one of the gardeners' cottages. The main house, with its magnificent seventeenth-century wood-paneled walls and ceilings, its great fireplaces (in one of which—yes *in*, not *by*—Eleanor keeps a chair for chilled visitors), has eighteen bedrooms and gives out on a variety of splendid views of downs, hills, and meadowlands. The house is filled with mementos and ancestral portraits of the Castle Stewarts, but one portrait seems to dominate the others, and that is the large portrait, by Sir William Orpen, of Solomon R. Guggenheim that hangs in the dining room and which Eleanor has willed to the Solomon R. Guggenheim Museum in New York. A staff of from fifteen to twenty, depending on the season, cares for the house and farm and for her ladyship, who has lived alone in Old Lodge since her husband committed suicide.

"Aye," the chauffeur will tell you, "his lordship was a fine man, a fine gentleman, he was in terrible pain. He would have wanted her ladyship to live here after he was gone, to take care of the place, as if he were with her."

Eleanor, Lady Castle Stewart, is determined to take care of the place until she dies, be there no doubt about that. Especially considering what happened to Stuart Hall, Stuartstown, Ulster, which passed to her eldest son upon the suicide of his father, and his accession to the family title.

Yes, that was something Solomon R. Guggenheim's daughter and grandsons will never forget, or forgive.

One morning in 1973 a large black limousine pulled up in front of Stuart Hall and two men got out carrying black suitcases, and rang at the front door. The housekeeper answered and they pushed her aside and burst in. Telling her to leave the building at once, they deposited the two black cases at strategic locations, one near the main staircase, another near the base of the tower, then ran out, got into the car, and left. A few minutes later the housekeeper saw the ancestral seat of the Castle Stewarts explode and collapse into a heap of smoking, crumpled masonry.

Her husband's two brothers killed in World War I, her two oldest sons killed in World War II, her husband killing himself, her husband's ancestral estate blown to smithereens by the I.R.A., yes, Eleanor has experienced her share of sorrow in this turbulent century.

"Now it is the young's turn," she says, nodding her head in a forceful gesture—it is clear from her decisive tone of voice and energetic manner that she has not let tragedy overwhelm her. "Perhaps they will be able to do a better job of things."

Yes, now it is the turn of King Solomon's grandsons, Arthur

Patrick Avondale Stuart, Earl of Castle Stewart; Simon Walter Erskine Stuart; Michael Wettach; Peter O. Lawson-Johnston—how ultraWASPian these names sound in a great Jewish family—now it is up to these heirs to some fifty or sixty million dollars to bear the heritage of the Castle Stewarts of Great Britain and the Guggenheims of the United States of America honorably and, one hopes, triumphantly through the last quarter of the twentieth century, and to help keep these last twenty-five years of the American century fruitful, and productive, and free of the killing of innocent men.

11

BENJAMIN'S OTHER DAUGHTER

TWO GUGGENHEIM HEIRS
DIE IN 13-STORY FALL

screamed the headline of a full-column article on page one of *The New York Times*, October 20, 1928.

Up until this date only Guggenheim triumphs—four decades of them—had attracted such a bold headline. This was the first tragedy to claim equal attention, and it shook the family to its roots. So there was a reverse side to the bright coin of American Success, to the Start-with-Nothing-and-Become-Rich-and-Famous American Dream. Become rich and famous, and not only your glories but also your agonies will be aired before the world.

What actually happened on the roof of the Surrey, an apartment hotel at 20 East Seventy-sixth Street, New York City, the afternoon of October 19, 1928, is still unclear. Only one person knows for sure and that is Hazel Guggenheim McKinley, the mother of the two "Guggenheim Heirs" who lost their lives that afternoon and the youngest daughter of Benjamin and Florette Guggenheim, Peggy's baby sister. And it is a matter about which Hazel does not wish to speak.

The publicly known facts are these: Hazel Guggenheim, a schoolgirl of seventeen, had married an Englishman by the name of Sigmund Kempner at about the same time her first cousin Eleanor married the son of the Earl of Castle Stewart. Two years later she divorced Kempner and married an American journalist living in England, Milton S. Waldman, by whom she had two sons, Terrence and Benjamin.

Hazel Guggenheim was not an easy person to live with. She was strong-willed, spoiled, and given to abrupt changes of mood. She suffered from the emotional instability that plagued many of the Seligmans, and this had, in turn, been aggravated by her father's drowning on the *Titanic*. Often she would have terrifying fantasies of that tragic night which had taken her beloved father from her when she was only ten years old. After five years of living with Hazel and her moods and her nightmares, Mr. Waldman sued for divorce.

Furious, humiliated, Hazel gathered up her two young sons and took the next ship for New York.

Once in Manhattan she checked into the Plaza Hotel. Then, after six or seven days of brooding on her broken marriage, with the innocent issue of that marriage constantly in her hair, she went to the Surrey on East Seventy-sixth Street with her two sons to visit a cousin, Mrs. Cornelius Ruxton Love, one of Isaac's granddaughters. The Loves had a penthouse on the sixteenth floor.

When Hazel and her two little ones, Terrence, four, and Benjamin, fourteen months, arrived at Mrs. Love's apartment a housekeeper greeted them and said Mrs. Love had gone out but would be back in a while.

After receiving this message Hazel went out on the roof with her two children. The Loves kept a landscaped plot on the roof, with garden furniture and a swing, surrounded by a picket fence. A double gate opened to the rest of the roof, which was protected from the sixteen-floor drop by a parapet, or coping, only two feet high.

For reasons Hazel herself could never satisfactorily explain, she did not remain within the safe confines of the picket fence. According to a house painter who was working on the roof, she resolutely opened both gates and strode out toward the low parapet.

It was a cool, breezy autumn afternoon and Terrence and Benjamin were full of life. Benjamin writhed in his mother's arms. Terrence pulled at his mother's hand.

Hazel walked over to the two-foot parapet and sat down. A few minutes later the two children lay mangled and dead on the roof of a neighboring apartment house on Madison Avenue, thirteen stories below.

Thus did Benjamin Guggenheim's two grandsons, including his namesake, meet as violent a death as he had, only sixteen years after the sinking of the *Titanic*.

Hazel was hysterical when she returned to the Loves' apartment. The housekeeper gave her a glass of water and tried to calm her down.

Shortly thereafter Mrs. Love arrived at the Surrey, encountered police and crowds in front of the entrance, was told what had happened by the doorman, rushed up to see Hazel, who by then was incoherent, called a doctor, and Hazel was quickly taken to the Park West Sanitarium, 170 West Seventy-sixth Street. Mrs. Love then notified the rest of the family of what had happened, not holding back her worst suspicions.

A day or two later there was a hurried gathering of the clan. The quadrumvirate—Dan, Sol, Murry, and Simon—met with their lawyers. According to a Guggenheim in-law living in New York today, some money, "perhaps a couple of million," changed hands and the event was buried. The Guggenheims, victims of injustices in Europe for centuries, could now buy their own justice, one of the infinite blessings of being in America.

The official investigation was reported in a full-column article on page one of *The New York Times*, October 28, 1928, with the headline STORY OF BOYS' FALL AS TOLD BY MOTHER.

According to the article, Hazel testified that she was "a little dazed" about what had happened but that she remembered sitting down on the low parapet for a minute to rest and "the next thing I knew the big boy started climbing up and pushing, and before I knew it, they had both disappeared over the side of the roof and it all happened so suddenly I just can't understand."

Two years after this episode Hazel met and married another Englishman, the intrepid Denys King-Farlow, by whom she eventually had two children, John, born in 1932, and Barbara Benita Mary, born two years later. The marriage with King-Farlow, however, did not last, and Hazel married a fourth time, to Charles McKinley, who eventually died in a plane crash in 1942.

Actually, and to put it mildly, Hazel, like Peggy, did not have a vocation for marriage. Both sisters have the reputation of having been voracious consumers of men all their long lives. Peggy will tell you that she and Hazel had a sort of standing competition over the "affairs" they had. Peggy says she reached one thousand before Hazel only because she "started earlier." After their one thousandth each sister "lost track." "Who knows," wonders Peggy, "who won in the end?"

Like Peggy, Hazel loved art, as well as men, but unlike Peggy she did not collect; she painted instead, first as an amateur, then professionally. Today Hazel maintains she is what Peggy really wanted to be, but didn't have the talent to be: a fully professional artist. Her curriculum vitae, in which she states "her age is just five years inferior to that of her sister, Peggy Guggenheim, and any resemblance between the two is purely coincidental," lists scores of one-man shows and private and museum collections that include her work.

Her painting has been described by the critics as "full of fantasy," "capricious," and "charmingly uninhibited." Their favorable judgment has not been echoed by sister Peggy, however. According to Hazel "she has always gone out of her way to tell mutual friends who admire my work that I am not a good painter. . . . Peggy did, however, stretch a point in my favor," she will concede, "and showed one of my paintings once in all the years she had galleries and included me in that fateful show of women painters at Art of This Century where her husband Max Ernst met Dorothea Tanning."

Hazel does not hide her sibling rivalry with her more famous sister (the middle sister, Benita, died young) and her feelings of not having been given her due. She is convinced of her worth as a painter and convinced that it is much more important and worthwhile to be a creative individual, an artist, than a mere patron, a collector, like her sister.

She admits, however, to being envious of her sister's wealth. Both she and Peggy inherited exactly the same legacies, but she, Hazel, has huge debts ("because I have to buy all my own materials") and does not possess a collection anywhere near as valuable as Peggy's $30 million hoard in Venice. ("You see, as an artist, I have spent all my time painting, whereas she has spent all her time collecting the works of people like me.")

Hazel Guggenheim McKinley, now in her mid-seventies, lives in New Orleans and likes to reminisce about her life and the lives of the other Guggenheims, including her sister Peggy.

She remembers her father, Benjamin, "who never failed to feed me my supper when he came home tired from a day's work at the office."

She remembers her first love affair and how it was broken up by her uncle Dan. "I was only a teenager and had accepted an engagement ring from a young man not much older than myself. I was a long, lanky girl and my short uncle very kindly sat me on his knee and told me I must not see the young man again for several years as we were both too young. My mother was very nervous and kept giggling all the time. I was forced to return a beautiful diamond ring that the young man had given me and have had many regrets since as this good-looking man became one of America's leading publishers."

Other reminiscences:

"Peggy once told Anaïs Nin to her face that she was too beautiful to be a writer and she should stop writing and just be beautiful."

Her aunt Leonie used to go down "to lunch near Wall Street every day to eat with her husband [Murry, donor of the children's dental clinic], she adored being with him so much."

Her uncle Solomon once sent her a "warm" Christmas present wrapped in fine tissue paper. "When I opened it I found a very warm limp duck that had been shot only a few hours before."

As for her uncle Daniel, who, for a while, substituted for her drowned father, "He must have been wedded to his business of mining as I would see in his suite at the Ritz in Paris a long wooden table with pegs on it which showed the exact location and depth of every mine he was interested in. Long-distance calls would come through from all parts of the world telling him where he should mark the depth of each peg in order to keep track of his mining interests."

On cousin Eleanor, Lady Castle Stewart:

"She was a marvelous mother and used to pour tea out of her teapot at her estate in Ashdowne Forest whilst giving one of her four sons his bottle with the other hand. . . . She was the least snobbish person I have ever met and the most down-to-earth and worthwhile of women."

Yes, Hazel Guggenheim McKinley has thousands of memories of her life and of the lives of the Guggenheims. But of her second husband, Milton S. Waldman, and of the two sons he fathered by her she will not speak.

"She put it all past her," says Barbara Loeb, Harold Loeb's widow. "It was a gruesome tragedy, but she overcame it, and went on to produce two more children and have a distinguished artistic career. . . . She's really to be congratulated. . . . Of course, it helped to be a Guggenheim."

CHAPTER

12

PEGGY IN VENICE:
THE LAST DOGARESSA

ALMOST EVERY SUMMER AFTERNOON AT ABOUT FOUR-THIRTY A
splendidly appointed gondola leaves the moss-stained steps of the
Palazzo Venier dei Leoni and glides out onto the Grand Canal.
Usually there are only two people aboard, the gondolier—in full
livery—and *la padrona*, a lively, white-haired lady in her late seventies. But sometimes, when *la padrona* feels lonely, which happens
more often now than ever, there are one or two other passengers: an
old friend, an old lover, a famous artist, an unknown artist, a critic,
a curator, a dealer, a cousin, a grandchild, her son.

It takes about an hour for Gino, the gondolier, to prepare the
gondola for her ride. An hour to bail out the gondola and wax its
varnished hull; to clean the frieze of carved black lions along the gun-
wales, affix the two carved black lions with their little brass collars to
the prow, and install the two prancing brass lions holding spears at the
sides; to lay the black carpet and put in place and wax the black
leather seats; to install the black leather chair and its great black
headrest with the boldly carved winged lion of Saint Mark flanked by
two lions rampant; to polish all the brass. Gino accomplishes it all
with consummate pride and skill. In the morning he is Venice's chief
corpse carrier, bearing the bodies of deceased Venetians through the
canals to the churches and cemeteries; a dreary, unprestigious occupation. But now, in the afternoon, in his white blue-buttoned sailor's
jacket, horizontal-striped shirt, white trousers, with blue waist sash
trailing in the breeze, he is the carrier of no less a personage than "La
Dogaressa" herself, and this fills him with a deep sense of importance.

Ecco, guarda, they exclaim from the bridges, as the boat glides below, *è la Guggenheim . . . sta facendo il giro in gondola.*

This afternoon La Guggenheim is taking her ride with one of her prized little Chinese Shih-Tsu terriers, and with her favorite grandson, the handsome Nicolas Helion, who is currently filming a TV documentary on his grandmother's life and times. These much-appreciated passengers are symbolic of the only things Peggy has ever really cared for in her life: her daughter, Pegeen, and her dogs, her "babies." And her art? The collection? Ah, Lord, how many paintings would she gladly dump into the canal to have her beloved Pegeen back again? Pegeen . . . her petite, charming, talented, blond artist darling, killed by her own hand at only forty-one years of age.

Quietly the gondola slips away from the green-splotched white palace steps, leaving all the Picassos, Pollocks, Ernsts, Légers, Braques to the tourists, and heads down the Grand Canal. Today Peggy has told Gino to go to the ancient district of San Polo, in the direction of the Rialto, one of the oldest sections of Venice.

. . . Under the great wooden Ponte dell' Accademia, past all the Bellinis, Tintorettos, Giorgiones, Titians, Tiepolos . . . past the vast, ornate Ca' Rezzonico, a former papal residence, where Robert Browning lived and died, past the three Gothic Giustiniani palaces, in one of which Richard Wagner wrote the second act of *Tristan und Isolde*, past the huge Ca' Foscari, once the palace of a doge; past the Palazzo Mocenigo, where Byron once resided in state and from whose balcony one of the poet's mistresses threw herself into the canal . . . past all the "cloud capp'd towers, the gorgeous palaces," the endless beauty of this, her Venice, the loveliness without end, "the loveliness," in the words of her former neighbor, Ezra Pound, "become a thing of tears."

. . . Into the Rio San Polo, the old red, orange, yellow, and brown buildings on either side blending, shimmering in the water, the water, in a sense, an artist, abstracting the shapes and colors, distilling their essences, composing moving rainbows, trembling pools of blue and red and brown. . . . Under the gently arched white marble and rose brick bridges . . . and into the little back canals, each one a delightful surprise: the Rio Terra Secondo, the Rio delle Muneghette, the Rio di San Cassiano. . . .

Peggy directs the gondola with a regal wave of her hand, never looking back at the gondolier, or uttering a word. If she wants to go into the next canal on the right she simply raises her right hand and waves in that direction. . . . Grandson Nicolas looks up at the parade of palaces, full of admiration, taking notes for his film, his grandmother smiling benignly on him, the shaggy little Shih-Tsu prancing about, the tall, muscular gondolier rowing on with a steady rhythm, keeping a sharp eye out for obstructions—mooring piles, other boats—his blue sash floating in the air behind him. . . . People are gaping from the *fondamente* as the gondola glides by. There are few, if any, gondolas like this, with such splendid regalia, remaining in Venice: The great old aristocratic families, anxious to appear up-to-date, succumbing, also, to Italy's growing egalitarianism, have been converting to *motoscafi*. . . . Most people do not know who is in the gondola, but a few do, and Gino acknowledges their recognition with a proud, calm smile. . . .

Two hours gliding through the narrow canals of San Polo, then back up the Grand Canal to the Palazzo Venier dei Leoni. . . .

The long black gondola bobbing up and down against the moss-fringed white steps. . . . The Shih-Tsu leaps out and shakes himself dry. Then La Guggenheim alights, followed by young Nicolas. Nicolas helps his grandmother up the steps while Gino begins dismantling the gondola. The black carpet is removed, along with the black leather chair, the black leather seats, the prancing brass lions, the black initialed headrest, the carved black lions with the little brass collars, and all is stored in the palace until the following afternoon.

The Palazzo Venier dei Leoni. Heavy, sepulchral, white marble structure stained green-black at the base, ivy dripping from the roof. The widest space of any palace on the Grand Canal, but only one story high. Started by the Veniers, a family with two doges in its long, distinguished history, with the intention of outdoing everyone else in splendor and magnificence on the Grand Canal, but never completed, the family having eventually run out of money. *Il Palazzo Non Compiuto.* Huge garden in back: laurels, lindens, magnolias, plantains, cedars of Lebanon, lime trees, overhanging the palace. One of the largest private gardens in Venice, good for displaying sculpture. And burying dogs. Lions once kept in the garden by the Veniers. Later another owner kept leopards and a black panther. Eighteen huge white marble lions' heads decorating the facade. Roof of the palace flat, a vast terrace, good for sunbathing. The entire palace a vast museum of modern art, a huge, waterlogged sarcophagus filled with the anguished remains of the 1930s, 1940s, and 1950s, older seeming, inside and out, than the nearby Accademia, with its ancient, glowing Bellinis, Giorgiones, Titians, Tiepolos. . . .

Peggy bought the *palazzo* for only $80,000 in still-depressed 1949 (the Venetians were afraid Tito would try to annex Venice to Yugoslavia), having to break one of her trusts to make the purchase. She had returned to Europe in 1946: "Much as I loved Art of This Century, I loved Europe more than America, and when the war ended I couldn't wait to go back." By now she had to admit she had become a confirmed expatriate. The previous Guggenheims had desperately wanted to be such *American* Americans, but she had none of that eagerness. She had become a European American, an international American, and was quite satisfied with that identity. With Peggy the Guggenheims had come full circle. One hundred years after Meyer and Barbara had abandoned their native Switzerland, their most celebrated granddaughter had come back to settle permanently only a few hundred kilometers from their birthplace. Furthermore, this granddaughter's own eight grandchildren were being raised not as Americans, but as Europeans—Sindbad's children as British citizens; Pegeen's as French.

Venice. Could there be a more fitting resting place for a Guggenheim? A powerful, exploitive commercial family, owners of mines of copper, silver, diamonds, and gold in Mexico, Chile, Africa; an imperial family, lavish patrons of the arts, in this imperial city built and adorned by some of the most ruthless exploiters of the world's wealth and some of the most generous patrons of the arts who ever lived.

The Palazzo Venier dei Leoni. As soon as Peggy was first shown the place she realized it would make the ideal repository and showcase for her paintings and sculptures. The rooms were airy and spacious, and, unlike so many other Venetian palaces, the walls and ceilings were unadorned. No gilded paneling, stucco friezes, or frescoes to distract from the paintings. And the little courtyard in front of the palace, and the large garden in back, seemed specially designed for displaying modern sculptures. Furthermore, where in America, or anywhere else for that matter, could she, with her relatively limited resources, buy a large eighteenth-century palace for only $80,000? Being one of the poor Guggenheims had always been a problem for Peggy. Unlike her more affluent cousins, she always had to settle for cut-rate elegance.

So install the works. For the little courtyard facing the Grand Canal, Marino Marini's ebullient "Horse With Rider," the squat horse bleating, the squat rider with arms spread out in ecstasy, phallus in full erection. "When Marini had it cast in bronze for me, he had the phallus made separately, so that it could be screwed in and out at leisure. . . . When the nuns came by to be blessed by the Patriarch, who, on special holy days went by my house on a motorboat, I detached the phallus of the horseman and hid it in a drawer. . . . Legend spread that I had several phalluses of different sizes, like spare parts, to use on different occasions."

Then, for the big garden in the back, place Paolozzi's contorted "Chinese Dog," Germaine Richier's macabre "Tauromachy," Giacometti's terrifying "Lion Woman" and "Woman With a Cut Throat, The Carotid Severed," Henry Moore's "Three Standing Figures," Max Ernst's "In the Streets of Athens," a couple of Jean Arps; finally place the immense composite Romanesque-Gothic-Renaissance throne, La Dogaressa's throne, her throne as the uncontested grande dame of the avant-garde, as the last and only true heiress of "La Serenissima."

Then, for the interior, hang the paintings, over two hundred of them. The great Picassos: "Girls With a Toy Boat," "The Poet," "Lacerba"; the great Max Ernsts: "The Entire City," "The Robing of the Bride," "The Anti-Pope"; the great Pollocks: "Moon Woman," "Eyes in the Heat," "The Enchanted Forest"; then the Braques, the Bazioteses, the di Chiricos, the Dalis, the Delaunay, the Duchamp, the Leonor Fini, the Gleizes, the Kandinskys, the Klees, the de Koonings, the Kupkas, the Légers, the Miró, the Mondrians, the Rothko, the Tanguys . . . the Vails, the Pegeens. . . .

And then install the furniture and all the *objets*. For the dining room: the long, narrow, fifteenth-century rustic Venetian oak table; the huge oak sideboard, made from two fourteenth-century Venetian chests; the small wooden African and Oceanic sculptures to complement the Braques, the Duchamp, the Gleizes, the Légers on the walls. For the bedroom: the silver Alexander Calder bedhead, a soaring, dancing silver fantasy against turquoise walls; the turquoise marabou coverlet; the collection of over one hundred earrings from all parts of the world; the gilt-framed antique Venetian mirrors; Lawrence Vail's decorated bottles; Lenbach's portrait of Peggy and sister Benita as young girls.

Yes, now she had added another landmark to her end of the canal.

Now the name of Guggenheim had taken its place on the canal along-side the names of Richard Wagner, Robert Browning, Titian, Ga-briele d'Annunzio, Henry James, Lord Byron, Ezra Pound. Ah, what a parade of geniuses had lived and worked along her end of the canal! Directly opposite the Venier dei Leoni, in the Casetta Rossa, D'An-nunzio had lived with La Duse and had written *Il Fuoco*, and a little farther down, in the Palazzo Barbaro, Henry James had written *The Wings of the Dove*. Titian once had a studio in the vicinity. And behind the Venier dei Leoni, a little to the east, another American expatriate, Ezra Pound, lived and worked during the last fifteen years before his death.

Another landmark indeed. And what more fitting landmark for the second half of the twentieth century? An American Jewish lady living by herself in a museum-palace on the Grand Canal of Venice. During the great age of the Venetian Republic such a thing would have been utterly inconceivable. Not only because America had not yet been settled, but principally because single women did not own and live in palaces on the Grand Canal in those patriarchal times, and the Jews were almost wholly confined to what was one of the original ghettos of Europe. How extraordinarily fitting it was in the Age of Jewish Emancipation, the Jewish Renaissance, the American Cen-tury, the Era of Women's Liberation, that the most famous contem-porary resident on the Grand Canal of Venice was an American Jewess who was a patron of the arts.

Let the old Venetian dowagers, the other grande dames, the *di-scendenti di dogi e dogaresse*—people like la contessa Marcello, la contessa Foscari, la contessa Grimani, and the rest of them—snub their noses at La Guggenheim, the upstart, the interloper, *L'Ebrea*, *L'Americana*. Peggy Guggenheim still remains the only Venetian on the canal, the last true dogaressa. The Venetians: "a people who lived wholly for gain," a materialistic people who nevertheless devoted a greater share of their wealth to the fine arts and to architecture than any other people in history.

A year before Peggy installed herself and all her paintings and sculptures in the Venier dei Leoni she was invited by Count Zorzi, then ambassador of Venice's Biennale Art Exhibition, to show her entire collection at the Twenty-fourth Biennale. The year was 1948, the one-hundredth anniversary of Simon and Meyer Guggenheim's emigration to the United States. The Biennale was at the time the most important international exhibition of contemporary art in the world. Each participating nation maintained its own pavilion in Venice's wooded Public Gardens, in the northeast section of town.

Peggy's show received enormous publicity and literally put her and her collection on the international map. Her remarks about the event in her *Confessions of an Art Addict* were a giveaway to her otherwise unacknowledged Guggenheimism: ". . . But what I enjoyed most was seeing the name of Guggenheim appearing on the maps of the Public Gardens next to the names of Great Britain, France, Holland, Austria, Switzerland, Poland, Palestine, Denmark, Belgium, Egypt, Czechoslovakia, Hungary, Rumania. I felt as though I were a new foreign country."

So well known, in fact, did the new foreign country become, that even Bernard Berenson, who loathed modern art, condescended to visit the new land and see what sort of fauna it contained. No sooner had he landed on Guggenheim soil than Peggy told him how thoroughly she had studied his books on art history and appreciation, and how much they had meant to her.

"Then why do you go in for all this?" he asked, waving somewhat contemptuously at her collection.

"I couldn't afford Old Masters and anyhow I consider it one's duty to protect the art of one's time."

Berenson then opined that Max Ernst's works were much "too sexual" for his taste (he did not approve of sex in art) and the Pollocks were not really paintings, but tapestries, a judgment Peggy confessed she had a difficult time disputing.

Another distinguished visitor, the princess Pignatelli, was even more blunt than Berenson about the collection. "If you would only throw all these awful pictures into the Grand Canal," she once told Peggy, "you would have the most beautiful house in Venice."

One thing leads to another, and so after the success at the Biennale, Peggy was invited to exhibit her collection at the Strozzina in Florence, and then at the Palazzo Reale in Milan. Yet all these shows were, in a sense, but a prelude to the great Pollock show she gave in the Sala Napoleonica of Venice's Correr Museum in 1950, the first exhibition of Pollocks ever held in Europe.

Peggy lent all her twenty-three Pollocks to the show, and since it was held in a room through which one had to pass in order to get into the much-frequented Correr Museum of Venetian painting and history, thousands upon thousands of people saw it. "It was always lit at night, and I remember the extreme joy I had sitting in the Piazza San Marco beholding the Pollocks glowing through the open windows of the Museum, and then going out on the balcony of the gallery to see San Marco in front of me, knowing that all the Pollocks were behind me. It seemed to place Pollock historically where he belonged, as one of the greatest painters of our time, who had every right to be exhibited in this wonderful setting. All the young painters were very much influenced by this show."

In the meantime, daughter Pegeen had married the French painter Jean Helion, a realist turned abstractionist who eventually turned realist again, and so it was all but inevitable that Peggy's next show would be for her son-in-law.

Pegeen had first met the talented Jean Helion in New York during World War II. Helion, a former soldier in the French army, had been captured by the Germans and had been interned in a Nazi work camp, from which he managed to escape and flee to America, an experience somewhat similar to Max Ernst's, which he later memorialized in his book *They Shall Not Have Me*. In 1944 he exhibited some of his work at Peggy's Art of This Century, met the gallery owner's artistic daughter, liked her—and what her mother could probably do for his artistic career—and married her.

They were an attractive couple, the young Helions, with a seemingly limitless future ahead of them. Pegeen Guggenheim Vail, the petite, charming painter-daughter of New York's most celebrated female avant-garde gallery owner and collector, grandniece of the renowned Solomon Guggenheim, who was rapidly asserting himself as the foremost patron of modern art in the world, great-granddaughter of the indomitable mining-empire builder, Meyer Guggenheim; and Jean Helion, handsome, intense young French painter, who had already made quite a name for himself in the art worlds of Paris and New York. As soon as the war ended the couple left their Greenwich Village walk-up and returned to Europe, first to a farmhouse in the South of France, then to Paris, where they both painted furiously and produced three sons, Fabrice, Nicolas, and Davide.

Peggy wanted her show for her son-in-law to be just as great a success as her show for Pollock. Pegeen was the most precious being in her life; she loved her three little grandsons almost as much as she loved Pegeen; and, she sincerely admired Helion's painting. But, almost as a prophecy of the tragedies to come, the show was a disaster from start to finish. Peggy had drastically cut the wordy catalogue, written by a friend, and the hypersensitive Helion had resented the cuts. The paintings were held up in Italian customs so long Peggy almost had to call the whole show off. The show was to be held in the glittering Sala dei Specchi in the Ca' Giustinian, headquarters of the Biennale, and two days before the show the haughty owner of the palace, one of those *discendenti di dogi e dogaresse*, removed the rich brocade from the walls (she feared *L'Americana* was going to ruin it) and Peggy had to replace it with sacking at the eleventh hour. "Then," Peggy wrote in her *Confessions of an Art Addict*, "as though the gods were against us, a terrible storm came and rain dripped from the crimson banner we had placed in the street to announce the show and ruined the dress of a girl passing beneath it. After that, the wind blew down the banner altogether. . . . As a result of all our troubles in connection with this show, I decided never again to do anything with works from abroad, or ever again to ask the local authorities for a gallery." To top it all off, the show was not even a critical or commercial success.

But Peggy, after all was said and done, was a Guggenheim, and Guggenheims were rarely daunted, least of all by their own fiascoes. (Buy a mine and find it peters out after twenty feet. All right, buy another.) Bouncing back from the Helion debacle, she eventually went on to hold very successful shows at the Biennale for Max Ernst and Jean Arp. (In the guest book for the Ernst show, Max had written: "An old friend has come back forever and ever and ever"—and "so finally," in Peggy's words, "peace was made.") Later she held a most successful show of Pollocks at the Museum of Modern Art in Rome.

Life was not all art, however; there was also love. Though well into her fifties, and the survivor of two unhappy marriages, several unhappy "unofficial marriages," and many inconclusive, frequently unhappy love affairs, Peggy still pursued love with a zest fully equal to the passion of her halcyon years.

Love . . . and patronage. Love and patronage had always gone together for Peggy in her youth and so again did they go together in her middle age. It was not always such a stable mixture, however, in her youth, and it proved to be an even more volatile compound in her fifties. Lovers may desperately need patronage in addition to love, but they almost always come to resent it.

Behold Peggy Guggenheim in her mid-fifties, in the mid-1950s. A lively, intelligent, sensual, trim, still-attractive multimillionaire (she now had around two and a half million in trust, plus the *palazzo*, and her collection was worth at least ten or fifteen million), with an international reputation as a patroness of modern art and a somewhat less widespread reputation as connoisseur and patroness of men. She is, as we have said, still undaunted. All her life she has reached out for art and life and love and she is not about to give any one of them up now.

If her Guggenheim luck would only hold, who knew what enthusiasms and successes might be hers in those often discouraging middle years? But, alas, luck has a way of drying up. We have seen how the Guggenheim mining luck dried up in the dusty nitrate fields of Chile. Peggy herself had been enormously lucky. To be the right catalyst at the right time with artists like Tanguy, Duchamp, Ernst, and Pollock? Yes, that was luck. If it hadn't been for the *Titanic*. . . . If it hadn't been for Hitler's war. . . .

But now, for Peggy, as with the Guggenheim family as a whole, luck was beginning to run out. Whereas once whatever a Guggenheim touched suddenly doubled, quadrupled, centupled, in value, whether it was a mine or a lover or a work of art, now what the family, and Peggy, touched, not only did not bloom and multiply, but often died before it was born.

Three people did Peggy love and patronize during her fifties and sixties and all three met violent ends. By a process of alchemy of unknown formula and justification, her Midas touch had begun to metamorphose into a distinctly unlucky caress.

There is a very famous small easel painting of Giorgione's called "The Tempest" in the Accademia, a few *palazzi* down the Canal from Peggy's place. A partially nude young woman, seated on a grassy embankment, suckles an infant. A handsome young man, spear in hand, stands at the opposite side of the canvas, ignoring the young woman. In the background: a village of stone houses, some ancient ruins, two stands of tall trees, a dark, gray-blue stormy sky rent by lightning. The mood is mysterious, ominous, enigmatic. Giorgione, like Max Ernst, had fine antennae. He was the first of the great Venetian painters to sense the rot that was slowly beginning to seep in and eat at the soul of "La Serenissima," the rot that would eventually destroy the Venetian state.

Now paint the sky above the Palazzo Venier dei Leoni silver and lead. Add a gray storm cloud, a streak of lightning. Color the tall, overhanging trees dark olive, dark brown. Make the ivy-hung white marble of the palace as cold and pallid as a Roman sarcophagus. Color the waters of the canal lead and blue. Paint in small white-crested waves, and make them slap at the sides of the black, dismantled gondola, the corpse carrier. Yes, prepare the scene for "La Tempesta."

La Signora Guggenheim, feeling lonely in the large, high-ceilinged rooms of her relatively uninhabited museum-palace, and with at least some of the sap of youth left, takes on a lover. His name is Raoul Gregovitch, a Venetian of Dalmatian extraction, an accountant by profession, though without permanent employment, and the son of a judge. He is handsome, vital, sexy, ten years younger than she, and, in Peggy's own words, "only interested in cars." During the war he had been a *partigiano,* raiding fascist convoys in Alpine passes, and immediately after the war he had continued his marauding, this time on innocent motorists, on the autostradas of the Veneto. During one escapade he killed someone and was thrown in jail. He eventually got out because his father was a judge.

Give him a key to the *palazzo.* Introduce him to a lot of high-class people. Buy him a snappy new car. Set him up in business. It is the early 1950s in Italy; *il miracolo economico* is just beginning to gain momentum. Italians are buying cars as never before. Fiat is now producing hundreds of vehicles a day. The ugly modern Venetian mainland suburb of Mestre badly needs a new garage. Raoul has the idea, but not the money. La Guggenheim has the money. Before long a new garage is born in Mestre.

Raoul Gregovitch, proprietor of a brand-new garage in Mestre, proprietor, also, of a fast new sports car, lover of no less a personage than La Milionaria Americana, "La Dogaressa" herself, a dashing young man with a bank account, a business of his own, and money in his pocket, feeling his new-found importance ("Raoul has discovered America," they gossip in Venice), begins to cut a wide swath on the Venetian mainland in his new car. La Guggenheim gets upset over the stories she hears. There are furious arguments in the Palazzo Venier dei Leoni. Shades of the War in the Brownstone. But Raoul has his garage now, and his long, shiny, fast new car. He got what he could get out of "La Dogaressa." Still, he was under some obligation to her, he had to admit. After one heated exchange he gets into his car, speeds out onto the flat, green plains of the Veneto, hurtles down long tree-lined lanes, and wraps himself and the car around a tree: dead on arrival at the Mestre hospital, Peggy's second protégé killed in an auto accident.

Go to Ceylon and India to forget: ". . . in the fall of 1954, after Raoul's death, I decided to get out of Italy and try to think of something else. Paul Bowles had invited me to Ceylon, where he had bought a little island. It was the southernmost inhabited spot in the

Indian Ocean, fantastically beautiful and luxuriant, with every conceivable flower and exotic plant in the east."

Several months wandering around Ceylon and India, continually besieged by aspiring painters, then return again to Venice, having presumably forgotten, and take on another lover, this time her newest protégé, the young Italian painter from Feltre in the Veneto, Tancredi Parmeggiani.

Peggy had begun to sponsor Tancredi in 1952 on recommendation from a friend. He was a quiet, sensitive young man in his early thirties, very talented, given to sudden fits of temper, and entirely without funds. Peggy put him on a monthly salary, just as she had done with Pollock, in exchange for two gouaches—his favorite medium at the time—per month. Eventually she also gave him use of a studio in the cellar of her *palazzo*. After a number of experimental starts, taking as full advantage as possible of his new freedom, Tancredi evolved a style of his own, becoming what the Italians call a "Spatialista," a spatial artist, painting highly original abstractions ("I *detest* objects," he used to tell everyone), somewhat in the manner of Pollock.

Tancredi was extremely temperamental and had a number of impossible eccentricities. He would drive Peggy's servants out of their minds by walking all over her *palazzo* "with his feet covered in paint of every conceivable color." Often, in one of his periodic fits, he removed all his paintings from the palace—and there were scores of them—only to bring them back in a few days. No sooner would Peggy give him money than he would spend it all on a sudden binge of eating, drinking, and buying, then, immediately after the spree, come back begging for more.

Nevertheless, despite these occasional lapses, Peggy fell for him—after all, he was eminently available: She had him right there in the *palazzo* all day—and patroness and protégé eventually became lovers. It was an old story for Peggy. All her husbands, official and unofficial, and almost all her lovers, had begun as protégés, with Peggy literally rescuing them from destitution.

Now things in the Peggy branch of the House of Guggenheim begin to get very complicated. Daughter Pegeen, as we know, was married to the French painter Jean Helion, whom she regarded as "a genius" (it had always been her ambition to marry a great genius). Soon Sindbad was married to a French lady by the name of Jacqueline Ventadour. The two couples were both living in Paris and saw a good deal of each other. In time, Jean Helion fell in love with Jacqueline Ventadour. There followed a double divorce and Helion married his ex-brother-in-law's ex-wife.

Shattered by this experience—after all, how often in life does a woman lose her husband to her sister-in-law?—small, thin, blond Pegeen moved to Venice with one of her sons, Nicolas, leaving the other two with Helion. Happy, at this critical moment in her life, to be near Mother, she soon met and married, on the rebound, a British painter by the name of Ralph Rumney, a man of whom Peggy disapproved, and by whom Pegeen soon had a son, Sandro, her fourth, born in Venice.

Pegeen was by now an excellent painter in her own right. While in Venice she worked in both her own studio-apartment, alongside Rumney, and at her mother's, in a small studio next to Tancredi's. Tancredi was so charming, interesting, and talented. It wasn't long before the unthinkable happened. Pegeen fell in love with her mother's lover and protégé.

Peggy was very proud of her painter-daughter, whom she often confessed she loved more than any thing, or any being, in the world, and apparently never suspected until it was too late that Pegeen's relationship with Tancredi was anything more than just friendship between two artists, even though Pegeen had shared other men with her mother before.

For Pegeen was always, in her mother's mind, very much the artist and, in a very real sense, Pegeen was, after Tancredi, Peggy's only other protégé. She bought her daughter canvases, brushes, and paints, showed her work to influential people, exhibited her paintings in her galleries, and, in general, promoted her as best she could. Pegeen, in turn, did well. During her brief career she held one-man shows in New York, Paris, Milan, Venice, Padua, Merano, Palm Beach, Vicenza, Stockholm, and Toronto.

Entirely self-taught (Peggy, strange as it seems, never gave her daughter formal art instruction, nor did her artist-father, Laurence Vail), Pegeen's work was almost "primitive." Disdaining abstraction, she produced naïve, infantile, naturalistic two-dimensional scenes of Venice and of little blond girls like herself in various settings and situations: in a bedroom, in a nursery, in a ballroom, on the terrace of a Venetian palace overlooking the Grand Canal. Sometimes the figures, almost always women, are dressed in Pegeen's own fantastic creations, sometimes they are nude. Almost always the people represented seem to have nothing to do with one another. In one painting two women are seated at a table together, one dressed, the other completely nude, each ignoring the other. She also produced little figurines of young women, again resembling herself, which she had made into colored-glass sculptures by a Venetian glassblower. Her style—childlike and full of fantasy, bold in the use of color—was very much her own, and won her many admirers. When Clare Boothe Luce, as United States Ambassador to Italy, visited Peggy's collection, she announced she liked Pegeen's paintings best of all, yes, even more than the Picassos, Pollocks, Ernsts. While the two American grande dames were examining the Pegeens, Peggy observed that in Pegeen's paintings "people never seem to be engaged in any conversation with each other, each going his own way." To which, Mrs. Luce sagely remarked, unwittingly commenting on the spiritual isolation in which Pegeen lived, "Maybe they have nothing to say." Later, Sir Herbert Read told Peggy that he thought Pegeen "remained as fresh and pure and still brought the same magical, innocent touch to her work as she did at age eleven." The compliment encouraged Pegeen, who was fragile emotionally and inclined to lose confidence in herself easily.

Not that there had not been other appreciators of her artistry. Henry Moore, an old friend of Mother's, who habitually referred to Pegeen as "Alice-in-Wonderland," liked her work, as did her step-father, Max Ernst, who, like her former husband, Jean Helion, often gave her a little instruction and could not get over the fact that she never tried to copy his style. And then her own mother had paid her quite a tribute in a magazine article, remarking on how wonderful it was that Pegeen was able to maintain such a childlike, innocent vision of reality, "a world in which people lived absolutely unconscious of mundanities."

At about the time Pegeen was beginning to take more than a sisterly interest in Tancredi, her mother completed the construction of her art pavilion in her garden, which she called her *barchessa*, after a certain type of building in the Veneto, usually a wing to a great villa.

Peggy's *barchessa* was modeled, on a smaller scale, after the great Palladian Villa Emo at Fanzole, and contained—among many elements, including a traditional tiled roof—a charming loggia with six arches facing her garden. Normally *barchesse* are used for storing grain and hay. Peggy used hers to house her collection of surrealists, her Dalis, Magrittes, Leonor Finis, Tanguys, her Max Ernsts.

After the completion of the building, Peggy held a *granzega,* or outdoor Venetian dinner party, in the garden of a favorite restaurant, for the architect, the builder, and all the workers. The six-course, three-wine affair, accompanied by guitars and mandolins, was a great success and Peggy was able to take time out from her troubles to write in her guest book, in a wobbly hand, "The nicest night of my life in Venice, 1948–58, Peggy G."

With all the surrealists now hanging in the *barchessa,* Peggy had more room in the *palazzo* for herself, her family, her protégés, her friends, or at least more of a feeling of space.

She had been holding a little salon for artists and writers and scholars in the Venier dei Leoni for the last few years; now she was able to include more people in these affairs, the only ones still held in Venice that are reminiscent of the great salons of the past.

To these salons came, of course, daughter Pegeen and protégé Tancredi. People who attended the parties noticed how nervous and ill at ease little Pegeen often appeared. The poor girl certainly had her problems at the time. The divorce from Helion had been a harrowing experience—especially losing her husband the way she did, to a sister-in-law and supposed friend—and the rebound marriage to Rumney was not working out. Now, just to add another problem to her life, she was in love with her mother's lover and protégé. And she had two young sons with her to raise, Nicolas Helion and Sandro Rumney, with very little support, moral or financial, from their fathers. Furthermore, she had to endure separation from her other two sons—Fabrice and Davide—who lived with Jean Helion. To top it off, she did not have much money: Her mother, though a generous supporter, as we know, of art and artists, kept both her children on very tight financial strings.

It was, all things considered, a tense family situation, and so Peggy was only too happy to make a trip to New York in the fall of 1959 to attend the grand opening of her uncle Sol's museum. She had been away from America for twelve consecutive years.

As it turned out, Peggy missed the continually postponed opening, but did have a chance to see the museum (with cousin Harry as guide), to visit several other Guggenheim cousins as well, and to take in the art scene in New York.

We have already reported Peggy's reactions to her uncle's museum. She didn't much care for it—"a huge garage," "the colors were ugly," and so on—and "much preferred" her "modest barchessa in Venice." "For the first time I did not regret the enormous fortune I had lost when my father left his brothers to go into his own business, a few years before he was drowned on the *Titanic.*"

As for the New York art scene, she was utterly repelled by it.

> I was thunderstruck; the entire art movement had become an enormous business venture. Only a few persons really care for paintings. The rest buy them from snobbishness or to avoid taxation. Prices are unheard of. People only buy what is the most expensive, having no faith in anything else.

A year later, in her *Confessions*, she wrote,

> I do not like art today—I think it has gone to hell, as a result of the financial attitude. . . . Eighteen years ago there was a pure pioneering spirit in America. A new art had to be born—Abstract Expressionism. I fostered it. I do not regret it. It produced Pollock, or rather, Pollock produced it. This alone justifies my efforts. As for the others, I don't know what got into them.

(Later, when the 1960s produced Pop Art and Andy Warhol, Peggy got her back up even higher. "Pop art," she declared, "has nothing to do with art. It is just the commercialization of a very stupid idea." No, she would not debase her collection with a Warhol.)

Concluding her melancholy thoughts on the contemporary art scene, at the end of her *Confessions of an Art Addict,* Peggy declared,

> . . . one cannot expect every decade to produce genius. The twentieth century has already produced enough. We should not expect any more. A field must lie fallow now and then. Artists try too hard to be original. That is why we have all this painting that isn't painting any more. For the moment we should content ourselves with what the twentieth century has produced. . . . Today is the age of collecting, not of creation. Let us at least preserve and present to the masses all the great treasures we have.

Among those great treasures, Peggy has distilled a list of the top ten modern masters. They are: Picasso, Miró, Kandinsky, Klee, Duchamp, Braque, Ernst, Matisse, Pollock, and Magritte.

As for Old Masters, her top ten is tilted heavily toward the great Venetians: Titian, Tintoretto, Giorgione, Carpaccio, Velásquez, Rembrandt, Giotto, Botticelli, Dürer, and Michelangelo.

Her disillusioning journey to America over, it was back to Venice and a much-appreciated letter, from Cousin Harry, waiting for her at the Venier dei Leoni:

> Before your arrival, and before we had a chance to become reacquainted after all these years, I had the general feeling that perhaps some

day you might want to leave your collection to the Foundation to be housed in the new Frank Lloyd Wright Museum. However, after thinking the matter through, I most sincerely believe that your Foundation and your palace, which has, thanks to your initiative, become world-renowned, should, after your death, be bequeathed, as you have planned, to Italy. I think that is the appropriate place for it, and I think from the family point of view—which I confess is always uppermost in my mind—this plan would be the most beneficial. I do hope while you were over here you were able to make progress with your plans.

May you continue, in great success, in your life dedicated to the progress of art, and also get lots of pleasure and fun from it.

"From a family point of view" Harry turned out to be quite correct in his approval of his cousin's intentions. The Guggenheims may have been well known in the United States, but they were relatively unknown in Europe. It was Peggy who put the family on the European map as well, who made them at the Venice Biennale into "a new country."

Yes, it was good to get back to her beloved Venice and to Harry's most reassuring letter, but unfortunately she also had to face a continuing and steadily worsening family crisis.

Son Sindbad Vail, having lost his first wife to his brother-in-law, and having had to bring up his two young sons, Clovis and Mark, alone, had recently married a lovely British girl by the name of Peggy Angela Yeomans, with whom he soon had two daughters, Karole and Julia. He was living and working in Paris, on very little money, as an insurance surveyor, something he never particularly wanted to be.

And daughter Pegeen, still having troubles with her marriage, and still very much enamored of her mother's darling Tancredi, was desperately trying to keep her head above water in her efforts to raise two sons on bits and pieces and scraps of money coming in sporadically, if at all, from Helion, Mother, and infrequent sales of her own work.

Peggy, at this point, could have well afforded to help her children financially—she now had over $3 million, having inherited additional trusts from her sister Benita, and a cousin, Nettie Knox—but she continued to keep both son and daughter begging. Not that she did this intentionally; it was just that she was so immersed in her role as Grand Patroness of modern art as to have only leftover thoughts for her children's needs. Her palace and *barchessa* were now open to the public three afternoons a week, from three to five, and the crowds were often enormous. In season she was receiving eight hundred visitors a day—mostly Americans and Japanese—and selling eighty catalogues at five thousand lire each, for a total daily take of six hundred and fifty dollars, not bad at all.

This was in addition to the exhibitions of her collection she was intermittently holding in Turin, Milan, and Rome, and the shows she was holding for artists like Pollock, Ernst, Arp, Tancredi, and others.

The collection, and the role that went with it, was, after all, a tremendous responsibility, a persistent commandment, and a constant worry. Especially in an Italy gradually but inexorably descending into anarchy and chaos. As it turned out, she was robbed twice. Once a man sauntered into the *barchessa*, handed a bystander an empty bag, telling him to hold it open, then calmly took a Tanguy off the wall, plopped it into the bag, took the bag, and left.

Later, no fewer than twenty-six paintings, worth over $2 million, were stolen from the palace and the *barchessa* one night while Peggy was sleeping. They were eventually recovered upon payment of a ransom. Now every painting in both the palace and the *barchessa* is wired to central police headquarters. If a painting is removed, the Venetian police are at Peggy's in six minutes. Or, as Peggy says, "they're *supposed* to be."

A commandment stone, a prison, that collection. A cruel master. I must be looked after. I must be protected. I must be served. I must be shown to the world. How many times had Peggy's attention been diverted from her family by her tyrannical collection?

Several times too often. For amid the triumphs of the grande dame of modern art there persisted the unhappiness of her children. Sindbad, a man who was raised as a prince, having to pound the pavements of Paris as an *insurance* surveyor. And Pegeen, her first husband taken from her by her sister-in-law, two of her sons taken from her by terms of the divorce settlement, unhappy in her second marriage, a marriage of which her mother disapproved, unhappy in her hopeless relationship with Tancredi, with two young sons to raise, and no money.

Sindbad, with two sons and two daughters to support and educate on his earnings as a free-lance insurance surveyor in Paris, gently requests, in vain, that his mother give him, or bequeath him, at least two or three paintings—a Picasso, one of the Pollocks, an Ernst—to help care for and educate his four children, now, when they need help the most, and also cushion his oncoming old age. No, the collection says. No, I am sacred. I must remain intact.

Pegeen. Pegeen . . . Pegeen needing money desperately. Her sons. The two with Helion she rarely sees. The two with her and Rumney she must support herself. On what? Mother, disapproving of her daughter's life, holds onto her money. Tancredi. Yes, Pegeen loves Tancredi. Now Peggy is jealous of that love. The two women contend for Tancredi. Rumney knows what is going on and moves Pegeen, Nicolas, and Sandro to Paris.

The sensitive, temperamental Tancredi, torn between two hopeless loves, resentful of Peggy's financial hold over him, suffering from Pegeen's move to Paris, goes to Rome, and in a sudden fit of despair, throws himself into the Tiber and drowns.

Now little Pegeen, too, begins to drown. She has lost Jean Helion. She has lost possession of two of her sons. She does not love her husband. She has lost Tancredi forever. Now *he* was a true genius. She has no money. One evening in 1967 she is finally overwhelmed, and, after a drunken spree, takes an overdose of sleeping pills in her apartment in Paris. The French police rule it a suicide. Peggy receives news of her daughter's death the following morning. Four times before had Pegeen tried to kill herself. Now, at last, she is successful.

After the funeral, held in Paris, with the yellow press hovering about, son Nicolas goes to live with his father, Jean Helion, and his brothers, Fabrice and Davide. Sandro Rumney goes to live with an "aunt," Katy Vail, Laurence Vail's daughter by his second wife, the writer Kay Boyle.

Usually the most dreaded things do not happen. But now, for Peggy, the very worst has happened. Yes, nothing could have been worse than this. Losing first Tancredi, to whom she had given so much support, so much love, and on whom she had pinned such high artistic hopes. And then Pegeen.

There is a small room in the crypt of the Palazzo Venier dei Leoni dedicated to the memory of Pegeen. The walls are hung entirely with Pegeens. Many are self-portraits. A little blond girl in her bedroom. A little blond girl walking by the Venetian lagoon. A little blond girl looking out over the Grand Canal from the terrace of a Venetian palace. . . . Duplicates, in a way, of all the little glass figurines of wide-eyed little blond girls staring at nothing which stand in a glass case against another wall.

A photograph of Pegeen sitting on her mother's throne hangs on the wall directly opposite the door. Underneath the photograph a small plaque:

PEGEEN GUGGENHEIM
1925–1967

Pegeen Guggenheim, only daughter of Peggy Guggenheim and her first husband, Laurence Vail, was born in Ouchy, Switzerland in 1925 and died in Paris in 1967. Studied in England, France, and the United States. Self-taught and had painted since childhood. One-man shows in New York, Paris, Milan, Venice, Padua, Merano, Palm Beach, Vicenzo, Stockholm, Toronto, the Museum of Modern Art, Venice, the Fine Arts Gallery of San Diego.

Peggy, returning to the Venier dei Leoni, is terribly distraught, but she is a Guggenheim of the old stamp and such Guggenheims do not allow themselves to be defeated; they bounce back. They are of hearty stock. They are survivors. Peggy Guggenheim, at sixty-eight, still has much to do for and with the collection. Her greatest achievements and triumphs are still awaiting her: the creation of her foundation in 1968; the showing of almost her entire collection at Uncle Solomon's museum in New York in 1969; and then the spectacular showing of the entire collection at the Orangerie in Paris in 1974.

And so, a year after Pegeen's death, the Peggy Guggenheim Foundation is born in Venice. The Palazzo Venier dei Leoni, the *barchessa,* and all the paintings and sculptures in them—over 250 works of art, worth over $30 million—are donated "in perpetuity" to the new foundation. Later, in accordance with an agreement worked out with her cousin Harry, they are willed to the Solomon R. Guggenheim Foundation in New York, with the proviso that they are to remain forever in Venice, "unless Venice sinks," in which case they may be removed to New York. Peggy's pride in her achievement is immense. In her generation the only Guggenheims who created foundations were herself and Harry, and she started with less money than any of the others.

Then, in 1969, the great triumph in New York. Almost the entire collection crated, insured, and shipped to Uncle Sol's museum. Nationwide attention from the press. A Guggenheim family reunion— the last the family has had—at the museum for the opening: Peggy, Harry, Gladys, Uncle Sol's daughters, Harry's daughters, the Strauses, Lawson-Johnston, others, on hand for the festivities.

Peggy was particularly gratified by Harry's noble statement in the official catalogue of the exhibition:

> In the 1920's the interests of my uncle, the benefactor of the Solomon R. Guggenheim Foundation, were turning from the traditional art forms to the first acquisition of those objects of modern art that today comprise the great collection bequeathed to this museum. At about the time of their transfer in the late 1930's, his niece, Peggy Guggenheim, the "enfant terrible" of the family, was indulging in a modern art spree of her own. She was plunging into intensive art collecting even as the war-clouds were gathering throughout the world, barely managing to keep her newly acquired treasures and herself a mere step ahead of the approaching enemy armies. She subsequently started a gallery in New York that depended heavily upon the normally unsold creations of "young talent." These and many other such acts at the time seemed daring in the extreme. Somehow, however, Peggy always emerged on top, invariably leaving in her wake, after much sound and fury, a valid and far-reaching result of quiet distinction. Her early recognition of Jackson Pollock's genius, and her active support of this painter during the most crucial years of his development, is now a matter of record. So too is Peggy's early sponsorship of little-known American artists whose group emergence after the war owes much to her prescient and courageous advocacy.

From the triumph in New York to the triumph in Paris in December, 1974, the great revenge exhibition at the Orangerie, which she called "Twentycento." Revenge because, it will be recalled, back in 1941, when the Germans were about to invade France and Peggy was compelled to flee to the United States, the Louvre had turned down her request to leave her paintings in their secret hideaway on the grounds that they "were not worth saving." Two hundred thousand visitors to "Twentycento," paying nine francs a head, the name of Guggenheim emblazoned over all the newspapers and magazines of France. Peggy, now seventy-five, present at the opening wearing Chinese-red tights, knee-high boots, and a blue shift with crimson embroidery. Yes, she had shown those snobbish museumocrats what was not worth saving!

Yes, Peggy was a true Guggenheim. The poor relation, overwhelmed in her youth by the power and wealth of the uncles and their children, those uncles who had done her out of all that Chile Copper money, who had bought up all those copies of *Out of This Century,* the poor relation had come out on top. The uncles were all dead and their children, though wealthier than she, had not, with the exception of Harry, accomplished half of what she had accomplished.

This accomplishment was officially consecrated by Alfred H. Barr, Jr., of the Museum of Modern Art in New York, when he wrote:

> Courage and vision, generosity and humility, money and time, a strong sense of historical significance, as well as aesthetic quality—these are the factors of circumstances and character which have made Peggy Guggenheim an extraordinary patron of twentieth-century art.
>
> The collection is Peggy Guggenheim's most durable achievement as an art patron but it is quite possibly not her most important. I have used the threadbare and somewhat pompous word "patron" with some misgivings. Yet it is precise. For a patron is not simply a collector who gathers works of art for his own pleasure, or a philanthropist who helps artists or founds a public museum, but a person who feels responsibility towards both art and artists together and has the means and will to act upon this feeling. Thanks largely to the influx of refugee artists and writers from Europe, New York during the war supplanted occupied Paris as the art center of the Western world. In their development, Peggy Guggenheim, as patron, played an important, and in some cases a crucial, role.

An accolade more flattering than that Peggy could not have demanded. Now, in the year 1976, in her own seventy-seventh year, she could quite easily lean back on her white leather settee with white sheepskin cover with her beloved dogs all over her and rest on her achievements. But no, she still had lots of ambitious things to do. She had to update her autobiographical *Out of This Century* with fifty fresh new pages on her life in Venice; she was collaborating with scholar Virginia Dorazzo of Little Rock, Arkansas, and with Viking Press, on her official biography; she was also collaborating with grandson Nicolas Helion on that fifty-minute television documentary on her life and times; and she was making plans to exhibit her collection in Zurich, and in other European cities. In addition, she collaborated with the new Centre National d'Art et Culture Georges Pompidou in Paris in its recent duplication, down to the last baseball-bat easel, of her Art of This Century gallery of the 1940s in New York.

Her life now in Venice? A settled, disciplined routine. In the morning she works at her desk, in close cooperation with her curator and secretary, John Hohnsbeen, answering her immense correspondence and attending to the infinite demands of the collection. Then she takes a short walk with the dogs, sometimes stopping at her dogs' cemetery in the garden: "Here lie my beloved babies: Cappucino, Pegeen, Peacock, Toro, Foglia, Madam Butterfly, Baby, Emily,

White Angel, Sir Herbert. . . ." Then lunch in her rustic Renaissance dining room, surrounded by all the Braques, the Duchamp, the Delaunay, the Gleizes, the African and Oceanic sculptures. Then a brief "snooze" on her silver Alexander Calder bed. Then present at the thrice-weekly opening of the Fondazione Peggy Guggenheim, sometimes allowing herself to be photographed by the visitors next to the Marino Marini horse with rider in full erection. Then, at four-thirty, the daily gondola ride. Then back to the palace to collect the take from the sale of catalogues, something which she, as a good Guggenheim, especially enjoys doing (delightedly she counts the bills which John Hohnsbeen places in her hand—"Four hundred thousand lire, well, it's been a good day, hasn't it?").

Another rest, then she is ready for entertaining, or being entertained. She gives a cocktail party for what is left of her salon. Or dines with a friend at Angelo's, Colomba, Antico Martini's, or her favorite, Harry's Bar. Avoiding, as much as possible, the stuffy affairs of the old Venetian aristocracy, the sclerotic parties of people like the countess Marcello, who periodically gets all the descendants of doges and dogaressas together, or that other countess, who likes to refer to Peggy contemptuously as "Il Mercante di Venezia," or as "the horse trader."

In the summer her grandchildren come to visit, and this is always a most happy time. Pegeen's three French sons, Nicolas, Davide, and Fabrice Helion, and one British son, Sandro Rumney. Sindbad's sons from Jacqueline Ventadour, Clovis and Mark; his daughters from Peggy Yeomans, Karole and Julia. How proud of, and interested in, all of them she is. Long-haired Nicolas, twenty-five, with his own art gallery in Paris and beginning to get interested in film production. Davide, twenty-nine, a student at the Sorbonne. Fabrice, thirty, a film director living in Caracas, married with two children. Sandro, nineteen, who is studying agriculture and wants to be a farmer. Clovis Vail, a publicity agent for a French newspaper. Mark Vail, twenty-seven, a farmer in Normandy, raising cattle and sheep. Julia Vail, doing well at a French school at St. Joseph du Barchamp. And the beautiful Karole Vail, studying at Bedales School in Britain, preparing for her exams to get into King's College, Cambridge. Karole, with such high tastes—a lover of Bach, Beethoven, and Wagner—who spends her free time playing Beethoven sonatas and weaving rugs. Ah, yes, not only has she created the collection, but there are also those eight beautiful young people she has helped create, ten if you include the great-grandchildren.

The grandchildren leave at the end of summer. A brief respite, then in the early fall the journalists and writers begin to descend, perennially hungry for her views. On modern art, on American civilization, on women's liberation, on herself. She obliges. None of this false privacy snobbism for her, this "An interview? I'd rather not," no I-want-to-be-alone escapism. She is public property and accepts it. She is a historical personage, one of the great buccaneers of modern art. She is a historical monument. Let her views be known in her time.

Contemporary art. We have already reported her views. It has gone to seed, to hell. Pop art "the commercialization of a very stupid idea." The most recent manifestations of the abstract expressionist movement, a negation of art and life. The contemporary Venetian Biennale: "A communist insult to painting and the human spirit."

American civilization. Almost as uninspiring as contemporary art. Peggy finds American life and culture at the country's two-hundredth anniversary "narrow," "drab," "faddish," "racist" ("very anti-Semitic"), and "commercial." "There is simply nothing of enduring value being created."

Women's liberation. "I was the original liberated woman, fifty-five years ago," she will tell you, straightening her skirt and hiking up her boots.

> I did everything, was everything; I was totally free financially, emotionally, intellectually, sexually. I believe in equal employment opportunities and equal pay for equal work for women. But I deplore the bad taste of the so-called Women's Movement. Friedan, Millet, Greer, Steinem, et cetera, they're all so unattractive, strident, and tasteless. It's such an awful bore the way they go about their so-called mission. And they all commit one of the worst crimes in the world: They pit women against men, and men against women. We can never forgive them that. Relations between men and women are seventy-five percent of life.

Herself. Yes, she knows where she and her family stand in the twentieth century, and makes no bones about it. "The Guggenheims are a twentieth-century royal family" (if she had used the word "imperial" she would have been more accurate), comparable, in many ways, to "the great noble houses of pre-French Revolutionary Europe." And she is the Isabella d'Este, the Beatrice d'Este, the Catherine de Médicis of our time. No other female patron in Western Europe, or the Americas, has had a greater impact on the visual arts of her time than she. "I have supported the greatest geniuses of our times.

I have put together a complete survey of nonrealistic art of our times. All the valid tendencies are represented in my collection."

Her regrets? Yes, she has her regrets . . .

She is not as rich as most of her Guggenheim female cousins. Dan's daughter, Gladys Straus, for instance, or Solomon's two daughters, Barbara Obre and Lady Castle Stewart, each of whom has four or five times as many millions as she has. "It's not that I need the money: I have more than I can spend, but I would like to be as rich as some of my cousins so I could leave more to my grandchildren."

Another regret. The Pollocks. She sold or gave away far too many Pollocks. "Blue Poles," she will tell you, with a hint of despair in her eyes—the kind of temporary despair Guggenheims used to display when they learned somebody else was earning huge profits from a mine they had not bought in time or had prematurely sold—"Blue Poles" was bought by the Australian government for no less than $2 million! Peggy had never owned "Blue Poles" but regards its price as representative of what Pollocks now bring.

And she is still very angry about her Guggenheim uncles not dividing the profits of Chile Copper with her and her sisters, and for confiscating all those copies of *Out of This Century*. "A censorship worse than the Russians'."

Then, going beyond mere regrets . . . the nightmares about her father going down with the *Titanic*. And about Pegeen . . .

What is left? There remains her $4.5 million plus in trust (wistfully she will sigh that she guesses she just got her "last inheritance," a legacy from one of father Ben's mistresses), destined to be split among Sindbad and his four children, and Pegeen's four sons. Constantly is she making out new wills. "One thing is certain," she will tell you, "no one is going to end up with a fortune. . . . Oh, if only my sisters and I had gotten in on Chile Copper!"

For, alas, the $35 million Peggy Guggenheim Foundation, comprising the palace, the *barchessa*, and the collection, is not even her property anymore. Legally it belongs to the Solomon R. Guggenheim Foundation of New York and could not become her property again unless her cousin, Peter Lawson-Johnston, and the other trustees of the S.R.G. foundation give it back to her, something they are highly unlikely to do.

Sindbad remains understandably upset. If she had only given him just *one* Pollock, *one* Picasso, *one* Ernst . . .

"And so now," the interviewer remarks, "your foundation is much richer than you are, much, much richer . . ."

And the true-blood Guggenheim looks up from her white leather settee, adjusts her Max Ernst dark glasses, pats a dog on the head, and replies (in her half-Philadelphia, half-British accent): "Well, isn't that the way it should be?"

The collection, the foundation, the monument, get almost everything.

Yes, if Venice is saved from sinking back into the mud from which it rose, then her monument, along with the Doge's Palace, San Marco, La Salute, San Rocco, I Frari, San Giorgio, will also endure down through the centuries, proclaiming to all that one hundred and fifty years after the fall of the Venetian Republic an American Jewess by the name of Guggenheim had helped keep the great flame of Western art alive, had nurtured it, and had brought it down into the last quarter of the twentieth century, forging a five-hundred-year link between Giovanni Bellini, Carpaccio, Titian, Giorgione, Tintoretto and Max Ernst, Wassily Kandinsky, Jackson Pollock.

La Fondazione Peggy Guggenheim, Palazzo Venier dei Leoni, Venezia. Yes, there it will stand, along the Grand Canal, as long as Venice itself will stand. Never mind the cost. The foundation will endure. The monument will stand . . . yet how many times in the silence of the Palazzo Venier dei Leoni, with the only sounds the waters of the canal slapping at its sides, has she echoed her uncle Simon's anguished cry and called out into the darkness: "Tancredi, Tancredi . . . Pegeen, Pegeen . . . Pegeen"?

CHAPTER

13

HARRY THE MAGNIFICENT: THE LEGACIES

TOWARD THE END OF HIS LONG, VARIED, AND PRODUCTIVE LIFE HARRY Guggenheim was frequently overwhelmed by the problem of what was going to happen to the Guggenheim heritage after his death.

He was also deeply concerned with the fate of the Guggenheim reputation. Somewhere in the depths of his aging heart he felt that the Guggenheim achievements had largely gone unrecognized, that his family's contributions to American civilization had not been fully appreciated by his countrymen.

And so, in the last decade of his life, from 1960 to 1970, as his once very considerable powers declined, and death gradually began to overtake him, he came to reflect more and more on his family's achievements and, at the same time, began to set his mind to ways of perpetuating and memorializing them. The fate of well over a century of struggles, failures, victories, and incredibly farsighted accomplishments—often on a heroic scale—was at stake.

It was principally at Falaise, his splendid Long Island estate, that Harry, alone since his third wife's death in 1963, began spending more and more time contemplating his own and his family's past and what he could do to enhance its influence and memorialize it.

He had had a great career, one so multifaceted as to seem unattainable in mid-twentieth-century America with its insistence on specialization at all costs, including the cost of full development of human personality. Harry was well aware that a career such as he had enjoyed was possible only in a family possessing great wealth. For, alas, versatility, Renaissance universality, was a luxury very few could afford in the most competitive society the world has ever known.

Harry had been fortunate to have benefited from an independent income since his twenty-first year. First from the multimillion-dollar trust Daniel had established for his three children during his lifetime; then from the $2 million-plus legacy, clear of taxes, he had received from Dan in his thirty-ninth year, and the additional millions he got from his mother, Florence, upon her death in 1944. By the time he was fifty-five in 1945 his unearned income from securities that were conservatively invested was around $500,000 a year, quite enough on which to pursue one's interests and passions unhampered by economic need. Still later, in his sixties and seventies, he had seen his wealth quintuple, so that by the late 1960s he knew he would be able to leave something in the neighborhood of $50 million to his heirs.

Yes, his family's wealth had enabled him to lead a unique career, one with infinite facets and implications, one as varied and exciting as several members of the Medici family had been able to lead in Renaissance Florence five hundred years before.

There had been his patronage of aeronautics and rocketry and his relationship with Robert H. Goddard. No, he had never lost faith in Goddard, had renewed his grants, over and over again, often in the face of strong opposition. What satisfaction he had had in helping to dedicate NASA's Goddard Space Flight Center in Maryland in March, 1961, and, eight years later, in beholding Apollo XI powered by rockets once infringing Goddard-Guggenheim patents, carrying the first men to the moon.

Then there had been his relationship with that other American genius, Frank Lloyd Wright, a relationship documented by hundreds of letters and memoranda he had been most careful about preserving. What a glorious day that had been, October 21, 1959, when, after ten years of unremitting struggles, with both donor and architect dead, he stood there in the museum's vast circular atrium with Henry Cabot Lodge, and formally opened the most daring temple of art in the world.

Subsequently as president of that museum he had had the satisfaction of receiving, in behalf of his Uncle Solomon's foundation, the magnificent Justin K. Thannhauser collection consisting of seventy-five masterworks from the impressionist and post-impressionist periods, among them four Cézannes, two Van Goghs, two Gauguins, two Modiglianis, and thirty-four Picassos.

But, as it turned out, his last career, that of newspaper publisher, had given him the most satisfaction of all. That career had begun with his third, and most fortunate, marriage—to Alicia Patterson—had taken off like one of Goddard's later rockets—*Newsday* soon becoming the fastest-growing and most profitable daily started in the United States in twenty years—and ended with offers to buy the paper that promised a hundredfold profit on his original investment.

Harry had to admit that his marriage to Alicia Patterson in 1939 had been a rare bonanza for a family that had been steadily running out of luck for the past ten years. What a bright, talented girl she had been. And what a background. Great-grandfather Joseph Medill, founder of the *Chicago Tribune*. Grandfather Robert Patterson, editor-in-chief of the same paper. Father Joe Patterson, founder and editor-in-chief of the New York *Daily News*.

Soon after the marriage—he was forty-nine; she was thirty-two— Harry realized Alicia could never be happy merely as the mistress of Falaise. She was too high-strung, too bright to spend all her time and talents looking after servants, antiques, Guggenheims, and peacocks. And so he had decided to give her a newspaper of her own, if only to give her something with which to occupy her time and her mind. But he had been clever. He hadn't given it to her entirely. Shrewdly he had kept 51 percent of the stock, letting her have 49 percent. The year was 1940. Then what a beginning she made. Set right out to violate every canon of sedate, well-mannered suburban journalism and produced a paper that looked like no other paper on earth, a tabloid format with only two front-page columns, yet somehow with the look of a serious newspaper, "a big-city paper," in her words, "that just happens to be published in the suburbs." During its first seven years the paper operated in the red. Harry had had to pour $750,000 into it. And then, miraculously, it began to turn around. The mass exodus of New Yorkers to the suburbs, especially Long Island, after World War II was the cause. What a time of change that had been for Long Island. The great old private estates of people like the Pratts, the Whitneys, the Phippses, the Vanderbilts, the Guggenheims were being sold, one by one, often to institutions like the Russian government, which bought the Pratt estate for $120,000, and IBM, which bought Uncle Sol's estate for a lot more. And while the millionaires were giving up, the big developers and new industries were moving in. Levittown. Grumman Aircraft. Republic Aircraft. Followed by hundreds of lesser developers and lesser industries. The gradual suburbanization and industrialization of once-rural Nassau County. Climaxing in the 1960s in that vast, and often ugly, sprawl of housing developments, shopping centers, parking lots, billboards, hamburger joints, superhighways, and small factories. Not very attractive aesthetically, but more than gratifying financially, for the bigger the suburban sprawl, the bigger the sales of *the* suburban newspaper. Anyway, Falaise was protected from the sprawl by the blue Sound on one side and by ninety acres of woods and fields on the other.

Yes, it had been a great adventure, *Newsday*. Harry had enjoyed seeing his investment grow and grow and grow, especially after seeing his family's investment in nitrates go to pieces, had enjoyed seeing Alicia happy in her work, and enjoyed having a chance to get his own two cents in now and then in an editorial, which he often placed next to one of Alicia's expressing a diametrically opposing viewpoint. And then, he might as well admit it, he enjoyed being in full control of the paper after Alicia died of cancer of the stomach in 1963, and enjoyed no end the prospect of selling the paper for one hundred times what he paid for it (that, most certainly, was in the Guggenheim tradition) and at the same time selling it to an organization that shared his conservative political and economic philosophy.

But what to do about perpetuating all these achievements? Not simply his own, but those of his grandfather, father, uncles, and cousins. And about getting the record down, and publicizing it, about letting the world know what the Guggenheims had wrought during the past one hundred and twenty years?

Central to Harry's problem was, as we know, the search for a son and heir; for a strong, intelligent, dependable young man to succeed him as head of the family and perpetuator of its traditions. His first two marriages had given him nothing but daughters, three of them, and so he had been forced to cast around among various relatives, friends, and associates in his quest for a successor. One by one he had tried out candidates—his nephew Oscar Straus II, his 1960s' counterculture grandson, Dana Draper, his too liberal *Newsday* editor-in-chief (after Alicia's death) Bill Moyers—and one by one they all failed him, in various ways. Then, as we know, at literally the eleventh hour, he settled upon his uncle Sol's grandson, Peter O. Lawson-Johnston, to whom he simply gave the entire world.

Finding a son and heir to carry the Guggenheim businesses and foundations into the future was only one part of the solution to Harry's problem, however, albeit a very important part. While he searched for a son there remained the problem of memorializing the achievements of the Guggenheim past.

"Look at what we have done!" Harry seemed to cry out. "Look at what we have contributed . . . and nobody seems to know anything about it, or even care to know anything about it."

What was even worse, not even his own immediate family seemed to care. By the time he had begun to think seriously about disposing of his wealth and preserving the Guggenheim heritage, Harry had succeeded in alienating his closest kin to such an extent that they wanted to have little or nothing to do with him or what he stood for. It was that egotistic, authoritarian, dogmatic nature of his. With so much energy and family pride in his character, and so much money at his disposal, he simply could not accept opposing attitudes, opinions, wants, desires. If his wife of the moment, or one of his daughters, had a thought or wish contrary to his own, she was just wrong, that's all there was to it. His first marriage, to Helen Rosenberg, daughter of a New York businessman, had been a bitter, quarrelsome affair that took a severe toll on Nancy, one of the two girls born from it, who committed suicide in her forty-first year. His second marriage, to Caroline Morton, daughter of Paul Morton, Theodore Roosevelt's Secretary of the Navy, and member of the family that founded Morton Salt, was another quarrelsome union, ending in divorce, and one which must have had an unhappy influence on its one offspring, Diane, now Mrs. William Meek. Diane turned her back on her father and exiled herself to Ireland, where she has been living for the past twenty years, and where she is currently running a monastery school. As for Alicia, former friends and associates say she and Harry argued without let-up, that the marriage was a virtual marathon of quarrel, and that it was a combination of *Newsday* and Harry that led her to an early death at fifty-six.

Another factor, however, may have contributed even more to Alicia's premature demise. In 1976 it was revealed publicly that Alicia had been carrying on a secret love affair with Adlai Stevenson since 1947, the eighth year of her marriage to Harry. Details of the romance, one of the most passionate of Stevenson's life, including the publication of many love letters, were revealed in John Martin's 1976 biography of Stevenson. Judging from the letters, by the time of Stevenson's presidential campaign of 1952, Alicia, in the midst of her success with *Newsday,* was dreaming of divorcing Harry, marrying Stevenson, and becoming First Lady of the United States. After Stevenson's defeat the affair lingered on for a while, with somewhat reduced passion, then Stevenson advised Alicia by letter to remain with Guggenheim, which she did, but with a broken heart. It was from the time of the breakup of her relationship with Stevenson that Alicia began to drink more heavily than usual, and it was drink, according to her physicians, that caused Alicia's fatal cancer of the stomach.

Whether Harry was aware of all this at the time it was happening is not known for sure. More than likely he was too preoccupied with *Newsday*, his Cain Hoy stables, the Guggenheim Museum, his continuing support of aeronautics, and the problem of preserving and transmitting the Guggenheim heritage to devote much time and energy to the problem of Alicia.

Harry's niece-in-law, Dorothea Straus, has left us a vivid portrait of Harry at this time in a chapter entitled "The Master of Finistère" in her book *Showcases*.

In this work, Dorothea, sensitive to the feelings of her husband's family, disguises her characters and settings. Harry is called Rupert, and his estate, Falaise, is Finistère.

Finistère was the most romantic house I ever knew. . . . I see Rupert seated on the terrace at the back of the house high above the spread carpet of the Sound. Sea, sky, and sand seemed to repeat his own coloring as a symphony takes up a theme introduced by a few chosen instruments. Rupert kept his tan all year round, and his bald head and face were the color of tawny sand. His large eyes, the palest blue of distant waters, were set so deep in their sockets that they resembled aquamarines in dark cases. In the summer he wore a white suit contrasting with his sunburned skin, and a pastel blue shirt that imitated the extraordinary color of his eyes. . . .

. . . Rupert maintained a gracious formality at Finistère. . . . He treated his three daughters with distant chivalry. . . . He treated Candace [his wife, Alicia] like his daughters, with cool gallantry, but she, unable to accept the role of accessory as pliantly as they, grew to be a threat to the regime. Under the same roof she lived apart. Early in their marriage Rupert, fearing that she, much younger and childless, might grow bored, had bought a newspaper for her amusement. He had bestowed it upon her in the same spirit in which he had given her his mother's large black pearl. . . . For her, however, the newspaper was no bauble, and like one of Rupert's pedigreed fillies, she took the bit in her teeth, becoming a successful editor, the "boss lady" to the staff of her magazine and a total loss to her husband. . . .

After Candace's untimely death, two changes occurred at Finistère: Rupert took over her position as editor of *The Record* [*Newsday*], and his eldest grandson, Ian [Dana Draper], recently come of age, made his appearance as heir apparent. . . .

Ian was often his grandfather's guest. Though quiet, he was not ill at ease. . . . One sunny July noon the four of us met for cocktails on the terrace. From where I was sitting the interior of the house looked cool and dusky, more mysterious than ever: a suit of armor partly glimpsed was a silvery shape in the living room. . . . Rupert was saying jocosely but with pride of ownership in his voice, "You didn't know that the Passion Play was in town, did you?" referring to Ian's beard and hair. In his T-shirt and jeans he did look remote from his grandfather's impeccable whites. . . . "This grandson of mine is going to learn the newspaper business from the bottom up so he can take over when I'm gone. I always say to him 'Do as I say, not as I do.' He is also learning about horse breeding and the management of the estate." Ian made no protest, he remained passive, but his bright squirrel eyes mutely registered a concealed life of their own. It must be far from Finistère, I thought.

Rupert's fantasy of succession ended. On his office desk at *The Record* he found a letter from Ian. It began "Dear Commodore," [Harry was often addressed "Captain"] and its tone was mild, but it went on to say that he was resigning from the newspaper and that he renounced his interests in the breeding farm and the estate. He had decided, after much consideration, that this was not the life for him. He was going to be a painter. . . .

Rupert related the content of the letter to my husband [Harry's nephew, Roger W. Straus, Jr.], his fury the more passionate for being quiet. "I offered him everything and that's the gratitude he shows me. I have already consulted my lawyers about changing my will. He will be cut off without a penny—let him starve in his filthy studio!"

He never saw his grandson again nor spoke to him although Ian made several gentle futile attempts at reconciliation. In his place Rupert acquired a brash young journalist and former White House aide [Bill Moyers], stepping down to make him chief editor of *The Record* with part ownership. . . .

Rupert was growing old. I noticed that his deep-set eyes were a more faded blue than his shirt and his tonsure more brilliantly white than his white suit. He often spoke about his will which he altered constantly, his plans for a foundation to study man's lust for power, and his decision to make Finistère a public park. . . . It was shocking. . . . Rupert was preparing for his demise in elaborate detail. With the cooperation of his sycophantic lawyers, he was building, codicil by codicil, his funeral monument—his Castel Sant'Angelo, the aging ruler's bid to immortality. His daughters hovered, but he turned more and more to his trusty servants.

The last time I saw Rupert was not at Finistère but in Miami, where he went each spring for the races. . . . While he and my husband conversed [in Harry's bungalow on the beach] I listened to the surf breaking on the beach, so much more overpowering and noisier than the whispering subservient waves of Finistère. When I returned my attention they were talking about *The Record*. Rupert looked unhealthily animated, his blue eyes in their hollow sockets had a febrile glow. He was saying: ". . . so Frank [Bill Moyers] thought he could take over the policy of the newspaper in anticipation of my death—filling it with half-baked Red propaganda. Well, I have shown him who is still master! I have just sold it from under his nose to a Republican middlewestern newspaper chain. Thank heavens I was spared long enough to make the deal. Such impertinence! Such ingratitude! I raised him up, now he can go back to where I found him. Before coming down here I consulted my lawyers about my will—"

Impertinence and ingratitude. That is about all Harry had received from those closest to him during his last years. *Newsday*. Falaise. The Guggenheim heritage. Who cared? His wives didn't care. His daughters didn't care. His grandson didn't care. And who knew if that abstraction known as the General Public cared? It had been a long time since the Guggenheims had drawn front-page headlines. Was the mighty Guggenheim adventure in America destined to be forgotten or, worse yet, ignored?

Not if Harry could help it. He had already done something important to keep the Guggenheim name alive and that was to insist his uncle Sol's museum be called The Solomon R. Guggenheim Memorial rather than the Museum of Non-Objective Art, as was originally intended by his uncle. Now, he took further steps to enhance the Guggenheim image. He hired a writer, chiefly of children's books, one Milton Lomask, and commissioned him to write a panegyric on the Guggenheim foundations, which was given the title *Seed Money—The Guggenheim Story*, and which was published in 1964, at Harry's expense, by Harry's nephew, Roger W. Straus, Jr., whose publishing firm was then known as Farrar, Straus & Company. At least the story of the Guggenheims' benefactions would now be available in libraries and universities.

That bit of publicizing taken care of, Harry then turned his attention to creating two more memorials to himself and his family which he fervently hoped would last down through the ages. These were the gift of his estate, Falaise, and nearly everything in it, to Nassau County to be operated as a sort of museum of Guggenheim achievement after his death, and the establishment of his own foundation, the Harry Frank Guggenheim Foundation, dedicated to developing a program to improve "man's relation to man."

The Harry Frank Guggenheim Foundation, now possessing assets of $20 million, is the most daring and visionary, and also the most vague, of all the Guggenheim foundations. The premise, or assumption, from which its many programs derive is that in the area of "man's relation to man," "man has failed to keep pace with the extraordinary progress of this era in science, engineering, medicine and surgery, agriculture, industry, transportation . . . and other fields of human endeavor."

Harry's relations with his fellow human beings, whether they were wives, children, associates, had always been contentious and abrasive. He was not an easy man to get along with, and he knew it. Was it partly a gesture of atonement for the many injuries he inflicted on people during his lifetime that he became so obsessed with human relations he decided to dedicate the bulk of his fortune to studying the problem?

"Is it a dangerous over-simplification," he asked, in his booklet on his new foundation, "to say that man's clash with his fellow man stems from his competition for sustenance, sex, and domination? Can we go a step farther and conclude that science will, in a reasonable time, provide enough food and shelter to sustain the planned population of this planet? Can we also conclude that there is adequate population and communication on this planet to have removed to a great degree man's frustration from lack of sex satisfaction?

"If this is a logical conclusion," he went on, "we might then concentrate on the subject of man's instinctive or developed urge to domination, and where it all leads in his relations with his fellow man. Does it in one case develop a Christ, and in another case, a Hitler?"

What were the answers to these gigantic questions? Harry consulted with his old aviation friends, Jimmy Doolittle and Charles Lindbergh. He consulted with Robert Ardrey, author of *African Genesis* and *The Territorial Imperative*. He consulted with Henry Allen Moe, president of the John Simon Guggenheim Memorial Foundation (Moe suggested, in characteristic fashion, that Harry's foundation's basic job should be to "find and encourage genius"). Finally, he came up with something of a program. At present the research projects currently being sponsored are directed toward obtaining a better understanding of man and his nature, particularly his tendencies toward dominance, aggression, and violence.

Among the most interesting projects the foundation has funded thus far have been a program of primate studies on the island of St. Kitts; research on the behavior of adolescent chimpanzees at Dr. Jane Goodall's Gombe Stream Research Center in Tanzania; research on prehistoric man in Africa, and notably the work of Dr. L. S. B. Leakey and his family in East Africa; studies in "images of killing, aggression, and weapons in prehistoric cultures"; studies in "dominance interaction in early peer group formations among children"; studies in "the use of symbolic systems in the maintenance of hierarchy"; researches in the ritualization of violence in Ireland; studies of the "political and economic behavior of females in Israeli Kibbutzim"; a study of civil war throughout the world; and advanced research in "female hierarchies."

Other, far less rarefied, programs funded by the H.F.G. Foundation have been such charities as the United Jewish Appeal and the Federation of Jewish Philanthropies. The foundation also made an extensive grant to Nassau County for the maintenance of Falaise.

It was throughout the 1960s that Harry took all these steps to perpetuate the name and achievements and influence of the House of Guggenheim. Then, on March 12, 1970, he put the final seal on them in his last will and testament, which confirmed Nassau County in its possession of Falaise, all its contents, and its ninety acres, and named Peter O. Lawson-Johnston and the Harry Frank Guggenheim Foundation as his principal heirs.

A little less than a year later, on January 23, 1971, Harry F. Guggenheim died at Falaise, after a long fight with cancer, in his eightieth year. His funeral was held at Temple Emanu-El and later he joined his forebears in the huge Guggenheim mausoleum at Salem Fields.

Dorothea Straus, in her *Showcases,* described the burial:

> It was a raw gray February day. . . . Inside the tent erected before the mausoleum, electric heaters were unavailing against the damp, and the steady drip of thawing snow accompanied the solemn intoning of the rabbi. . . . The deafening explosion of a cannon shattered the hush, a last salute to the commodore from the Navy. . . . Then the massive doors of the mausoleum opened, revealing a black shaft, and the master of Finistère joined his forbears.

> After the funeral there was a great deal of scandalized discussion about the will. The foundation had triumphed. Marion, Diana, and Penelope [Harry's daughters, Joan, Nancy, and Diane] were left a pinched portion of their inheritance. Some relatives claimed that Rupert had been senile when he signed the final codicil, others said that his enlarged vanity had created the bloated amorphous foundation to outlast him like the Sphinx.

Although he had not enjoyed a particularly happy private life, Harry died proud of his achievements and content in the knowledge he had proved worthy of his heritage and had done his very best to preserve and propagate it in the future. Mercifully he was spared his daughter Nancy's suicide, for she killed herself two years after his death, but he had not been spared her son Dana's defection from what he felt were his Guggenheim responsibilities and this had embittered him grievously. It had been a sad day when he struck the young man out of his will.

His will. What a man ultimately believes in, or does not believe in, is usually reflected in his will. Harry did not believe in his own progeny. Nor did he believe in subsidizing the weak and indigent, simply because they were weak and indigent. Harry believed in himself, in excellence, in the accomplishments of his forebears, in his cousin, Peter Lawson-Johnston, and in the work he hoped his daring new foundation would accomplish in the years ahead. So be it. There had always been something Nietzschean in Harry's, and indeed in his family's, personality.

"Do love your neighbors as yourselves—but first be such as *love themselves*."

"My brothers, neighbor-love I do not teach you: I teach you the love of the farthest."

CHAPTER

14

HARRY THE MAGNIFICENT: THE GLORIFICATION

IN THE GREAT HALL OF THE VILLA MEDICEA AT POGGIO A CAIANO, situated in the soft green hills surrounding Florence, there is a series of wall frescoes expressing the glorification of the Medici family, and particularly the glorification of its most versatile and brilliant member, Lorenzo, son of Piero, called the Magnificent.

The scenes, painted by several of the foremost artists of the day, Andrea del Sarto and Jacopo da Pontormo among them, actually represent episodes from ancient Roman history, but the characters bear the likenesses of the Medici, and the episodes depicted can easily be translated into events of Florentine history at the time the Medici were in power.

Thus we see, in rich crimsons, browns, oranges, and golds, such resounding works as "The Return of Cicero from Exile," with Cicero bearing the exact likeness of Lorenzo's grandfather, Cosimo de' Medici, who had also been in exile (from Florence) and who later made a triumphant return; "Consul Flaminius Defeats the League," with the Roman consul the exact likeness of Lorenzo the Magnificent, who, at the Council of Cremona, had defeated, through agile diplomacy, the league the Venetians had organized against him; "Julius Caesar Receives Tribute from Egypt," with Caesar the exact likeness of Lorenzo the Magnificent, the episode alluding to the costly gifts the Sultan of Egypt had once sent Lorenzo . . . Other scenes, other glorifications. And then, in the adjoining dining hall the ultimate panegyric: Antonio Gabbiani's vast, blazing ceiling fresco depicting "Florence Presenting Cosimo de' Medici to Jove."

Other artistic glorifications of the Medici are scattered throughout

Florence, Tuscany, and the rest of Italy, some of the most notable of which are Vasari's frescoes in the Palazzo della Signoria dominating Florence's principal piazza. Here we see such flatteries as "Lorenzo the Magnificent with His Poets and Philosophers"; "The Virtues of Lorenzo the Magnificent"; "Brunelleschi and Alberti Presenting Cosimo de' Medici with a Model of the Church of San Lorenzo"; "Lorenzo the Magnificent with the Young Michelangelo"; "The Apotheosis of Lorenzo."

Lorenzo de' Medici, member of one of the two or three wealthiest families in fifteenth-century Europe, head of the Medici Bank, the largest bank in the world at the time, ruler of Italy's most civilized state, a poet of genuine talent, a philosopher as well, member and disputant in Florence's Platonic Academy, and the most enlightened patron of the arts of his time, or indeed of any time, now considered perhaps the most perfect exemplification of the "Renaissance man," died in 1492. In the same year another Renaissance man, Cristoforo Colombo, made his momentous voyage to what he thought was India, but which turned out to be America, so named after another Florentine Renaissance man, Amerigo Vespucci, an agent of the Medici Bank, who sailed and mapped some of the coasts of this New World in the years around 1500.

Four centuries later certain families had established themselves so mightily in that New World, and had become such lavish patrons of the arts and sciences, that they could, without exaggeration, be compared, admittedly in a somewhat lesser light, to the Medici, who have been called, perhaps with some exaggeration, "the greatest family of all time."

One need go no further than several of the principal centers of the arts and sciences in New York to discover who some of these families are. Carnegie Hall. The Rockefeller University. The Morgan Library. The Whitney Museum. The Frick Museum. The Guggenheim Museum.

Carnegie, Rockefeller, Morgan, Whitney, Frick, Guggenheim in New York; Du Pont, Mellon, and Ford in Delaware, Pittsburgh, and Detroit. It is these families, above all others, who by virtue of their great wealth and dedication to the highest achievements in the arts and sciences, do have some justification to claim parallels with the great houses of the Italian Renaissance, with the Este, the Visconti, the Gonzaga, the Sforza, the Borgia, the Medici. At least they had the money, the power, the prestige, the courage, the education, the taste . . .

But where, pray tell, among these mighty American families were the Renaissance men?

Andrew Carnegie a Renaissance man? No, too single-mindedly a businessman; no personal, creative involvement in either government or the arts and sciences of his day, to his death essentially a one-dimensional man. John D. Rockefeller, Sr., John D., Jr., the brothers David, John D., III, Laurance, Winthrop, Nelson, Renaissance men? No, one or two essential dimensions are always lacking. None of the Rockefellers—a peculiarly practical clan—has ever been personally involved with the artists and scientists they and their foundations have patronized, and none of them has ever written or painted or composed anything noteworthy himself. J. P. Morgan? Yes, a Renaissance prince in many respects, accumulator of the largest private collection of fine art in United States' history, and a competent draftsman himself, but never a holder of public office, and not a supporter of contemporary artists, his collection being limited to fully canonized artists from the shadowy grandeurs of the past. Henry Clay Frick? Another single-minded businessman, partner with, and like spirit to, Carnegie and Morgan, concerned only with collecting works of the long dead and buried. Cornelius Vanderbilt Whitney? It was his granddaughter, Gertrude Vanderbilt Whitney, who built the Whitney Museum, not him. The Du Ponts, Mellons, Fords? None, with the possible exception of the talented and versatile Andrew Mellon, comes close to being a genuine Renaissance prince, a "universal man" in the sense in which the term was understood in fifteenth-century Italy, and even Mellon, though a great collector, fails in the end to qualify because he had little personal involvement in contemporary art.

And then we come to Harry F. Guggenheim, and here, suddenly, and somewhat to our astonishment, all or almost all the dimensions of the Renaissance man appear to be present. For not only was Harry a businessman, a statesman, a soldier, a sportsman, a publisher, a patron of the arts and sciences, he also enjoyed an intimate, creative relationship with several beneficiaries of his patronage—with men like Lindbergh, Goddard, and Frank Lloyd Wright—and he was an author of considerable ability himself.

It is not in the American grain for wealthy families to indulge in the sort of self-glorification the Medici indulged in at Poggio a Caiano and elsewhere. Nor is it particularly in the American grain for artists to glorify the rich and powerful as barefacedly as did Vasari with the Medici in Florence's Palazzo della Signoria. Most of the great American families are of North European ancestry, possessing mixtures of English, Scottish, Irish, German, Scandinavian, Dutch, and French blood, and are predominantly of the Protestant faith. These people, for all their wealth and power, tend to be self-effacing, ascetic, and frequently consumed by a sort of diffuse, generalized guilt . . . especially guilt over having so much money.

The Guggenheims were, and are, different. First of all, their ancestral origins are central European and their religion is Judaism. These are roots quite different from those of the Scotch Presbyterian Carnegie and Frick, or the north German, originally Lutheran, Rockefellers. In this regard it is significant that Peggy Guggenheim claims she can only be happy and feel at ease in southern, preferably Latin, cities, and that her father and several of her uncles often claimed they felt more at home in Paris, Mexico City, and Valparaiso, than they did in their adopted New York.

No, the Guggenheims came out of far different soil, had far different racial and cultural roots than the likes of the Carnegies, Fricks, Whitneys, Rockefellers, Mellons. And so it was not above them, or beneath them, to glorify themselves in the manner of their predecessors of four and a half centuries before, the Medici.

There are many places in which the Guggenheims are glorified—in the offices of Guggenheim Brothers, in the Solomon R. Guggenheim Museum, in the offices of several of the Guggenheim foundations—but it is principally in Harry's Falaise, the Guggenheim counterpart to the Medici villa at Poggio a Caiano, that we behold the definitive apotheosis of the Guggenheim family.

The great house, built in the style of a sixteenth-century Norman *manoir*, is situated on a rising bluff overlooking Long Island Sound, not far from Sands Point, and gives the immediate impression of being a transplant, a structure charming and original for America, but alien to its setting. Ninety acres of woods and meadows slope southward from the bluff and the house, a gentle landscape of groves, glades, small hills, little valleys, paddocks, open fields, typical of the North Shore of Long Island. Orchards of apples, peaches, and plums are scattered throughout the estate, and there is a duck pond and a stream. The main approach is through huge iron gates, reminiscent of the great baronial estates of Britain, emblazoned with the initial "G," and the long driveway winds through two miles of woods and pastures filled with peacocks, pheasants, sheep, deer. Another iron gate, this one from sixteenth-century France, of twisted iron bars and with a frieze of gilded fleurons, guards the broad, paved French courtyard immediately before the house. Tall cedars of Lebanon shade the courtyard and over two hundred pots of geraniums flank the entrance to the house. The facade is of a mellow red-brown Dutch brick and the steep, French-style roofs are covered with a dark brown French tile. There are four arcaded openings along the landward side of the building, supported on Gothic capitals, and there is a circular tower two stories high on the south side with a squat, spire-topped roof, the whole giving the impression of a cross between a small French château and a large French country house. The exterior is partially covered with climbing trees and shrubs—wisteria, ivy, cordon magnolia—lending the great house a touch of mystery.

At the southeastern angle there is a swimming pool set in a sort of court enclosed by a Gothic colonnade, and here there is a "hortus conclusus" planted with honey locusts, white dogwood, oleanders, enchantment lilies, and orange trees in tubs. "The atmosphere in this court branching from the main court," observed Dorothea Straus in her *Showcases,* "was hothouse—a Roman bath fit for the Caesars." Four Ming dynasty marble fountains in the form of giant Chinese carps play into the pool and at the base of one of these there is a touch dear to Guggenheim hearts: small leaf ivy grown from cuttings taken from the graves of the Guggenheims' ancestors in the Endigen-Lengnau Israelite cemetery in Switzerland. At the far end of the emerald pool a marble cupid riding on a dolphin plays a lute.

Inside the house there is a mélange of everything, mostly French and Italian Gothic and Renaissance: tiled floors copied from a Renaissance house in Florence; a sixteenth-century French staircase; an extraordinarily beautiful fifteenth-century limewood statue of the Virgin; a rare ceramic by Paul Gauguin, called "La Femme Noire"; a "King Solomon" by Pedro Berruguete; a Giacometti bust; flamboyant Gothic fireplaces; Gothic millefleur tapestries; a lovely blue, white and gold Andrea della Robbia terra-cotta relief of Saint John the Baptist; some exquisite marble reliefs of King Louis XII and his queen, Anne of Brittany; a fifteenth-century Swabian Saint Catherine; some lovely Italian cassoni.

Some objects seem to reflect a Guggenheim identification with royalty and aristocracy: two magnificent seventeenth-century faïence ceramic lions painted purple and gold, the colors of royalty, decorating, where else? Harry's bedroom; a superb stained-glass window-pane of a plumed knight on horseback with the horse's saddle cloth displaying many letter G's; a commodious blue-tiled bathroom with a huge sunken bath styled after a bath of one of the French kings. Much of the interior is copied from the Renaissance Palazzo Davanzati in Florence. Almost all the works of art, and there are hundreds of pieces, are Christian. There is not one Jewish symbol in the house.

When Harry lived in Falaise he kept a staff of fourteen and insisted the estate be self-sufficient, on the lines of a European feudal manor. Pigs and cattle were slaughtered, hams and bacons were cured and smoked, milk, cream, and butter were produced in the estate's dairy, and all vegetables and fruits were grown on the premises. Protected by his ninety acres of woods and farmland, Harry was able to work at Falaise in peace, for it must be emphasized that Falaise was not only a showplace for a very wealthy man but also a base of operations for a very busy man.

The process of Guggenheim glorification at Falaise begins in a small tower detached from the main house to the right at the gate. There a brief film featuring Harry Guggenheim and Charles Lindbergh is shown over and over again to groups of visitors. We are reminded at the beginning of the film that Nassau County is "the cradle of aviation," then told of the Guggenheims' early promotion of flight, and, as we see Harry and Lindbergh strolling about Falaise, we are informed that Lindbergh and his wife made their first flight together from Falaise and that Lindbergh wrote the log of his historic flight across the Atlantic at the estate. No, a guide will tell you, Harry never let Lindbergh down; he stood by him to the end, even when he was flirting with the Nazis.

The film over, visitors are invited to observe a framed photograph and testimonial on a wall. It reads:

> To Harry F. Guggenheim whose farsighted support
> of Dr. Robert H. Goddard's work contributed so much
> to the success of Saturn V, with warmest regards.
>
> WERNHER VON BRAUN

From aviation and rocketry to statesmanship. Once inside the main house the visitor is immediately shown Harry's dining room, the table set with blue, gold, and white Minton ambassadorial china, displaying the Great Seal of the President of the United States.

Statesmanship and aviation are also symbolized in the large gold, brown, and beige living room, dominated by a huge stone Gothic mantelpiece at one end. Here, ranged on a long table, are signed photographs, with testimonials, of Herbert Hoover, Bernard Baruch, Robert H. Goddard, Charles Lindbergh, and James E. Doolittle. Beyond this display antique paintings, tapestries, and sculptures clamor for attention. But by far the most interesting object in the room is almost hidden. It is a small plaque to the right of the fireplace that may well be read with awe someday when Americans begin mining the planets, moons, and asteroids, and colonizing space satellites:

> Sitting before this hearth, in 1929, Carol Guggenheim [Harry's second wife] noticed and read aloud to Harry Guggenheim and Charles Lindbergh the New York Times article about Robert Goddard's abortive rocket experiment at "Aunt Effie's farm" in Massachusetts.
>
> Soon thereafter, Lindbergh arranged a meeting with Goddard which was the first step in the Guggenheim financing of Goddard's pioneering development in astronautics.

In the Gothic library with its oily dark woodwork, carved French Gothic screens, and collection of Lindbergh's books, there is still another item that will doubtless inspire awe in future Space Age visitors: an autographed six-volume set of *The Papers of Robert H. Goddard*, published at the expense of Harry F. Guggenheim. Among these papers is the original design for the first successful liquid-fueled, jet-propelled rocket devised by man, whose eventual construction was financed by the Daniel and Florence Guggenheim Foundation.

From rocketry to horses and thoroughbred racing. A narrow stairway leads down to the basement and Harry's Trophy Room. Horses became Harry's principal passion in his later years, even overshadowing his interest in newspaper publishing. Harry was good at most everything, what he did he did well, whether it was cattle breeding, timbering, or museum managing, and he turned out to be particularly good at horse breeding and racing, so good he eventually earned millions from it. And so in his glittering Trophy Room, where Harry used to take his gentlemen friends for after-dinner coffee and brandy, we see a painting of his Dark Star just nosing out Native Dancer to win the Kentucky Derby in 1953; a portrait of his other big money winner, Bald Eagle; a picture of his "Cain Hoy" stables; a set of leatherbound *Thoroughbred Sires and Dams*; a display of his jockey's blue and white silks; and scores and scores of flashing silver trophies. But even here among his racing mementoes Harry could not entirely get away from aviation: On a table under glass rests a small reliquary containing "two pieces from the wing of the plane flown at Kitty Hawk, North Carolina, December 17, 1903, Orville Wright."

Upstairs the master's bedroom remains exactly as he left it—we observe Harry's navy captain's hat and his racing meeting top hat on his closet shelf—and Alicia Patterson's bedroom remains exactly as she left it, the bed made with her favorite bedspread. Gilt-framed portraits of Daniel and Florence Guggenheim hang in the upper hall leading to the room in which Lindbergh lived while writing the log of his transatlantic flight. A letter of appreciation from Lindbergh, glorifying Harry's support of aviation, hangs on a wall.

There are other reminders of Guggenheim exploits here and there about the house—a photograph of Captain Harry, tail gunner ready to take off from the USS Nehenta Bay, near Okinawa, in 1945, a photograph of publisher Harry behind his desk at *Newsday*—but the final panegyric is reserved for the tower room near the gate. There, when the Lindbergh film is not being shown, we behold THE GUGGENHEIMS, photographic display showing immigrants Meyer and Barbara and their ten children; Meyer and his seven sons at the long mahogany table in the offices of M. Guggenheim's Sons; the A. Y. and Minnie mines in Leadville, the great copper mine at Bingham Canyon; one of ASARCO's refineries; the Solomon R. Guggenheim Museum; and a portrait of young John Simon Guggenheim whose early death gave rise to the foundation that bears his name.

"You see what we have done? . . . You see what we Guggenheims have wrought in one hundred and thirty years in this country? . . . You sense our passion for excellence? . . . You see the great gifts we have presented to the American people?"

The ghost of Harry Guggenheim fairly shouts from every room in Falaise.

And indeed what magnificent gifts this extraordinary family has bestowed, not only upon the American people, but upon all mankind.

Lorenzo appears to have laid the foundation of his glory and his fame by which he obtained the appellations of "Magnificent" and "Magnanimous" by universal consent, for he displayed great liberality towards all.

He was hardly out of boyhood when the ruler of Sicily, hearing of his love of fine horses, sent him one as a gift. Lorenzo acknowledged it by sending back presents worth three or four times that of the horse. When his tutor remonstrated with him for overgenerosity, Lorenzo replied that there was nothing so glorious as to outdo all men in generosity. That was true royalty.

That was true royalty. To take two hundred and fifty million dollars from the earth and give five or six hundred million back.

V

THE SURVIVORS

(1945-1978)

THE FIFTH AND SIXTH

GENERATIONS

A people which takes no pride in the most noble achievements of remote ancestors will never achieve anything to be remembered with pride by remote descendants.

—Macaulay

The longest wave is quickly lost in the sea.

—Emerson

THE GUGGENHEIMS

GENEALOGICAL CHART

(FOR PART V)

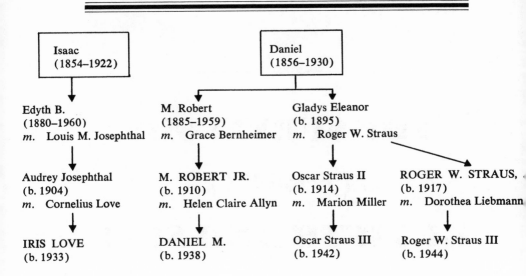

Isaac
(1854–1922)

Edyth B.
(1880–1960)
m. Louis M. Josephthal

Audrey Josephthal
(b. 1904)
m. Cornelius Love

IRIS LOVE
(b. 1933)

Daniel
(1856–1930)

M. Robert
(1885–1959)
m. Grace Bernheimer

M. ROBERT JR.
(b. 1910)
m. Helen Claire Allyn

DANIEL M.
(b. 1938)

Gladys Eleanor
(b. 1895)
m. Roger W. Straus

Oscar Straus II
(b. 1914)
m. Marion Miller

Oscar Straus III
(b. 1942)

ROGER W. STRAUS,
(b. 1917)
m. Dorothea Liebmann

Roger W. Straus III
(b. 1944)

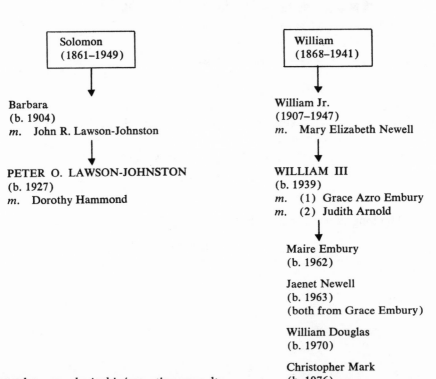

Solomon
(1861–1949)

Barbara
(b. 1904)
m. John R. Lawson-Johnston

PETER O. LAWSON-JOHNSTON
(b. 1927)
m. Dorothy Hammond

William
(1868–1941)

William Jr.
(1907–1947)
m. Mary Elizabeth Newell

WILLIAM III
(b. 1939)
m. (1) Grace Azro Embury
m. (2) Judith Arnold

Maire Embury
(b. 1962)

Jaenet Newell
(b. 1963)
(both from Grace Embury)

William Douglas
(b. 1970)

Christopher Mark
(b. 1976)
(both from Judith Arnold)

For complete genealogical information consult
genealogical tables on pages 541–544.

CHAPTER

1

AFTER HARRY:
A FAMILY IN FRAGMENTS

WITH HARRY GUGGENHEIM'S DEATH IN 1971, AND THE TRANSFOR-
mation of Falaise into a museum, the grand era of the Guggenheims
in America appeared to be over. Now there remained not much else
for the family to do but hold onto what they had and make sure
their various businesses, investments, and foundations did not go
astray.

To be sure, there was still money, energy, and talent in the family
for further creative achievement—as the extremely successful careers
of Roger W. Straus, Jr., in publishing, and Iris Love, in archaeology,
attest. And there was at least an outside chance that Harry's principal
heir, the personable and capable, and now affluent, Peter O. Lawson-
Johnston, could eventually revitalize the Guggenheim name, finances,
and influence. But the heroic days of empire building and daring,
innovative leadership in the arts and sciences did, nevertheless, seem
to be gone forever, as they may well have been gone forever for all
of the United States of America.

It was, in the end, a typically American family situation. In pre-
World War I Europe certain "great families," those who paid the
closest attention to such eugenic essentials as bloodlines, the right
marriage alliances, and the most promising legatees to last wills and
testaments, often managed to stay in power for centuries. The Medicis
dominated Florence and Tuscany, and much of Italy and Europe, for
over two hundred years. The Hapsburgs dominated Vienna and most
of Austria for six hundred years before losing their power in the
holocaust of World War I. The Bourbons, in their various branches,

remained in the forefront of European politics as rulers of France, Spain, and the Kingdom of the Two Sicilies for three centuries, and still have one of their number on a European throne. By contrast, in the United States of America great families usually begin losing their power and influence after the fourth generation.

Herein lies something of an irony. Thousands of Americans have struggled so mightily to enrich themselves and found what they hope are impregnable dynasties, to realize the classic American Dream of rising from poverty and obscurity to wealth and power, only to find their efforts undermined by certain leveling forces which, alas, are always at work, steadily eroding the financial bases of those who have attained economic power. The graduated income tax (Harry Guggenheim was once in the 89 percent bracket). Confiscatory estate and gift taxes (Murry Guggenheim, it will be remembered, paid in 1925 the then highest gift tax in U.S. history). Education of tender young heirs by underpaid liberal professors who resent their students' fathers' wealth. Other subversions. It is as if there are two separate Americas, each claiming to represent the American way: one moneyed, aristocratic, conservative, dynastic, and exclusive, involved almost wholly with the private sector, the other poorer, egalitarian, liberal, populist, involved more with, and looking more to, the public sector for salvation, and they are constantly at war with one another.

Who, and what, was left of the Guggenheim dynasty, and the institutions its founders had created, after Harry's death?

To begin with, it must be remembered that the fourth and fifth generations of Guggenheims were decimated generations. No fewer than eight Guggenheims from these generations died either premature or violent deaths before their forty-first year. John Simon Guggenheim, Senator Simon's firstborn son, the one after whom the foundation that distributes the fellowships was named, died at seventeen. Daniel Guggenheim II, Colonel Bob's first son, died at eighteen. Benjamin's two grandsons, Hazel's children Terrence and Benjamin II, died at four years and fourteen months respectively. William, Jr. died at thirty-nine. George Denver Guggenheim, Senator Simon's younger son, died a suicide at thirty-two. Pegeen Guggenheim died a suicide at forty. And Nancy Draper, Harry's middle daughter, died a suicide at forty-one.

Who, then, was left besides the vast number of men and women descended from Guggenheim females, people bearing surnames like Short, Smith, Meek, Johnson, and Butler, that legion of great and great great grandchildren of Meyer and Barbara, living off money the Guggenheim brothers had made but having little or nothing to do with the Guggenheim family or its institutions? Who were the survivors who by virtue of their wealth and activities could legitimately be called Guggenheims?

First of all, there was Harry's principal heir, Solomon's grandson Peter O. Lawson-Johnston, a slim, handsome, fair-haired young man in his early forties, firmly ensconced behind the principal desk in the Partners' Room of Guggenheim Brothers and behind many other desks besides. Then there was Colonel Bob's peppy, sixty-year-old son, M. Robert Guggenheim, Jr., and *his* capable, thirty-four-year-old son, Daniel M. Guggenheim, the two living luxuriously and productively at Newport Beach, California, far from the family power center in New York. There were Gladys Guggenheim Straus' offspring, the ebullient Roger W. Straus, Jr., and the quieter, more reserved Oscar Straus II, and their sons, Roger W. III and Oscar III, all of whom sat on the boards of one Guggenheim foundation or another. There were Harry's surviving daughters and grandchildren, who, with the exception of Harry's eldest daughter, Joan, did not much identify with the heritage Harry had spent the better part of his lifetime trying to conserve and promote. And then there was Isaac's talented great granddaughter, Iris Love, regarded by some as the most inspired female archaeologist in the world. Lastly, there was William's (Gatenby Williams') grandson, William Guggenheim III, a self-styled religious mystic, living in Florida with a wife and their infant son.

As for what was left of the Guggenheim institutions, there remained a number of relatively small businesses, bits and pieces of the former mining and smelting empire, such as Guggenheim Brothers, the Feldspar Corporation, the Anglo Company, and Pacific Tin Consolidated, and then five foundations, the John Simon Memorial, the Daniel and Florence, the Solomon R., the Harry Frank, and the Peggy. The foundations, with combined assets of approximately $700 million, including two museums and thousands of paintings, were worth more than all the surviving Guggenheims put together. Peter O. Lawson-Johnston is currently head of all the businesses and two of the foundations.

A fragmented, diminished family, a handful of small companies, and five foundations facing the new America of the last quarter of the American century.

A new America indeed. Gone the open frontier, with its promise

V / THE SURVIVORS—1945-1978

of unlimited opportunities. Gone the feeling of uniqueness, the sense of being new, revolutionary, exceptional, different. Gone "the impenetrable forests full of wild beasts and Indians." Going the "rolling hills, untouched plains, the brawling streams, the lakes spread like tablecloths beneath the trees." Gone the illusions. Gone the innocence. Gone the bonanzas. Gone the feeling of special historical mission. Going individual initiative. Going free enterprise. Going individual liberties.

For, alas, by the mid-1970s the American empire had been firmly established and was now governed by a few score giant multinational corporations, each acting like a sovereign state unto itself, each seeking to limit the play of the free market, each suppressing individual liberties in its own way, each committed to endless growth in a world in which endless growth is no longer possible, except at the expense of other people and the environment. In a mere two hundred years of independence from the British Empire the American empire builders had all but exhausted their country's possibilities. Now, all of a sudden, America was the ancien régime. Now, all of a sudden, the Coca-Colonization of the world had been completed beyond its founders' wildest dreams; the pause that refreshes could at last wash down a sandwich from the Amazon to the Himalayas, from Pitcairn Island to Lapland. Sherwin-Williams paints did at last cover the earth, and there was now a Holiday Inn on Madagascar in which one could reserve a room by picking up one's phone in Kansas City and dialing a toll-free number. Soon there would be little left for the empire builders to do but attempt to sell the Imperial hamburger on Tasmania and Baffin Island. "The sun never sets on McDonald's hamburgers" would be the final consummation.

Yes, the empire had been firmly founded. But the strange thing was that most Americans, unlike their counterparts in the Rome of two millennia ago, did not seem to be particularly proud of having created the greatest commercial empire in world history. In fact, many Americans were even reluctant to admit that the United States of America *was* an empire.

And as the popular response to the war in Vietnam proved, they certainly were not ready to die for the stockholders of Coca-Cola, ITT, McDonald's hamburgers, and Sherwin-Williams paints.

A whole new America. An overbuilt America afflicted with gigantism. An America in which a small partnership like Guggenheim

Brothers could no longer compete successfully with the corporate giants it had spawned. An America in which gigantic government was steadily encroaching on the private sector, which had been the Guggenheims' arena for so long, regulating and preempting more and more of its activities. A despoiled America, a land crying out against the sort of exploitation the Guggenheims had engaged in for over half a century, a land whose major natural resources, excluding coal, might all be used up by the second decade of the twenty-first century. An America, also, in which the work ethic that had guided people like the Guggenheims to such extraordinary financial heights was steadily losing favor, especially among the young. Above all, an America that seemed already overdeveloped, already exhausted, a nation that had largely consumed itself, one that seemed to have already spent, or used up, its future. Where could the country go now?

Where indeed? And where could the Guggenheims go now? By the Bicentennial year the Guggenheims had done practically everything, been practically everything it was possible to do or be in the freedom of America. They had even become so assimilated into the mainstream of American society that most of them were no longer Jewish. Peter O. Lawson-Johnston, M. Robert Guggenheim, Jr., Daniel M. Guggenheim, Iris Love, and William Guggenheim III were, with the exception of Robert, half WASP by blood, and all, including Robert, had been brought up in the Christian faith. Not only had the family realized the American Dream a hundredfold, it had even succeeded in liberating itself from its often inconvenient Jewishness. What was there to be, what was there to dream, where was there to go, now?

The American Dream had always been one of upward mobility. Now many Americans were faced with the American nightmare of downward mobility. Indeed, as other countries, notably China and the Soviet Union, grew in power, the entire nation was faced with it.

As for the fifth and sixth generation of Guggenheims in the Bicentennial year (one of whose chief events, the Viking landing on Mars, could be traced back to the Guggenheims' support of Robert Goddard), they were not necessarily going up, or down; they, like the nation, were just about holding their own.

But where to go from 1976, other than to the planets beyond Mars?

For Roger W. Straus, Jr. and his cousin Iris Love there was not much of a problem. Both were fortunate to have had very clearly defined vocations since their teens, which, partly thanks to the money behind them, and mostly thanks to their own exceptional talents, they have pursued successfully and give every indication of pursuing successfully for many years to come.

For the Guggenheims of the West Coast, M. Robert, Jr. and Daniel M., it was a slightly different situation. Neither was involved in a calling as specialized and glamorous as publishing or archaeology. Life and work for them in the mid-seventies consisted of making money, putting what Robert had inherited, which was considerable, and what Daniel was currently earning, which was also considerable, to work, hoping by hard work and shrewd investment to bring their share of the family fortune back to where it had been during the lifetime of their extraordinary forebear, the bold and visionary Mr. Dan.

Peter Lawson-Johnston, of course, faced the most formidable challenge of all. As Harry's principal heir, not only to his fortune but also to "the Guggenheim heritage," it was up to him to pick up the pieces of the fragmented Guggenheim empire and try to put them back together again. It was up to him to revitalize moribund Guggenheim Brothers, up to him to lead the other Guggenheim businesses, like Anglo Company and Pacific Tin, to ever brighter futures, up to him to see that the Guggenheim Museum remained solvent and continued to be a vital, innovative artistic force, up to him to do something constructive with that biggest Guggenheim question mark of all, the Harry Frank Guggenheim Foundation, up to him to choose a successor to carry on in the next century. All this in a time of steadily increasing competition from the multinationals, ever-burgeoning and ever-interfering big government, steadily diminishing acceptance of the work ethic, steadily diminishing natural resources.

Such monumental challenges were the price Lawson-Johnston had to pay for being Harry's heir. They were certainly quite remote from the dividend and interest collecting that had become the principal challenge of most of the other members of the family. Even more remote were these challenges from the world of the young man who might be called, without melodrama or exaggeration, "the last of the Guggenheims," William Guggenheim III, the only male left in the family bearing the name Guggenheim who possessed sons. For Will III was not only the last Guggenheim with offspring capable of perpetuating the Guggenheim name, he was also the only member of the family headed in a radically new direction. To come from a family that had made its fortune exploiting the natural riches of the earth, then used that fortune to support themselves in royal style, and support the arts and sciences in exceptionally daring ways . . . and then turn one's back on all that came before, and embark upon the lonely path of religious mysticism, that, for a Guggenheim, was indeed a new direction.

Almost one hundred years before Peter Lawson-Johnston took up his responsibilities as Guggenheim standard-bearer in the 1970s, and M. Robert Guggenheim, Jr. established himself so luxuriously at Newport Beach, and Roger W. Straus, Jr. enjoyed the thirtieth anniversary of his New York publishing house, Farrar, Straus & Giroux, and Iris Love discovered the Temple of Aphrodite on Knidos, and William Guggenheim III discovered in Florida his vocation as a religious mystic, their great grandfather, Meyer Guggenheim, had gathered his seven sons around that long mahogany table in his office and acted out the parable of the sticks and bundle of sticks.

"You see, my boys, singly the sticks are easily broken, together they cannot be broken. So it is with you. Together you are invincible. Singly each of you may be easily broken. Stay together, my sons, and the world will be yours. Break up and you will lose everything."

This philosophy was heeded by all the brothers, with magnificent results, for several decades, then it was abandoned, gradually by the brothers themselves, then precipitously by their children, grandchildren, and great grandchildren. By 1976 many Guggenheims had been broken. The family had by no means "lost everything," but it had lost much, and it was now far from "invincible." Now there was really no such thing anymore as the Guggenheim family. There were, instead, several different families, each stemming from one of the original seven brothers, and each going in a different direction from the other. There were no more big family reunions embracing everyone. It was a family in fragments and though it might well continue to produce men and women of ability, it most certainly would never regain the strength and sense of purpose it had enjoyed in those exuberant days when seven young men, sons of a poor refugee from a European ghetto, boldly set out together to conquer the mineral wealth of the new world.

CHAPTER

2

PETER O. LAWSON-JOHNSTON: THE ANOINTED

HE IS AT HIS DESK IN THE VAST, WOOD-PANELED PARTNERS' ROOM of Guggenheim Brothers almost every weekday morning at nine.

To arrive there by that hour he has awakened at his home in Princeton at six-fifteen, jogged, breakfasted, has taken a commuter train from Hopewell to New York, then a subway to Wall Street.

His desk is the principal one, in the center of the room, facing the entrance, his back to a view of the World Trade Center, the Hudson River, and the Jersey meadows. The other desks, once occupied by his grandfather and granduncles and cousin Harry, and now claimed by his aging partners, are usually empty.

It is nine-thirty on a typical weekday morning. Not much is going on. But from his desk Lawson-Johnston can see all the protagonists of the tumultuous activities that went on for decades in what has now become *his* room.

On the dark walnut walls near him hang portraits of the immigrant tailor from Lengnau, Switzerland, Simon Guggenheim, and his son, Meyer. On the far walls in front of him, to the right and left of the main entrance, hang granduncles Daniel, Murry, Simon, Isaac, Benjamin, grandfather Solomon, and cousin Harry. On a small table not far from his desk is the framed National City Bank check dated March 1, 1923, made out to Guggenheim Brothers in the amount of $70 million and signed by Anaconda Copper. On another table nearby is the photograph of grandfather Solomon hunting grouse in Scotland with his son-in-law, the Earl of Castle Stewart, and the reliquary containing the "true piece of the first hangar in the world at Kitty Hawk."

Here and there over other tables are scattered the company reports relating activities in Angola, Malaysia, Brazil, Thailand, Canada, Alaska. And the reports of the foundations depending partly on those activities: the Solomon R. Guggenheim Foundation and Museum, the Daniel and Florence Guggenheim Foundation, the Harry Frank Guggenheim Foundation.

Now and then something happens. The phone rings. Or a clerk or a secretary comes in with a letter to sign. Or one of the other partners, most of whom are over seventy-five, saunters in to look over his mail. But usually all is very quiet. Gone the days when the reception rooms were crammed with prospectors, investors, miners, grubstakers, bankers, explorers, inventors, bums, and impostors waiting to set their tremendous deals before one of the brothers. Gone the days when the brothers, meeting around the long partners' table, discussed and discussed and discussed, and then decided to build a $25 million railroad over a moving glacier in Alaska, or invest an equally impressive sum in a barren mountain nine thousand feet up in the Chilean Andes. Gone the excitement of finding gold in the Yukon, copper in Alaska, copper in Utah, silver in Mexico, diamonds in Angola, tin in Bolivia. Gone the big gambles. Gone the bonanzas. Gone the days when the brothers controlled 75 percent of all the copper and lead in the world. Gone the chutzpah. Gone the days when Daniel Guggenheim, heady with the prospect of cornering all the natural nitrate on the planet, would come before his brothers and emit enthusiasms such as: "Nitrates will make us rich beyond the dreams of avarice!"

This is not to say, however, that there is nothing to do. Bits and pieces of the former Guggenheim empire remain, and they are solvent. There is the Anglo Company, an outgrowth of Murry's brainchild, the Anglo-Lautaro Nitrate Company of Chile; there is the New York Stock Exchange-listed Pacific Tin Consolidated Corporation, an outgrowth of the old Yukon Gold. There is the Feldspar Corporation. There is Diamang, the Angolan diamonds concern. There is the Brazilian Mining and Dredging Company. There are still hundreds of thousands of shares of Kennecott Corporation to think about. There are other, smaller concerns, like Elgebar, the South Carolina timber and cattle operation. And there are all the foundations and trust funds that depend, partly or entirely, on these businesses.

Yes, although the economies and governments of entire nations no longer rise or fall because of what is decided in the Partners' Room of Guggenheim Brothers, there is still quite a lot for the occupant of the principal desk to do.

The occupant, Peter O. Lawson-Johnston, landed at this desk in this room thanks, as we know, to his cousin Harry, who, as he lay dying of cancer at the Sloan Kettering Institute in New York, passed over his employee Bill D. Moyers and his grandson Dana Draper to make Peter his chief heir and trustee.

Well does Peter remember the events leading to his investiture. Albert Thiele giving him the job at Guggenheim-controlled Feldspar Corporation in 1956. Harry gradually taking notice of him, inviting him to be a partner at Guggenheim Brothers, then, in 1960, sending him off to Malaysia with Pacific Tin. His becoming a member of the board of Kennecott Corporation upon Albert Thiele's retirement in 1965. Harry putting him on the board of the Guggenheim Museum. That trustees meeting at the museum when he made that ringing speech about the necessity of living up to his grandfather's ideals, and Harry congratulating him when the meeting was over. Then, December 10, 1969, Harry suddenly making him vice-president for finance at the museum and putting him in charge of all future development. Harry then taking such a strong new interest in him. The phone calls, the luncheons, the meetings. Culminating in Harry appointing him president of the museum and telling him he wanted him to be president of his own foundation after he died. And then that fateful day in 1970 when Harry called him up from Sloan Kettering and asked him to pay him a visit, telling him that George Fountaine of Guggenheim Brothers had a large envelope for him.

Since Peter had by then grown accustomed to going over business affairs with Harry, he did not have more than a "modicum of curiosity about the contents of the package."

But soon he realized the contents were probably quite important, because immediately after his arrival at Harry's bedside Harry asked him to open the envelope and read its contents.

There was not a sound in the hospital room but the tearing open of the manila envelope and the labored breathing of the cancerous old man.

When Peter read that Harry had made him heir to a multimillion-dollar trust fund that would guarantee him at least $500,000 income a year for the rest of his life, had made several other substantial bequests to him besides, and had also entrusted him with the responsibility of carrying on the Guggenheim tradition, he was utterly overwhelmed.

"I can't believe it," he gasped.

Harry looked at him steadily and smiled. "Peter, you have good common sense," he said, "good judgment, you have a wonderful wife and family, but the main reason for this is that you are a gentleman."

Harry was no fool. He, like his father and uncles, had always been a shrewd judge of character, and in selecting Peter as his heir and trustee he had made a particularly good choice.

Peter Lawson-Johnston belies all the standard clichés about fifth-generation American scions of wealthy families. He is not decadent. He is not self-indulgent. He is not a spendthrift. He is not self-satisfied about his wealth and social position. He is not spoiled. He is, rather, a steady, balanced, dedicated, intelligent, hardworking young man.

The American rich, so exposed to democratic social pressures, are usually not as spoiled as their European and Latin American counterparts. Certainly they are nowhere near as spoiled as the Greek, Italian, Mexican, or Spanish rich, whose wealth has a tendency to place them in a caste by themselves. And Peter is no exception. He is not self-important. He does not tyrannize over his subordinates. He is considerate of others. He is not ostentatious. He works as hard, if not harder, as any man in the many organizations in his charge. Furthermore, he possesses a strong sense of obligation toward his fellowman.

Much of the credit for the way he has turned out must go to his grandfather and his mother. Neither Solomon nor Barbara Guggenheim ever gave him very much money and both let him know early in life that if he was to receive any money he would have to earn it by performing some useful chore. And after he graduated from college there wouldn't be much money forthcoming either, unless he worked hard and succeeded at whatever job he took. And there were never graduation or birthday presents of fancy sports cars. Or "wonderful little cheques" suddenly and miraculously floating his way from Kennecott Mountain or the nitrate fields of Chile.

Yes, Barbara raised him well. The boy grew up in the Maryland countryside where Barbara had gone to live with her second husband, the champion horseman Fred Wettach. It was a boyhood spent mostly outdoors, helping out at his mother's farm, working alongside the hired hands, and riding, hunting, and fishing.

It was a boyhood, however, without a real father, for Barbara had divorced John Robert Lawson-Johnston after only three years of marriage. Peter did not then see his father again for twenty-one years.

John Robert, it appears, was somewhat of a playboy and a ladies' man. The son of John Ormond Lawson-Johnston of Edinburgh, founder, as we have mentioned, of Bovril, the company that makes the famous beef-soup concentrate, and Fannie Roberta Dunlop of Savannah, he was brought up as an American citizen but was educated at Eton. He eventually had five wives, of whom Barbara Guggenheim was the second.

To compensate for Peter's lack of a father, Barbara tried to have him see his grandfather as often as possible, sending him off regularly to Sol's plantation in South Carolina and ranch in Idaho, and arranging for him to visit the old man now and then in New York and Long Island.

Peter enjoyed a close relationship with Solomon Guggenheim. He remembers hunting with him at Big Survey, fishing with him at Island Park, visiting him at his Plaza suite and being bewildered by all the Bauers and Kandinskys in heavy gilt frames (which contrasted so glaringly with the collection of Old Masters Aunt Irene kept in her room), going with Sol to Mount Vernon, where Solomon made a point of "watering George Washington's lawn." He also remembers how thrilled he was to go out on Sol's gigantic yacht, the *Trillora,* and how delighted Sol was when the vessel sank. Apparently Solomon wanted to sell the converted destroyer and could not find a buyer. The ship was insured, so the best thing that could have happened to it was for it to sink. Which it did, in Roslyn harbor, during the great hurricane of 1938. Peter and his mother were staying at Trillora Court at the time, and Peter remembers his grandfather announcing, with a broad grin, that the yacht had been declared a total loss.

What qualities of his grandfather does Peter remember the most? Two: his manliness and his love of art. "He had phenomenal courage and assurance. As a child I always felt extremely secure around him and looked up to him. And I remember that the greatest joy in his life, beside his family, was contemplating his paintings."

If his grandfather was a beneficial influence on him, one person who was not was his nurse. Peter blames his nurse for giving him a complex about his Jewishness. During the late thirties and early forties she would repeatedly tell him to be good because if he wasn't, he, as a Jew, would be killed by Hitler. It was the first time he had ever been told outright he was a Jew—he had been raised an Episcopalian, the religion of his father—and since he did not want to be killed by Hitler he consciously tried to hide his Jewishness. Later he overcame the complex and now maintains he is exceedingly proud of his Jewish origins.

He still had the complex, however, when he went to prep school at Lawrenceville at the age of fourteen. The Second World War was on and reports were coming in from Europe that Hitler had sworn to exterminate the Jews and was even beginning to carry out his pledge. So at Lawrenceville he did not go around telling his schoolmates he was a Guggenheim. As it turned out, it might not have made much difference what he told them at Lawrenceville, for he became exceedingly popular there. In his senior year he was elected president of the student body and voted "the best all-around fellow" in the school.

Two weeks after graduating in 1945 Peter joined the Army and served a year with the U.S. occupation forces in Italy. This was an exciting time. He was stationed in Rome, Rome right after the *liberazione*. Before long his managerial skills were recognized by his superiors and he was put in charge of the Excelsior Hotel on the Via Veneto, then being used as a residence for field-grade officers. One of his duties was to see that women did not go upstairs to the officers' quarters. Peter stationed guards at all the elevators and stairways, but somehow the women got up anyway. He found out they were going up the dumbwaiters.

College came next, at the University of Virginia, and though it was a bit of a letdown after managing the Excelsior Hotel in Rome, Peter survived it to graduate with honors in 1951.

It was during his sophomore year at Virginia that he met his father for the first time in over twenty years. The meeting was set for the Palm Court of the Plaza in New York. Both were there at the appointed hour, sitting near each other and not having the nerve to identify themselves. The older man was looking at his watch nervously. Finally Peter went up to him and asked, "Who are you waiting for?" To which the older man replied, "None of your goddamned business." Peter then identified himself and the two laughed and embraced. They have since become good friends.

What to do after college?

Peter did not know. He had no clear, unmistakable vocation. And so he took a number of jobs in journalism and public relations in and around Baltimore, hoping somehow to find himself. He became a reporter for the Baltimore *Sun*. He worked as a PR man for the Maryland Classified Employees Association and the Maryland Civil Defense Agency. He became a roustabout in New Mexico, working for a Texas oil company ("That experience cured me of any desire to ever have a job again as a laborer"). During this relatively unsettled period he felt compelled to deny his Guggenheim origins entirely, rarely telling any of his coworkers who he was. Certainly he never breathed a word about being a Guggenheim to his fellow roustabouts on the oil rigs in New Mexico.

Meanwhile he had gotten married to Dorothy "Didi" Hammond of Baltimore and had fathered the first two of his four children.

He was now a married man with two children and no clear direction to his life, no exceptional opportunities on his horizon. Not the best situation to be in. He began to reconsider his position in regard to the Guggenheims. Might there be interesting opportunities in his own backyard?

Harry was quick to come forward with an offer. He would give Peter a job with Anglo-Lautaro in the nitrate fields of Chile. Peter was receptive to the offer, but his wife's family was dead against it. The Hammonds did not want their Didi living in a mining camp on the Chilean desert. When Peter told this to Harry, Harry was disgusted. Harry had put in his mining apprenticeship on the parched slopes of Chuquicamata Mountain and had been married at the time. Promptly he crossed Peter off his list. For a while it appeared that the Hammonds had scotched forever Peter's chances to cash in on his Guggenheim connections.

Finally Albert Thiele, a Guggenheim Brothers partner, formerly Solomon Guggenheim's personal assistant, came to the rescue and gave Peter a job with the Feldspar Corporation, a wholly owned subsidiary of Pacific Tin, for the purpose of familiarizing Peter with the processes of mining and milling feldspar and mica, and, lo and behold, Peter was on his way.

From Feldspar Peter graduated to the parent company, Pacific Tin, which sent him to the Far East to study placer dredge mining of tin in Malaysia. After a while he knew something about dredging tin from jungle rivers. He remained at Pacific Tin, in various capacities, until Harry's death in 1971, after which he came into a dozen or so more positions, a veritable bonanza.

Among the hats he was wearing in 1978 were:

> Partner of Guggenheim Brothers
> Chairman and Director, Anglo Company
> Chairman and Director, The Feldspar Corporation
> Chairman and Director, Brazilian Mining and Dredging Company
> Chairman and Director, Pacific Tin Consolidated Corporation
> Director, The Kennecott Copper Corporation
> Director, McGraw-Hill, Inc.
> Director, Minerec Corporation

Director, Nabors Drilling Company
Director, Printex Corporation
Vice-President and Director, Elgebar Corporation
President and Trustee, The Solomon R. Guggenheim Foundation
Chairman and Director, The Harry Frank Guggenheim Foundation

And his clubs in 1978 were:

Century Association (New York City)
Bankers Club (New York City)
American Club (London)
Beden's Brook Club (Princeton, N.J.)
Green Spring Valley Hunt Club (Garrison, Md.)
Pretty Brook Tennis Club (Princeton, N.J.)
Maryland Club (Baltimore, Md.)
Edgartown Yacht Club (Edgartown, Mass.)
The River Club (New York City)
The Jupiter Island Club (Hobe Sound, Fla.)
Seminole Golf Club (North Palm Beach, Fla.)
Nassau Gun Club (Princeton, N.J.)

Can anything more be said about the importance of being intelligent, polished, honest, hardworking, and well-behaved . . . and having the right grandfather, mother, and cousin?

And never let it be said again that in the United States of America a son of a Jewish mother cannot get into the best clubs.

Impressive as Lawson-Johnston's 1978 curriculum vitae is, the businesses over which he presides are nevertheless small potatoes compared to those over which his grandfather and granduncles once presided. What remains in Peter's custody is but a few scraps left over from a table once piled high with the riches of the earth. But, starting with these scraps, who knows, perhaps Peter can construct a brand-new empire. People have started with less. People like his great grandfather Meyer.

Peter's biggest scrap is Anglo Corporation, formerly the Anglo-Lautaro Nitrate Company, now a diversified holding company with gross revenues in 1976 of $56,785,000 from which a net profit of $2,162,000 was realized. (Compare this to the net profits in 1917 of Guggenheim-controlled Utah Copper: $23,000,000; Kennecott Copper: $16,000,000; and ASARCO: $25,000,000.)

In 1971, during the short-lived administration of Salvador Allende, Anglo-Lautaro Nitrate was compelled to sell its remaining assets in Chile to an agency of the Chilean government for a mere pittance,

$7,885,590, and in so doing got out of the nitrate business for good. The company's net loss, as a result of Allende's nationalization of the nitrate industry, amounted to $25,912,596.

It was after payment of the $7,885,590 that Anglo Corporation was established, a new company altogether, incorporated in the Bahamas.

Today, as a result of Lawson-Johnston's acquisition policies, Anglo owns 52.6 percent of Nabors Drilling, an oil drilling company based in Canada and currently active on Alaska's North Slope; 100 percent of Minerec, which produces mining chemicals to maximize metallic extraction, such as reagents for use in copper flotation; 100 percent of Printex, which makes circuit boards for computers; and 100 percent of Motor Parts Industries, which specializes in replacement parts for jeeps.

The germ of another globe-girdling conglomerate? Another AS-ARCO? Another Kennecott? Possibly. Lawson-Johnston plans a steady program of acquisitions (he plans, among other things, to purchase the rest of Nabors), and sees considerable potential in both Nabors and Printex.

The next-biggest scrap of empire is Pacific Tin Consolidated, formerly Guggenheim-controlled Yukon Gold, now 36.8 percent owned by Denison Mines of Canada. Pacific Tin is chiefly a Malaysian tin operation, where huge dredges once used in the Yukon are now active in the Batang Berjuntai delta, but it is also involved in feldspar mining and processing, diamond dredging in Brazil (it owns part of Brazilian Mining and Dredging), and tin drilling in Thailand and Venezuela, and more recently the mining of low-sulphur coal in Tennessee. The company currently earns around $1,500,000 a year for its stockholders from revenues of around $17,700,000 and is seriously threatened because the Malaysian government wants Malaysians to own 70 percent of the country's natural resources. The Malaysian operation is Pacific Tin's major money-maker.

Then there is, of course, good old Guggenheim Brothers, a curious little partnership functioning like Anglo as a small, diversified holding company. At present Guggenheim Brothers owns a great many shares of Kennecott Corporation (it once owned almost the entire company), a small copper mine in Canada, a percentage of Diamang in Angola, a healthy percentage of the Brazilian Mining and Dredging Company, and a healthy percentage of Pacific Tin. Like Pacific Tin, Brazilian Mining and Dredging is also gravely threatened. Ever since the company, which is partly owned by Brazilians, began dredging as many as 72,661 carats a year out of the Jequitinhonha River in the state of Minas Gerais, earning profits of as much as $100,000 a month, the Brazilians have been demanding a greater share of ownership.

The direction Guggenheim Brothers has taken, sticking with the development of natural resources in underdeveloped countries, was mostly Harry's idea, and it has proved to be a mistaken one.

Renaissance versatility may provide the renaissance man with scores of stimulating opportunities to develop the many sides of his personality, but it is not always a great asset in business. Harry was always so busy with his horse breeding and racing, his aeronautical pioneering, his writing, his art museum overseeing, his public-service jobs, his cattle raising, his timbering, his foundation creating, his newspaper publishing, that he did not really have the time to devote to a serious consideration of what direction Guggenheim Brothers should take in the sixties and seventies. He decided, rather hastily, that it should merely try to do what it had always done, develop natural resources in underdeveloped countries. In deciding this he overlooked two late-twentieth-century phenomena: the rise of the giant multinationals, such as Tenneco and Engelhard Minerals & Chemicals, against which Guggenheim Brothers could not possibly hope to compete, especially in the field of exploration, and the ardent desire of underdeveloped nations to own and develop their own natural resources.

Harry therefore left Lawson-Johnston with a Guggenheim Brothers that was little more than a museum piece in the new economic order of the mid-1970s.

Peter is fully aware of this and intends to do something about it. "I have been giving consideration," he declares, "to the idea that Guggenheim Brothers be revitalized by my bringing in new partners who will share my interest in newspaper or magazine publishing. I have no desire to get back into mining exploration because this has become too expensive an undertaking for individuals in competition with the major mining companies. It would, in my view, be very rewarding to launch or acquire one or perhaps more publications which would have an impact on current events. It would be, I think, in line with one of Harry's major interests (*Newsday*) and a type of venture compatible with my interests."

If Harry left Peter little more than a museum piece in Guggenheim Brothers, what did he leave him in the way of foundations?

More besieged institutions. The Solomon R. Guggenheim Foundation and Museum, hit by the Allende takeover in Chile, the world-wide drop in the price of copper, and the Angolan civil war, cost $2,500,000 a year to run and their original endowment no longer covers this expense. To make up its annual deficit of approximately $250,000, the museum must resort to various fund-raising schemes: operating a restaurant and a bookshop, soliciting gifts, soliciting aid from the federal government, and throwing parties for patrons.

Most Americans are under the illusion that foundations are some-how miraculously immune to the vicissitudes of empire, but they are not. The Solomon R. Guggenheim Foundation owned a good many shares in the Anglo-Lautaro Nitrate Company of Chile, and when Salvador Allende virtually expropriated the company those shares suddenly became next to worthless. At present the foundation owns 12,342 shares of Diamang. Before the Angolan civil war these were worth $1,357,620. Now they are worth $123,420. If it weren't for their 157,000 shares of Kennecott, valued in 1977 at $4,396,000, the foundation and museum would be in serious trouble.

Fortunately, Solomon Guggenheim's daughters, Eleanor and Barbara, still possess substantial fortunes and have earmarked significant bequests to their father's museum in their wills. In June, 1977, Barbara, responding to her son Peter's most recent fund-raising campaign, gave a substantial trust to the museum.

It is still a bit too early to determine the extent and quality of the Solomon R. Guggenheim Museum's influence on the painting and sculpture of our time. The museum is currently under the direction of the Czechoslovakian-born art historian Thomas M. Messer, who, in a mere twenty years, has carved out an impressive domain for himself in the art world of the United States.

As director of the Guggenheim he has pursued an acquisitions policy that only time will justify or condemn, selling some fifty Kandinskys and purchasing, among many paintings, five Dubuffets from Baron Elie de Rothschild, $1 million worth of paintings from the Hilla Rebay estate, and important works by such modern abstraction-ists as William Baziotes and Robert Motherwell. He has also put on several very impressive shows. Thus far Messer has held exhibitions of the work of Arp, Malevich, Ernst, Giacometti, Lichtenstein, and Kupka, among others. His vast Max Ernst retrospective, which opened to much fanfare in February, 1975, was the most complete exhibition of the works of that painter—so intimately connected with the Gug-genheim family—ever held. Messer is unsparing in his efforts to put together exhaustive shows. It took him seven years to arrange the highly successful show of his fellow Czech Frantisek Kupka in 1976.

Messer and his curators have also been very adept at turning out large, handsome, heavily footnoted catalogues of the museum's exhibits and permanent collections. The first two volumes of a monumental work to cover the museum's most important holdings, compiled by research curator Angelica Z. Rudenstine, won such widespread acclaim in the world press that one would have thought Kandinsky had come back from the dead and painted ten more masterpieces. The catalogue was generally representative of the collection, with two exceptions: It contained only thirteen Bauers and four paintings by the baroness Hilla Rebay von Ehrenwiesen out of literally hundreds by these two available in the storerooms. Another volume is due from Mrs. Rudenstine and still another will be compiled of the holdings of the Peggy Guggenheim Foundation which, as we know, will become the property of the Solomon R. Guggenheim Foundation upon Peggy's death.

With all this scholarly cataloguing going on, have the Solomon R. Guggenheim Foundation and Museum, those daring leaps into the unknown, entered upon their Alexandrian phase? It would appear so. Certainly the freewheeling, buccaneering days of Hilla and Sol and Bauer and Kandinsky are long since gone, and they are not likely to return in any guise.

As for the other foundation Harry left in Peter's charge, the one bearing Harry's name, it is still anyone's guess whether it will make a valuable contribution to our civilization.

Shortly before his death Harry had informally expressed to Peter the rationale behind his "Man's Relation to Man" foundation by exclaiming one day: "You know, Peter, it bugs me we can get a man on the moon, but we can't stop these goddamned wars."

So far the results of research conducted by the Harry Frank Guggenheim Foundation "to explore patterns of social dominance in man," have suggested, as in a report by a recent recipient of one of the foundation's grants, Prof. Sherwood Washburn, that the social systems of animals and humans will not work without violence, and that individuals in their relations with one another must inevitably get hurt. Judging from this finding, which is far older than the Harry Frank Guggenheim Foundation, having been prevalent wisdom in the ancient world, it looks as if we shall put men on Mars but will still not "stop these goddamned wars." And when we have populated Mars sufficiently so that there are different communities on the Red Planet, there will probably be wars on Mars.

In any case, Peter Lawson-Johnston, as chairman and director, and as of November, 1977, chief executive officer of the Foundation, is working on the age-old problem of man's relation to man with about $20 million in capital, much of it Times Mirror Company stock received from the sale of *Newsday*. Recent grants have gone to a team of researchers at Columbia studying patterns of learning in chimpanzees, to the Department of Anthropology at Pennsylvania State University for a study entitled "Population Expansion and Group Selection in South American Tribal Populations" (which has found that the most warlike tribes are also the most reproductive), and to Alexander Marshack of the Peabody Museum at Harvard for the study "Symbolism and Cognitive Contents of Killing, Aggression, and the Weapon in the First Homo Sapiens Cultures," notably the cave-dwelling cultures of southern Europe.

But Lawson-Johnston still remains somewhat perplexed about what to do with the Harry Frank Guggenheim Foundation. Fortunately he has a great deal of latitude in which to operate. Not long ago, for instance, he departed from research into "man's relation to man" to erect another monument to his benefactor, donating $500,000 to "The Harry Frank Guggenheim Hall of Minerals and Gems" at the American Museum of Natural History.

Peter's ultimate hope for the foundation is, in his words, for it "to become almost a household word in its field of research concerning 'man's relation to man.' "

With two important foundations to look after, as well as all the businesses, Lawson-Johnston is not only a busy, but a most fortunate man, a man in a position to enjoy the best of two worlds. Most businessmen are condemned to be just businessmen. Most foundation heads are condemned to be just foundation heads. Peter is both. And this gives heightened meaning to his work, for one feeds the other. The businesses feed the foundations and the foundations justify the businesses. With all the wide-eyed enthusiasm of a child Peter will lean over his desk at Guggenheim Brothers and say: "I tell you, I *can't wait* to get to the office every day, I enjoy my work so much!"

He is fortunate also in his family life, which centers mainly in his lovely old house and farm in Princeton, and at his summer place in Edgartown, Mass. He and his tall, blond, rather imposing wife, Didi, have been married for twenty-six years and have four children: Wendy, twenty-four in 1977, married and the mother of a daughter; Tania, twenty-two and just married; Peter, Jr., eighteen, a graduate of St. George's, now at Trinity College in Hartford, Conn.; and Mary, ten, currently attending Princeton Day School.

In addition to their Princeton estate and the house in Edgartown, the Lawson-Johnstons also own a house at Hobe Sound, Florida, where they spend a few weeks each winter, and have the use of grandfather Solomon's plantation Big Survey in South Carolina, now owned by the Elgebar Corporation, and also mother Barbara's ranch in Idaho. As if that were not enough, they also use Harry's Cain Hoy plantation in South Carolina every Thanksgiving, Christmas, and New Year's. And then, when the Lawson-Johnstons are in Europe, as they frequently are, they have Lady Castle Stewart's magnificent Old Lodge at their disposal in England and the use, when they want it, of cousin Peggy's splendid Palazzo Venier dei Leoni in Venice.

Summers the entire Lawson-Johnston family gathers at Edgartown and Peter usually takes a month off in July or August to be with them.

Neither Hobe Sound nor Edgartown has ever been noted for its pro-Semitism. However, the Lawson-Johnstons have fitted into both communities very smoothly, belonging to the extremely exclusive Jupiter Island Club in Hobe Sound, and the equally exclusive Edgartown Yacht Club. As daughter Wendy puts it to her young WASP friends in Edgartown: "O.K., we're one-quarter Jewish, but we're proud of it, because that's where all the money comes from."

No, there is not much Jewishness left, besides the ancestry of the money, in these present-day descendants of one of the wealthiest and most influential Jews in American history. Certainly no one would ever take Peter Lawson-Johnston for a Jew on first sight, least of all would they take his children to be Jews. Something has been gained—admittance into WASP upper-class society, among other things—but something has also been lost. These attractive, polished, Ivy-Leaguish fifth- and sixth-generation descendants of Jewish immigrants do not appear to possess anything remotely resembling the chutzpah of Meyer, Daniel, Simon, Solomon, or Harry.

And chutzpah may be one of the qualities Peter Lawson-Johnston will need if he is going to bring Guggenheim Brothers and the other family-owned businesses in his charge back to life, as he has vowed to do.

Peter himself has a clear understanding of his mission. And he will need Anglo-Saxon prudence and common sense at least as much as Jewish chutzpah to accomplish it. He sees his task as "not to 'trailblaze,' but to make our forebears proud of the vehicles which bear their names, by insuring they have imaginative, high-caliber leadership. One might say that my responsibility is to see a maintenance of excellence."

Toward that noble end Peter must, among other things, choose and groom a successor to carry on after he retires. Presently he is leaning toward his cousin Oscar Straus III, a capable young man now serving as corporate secretary of Pacific Tin.

But Peter has little intention of retiring in the near future. If his health holds up, he should have another twenty years of work ahead of him. That gives him until the end of the American century to prove he was worthy of the immense faith Harry Guggenheim placed in him in 1971.

3

THE CALIFORNIA GUGGENHEIMS: BOB, JR. AND DANIEL M.: NEW BEGINNINGS

THE SECURITY IS THE BEST IN NEWPORT BEACH, IF NOT IN ALL OF Orange County, for there is only one way Linda Isle in Newport harbor can be reached by land, and that is over a narrow causeway at which is stationed a twenty-four-hour armed guard. Only persons showing proper identification are allowed past, and no outsider, even with proper identification, is admitted without his first being checked on the intercom with the resident he is supposed to see.

Security is very important to the residents of Linda Isle, even more important than the shimmering lotus-land beauty of the place. For nowadays on the southern California mainland, even with round-the-clock police patrols, no one is really safe anymore in his own house, especially if his name is Guggenheim.

It was not so far from Newport Beach, and not so long ago, that Sharon Tate and her friends, and then Leno and Rosemary LaBianca, were butchered in their homes by the followers of Charles Manson.

What happened to M. Robert Guggenheim, Jr. at his former home on the mainland was so mild in comparison as to hardly bear mentioning, but still it was very distressing. It left him with a sort of permanent queasy feeling, especially at night.

One of Bob Guggenheim's passions was raising koi fish. He was, in fact, the owner of almost all the champion kois in southern California, regularly winning the koi competitions in Gardena each year.

Raising the brilliantly hued kois, an aristocratic member of the carp family, is one of the great pastimes of the Japanese rich. Among the most favored varieties are the red-and-white Kohato, the red-and-black Sanke, and the black, red, and white Skowa. These gorgeous fish, usually about ten or twelve inches long, can live to be forty or fifty years old and can cost as much as $40,000 apiece in Japan.

Bob Guggenheim's kois were the talk of Newport Beach. People came to his lovely home on Galaxie Drive in Dover Shores just to admire them.

There the koi fish would be in his garden pool, swimming among the water grasses, frolicking under the little artificial waterfall. Flashes of white, red, black, orange in the deep blue water, the bright green water grass . . .

There they were, the most beautiful fish in all southern California. And then, suddenly one morning, fifteen of them, worth $75,000, were floating on the pool's surface, whitened, bloated, and dead.

An investigation was conducted; the pool carefully examined. Verdict: The pool had been deliberately poisoned. Vandalism. The poison destroyed the algae on which the fish depended for nourishment. Vandals, or a vandal, were systematically attempting to kill M. Robert Guggenheim, Jr.'s prize koi fish. Who? Why? For what? You don't ask why of a vandal. When that barbaric tribe from Germany, the original Vandals, began raiding the villas of the Roman rich during the declining years of the Roman Empire, what struck the Romans most at the time was the random, senseless nature of their pillage. Often they would just wreck and not even bother to steal.

"What should I do?" Mr. Guggenheim asked the chief of police.

"You better move, sir," was the reply.

Move? Yes, the chief was right. Here on Galaxie Drive anyone could walk across Duke Wayne's fields, arrive at Robert Guggenheim, Jr.'s lawn, climb over a relatively low stone wall, and get to not only Robert Guggenheim, Jr.'s koi pool, but to everything else on his property, including himself and his beautiful young wife.

Yes, move. Linda Isle was the solution. One must face realities. It is the year 1977. America is over two hundred years old. The American republic has been faltering. The American empire is besieged. The Vandals, the Huns, the Goths, are waiting in the wings. Whenever they get an opening they take what they can take, they destroy what they can destroy.

There are 107 homes of varying degrees of luxury, priced from $200,000 to $1,250,000, on man-made Linda Isle in Newport Beach harbor. The M. Robert Guggenheims own one of the most luxurious, a two-story, eleven-room, eight-bathroom structure in "French Regency" style facing the water on two sides, in a setting not unlike that of cousin Peggy's palace in Venice, also on a man-made island.

Each floor of the house has its own laundry room and kitchen. Each room, and many of the bathrooms, has its own stereo and color TV. The main kitchen boasts, in addition to the conventional conveniences, two refrigerator-freezers, a large microwave oven, and a see-through refrigerated pastry keeper. There is a basement-to-attic elevator and the entire house is climate controlled. In the garage, which is incorporated into the house, rest the Rolls and the Continental Mark IV. In the slip below the broad waterfront terrace floats Bob junior's version of his father's *Firenze*, a sixty-foot, twenty-five-ton Pacemaker that costs $65,000 a year to run, can sleep eight, has color TV in each stateroom, and is called, after Bob and his wife, Shirlee, the *Shirrob*. ("It's nothing compared to Duke Wayne's *Wild Goose*," Bob will tell you, gesturing across the harbor to where the actor's 126-foot yacht is moored.)

To enter the house one walks through an iron gate and up a brick path that divides a swimming pool into two sections. Rosebushes, flowering pears, miniature lemon and lime trees, beds of pink, white, and red begonias, surround the pool. Four potted cypress trees stand by the main entrance. The two entrance doors are an imposing twenty-two feet high and can be opened and closed by pressing a button. Pressing a button will also raise or lower the huge hall chandelier.

Once inside the elegant, high-ceilinged, white marble foyer and hallway, one looks directly at a formal French stairway leading to the second floor.

Great grandfather Meyer, in a huge, gilt-framed, full-length portrait, is in the center of the stairway wall looking down, as if he were presiding over the entire house. On his left is great great grandfather Simon, and on his right is grandfather Daniel. Opposite Daniel, near Simon, is father M. Robert, Sr. in full-dress colonel's uniform with ambassadorial sash and tassel. On a table in the hallway stands a framed photograph of Ambassador M. Robert Guggenheim shaking hands with Prince Juan Carlos de Borbón of Spain.

It is a good life, the life Meyer Guggenheim presides over at Linda Isle. It is to this house, in this place, that his and his father's dreams in a European ghetto have led. Now, 128 years after those dreams, his great grandson is living here, in this beautiful house, in this beautiful corner of southern California, living on the wealth Meyer and his seven sons accumulated while assembling one of the great industrial empires of all time.

Yes, it is a good life, the life of the M. Robert Guggenheims at Newport Beach. Newport Beach, one of the most desirable communities in America, the fourth most expensive real estate in the country, the largest concentration of pleasure craft—9,500 boats—in the West. Weather consistently fair. One can swim, sail, and play golf and tennis all year round. And Bob, his son Dan, and Bob's beautiful, young third wife, Shirlee, as members of all the top country clubs in the area—the Big Canyon, the Balboa Bay, the Irvine Coast—are able to take full advantage of all these activities far from the madding crowds.

Things have not always been so sweet and easy for Bob Guggenheim, Jr., however. His parents' divorce when he was only ten years old had been hard on him. He loved his father, the ebullient *bon vivant* Colonel Bob, but the court awarded him and his brother to his mother. He therefore grew up somewhat outside the Guggenheim orbit. Then his beloved older brother, Daniel II, dropped dead of a heart attack at only eighteen years of age, the first of all those Guggenheims of his generation to die young. For Bob, Jr. the sudden death of his big brother was an event he never got over. It taught him, at a very early age, how fragile life was, how irretrievable.

After an unsettled childhood during which he was constantly shuttling back and forth between his divorced parents, between great wealth and comparative modesty, now spending some time at his mother's not-so-large apartment, now visiting his father at one of his sumptuous Firenzes, or at his 1,500-acre South Carolina plantation, or on his 170-foot yacht, he was sent to prep school at Penn Charter, near Philadelphia, and then to Dartmouth where he took his B.A. in English in 1933.

While at Dartmouth Bob became very interested in the theater and it was this interest that eventually brought him into sharp conflict with his father and radically affected his life.

M. Robert Guggenheim, Sr. had realized too late in life that he had made an enormous mistake in not staying with the family mining and smelting business, and hence insisted, with all his powers of persuasion, that son Bob not make a similar error.

Bob junior was therefore compelled by his father to enter American Smelting and Refining immediately after graduating from Dartmouth, even though he did not feel any marked vocational inclination toward the work. Uncle Simon, then president of ASARCO, gave him a job:

ore buyer in Mexico. Later he graduated to ore buyer and assistant manager of the ASARCO office in Salt Lake City.

While at Salt Lake Bob married Helen Claire Allyn, a Protestant Canadian from Montreal, who was to bear him two children, Grace Anne and Daniel M. He also gravitated again toward the dramatic arts, becoming the moving spirit behind the Salt Lake Little Theater.

Soon his after-hours work at the theater began to absorb him more and more, and his job at ASARCO became a bore and a burden.

For, alas, the business of mining and smelting had changed since the freewheeling days of Leadville, Kennecott, Bingham Canyon, and Chuquicamata. It was not nearly so exciting as it used to be. Gone the big gambles. Gone the big bonanzas. Now the business was just like any other industrial routine.

Bob longed to do something more exciting with his life than buy and smelt ores. So what if his family had been in the mining business for over half a century? It was time a Guggenheim did something different. His conflict was brought to a head when the company offered him the position of assistant manager at the important ASARCO plant in Helena, Montana. Bob realized then that if he accepted that job he would be in ASARCO for the rest of his life. So he made the decision to get out and, on the strength of his success with the Salt Lake Little Theater, landed a job with David O. Selznick's studios in Hollywood as a production assistant. He was twenty-six years old.

When Robert, Sr. was informed, he was so upset he flew out to the West Coast to make his son change his mind. He was the last hope of his generation, he told him. Uncle Simon's son was suicidal. William, Jr. was infirm. There were no other Guggenheim males in his generation capable of running ASARCO some day but him. He would regret leaving the family business for the rest of his life.

But Bob senior's protests were to no avail. Bob junior was firmly ensconced at Selznick International Pictures and would not budge. Mining was a bore, he told his father. The excitement, the bonanzas were now in movies. Newspapers across the nation headlined: GUGGENHEIM SCION HEADS FOR MOVIES, MINING TO MOVIES FOR SMELT,- ING HEIR, MINES TO MIMES FOR GUGGENHEIM.

And so M. Robert Guggenheim, Jr. settled down to making movies as an assistant director for the brilliant and imperious David O. Selznick, working on such films as *The Prisoner of Zenda* with Ronald Colman, Madeleine Carroll, and Raymond Massey, and *A Star Is Born* with Fredric March and Janet Gaynor.

But no sooner had he achieved his ambition of getting into the film business than the peppery litle Bob began to clash with Selznick's directors. It was not so easy for a Guggenheim, the grandson of Daniel Guggenheim at that, to take orders from others. One quarrel led to another and before long Bob no longer had a job with Selznick. Quickly he secured a better position as an associate producer at Twentieth Century-Fox. Working with Kenneth MacGowan, he helped produce *Four Men and a Prayer* with Loretta Young and David Niven, Robert Louis Stevenson's *Kidnapped* with Freddie Bartholomew, and *Hold That Co-ed* with John Barrymore and Joan Davis.

For a while Bob was reasonably happy at Twentieth Century-Fox, but then he began quarreling again with his superiors. He found movie people a very special breed, and he did not much like the breed. They were not exactly the kind of people with whom he had been brought up or with whom he had gone to school. In the end Twentieth Century-Fox did not work out and he left it to take a job as a staff producer with radio station KNX of the Columbia Broadcasting System. And, of course, Bob, Sr. had the pleasure of telling his son: "I told you so. You should have stuck with ASARCO. You could have been president of the goddamned company some day."

Came the war and Bob left CBS to go to Naval Officers Training School. For eighteen months he served in the southwest Pacific, on the staff of Admiral Kinkaid, then was assigned to shore duty in California. By the time of his discharge he had risen to the rank of lieutenant commander and had somewhat regained the esteem of his military-minded father.

Temporarily regained it, at least. For he still adamantly refused to reenter mining and smelting after the war, and he probably could have, under the aegis of the president of the company, his uncle Roger Straus. Instead he went into the promising new field of television, becoming manager of film operations at KRCA in Hollywood, West Coast headquarters of NBC. It was a pioneering job, showing vintage feature films on TV for the first time, and Bob did very well at it.

While working for KRCA Bob also founded Guggenheim Enterprises and launched Wackie Pictures, a novelty item featuring three-dimensional pictures, some created by Walt Disney cartoonists, whose characters burst out of their frames. The venture was moderately successful, but in the end, Wackie Pictures never really caught on.

By this time Bob was married again—to Harriet Boyle—was still supporting his first wife and their two children, and needed all the money he could get his hands on. So he switched careers a fourth time and entered advertising, becoming, after a while, vice-president and West Coast general manager for MacManus, John and Adams, one of the biggest advertising firms in the country. While at Mac-Manus, Bob was instrumental in producing NBC-TV's *Medic* series for Dow Chemical and the *Jack Carson Show* for Pontiac. He also produced TV telethons to help raise money to wipe out multiple sclerosis.

Bob was doing well, but it did not make much of an impression on his father. Bob senior never forgave his son for not sticking with American Smelting and Refining and refused to help him out financially, even in emergencies, although he himself had been heavily subsidized by *his* father while not working at all. Once, when Bob junior needed $5,000 to tide him over a period between jobs and asked his father for a loan in that amount, Bob senior told him to go to a bank.

But, in the end, Senior did leave Junior well off in his will. So well off, in fact, that after the fun-loving Colonel died, Bob was compelled to quit his job at MacManus, John and Adams to dedicate himself exclusively to settling his father's large and complex estate. This process lasted eight years and when it was over M. Robert Guggenheim, Jr. ended up the possessor of a multimillion-dollar fortune. He now owns the highly profitable Lucky Market Shopping Center in Newport Beach, and a healthy portfolio of stocks and bonds, which includes substantial holdings in such Guggenheim-spawned businesses as Anglo and Kennecott. In late 1976 Bob received an unexpected windfall when his father's home in Washington, Firenze House, was sold to the Italian government for $4.5 million. Bob received 79 percent of the proceeds from the sale and the remainder went to his stepmother, Polly Logan.

Not long after getting control of his patrimony, Bob Guggenheim took himself a new wife. She was Shirlee Weatherford, an attractive redhead from Florida, twenty-five years younger than he.

Promptly Bob took his pretty young bride east to introduce her to the rest of the family. He was feeling good. He was rich and healthy and had a beautiful new wife.

Shirlee's first encounter with the family was something she never will forget. She has told the story in Newport Beach hundreds of times.

One of Bob's aunts, the former Alva Bernheimer (his mother's sister), was the wife of Bernard Gimbel, chairman of Gimbel Brothers and Saks Fifth Avenue, and she decided to give a tea for the newlyweds.

An assembly of imposing older ladies was present and Alva Gimbel held court over the great silver kettle as she poured tea.

After chatting about this and that she suddenly paused, and turning to Shirlee, said, in a loud voice so all could hear: "Oh, Shirlee, my dear, there's one thing the family has forgotten to tell you. Robert has syphilis."

Whereupon Shirlee, believing it, almost collapsed into the arms of one of the imposing older ladies.

Later, Bob had to "demonstrate" he was really all right.

Since coming into his inheritance, Bob junior has found a new vocation, and it is a typically Guggenheim one: giving his money away, as generously and wisely as he can.

Just as his father had wanted Bob to make up for what he had not done by sticking with ASARCO, now Bob wanted to make up for what his father had not done with the enormous financial resources at his command.

Bob Guggenheim, Jr.'s generosity has expressed itself more in supporting causes that lie close to his heart than in establishing foundations, which inevitably come to be dominated by other people, and thereby lose the quality of personal charity.

One cause that lies particularly close to his heart is multiple sclerosis research. A year after Bob married Shirlee Weatherford, Shirlee discovered she had multiple sclerosis. Bob had raised money for MS in the past as a TV producer and advertising man. Now he set himself to giving money to MS out of his own pocket. Over the past seven years he has contributed abundantly to the National Multiple Sclerosis Society, of which he is on the board of directors for southern California, and especially to MS research at the University of California at Irvine. Other causes to which he has given substantial sums include the Children's Hospital of Orange County, of which he is a director, Chapman College in Newport Beach, of which he is a trustee, Big Brothers of Orange County, of which he is president, the Orange County Philharmonic Society, the Newport Harbor Art Museum, the Hoag Memorial Presbyterian Hospital of Newport Beach, the Newport Spastic League, the Newport Harbor YMCA, and the Girl Scouts of Orange County. In addition, he continues to sit on the board of his grandfather's foundation, the Daniel and Florence Guggenheim Foundation, where he energetically champions his own pet charities, particularly the New Horizons Boys Ranch in Oregon, an institution for the rehabilitation of delinquent youths, also championed by his son, Dan.

What Bob did for the Big Brothers of Orange County was typical of his manner of giving. First the organization had wanted him to be a Big Brother himself, but he felt, in his own words, that "if Little Brother saw my standard of living he might get envious," and so it would be better if he helped out in other ways. Whereupon the board promptly elected him its president. When he took over the agency it was $4,000 in the red. In four years he put it $84,000 in the black and presented it with a matching gift of his own.

In 1973 the citizens of Newport Beach conferred upon Bob the community's highest honor, the King Neptune Award, "for distinguished service to the people of Newport Beach."

Today, at a healthy sixty-six, Bob Guggenheim, Jr., a buoyant, scrappy little man who has inherited the energy of his grandfather "Mr. Dan," keeps himself busy while at the same time enjoying what is perhaps the sweetest life in all the United States of America. Maintaining an office and a secretary at his house on Linda Isle, he spends his mornings at his desk attending to his shopping center, his other investments, and the dozen or so organizations of which he is a board member, today Chapman College, tomorrow Big Brothers, the next day the Multiple Sclerosis Society, devoting from fifty to sixty percent of his time to civic activities. Then he has lunch, usually with one of his committees, either at home, at the Balboa Bay Club in Newport Harbor, or at the Big Canyon Club inland, followed by a swim, a sail, or a spin on the yacht. In the evening there are always plenty of cocktail parties, receptions, dinners, should the Guggenheims wish to accept the scores of invitations that reach them each week. On weekends there is often a day-long trip on the *Shirrob*—to nearby Santa Catalina Island or down the coast toward San Clemente—with Hollywood cronies Duke Wayne and Claire Trevor aboard.

His koi collection? Bob has given it up—his remaining kois are up for sale—as he has also given up his once-celebrated bonsai collection. They were targets for vandals and thieves, and he has decided he can put his money to more constructive uses than raising $15,000 fish and growing $10,000 trees.

Regrets about leaving American Smelting and Refining, about being the last male with the name Guggenheim to work for the family's foremost business creation? None whatsoever. "A man must follow his inclinations. My grandfather may have been a virtual genius as a mining industrialist, but I am something else, my interests have always lain in communications and the dramatic arts and there is no reason why I should have pretended to be a mining magnate when I wasn't."

And what about Guggenheim Brothers? How does he feel about the old family firm, and did Harry ever invite him to help in the reorganization of the firm in 1956? "Guggenheim Brothers became a defunct organization after the big nitrate gamble didn't work out. Uncle Harry never asked me to join Guggenheim Brothers when it was reorganized, and if he had asked me I would have refused. I was then with the advertising agency and enjoyed my work very much. I did not want to work with Harry and I did not want to live in New York."

And cousin Peter Lawson-Johnston and the responsibilities Harry entrusted him with to carry on the Guggenheim tradition and businesses? A smile, and, "I wish him luck."

*   *   *

Not the least of Bob Guggenheim, Jr.'s achievements has been the raising of his only son, Daniel, one of the last males in the family bearing the name Guggenheim and a most engaging young man, trim, athletic, sandy haired, clear headed, hardworking. Bob enjoys a close relationship with his son and has justifiably great hopes for him.

Like his cousin Peter Lawson-Johnston, Dan Guggenheim belies the stereotype of the (in his case) sixth-generation son of a family of great wealth.

It would be difficult, in fact, to imagine a more solid, balanced, and unspoiled young man.

Raised in somewhat straitened financial circumstances—his father was living wholly off his salary, not receiving a penny from Colonel Bob—this great grandson of Mr. Dan took his first job, running a paper route, at the age of ten, on the south side of Beverly Hills, went on to do gardening for seven Beverly Hills homes at age twelve, and at fourteen worked in a machine shop after school for seventy-five cents an hour.

While in prep school Dan was confirmed an Episcopalian, became an altar boy in his mother's church, and was seriously considering entering the Episcopalian priesthood at one point in his life.

By the time he was eighteen, however, he had given up the idea of a religious vocation and had taken a summer job as a draftsman at Northrop Aviation, earning $1.86 an hour. It was while holding down this job that he took time off to visit his grandfather for the first time at Colonel Bob's palatial Firenze House in Washington.

When the spendthrift, nonworking Colonel, habitually oblivious to the financial plight of his offspring, heard that his grandson was working, he was much surprised and asked him, "What are you working for?"

"I need the money," said Dan.

"How much are they giving you?"

"A dollar eighty-six an hour."

"Well, son, I'll pay you a dollar eighty-six an hour just to stay with me for the summer."

Dan declined, and, after a couple of weeks of being catered to by chauffeurs, chefs, butlers, and other servants—there were eighteen on the Colonel's household staff, and thirteen on the crew of the *Firenze* —he went back to his job in California.

One day, not long after he returned to work, he was toiling away at Northrop when he was summoned by a foreman and told there was a man outside the plant who wanted to see him. The man turned out to be a car salesman. As the salesman shook hands with young Dan he handed him a pair of car keys and a note. The note was from grandfather Bob and it read: "I think Daniel Guggenheim III ought at least to own a Ford." The shiny new car was parked nearby.

The Northrop job was a summer occupation. The rest of the year Dan went to the University of California at Berkeley, where he took a B.S. degree at the College of Business Administration, majoring in money and banking. A tour of duty as an army officer came next, then he became a stockbroker with William R. Staats & Company.

By 1966 he was working as a stockbroker for Goodbody & Company and averaging around $50,000 a year in income. During his last four years at Goodbody he was the top producer for the Newport Beach office and was among the top twenty-five producers out of Goodbody's two hundred and fifty salesmen in the entire Pacific Coast region. In 1968, at the height of the bull market, he was the fifth-highest producer in the region.

On the strength of this success he founded, in 1971, Guggenheim and Davenport, licensed investment counselors. It was a bad time to found such a company; the bull market had turned bear, and, although he succeeded in bringing in around four million dollars in accounts in eighteen months, he was compelled to dissolve the firm in October, 1972 "due to lack of profitability." For the past four years he has been a salesman of commercial and industrial property for the Coldwell Banker Company, a real estate development and brokerage company with gross annual revenues of close to eighty million. He also spends a good deal of time scouting promising real estate investment opportunities for his father. So far business has been excellent. In 1976 Dan was the thirteenth-highest producer among Coldwell Banker salesmen, and earned over $150,000 in commissions. And it was Dan who got his father to buy the lucrative Lucky Market Shopping Center.

Dan's ambitions? Short range: "to develop a 50,000-square-foot neighborhood shopping center and put up a couple of high-rise apartment buildings, and own and operate them as well." Long range: "to build the family fortune back up again to something in the neighborhood of where it was in the days of my great grandfather."

Meanwhile, as he tries to progress toward that formidable goal, Dan and his pretty second wife, the former Susan Winchester of England, and their young daughters, Sara and Beth, enjoy the sweet life of Newport Beach. Dan's house is right on the water—his girls can walk from their bedroom onto the sand—and he keeps a small boat at the yacht club. Since Dan also has two daughters from his first wife, he has, like many Guggenheims before him, daughtered out, so that unless current wife Susan produces a son in the near future ("an unlikely event," says Dan) the name of Guggenheim will die out altogether in the line founded by the first Daniel.

In keeping with the philanthropic traditions of his family, Dan III sits on the board of his great grandfather's foundation and takes a special interest in one of its major benefactions, the New Horizons Boys Ranch in Bly, Oregon.

This institution for the rehabilitation of juvenile delinquents was founded in 1970 by one Gus Valencia, former professional boxer, sea captain, and engineer. It is located on a ranch in Oregon to which Gus Valencia had intended to retire but later decided to use to help wayward boys.

What persuaded Valencia to use his ranch for this purpose was certain alarming facts about juvenile crime that came to his attention: that crime in America increased 174 percent between 1964 and 1974, that nearly ten million crimes were committed in 1974 by juveniles between the ages of eight and twenty, that of those juveniles who have been apprehended and incarcerated in youth facilities more than 74 percent are repeaters, and that about two million known juvenile delinquents emerge on the American scene every year.

At first Valencia's efforts to combat this frightening situation were limited to taking a few boys into his house and trying to straighten them out. When his initial efforts proved successful he was encouraged to appeal for funds to create a full-fledged center for juvenile rehabilitation.

Mainly due to the insistence of young Dan, the Daniel and Florence Guggenheim Foundation responded with enough money to build the Daniel and Florence Guggenheim Vocational Training Center at the ranch and to provide a number of scholarships each year to enable delinquent boys to attend the center. Today the center is a model for juvenile delinquent rehabilitation in the United States, with a record second to none among institutions of its kind.

Dan Guggenheim is understandably proud of the center and is hopeful that it will influence the creation of similar institutions throughout the country in the years to come.

Hopeful, but not optimistic.

For although he, at thirty-nine in 1977, has had a successful record and has everything to look forward to, including a substantial inheritance someday, he remains fundamentally pessimistic about America's future, especially its economic future.

> My biggest cause for pessimism, [he writes] over our economic future is the tremendous lack of education of the American people in the workings of free enterprise and the capitalistic system. This educational shortcoming has resulted in a total lack of understanding of, and appreciation for, our economic system and why this country has provided us with the highest standard of living any nation has ever known. This lack of knowledge does not just rest with the average man on the street but, unfortunately, it is my opinion it is equally prevalent in Washington with our politicians. The legal background of the majority of our legislators provides them with little assistance in guiding our nation's economic future. As a result, the public and politicians, alike, are quick to point the finger at the big businessman every time the economy runs into trouble. Profits to too many people have an evil connotation, and the word capitalism, to many, raises thoughts of greed and selfishness.
>
> The profit motivation is the root of the success of our economic system. Only through increasing profits will businessmen have the incentive for increasing investment in plant and equipment. Only through increased investment in plant and equipment will we create new jobs and greater productivity to increase our standard of living further. Dur-

ing times of economic stress, unfortunately too many people, through lack of understanding, blame big business and choose, instead, to turn to big government for solutions.

Government's answers for our economic problems, unfortunately, are too often dictated by short-term considerations. A politician, whether through a lack of understanding or short-term political considerations, prescribes remedies which tend to aggravate the long-term economic stability.

Federally created jobs tend to aggravate our inflation problems due to the unproductive nature of many of these jobs, bureaucratic red tape, and increased federal deficits. Changes in our tax laws to give greater incentives to private industry to expand, and a greater awareness in Washington of the need for business to earn a decent rate of return on invested capital, would result in private industry expanding and creating new jobs which are both more productive and less inflationary than short-term government programs.

Unfortunately, the steps necessary to give business greater incentives to expand are not politically popular due to a lack of understanding among the electorate of economics. Contrary to popular opinion, corporate profit as a percentage of the sales dollar, and return on invested capital has been in a steady decline for years. Only by reversing these trends can private industry continue to provide us with the ever-increasing standard of living it has so ably been able to accomplish since this country's founding.

If our politicians continue to sell us out for short-range political expediency, we will go the way of England, and more recently Canada. In both cases, the government has continually promised the electorate more and more for doing less and less with the resulting socialization of one industry after another. The end result is ever-increasing rates of inflation with concurring lower standards of living.

We must educate the electorate in the workings of our free enterprise system, or I fear our politicians will continue to push us the way of England with increased government control over more and more phases of our lives. The results of socialism are always the same: a lower standard of living for all with less and less freedom for all.

Echoes of his great grandfather? A chip off the old block? Most decidedly yes. Daniel M. Guggenheim's economic thinking is certainly more or less the same as that of Mr. Dan. But whereas young Dan's general outlook is basically pessimistic, Mr. Dan's general outlook never was. Mr. Dan was always positive, hopeful, optimistic. He *never* lost faith.

Is not the difference between the two Daniel Guggenheims' views emblematic of the essential difference between the America of the first quarter of the twentieth century and the America of the last quarter?

In 1923, after the Guggenheims had sold Chile Copper to Anaconda for $70 million, Daniel Guggenheim, in his unguarded Hempstead House, looked out upon an America of limitless economic growth. In 1977 his great grandson and namesake looked out from an ultrasecurity compound upon a nation whose economic future was in doubt, or at least seemed far from limitless.

However, although young Daniel Guggenheim is pessimistic about the future of the American economy, there are some things about the United States he is optimistic about and one of these is the space program. America may have almost exhausted her geographical frontier, Daniel asserts, but she still may have a glorious mission and future in the new frontier of space. Recently he attended the International Academy of Astronautics meeting of leading aerospace scientists from all over the world at Anaheim at which the annual Daniel and Florence Guggenheim aeronautics award was given and felt an understandable surge of pride that his Guggenheim forebears were among the first pioneers in the great new enterprise of interplanetary exploration, and space colonization.

4

ROGER W. STRAUS, JR., PUBLISHER

By AROUND SEVEN-THIRTY THE PARTY IS USUALLY IN FULL SWING, surging back and forth between the long black, beige, and brown dining room and the large black, beige, brown, and gold living room, between the bar and the buffet and the author and his idolizers, a crowd of a hundred or more, gathered this winter night in the publisher's elegant four-story East Side townhouse to celebrate the appearance of yet another volume bearing the imprint Farrar, Straus & Giroux.

The crowd is extremely talkative; most everyone either knows, or knows of, everyone else. In addition to the author, his relatives and friends, the publisher, his relatives and friends, the editors and officers of the firm, other authors and their spouses and friends, there is a great slew of people from the publishing business who might possibly be useful to the book (for this is not merely a social gathering, it is a *working* session as well): paperback publishers, book club editors and judges, *Publishers Weekly* editors, distinguished critics, magazine reviewers, radio and TV talk show scouts and hosts, gossip columnists, publicity agents, newspaper men and women, TV camera operators (if there's going to be a filming), a literary agent (if the author has one), librarians, book dealers, television and film producers, professors, representatives of European publishers . . . Ernest Hemingway once characterized this world with typical ingratitude as "a can of tapeworms feeding on each other."

There, moving expertly through the crowd, slipping from the dining room to the living room, from the living room to the dining room, shaking hands, bestowing smiles and kisses, is the publisher's svelte, quick, pale, wide-eyed wife, Dorothea, wearing her usual winter publication party uniform: wide-brim black hat with black veil, longish black dress, black gloves, black handbag, and black boots. Now she is kissing Carlos Fuentes, just up from Mexico City, now she is greeting Marc Jaffe of Bantam, now she is shaking the hand of Book-of-the-Month Club's Al Silverman, now she is passing on to *Publishers Weekly*'s Arnold Ehrlich, always smiling, smiling softly under her black veil, deftly maneuvering her wide-brim Mr. John hat among all the jostling shoulders and coiffures. Most people are on their feet, milling around with drinks in hand, but a few are sitting, just taking it all in. There, for example, on the gold couch under the black, white, beige, brown, and gold abstract painting by Francis Scott Bradford, sits Susan Sontag in plain sweater and skirt, no makeup or jewelry, attentively observing the scene. Now and then she leans toward her friend, points with her cigarette to someone in the crowd and says something that makes her friend laugh. Then she looks around for another target. She has no end of material. There, not far from where the author is accepting homage, lurks sleepy-eyed, moustached Kurt Vonnegut, Jr., looking like an undernourished walrus, his pretty friend, the photographer—specializing in authors—Jill Krementz, at his side. Another author-and-friend combination, the lean, tense Jerzy Kosinski and Kiki Von Fraunhofer, are deep in discussion nearby. There, by the fireplace, talking to Maurice Sendak, is the short, inconspicuous, funny two-time National Book Award winner, one-time Pulitzer winner Bernard Malamud, looking like a composite of his own characters. Over by the gold curtains obscuring the view of East Seventieth Street is the jovial, florid, white-haired, fatherly Bob Giroux talking to an editor from New American Library and someone from the Literary Guild. A distinguished New York book critic, tall and lean and bloodless, and standing slightly apart from the crowd, looks on the scene with apparent contempt. Another day, another book, he seems to be saying to himself, they just keep on scribbling them, don't they? One after another, now it's this Barry Boywoody, or whatever his name is, tomorrow it will be some other self-deceived creature, think they're all Melvilles or somebody, will it ever end? He leans over toward a fellow critic and whispers a comment. The fellow critic sneers. "A toast to the author!" someone suddenly shouts, "a toast to the book!" And, raising their glasses, everybody cheers. As the tumult subsides the publisher's trim, energetic, six-foot-five son, Roger III, suddenly breaks from his cover, collars an editor from Pocket Books, drags him over to meet the author. The bustling author and former Book-of-the-Month Club judge Paul Horgan follows quickly upon Roger III's heels to pay *his* respects. The author has, by now, forgotten most of the names and professions of the seventy-eight people thus far introduced to him and, dazed by the klieg lights and abetted by the generous vodka martinis the publisher's son has been pressing on him, is beginning to commit a few faux pas. He tells someone from the Literary Guild how much he has always admired the wisdom of the Book-of-the-Month Club judges. He says to a paperback publisher: "Excuse me, I forgot the name of the magazine you work for." And so it goes. . . . But he survives. Most of the people he confuses are enjoying themselves too much to be offended anyway. Whatever he says or does, he still remains the Star.

Until he is upstaged. And upstaged, for a while, he will be, as nearly every FS&G author is, by a certain member of the fold. Here he is now, yes, someone has just come in who has made all heads and all cameras turn in his direction. See him swaggering among the black and gray suits and dresses in his wide-lapel, white, Mississippi riverboat gambler suit with string bow tie, vest, watch chain, trousers breaking over white shoes. Who the hell does he think he is anyway, Mark Twain? "Hi, Tom, how are you?" "Hello, Tom, glad to see you." No, it's just that erstwhile country lad from the Deep South taking time out from the new book he's doing for FS&G, taking a little time out to survey a bit of literary chic, taking note of who seems to be in and who seems to be out, promising the man from *New York* magazine a piece on Marilyn Chambers' DAR mother, the woman from *Harper's* something on Leonard Bernstein's recent break with the Hanafi Muslims. The author is visibly relieved when, after completing his crowd-catching tour of the living room, the riverboat gambler recedes toward the bar to pick up a drink. Now the gray suits and black dresses are left with only other gray suits and black dresses to look at. Isn't that Donald Barthelme over there? He *rarely* comes to these things. And isn't that Isaac Bashevis Singer talking to Harvey Shapiro of *The New York Times Book Review*? Singer's up for a Nobel, isn't he? And isn't that Philip Roth? And isn't that Vera Stravinsky? And isn't that Erica Jong talking to Nora Ephron? Other authors, other editors, critics, agents, journalists, professional celebrities, librarians, publishers, professors, book-chat people, talk show people—isn't that Gene Shalit?—and then, omnipresent, presiding over all, with his watchful, protective secretary, Peggy Miller, not far away, the man responsible for it all, Daniel Guggenheim's grandson, the most distinguished Guggenheim of his generation, Roger W. Straus, Jr., in a black velvet jacket, founder and president of the foremost literary publishing house in the world today, his own Farrar, Straus & Giroux.

If heredity is as important in the formation of a human being as the aristocrats of the past and the geneticists of the present have claimed it is, then Roger W. Straus, Jr. must be considered at least six times blessed. Two of his great grandfathers remarkable self-made men. One grandfather a cabinet member, ambassador, and author, the other an industrial giant and pioneer patron of aviation and rocketry. Father president of American Smelting and Refining; mother one of the leading women of her generation and president of her parents' foundation. Not to mention all the distinguished collateral relatives: granduncles and uncles Isidor and Nathan Straus, Solomon, Simon, and Harry Guggenheim, cousin Peggy. And let us not neglect the fact that being Jews in a fundamentally anti-Semitic society his great grandparents, grandparents, parents, and other relatives had to be twice as competent as their Gentile counterparts to arrive where they did.

Yes, background Roger Straus most certainly has. Not a weak root or branch discernible on either tree for as many generations back as have been identified. On both sides high intelligence, phenomenal energy, strong character, and, above all, boldness, daring, willingness to go out on a limb, to head into the unknown, to take the big risk . . . and live with it.

A fortunate inheritance combined with a fortunate inclination. For, unlike most people, Roger Straus never had the slightest doubt about what he wanted to do in life. From his late teens on he wanted to be a publisher.

After a carefree, distinctly overprivileged youth romping around magnificent estates, his grandfather Straus's splendid thirty-acre Sarosca Farm in Purchase, New York, and his grandfather Guggenheim's imperial three hundred fifty-acre Hempstead House at Sands Point, Long Island, young Roger was sent away to prep school at ultrafashionable St. George's in Newport, then entered Hamilton College.

It was while he was at Hamilton that he realized he wanted to go into publishing someday and upon that realization promptly dropped out, took a job on a newspaper, then entered the University of Missouri School of Journalism, from which he graduated in 1939. After college he became a reporter and feature writer for the *White Plains Daily Reporter,* an associate editor of *Forum* and *Current History* magazines, and the founder of a book-packaging firm, Book Ideas. A four-year stint as an enlisted man in the Navy came next, during which he became head of the magazine and book section of the Navy's Office of Public Information in New York, and then, in 1945, at twenty-eight, he embarked on the venture that was to determine the course of the rest of his life.

By then Roger had decided to take the giant step of founding his own publishing house, one that he hoped would publish the best writing of his time. Toward this end he persuaded his parents to back him to the tune of $80,000 and persuaded John Farrar, formerly of Farrar and Rinehart and then without a job, to become his partner. Later more backers were secured—notably Julius Fleischman and James Van Allen—whose contributions brought the total capital invested in the new firm to $160,000. Farrar, Straus & Company was then incorporated in New York City on November 21, 1945. Since then its name has changed several times to accommodate new partners: first to Farrar, Straus & Young, then to Farrar, Straus & Cudahy, then to its present Farrar, Straus & Giroux. In its final format it became perhaps the most ecumenical firm in publishing. The late John Farrar was a High Church Episcopalian, Roger Straus is a Jew, and Robert Giroux is a Roman Catholic.

From its very beginnings the firm emphasized literary quality first and foremost, a policy from which it has never wavered. During its first twenty years Farrar, Straus published Carlo Levi, whose *Christ Stopped at Eboli* was the house's first major success, Robert Graves, T. S. Eliot, Alberto Moravia, Edmund Wilson, Martin Buber, François Mauriac, Jean Stafford, Bernard Malamud, Salvatore Quasimodo, Nathanael West, Robert Lowell, Paul Horgan, Flannery O'Connor, Isaac Bashevis Singer, and John Berryman. By its thirtieth anniversary in 1975 the firm had also added to its lists Pablo Neruda, Christopher Isherwood, Hermann Hesse, Randall Jarrell, Walker Percy, and Alexander Solzhenitsyn, whose *August 1914* was one of the house's most recent major successes.

Ten times Farrar, Straus & Giroux books have been National Book Award winners and an equal number of times the Nobel Prize has been given to writers published by the firm. And in most cases these awards were given to the authors *after* they had already been published by Farrar, Straus, and were thus a confirmation of Roger's judgment of them rather than a mere cashing-in on an already established reputation.

By 1976 Farrar, Straus & Giroux had acquired Noonday Press (now its paperback subsidiary), Hill and Wang (college-oriented books), Octagon Books (scholarly reprints), and was doing a business of around six or seven million dollars a year, not at all bad for a literary publisher. Roger Straus holds 60 percent of the stock, his partners, a few friends, and his son, Roger III, hold the rest. As such the firm remains one of the very few independent houses left in U.S. publishing, a status Roger wishes to maintain at all costs: "Although no month goes by that we don't get some offer to buy us . . . I have no desire to be a division of Kleenex, or whatever."

Roger's ability to remain independent—a key factor in his ability to maintain such high standards—is, of course, partly due to the twin blessing that he is a Straus and a Guggenheim. Not because the Straus or Guggenheim fortunes actually help float Farrar, Straus & Giroux (they contributed only to the original $160,000 investment), but because Roger himself, given his own independent wealth, which is not enormous but comfortable enough, does not have to depend on either his salary as president or his dividends as chief stockholder for his livelihood. He enjoys more than ample income from sources other than Farrar, Straus & Giroux. And he is further comforted by the assurance that if worse came to worst—which has not yet threatened to happen and does not seem likely to happen—his mother, Gladys, who has occasionally come to her son Oscar's rescue, would certainly not hesitate to use her considerable fortune to see her other son and his firm through a difficult period.

Be that as it may, it is still an extraordinary feat, in this age of high-schlock writing and fast-buck publishing, for an American publishing house to survive on lists featuring such high quality but rarely best-selling authors as Alberto Moravia, Paul Horgan, Robert Lowell, Isaac Bashevis Singer, Bernard Malamud, Pablo Neruda (for whom Roger controls most world English rights), and John Berryman. And let there be no doubt about it. Roger Straus has not, and will not ever, publish schlock, no matter who writes it, whether it be a Harold Robbins, an Irving Stone, a Jackie Susann, or a Leon Uris ("push-cart novelists" Dorothea Straus calls these practitioners who are not particularly known for their ceaseless search for *le mot juste*). Schlock is one thing. Literature is another. Farrar, Straus & Giroux publishes literature, and that's all there is to it.

How does Roger do it, and survive financially?

First of all, some of his writers, despite their high quality, do make the best seller lists now and then. Tom Wolfe occasionally does. Alexander Solzhenitsyn nearly always does: His *August 1914* climbed to the number two slot on *The New York Times* best seller list in 1972. Second, Roger is not above publishing some commercial non-fiction now and then. He publishes health writer Gayelord Hauser, for example. And he put out Sammy Davis, Jr.'s autobiography, *Yes, I Can.* More recently he published an informational potpourri entitled *The Best,* which had no pretensions to be anything but a money-maker. Third, incredible as it seems, some books of genuine literary merit do occasionally make a little money in the Age of High Schlock—not much, but enough to earn out their advances and show a modest profit. Who, for example, would have ever thought Paul Horgan's *Lamy of Santa Fe* would have sold over thirty thousand copies in hardcover, but it did. Fourth, Roger publishes a higher percentage of authors who don't have agents than any other major publisher. This saves him money because, since so many of his authors don't have to give 10 percent of their earnings to an agent, they will accept advances that are 10 percent smaller than what he would have had to give them had they had agents. Fifth, in recent years, FS&G has begun to take advantage of the mass market paperback boom and made some very healthy paperback sales. Walker Percy's *Lancelot* went for $300,000. Solzhenitsyn's *Lenin in Zurich* was sold for $400,000. Sixth, Roger has occasionally realized unexpectedly whopping profits by buying the rights to classics cheap and selling them dear. He calls this "cannibalizing" his list. The twelve Hermann Hesse novels he bought from the German publisher Suhrkamp for $12,500 when the German author was out of favor, six of which he then sold to Bantam for $1,200,000 when Hesse had become the rage of the campuses, are a case in point. But it is perhaps mostly by running an exceptionally tight ship that Roger has been able to make his unique pursuit of literary excellence pay its way.

The formula boils down to low rent, low salaries, low advances, and low publicity budgets to make publishing quality writing possible.

Low rent: Farrar, Straus & Giroux occupies two floors of unpretentious, plainly furnished, drab offices in a modest little building on Union Square West in New York City, just a few blocks north of the West Village. An unfashionable address. A not very attractive neighborhood. No frills, no plush. At first glance the place could easily pass for the offices of a Seventh Avenue zipper manufacturer.

Certainly few would take it for what it actually is, the vital center of the publication of literature in the Western world today.

Low salaries: An editor at FS&G can make up to $40,000 a year, but if he wants more than that he has to look for another job—even if Roger regards him highly. One of Roger Straus' top senior editors demanded more than the FS&G top and was unceremoniously let go. Other employees—for example, the director of subsidiary rights, a big job, the director of publicity, another big job—do not fare much better than the editors, though, as Roger puts it, salaries for these positions tend to be "a little more competitive."

This salary policy stands out in glaring contrast to that of Roger's extraordinary grandfather. It was, as we know, a cardinal rule of Daniel Guggenheim's that you had to spend money to make money, and that, if necessary, you had to be prepared to pay the highest salaries in your business, as Mr. Dan did with John Hays Hammond, to whom he once paid the highest salary in the world. But, of course, Daniel was dealing in metals not novels.

Low advances: Yes, at Farrar, Straus & Giroux there is simply no such thing as the staggering advances the high- and low-schlock novelists receive from other publishers (for example, Joseph Heller recently receiving a reported two million dollars from Simon and Schuster for his next novel). And since Roger refuses to publish high schlock, and the high schlockers resolutely stay away from him, he doesn't have to give out these advances. FS&G authors like Isaac Bashevis Singer, Robert Lowell, Bernard Malamud, and Alexander Solzhenitsyn simply do not demand huge advances. They are primarily interested in getting their books published well, not making immense fortunes from them. And because most FS&G authors are so well known, Roger doesn't need to spend much money publicizing them. Low advertising budgets are another element in the FS&G publishing formula.

No, it is not big money that makes FS&G authors loyal to Roger Straus. It is primarily Roger's engaging personality and high literary standards. For Roger, unlike many other publishers today, enjoys a close personal relationship with his authors. He has lunch with them. He invites them to his dinner parties, his publication parties. He phones them regularly and encourages them, cheering along the work in progress. He amuses them with his salty literary gossip, liberally spiced with his favorite four-letter words. (Nothing effete about Roger's speech. The proverbial truck driver would feel perfectly at home with him.) Furthermore, all FS&G authors have the satisfaction of knowing that when they are dealing with Roger they are dealing with a peer, a man who understands, appreciates, and respects their work.

They are also dealing with a man of panache, style, of a certain éclat, a personality that comes on strong, and this is one of the things an author usually looks for in a publisher. As Tom Wolfe puts it: "When I came to New York from the South, Roger Straus was the only man in publishing I met who was what I expected a New Yorker and an important publisher to be. Compared to him all the others were just dim gray types scurrying around in fedoras and trench coats."

So respected, in fact, is Roger Straus today on the New York publishing scene that when *The New York Times* wants an opinion from a publisher on literary or publishing matters it inevitably turns to him, just as it inevitably turned to his grandfather Daniel for comments on the economic scene fifty years before. He has thus become, without having sought the office, the most outspoken of all the New York publishers. Hardly a week goes by when a statement of his does not appear in the papers. Roger enjoys the role. Especially since he has so little regard for other publishers. "Most publishers seem like wallpaper," he told *Publishers Weekly* in a 1977 interview, "most of them today are either promoted bookkeepers or ambitious men and women who care only for power and couldn't care less what they actually publish."

A fearless statement and one the publishing-literary jungle badly needed. Equally fearless have been Roger's statements on such lamentables as the best-seller list racket (epitomized not long ago by Paramount Pictures' buying huge quantities of Erich Segal's *Love Story* to catapult it quickly onto the lists)—"bookstores report some titles as best sellers before they have the books in the stores," says Roger—and the "awful state of reviewing in this country," with "not nearly enough reviewers around with sufficient backgrounds to discuss the best books adequately."

But publishing is not Roger's only activity. He is also very active on a number of family foundations. He is president of the Roger Williams Straus Foundation, which, among other things, maintains a chair in history at Princeton. He is the only member of the Guggenheim family on the board of the John Simon Guggenheim Foundation, of which his father was once president and guiding spirit, and he is a board member, also, of the Harry Frank Guggenheim Foundation. (The seat on the John Simon board often comes in handy to him as a publisher. If he is unable, or unwilling, to give a promising new author a decent advance, he will encourage him to compete for a Guggenheim fellowship, and between the fellowship which he might win and the meager advance, the young man may have enough to live on while he completes his book.)

Roger is also very much a Guggenheim. He and cousin Peter Lawson-Johnston are quite close and it is they who constitute the new Guggenheim family focal point and power center of the 1970s . . . at least in the East. Between them they run five companies and either sit on the boards of, or run, four major foundations. The combined assets they manage or influence are considerable, and from their respective positions on the Solomon R., the Daniel and Florence, the John Simon, the Harry Frank, and the Peggy Guggenheim foundations, and with the publishing firms of McGraw-Hill and Farrar, Straus & Giroux, their combined influence on literature, the sciences, and the arts is large indeed. If a young, aspiring writer, painter, scholar, or scientist knows Roger Straus and Peter Lawson-Johnston, and holds their respect, a good part of his battle for financial assistance and professional recognition is already won.

It may be noted, in passing, that Roger Straus and Peter Lawson-Johnston constitute the third consecutive generation of patrons of the arts in the Guggenheim family. First it was Solomon in painting and Simon in literature. Then in the next generation, it was Peggy in painting and Harold Loeb (the first publisher in the family) in literature. And today it is Roger and Peter. Is there another family in America that has influenced the lives and works of as many painters and writers of distinction as the Guggenheims? There is scarcely a major figure in either field since the 1920s who has escaped the influence of the family.

At sixty years of age in 1977, and with over thirty years of uniquely successful book publishing behind him, Roger Straus is a sort of object lesson to the sons of the very rich. Here he is a millionaire son of two of America's richest and most influential Jewish families, a man who has already inherited and received as gifts more than enough money to live on without having to work and stands to inherit much more someday, who has worked hard every day of his life, not simply at making more money but at something he fervently believes in and thinks plays an essential role in the preservation of our civilization. How many great grandsons, grandsons, and sons of American millionaires have achieved as much? And is there a more convincing argument for the importance of a nation maintaining a privileged class, an occasional Colonel Bob notwithstanding, than a Roger Straus? For in the last analysis, it is chiefly because he is a Guggenheim and a Straus, a man with several generations of education and independent wealth behind him, that he can afford to publish the best writing in the world today. Certainly if he had to rely wholly on his salary as president of FS&G to survive, there would be fewer Singers and Nerudas on his lists and more Wallaces and Robbinses.

However, let us not foster a wrong impression. Although he leads a nine-to-five business life, rarely missing a day at the office, and loves his work, Roger Straus is still a Straus and a Guggenheim, and Strauses and Guggenheims have had a way of living grandiosely for over three-quarters of a century. Behold Roger's opulent, four-story, fourteen-room Manhattan townhouse, the locus of many of the top literary parties in New York. Behold his sumptuous thirty-acre Sarosca Farm in Purchase, New York, with its three houses, elaborate Italian gardens, its baroque fountains and statues, its huge terraces overlooking all, it seems, of Westchester County. Is there a man in all U.S. publishing, including the most blatant purveyors of high schlock, outside of the Hearst brothers, who lives as well?

Yet it must also be observed, in all fairness, that the Strauses lead far from lavish lives in their splendid residences. Guests at Sarosca Farm, which have included people like Father Teilhard de Chardin, the Jesuit philosopher, who used to spend peaceful weeks at a time with the Strauses, have observed that the atmosphere of the great estate is almost "monastic": Roger Straus in his study reading manuscripts; Dorothea in her study, working on her latest book.

But there are other Strauses, descended from Guggenheims or related to Guggenheims by marriage, besides Roger, and they must also be given their due.

There is Roger's handsome brother, Oscar Straus II, a distinguished-looking gentleman of sixty-four who has trodden a path much closer to that of his mother and father than Roger has, working his way up to the number three slot at American Smelting and Refining before he was pushed out by one of his father's enemies, joining Guggenheim Brothers, then fighting bitterly with Harry, founding Straus Minerals, a not particularly profitable venture which, it is said, has eaten up a good deal of his mother's money, becoming a trustee of Temple Emanu-El, president of the Guggenheim-financed Institute of Man and Science at Rensselaerville, New York, and now, in 1977, president of the Daniel and Florence Guggenheim Foundation.

There is Roger's acutely intelligent wife, whom he married when he was twenty-one and she eighteen, the former Dorothea Liebmann, granddaughter of Samuel Liebmann, German-Jewish immigrant founder of Rheingold Beer (named after the Wagner opera and recently sold to Chock Full O' Nuts), Dorothea, who remembers the days when horses named after Wagnerian gods and heroes—Wotan, Fricka, Donner, Fasolt—pulled her family's beer trucks through New York City, and who, besides presiding as an exquisite hostess over her husband's literary parties, has herself contributed to the literature of her times by writing three Proustian volumes of memoirs—*Showcases, Thresholds,* and *Palaces and Prisons*—published by Houghton Mifflin, in which she limned portraits of two of her Guggenheim in-laws, Harry, the Master of Finistère, and Peggy, whom she characterized as a prisoner in her Venetian palace.

And there is Oscar II's son, young Oscar III, who is married to Geraldine Coors of the Coors Beer family, has two sons and works high up in Pacific Tin under the vigilant eye of his cousin chairman Peter Lawson-Johnston, who, we have already indicated, regards him as *the* comer in the family and the possible successor as Guggenheim standard-bearer in the twenty-first century.

And finally there is Roger and Dorothea's only son, Roger III, a tall, energetic, and hardworking young man, who, after apprenticing for a while in his father's firm as director of marketing, is now wearing the same hat at Harper & Row, and is, therefore, actually in competition with Farrar, Straus & Giroux, more than 60 percent of whose stock he is due to inherit upon his parents' deaths. Young Roger is married, has three daughters, has a house on his father's estate in Purchase, and, like his cousin Oscar III, sits on the board of the Daniel and Florence Guggenheim Foundation.

Let it further be mentioned, in passing, that the Straus clan includes the *only* living male Guggenheim descendants who continue to observe Judaism. Oscar II, we have mentioned, is a trustee of Temple Emanu-El, just as Roger, Sr. was. And Roger, Jr. made sure his son, Roger III, was bar mitzvahed, making him and Oscar III, and their fathers, the only male descendants of Meyer and Barbara Guggenheim who can still justly be called "Jewish." All the others—the Guggenheims of the West Coast, Lawson-Johnston, William Guggenheim III—have crossed over into other religious and ethnic realms.

* * *

The hot June sun is reddening as it dies in the smoggy haze above the Hudson Valley. Now the fountains and statues and urns on the broad, open terraces of Sarosca Farm are turning pink and orange, and a welcome cool is beginning to soothe the one hundred and fifty guests assembled to celebrate the appearance of yet another book bearing the imprint Farrar, Straus & Giroux.

Standing on one of these large, elegantly landscaped terraces, with their bright, geometrical Italian gardens bordered by boxwood hedges, and their immense hazy views of Westchester County, one could almost be on the terrace of one of the great patrician villas of the Tuscan countryside overlooking Florence. The same pink-red-orange light suffusing the valley below. The same enormous open vistas, the same dark green hedges enclosing carefully manicured beds of roses, marigolds, and zinnias, the same mossy statues, urns, and fountains glowing in the waning light.

There by the urn fountain the splendidly attired Simonetta Vespucci is having a little chat with Giuliano de' Medici and the painter Botticelli, who has recently finished a work depicting Simonetta and Giuliano, along with other figures, which he has called "Primavera."

There, by the urn fountain, surrounded by rosebushes, is Dorothea Straus in her long white dress and white gloves, carrying a white handbag, wearing white shoes, talking to Robert Silvers, editor of *The New York Review of Books,* and someone from *Saturday Review.* Before long they are joined by Paul Horgan, just down from his place in Middletown, Connecticut, and by the sculptor Frederick Shrady and his beautiful Viennese wife, Maria, just down from Monroe, Connecticut. The conversation has been turning on the evening's author but now turns to Italy where Shrady has his sculptures cast and from which he has just returned. Dorothea, never at a loss on any subject, is well acquainted with Italy. She accompanies Roger to Rome almost every year and has known a few of the most eminent Italians of her time: Carlo Levi, Salvatore Quasimodo, and Alberto Moravia among them. After a while the talk drifts to the book Roger is putting together on the futurist Filippo Marinetti's writings. Roger and Dorothea are good friends of Marinetti's daughter Luce, who lives in Venice and knows cousin Peggy quite well, and soon the talk drifts toward Peggy.

Dorothea never remains in one place very long at Farrar, Straus & Giroux parties, especially when she finds herself trapped by too many people, and so she is soon off through the garden to console John Canaday of the *Times,* just up from sweltering Manhattan. A kiss, a most decisive handshake, a few pungent remarks, and Dorothea is off again to greet sister author Laura Huxley, just tripping down the mossy brick steps from the upper terrace, bringing her over to meet the author of the evening.

The author this evening is, like her hostess, a woman. Here she is wearing a silver lamé miniskirt, her long dark hair falling to the break of her bare back, surrounded by hedges, rosebushes, and well-wishers. Roger III has been up to his old tricks and has buttressed her with enough vodka martinis to enable her to confront even the New York critics. It is not always easy being the author on publication day. It is, of course, consoling to receive so much attention, after all the loneliness, self-doubt, and hard work endured during the writing of the book. But it is such a change from the solitude of writing that the experience can be confusing. A writer being celebrated on publication day can get the feeling his book has been successful before the public has even read it and may become prematurely complacent about it. In reality much hard work still lies before him. Now he must get out and sell the book.

Sell it. That is really the whole point of the party. That is why Bob Giroux, and Roger III, and Dorothea are bringing the lady from the Literary Guild and the editor from Fawcett over to meet the author. The book has not yet been selected by a book club, or sold to a reprinter, nor have first serial rights been sold to a magazine yet.

Book club and paperback editors, critics, magazine people, publicists, authors. Yes, it is more or less the crowd Dorothea is used to seeing much more often during the winter season on East Seventieth Street. (For summer parties at Sarosca Farm are now rare.) There, munching those crudités, is Bernard Malamud telling yet another Jewish joke to Bob Giroux, who has heard several during his career. There, near that great mossy urn, which looks as if it had been lifted from a villa in Fiesole, one of *The New York Times* critics talks to an editor from *Publishers Weekly*. And there, a few marigold beds away, yes, it's Tom Wolfe, ever in white, white as Dorothea, white as a stork, just a smudge of green above the soles of his otherwise immaculate white bucks, Tom promising some magazine type an article on the lost art of Ethel Scull. And there, on a grassy eminence, looking up at the great house, the house three generations of Strauses have lived in, is Kurt Vonnegut, Jr. with Jill Krementz at his side, and, just beyond them, Oscar Straus II and III looking somewhat out of it. These literary types. A bit removed from Pacific Tin and Straus Minerals.

But where's Roger? Dorothea hasn't seen him for a while. Not that he wouldn't be faring well. But still, he's supposed to be toasting the author shortly, or at least getting someone to toast her. Ah, there he is, not far from the bar, doing what he does best after publishing books, celebrating the publication of books.

Yes, there he is, tall, trim, tanned, gray-haired, in one of his light summer suits, pouring drinks, serving drinks, smiling, hugging, kissing, shaking hands, juggling as many as five conversations at once while trying to compose his toast to the author, yes, there he is, the man responsible for it all, responsible for thirty years of the highest quality book publishing in the United States, if not the entire world, Daniel Guggenheim's grandson, adding yet more glories to the already overcrowded blazonry in the Guggenheim coat of arms.

Dexter chief, lion rampant, with body in the form of a rocket, holding bars of copper, silver, lead, and gold in each claw. Center and sinister chiefs: emblems of Colorado, Mexico, Alaska, Chile, the Congo; a Star of David. Dexter flank, a miniature Pollock. Fess point, a scholar at his desk. Sinister flank, a child in a dental chair. Honor point, an art museum resembling a cement mixer. Nombril point, a hospital in Jerusalem. Dexter base, a palace in Venice. Center base, a miner's pick and shovel. Sinister base, a book bearing the minuscule Farrar, Straus & Giroux logo of three fishes, two swimming to the right, one to the left—"That's me," says Roger.

CHAPTER

5

IRIS LOVE:
BONANZA ON KNIDOS

FOR OVER SIX HUNDRED YEARS THE GODDESS OF LOVE STOOD IN HER temple on Knidos facing the sea. The temple was on high ground, above a succession of rugged cliffs, and so it could be seen over great distances by sailors, who regarded it as their special shrine. The statue it enclosed was so beautiful—it was the first nude statue of Aphrodite ever wrought—that emperors, kings, and poets came from all over the world to see it. So prized did it eventually become that King Nikomedes of Bithnya offered to pay off the entire debt of the city of Knidos, which was considerable, in exchange for the statue. The Knidians preferred to remain in debt. Years later, the Roman historian Pliny wrote: "With this statue Praxiteles made Knidos a famous city." The work had, by then, attained the reputation of being the most beautiful statue ever made. In time, the larger-than-life-size work was copied and copied and copied so that by the fourth century A.D. it had become the most copied statue in the Greco-Roman world. For at least six centuries, perhaps more, the Knidian Aphrodite excited the passions of pagan civilization. Then, with the decline of Greece and Rome, the Theodosian decree ordering the destruction of all pagan temples throughout the Roman Empire, and the rise of Islam, Knidos suffered depredations, the temple fell into ruin, and Praxiteles' incomparable statue disappeared.

Well over a thousand years later, in October, 1970, Iris Cornelia Love, tall, blond, husky-voiced great granddaughter of Isaac Guggenheim, attracted worldwide attention by announcing she had found the head of the statue in the basement of the British Museum.

For the past three years Miss Love, a professional archaeologist, had been excavating what was left of the ancient Greek city of Knidos, now Tekir, on the southwestern coast of Turkey. Hoping she would find Praxiteles' statue, fifty-two known copies of which are still in existence, and largely frustrated in that hope (although she thought she had discovered the foundation of the temple), she went to the British Museum with a cousin, Margot Love Marshall, to inspect its large collection of Knidian antiquities, which had been lifted from the ancient site by a British archaeological expedition led by Sir Charles Newton in 1858. Perhaps this hoard of over three hundred and fifty pieces would contain some important clues to what was left on Knidos.

Again she was frustrated. Nothing on display proved particularly enlightening. So, catalogue of the Sir Charles Newton collection in hand, she and her cousin descended into the museum's enormous, crowded basement to see what pieces of the collection had been stored there. "It was dark and dank, with bare electric light bulbs breaking into the gloom at long intervals," Iris later told the press, "and spooky too, with all those white faces in tiers of shelves looming." At length she came upon a head, catalogued as number 1314, "covered with a cloth and the dust of ages." Iris pulled it out, took away the cloth, looked at it, and screamed, "Margot, it's here! It's here!"

According to Miss Love, the head, which was missing its mouth, chin, nose, most of its hairdo, and a good part of the back of its skull, was carved of the same fine-grained white Parian marble favored by Praxiteles, and the quality of workmanship, the late-classical style and type of hairdo, "the delicate folds in the neck," and the slightly larger-than-life dimensions, all indicated it came from the chisel of the supreme master.

The curators of the British Museum were not all that convinced. Or pleased. They maintained that the head had been found originally at the Temple of Demeter, goddess of agriculture, about a mile from where the Temple of Aphrodite was supposed to have been. And they were very upset at the implication in Miss Love's sensational announcement that they neither knew nor appreciated the value of the thousands of artifacts stored in their basement. "To imply that we didn't know we had this piece, and that it was unstudied," said Denys Haynes, Keeper of Greek and Roman Antiquities, and custodian, among other things, of the Elgin Marbles and the Rosetta Stone, "is simply untrue. We're overcrowded with material, but we know what we have. . . . I'm very cross at her," he went on, "if she wants to put her points down on paper we shall examine them, as we should arguments of any member of the public."

Undaunted, Iris hurled back more reasons why she knew the head was what she claimed it was. "The slight burnishing that gives the impression of flesh," she elaborated, "the folds in the neck, they all agree with copies I have examined in the Louvre and the Vatican Museum."

Undaunted as well, the British Museum, hauling the head out of the basement, dusting it off, and putting it on display, marshaled evidence that it was the head of Persephone, daughter of Demeter, and got the noted Austrian archaeologist Prof. E. Schwarzenberg to back them up. The dispute has never been resolved.

The controversy over the head of Praxiteles' Aphrodite of Knidos was not the first archaeological dispute Iris Love had been engaged in.

As a young girl in New York she had become interested in Greek and Roman history and mythology, chiefly due to the influence of her English governess, the late Katie Wray, and from an early age became a steady visitor at the Metropolitan Museum of Art. There she spent many hours studying, among other things, the three huge "Etruscan Warriors," among the most prized treasures in the museum. Later, while spending her junior year (at Smith College) at the University of Florence, she frequently visited Florence's Museo Archeologico, which contains one of the finest collections of Etruscan art in the world. Struck by the great differences between the figures in the Metropolitan and those in the Archeologico, she came to the conclusion that the ones in the Metropolitan were fakes.

Returning to Smith, she wrote her thesis for the bachelor's degree on the subject, then held off publication of her findings out of consideration for the feelings and reputations of the Metropolitan's curators, many of whom had been frequent visitors to her parents' Park Avenue apartment (which, Iris likes to point out, was a virtual museum itself, since the Loves were ardent collectors). Gisela M.A. Richter, the Met's curator of Greek and Roman art, had been one of those frequent visitors and had written up the Etruscan statues as masterpieces, and spent years of her career defending their authenticity in scholarly journals.

Finally in 1960, Iris decided to publish. Three months before the publication date she spoke with James Rorimer, the director of the Metropolitan and an old friend of the family, and told him she was going to reveal his treasured Etruscan warriors as forgeries. She even offered to let him have her paper for the museum to publish, under her authorship and the museum's imprint. Rorimer did not take her up on it. After a while, not long before publication day, Rorimer invited Iris for lunch at his office, asked her a lot of questions, then called in Joseph V. Noble, the operations administrator, and said: "Joe, did you know that the 'Etruscan Warriors' are forgeries?" "I've thought they were fakes for a year," replied Noble. Rorimer then called up Iris' mother and said Iris could do what she wanted with her paper. The day before it was due to be published, the museum announced the forgeries to *The New York Times* with no mention of Iris Love. When Iris called up Rorimer to protest, the Met director admitted that he had treated her "rather shabbily."

Shabbily indeed. But it taught her a valuable lesson. Now, when she makes an important discovery, she does not give away her hand in advance . . . no, not to *anyone,* sometimes not even to her closest collaborators. And important discoveries she has since made, scores of them, in her nine years as director of the excavations at Knidos, one of the most important archaeological expeditions being conducted in the world today.

How did it all come about? How did this great great granddaughter of Meyer and Barbara Guggenheim become perhaps the foremost female archaeologist in the United States, if not in the entire world?

The story of Iris Love in relation to the Guggenheim family is almost too appropriate to be true. For three-quarters of a century the Guggenheims had mined the globe for the metals of the earth. Then, at a certain point, they stopped digging, and, for the most part, sat back and lived off the dividends of their efforts. At precisely this juncture a member of the sixth generation came forward to dig again, not for metals, but for antiquities, not for financial gain, but for knowledge. At precisely the time when the mining bonanzas ceased, the archaeological bonanzas began.

But to get at the phenomenon of Iris Love, we must go back a few decades to her great grandfather Isaac, who, it will be remembered, was the eldest and perhaps the least effective of the seven sons of Meyer and Barbara Guggenheim.

Isaac died in 1922, leaving each of his three daughters $2 million. One of these daughters, Helene, married Lord Melvill Ward, becoming the second Guggenheim daughter to marry into the British aristocracy. Another, Beulah, married William Spiegelberg (it was their offspring, William, Jr., who was bribed to change his name briefly to

Isaac Guggenheim II). The third daughter, Edyth, it will be recalled, married the banker and naval officer Louis M. Josephthal, who eventually became Admiral Josephthal, commandant of the Naval District of New York. Admiral and Mrs. Josephthal had, in turn, two daughters, one of whom, Audrey, became the mother of Iris Love.

Audrey Love, a keenly intelligent woman, summa cum laude and Phi Beta Kappa at Smith, and her husband, Cornelius Ruxton Love, brought up their precocious daughter in a museumlike atmosphere in their opulent New York maisonette. As a child Iris found herself surrounded by priceless collections; there was scarcely a corner of the two-floor apartment that was not occupied by an important work of art. Among the many collections were a rare group of ancient Greco-Buddhistic heads, a superb array of Chinese cloisonné dragons, incense burners, and pagodas, a group of giant seventeenth-century late Ming Fou dogs, and the most extensive private collection of Napoleonic furniture, vermeil, and memorabilia in existence. Young Iris absorbed these influences, made a point of learning their history, and, according to her mother, dreamed of discovering similar treasures herself one day.

Audrey Love's mother, Edyth Guggenheim Josephthal, besides inheriting that $2 million from her father, went on to inherit substantial sums also from her mother and her husband, becoming in her later years an extremely wealthy old lady. She was, in her granddaughter Iris' words, "an incredibly domineering person . . . a woman of frightening energy, known everywhere for her temper tantrums." Once, when Iris was staying with her grandmother and mother at the Hotel San Domenico, a converted monastery in Taormina, Sicily, Edyth threw such a fit over some minor lapse in service that she had "the manager, his clerks, and half the chambermaids cowering in a corner of the cloister in utter terror." But she was always good to Iris. Recognizing her granddaughter's precocious sense of history and markedly superior intellectual curiosity, she singled her out among her grandchildren and left her a substantial trust fund in her will, which was sufficient to guarantee Iris financial independence for life.

As it turned out, it was a most fortunate bequest, because Iris' father, Cornelius Love, an Episcopalian, a stockbroker, and an art collector, was not all that well-off himself, even though he claimed to be a direct descendant of Alexander Hamilton and King George IV, both of whom had a little money in their day. Furthermore, Iris' mother, Audrey, one of the first patrons of Lincoln Center and a major supporter of the Metropolitan Opera and the theater, was too much committed to support of the theater to be able to provide Iris with more than just token financing.

Grandmother Edyth died in 1960 and was given an Episcopalian funeral, in accordance with her testamentary wishes, even though she was Jewish on both sides of her family. Immediately thereafter, Iris came into her trust fund. She was only twenty-five and she was free to dedicate herself, with no financial impediments, to her great passion, classical archaeology.

That passion had manifested itself remarkably early in her life.

Iris claims she made her first archaeological discovery at the Brearley School in New York at the age of six. Her teacher, a Miss Waldren, drew some large tracks on the blackboard and asked the students to identify them. None of the other little girls had a clue, but Iris correctly identified them as *Tyrannosaurus rex,* a skeleton of which she had recently seen in the American Museum of Natural History with her parents.

While at Brearley little Iris devoured all the school's courses in prehistory and history and spent much of her free time exploring the museums of New York, especially the Natural History and the Metropolitan. So enamored of history did she become that the only way her governess, Miss Wray, also a history buff, could persuade her to eat certain vegetables was to make a historical association with the vegetable in question. Iris hated all green vegetables, especially brussels sprouts. To get Iris to eat brussels sprouts Miss Wray told her that Charlemagne loved green vegetables and that once, during a winter campaign in Belgium when there was snow on the ground and there were no green vegetables available, the emperor ordered his men to clear the snow away, in the hopes that they would find some green vegetables, and all they found were some withered cabbages with small sprouts on them. So they cut off the sprouts and served them gingerly to the emperor. To their immense relief Charlemagne liked them. "Where are we?" he demanded. "Near Brussels, my Lord." "Well, let these hereafter be called Brussels sprouts," said Charlemagne. After Iris was told this story she could never have enough of the vegetable.

From Brearley and Miss Wray Iris, at fifteen, was sent away to boarding school at fashionable and ultraexclusive Madeira in Virginia. At first Iris felt herself somewhat at a loss in her new school because she could no longer pay regular visits to her beloved museums. But fortunately there were some good history courses at Madeira and she gobbled them up like brussels sprouts.

It was at Madeira that, strange as it may seem, she first found out she was Jewish. Iris' mother, Audrey, never so much as intimated to her younger daughter that she had Jewish blood.

One day Iris and some of her Madeira roommates were sitting around in the dormitory gabbing when one girl got up and bluntly asked Iris, "Are you Jewish?" "No, Episcopalian," said Iris, which was true. "Are you sure you're not Jewish?" the girl insisted, adopting, according to Iris, a "third-degree attitude," and suddenly establishing "a sort of kangaroo court." "Absolutely sure," said Iris. "My father had me confirmed in the Episcopal Church." A brief silence . . . then the girl announced to all the others: "She's lying, you know. We know what you are, Iris, my mother told me your mother is a Guggenheim and everybody knows the Guggenheims are *Jewish!*" Whereupon all the girls got up and walked out of the room, leaving Iris alone to cry her eyes out. As soon as she recovered, she went to the phone and called up her older sister, Noel. "Are we Jewish?" she cried. "A girl here at school said I was Jewish." "Of *course* you're Jewish, silly," Noel replied. "You know Granny was a Guggenheim."

Being a Guggenheim was, Iris later found out time and again, not always an asset. When she began trying to raise funds for her archaeological campaigns, individuals and foundations to which she appealed for money would often say, "But you're a Guggenheim, why are you asking *me* [or *us*] for money?"

It was not always easy for Iris to explain that though her Guggenheim grandmother did leave her a handsome trust fund, it netted her no more than $25,000 to $30,000 a year before taxes, or just enough to meet her personal expenses, certainly not enough to finance major archaeological expeditions. (A three-month campaign on Knidos costs a minimum of $50,000.) In addition, she could not count on significant financing from the living members of her family. Furthermore, she would be compelled to explain, just because she was a great grandniece of foundation founders Daniel, Solomon, Murry, and Simon Guggenheim, did not mean she had access to funds from their foundations. In fact, she would probably be the *last* person the Daniel, Solomon, or John Simon Guggenheim foundations would finance.

No, the only real advantage for Iris in being a Guggenheim was, besides inheriting the trust fund, sharing in what can only be called the Guggenheim genius. For among all the members of her generation, the generation immediately following that of Peter Lawson-Johnston, Bob Guggenheim, Jr., and Roger Straus, she alone possessed the imagination, the boldness, the adventurousness, the willingness to take big risks, to plunge into the unknown, that made the first generations of Guggenheims the most daring, innovative mining industrialists and patrons of the arts and sciences in the world.

Imagination. Boldness. Adventurousness. We have already mentioned Iris' bold and precocious exposé of the fake "Etruscan Warriors" and her sensational attempt at identifying the dusty marble head in the basement of the British Museum as the head of Praxiteles' statue of Aphrodite. But these were mere preludes, or rehearsals, to the extraordinary adventures of Iris to come on Knidos.

Knidos was one of the most important communities of ancient Greece. Located in the eastern Aegean just south of the islands of Lesbos, Chios, and Samos, it was close to the greatest centers of Greek civilization and within less than one hundred miles of three of the seven wonders of the ancient world—the Temple of Artemis at Ephesus, the Colossus of Rhodes, and the tomb of Mausolus. In its heyday during the fourth century B.C. it was the capital of the Dorian Hexapolis, a confederation of six cities that included nearby Rhodes and Halicarnassus. The city had two excellent harbors, a large commercial one to the south, from which the famous Knidian wine was exported all over the Mediterranean, and a smaller naval station facing north that could berth as many as twenty triremes at a time, and once accommodated the entire Spartan navy during the Peloponnesian War. A dozen huge towers guarded these harbors from enemy attacks and pirate raids. The city also boasted an advanced medical school and an astronomical observatory run by Eudoxus, a friend of Plato's. And there were many important temples scattered about—dedicated to Demeter, to Dionysius, to the muses—the most famous of all being the Temple of Aphrodite Euploia, a graceful, circular structure supported by eighteen slim white marble columns of the Doric order, and housing, at its center, Praxiteles' immortal statue of the goddess of love and beauty.

Iris first saw Knidos from the prow of a caïque in the summer of 1966. She was traveling with Askidil Akarca, a granddaughter of the last sultan of Turkey and a fellow classical archaeologist at Istanbul University. For the past nine summers Iris had been a jack-of-all-trades at the New York Institute of Fine Arts expedition on Samothrace. Now she had begun looking around for a site to excavate herself.

Landing on the little peninsula, she was immediately awestruck by the ancient city's great walls with their more than thirty towers, all still in an excellent state of preservation. Within the walls she was charmed to find farmers were growing cotton, tobacco, and sesame among the ancient ruins, oblivious to their significance, as if they were only so many stones in a field. Interspersed among the stones grew oregano, thyme, sage, and rosemary. Flocks of geese and turkeys were wandering in and out of a crumbled Greek theater and there were goats grazing among the ruins of the ancient agora. Then and there she made up her mind to excavate Knidos.

Iris at the time was an assistant professor of art history and archaeology at C. W. Post College, Long Island University. When she returned from her summer in Greece for the fall term, she screwed up her Guggenheim courage, and, after a series of impassioned pleas reminiscent of her great granduncle Daniel's petitions to J. P. Morgan to raise money to develop Kennecott Mountain, she succeeded in persuading Long Island University and the steamship magnate Jakob Isbrandtsen (who was fascinated by the trireme harbor and what it might yield) to finance a full-fledged archaeological expedition to Knidos for the summer of 1967. The following year Iris won additional financial backing from the Old Dominion Foundation, the Ingram-Merrill Foundation, and two archaeology buffs who were friends of hers, Win Nathanson and David Fromkin.

And so, beginning in the summer of 1967 and continuing to the present time, Iris Love has been pitching her "smelly, hot U.S. Army tents" among the stones and potsherds and flowers of ancient Knidos, living and working, sometimes in 120-degree heat, with her dachshunds, Heinrich and Phryne (the latter named after Praxiteles' mistress, the model for the statue of Aphrodite), and a small professional staff, and overseeing a force of Turkish laborers that has grown from thirty to one hundred.

And Iris is most emphatically boss of her expeditions. She raises the money, starting from scratch for each expedition. She writes up all the reports for the Department of Turkish Antiquities, sees to it that the objects she recovers reach the museums the Department designates, takes roll call, is the paymaster on payday, makes sure the water arrives at camp (there is only one freshwater spring on Knidos), buys all the food—she picks up okra, peppers, tomatoes, melons, eggplant, grapes, figs at the local market in her Land Rover—and even does the cooking, her specialty being barbecued wild boar with orange sauce. She also buys all the wine, which is very good at

Knidos, as it has been for millennia, because, as Iris likes to point out, "the vine is native to Turkey, not Greece, contrary to what most people think."

Iris' first summer on Knidos was primarily exploratory, and so it was not until the second summer that she began to make important finds.

Her first spectacular bonanza came during the first week of August, 1968, when a group of workers under the supervision of staff member Marie Keith, an indexer at the Frick Art Reference Library in Manhattan, unearthed a small marble sarocophagus inside of which gleamed a magnificent gold funeral crown, in perfect condition, not even tarnished, along with gold ornaments, and a rare two-handled glass wine goblet.

Immediately the workers began circulating rumors that the expedition had found a *pithos*, or enormous storage jar, filled with gold coins, and that the streets of ancient Knidos were flowing with gold. The rumor was circulated as far as three hundred miles away and caused a stampede of farmers who owned what they had thought was worthless, unproductive property in the area. Scores of these humble folk, many of whom were very poor, descended on the little peninsula demanding their share of "the treasure." Eventually the Turkish commissioner of antiquities for the district had to be called in to persuade these people that there really were no rivers of gold in the streets, and that, according to Turkish law, everything that was found would automatically become the property of the Republic of Turkey anyway. No one, not even Professor Doctor Directress Love, would be allowed to profit financially from the excavations at Knidos.

The second bonanza came in the summer of 1969 when Iris and her crew unearthed, in rapid succession, a beautiful bronze statuette of Priapus, a perfectly preserved marble statue of a woman, an exquisitely carved Hellenistic bone portrait ring of a matron, a marble head of a boxer, and a splendid larger-than-life-size statue of a young woman, possibly a goddess. They also discovered a strange round temple which Iris—holding her breath—intimated, but did not state at the time, might be the fabled Temple of Aphrodite.

Meanwhile, the expedition suffered the usual vicissitudes of archaeological expeditions.

The first time Iris went to meet the Knidos lighthouse keeper, a very important man on the peninsula it seems, her dachshund Heinrich bit him.

Later, good relations were restored when Iris administered an aspirin to the man's favorite goat, after the animal had been bitten by a poisonous snake, and, not long after the medication, the goat recovered.

Sometimes a *melteme*, a fierce north wind from the Aegean, would arrive with such force that it would blow away Iris' tents and even knock her people down. "It would come from nowhere, like a bolt of lightning, sometimes in the middle of the night, and we would suddenly find ourselves free of our smelly tents, lying on potsherds looking at the stars."

And scorpions were always lurking among the ruins, some varieties of which in Turkey have been known to inflict fatal bites. "In searching the ruins it soon became second nature to lift stones outward so the scorpions wouldn't spring at you." Nevertheless, some workers and staff members did get bitten and suffered terrible pain, even convulsions. And "aspirin didn't help."

One of the more pleasant things that happened on the expedition took place on Iris' birthday, August 1, in 1968. On that morning seven geese waddled into her tent "in single file, stood there cackling for a while, then turned around and waddled out again single file." Iris interpreted this as an exceptionally good omen since the goose, along with the dolphin, was one of Aphrodite's holy animals—she was often depicted riding one—and the number seven was sacred to the ancient gods.

A good omen indeed. For Iris' principal ambition on Knidos was to find the Temple of Aphrodite and, she hoped, Praxiteles' statue, or at least a part of it. In 1970 she finally reached her goal. It was her biggest bonanza and it landed her at age thirty-seven on the front pages of the major newspapers of the world.

The discovery of the temple actually took place on July 20, 1969, but Iris was not a hundred percent sure it was Aphrodite's sanctuary that she discovered at the time, although she had a strong hunch it was.

On that torrid July morning Iris and a member of her staff, Rolf Stucky, a Swiss archaeologist and mountain climber, struck out for a steep height they had not yet explored and which had not been assigned any importance on Sir Charles Newton's 1858 map of ancient Knidos. Climbing northward through steep, rocky fields covered with holly oak, thistles, yellow gentian, and stinging nettles, they eventually came to the base of a sort of terrace, and immediately felt a soft, refreshing breeze from the sea. The view was magnificent: to the north a series of steep cliffs plunging into the blue Aegean; to the south, far below, the two harbors, and then, immediately behind them, the parched white stones of ancient Knidos.

Climbing up the rock terrace wall, Iris' keen eye spotted something at eye level that took her breath away and made her tremble: a spill of stones, in what appeared to be a circular configuration, the remains, perhaps, of some collapsed structure.

What sort of structure would the Greeks have built on such a high eminence as this? Only a temple. A temple to a very important deity. Immediately Iris began poking about in the holly oak bushes that covered the terrace and found in one bush the top of what appeared to be a statue base. Was this the base of Praxiteles' statue of Aphrodite?

That evening, on returning to camp, she confided her hunch that she had at last found the Temple of Aphrodite and announced her intention to dig an exploratory trench on the site the following day.

Iris will never forget that hot July day. It was, among other things, the day the Apollo astronauts first landed on the moon and she had mused after returning to camp on how gratified her cousin Harry must have been by that event: Another Guggenheim hunch had paid off.

Iris arrived at the site charged with almost unbearable emotion. It was a scorching morning and the rocks blazed in the sun. The scent of sage and thyme was heavy in the warm air. Carefully she and her workers began digging the exploratory trench.

Before long it became apparent that the structure she had had only a dim hint of the day before was indeed circular. Iris knew from ancient literary sources that the Temple of Aphrodite at Knidos was circular and so, as the dimensions of the marble courses were gradually revealed, she knew she had found what she had been searching for for three years.

That conviction was confirmed in the summer of 1970 when she unearthed the statue base she had discovered the summer before and found it contained the partial inscription: "PRAX . . . NUDE . . . ABOVE." Examination of the base revealed its construction was contemporary with that of the temple. The inscription had probably been etched much later, possibly as a guide to pilgrims and tourists. Later on, beneath a staircase leading to a terrace below the temple, Iris found a slightly larger-than-life-size fragment of a Parian marble hand, the dimensions of which almost exactly matched those of the known copies of the Aphrodite of Praxiteles. And not far away she also found "an overlifesize Parian marble female finger" and "an exquisite fragment of Parian marble drapery, both of which may have been parts of the original statue."

Iris made the official announcement of her discovery of the temple at the annual meeting of the Archaeological Institute of America in San Francisco, and a day later a photograph of her standing in a miniskirt alongside a Greek statue (having nothing to do with Aphrodite) was on the front page of *The New York Times*, accompanied by an article headlined "TEMPLE OF APHRODITE FOUND IN TURKEY."

Other publications had great fun with the event. "LOVE FOUND LOVE," "A LOVELY COUPLE," "MISS LOVE FINDS LOVE ON TURKISH COAST" ran some of the headlines. "THE LOVE AFFAIR" was *Time* magazine's headline. Only *The New Yorker* did not attempt a pun on Iris' surname. "Archaeologist" was the title of their subdued article on the find.

After the sensational discovery—one of the two or three most important Greek archaeological discoveries since World War II—and specifically during the campaigns of 1971 and 1972, Iris went on to make still more sensational discoveries. Excavating very carefully within the precincts of the temple itself in 1971, she found scores of beautiful terra-cotta female heads dating from the archaic through the Hellenistic periods. Many were heads of young women at the zenith of their beauty. Some depicted groups of young women. One group represented the birth of Aphrodite aided by Horae. There were representations, also, of Aphrodite's son, Eros. The find was so large and varied that Iris was able to introduce an entirely new school of coroplastic sculpture to the archaeological world, which she has named the Knidian School.

Then, the following year, in a trench dug southeast of the altar of Aphrodite, a cache of several hundred terra-cotta statuettes, some intact, some fragmentary, was unearthed. Most depicted young females clutching their breasts. One was a double figurine showing two nude reclining figures, perhaps a bride and a groom. Another group included divine female musicians carrying lyres and kytherai, playing double flutes and carrying tambourines. And in the supposed gardens of Aphrodite to the northeast of the sanctuary, wherein aphrodisiacs were once grown, other appropriate items, such as "a jug with its spout in the form of a phallus, as well as phalli of all sizes" (some as long as four feet), were found. It was not for nothing that Pseudo-Lucan had written in the second century: "I took two authorities on love and went about Knidos, finding no little amusement in the wanton products of the potters, for I remembered I was in Aphrodite's city."

With the discovery of the temple in 1969, the discovery of fragments of Praxiteles' statue and its pedestal in 1970 and 1971, all the terra-cotta heads discovered in 1971, all the figurines in 1972, and the discovery, as well, of four other Hellenistic and Roman temples, two theaters, a council house, a colonnaded marketplace, a stoa, and scores of pieces of gold jewelry and painted pottery, Iris had made a strike on Knidos comparable, in archaeology, to the Bonanza Lode above Kennecott Creek. It was that latter strike, of course, made in the first decade of the twentieth century, that was partly responsible for the financial independence which has enabled Iris to engage in such nonremunerative pursuits as excavating ancient Greek cities.

Today the work goes on: In 1976 Iris made several sensational finds of female statues, one of which, a terra-cotta head of Aphrodite, ranks as a masterpiece. Meanwhile the honors and awards poured in. In 1973 Iris was cited for "exceptionally valuable work regarding Turkish culture" by the Turkish minister of state, upon the fiftieth anniversary of the Republic of Turkey. In 1974 she was appointed John Hamilton Fulton Lecturer at Middlebury College in Vermont. Invitations to lecture continue to reach her from all over the United States. And she has won much acclaim from members of her own family. Peggy Guggenheim considers her "the foremost Guggenheim of her generation." Which she most decidedly is, and appropriately so in this era of women's liberation (in the first two generations, the achievers were all men, in the later generations the women have come into their own). All this has been most gratifying, of course, but still Iris frets occasionally over the fact that the official archaeological community has never fully accepted her. Archaeology's *enfant terrible*. No, there are certain things they simply will not forgive or condone. For one, she never got her Ph.D. Now, for all those Ph.D.-holders to accept someone who did not go through what they had to go through is a bit much to ask. For another, she has had the blatant audacity time and again to challenge—publicly!—such eminent Ph.D.'s, people twice her age, as the heads of the Metropolitan and British museums, about matters she really knew very little about—after all, she never wrote a doctoral thesis—which, of course, has been and continues to be absolutely unforgivable.

In addition to not having been fully accepted by her so-called peers, Iris has also continued to take her knocks from other directions.

One of the biggest jolts came from Alexander Liberman, sculptor and editorial director of *Vogue*. Liberman, it seems, invited her to write the text and captions for a book he was pasting together about Greece, under the imprint of Viking, entitled *Greece, Gods, and Art*. After she accepted, he gave her much encouragement and an advance of $1,000, in two installments, assuring her she would be given full credit for her work. For months she slaved over both text and captions. Then, when the book came out, she was appalled to find only Liberman's name on the jacket, when all he had done was take the photographs.

But despite the envy and skepticism and false snobbery of many of her colleagues in the profession, and the knocks she has had to take from the likes of Messrs. Rorimer of the Metropolitan and Liberman of *Vogue*, Iris still wears that delightful air of perpetual wonder (and vulnerability) on her face that has endeared her to her friends, her staff members, and her workers for many years. And no one, regardless of where his Ph.D. is from, not even the heads of the Metropolitan or British museums, can diminish the remarkable achievements that have been hers at such a young age, achievements that rank her alongside her great granduncle Daniel, her cousins Harry, Peggy, and Roger, as one of the ablest Guggenheims of all.

It remains for Iris to complete her excavations at Knidos—the trireme harbor is next—and then make some sense out of them. For, although her finds have been spectacular, she has yet to interpret them and place them in some sort of historical, religious, and philosophical perspective. But that will undoubtedly come.

In the meantime, bring out that old Guggenheim escutcheon from the basement of Falaise. Take away the cloth. Dust it off. Now find some space for the latest contribution of the family. The great shield is very crowded. But, yes, perhaps there is a place between Dexter base and Center base, between the palace in Venice and the miner's pick and shovel. Yes, now put in that space, in bold sculptural relief, an archaeologist's pick and shovel, and a miniature of the Aphrodite of Knidos.

CHAPTER

6

WILLIAM GUGGENHEIM III:
AMEN

On April 24, 1974, William Guggenheim III attended an evening service of the Spiritualist Church of Orlando, Florida, at which an elderly female medium told him, during the "message session," that he should "rid himself of many boxes" when he and his wife, Judy, moved into their new home.

The advice momentarily stunned him because he and Judy had just moved from their estate in Cresskill, New Jersey, to a rented house in Jupiter, Florida, and, in addition to many trunks and suitcases of clothing, and much furniture, they had brought with them no fewer than 125 large cardboard boxes filled with William's books, knick-knacks, and various collections. And there was no way, except through clairvoyance, that the medium could have known about the move.

When William and Judy returned home after the service, William immediately began sorting through his books and collections to decide what he was going to keep and what he was going to give away.

It wasn't long before he decided to give away practically everything. That week he donated most of his books to the local library, "always," in his own words, "being sure I obtained receipts so as to take them as a charitable deduction on my income tax return—evidence of 'high spirituality'!"

He had imagined the giveaway process would be painful, but immediately after he commenced it he began to feel better, "lighter, . . . as though a weight was being removed from me." After a while he became "addicted to this feeling (joyfully)" and turned his attention to disposing of his many collections. "Out went more books, records, guns, *Mad* magazines, excess photographic equipment, art objects, stamps, coins, rocks, sea shells, matchbooks (over five thousand, all unusual), Agatha Christie books (had every one she wrote), comic books (Disney-type only), Little Golden Books, small wood carvings, paintings, antiques," some of which he had inherited from his father and grandparents, "all the things I hadn't used for years and probably never would read, hear, or use again."

Later, after he had disposed of most of his worldly possessions, he found that things that had once virtually constituted his very identity no longer had any value for him. "I found I could not only live without them, but could live far better, far more happily, without them. I even began enjoying giving away my formerly precious records to my baby-sitter and my revered science fiction books to her mother. The feeling was quite intoxicating, exhilarating, a feeling of freedom." Later still he realized that "it was not the 'things' I gave away that were important, but rather that I was able to shed my attachment to them—that's what made the difference! That is what enabled me to live more in the present and allowed me to begin 'to flow.' "

"To flow," for young William, was to become, shortly after this shedding experience, an intermediary between the living and the dead.

For since Sunday, May 12, 1974, eighteen days after the medium in the Spiritualist Church told him to rid himself of those boxes, William Guggenheim III, a slight, sharp-featured, dark-haired young man of medium height, has been receiving writings from the spirit world, particularly from the souls of the departed, and he is still receiving them. By 1976 he had taken down over four hundred pages of what he calls "automatic writing." So powerful and insistent are the voices William hears, and so rarefied is the philosophy they express, that William has come to consider himself a genuine religious mystic.

The time is short and you have not many years left, [he writes, or rather takes down, from a creature he calls White Dove] for you have created a weapon even more powerful than your strongest bombs and missiles. You have created ignorance. You have created spiritual blindness. The surest, swiftest path to self-destruction. You have come to believe that the things of the earth are more important than the earth itself. That products from the lands are more valuable than the lands. You believe you have opened a bottomless treasure chest of trinkets which you mistake for diamonds. And, in your pride, your blind satisfaction, you believe that what you term "progress" is the greatest force, the greatest value, in the universe. O my brothers, we weep for you with all our hearts, for in your haste you have lost the true meaning of the lands, of life, of death. And like a deluded fool who drinks of salt water, you have become addicted to your own blindness and folly. Like a child with a little red wagon, you bring your cars to your stores, load them up with trinkets, and hurry home to be amused by them. And when the glitter rubs off, you hurry again to other stores for more baubles, each time believing these toys will make you happy and fulfill your deepest needs. If that is true, why do you discard them so readily, only to replace them with others—newer ones, shinier ones, "perfected" ones?

Some among you have understood this madness and rejected it. Others, having glimpsed this insanity, this cult of material things, have begun to question it aloud. They know the treasure chest is not bottomless, even if they have not yet found out that it contains but bits of glass and other fake imitations. Particularly your children have seen through the delusion and sought other, truer paths. But few among you are brave enough to hear their questions, let alone seek answers from deep within their being. Few among you will pause long enough in your mad race towards destruction to still their minds and listen to the quiet voice within. Faster, ever faster they spin, never daring to question what it is they are riding on and where it will lead them.

I beg you, I implore you, to slow down long enough to create a stillness of your thoughts, and by doing so, to begin to listen to the truth from within. Every answer to every question that you honestly seek is already within you. Everything that you ever need to know has been placed within your being from the moment of your creation. You need not turn to others for answers, for knowledge, for truth—all these have already been revealed to you. All you need do is go within your own self for this knowledge. You need not take another's word, believe in another's experiences to find this knowledge. It is already within you and has been as long as you have existed. Merely establish the stillness, the quietness, and go within your own being and you will discover for yourself the truth of my words. Do not wait for miracles to save you from your own self-destruction. No such miracles ever have occurred or ever will occur. Each one among you can perform what you regard today as "miracles," but you can only do this for yourself; no one can perform a miracle for you.

I leave you now my little brothers, with these words so that you may begin to think for yourselves, question for yourselves, and turn inward to yourselves for the true answers that you already have within you.

WHITE DOVE

The author of these words, or rather, the receiver of them, occupies a special position in the Guggenheim family today because, as we have already indicated, he is the only male bearing the Guggenheim name who has sons. And so if the name of Guggenheim is going to survive in more than foundation mastheads and institutional lettering, it will be through William III's sons, and through them alone.

The situation is ironic, considering the fact that William III descends from the youngest and least-Guggenheim of the seven Guggenheim brothers, William, Sr., alias Gatenby Williams, the first to drop out of the family business, the first to marry a Gentile girl, the first to divorce, the first to write a book, the first to stray from Judaism, and the first to open a rift in the family ranks, by bringing that $10 million suit against his brothers over Chile Copper.

How happy William, Sr. had been when he received news of the birth of his first and only grandchild, William III. How proud it had made him feel in front of those older brothers of his, who had always made him feel so inadequate and foolish. Solomon, Murry, and Simon may have held all the power, but not one of them had a grandson with the name of Guggenheim. That was one thing he now had that they did not.

Will senior's estranged wife, Aimee, was also very proud of her grandson who, after her son died, became the apple of her eye. She hated her husband's brothers, had spent most of her married life trying to turn William against them, which proved not to be difficult, and was only too delighted that her grandson might be the only offspring in the family capable of perpetuating the Guggenheim name. Not only did it make her one up on the brothers, but also one up on their *wives*.

Aimee Guggenheim was no fool. She looked out for herself and her own. At the time of her estrangement from William, Sr., when she began to notice how much attention her husband was paying to showgirls and other fortune hunters, she took care to have a goodly portion of William, Sr.'s property put in her name. And so she was by no means left destitute when William, Sr. died, leaving the bulk of his depleted estate to Miss America of 1929, Miss Connecticut of 1930, and two other former showgirls. Besides making sure that she got her legal share of that estate, by taking the young ladies to court, she had by that time squirreled away under her own name over $2 million of her late husband's assets. These assets eventually passed to her son, William, Jr., and then to his wife, now Mrs. Elizabeth Broadhurst of New York, and their son, William Guggenheim III.

But these funds were not the only ones available to the line of William, Sr. There was also that $1 million "iron trust" set up for William and his heirs by Simon Guggenheim after the settlement of the Chile Copper dispute. It was, as we know, a trust the principal of which could not be invaded and against which one could not borrow. Upon William, Sr.'s death it passed to William, Jr., and upon his death, to William III.

William III, then, like his cousin Iris Love, was financially free to pursue his own interests from an early age. Unlike Iris, however, it took quite a while for those interests to manifest themselves, but when they did he knew he had finally found his way. It was a way no other Guggenheim had ever taken, a radical departure from what the family had always stood for, a virtual contradiction of what had been the family ethos so far.

Turning one's back on getting and spending, on technological progress, on exploiting the natural resources of the earth, on industrial civilization, on the consumer society, and embracing renunciation, mysticism, Eastern religions, the occult, communicating with spirits, yes, this indeed was a radical departure from what the name of Guggenheim had meant to the world for the past one hundred years.

Will III was, of course, not alone in his attitudes and pursuits. Tens of thousands of young Americans had adopted similar orientations during the 1960s and 1970s. Nor was it a particularly new phenomenon, or episode, in the history of Western civilization. At the time of the decline of the Roman empire in the third and fourth centuries, the sons and daughters of the Roman patriciate gradually turned away from making war and money and turned toward Eastern mystery cults, pacifism, Oriental philosophies, and the new Christian religion, which also came from the East.

Was William Guggenheim III roughly in the same position as the son of a Roman patrician of the fourth century?

More or less, yes. His mother's and father's families, especially his mother's, had been patricians for generations, with all that implies for the development of personality. The former Mrs. William Guggenheim, Jr. is, as we know, a direct descendant of Wilhelmus Beekman, Dutch burgomaster of New York, then Nieuw Amsterdam, in the seventeenth century, and counts among other illustrious ancestors, Theophilus Parsons, one of the earliest chief justices of the Supreme Court of Massachusetts, Theophilus Parsons, Jr., one of the earliest deans of Harvard Law School, and Dr. Charles Chauncy, second president of Harvard College. With his mother's family in America for 340 years, and his father's for 130, Will III is, on his mother's side, a twelfth-generation American and on his father's side, a fifth-generation American.

Americans with five or more American generations behind them are generally quite different from second-, third-, and fourth-generation Americans, who constitute the majority. They are not likely to be such go-getters as the later arrivals. They are not so obsessed with "making it." Their families made it a long time ago. They also feel much more secure in their social status and therefore do not feel compelled to push. "We do not have to keep up with the Joneses," they seem to say, "because we *are* the Joneses."

As for Will Guggenheim III, who was in his twenties at the time of the Vietnam War, and thirty-five at the time of his first mystical experience, what was there left to be or do when your ancestors had been burgomasters of New York, presidents of Harvard, founders and presidents of major industrial corporations, founders and presidents of major philanthropic institutions, ambassadors, authors, senators, publishers, aeronautical pioneers, museum donors, art patrons, great princes of the American empire? Especially if you had come to believe, as Will III had, in the essential futility of most of these offices and functions? (In one of his automatic writings Will had had revealed to him these opinions of the prevailing establishment: ". . . some were called 'universities,' others 'hospitals,' and yet others 'social institutions' or 'churches' or 'temples' or 'government agencies' —it didn't matter what the label said, they were basically all the same, men in darkness leading men in blindness.")

Yes, America in the last quarter of the century of her world dominance had, in many ways, come to resemble ancient Rome in the last centuries of her world dominance. So we have conquered the world. So now there *is* a Holiday Inn on Madagascar, a McDonald's in Hamburg, a U.S. naval base in the middle of the Indian Ocean. So some U.S. corporations, like Exxon with revenues of $52,584,821,000 in 1976, draw income from one hundred countries and are richer than many of the nations in which they operate. So the Romans did have outposts in Scotland in which the Roman legionnaires enjoyed more luxuries than the Scots. So there were Roman temples in Athens, Baalbeck, and Carthage that were bigger than anything the Athenians, Syrians, and Carthaginians had. So Roman engineers did build gigantic aqueducts and sports arenas in Spain and France and North Africa. Was the world any better off when gladiators could at last fight lions in the arena in Nîmes? Is the world any better off now that you can buy a Coke in New Zealand? What has happened to the inner life of man during all this frantic empire building? What has happened to the life of the spirit? What has happened to the ideals of truth and love and beauty and justice? Has the cause of truth and love and beauty and justice been served by erecting yet another Roman amphitheater in Gaul, another Roman wall in Britain, another Holiday Inn in the Cayman Islands, another Coca-Cola bottling plant in Sri Lanka? These were the questions that young Romans in the third century and young Americans in the late twentieth century had begun to ask.

And what, these same young Americans were beginning to ask, what was the much-vaunted American Dream anyway? Was it a dream of truth and beauty and justice, and the promotion of a higher type of human being, or was it just a dream of wealth and power and fame? Or, worse yet, a dream of mere security, comfort, and pleasure, a dream of the greatest ease for the greatest number?

And so here is the great empire builder Meyer Guggenheim's great grandson, his only descendant with sons bearing the name Guggenheim, now living in Florida, caring for his little family, caring for his capital, which, of course, had originally been accumulated by the empire builders he now rejects, attending spiritualist séances, consulting mediums, taking down messages from the spirit world, attending a seminar on faith healing by the medium and psychic Anne Gehman, a seminar on death and dying by the Swiss psychiatrist and faith healer Dr. Elisabeth Kübler-Ross, who claims she was visited by a former patient a year after the patient died. Here is Will Guggenheim III thinking of spending some time at Peter Caddy's New Age religious commune in Findhorn, Scotland, where they grow forty-pound cabbages on sand dunes using only love and prayer as fertilizer; William Guggenheim III thinking also of founding his own New Age religious commune in Florida someday, using part of his inheritance as seed money.

The route which William Guggenheim III took to arrive in this place and at these activities and intentions has been a circuitous one, to say the least.

After graduating from the Browning School for Boys in New York, Will, an only child, went to Yale, from which he dropped out after his sophomore year because the place was too big and impersonal after Browning and made him "unstable," and, after all, he did not *have* to take all that "nonsense" from a bunch of professors in order to make his living someday. Short stints at the Stanford University Radio and Television Institute, Announcers Training Studios in New York, the New York Institute of Finance, and the New York Institute of Photography, followed in rapid succession. From Announcers Training Studios he went to work as a time salesman, engineer, and announcer for several small radio stations (he had always been a ham radio operator). Soon, however, because taking care of his investments began to absorb more and more of his attention, he became "fascinated with Wall Street," abandoned radio "and took virtually every course offered at the New York Institute of Finance," after which he became a stockbroker and later a securities analyst for two New York brokerage houses, Correau, Smith and Hoppin, Watson. This activity he found very useful, and because of it he does not have to rely on a financial advisory service to manage his investment portfolio. But being a stockbroker did not hold young Will for long (it was "too materialistic a trip" for him), and soon he was working for his mother's second husband as an industrial security consultant, a job he left after a year "to open and operate and close New York's only all-paper dress store, Indispensable Disposables, on East Sixtieth Street, opposite Serendipity."

From Indispensable Disposables, a shorter "trip" than he had supposed it would be, and one whose frivolity made him feel a bit guilty, he went on to expiate his guilt by becoming a full-time volunteer social worker at the Forum School, Paramus, New Jersey, a private school for autistic and schizophrenic children, and then a full-time unsalaried social worker at the Englewood Narcotic and Drug Abuse Center, Englewood, N.J.

Meanwhile he had married Grace Embury and had two daughters with her, Maire and Jaenet, and had bought a three-hundred-acre estate at Clinton Corner, near Millbrook, N.Y., to settle his family in. Then he divorced Grace, who took custody of the two daughters, and a year later married Judith Arnold, who has since presented the Guggenheim family with two male heirs, William Douglas Guggenheim, born in 1970, and Christopher Mark Guggenheim, born in 1976.

After marrying a second time, William collaborated with his new wife to write what Will calls a "book/game," titled *The Love Game,* which was published as a paperback by Pinnacle Books, publisher of Linda Lovelace's autobiography, in 1973.

The Love Game, "The Ultimate Game for Sensuous Partners,

created by Judy and Bill" (so proclaims the cover, which omits Judy and Bill's last name), is a curious document. On the back cover it is described as follows:

> It's a romantic and sexual game for lovers . . . the sensuous way to share a new excitement in a look, a word, a touch, a moment of ecstasy!
>
> Partners experience total sensuality together as play progresses from love-talk to love-making, guided by the cards in this unique book.
>
> It's the fun game, the sexy game to play for an evening or an entire weekend with your favorite lover!

Under "Suggestions for Play" in the first pages of the book, Judy and Bill Guggenheim have this to say:

> Sensuous clothing is recommended for both partners. Women may apply perfume, cologne or bath oils to their bodies; different scents might be used on different areas.
>
> Soft, subdued lighting suggests intimacy and romance. Try substituting colored light bulbs, particularly pink or red ones, for regular bulbs. Experiment with firelight and candlelight to evoke mystery and sensuality.
>
> Textures offer a variety of experience. Consider playing on a water bed, a fur rug, inflatable furniture, assorted pillows, carpeting, and puffy quilts or downy blankets.
>
> After each partner answers a question *both* partners remove one article of clothing. Players may remove the clothing from each other if this is mutually agreeable. By the time all the green cards have been played, both partners should be nude. If not, they should remove whatever clothing they are still wearing.
>
> After playing *The Love Game*, you may find it very relaxing and romantic to shower or bathe together.

The cards in the book, all of which are detachable, are divided into three parts, each with its own color: Part I, Talking together; Part II, Touching together; Part III, Loving together.

A typical card in Part I reads: "How many times would you like to make love to your partner during one night? . . . Would you like a chance to do it?"

In Part II we find: "Caress all areas of his fascinating body using only your breasts."

And in Part III we find such suggestions as: "Explore all of her very sensuous body with your tongue."

After the book came out Judy and Will Guggenheim were a bit

disconcerted to see the newspapers describe it as "pornographic," when they resolutely claim it wasn't. The purpose of the book, Will claims, was simply to instruct people on "how to improve communication between man and woman, especially on the sexual level." They were also a bit disconcerted to see another, far more explicit how-to sex book, *The Sensuous Woman* by "J," come out at the same time and far exceed *The Love Game* in sales. But Will claims he never expected the book to become a best seller. "It was just a fun trip, that's all," he explains.

By the time *The Love Game* came out, the William Guggenheims had moved to Florida and Will was only a short time away from receiving the advice about the boxes from the medium.

In the meantime, as if to anticipate the shedding of the boxes, he began shedding his clubs, giving up his memberships in the Sands Point Bath and Tennis Club, the Yale Club of New York, the English-Speaking Union, and the Sons of the American Revolution. The memberships were just "status trips," he explains.

The stage was now set for William's second birth, his "spiritual awakening" as he puts it, which occurred in May, 1974.

> Though I had no belief in an "afterlife" [he writes] and definitely did not believe in communication between "the living" and "the dead," I spontaneously began a form of mediumship which I now term "telepathic writing" (some people call it "automatic" or "inspirational" writing). In any case, I "receive" thoughts, translate those thoughts to words and either write them down myself or, more recently, dictate them to my wife, Judy. Thus far I have received over 400 typewritten pages of short stories, philosophy, poetry, parables and messages from a wide variety of "sources." Thus May 12, 1974, was not only my "psychic" beginning, it was also my spiritual awakening—and since that date my life has literally changed in many, many ways. Though Judy and I do not belong to any church or religious organization (we have no labels of any kind) [He was raised an Episcopalian, then converted to Catholicism.], we have already begun an informal "ministry" that has a number of facets, i.e, each Friday night we have "open house" during which we play tapes of various spiritual teachers and leaders (Eastern, Western, conservative, radical—almost anyone!): about twenty adults attend our Friday night sessions. We are very much into New Age "thought, philosophy and religion," not conventional theology. If I had to describe myself in one word, that word would be "mystic" and my personal cosmology is a synthesis of Mystical Chris-

tianity and Spiritualism. . . . I believe that Judy and I are "in training" at this point in our lives, and that we will eventually join (or possibly even found) a spiritual New Age community.

By 1977, three years after his spiritual awakening, William, now thirty-eight years old, was still receiving messages occasionally, but not nearly as many as he received in the sudden rush of 1974.

William describes his writing process as follows:

I am usually alerted to expect an "incoming message" by "hearing" such words as "Peter calling" followed by the first few words of the message itself. In a couple of instances I've been alerted by Willy [his son], directly or through Judy, who sensed that Willy was trying to attract my attention and get me to "tune in."

The easiest way to understand this process is to view me as a "translator" and a "transcriber." I receive thoughts in much the same manner as a secretary receives dictation.

In all honesty I do not yet *know* the *source* of this material, though for me there are only two possibilities or explanations:

1. All the messages are actually communicated to me from deceased persons who are living a continuous life beyond what we term "death."
2. All the messages are derived from my own subconscious mind, by a process or means completely unknown to me and for reasons of which I have no knowledge.

Of all the hundreds of inspirational writings William has received, the one he feels most deeply about is a short poem that came to him one morning, which he has called "My Pledge of Love":

> I pledge my love to the brotherhood of man
> and to the Earth on which we live,
> One world under God, indivisible,
> With compassion and harmony for all.

William feels that the time has come for this pledge, "which might be termed the macroscopic or astronaut's view of man and the planet earth . . . to replace our current pledge of allegiance, which is nationalistic and divisive."

Meanwhile, in anticipation of that unlikely event, William and Judy Guggenheim and their two little boys continue to live quietly and comfortably in their new home (bought in 1977) in Longwood, Florida, not far from Orlando, in nearly total opposition to what has been conventionally understood to be the American way of life, and in opposition, as well, to almost all that the Guggenheim family has stood for ever since Meyer began peddling stove polish in Pennsylvania nearly one hundred and thirty years ago.

The Guggenheims' house in Longwood is in a subdivision called the Woodlands in which there are some five hundred homes. Security is excellent, and nearby there are two large shopping malls, Longwood Village and Altamonte Mall, the latter, according to William, "a double-deck affair which is the largest, most deluxe mall in Florida."

The house itself is a rambling one-story "pool home" of cement-block construction, containing four bedrooms, four bathrooms, a family room, a living room, a dining room, and a large kitchen. The living room and dining room have large, sliding glass doors that lead to the screened-in pool, which can be heated in winter. Beyond the pool there is a half acre of land planted, in Will's words, with "tall, stately oak trees which provide a 'cathedral' effect." In this area Will plans to hold meditation sessions for groups of thirty persons.

The decor and feeling of the house is light, airy, open, and cheerful. No formality. None of the pretentious stuffiness that characterized his grandfather's opulent residences. The dominant colors are white, green, and yellow. There are no "heavy pieces of furniture or clutter of antiques." Light, colorful paintings of flowers and butterflies adorn the predominantly white walls. Although the rooms are furnished with a few chairs and sofas, there is an abundance of large pillows on the floor, on which both residents and guests sit most of the time at social gatherings. There are lots of candles everywhere, which the Guggenheims prefer to electric lights, and dozens of houseplants, many hanging from the walls and ceilings.

William calls the living room "The Butterfly Room." A motto greets the visitor to this precinct: "All ye who enter be prepared to change and grow and unfold." The walls here are decorated with New Age religious art "implying metamorphosis." There is an elaborate stereo system with four large speakers for playing New Age spiritual music. Very little furniture, but lots of pillows, candles, and plants. The Guggenheims hold informal, on-the-floor gatherings in this room where the guests engage in meditation, healing, and listening to cassettes of New Age spiritual music and the teachings of New Age prophets and healers. All the Guggenheims' friends, Bill asserts, are on "consciousness trips" and are not interested in "small talk, gossip and trivia."

The large kitchen is Judy Guggenheim's domain. According to Bill, she is very much "into nutrition, vitamins, health foods, and plants." She has planted a vegetable garden in the yard near the kitchen door and is thus able to serve her family fresh produce every day. Judy and Bill are also "into birds" and have installed many bird feeders around the house. It was Judy, again according to William, who "received the inner guidance to settle in the Orlando area." She apparently had two successive visions, one of Orlando, the other of the Woodlands, and that settled it. Against Bill's initial objections, they moved there from their rented house in Jupiter, Florida.

What does William Guggenheim III, who does not hold a job or office of any kind, do with his time?

Many things, all related to his spiritual concerns. For one, he has financed and overseen the development of the Greun Madainn Foundation ("Sun of the Morning" in Gaelic), a New Age religious community in North Carolina serving as a center for "living, healing and meditation," and as a "universal pathway" to God.

Recently he has become very interested in thanatology, particularly in the care of terminally ill patients and their families. Will has been especially interested in the work of Dr. Elisabeth Kübler-Ross, the Swiss psychiatrist whose work in the field of death and dying has attracted a good deal of attention in recent years. After attending a seminar by Dr. Kübler-Ross in Florida, William came to the conclusion that the "twentieth-century spiritual mission of Dr. Elisabeth Kübler-Ross is to announce publicly in the Western scientific, rational, intellectual idiom the same message that Jesus of Nazareth sought to deliver almost two thousand years ago, that life continues after death." In time, Bill, who believes he has a "healing mission" and is destined for a "healing ministry," would like to establish a hospice for terminally ill persons.

But William's principal ambition is to establish "a small, nonprofit, tax-exempt foundation for use as a vehicle for various small-scale spiritual 'works,' " which he intends to call the Butterfly Foundation, and which may someday become the parent of a New Age spiritual community in Florida.

"The Western world," William declares, "is searching for alternatives to their present culture, which is grounded upon materialism." It will be the ultimate purpose of the Butterfly Foundation to help provide some of those alternatives.

But, Will admits, "the real work, though, is on oneself—growing, unfolding, changing, becoming more loving and compassionate. The money I inherited from my family makes it possible to share this with others, in a variety of ways, so they may do likewise."

William III may be able to live the way he does thanks to the freedom his Guggenheim inheritances have given him, but he is nevertheless almost wholly isolated from the family that provided him with his money.

In fact, Will has become so isolated from the rest of the Guggenheim family that when his second son, Christopher Mark, was born in November, 1976, he did not know of a single Guggenheim to mail an announcement to, with the exception of Peter Lawson-Johnston, and even in his case he had to use c/o Guggenheim Brothers, 120 Broadway, New York City, as an address.

Will, however, is not without his views on the Guggenheim family as a whole.

Basically I feel that they did what felt right and comfortable for them to do [he says], that their accumulation and distribution of wealth was based on an inner expression or drive, perhaps a creative expression of their family or "group" consciousness in which the whole was greater than the sum of its parts. Though not a student of "great American families," to my knowledge the Guggenheims are unique in the fact that virtually the entire family participated in their activities, not merely one or two exceptional men as in the case of [the families of] John D. Rockefeller or Henry Ford or J. P. Morgan. . . . Perhaps another way of saying this is that the Guggenheims were a uniquely *creative* family, even down to the third generation and beyond—and I have Peggy and Harry in mind, and perhaps myself too, though in a far more limited way in the latter case. Esoterically, there is a theory that a "group of souls" will choose to incarnate together in order to carry out some special plan or project. Could it be possible that the purpose of the Guggenheims was to establish the many foundations etc., and in order to do so they had to accumulate a sizable fortune to finance these projects? I realize that this is a reversal of the traditional view that first you make it, then you spend it, but why not the other way around? This does not imply that they were conscious or aware of their intentions before they built their empire, but who is to say that they too, in their own way, were not acting upon "inner guidance" or "higher guidance," or whatever term you may prefer?

As for William's own contribution to the Guggenheims, he is understandably proud that he has been able to give the family two more sons. "Indeed the Guggenheim name," he exults, "seems destined to go on for yet a little while longer, and hopefully for several more generations."

Wife Judy, however, is a bit less sanguine about perpetuating names. After their first son was born, she and William had quite a discussion over what to name the infant. Will wanted to name him William Guggenheim IV. But Judy wanted to give him a middle name, Douglas, after an autistic child they had both helped, even though this would make it impossible to refer to the boy as William IV. Will pleaded his case as eloquently as he could, emphasizing the appropriateness of it all, four consecutive generations of William Guggenheims and so forth. But what could be more appropriate, Judy countered, than to give their boy the name of that darling little child they had assisted? In the end Judy's will prevailed.

"But why, why don't you want to call him William IV?" Will III had cried out in exasperation, at the height of the argument.

"Oh, because it's much too dynastic, that's why," Judy replied.

THE GUGGENHEIMS
GENEALOGICAL TABLE
(NUMBER 1)

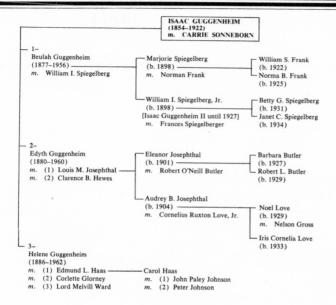

ISAAC GUGGENHEIM
(1854–1922)
m. CARRIE SONNEBORN

1–
Beulah Guggenheim
(1877–1956)
m. William I. Spiegelberg

Marjorie Spiegelberg
(b. 1898)
m. Norman Frank

William S. Frank
(b. 1922)
Norma B. Frank
(b. 1925)

William I. Spiegelberg, Jr.
(b. 1898)
[Isaac Guggenheim II until 1927]
m. Frances Spiegelberger

Betty G. Spiegelberg
(b. 1931)
Janet C. Spiegelberg
(b. 1934)

2–
Edyth Guggenheim
(1880–1960)
m. (1) Louis M. Josephthal
m. (2) Clarence B. Hewes

Eleanor Josephthal
(b. 1901)
m. Robert O'Neill Butler

Barbara Butler
(b. 1927)
Robert L. Butler
(b. 1929)

Audrey B. Josephthal
(b. 1904)
m. Cornelius Ruxton Love, Jr.

Noel Love
(b. 1929)
m. Nelson Gross

Iris Cornelia Love
(b. 1933)

3–
Helene Guggenheim
(1886–1962)
m. (1) Edmund L. Haas
m. (2) Corlette Glorney
m. (3) Lord Melvill Ward

Carol Haas
m. (1) John Paley Johnson
m. (2) Peter Johnson

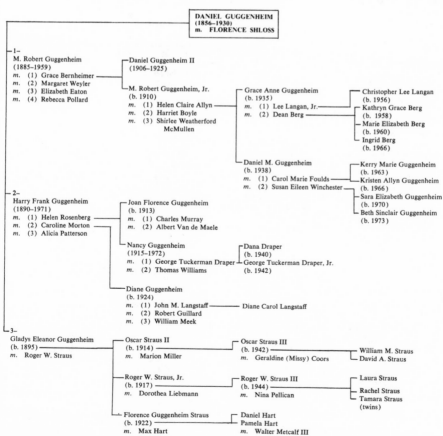

DANIEL GUGGENHEIM
(1856–1930)
m. FLORENCE SHLOSS

1–
M. Robert Guggenheim
(1885–1959)
m. (1) Grace Bernheimer
m. (2) Margaret Weyler
m. (3) Elizabeth Eaton
m. (4) Rebecca Pollard

Daniel Guggenheim II
(1906–1925)

M. Robert Guggenheim, Jr.
(b. 1910)
m. (1) Helen Claire Allyn
m. (2) Harriet Boyle
m. (3) Shirlee Weatherford
McMullen

Grace Anne Guggenheim
(b. 1935)
m. (1) Lee Langan, Jr.
m. (2) Dean Berg

Christopher Lee Langan
(b. 1956)
Kathryn Grace Berg
(b. 1958)
Marie Elizabeth Berg
(b. 1960)
Ingrid Berg
(b. 1966)

Daniel M. Guggenheim
(b. 1938)
m. (1) Carol Marie Foulds
m. (2) Susan Eileen Winchester

Kerry Marie Guggenheim
(b. 1963)
Kristen Allyn Guggenheim
(b. 1966)
Sara Elizabeth Guggenheim
(b. 1970)
Beth Sinclair Guggenheim
(b. 1973)

2–
Harry Frank Guggenheim
(1890–1971)
m. (1) Helen Rosenberg
m. (2) Caroline Morton
m. (3) Alicia Patterson

Joan Florence Guggenheim
(b. 1913)
m. (1) Charles Murray
m. (2) Albert Van de Maele

Nancy Guggenheim
(1915–1972)
m. (1) George Tuckerman Draper
m. (2) Thomas Williams

Dana Draper
(b. 1940)
George Tuckerman Draper, Jr.
(b. 1942)

Diane Guggenheim
(b. 1924)
m. (1) John M. Langstaff
m. (2) Robert Guillard
m. (3) William Meek

Diane Carol Langstaff

3–
Gladys Eleanor Guggenheim
(b. 1895)
m. Roger W. Straus

Oscar Straus II
(b. 1914)
m. Marion Miller

Oscar Straus III
(b. 1942)
m. Geraldine (Missy) Coors

William M. Straus
David A. Straus

Roger W. Straus, Jr.
(b. 1917)
m. Dorothea Liebmann

Roger W. Straus III
(b. 1944)
m. Nina Pellican

Laura Straus
Rachel Straus
Tamara Straus
(twins)

Florence Guggenheim Straus
(b. 1922)
m. Max Hart

Daniel Hart
Pamela Hart
m. Walter Metcalf III

THE GUGGENHEIMS

GENEALOGICAL TABLE

(NUMBER 2)

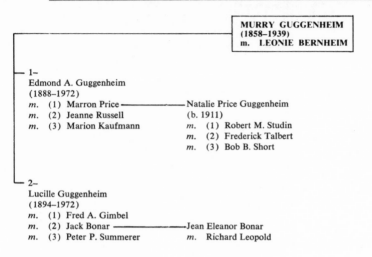

MURRY GUGGENHEIM
(1858–1939)
m. LEONIE BERNHEIM

— 1—
Edmond A. Guggenheim
(1888–1972)
m. (1) Marron Price ——————— Natalie Price Guggenheim
m. (2) Jeanne Russell   (b. 1911)
m. (3) Marion Kaufmann   *m.* (1) Robert M. Studin
                                 m. (2) Frederick Talbert
                                 m. (3) Bob B. Short

— 2—
Lucille Guggenheim
(1894–1972)
m. (1) Fred A. Gimbel
m. (2) Jack Bonar ——————————Jean Eleanor Bonar
m. (3) Peter P. Summerer   *m.* Richard Leopold

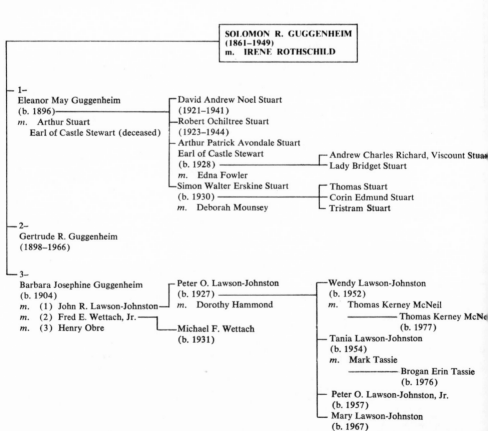

SOLOMON R. GUGGENHEIM
(1861–1949)
m. IRENE ROTHSCHILD

— 1—
Eleanor May Guggenheim   ┌ David Andrew Noel Stuart
(b. 1896)——————————   │ (1921–1941)
m. Arthur Stuart   ├ Robert Ochiltree Stuart
    Earl of Castle Stewart (deceased)   (1923–1944)
                              ├ Arthur Patrick Avondale Stuart
                              │ Earl of Castle Stewart   ┌ Andrew Charles Richard, Viscount Stuart
                              │ (b. 1928) ——————   └ Lady Bridget Stuart
                              │ *m.* Edna Fowler
                              └ Simon Walter Erskine Stuart ┌ Thomas Stuart
                                (b. 1930) ——————   ├ Corin Edmund Stuart
                                m. Deborah Mounsey   └ Tristram Stuart

— 2—
Gertrude R. Guggenheim
(1898–1966)

— 3—
Barbara Josephine Guggenheim ┌ Peter O. Lawson-Johnston   ┌ Wendy Lawson-Johnston
(b. 1904)   │ (b. 1927) —————   │ (b. 1952)
m. (1) John R. Lawson-Johnston── *m.* Dorothy Hammond   │ *m.* Thomas Kerney McNeil
m. (2) Fred E. Wettach, Jr. ┐   │ ——————————— Thomas Kerney McNe
m. (3) Henry Obre   │   │   (b. 1977)
                                └ Michael F. Wettach   ├ Tania Lawson-Johnston
                                  (b. 1931)   │ (b. 1954)
                                                             │ *m.* Mark Tassie
                                                             │ ——————————— Brogan Erin Tassie
                                                             │   (b. 1976)
                                                             ├ Peter O. Lawson-Johnston, Jr.
                                                             │ (b. 1957)
                                                             └ Mary Lawson-Johnston
                                                               (b. 1967)

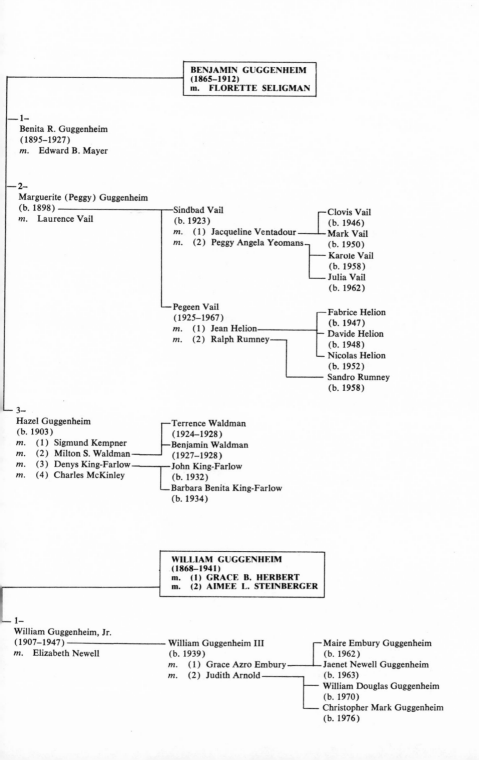

**BENJAMIN GUGGENHEIM
(1865–1912)
m. FLORETTE SELIGMAN**

—1—
Benita R. Guggenheim
(1895–1927)
m. Edward B. Mayer

—2—
Marguerite (Peggy) Guggenheim
(b. 1898) ————————— Sindbad Vail
m. Laurence Vail (b. 1923)
                       m. (1) Jacqueline Ventadour ——— Clovis Vail
                       m. (2) Peggy Angela Yeomans (b. 1946)
                                           Mark Vail
                                           (b. 1950)
                                           Karole Vail
                                           (b. 1958)
                                           Julia Vail
                                           (b. 1962)

                     Pegeen Vail
                     (1925–1967)
                     m. (1) Jean Helion ——— Fabrice Helion
                     m. (2) Ralph Rumney (b. 1947)
                                           Davide Helion
                                           (b. 1948)
                                           Nicolas Helion
                                           (b. 1952)
                                           Sandro Rumney
                                           (b. 1958)

—3—
Hazel Guggenheim
(b. 1903)   Terrence Waldman
m. (1) Sigmund Kempner (1924–1928)
m. (2) Milton S. Waldman ——— Benjamin Waldman
m. (3) Denys King-Farlow (1927–1928)
m. (4) Charles McKinley ——— John King-Farlow
                                           (b. 1932)
                     Barbara Benita King-Farlow
                     (b. 1934)

**WILLIAM GUGGENHEIM
(1868–1941)
m. (1) GRACE B. HERBERT
m. (2) AIMEE L. STEINBERGER**

—1—
William Guggenheim, Jr.
(1907–1947) ——————— William Guggenheim III
m. Elizabeth Newell (b. 1939)
                     m. (1) Grace Azro Embury ——— Maire Embury Guggenheim
                     m. (2) Judith Arnold (b. 1962)
                                             Jaenet Newell Guggenheim
                                           (b. 1963)
                                           William Douglas Guggenheim
                                           (b. 1970)
                                           Christopher Mark Guggenheim
                                         (b. 1976)

THE GUGGENHEIMS

GENEALOGICAL TABLE

(NUMBER 3)

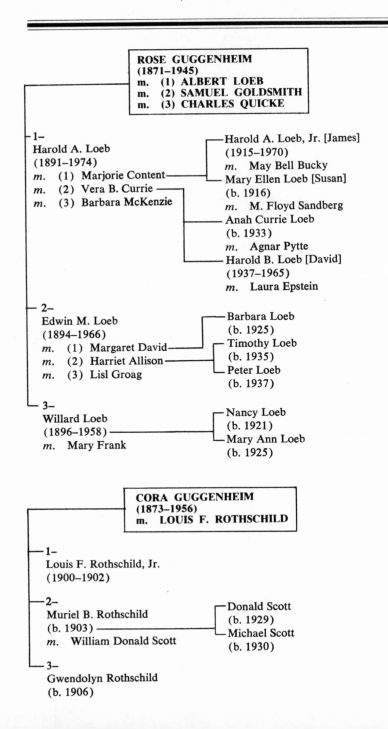

**ROSE GUGGENHEIM
(1871–1945)
m. (1) ALBERT LOEB
m. (2) SAMUEL GOLDSMITH
m. (3) CHARLES QUICKE**

–1–
Harold A. Loeb
(1891–1974)
m.   (1) Marjorie Content
m.   (2) Vera B. Currie
m.   (3) Barbara McKenzie

Harold A. Loeb, Jr. [James]
(1915–1970)
m.   May Bell Bucky
Mary Ellen Loeb [Susan]
(b. 1916)
m.   M. Floyd Sandberg
Anah Currie Loeb
(b. 1933)
m.   Agnar Pytte
Harold B. Loeb [David]
(1937–1965)
m.   Laura Epstein

–2–
Edwin M. Loeb
(1894–1966)
m.   (1) Margaret David
m.   (2) Harriet Allison
m.   (3) Lisl Groag

Barbara Loeb
(b. 1925)
Timothy Loeb
(b. 1935)
Peter Loeb
(b. 1937)

–3–
Willard Loeb
(1896–1958)
m.   Mary Frank

Nancy Loeb
(b. 1921)
Mary Ann Loeb
(b. 1925)

**CORA GUGGENHEIM
(1873–1956)
m. LOUIS F. ROTHSCHILD**

–1–
Louis F. Rothschild, Jr.
(1900–1902)

–2–
Muriel B. Rothschild
(b. 1903)
m.   William Donald Scott

Donald Scott
(b. 1929)
Michael Scott
(b. 1930)

–3–
Gwendolyn Rothschild
(b. 1906)

NOTES AND SOURCES

*(For complete publishing information
consult the Bibliography)*

PROLOGUE

A GUGGENHEIM WILL

1. Last will and testament of Harry F. Guggenheim, dated March 12, 1970, first codicil, dated May 8, 1970, was given to the author by Mr. George Fountaine, formerly administrative assistant to Harry F. Guggenheim, now administrative assistant to Peter O. Lawson-Johnston, senior partner of Guggenheim Brothers.

2. After Guggenheim Brothers sold two million shares of their Chile Copper Company to the Anaconda Company for $70 million in 1923, the Guggenheims' collective wealth was variously estimated as being anywhere from $200 million to $500 million (the *Encyclopaedia Judaica* put it at $500 million, a grossly exaggerated figure). What is known for certain is that in addition to the $70 million from the sale to Anaconda, they still held stock in Chile Copper worth around $33 million, stock in Kennecott Copper and other domestic copper producers worth approximately $100 million, and miscellaneous assets, including stock in American Smelting and Refining, diamond mines in the Belgian Congo and Angola, and real estate and works of art, worth another $50 million, giving the seven brothers and two surviving sisters, and several of their children, a total worth of around $253 million in 1923. Although the paper value of these assets undoubtedly increased during the bull market of the late twenties, I doubt if the Guggenheims' collective wealth ever exceeded this sum by very much. Certainly I do not think it ever exceeded $300 million. Still the size of the fortune was substantial enough to make it the largest ever amassed by a Jewish family in America. In terms of the relative purchasing power of the U.S. dollar in 1923 and 1976, calculated on the basis of the consumer price index for those years, the fortune was worth nearly 850 million 1976 dollars in 1923, probably a lot more when one considers that on an annual income of around $600,000 in 1921 Isaac Guggenheim was

able to afford over one hundred servants and groundskeepers at his $2 million Long Island estate.

It is more difficult to state authoritatively that the Guggenheims' fortune is the largest private fortune ever made from mining and metallurgy in history, but it appears reasonably certain that it was. Cecil Rhodes, who also made a huge fortune from mining, left only £6 million (about $27 million) in 1902. Simon Patiño (1862–1947), the Bolivian tin mine owner, was reputed to have been worth around $100 million in 1925, or less than half of what the Guggenheims were worth at the time. It is not known how much he left to his heirs in 1947, but the amount is thought to approach the Guggenheims' collective wealth. Sources: for the Guggenheims: archives of Guggenheim Brothers, 120 Broadway, New York, hereafter referred to as GB; Moody's Industrials, 1910–1927; Federal Trade Commission, *Report on the Copper Industry, Part II, Concentration and Control by Three Dominant Companies,* Washington, 1947; O'Connor, Parsons, and Baruch. For Rhodes and Patiño: Sir Sidney Lee, ed., *The Dictionary of National Biography* (January, 1901–December, 1911), Oxford, Oxford University Press, 1912; Anne Rothe, ed., *Current Biography,* New York, H. W. Wilson, 1947.

3. The discussion of Harry F. Guggenheim and his last years is based chiefly on the author's conversations on numerous occasions throughout 1975, 1976, and 1977, with Harry's nephew, Roger W. Straus, Jr.; Harry's former secretary and administrative assistant, George Fountaine; his cousin and principal heir, Peter O. Lawson-Johnston; his former lawyer, Leo Gottlieb; former Guggenheim Brothers partner, Albert E. Thiele; daughter Joan Van de Maele; and Phyllis Braff, curator of fine arts at the Nassau County Museum and presently in charge of Harry's former Long Island estate, Falaise. Additional material on Harry has been drawn from Harry's own writings in the archives of Guggenheim Brothers, his *Newsday* Policy Papers, his obituary in *The New York Times,* January 23, 1971, and from Lomask.

Harry F. Guggenheim's office memorandum "to the Partners of Guggenheim Brothers," February 16, 1959, was given to the author by George Fountaine.

4. The letter from Harry F. Guggenheim to Nancy Draper is quoted in Hoyt, page 347.

5. The description of the Partners' Room and offices of Guggenheim Brothers, 120 Broadway, New York, is based on the author's personal observations during numerous visits throughout 1975, 1976, and 1977.

I

MEYER AND BARBARA
1828–1905
FOUNDING AN AMERICAN DYNASTY

1 / OUT OF THE GHETTO

1. The description of Lengnau is based on impressions of the village the author received during a visit in April, 1975.

2. Most of the information on the Jews and the Guggenheims in Switzerland was derived from conversations with Mr. Jacques Oppenheim of Lengnau, president of the Society for the Preservation of the Endigen-Lengnau Synagogues and Cemetery, and Dr. Florence Guggenheim-Grunberg of Zurich, historian of the Jews in Switzerland and of the Guggenheims before they emigrated to the United States. Mr. Oppenheim allowed the author to consult the All-Families Book of the cantonal records of Lengnau in which the births, marriages, and deaths of the Swiss Guggenheims are registered. He also brought the author to the Schweizerisches Israelitisches Alterasyl. Dr. Guggenheim-Grunberg, who has thoroughly researched the Guggenheims' origins in Switzerland, discussed with the author in April, 1975, her article on the subject, *Die Lengnauer Vorfahren der Kupfer-Guggenheim in Amerika,* which appeared in the *Israelitisch Wochenblatt* on August 7, 1953.

3. Background on the Jews in Switzerland was derived from Guggenheim-Grunberg, *Die Juden in der Schweiz,* Zurich, Verlag Judische Buch-Gemeinde, 1961, and from O'Connor and Lomask.

2 / THE HAVEN CITY

1. The only source for the story of the Guggenheims' and the Meyers' voyage to America and subsequent settlement in Philadelphia is William Guggenheim's autobiography. His account is apparently based on stories his father and mother told him.

2. Background on Philadelphia in the mid-nineteenth century is derived principally from Struthers Burt, *Philadelphia—Holy Experiment,* New York, Doubleday, 1945.

3. Most of the information on the Guggenheims' and Meyers' first years in Philadelphia is derived from Williams, O'Connor, and Marcosson. O'Connor researched the two families' frequent changes of business and home addresses. Williams provides a firsthand account of Guggenheim business and family life in Philadelphia in the 1870s and 1880s. Marcosson interviewed Solomon R. Guggenheim on the subject for *Metal Magic.*

4. It is uncertain how many Guggenheims and Meyers emigrated from Switzerland to the United States in 1847. According to O'Connor, Rachel Meyer brought all her seven children with her, three sons and four daughters. However, only three of these have been identified from Philadelphia records: Barbara, who married Meyer Guggenheim, and Lehman and Benjamin. According to the All-Families Book of Lengnau, Simon Guggenheim (1792–1869) had six children: Vugeli, b. 1824, Babbetta, b. 1825, Rachel, b. 1826, Meyer, b. 1828, Rebecca, b. 1829, Zirreler, b. 1832. Of these only Rachel, Meyer, Rebecca, and Zirreler show up in Philadelphia records.

It is not known what happened to Barbara Meyer's brothers and sisters and Meyer Guggenheim's sisters. No living member of the Guggenheim family has any knowledge of them and there are no family records of them. Since Meyer left $10,000 in his will to a "nephew" named Leon Beyle, it is assumed one of his sisters married a man by the name of Beyle. A search for Beyle's descendants, however, has proved fruitless.

Some Swiss relatives of the American Guggenheims have been positively identified. Simon Guggenheim had a brother, Daniel Guggenheim, who remained in Switzerland and fathered nine children. A great-grandson of Daniel's, Felix Guggenheim, born in 1897, is a retired businessman living in St. Gallen, and is aware he is distantly related to the American Guggenheims. Sources: All-Families Book, Lengnau, and letter to the author from Felix Guggenheim, May 24, 1976.

3 / ROASTED PIGEONS DO NOT FLY INTO ONE'S MOUTH

1. The portraits of Meyer and Barbara Guggenheim are derived almost wholly from Williams. A few embellishments on Meyer were provided by Peggy Guggenheim and Gladys Guggenheim Straus, both of whom remember him. The quotations are from Williams.

2. The account of Meyer Guggenheim's early business ventures is derived from Williams, O'Connor, and Marcosson.

4 / BONANZA IN COLORADO

1. The Shakespeare quotation is from *Julius Caesar.*

2. The story of Meyer Guggenheim's mining ventures in Colorado, subsequent reorganization of M. Guggenheim's Sons, entry into the smelting business, and expansion into Mexico is derived from Williams (William Guggenheim participated in most of these events), O'Connor, Marcosson, and documents pertaining to the A. Y. and Minnie mines the author consulted in the Western History Room, Denver Public Library, and the Colorado Historical Society, Denver. A most detailed and comprehensive account of this period is contained in Hoyt. Hoyt claims to have checked all the pertinent records in Leadville and Denver.

5 / THE CONQUEST OF MEXICO

1. The account of the Guggenheims' early ventures in Mexico is derived principally from Williams (William Guggenheim erected the family's first two smelters in Mexico). Further information was derived from Marcosson, O'Connor, and Bernstein. Bernstein has a complete bibliography of the Mexican mining industry from 1890 to 1950.

6 / STRUGGLE FOR POWER

1. The account of the struggle for control of the American Smelting and Refining Company (ASARCO) is derived principally from Marcosson, historian of ASARCO. Additional information comes from O'Connor and GB.

7 / THE GOOGS OF NEW YORK

1. The account of the Guggenheims' move to New York is related in Williams.

2. The Sidney Fisher quotation is taken from Burt.

3. The account of the Seligman-Hilton affair is related in Birmingham.

4. Information on the Guggenheims' first decade in New York, and their gradual penetration into New York's German-Jewish elite is drawn from Williams, Loeb, Peggy Guggenheim, *Out of This Century,* O'Connor, and Birmingham.

5. Barbara Guggenheim's death, the effect it had on the family, and the charities it gave rise to, are related in Williams.

8 / DEATH OF A PATRIARCH

1. The account of the declining years of Meyer Guggenheim is derived principally from Williams and O'Connor (William Guggenheim lived with his father during those years; O'Connor interviewed three of Meyer's sons). Peggy Guggenheim and Gladys Guggenheim Straus have provided some reminiscences.

2. The account of William Guggenheim's marriage to Grace Brown Herbert, and their divorce, is derived wholly from O'Connor and from articles in *The New York Times,* November 1, 1908, and July 17, 1913. The matter is not mentioned in Williams.

3. The account of Hanna McNamara's suit against Meyer Guggenheim is derived from O'Connor, and Peggy Guggenheim, *Out of This Century.*

4. The last will and testament of Meyer Guggenheim, signed by him on July 5, 1904, was obtained from the archives of the Surrogate's Court, County of New York. Details of the settlement of Meyer's estate were reported in *The New York Times,* July 1, 1905.

5. The description of the Schweizerisches Israelitisches Alterasyl is based on the author's observations of that institution during a visit to Lengnau in April, 1975. The author assisted at the discussion which closes the chapter. Some information on the Alterasyl is derived from *50 Jahre Schweizerisches Israelitisches Alterasyl, Lengnau, 1903–1953,* Zurich, Buchdrukerei Neumann, 1953.

II

LORDS OF THE EARTH
1905–1923
BUILDING THE GUGGENHEIM EMPIRE

1 / ON THEIR OWN

1. The opening portraits of Meyer and his sons are derived principally from Williams, with some embellishments drawn from O'Connor, Marcosson, and Hammond.

2. The characterization of Daniel Guggenheim is based on Williams, Hammond, Marcosson, and Baruch.

3. The account of John Hays Hammond's association with the Guggenheims is derived from Hammond and O'Connor.

2 / GUGGENMORGANS AND MORGANHEIMS

1. Most of the account of the Guggenheims' ventures in Alaska, in association with J. P. Morgan, is derived from O'Connor, who interviewed the surviving brothers active in the business—Solomon, Murry, and Simon—in 1936.

2. Arnold Bratnober's account of the meeting between Daniel Guggenheim and J. P. Morgan was reported in Henry Alloway, "Guggenheim, Scientist of Big Business," *The Wall Street Journal*, September 27, 1930.

3. Background on Alaska prior to the arrival of the Guggenheim-Morgan Alaska Syndicate is derived from Alberto Ronchey, *La Crisi Americana*, Milano, Garzanti, 1975.

4. The cartoons on the Guggenheims and J. P. Morgan in Alaska appeared in the Minneapolis *Journal* and *The Best of Art Young*, New York, Vanguard Press.

5. The story of the mining of Kennecott Mountain is derived from Fred Rockwood and The Boston Consulting Group, "Formation of the Ken-

necott Copper Corp.," Boston, July 15, 1974 (unpublished report for Kennecott Copper containing a detailed section on the Guggenheims entitled "The Guggenheim Copper Interests"). Some embellishments are from O'Connor.

6. The Ballinger-Pinchot controversy over the exploitation of Alaska's natural resources is derived from Federal Trade Commission, *Report on the Copper Industry, Part II, Concentration and Control by Three Dominant Companies,* Washington, D.C., 1947, and from O'Connor.

3 / MINING THE GLOBE

1. The Guggenheims' worldwide mining ventures are related in Marcosson, O'Connor, Parsons, and Rockwood, "Formation."

2. John Hays Hammond related the episode on page 111 in his auto-biography.

3. Albert E. Thiele, partner of Guggenheim Brothers and former secretary and special assistant to Solomon R. Guggenheim, gave the author a full account of the Guggenheims' mining activities in the Belgian Congo, Angola, and Chile during three interviews held in East Hampton, Long Island, in July, 1975.

4 / HARVEST OF WAR

1. The account of the business activities of the Guggenheims during World War I is drawn from GB, Marcosson, O'Connor, and Parsons. The quotations of Daniel and Isaac Guggenheim are from O'Connor.

2. The estimate of the Guggenheims' net worth of from $200 million to $300 million after World War I is based on the family's holdings in Utah Copper, Chile Copper, Kennecott Copper, and American Smelting and Refining in 1920, documented in GB and reported by O'Connor. By the end of 1923 the value of the Guggenheims' holdings was, as reported in the notes to the Prologue, about $253 million.

3. Henry Ford's attack on the Guggenheims is reported in O'Connor and Birmingham.

5 / THE GREAT SCHISM

1. William Guggenheim's suit against his brothers over Chile Copper is documented in testimony and depositions in *Guggenheim v. Guggenheim* (court papers are on file in GB), in GB, and in *The New York Times* throughout 1916. The 1893 partnership agreement of M. Guggenheim's Sons is also in GB. In an interview in January, 1977, Mrs. William J. Broadhurst (formerly Mrs. William Guggenheim, Jr.) stated that she had heard that William senior received "about five millions" in settlement.

2. Daniel Guggenheim's retirement from his position in American Smelting and Refining and the accession of Simon Guggenheim to the presidency of the company is reported in O'Connor and Marcosson.

3. Details on the sale of Chile Copper to the Anaconda Company in 1923 are on file in GB.

4. The wealth of the Guggenheims at the time of the sale is discussed in the notes to the Prologue.

III

SEVEN BROTHERS AND TWO HUNDRED FIFTY MILLIONS
1918–1959
ON THE USES OF WEALTH

1 / A FORTUNE TO SPEND

1. Information on William Guggenheim's estate at Sands Point comes from Mrs. William J. Broadhurst (formerly Mrs. William Guggenheim, Jr.).

2. Information on Isaac's estate at Sands Point, Villa Carola, later Solomon's Trillora Court, comes from Kenneth Gross, "IBM's School for Success," *Newsday*, July 13, 1975, and interviews with Mr. Chauncey Newlin, Solomon Guggenheim's former attorney, and Mrs. Henry Obre (née Barbara Guggenheim).

3. Information on Hempstead House was provided by Miss Phyllis Braff, fine arts curator of the Nassau County Museum, current owner of Hempstead House.

2 / ISAAC: ON DAUGHTERING OUT

1. The characterization of Isaac Guggenheim is based on Williams and Baruch. O'Connor reported Isaac's nervous breakdown over Nipissing, his persuading William Spiegelberg, Jr., to change his name to Isaac Guggenheim II, and the settlement of his estate.

2. Information on Isaac's daughters and their families was given the author by Isaac's great granddaughter, Miss Iris C. Love, in an interview held on January 11, 1976.

3. Information on Isaac's Sands Point estate, Villa Carola, was drawn from Gross, "IBM's School for Success," interviews with IBM personnel on the estate, and reminiscences of Solomon Guggenheim's daughters Eleanor Castle Stewart and Barbara Obre.

4. Chauncey Newlin of White and Case, former attorney for Solomon R. Guggenheim, told the author the story of Isaac having been turned down for membership in the Sands Point Bath and Golf Club.

5. The description of Isaac's estate is based on the author's impressions during a visit in July, 1975.

6. Some information on Isaac Guggenheim's life and death is drawn from Isaac's obituary in *The New York Times*, October 17, 1922.

3 / DANIEL AND FLORENCE: A FIRST STEP INTO SPACE

1. The characterization of Daniel Guggenheim is based essentially on Baruch, Hammond, and Williams, and contemporary newspaper articles. Daniel's daughter, Mrs. Gladys Guggenheim Straus, has supplied some reminiscences.

2. Information on Daniel Guggenheim's life is drawn from Baruch, O'Connor, Williams, and his obituary in *The New York Times*, September 29, 1930.

3. Information on Daniel Guggenheim's financial support of aviation and rocketry is drawn from Cleveland, Emme, Harry F. Guggenheim, *The Seven Skies,* Goddard and Pendray, Hallion, Lehman, Lomask, and from Phyllis Braff, "A Chronology of the Guggenheim-Goddard Relationship," unpublished paper for use in Nassau County museum system.

4. Daniel Guggenheim's remarks on pages 153–154 are reported in O'Connor.

5. Information on Daniel Guggenheim's Long Island estate, Hempstead House, is from Miss Phyllis Braff, under whose supervision the estate is now managed. Description of the estate is based on the author's impressions of it during several visits in 1975, 1976, and 1977.

6. Letter of Daniel Guggenheim to Harry F. Guggenheim quoted on page 157 is dated April 12, 1911, and is on file at GB.

7. History of the Daniel and Florence Guggenheim Foundation is drawn from *Report of the President, 1961,* The Daniel and Florence Guggenheim Foundation, New York (unpublished report under the presidency of Harry F. Guggenheim), and *Report of the President, 1974,* The Daniel and Florence Guggenheim Foundation, New York, 1974 (unpublished report on the fiftieth anniversary of the foundation, under the presidency of Mrs. Gladys Guggenheim Straus), and from Lomask.

8. Details of the life and work of Robert H. Goddard are drawn from Goddard and Pendray, and Lehman.

9. Description of Daniel Guggenheim's funeral as reported in *The New York Times*, October 1, 1930. Details of the settlement of Daniel

Guggenheim's estate reported in *The New York Times*, October 4, 1930. Further information on the settlement of his estate from Mr. Chauncey Newlin of White and Case.

10. The use of Hempstead House after Daniel's death as a home for British war orphans was reported in an article in *Life* magazine, July 22, 1940. Information on subsequent uses of Hempstead House was supplied by Miss Phyllis Braff.

4 / MURRY AND LEONIE: CHILEAN NITRATES AND THE CHILDREN OF NEW YORK

1. The characterization of Murry Guggenheim is based on Baruch, Lomask, O'Connor, and Williams.

2. Information on Murry's life is drawn principally from Lomask, and from Murry's obituary in *The New York Times*, November 16, 1939.

3. Murry's trusts for Edmond and Lucille are reported in O'Connor and Lomask. Further information on Murry's immediate family comes from Hoyt, O'Connor, and from Mrs. Edmond A. Guggenheim.

4. Most of the information on the Murry and Leonie Guggenheim Foundation and Dental Clinic comes from Lomask and Mrs. Edmond A. Guggenheim.

5. Murry's business activities, and specifically his involvement with Chilean nitrates, are reported in considerable detail in Hoyt, Lomask, and O'Connor.

6. Information on Edmond A. Guggenheim was given to the author by Mrs. Edmond A. Guggenheim in letters dated May 30, 1976, and June 26, 1976.

7. Donations of the Murry and Leonie Guggenheim Foundation to the Mount Sinai Medical Center were reported to the author in a letter from Milton Seldin, director of public information at Mount Sinai Medical Center, January 26, 1977. In his letter Mr. Seldin stated that the Murry and Leonie Guggenheim Memorial Endowment at Mount Sinai was "the largest contribution ever received in the 125-year history of the Mount Sinai Hospital."

5 / SOLOMON'S SECOND SPRING

1. Most of the characterizations of Solomon R. Guggenheim and Hilla Rebay, and information on the Guggenheim-Rebay relationship are derived from interviews conducted throughout 1975 and 1976, and part of 1977, with members of the Guggenheim and Rebay families and people who were associated with them, and from the Hilla von Rebay Foundation archives in New York (hereafter referred to as HR). The following persons were interviewed: Solomon R. Guggenheim's two

surviving daughters, Mrs. Henry Obre (Barbara Guggenheim) and Lady Castle Stewart (Eleanor Guggenheim), Solomon's two American grandsons, Peter O. Lawson-Johnston and Michael Wettach, Solomon's niece and grandnephew, Gladys Guggenheim Straus and Roger W. Straus, Jr., Thomas M. Messer, director of the Guggenheim Museum, Chauncey Newlin, former attorney for Solomon Guggenheim, Albert E. Thiele, former secretary and administrative assistant to Solomon Guggenheim, James Johnson Sweeney, former director of the Guggenheim Museum, Francis P. Schiarolli, senior partner of Cummings and Lockwood and trustee of the Hilla von Rebay Foundation, Baron Franz Hugo Rebay, brother of Hilla Rebay, and Dr. Roland Rebay, nephew of Hilla Rebay.

2. Details of the first meeting between Solomon R. Guggenheim and Hilla Rebay are from Barbara Obre.

3. Details of the first meeting between Solomon Guggenheim and Wassily Kandinsky are reported in Lomask.

4. Biographical information on Hilla Rebay is drawn from the curriculum vitae of Hilla Rebay on file in HR, and from interviews with Baron Franz Hugo Rebay and Dr. Roland Rebay at Wessling-am-See, West Germany, in August, 1976.

5. Instances of Solomon R. Guggenheim's free spending on page 203 were given to the author in an interview with Barbara Obre, and in a letter from Hazel Guggenheim McKinley.

6. Solomon's advice to his nephews is reported in Lomask.

7. Hilla Rebay's essay on nonobjective art, "New Age," is on file at HR.

8. All letters of Hilla Rebay, Rudolf Bauer, Solomon Guggenheim, and Irene Guggenheim quoted or referred to are on file at HR.

9. Remarks by art critics on Hilla Rebay's catalogues and shows are reported in Lomask. Some are on file at HR.

10. That Hilla Rebay was in love with Rudolf Bauer is documented by correspondence between Hilla and Bauer on file at HR.

11. The article on Hilla in *Palm Beach Life* is at HR.

12. The story of Hilla Rebay and Franz Hugo Rebay aiding Bauer to escape from the Nazis was told to the author by Franz Hugo Rebay and Roland Rebay at Wessling-am-See, in August, 1976.

13. An account of the Hilla Rebay-Rudolf Bauer conflict is given in Lomask.

14. Hilla Rebay's difficulties with the FBI during World War II were related to the author by Mr. Chauncey Newlin of White and Case, Solomon Guggenheim's lawyer at the time, and Francis P. Schiarolli of Cummings and Lockwood, Hilla Rebay's former lawyer and ex-

ecutor of her estate. It was Mr. Newlin who told the author that Solomon Guggenheim went to President Roosevelt on the matter.

15. Solomon Guggenheim's letter to Attorney General Francis Biddle, dated February 12, 1943, is on file at HR.

16. Most of the information on Frank Lloyd Wright is derived from Frank Lloyd Wright's own writings collected in Edgar Kaufmann and Ben Raeburn, *Frank Lloyd Wright—Writings and Buildings*, New York, New American Library, 1960.

17. Correspondence between Frank Lloyd Wright and Hilla Rebay and Solomon Guggenheim is on file at HR, GB, and the Solomon R. Guggenheim Foundation, New York, hereafter referred to as SRG.

18. Solomon Guggenheim's declaration of faith in nonobjective art and his projected museum was written in April, 1949, and is on file at HR.

19. Solomon R. Guggenheim's last will and testament, dated November 3, 1949, was given to the author by Mr. Chauncey Newlin of White and Case.

20. The summary of securities willed to Hilla Rebay is given in a memorandum dated January 7, 1949, on file at HR.

6 / KING SOLOMON'S MUSEUM

1. Details of the conflict between Harry F. Guggenheim and Hilla Rebay are drawn from letters and memoranda on file at HR.

2. Mr. Chauncey A. Newlin of White and Case, Solomon Guggenheim's former attorney, and Mr. Francis P. Schiarolli, Hilla Rebay's former attorney, provided the author with information on Hilla's retaliatory confiscation of paintings and sculptures loaned to her by Solomon R. Guggenheim.

3. Details of the relationship between Harry F. Guggenheim and Frank Lloyd Wright and their efforts to realize the building of the Solomon R. Guggenheim Museum are drawn from the Frank Lloyd Wright historical file, SRG. Frank Lloyd Wright, in a letter to Harry Guggenheim dated December 27, 1958, declared that their letters would one day be read "in every school and museum in the world." Reacting to this assertion, Harry collected some seven hundred letters he and Mr. Wright had written to each other and commissioned Miss Mamie Schweppenheiser to arrange them in four leather-bound volumes, index them, and place them in a vault in the museum's archives.

4. Further information on the realization of the museum is drawn from SRG, HR, Wright, Caso, and from Solomon R. Guggenheim's scrapbook located in the Archives of American Art, 41 East 65 Street, New York.

5. James Johnson Sweeney discussed his conflict with Frank Lloyd Wright in an interview with the author held on January 13, 1976.

6. Description of the gala opening of the museum and press reactions to the museum are drawn from SRG, HR, and Lomask.

7. Details of the settlement of the dispute between Hilla Rebay and the Guggenheim Museum and of the settlement of Hilla Rebay's estate are from Chauncey A. Newlin and Francis P. Schiarolli. Mr. Schiarolli gave the author the last will and testament of Hilla Rebay, dated July 18, 1967.

8. Information on Hilla's relatives and legatees in Germany came from an interview with Baron Franz Hugo Rebay and Dr. Roland Rebay in Wessling-am-See, in August, 1976.

7 / BENJAMIN: ON DROPPING OUT, PART I

1. Description of the portrait of Benjamin in the Partners' Room of Guggenheim Brothers is based on the author's first visit to Guggenheim Brothers in July, 1975.

2. Details of the life and career of Benjamin Guggenheim are from Peggy Guggenheim, *Confessions of an Art Addict,* and *Out of This Century,* and from Loeb, Lomask, O'Connor, and Williams, with some reminiscences supplied in letters to the author from Hazel Guggenheim McKinley and in interviews with Peggy Guggenheim conducted in Venice in May, 1975, and September, 1976.

3. Description of Benjamin's townhouse in New York and portrait of the Seligman family from Peggy Guggenheim, *Out of This Century.*

4. Most of the details of the *Titanic* disaster are taken from Walter Lord, *A Night to Remember,* New York, Holt, Rinehart & Winston, 1955. The story of Benjamin's wife and daughters first hearing of the tragedy was given the author in correspondence with Hazel Guggenheim McKinley.

5. Details of the settlement of Benjamin Guggenheim's estate were related to the author by Peggy Guggenheim in an interview with her held in Venice in September, 1976.

8 / SENATOR SIMON, OR DEMOCRACY IN AMERICA

1. The celebration of Simon Guggenheim's election to the U.S. Senate in Denver's Brown Palace was described in *The Denver Post,* January 16 and 17, 1907.

2. Information on how Simon Guggenheim was elected to the U.S. Senate is derived from articles in the T. F. Dawson scrapbooks, Colorado Historical Society, Denver, articles in *The Denver Post* throughout December, 1906, and January, 1907, and from O'Connor.

3. Reactions to Simon Guggenheim's election to the U.S. Senate and the summary of his Senate career are derived from articles in *The Denver Post* throughout Simon's term of office—1907–1913—and from Hoyt, Lomask, and O'Connor.

9 / ALL SIMON'S SONS

1. The suicide of George Denver Guggenheim was reported in *The New York Times* on November 10, 1939. Other details on the suicide, and on the personality of George Denver, were given to the author by Gladys Guggenheim Straus, M. Robert Guggenheim, Jr., and Mr. James F. Mathias, vice-president of the John Simon Guggenheim Memorial Foundation.

2. Details of Simon Guggenheim's early life and career are from Loeb and Williams.

3. The story of the creation of the John Simon Guggenheim Memorial Foundation is derived from interviews with Gordon N. Ray, president of the foundation, James F. Mathias, vice-president, Peach and Reeves, and from Betty Gerstein, Mary A. Judge, and Mary Ellis Woodring, eds., "Reports of the President and Treasurer," John Simon Guggenheim Memorial Foundation, New York, 1975 (the fiftieth anniversary).

4. Simon Guggenheim's 1925 letter of gift to the John Simon Guggenheim Memorial Foundation and the charter, constitution, and bylaws of the foundation are on file at the John Simon Guggenheim Memorial Foundation in New York, hereafter referred to as JSGM.

5. Information on Guggenheim fellows who have received the Nobel Prize, the Pulitzer Prize, and the National Book Award was given to the author by Mr. James F. Mathias, vice-president of the foundation.

6. The statements of appreciation by Mrs. Stephen Vincent Benét, Gian Carlo Menotti, Katherine Anne Porter, and Willard F. Libby are quoted in Peach and Reeves.

7. The other statements of appreciation were given the author in letters as follows: Aaron Copland, October 20, 1975; John Kenneth Galbraith, November 4, 1975; Linus Pauling, October 30, 1975; Alfred Kazin, October 18, 1975.

8. The quotations of Henry Allen Moe are from Lomask and Peach and Reeves.

9. The story of Hart Crane's year on a Guggenheim fellowship is derived from John Unterecker, *Voyager: A Life of Hart Crane*, New York, Farrar, Straus & Giroux, 1969.

10. The story of the rejection of Arnold Schoenberg for a Guggenheim fellowship comes from James F. Mathias.

11. The rejections of Gore Vidal and Truman Capote are reported in Gore Vidal, *Matters of Fact and Fiction*, New York, Random House, 1977.

12. The story of the rejection of Henry Miller is told in Henry Miller, *The Air-Conditioned Nightmare,* New York, New Directions, 1945.

13. Roger W. Straus, Jr., a trustee of the John Simon Guggenheim Memorial Foundation, told the author the reason why Miller was rejected in an interview in September, 1975.

14. Henry Allen Moe's remarks on "grubstaking" are quoted in Peach and Reeves.

15. Simon Guggenheim's second letter of gift is on file at JSGM.

16. Information on the deterioration of George Denver Guggenheim and on Simon Guggenheim's mistresses was given the author by Gladys Guggenheim Straus, Peggy Guggenheim, M. Robert Guggenheim, Jr., and Roger W. Straus, Jr.

17. Details on Olga Guggenheim's fund for the Museum of Modern Art are taken from Lyon.

18. Information on the Simon Guggenheim Memorial collection, the Denver Art Museum, was given to the author by the museum.

19. Mr. Chauncey Newlin of White & Case, former attorney for Solomon and Simon Guggenheim, claims that Simon's estate was the largest of the seven Guggenheim brothers'.

20. Information on finances of the John Simon Guggenheim Memorial Foundation comes from James F. Mathias and JSGM.

21. Details on congressional investigations of the John Simon Guggenheim Memorial Foundation come from the reports of the president and treasurer for 1967 and 1968, compiled and edited by Mary Ellis Woodring and Susan Park Norton, and from Peach and Reeves, Lomask, and JSGM.

22. Professor Brand Blanshard's remarks on the foundation are quoted in Lomask, p. 248.

10 / WILLIAM, OR GATENBY WILLIAMS: ON DROPPING OUT, PART II

1. The characterization of William Guggenheim is almost wholly derived from his autobiography, referred to throughout this book as Williams.

2. William Guggenheim's marital difficulties are related in O'Connor. Grace Herbert's letter is quoted in O'Connor, p. 149.

3. Details on the personality and life of Aimee Guggenheim were given

the author by her daughter-in-law, Mrs. William J. Broadhurst, formerly Mrs. William Guggenheim, Jr.

4. The story of the last years of William Guggenheim's life is derived from Lomask, O'Connor, Williams, interviews with Mrs. Broadhurst and her son, William Guggenheim III, William Guggenheim's obituary in *The New York Times*, June 28, 1941, and the Associated Press release of June 27, 1941, quoted in the text.

IV

REBELS AND ANGELS
1923–1977
THE FOURTH GENERATION

1 / EMPIRE IN DECLINE

1. This introductory chapter is essentially retrospective and as such the many sources on which it is based have already been cited in the notes to Books I, II, and III.

2 / COLONEL BOB

1. The characterization of M. Robert Guggenheim is derived from interviews with his fourth wife, Mrs. John A. (Polly) Logan, held in Washton, D.C. in September, 1975; with his son, M. Robert Guggenheim, Jr., held in Newport Beach, Cal. in September, 1975, and April, 1977; and with his friend Mr. Robert Woolforth, held in New York, May, 1977. Embellishments were provided by his sister, Gladys Guggenheim Straus, and nephew, Roger W. Straus, Jr.

2. Details of M. Robert Guggenheim's life come from the above sources and O'Connor, Lomask, and contemporary newspaper accounts of his escapades, especially in the Washington and New York newspaper society columns.

3. The descriptions of the yacht *Firenze*, Firenze House in Washington, D.C., and the Poco Sabo plantation were given the author by Polly Logan, M. Robert Guggenheim, Jr., and Robert Woolforth. The author also visited Firenze House in September, 1975.

4. The story of M. Robert Guggenheim's career as U.S. ambassador to Portugal was related to the author by his son, M. Robert Guggenheim, Jr. It is also reported in *Confidential* magazine, September, 1954, and in Lomask.

5. The account of M. Robert Guggenheim's last years comes from Polly Logan and M. Robert Guggenheim, Jr.

6. The description of Firenze House today is based on the author's impressions of the estate during a visit in September, 1975.

7. The story of what happened to the yacht *Firenze* was told to the author by Polly Logan, who visited The South Seas on a trip to Miami.

8. M. Robert Guggenheim, Jr., reported to the author the sale of Firenze House to the Italian government.

3 / AMBASSADOR HARRY: GUGGENADO AND MACHADOHEIM

1. The characterization of Harry F. Guggenheim is a composite drawn from interviews with his sister, Gladys Guggenheim Straus, his nephews Roger W. Straus, Jr., and M. Robert Guggenheim, Jr., and his second cousin Peter O. Lawson-Johnston.

2. The account of Harry F. Guggenheim's career as U.S. ambassador to Cuba was drawn from two principal sources: The Harry Frank Guggenheim Papers, Library of Congress, Washington, D.C., and Kraeutler. (Mr. Kraeutler, who served for a year as researcher for this book, made a complete investigation of Harry Guggenheim's career as U.S. ambassador to Cuba, including an inspection of pertinent records in the archives of the U.S. State Department.)

3. Some illumination of Harry Guggenheim's career in Cuba is derived from Harry F. Guggenheim, *The United States and Cuba*, New York, Macmillan, 1934.

4 / PEGGY: LIBERATED IN EUROPE

1. All the details of Peggy Guggenheim's early life in this chapter were either related to the author by Peggy Guggenheim or drawn from her autobiography, *Out of This Century, The Informal Memoirs of Peggy Guggenheim*. The author's interviews with Miss Guggenheim took place in Venice throughout May, 1975, and September, 1976. Some information may have been gathered during the spring of 1972 when the author lived in Venice and was a frequent guest at Miss Guggenheim's palazzo.

2. Peggy Guggenheim disguised almost all of her characters in *Out of This Century* by giving them fictional names. She revealed their true identities to the author in September, 1976.

5 / PEGGY AND GUGGENHEIM JEUNE

1. Almost all the material in this chapter was derived, as in the preceding chapter, from the author's interviews with Peggy Guggenheim and from *Out of This Century*. A few details were provided by Peggy's sister,

Hazel Guggenheim McKinley, in correspondence, and by Peggy's son, Sindbad Vail, in an interview with the author in Paris, November, 1976.

2. All the quotations of Peggy Guggenheim were taken either from interviews or from *Out of This Century*.

6 / PEGGY IN NEW YORK: ERNST, POLLOCK, AND ART OF THIS CENTURY

1. Most of the information on Peggy Guggenheim's life in this chapter, as in the preceding two, was drawn from interviews with Peggy Guggenheim and from *Out of This Century*. A few details were supplied by Hazel Guggenheim McKinley and Sindbad Vail.

2. Information on Max Ernst comes from John Russell, "The Artistic Legacy of Max Ernst," *International Herald Tribune*, Paris, April 3–4, 1976, and from *Max Ernst: A Retrospective Exhibition*, New York, The Solomon R. Guggenheim Foundation, 1975.

3. Information on Jackson Pollock not given the author by Peggy Guggenheim comes from B. H. Friedman, *Jackson Pollock*, New York, McGraw-Hill, 1972.

4. The story of the Art of This Century gallery is almost wholly derived from Peggy Guggenheim, *Confessions of an Art Addict*. Some details were provided by Hazel Guggenheim McKinley, who visited the gallery and had some of her paintings exhibited in it.

5. Peggy's first cousins Gladys Guggenheim Straus, Eleanor Castle Stewart, and Barbara Obre, told the author how scandalized the Guggenheim family was by *Out of This Century*, and how an effort was made to suppress it.

7 / HAROLD LOEB: *THE WAY IT WAS*

1. The quotations from Ernest Hemingway's *The Sun Also Rises* are from the paperback edition published by Charles Scribner's Sons, New York, 1970.

2. Most of the information on the life of Harold Loeb in this chapter is derived from Loeb's autobiography, *The Way It Was*, hereafter referred to as *Way*. Many details were also supplied by Loeb's widow, Barbara McKenzie Loeb, in an interview with the author in September, 1975, or were taken from Loeb's curriculum vitae, supplied by Mrs. Loeb.

3. Quotations from Harold Loeb's essays "Foreign Exchange" and "The Mysticism of Money" are taken from Harold Loeb, ed., *The Broom Anthology*, Boston, Milford House, 1969.

4. Loeb's reaction to the reception of his autobiography is quoted in "The

Bull, Notes on Princeton University's Class of 1913 47th Reunion" in 1960.

5. Loeb's interpretation of Hemingway's personality comes from Loeb's autobiography and from his article "Hemingway's Bitterness" published in the *Connecticut Review*, Connecticut State College, October, 1967.

8 / GLADYS GUGGENHEIM STRAUS: CARRYING ON

1. The characterization of Gladys Guggenheim Straus is derived from the author's interview with Mrs. Straus in August, 1975, and from interviews with her son, Roger W. Straus, Jr., first cousins Lady Castle Stewart, Barbara Obre, and Peggy Guggenheim, and from Mr. George J. Fountaine of Guggenheim Brothers, who served as secretary and member of the board of the Daniel and Florence Guggenheim Foundation when Mrs. Straus was president of that foundation.

2. Information on the Straus family comes from the official Straus family tree given to the author by Roger W. Straus, Jr.; interviews with Mr. Straus; Geoffrey Hellman, "Straightening Out the Strauses," *The New Yorker*, March 21, 1953, and Madison. According to the official Straus family tree, the American Strauses descend from Lazarus Straus, 1809–1898, of Otterberg in the Rhenish Palatinate, and his second wife and cousin, Sarah Straus, 1823–1876.

3. The description of the marriage of Gladys Guggenheim and Roger W. Straus is derived from *The New York Times*, January 11, 1914. Some embellishments come from O'Connor.

4. Information on Roger W. Straus comes from interviews with Gladys Guggenheim Straus and Roger W. Straus, Jr., and from Marcosson.

5. Descriptions of the benefactions with which Gladys Guggenheim Straus has been associated are given in *Report of the President, 1961*, and *Report of the President, 1974*, of the Daniel and Florence Guggenheim Foundation, New York.

6. The observations of Mrs. Straus on the recent history of the Guggenheim family were given the author during an interview with Mrs. Straus in Greenwich, Connecticut in August, 1975.

9 / THE QUIETER ONES: EDMOND AND WILLIAM, JR.

1. The characterization of Edmond A. Guggenheim and information on his life are derived from Lomask and from letters of Mrs. Edmond A. Guggenheim, dated May 30, 1976, and June 26, 1976. A few details come from his obituary in *The New York Times*, March 15, 1972.

2. The characterization of William Guggenheim, Jr., and all information on his life, comes from the author's interviews with Mrs. William J. Broadhurst, the former Mrs. William Guggenheim, Jr., and with her

son, William Guggenheim III, throughout 1975, 1976, and the first half of 1977.

10 / KING SOLOMON'S DAUGHTERS

1. Information on Eleanor Guggenheim, later Lady Castle Stewart, and her immediate family comes from the author's interviews with her in London, April 2, 1976, and at Nutley, Sussex, December 7, 1976.

2. Information on Barbara Guggenheim, now Mrs. Henry Obre, and her immediate family comes from the author's interview with her in Monkton, Maryland, on September 12, 1975, and from a letter to the author dated June 20, 1976.

3. The description of Old Lodge is derived from the author's impressions of the estate during a visit on December 7, 1976.

4. All quotations are from the interviews above mentioned.

11 / BENJAMIN'S OTHER DAUGHTER

1. The story of the fall of Hazel Guggenheim's two children from the roof of the Surrey is derived from two *New York Times* articles on the subject, dated October 20, 1928, and October 28, 1928, and from interviews with Roger W. Straus, Jr., Dorothea Straus, and Iris Love (from whose mother's roof the children fell).

2. The story of the gathering of the Guggenheim clan over the tragedy and the money that reputedly changed hands is from Dorothea Straus.

3. Information on the life of Hazel Guggenheim McKinley comes from a biographical sketch with reviews of her paintings which Mrs. McKinley gave the author, and from a letter from Mrs. McKinley to the author dated Dec. 31, 1975. All the quotations come from the same letter.

4. Barbara Loeb's remarks at the end of the chapter were made in an interview with the author held in September, 1975.

12 / PEGGY IN VENICE: THE LAST DOGARESSA

1. Description of Peggy Guggenheim's gondola and her gondola trip is derived from the author's impressions during a visit in September, 1976. The author rode with Miss Guggenheim in her gondola at the time.

2. Description of the Palazzo Venier dei Leoni and its garden furnishings and works of art is based on the author's observations during several visits to the palazzo in May, 1975, and September, 1976.

3. Almost all the information on Peggy Guggenheim's life in Venice from 1948 to 1977 is derived from the author's interviews with Miss

Guggenheim in Venice during May, 1975, and September and October, 1976, and with Mr. John D. Hohnsbeen, curator of the Peggy Guggenheim Collection, also during 1976. A few details were taken from *Confessions of an Art Addict.*

4. Information on Pegeen Guggenheim comes from interviews with Peggy Guggenheim and John D. Hohnsbeen in Venice in 1976, and from an interview with Pegeen's brother, Sindbad Vail, in Paris, December, 1976. Many details were also supplied by Peggy's grandson, Nicolas Helion, in September, 1976.

5. Peggy Guggenheim mentioned her affair with Raoul Gregovitch in *Confessions of an Art Addict.* Additional information on him was supplied by Mr. Hohnsbeen.

6. The story of Peggy Guggenheim, Tancredi Parmeggiani, and Pegeen was told to the author by John D. Hohnsbeen, and by Signora Bonna de Pisis, a friend of Peggy Guggenheim's, in Paris, December, 1976, and has been confirmed by four other people the author met in Venice. Some details of the story were related to the author by Sindbad Vail in Paris in December, 1976.

7. Peggy Guggenheim's remarks on modern art were either made to the author during interviews throughout September, 1976, or were taken from her *Confessions of an Art Addict.* The list of top ten modern masters, and top ten Old Masters was given to the author by Miss Guggenheim in September, 1976. The list has since appeared in David Wallechinsky, Irving Wallace, and Amy Wallace, *The Book of Lists,* New York, William Morrow, 1977.

8. Harry Guggenheim's letter to Peggy is quoted in *Confessions of an Art Addict.*

9. Peggy Guggenheim discussed the thefts of her paintings with the author in September, 1976.

10. Harry Guggenheim's statement on page 431 is from *Works from the Peggy Guggenheim Foundation,* New York, The Solomon R. Guggenheim Foundation, 1969.

11. The description of the "Twentycento" exhibition in Paris is from Pierre Cabanne, "Peggy Guggenheim présente son Twentycento," *Paris Match,* December, 1974, and from Jean Legmarie, "Art du xxe Siècle Fondation Peggy Guggenheim, Venise," *Le Petit Journal des Grandes Expositions,* Paris, 30 Novembre, 1974.

12. Alfred H. Barr, Jr.'s accolade is quoted in *Confessions of an Art Addict.*

13. All Peggy Guggenheim's comments toward the end of the chapter were made to the author in Venice during interviews held throughout September and October, 1976.

13 / HARRY THE MAGNIFICENT: THE LEGACIES

1. The characterization of Harry F. Guggenheim and the account of his activities are derived from the author's interviews with the following people: Harry's second cousin and principal heir, Peter O. Lawson-Johnston, and Harry's former administrative assistant, George J. Fountaine (currently executive director of the Harry Frank Guggenheim Foundation), held in July, 1975; Harry's sister, Gladys Guggenheim Straus, held in August, 1975; his nephew, Roger W. Straus, Jr., and his daughter, Joan Van de Maele, in October, 1975; Phyllis Braff, fine arts curator of the Nassau County Museum and coordinator for the historic interpretation of Harry's estate, Falaise, in August, 1975; Albert E. Thiele, partner of Guggenheim Brothers, in August, 1975; Thomas M. Messer, director of the Guggenheim Museum, in October, 1975; Chauncey Newlin, Guggenheim family attorney, August, 1975; Hal Burton, book editor at *Newsday*, January, 1976; and Leo Gottlieb, Harry's former attorney, February, 1976.

2. Many details of Harry Guggenheim's life were taken from "Biographical Information, Harry Frank Guggenheim," a document furnished to the author by George J. Fountaine, and from *The New York Times* obituary of Harry, January 23, 1971.

3. Most of the information on Harry and *Newsday* was given the author by George J. Fountaine, Roger W. Straus, Jr., and Hal Burton. Details on the family and life of Alicia Patterson come from the above-cited interviews and from "Alicia in Wonderland," *Time*, September 13, 1954, and Alicia's obituary in *The New York Times*, July 3, 1963.

4. Harry F. Guggenheim's views on everything from Latin-American relationships to desalinization to wiretapping to President Johnson are contained in his forty-two-page booklet "Policy Papers," *Newsday*, September 6, 1966, revised in 1967.

5. Information about the Harry Frank Guggenheim Foundation is derived from interviews with the foundation's chairman, Peter O. Lawson-Johnston, and executive director and secretary-treasurer, George J. Fountaine, throughout 1975, 1976, and part of 1977, and from "The Man's Relation to Man Program of the Harry Frank Guggenheim Foundation," undated publication of the foundation, and "Report of the Harry Frank Guggenheim Foundation," New York, 1974.

14 / HARRY THE MAGNIFICENT: THE GLORIFICATION

1. The description of the Villa Medicea at Poggio a Caiano is based on the author's impressions during a visit in January, 1965, and *Firenze e Dintorni,* Touring Club Italiano, Milano, 1974.

2. The description of Falaise is based on impressions the author received during visits to the estate in August, 1975, March, 1976, and July,

1977. Some information about the estate was taken from John Hunt, "Falaise," a fifty-six-page descriptive booklet on the estate, undated, prepared at the behest of, and financed by, Harry F. Guggenheim. Much information was provided by Phyllis Braff.

3. The quotation attributed to Lorenzo the Magnificent appears in Hugh Ross Williamson, *Lorenzo the Magnificent*, New York, G. P. Putnam's Sons, 1974.

4. The quotations from Nietzsche are from Walter Kaufmann, *The Portable Nietzsche*, New York, Viking, 1954.

V

THE SURVIVORS
1945–1978
THE FIFTH AND SIXTH GENERATIONS

1 / AFTER HARRY: A FAMILY IN FRAGMENTS

1. This chapter is essentially an essay on the status of the Guggenheim family in the 1970s. The information is derived largely from sources already cited, and sources cited in the following notes.

2 / PETER O. LAWSON-JOHNSTON: THE ANOINTED

1. The characterization of Peter O. Lawson-Johnston and the description of his daily routine and his office are based on the author's interviews with Mr. Lawson-Johnston in his office throughout 1975, 1976, and part of 1977, and a visit to Mr. Lawson-Johnston's estate at Princeton in January, 1976.

2. The steps leading to Mr. Lawson-Johnston's designation by Harry as his principal heir and perpetuator of the Guggenheim tradition were related to the author in a letter from Mr. Lawson-Johnston dated March 30, 1977, and in an interview on May 4, 1977.

3. Information on the Lawson-Johnston family was given the author by Barbara Obre and Peter O. Lawson-Johnston in several interviews conducted throughout 1975, 1976, and part of 1977.

4. The list of Peter O. Lawson-Johnston's business and foundation positions and club memberships is given in Mr. Lawson-Johnston's curriculum vitae, furnished to the author by Mr. Lawson-Johnston.

5. The description of the business of Anglo Company, Pacific Tin Consolidated, and Guggenheim Brothers comes from interviews with Mr. Lawson-Johnston, and from the annual reports of those companies for 1974, 1975, and 1976. Mr. Lawson-Johnston's remarks on his business

concerns were made to the author in correspondence and interviews in April, May, and June, 1977.

6. The description of the plight and activities of the Solomon R. Guggenheim Foundation and the Harry Frank Guggenheim Foundation is derived from the author's interviews with Mr. Lawson-Johnston throughout 1975, 1976, and the first half of 1977.

7. Alexander Marshack's research in the Ice-Age painted caves of southern France, which is now being financed by the Harry Frank Guggenheim Foundation, is reported in Calvin Tomkins, "Thinking in Time," *The New Yorker,* April 27, 1974.

8. Information on Thomas M. Messer, director of the Guggenheim Museum, comes from his curriculum vitae, given to the author by Mr. Messer, and from Diamonstein.

9. The description of Peter Lawson-Johnston's family life comes from the author's interviews with Mr. Lawson-Johnston in 1976 and 1977. The remark by daughter Wendy was made to the author at the gala opening of the Frantisek Kupka exhibition at the Guggenheim Museum in October, 1975.

3 / THE CALIFORNIA GUGGENHEIMS: BOB, JR. AND DANIEL M.: NEW BEGINNINGS

1. The description of Linda Isle, Newport Beach, M. Robert Guggenheim, Jr.'s home and yacht, and the discussion of Mr. Guggenheim's koi collection are based on the author's observations and interviews with Mr. Guggenheim during a visit to his Linda Isle home in April, 1977.

2. The story of M. Robert Guggenheim, Jr.'s life is based on "Biographical Data, Robert Guggenheim, Jr.," and "Resumé of Activities of Robert Guggenheim," given the author in October, 1975, and April, 1977, respectively, and interviews with Mr. Guggenheim at those times. Some information was also taken from newspaper clippings in Mr. Guggenheim's scrapbooks, which Mr. Guggenheim lent to the author. Some episodes, such as the story of M. Robert Guggenheim, Sr.'s disapproval of his son's leaving ASARCO, come from an interview with M. Robert Guggenheim, Jr.'s stepmother, Mrs. Polly Logan, in Washington, D.C., October, 1975.

3. Most of the information on the benefactions of M. Robert Guggenheim, Jr., was given to the author by Mr. Guggenheim. Some of it was taken from Orange County newspapers. A summary of Mr. Guggenheim's charitable activities was reported in Gary Granville, "Newport Man Named to Panel," *Daily Pilot,* Newport Beach, October 1, 1976.

4. Details of the life of Daniel M. Guggenheim were related to the author by M. Robert Guggenheim, Jr., and Daniel M. Guggenheim during inter-

views with both men in October, 1975. Some information is taken from Mr. Guggenheim's curriculum vitae.

5. Information on the New Horizons Boys Ranch comes from Gus Valencia, "New Horizons Boys Ranch," Bly, Oregon, an undated solicitation for funds in form of a pamphlet, and "New Horizons Boys Ranch, 1972–1973 Year Report to the Daniel and Florence Guggenheim Foundation." Both pamphlets were given to the author by Daniel M. Guggenheim.

6. The long quotation of Daniel M. Guggenheim comes from Mr. Guggenheim's letter to the author dated January 6, 1977.

4 / ROGER W. STRAUS, JR., PUBLISHER

1. The description of a publication day party at the New York home of Mr. and Mrs. Roger W. Straus, Jr., is derived from impressions the author has received during attendance at many such parties including the one Mr. Straus gave for the author in April, 1969, upon publication of *The Bouviers.*

2. Details of the life of Roger W. Straus, Jr., and of the history of Farrar, Straus & Giroux come from interviews with Mr. Straus held in October, 1975, January, 1976, and May, 1977; from "Biographical Data, Roger W. Straus, Jr.," and "Brief History of Farrar, Straus & Giroux," dated May 12, 1971, and given to the author by Peggy Miller, secretary to Mr. Straus; and from "Roger W. Straus, Jr., Reflects."

3. Much of the information on Farrar, Straus & Giroux is derived from the author's own experience with that publishing house. Farrar, Straus & Giroux published the author's book *The Bouviers* in April, 1969. For two years during the writing of that book, the author was in constant association with Mr. Straus and with Farrar, Straus & Giroux.

4. The description of the publication day party at Sarosca Farm is based on the author's impressions of a party the author attended there in the summer of 1968.

5 / IRIS LOVE: BONANZA ON KNIDOS

1. Information on the Temple of Aphrodite on Knidos and, later on in the chapter, on the ancient city of Knidos, comes from interviews with Iris Love, January, 1976, and May, 1977, and from Foster.

2. The story of the identification of the head of Aphrodite in the British Museum was told to the author in the above interviews and was reported in *The New York Times,* November 8, 1970, and *Time,* November 23, 1970.

3. Almost all information on the life, family background, and archaeological career of Iris Love comes from the above-mentioned interviews

with Miss Love. Many details were taken from "Biographical Data Sheet, Iris Cornelia Love," given the author by Miss Love. All quotations of Miss Love come from the above interviews.

4. Information on Iris Love's archaeological expeditions on Knidos come from the above-cited interviews with Miss Love, especially the interview in May, 1977, and from the following publications: Iris Love, "Preliminary Excavations at Knidos in Karia," *American Journal of Archaeology,* 1968; and annual reports on the excavations at Knidos, printed in *American Journal of Archaeology* from 1969 through 1973. Some information on the discovery of the Temple of Aphrodite comes from "Archeologist," *The New Yorker,* March 28, 1970, and from the above-cited article by Foster.

6 / WILLIAM GUGGENHEIM III: AMEN

1. The entire chapter is based on interviews with Mrs. William J. Broadhurst (the former Mrs. William Guggenheim, Jr.) and interviews and correspondence with William Guggenheim III as follows: with Mrs. Broadhurst, interviews in October, 1975, February, 1976, February and June, 1977; with Mr. Guggenheim, interview in October, 1975, letters dated August 15, 1975, December 23, 1975, January 25, 1977, February 7, 1977, March 15, 1977, and April 15, 1977.

2. Quotations from Mr. Guggenheim's writings are from Judy and Bill [Mr. and Mrs. William Guggenheim III], *The Love Game,* New York, Pinnacle Books, 1973, and Guggenheim, Bill [William Guggenheim III], *The Book of Circles,* a collection of telepathic writings and other experiences received and edited by Mr. Guggenheim, still in manuscript.

3. The quotation from Judy Guggenheim at the end of the chapter was given to the author by William Guggenheim III in the October, 1975, interview.

BIBLIOGRAPHY

WORKS BY MEMBERS OF THE GUGGENHEIM FAMILY CONTAINING PORTRAITS OF THE GUGGENHEIMS

GUGGENHEIM, PEGGY. *Confessions of an Art Addict*. New York: Macmillan, 1960.

————. *Out of This Century, The Informal Memoirs of Peggy Guggenheim*. New York: Dial, 1946.

LOEB, HAROLD. *The Way It Was*. New York: Criterion Books, 1959.

STRAUS, DOROTHEA. *Palaces and Prisons*. Boston: Houghton Mifflin, 1976.

————. *Showcases*. Boston: Houghton Mifflin, 1974.

WILLIAMS, GATENBY [pseudonym of William Guggenheim], and CHARLES MONROE HEATH, *William Guggenheim*. New York: Lone Voice Publishing, 1934.

WORKS CONTAINING FIRST-HAND PORTRAITS OF THE GUGGENHEIMS BY CONTEMPORARIES

BARUCH, BERNARD M. *My Own Story*. New York: Holt, Rinehart and Winston, 1957.

GODDARD, ESTHER C., and G. EDWARD PENDRAY. *The Papers of Robert H. Goddard*, 6 vols. New York: McGraw-Hill, 1970.

HAMMOND, JOHN HAYS. *The Autobiography of John Hays Hammond*. New York: Farrar and Rinehart, 1935.

HEMINGWAY, ERNEST. *The Sun Also Rises*. New York: Charles Scribner's Sons, 1926. The portrait of Robert Cohn is modeled after Harold Loeb.

LINDBERGH, ANNE MORROW. *The Anne Morrow Lindbergh Diaries*, 3 vols. to date. New York: Harcourt Brace Jovanovich, 1971–1973.

MARCOSSON, ISAAC F. *Metal Magic, The Story of The American Smelting and Refining Company*. New York: Farrar, Straus, 1949.

WRIGHT, FRANK LLOYD. *An Autobiography*. New York: Duell, Sloan, & Pearce, 1943.

WORKS IN GERMAN ON THE JEWS IN SWITZERLAND AND THE GUGGENHEIMS BEFORE THEY EMIGRATED TO THE UNITED STATES

GUGGENHEIM-GRUNBERG, FLORENCE. *Die Altesten Grabsteine des Friedhofes Endigen Lengnau*. Zurich: Verlag Judische Buch-Gemeinde, 1958.

————, *Die Altesten Judischen Familien in Lengnau und Endigen*. Zurich: Verlag Judische Buch-Gemeinde, 1954.

————, *Die Juden in der Schweiz*. Zurich: Verlag Judische Buch-Gemeinde, 1961.

————, *Pfarer Ulrich als Missionar im Surbtal*. Zurich: Verlag Judische Buch-Gemeinde, 1953.

————, *Die Sprache der Schweizer Juden von Endigen und Lengnau*. Zurich: Verlag Judische Buch-Gemeinde, 1950.

ULRICH, JOHANN CASPAR. *Sammlung Judischer Geschicten welche sich mid diesem Volk in XIII und folgenden Jahrhunderten bis auf 1760 in der Schweiz von Zeit Zu Zeit Zugtragen*. Basel, 1768. This collection of Jewish narratives presents a full account of the history of Swiss Jewry from the thirteenth century to 1760, including a portrait of Parnas Jakob Guggenheim and other ancestors of American Guggenheims.

ARCHIVES AND SPECIAL COLLECTIONS

Archives of Guggenheim Brothers, 120 Broadway, New York, N.Y. 10005. (GB)

Archives of the Kennecott Copper Corporation, 161 East 42nd Street, New York, N.Y. 10017. (K)

Archives of the American Smelting and Refining Company, 120 Broadway, New York, N.Y. 10005. (ASARCO)

Archives of the Solomon R. Guggenheim Foundation, Solomon R. Guggenheim Memorial Museum, Fifth Avenue and 89th Street, New York, N.Y. 10028 and 120 Broadway, New York, N.Y. 10005. (SRG)

Archives of the John Simon Guggenheim Memorial Foundation, 90 Park Avenue, New York, N.Y. 10016. (JSGM)

Archives of the Daniel and Florence Guggenheim Foundation, 120 Broadway, New York, N.Y. 10005. (DFG)

Archives of the Harry Frank Guggenheim Foundation, 120 Broadway, New York, N.Y. 10005. (HFG)

Archives of the Hilla von Rebay Foundation, 1083 Fifth Avenue, New York, N.Y. 10028. (HR)

The Daniel Guggenheim Papers (including papers of the Daniel Guggenheim Fund for the Promotion of Aeronautics), Library of Congress, Washington, D.C. (DGP)

The Harry Frank Guggenheim Papers, Library of Congress, Washington, D.C. (HFGP)

The All-Families Book, Office of the Society for the Preservation of the Endigen-Lengnau Synagogues and Cemeteries, Lengnau, Canton Aargau, Switzerland.

PUBLICATIONS OF GUGGENHEIM FOUNDATIONS

1. The Daniel and Florence Guggenheim Foundation:
   Report of the President, 1961. Publication issued under the presidency of Harry F. Guggenheim with sections on the flight sciences, musical, educational, medical, civic, and philanthropic projects, and appendices on the Daniel and Florence Guggenheim Fellows 1949–50 to 1961–62, and organizations aided by major grants, 1924–1960.

   Report of the President, 1974. Fiftieth anniversary publication issued under the presidency of Gladys Guggenheim Straus with sections on social and educational projects, health and medical projects, aviation and space flight, the Guggenheim Memorial Concerts, civic, educational, and religious grants, and an appendix on organizations aided by major contributions from April 1, 1924, to March 31, 1974.

2. The Daniel Guggenheim Fund for the Promotion of Aeronautics:
   Reports of the President, January, 1926 to January, 1930, and various bulletins contained in the Daniel Guggenheim Papers, Library of Congress, Washington, D.C. An example of the latter is "Guggenheim Fund Makes Grants to Finance Study and Experiments in Aeronautics." Bulletin of The Daniel and Florence Guggenheim Fund for the Promotion of Aeronautics, New York, August 14, 1926.

3. The Harry Frank Guggenheim Foundation:
   The Man's Relation to Man Program of the Harry Frank Guggenheim Foundation. Booklet relating history and purposes of the foundation.

   Report of the Harry Frank Guggenheim Foundation, 120 Broadway, New York, N. Y., 1974. First published report of the foundation giving general history of the foundation and projects financed through June 30, 1974.

4. The John Simon Guggenheim Memorial Foundation:
   Charter, Letter of Gift, Constitution, and By-Laws, New York, 1925.

   Report of the Educational Advisory Board and Treasurer's Report, 1925–1926, New York, 1926.

   Reports of the Secretary and Treasurer, New York, 1927–1976.

   Directory of Fellows 1925–1967, John Simon Guggenheim Memorial Foundation, New York, 1968.

   Directory of Fellows 1925–1974, John Simon Guggenheim Memorial Foundation, 1975.

5. The Murry and Leonie Guggenheim Foundation:
   Annual reports of the Murry and Leonie Guggenheim Foundation, New York, 1932–1969. Archives of Mr. Neal M. Welch, former attorney for the Murry and Leonie Guggenheim Foundation, 102 Robinson Street, Georgetown, Delaware.

6. The Peggy Guggenheim Foundation:
   Catalogue of the Peggy Guggenheim Collection, Palazzo Venier dei Leoni, Venice, The Peggy Guggenheim Foundation, 1965. This catalogue was reproduced and published in the U.S. as: Calas, Nicolas and Elena. *The Peggy Guggenheim Collection of Modern Art.* New York: Abrams, 1967.

7. The Solomon R. Guggenheim Foundation:
   [A selection of publications in chronological order.]
   A Handbook to the Solomon R. Guggenheim Museum. New York, 1959. [A selection of painting, sculpture, and drawing in the museum collection to 1959, the date of the opening of the Frank Lloyd Wright museum building. Preface by Harry F. Guggenheim, Introduction by James Johnson Sweeney.]

   Acquisitions of the 1930's and 1940's. New York, 1968. [Exhibition in tribute to Baroness Hilla von Rebay, first director of the Guggenheim Museum. Foreword by Thomas M. Messer.]

   Works from the Peggy Guggenheim Foundation. New York, 1969. [Preface by Harry F. Guggenheim, Foreword by Thomas M. Messer, Introduction by Peggy Guggenheim.]

   Masterpieces of Modern Art. New York, 1972.
   [Picture book published on occasion of the reopening of the Justin K. Thannhauser Wing at the museum.]

   Kandinsky at the Guggenheim Museum. New York, 1972.
   [Picture book published on occasion of exhibition of the museum's entire holdings of Kandinsky oils, watercolors, and prints.]

   Jean Dubuffet: A Retrospective. New York, 1973.
   [The largest exhibition assembled to date at the Guggenheim Museum. Introduction by Thomas M. Messer. Essay by Margit Rowell.]

   Max Ernst: A Retrospective Exhibition. New York, 1975.
   [Essay by Diane Waldman, curator of exhibitions, Guggenheim Museum, with chronology and selected bibliography.]

   The Solomon R. Guggenheim Museum, New York, Frank Lloyd Wright, Architect. New York, 1975.
   [Picture book with introduction by Peter O. Lawson-Johnston and Thomas M. Messer. Statement and letter on the building by Frank Lloyd Wright.]

   The Guggenheim Museum Paintings 1880–1945, 2 vols. New York, 1976.
   [Definitive catalogue of the museum painting collection 1880–1945 by Angelica Zander Rudenstine, research curator. Foreword by Peter O. Lawson-Johnston, Preface by Thomas M. Messer.]

NONAUTOBIOGRAPHICAL WORKS MENTIONED IN THE TEXT, BY MEMBERS OF THE GUGGENHEIM FAMILY

GUGGENHEIM, HARRY F. *The United States and Cuba.* New York: Macmillan, 1934.

LOEB, HAROLD, ed. *The Broom Anthology.* Boston: Milford House, 1969. Contains original works published by *Broom* magazine and an introduction by Harold Loeb.

LOEB, HAROLD. "Hemingway's Bitterness." *Connecticut Review,* Connecticut State College, October, 1967.

MISCELLANEOUS WORKS BY MEMBERS OF THE GUGGENHEIM FAMILY

LOEB, HAROLD. *Capacity Vs. Rapacity.* New York: Continental Committee, 1934.

———. *The Chart of Plenty.* New York: Viking, 1935.

———. *Doodab.* New York: Boni & Liveright, 1925.

———. *Full Production without War.* Princeton: Princeton University Press, 1946.

———. *Life in a Technocracy, What It Might Be Like.* New York: Viking, 1933.

———. *The Non-Production of Wealth.* New York: Continental Committee, 1933.

———. *Production for Use.* New York: Basic Books, 1936.

———. *The Professors Like Vodka.* New York: Boni & Liveright, 1927.

———. *Stupidity of Poverty.* New York: Continental Committee, 1934.

———. *Tumbling Mustard.* New York: H. Liveright, 1929.

LOVE, IRIS. "Excavations at Knidos, 1972." *American Journal of Archaeology* (1973): 413–24.

———. "Excavations at Knidos, 1971." *American Journal of Archaeology* (1972): 393–405.

———. "Excavations at Knidos, 1970." *American Journal of Archaeology* (1971): 61–76.

———. "Excavations at Knidos, 1969." *American Journal of Archaeology* (1970): 149–55, 170–71.

———. "Excavations at Knidos, 1968." *American Journal of Archaeology* (1969).

————. *Greece, Gods, and Art.* New York: Viking Press, 1968. (Text and captions by Iris C. Love; photographs by Alexander Liberman; preface by Robert Graves.)

————. "Preliminary Excavations at Knidos in Karia." *American Journal of Archaeology* (1968).

————. "Preliminary Excavations at Knidos in Karia." *Anatolian Studies* XVIII (1968).

STRAUS, ROGER W., JR. *The New Order.* New York: G. P. Putnam's Sons, 1941.

————. *War Letters from Britain.* New York: G. P. Putnam's Sons, 1941.

BIOGRAPHIES OF THE GUGGENHEIM FAMILY

HOYT, EDWIN P., JR. *The Guggenheims and the American Dream.* New York: Funk and Wagnalls, 1967.

LOMASK, MILTON. *Seed Money, The Guggenheim Story.* New York: Farrar, Straus, 1964. [Primarily about the foundations]

O'CONNOR, HARVEY. *The Guggenheims, The Making of an American Dynasty.* New York: Covici Friede, 1937.

THE GUGGENHEIMS AND AVIATION AND ROCKETRY

CLEVELAND, REGINALD M. *America Fledges Wings, the History of the Daniel Guggenheim Fund for the Promotion of Aeronautics.* New York: Pittman, 1942.

EMME, EUGENE M. *Aeronautics and Astronautics, An American Chronology of Science and Technology in the Exploration of Space, 1915–1960.* Washington, D.C.: National Aeronautics and Space Administration, 1961.

GODDARD, ESTHER C., and G. EDWARD PENDRAY. *The Papers of Robert H. Goddard,* 6 vols. New York: McGraw-Hill, 1970. Publication financed by Harry F. Guggenheim.

GUGGENHEIM, HARRY F. *The Seven Skies.* New York: G. P. Putnam's Sons, 1930.

HALLION, RICHARD P. *Legacy of Flight, The Guggenheim Contribution to American Aviation.* Seattle: University of Washington Press, 1977. Contains a complete bibliography of the subject.

LEHMAN, MILTON. *This High Man, The Life of Robert H. Goddard.* New York: Farrar, Straus, 1963.

MILLIKIN, ROBERT. *The Guggenheim Aeronautical Laboratory of the California Institute of Technology, The First Twenty-five Years.* Pasadena: California Institute of Technology, 1954.

PENDRAY, G. EDWARD. *The Coming Age of Rocket Power*. New York: Harper & Bros., 1945.

PENDRAY, G. EDWARD, ed. *The Guggenheim Medalists, Architects of the Age of Flight*. New York: The Guggenheim Medal Board of Award, the United Engineering Trustees, 1964.

REYNOLDS, QUENTIN JAMES. *The Amazing Mr. Doolittle*. New York: Appleton-Century-Crofts, 1953.

THE GUGGENHEIMS AND MINING AND METALLURGY

BERNSTEIN, MARVIN D. *The Mexican Mining Industry, 1890–1950*. New York: State University of New York, 1965. Contains a complete bibliography of the subject.

DORSET, PHYLLIS FLANDERS. *New Eldorado*. New York: Macmillan, 1970.

HAMMOND, JOHN HAYS. *The Autobiography of John Hays Hammond*. New York: Farrar & Rinehart, 1935.

HAYNES, WILLIAM. *Chemical Pioneers:* Freeport, N. Y.: Books for Libraries Press, 1939.

JACKSON, SAMUEL B. *Two Hundred Trails to Gold*. Garden City, N.Y.: Doubleday, 1976.

JORALEMON, IRA B. *Romantic Copper, Its Lure and Lore*. New York: Appleton-Century, 1934.

MARCOSSON, ISAAC. *Metal Magic, The Story of the American Smelting and Refining Company*. New York: Farrar, Straus, 1949.

PARSONS, A. B. *Porphyry Coppers*. New York: American Institute of Mining and Metallurgical Engineers, 1933.

RICKARD, T. A. *A History of American Mining*. New York: McGraw-Hill, 1932.

SLOANE, HOWARD N., and LUCILLE L. SLOANE. *A Pictorial History of American Mining*. New York: Crown, 1970.

NOTE: Annual reports of formerly Guggenheim-controlled corporations, and corporations currently controlled by the family, are an excellent source of information on the Guggenheims and the mining industry.
These are:

American Smelting and Refining (ASARCO), 120 Broadway, New York, N. Y. 10005.

Kennecott Copper, 161 East 42nd Street, New York, N. Y. 10017.

The Anaconda Company, 1271 Avenue of the Americas, New York, N. Y. 10019.

Anglo Company, 120 Broadway, New York, N. Y. 10005.

Pacific Tin Consolidated Corporation, 120 Broadway, New York, N. Y. 10005.

There are no published reports of the private partnership of Guggenheim Brothers, formerly M. Guggenheim's Sons. Records of Guggenheim Brothers are on file at Guggenheim Brothers, 120 Broadway, New York, N. Y. 10005.

GENERAL WORKS ON JEWISH HISTORY AND THE JEWISH PEOPLE

BAMBERGER, BERNARD J. *The Story of Judaism.* New York: Schocken Books, 1964.

BIRMINGHAM, STEPHEN. *Our Crowd.* New York: Harper & Row, 1967.

CUDDIHY, JOHN MURRAY. *The Ordeal of Civility: Freud, Marx, Levi-Strauss and the Jewish Struggle with Modernity.* New York: Basic Books, 1975.

DIMONT, MAX I. *Jews, God and History.* New York: New American Library, 1962.

GRAETZ, HEINRICH. *History of the Jews,* 6 vols. Philadelphia: Jewish Publication Society of America, 1898.

GRAYZEL, SOLOMON. *A History of the Contemporary Jews.* New York: Meridian Books, 1960.

HERBERG, WILL. *Judaism and Modern Man: An Interpretation of Jewish Religion.* New York: Farrar, Straus & Cudahy, 1951.

HIRSCHLER, ERIC E., ed. *Jews From Germany in the United States.* New York: Farrar, Straus & Cudahy, 1955.

HOROWITZ, GEORGE. *The Spirit of Jewish Law.* New York: Central Book Company, 1973.

KAUFMANN, WALTER. *Religions in Four Dimensions.* New York: Reader's Digest Press, 1976.

MADISON, CHARLES A. *Eminent American Jews, 1776 to the Present.* New York: Frederick Ungar, 1970.

ROTH, CECIL. *The Jewish Contribution to Civilization.* New York: Harper & Bros., 1940.

VAN DEN HAAG, ERNEST. *The Jewish Mystique.* New York: Stein & Day, 1969.

NEWSPAPER AND MAGAZINE ARTICLES ON THE GUGGENHEIM FAMILY, BUSINESSES, AND FOUNDATIONS

ARONSON, HARVEY. "The Captain and the Kid." *New York,* March 30, 1970. About Harry Guggenheim and Bill Moyers.

CHATWIN, BRUCE. "The Guggenheim Saga." *The Sunday Times Magazine* [London], November 23, 1975. Fourth in the London *Times* series "on seven families who have influenced American life over the past 200 years."

DIAMONSTEIN, BARBARALEE. "Thomas Messer: From the Bohemian Musical Life to the Guggenheim." *Art News,* October, 1975.

DOHERTY, EDWARD. "The House of Guggenheim, An Epic of Seven Sons." *Liberty,* November 8, 1930.

DONOVAN, MARIA KOZSLIK. "An American in Venice." *Holiday,* January–February, 1974. About Peggy Guggenheim.

FOSTER, JOHN. "LIU Expedition to Knidos, Iris Love Excavates an Ancient Greek City." *The Long Island University Magazine,* Greenvale, April 20, 1970.

GUGGENHEIM, HARRY F. "Aviation and Confidence." *Aviation,* February, 1927.

———. "Policy Papers: *Newsday,*" revised. *Newsday,* January, 1967.

"Guggenheim Visions Sky Full of Ships." *New York American,* April 29, 1926.

"The Guggenheims." *Fortune,* July, 1930. No author given.

GUGGENHEIM-GRUNBERG, FLORENCE. "Die Lengnauer Vorfahren der 'Kupfer-Guggenheim' in Amerika." Zurich, Israelitisch Wochenblatt, 1953.

HELLMAN, GEOFFREY. "Getting the Guggenheims into Focus." *The New Yorker,* July 25, 1953.

HESS, THOMAS B. "The Good Old Guggenheim." *New York,* June 21, 1976.

HOYT, EDWIN P. "The Guggenheims, Giants of Mining." *Empire* magazine, *The Denver Post,* December 4, 11, 18, 1966.

LYON, PETER. "The Adventurous Angels." *Horizon,* May, 1959. About the Guggenheim foundations.

MOK, MICHAEL. "If You Had Millions to Spend." *Popular Science Monthly,* February, 1929.

PEACH, BERNARD, with PASCHAL REEVES. "The John Simon Guggenheim Memorial Foundation: Investment in Free Individuals." *The South Atlantic Quarterly,* Spring, 1961.

"Roger W. Straus, Jr., President of Farrar, Straus & Giroux, Reflects on His Firm's 30-Year Pursuit of Literary Excellence." *Publishers Weekly,* February 7, 1977.

SHIRER, DAVID L. "Peggy's Back in Town." *Newsweek,* January 27, 1969.

MISCELLANEOUS WORKS CONTAINING REFERENCES TO THE GUGGENHEIMS OR TO GUGGENHEIM INSTITUTIONS

CARO, ROBERT A. *Robert Moses and the Fall of New York.* New York: Alfred A. Knopf, 1975.

FRIEDMAN, B. H. *Jackson Pollock.* New York: McGraw-Hill, 1972.

LORD, WALTER A. *A Night to Remember.* New York: Holt, Rinehart & Winston, 1955.

MILLER, HENRY. *The Air-Conditioned Nightmare.* New York: New Directions, 1945.

UNTERECKER, JOHN. *Voyager: A Life of Hart Crane.* New York: Farrar, Straus & Giroux, 1969.

GENERAL REFERENCE WORKS

Encyclopaedia Judaica. Jerusalem: The Ketter Publishing House, 1971.

The Foundation Center. *The Foundation Directory,* 4th ed. New York: Columbia University Press, 1971.

LANGER, WILLIAM L., ed. *An Encyclopedia of World History.* Boston: Houghton Mifflin, 1940.

The Standard Jewish Encyclopedia. Garden City, N.Y.: Doubleday, 1959.

Who's Who in World Jewry, A Biographical Dictionary of Outstanding Jews. New York: Pitman, 1972.

UNPUBLISHED WORKS

50 Jahre Schweizerisches Israelitisches Alterasyl Lengnau, 1903–1953. Zurich, 1954. History of the Alterasyl, mentioning the Guggenheim contribution. No author given.

HUNT, JOHN. "Falaise." New York, n.d. An illustrated guide to *Falaise.*

KRAEUTLER, ERIC. *The Indifferent Colossus and the Good Neighbor: America's Cuban Policy, 1929–1933.* Department of History, Princeton University, 1976. Thesis for partial fulfillment of the requirements for the degree of Bachelor of Arts.

NASSAU COUNTY MUSEUM. "Preliminary Interpretation Plan, Falaise, Sands Point Park and Preserve." Nassau County Museum, February, 1973.

AUTHOR'S NOTE AND ACKNOWLEDGMENTS

THIS BOOK IS THE RESULT OF FORTUNATE CIRCUMSTANCES. AT THE time the subject was suggested to me, I was living in Italy and beginning a book on Italian civilization with emphasis on the Renaissance. I had just completed a tour of some of the palaces of great Italian families of the Renaissance—the Reggia of the Gonzagas of Mantua, the Palazzo Ducale of the Estes of Ferrara, the Castello Sforzesco of the Sforzas of Milan—when the possibility of doing a book on the Guggenheims was conveyed to me by my agent, Carl D. Brandt. The prospect interested me immediately, as I already knew three members of the family quite well—Roger W. Straus, Jr., who published my book on the Bouvier family, Iris Love, a friend of my sister's, and Peggy Guggenheim, whom I had gotten to know while writing a book on Venice—and I had always been curious about their Guggenheim background. After some preliminary reading on the family I concluded that the Guggenheims were about the nearest thing America had to a great family of the Italian Renaissance. Bold and adventurous in making their fortune, they had been equally bold and adventurous in spending it on such hitherto unfertilized causes as abstract art, individual creative work in the arts and sciences, and aviation and rocketry. (I could not help thinking of the Sforzas' support of Leonardo's then avant-garde painting and advanced mechanics, which included a design for a flying machine.) To be brief, one thing led to another, and, before long, I had abandoned the book on Italian civilization and was deep in research for *The Guggenheims*.

I mention all this to explain my principal debts of gratitude. They are first to my editor, James Landis, Editorial Director of William Morrow & Company, whose idea it was for me to write this book and who has since given me unflagging encouragement and most perceptive editorial advice, and second to Carl D. Brandt, who suggested me to Mr. Landis when Mr. Landis first proposed the book, and who has also given me much-appreciated encouragement and advice.

My next debts go to the many members of the Guggenheim family who provided me with information on themselves, their relatives, and their ancestors. First of these, in order of gratitude, is Roger W. Straus, Jr., who not only provided me with a great deal of information on the Guggenheims, but also introduced me to many members and employees of the family I had not yet met: Peter O. Lawson-Johnston, Joan Van de Maele, George Fountaine, Gladys Guggenheim Straus, Oscar Straus III, Lady Castle Stewart, Barbara Obre, and Michael Wettach. To them and to Roger I am sincerely grateful.

Further debts of gratitude go to members of the Guggenheim family I either already knew or contacted on my own: Mrs. William J. Broadhurst (the former Mrs. William Guggenheim, Jr.), Polly Logan (the former Mrs. M. Robert Guggenheim), Dorothea Straus, Sindbad Vail, Nicolas Helion, Hazel Guggenheim McKinley, Mrs. Edmond A. Guggenheim, and William Guggenheim III, all of whom have been most helpful. Particularly deep thanks go to Mr. and Mrs. M. Robert Guggenheim, Jr., Mr. and Mrs. Daniel M. Guggenheim, Iris Love, and Peggy Guggenheim, for the long hours, and, in some cases, days, they spent talking with me about the Guggenheims.

This book would have been much less complete if it had not been for the cooperation I received from many people who, in one capacity or another, had been associated either with members of the Guggenheim family or with certain Guggenheim businesses and foundations. They were: Phyllis Braff, fine arts curator, Nassau County Museum (custodian of the Guggenheim estates on Long Island); John D. Hohnsbeen, curator, the Peggy Guggenheim Collection, Venice; Leo Gottlieb, former attorney for Harry F. Guggenheim; Chauncey A. Newlin, former attorney for Solomon R. Guggenheim; Francis P. Schiarolli, former attorney for the baroness Hilla Rebay; Thomas M. Messer, director of the Solomon R. Guggenheim Museum; Peggy Miller, secretary to Roger W. Straus, Jr.; Albert E. Thiele, partner of Guggenheim Brothers; James F. Mathias, vice-president of the John Simon Guggenheim Memorial Foundation; Gordon N. Ray, president of the John Simon Guggenheim Memorial Foundation; Dr. Florence Guggenheim-Grunberg of Zurich, historian of the Guggenheim family in Switzerland; Jacques Oppenheim, president of the Society for the Preservation of the Endigen-Lengnau Synagogues and Cemeteries, Lengnau, Switzerland; Baron Franz Hugo Rebay and Dr. Roland Rebay of Wessling-am-See, West Germany; and Joan Lukach, custodian of the Hilla von Rebay Foundation archives. My deep thanks to all.

Many thanks, also, to my most capable researchers, Joanna Hughbanks, Doris Landmann, Eric Kraeutler, and Ellen Yager, and to Daniel C. Cochran, Financial Analyst, Exxon Corporation, for assistance in making dollar conversions.

Special thanks to Sara K. Stillman and Wes Kirk, who typed the entire manuscript.

I am also very grateful to Robert Bender, copy editor at William Morrow, for his many suggestions toward improving the book.

My final thanks go to certain friends and relatives who, in one way or another, encouraged me and helped sustain me during the writing: Eric F. Goldman, Lya Haby, Angelika Fischer, Monica Rotelli, Theresa Lewis, Petunia Camero, Max Vairo, Maude B. Davis, and Nancy W. Davis, the last a source of strength from start to finish.

JOHN H. DAVIS
New York
August, 1977

INDEX

A. Y. mine, 58-60, 90, 233
Aeronautics, *see* Daniel and Florence Guggenheim Aeronautical Laboratories and Jet Propulsion Centers; Daniel and Florence Guggenheim Foundation; Daniel Guggenheim Fund for the Promotion of Aeronautics; Guggenheim, Daniel; Guggenheim, Harry Frank
Affluent Society, The (Galbraith), 261
African mines, 111-113
  labor exploitation at, 113
  Ryan and, 112-113
Aiken, Conrad, 258, 353
Air-Conditioned Nightmare, The (Miller), 266-267
Akarca, Askidil, 518
Alaska Syndicate, 102-104
Albert Einstein Award, 260
Albright, Joe Patterson, 26
Aldrich, Nelson W., 248
Alexander, Morton, 247
Allende, Salvador, 132
Allyn, Helen Claire, 485
American Concentrated Lye Company, 53
American Congo Company, 112
American Federation of Labor (AFL), 123
American Smelters Securities, 251
American Smelting and Refining Company (ASARCO), 23, 24, 82, 87, 90-91, 167, 195, 234, 248, 257, 289, 290
  Guggenheim Brothers and, 130-131
  the Guggenheims and, 74-76, 95-99, 143, 172, 251, 253, 484-490
  Straus and, 365, 368
American Women's Association, 157
Anaconda Copper Corporation, 193, 194, 257
  sale of the Chuquicamata copper mine to, 33, 131-133, 165
Anderson, Sherwood, 353
Anglo Corporation, 461, 464, 467, 473-474
Anglo-Chilean Nitrate Company, 193
Anglo-Lautaro Nitrate Company, 193, 467
Anti-Semitism
  in American business, 74
  Ford and, 125
  Hemingway and, 349-350, 358-364
  Isaac and, 145, 146
  Miller and, 267-268
  in Philadelphia (1800s), 46-47, 63

the Seligman-Hilton affair, 78-80
  in Switzerland, 38-40
  World War I and, 121-122
Apollo XI space flight, 32, 438
Aragon, Louis, 353
Ardrey, Robert, 445
Arp, Jean, 321, 419
Art, *see* Guggenheim, Peggy; Guggenheim, Solomon R.; Peggy Guggenheim Foundation; Rebay von Ehrenwiesen, Hilla; Solomon R. Guggenheim Collection of Non-Objective Painting, The; Solomon R. Guggenheim Foundation; Solomon R. Guggenheim Museum
Art News and Review, 228
Art of This Century gallery, 340, 342-347
Astor, John Jacob 4th, 238
Auden, W. H., 258
Aydelotte, Frank, 256, 257, 275

Balbo, Italo, 283
Balzac, Honoré de, 90
Bantam Books, 22, 502
Baranov, Aleksandr, 103
Barbara Guggenheim Memorial fund, 85
Barber, Samuel, 258, 266
Barnes, Djuna, 338
Barr, Alfred H., Jr., 271, 343, 344, 432
Barron's, 206
Barthelme, Donald, 498
Baruch, Bernard M., 111, 144, 152, 167, 172, 227
Bauer, Rudolf, 200, 202, 205, 207-215
Baziotes, William, 343, 476
Beckett, Samuel, 321-322, 324
Beecher, Henry Ward, 80
Benét, Stephen Vincent, 258, 259, 270
Bennett, Floyd, 161
Berenson, Bernard, 417
Bernheim, Jacques, 196
Bernheim, Leonie, 81
Bernheimer, Grace, *see* Guggenheim, Grace Bernheimer
Berryman, John, 258, 500, 501
Beyle, Leon, 90
Biddle, Francis, 213
Bingham Canyon copper mine, 115-117
  labor exploitation at, 115-116
  value of, 116
  World War I and, 120

Blanshard, Brand, 275
Bonar, Jack E., 175
Bonar, Jean, 175, 196
Bowles, Paul, 421
Boyle, Harriet, 486
Boyle, Kay, 260-261, 429
Bradley, Omar, 299
Brancusi, Constantin, 321
Braque, Georges, 321
Bratnober, Arnold "Arctic," 101
Brazilian Mining and Dredging Company, 467
Breton, André, 323, 329, 343, 347
"Broken Tower, The" (Crane), 264-265
Broom, 255, 311, 350-356
Brownell, Francis H., 167
Bryan, William Jennings, 246
Buber, Martin, 500
Bundy, McGeorge, 274
Butterfly Foundation, 538
Byrd, Commander Richard E., 160

Calder, Alexander, 321, 340
California Institute of Technology, 161, 169, 170
Canaday, John, 508
Capote, Truman, 265, 266
Caracoles Tin Corporation, 147
Carnegie, Andrew, 450
Carnegie Endowment, 273
Carrington, Leonore, 336, 338
Carter, Elliott, 258
Castle Stewart, Earl of, 379, 380-382
Castle Stewart, Lady, *see* Guggenheim, Eleanor May
Cerruti, Marquise de, 236, 237
Chagall, Marc, 202, 210
Chase National Bank, 304, 305
Chicago Tribune, 439
Chile Copper Company, Chuquicamata copper mine, 21, 117
    sold to Anaconda Copper Corporation, 33, 131-133, 165
    World War I and, 120
Cité Universitaire, 196
Clark, Sir Kenneth, 327
Clark University, 161
Clarke, Mary Mowbray, 352
Coates, Robert, 343
Cochran, Thomas, 219
Cocteau, Jean, 321
Colorado, University of, 247
Colorado School of Mines, 247, 253, 292
Compañía de La Gran Fundición Nacional Mexicana, 70
Compañía de Salitre de Chile (Cosach), 193-195
Compton, Arthur, 270, 271
Compton, Dr. Carl T., 167
Concerning the Spiritual in Art (Kandinsky), 209
Confessions of an Art Addict (Guggenheim), 347, 348, 417, 419, 426
Connecticut Review, 364
Consul, The (Menotti), 259

Coolidge, Calvin, 152, 160
Copland, Aaron, 258, 261, 273
Corbin, Austin, 80
Corman, A. Y., 60
Corman, Minnie, 60
Cowley, Malcolm, 264, 353
Cowley, Peggy, 264
Crane, Hart, 258, 263-265, 353
Cuban Patriotic League, 306
cummings, e. e., 353
Curtis, George William, 49
Curtis, William, 97

"Dada Manifesto" (Tzara), 334
Daniel and Florence Guggenheim Aeronautical Laboratories and Jet Propulsion Centers, 169-170
Daniel and Florence Guggenheim aeronautics award, 495
Daniel and Florence Guggenheim Foundation, 30, 169, 461
    bequest from Daniel's will, 168
    established, 156-157
    Goddard and, 161-164, 168
    grants made by, 157
    space exploration program and, 150-151, 454
    Straus (Gladys) and, 368-370
Daniel and Florence Guggenheim Vocational Training Center, 493
Daniel Guggenheim Fund for the Measurement and Investigation of High Altitudes, 164
Daniel Guggenheim Fund for the Promotion of Aeronautics, 158
    bequest from Daniel's will, 168
    established, 160
    Harry and, 160-161, 302, 303
    projects funded by, 161
    schools of aeronautical engineering established by, 160
Dante, 97
Davidson, Henry, 152
Davis, Harold L., 270
Davis, Sammy, Jr., 400-401, 502
Democracy in America (Tocqueville), 243-244
Denver Art Museum, 271
Denver Post, 245, 247, 248
Diamang (Angolan diamond company), 113, 131, 195, 467
Díaz, Porfirio, 68
Doolittle, Lt. James H. (Jimmy), 161, 445
Dos Passos, John, 353
Douglas, Norman, 311
Draper, Dana, 24-26, 440, 447
Draper, Nancy, 24, 28
Du Pont, Henry, 248
Duchamp, Marcel, 321, 322, 327, 342, 343, 347

Eaton, Elizabeth, *see* Guggenheim, Elizabeth Eaton
Edel, Leon, 258
Edward VII, King, 73

Ehrenburg, Ilya, 353
Ehrlich, Arnold, 497
Eisenhower, President Dwight D., 227, 293, 296
M. Robert and, 296, 298, 299
Elgebar Corporation, 379
Eliot, T. S., 327, 500
Embury, Grace, 533
Ephron, Nora, 498
Ernst, Jimmy, 336, 341
Ernst, Max, 321, 331, 343, 347, 348, 424, 476
Peggy and, 209, 328-341, 419
surrealistic art of, 334-335
Explorer I satellite, 170

Farrar, John, 500
Farrar, Straus & Giroux, 369, 465, 496, 499, 508, 510
authors published by, 500, 501
founding of, 500
high standards of, 500-501
success of, 502-504
See also Straus, Roger W., Jr.
Farrell, James T., 258
Federation of Jewish Charities, 147
Federation of Jewish Philanthropies, 446
Feldspar Corporation, 27, 461, 467, 468, 472
Fini, Leonor, 336
Finnegans Wake (Joyce), 321
Firenze (yacht), 291, 294, 295, 300
Fisher, Sidney, 78
Fitzgerald, F. Scott, 138, 154, 255, 356, 360, 364
Fleischman, Julius, 500
Flemming, Arthur S., 227
Forbes, 152, 206
Ford, Ford Madox, 360
Ford, Henry, 46, 125
anti-Semitism and, 125
Ford Foundation, 274
"Foreign Exchange" (Loeb), 356-357
Foundations, *see* Guggenheim foundations
Fountaine, George, 28, 468
Frick, Henry Clay, 450
Fromkin, David, 519
Fuentes, Carlos, 497
Full Flight Laboratory for the Study of Fog-Flying, 161

Galbraith, John Kenneth, 258, 261
Garman, Douglas, 317-318
Genauer, Emily, 228
Genealogical charts and tables, 36, 136, 288, 458, 541-544
General Cable Corporation, 254
George VI, King, 377, 402
Georgia Tech, 161
Gerstle, Nettie, 70
Giglio, Victor, 238
Gimbel, Alva, 488
Gimbel, Fred A., 175
Giroux, Robert, 497, 500, 509

Gleizes, Albert Léon, 202
Goddard, Esther C., 150
Goddard, Robert H., 29, 33, 150, 166, 438, 450
Daniel and Florence Guggenheim Foundation and, 161-164, 168
Goddard Space Flight Center, 438
Godfather, The (motion picture), 29
Gompers, Samuel, 123-124, 152
Daniel and, 123-124
Gottlieb, Adolph, 343
Gottlieb, Leo, 28, 174
Gould, Howard, 138, 154
Gould, Jay, 55
Gourmet, 368
Graham, Charles D., 58
Gran Fundición Central Mexicana, 72
Graves, Robert, 500
Great Gatsby, The (Fitzgerald), 138, 154
Greece, Gods, and Art (Liberman), 525
Greenberg, Clement, 344
Gregovitch, Raoul, 421
Greun Madainn Foundation, 538
See also Guggenheim, William III
Grosz, George, 353
Guggenheim, Aimee Lillian, 281-286, 374, 375
Guggenheim, Barbara, 201, 221, 399-402
childhood of, 379-380
homes of, 400-401
horse breeding of, 401
inheritance of, 379
marriages of, 399-400
son of, 400-402
Guggenheim, Barbara Meyer, 45
charitable activities of, 52, 85
children born to, 52
death of, 84-85
health of, 83, 84
marriage of, 48
maternal role of, 51-55, 65, 85
New York social life and, 80-83
religion and, 55, 81
Guggenheim, Benita, 128, 234, 235, 239, 241, 409
Guggenheim, Benjamin, 33, 56, 232-242
ASARCO and, 74-76
birth of, 52
breaks partnership with brothers, 74, 127-128, 234
drowning of, 128, 239
heroism of, 239
education of, 232
effect of mother's death on, 84
expatriate life of, 236-238
financial failure of, 240-241
marriage of, 82
romantic affairs of, 235-237
townhouse of, 234-235
Guggenheim, Beth, 492
Guggenheim, Beulah, 144, 145, 147
Guggenheim, Carrie Sonneborn, 81, 144, 146
Guggenheim, Christopher Mark, 376, 533, 539

Guggenheim, Daniel, 31, 33, 55, 56, 62, 64, 150-170
  aeronautics and, 150-167
  established first school in U.S., 159
  ASARCO and, 74-76, 95-98, 130-131
  assumes role as family leader, 96
  birth of, 52
  on the business strategy of the Guggenheims, 109-110
  communism and, 153-154
  death of, 166
  education of, 152-153
  Gompers and, 123-124
  Guggenheim Exploration Company and, 73-98
  Harry and, 156, 157, 165, 168
  health of, 165
  Hempstead House of, 138, 154-156, 169
  as the ideal business man, 151-152
  Lindbergh and, 163-164
  magnanimity of, 153
  marriage of, 81
  Morgan and, 101-108
  "Napoleonic" nature of, 97
  tributes to, 167
  will of, 168
  See also Daniel and Florence Guggenheim Foundation
Guggenheim, Daniel II, 293, 484
Guggenheim, Daniel M., 32, 461, 463, 464, 485, 490-495
  on America's economic future, 493-495
  business career of, 491-492
  childhood of, 490-491
  education of, 491
  philanthropies of, 492-493
Guggenheim, Edmond, 121, 131, 196, 290, 371-373
  Guggenheim Brothers and, resigns from, 133, 174
  love of sports, 174, 372
  marriages of, 174-175, 372
  Murry and Leonie Guggenheim Foundation and, 196-197, 372
  philanthropies of, 373
  trust fund established for, 173-174, 371-372
  will of, 373
Guggenheim, Edyth, 144, 145, 147, 148
Guggenheim, Eleanor May, 203, 221, 377-382, 402-405
  childhood of, 379-380
  English estate of, 382, 403-404
  on Guggenheim money, 403
  inheritance of, 379
  marriage of, 377-379, 381
  philanthropies of, 402
  sons of, 382, 402
  tragedies in life of, 402-404
Guggenheim, Elizabeth Eaton, 294, 295
Guggenheim, Elizabeth Newell, 374
Guggenheim, Florence Shloss, 81, 120, 156, 166-169
Guggenheim, Florette Seligman, 82, 233,

235-241, 310-311
Guggenheim, George Denver, 249, 252-255, 270-272, 290
Guggenheim, Gertrude, 382-399
  charities of, 399
  childhood of, 379-380
  English home of, 382
  inheritance of, 379
Guggenheim, Grace Ann, 485
Guggenheim, Grace Bernheimer, 293
Guggenheim, Grace Herbert, 280-282, 284
Guggenheim, Harry Frank, 21-32, 121, 131, 156, 290, 301-307, 437-456
  aeronautics and rocketry and, 158-170, 438
  birth of, 81
  Daniel and, 156, 157, 165, 168
  Daniel Guggenheim Fund for the Promotion of Aeronautics and, 160-161, 302, 303
  death of, 31-32, 446
  education of, 303
  the Falaise estate of, 437, 444, 446, 451-455
  Guggenheim Brothers and, resigns from, 133, 305
  horse breeding of, 454-455
  inheritances of, 438
  Lindbergh and, 161, 306, 450, 453
  the many careers of, 28, 302
  marriages of, 439, 441
  newspaper publishing and, 438-439
  Peggy and, 426-427, 430
  the philosophy of, 22-23, 301, 441
  Rebay and, 223-225
  as a Renaissance man, 437-438, 448-456
  search for a male heir, 23-28, 440
  the Solomon R. Guggenheim Museum and, 223-227, 444
  as U.S. Ambassador to Cuba, 165, 302-307
  will of, 21-32, 446-447
    Lawson-Johnston and, 446, 447, 468-469
  See also Harry Frank Guggenheim Foundation
Guggenheim, Helene, 144, 145, 147
Guggenheim, Irene, 198, 199, 215, 221
  Rebay and, 205-206, 221
Guggenheim, Isaac, 33, 42-43, 55, 56, 62, 64, 142-149
  anti-Semitism and, 145, 146
  ASARCO and, 75, 98-99, 143
  birth of, 52
  death of, 131, 147
  as the family victim, 142-144
  grandson of, 145, 147
  nervous breakdown of, 114-115, 144
  marriage of, 81
  the Villa Carola of, 138, 142, 145-149
  wife of, 144
  will of, 147
Guggenheim, Isaac (Meyer's uncle), 42-43
Guggenheim, Isaac II, *see* Spiegelberg, William I., Jr.

Guggenheim, Jacob, 41-42
Guggenheim, Jeannette, 52, 56, 85
Guggenheim, John Simon, 249, 252-257
Guggenheim, Joseph, 42
Guggenheim, Judith Arnold, 526, 533-535, 536-538, 540
Guggenheim, Leonie Bernheim, 171, 196
Guggenheim, Lucille, 173-174, 175, 196, 197
Guggenheim, M. Robert, 156, 168, 169, 290-300
  appraisal of career, 299
  childhood of, 292
  converts to Catholicism, 293-294
  death of, 299
  early business career of, 292-293
  education of, 292, 293
  Eisenhower and, 296, 298, 299
  father's will and, 294
  income of (1940s), 296
  the leftist press and, 295
  marriages of, 293-295
  the philosophy of, 291
  romantic affairs of, 298-299
  as U.S. Ambassador to Portugal, 296-297, 307
  World War I and, 293
Guggenheim, M. Robert, Jr., 31, 32, 293, 299, 401, 463, 464, 465, 481-490
  ASARCO and, 484-490
  business career of, 485-487
  childhood of, 484
  education of, 484
  inheritances of, 487
  life-style of, 482-484, 489
  philanthropies of, 488-489
Guggenheim, Margaret Weyher, 293-294
Guggenheim, Marion Kaufmann, 175, 372-373
Guggenheim, Meyer, 32, 34, 37-64, 86-92
  ancestry of, 38-44
  appraisal of career, 89-90
  children born to, 52
  Colorado mining and smelting speculation, 58-64
  death of, 89
  early business successes of, 47-48, 52, 53
  emigrates to America, 45-47
  family unity in business and, 56-57, 61-63, 74, 87, 95-96
  first job of, 47
  import business of, 53-54, 56-57
  last years of, 86-89
  love of money and, 50-51
  marriage of, 48
  moves family from Philadelphia to New York City, 63-64, 77
  New York social life and, 80-83
  philanthropies of, 88
  physical description of, 50
  religion and, 55, 81, 83
  Wagner and, 86-87
  will of, 90-91
  See also M. Guggenheim's Sons

Guggenheim, Murry, 33, 55, 56, 62, 171-197
  ASARCO and, 75, 99, 172
  birth of, 52
  business forte of, 171-172
  the Chilean nitrate business and, 193-196
  death of, 195
  establishes trust funds for children, 173-174
  marriage of, 81
  philanthropy of, 172, 195-197
  will of, 196
  See also Murry and Leonie Guggenheim Foundation
Guggenheim, Nancy, 441, 447
Guggenheim, Natalie, 174, 175, 196, 197, 373
Guggenheim, Olga Hirsch, 81-82, 246, 248, 249, 252-253, 271, 273, 275
  as art patron, 271-272
  sons' deaths and, 245
  will of, 272
Guggenheim, Peggy, 21, 83-84, 128, 232, 235, 237, 239, 242, 308-349, 411-436
  art collection of, 415-418, 428
  beginning of, 323-324, 328
  critical appraisals of, 431, 432
  showings of, 430-431
  value of, 21-22, 241, 430
  World War II and, 328-329
  Art of This Century gallery of, 340, 342-347
  Beekman Place townhouse of, 331
  on contemporary art, 426, 434
  Ernst and, 209, 328-341, 419
  father's drowning and, 240, 241, 326, 335-336
  the Guggenheim Jeune art gallery of, 320-326
  Harry and, 426-427, 430
  Hazel and, 408-409
  Holms and, 314-317
  inheritances of, 308, 320, 327, 335, 427, 435
  life-style of, 309-311, 313-314, 324-325, 338-339, 419-422, 432-436
  on Love (Iris), 524
  the Palazzo Venier dei Leoni, 411-416, 424-425, 427-428
  Pollock and, 343-347, 417-419
  Rebay and, 322-323, 327
  the Solomon R. Guggenheim Museum and, 228, 425, 430-431
  Straus (Gladys) and, 369-370
  Vail and, 309-316, 339, 347
  on women's liberation, 434
  World War II and, 328-330
  writings of, 347-348
  See also Peggy Guggenheim Foundation; Vail, Laurence; Vail, Pegeen; Vail, Sindbad
Guggenheim, Polly, 295-300, 487
Guggenheim, Robert, 52, 56
Guggenheim, Sara, 492

Guggenheim, Shirlee Weatherford, 483, 487-488
Guggenheim, Simon, 33, 54, 62, 243-276
  ASARCO and, 75, 131, 251, 253
  birth of, 52
  death of, 272
  marriage of, 81-82, 246
  religion and, 272
  romantic affairs of, 249, 271
  sons' deaths and, 252-256, 276
  as U.S. Senator, 99, 108, 115, 249-251
  campaign for, 245-248
  will of, 272
  See also John Simon Guggenheim Memorial Foundation
Guggenheim, Simon (Meyer's father), 38, 43, 45, 47, 49
Guggenheim, Solomon R., 33, 55, 56, 62, 64, 198-231
  art collection of, pre-Rebay, 200, 205
  ASARCO and, 75, 99
  birth of, 52
  death of, 218
  homes of, 83, 138, 198, 380
  Lawson-Johnston and, 470
  life-style of, 198-199, 203
  marriage of, 82
  outstanding qualities of, 220
  Rebay and, 199-221
  romantic affairs of, 203-204
  will of, 221-222
  Wright and, 216-218, 221
  See also Solomon R. Guggenheim Foundation; Solomon R. Guggenheim Museum
Guggenheim, Susan Winchester, 492
Guggenheim, William, 54-56, 277-286
  artistic temperament of, 278, 283-284
  ASARCO and, 74-76
  birth of, 52
  breaks partnership with brothers, 74, 127-128
  compared to other brothers, 278, 279, 282, 286
  death of, 285
  education of, 278
  effect of mother's death on, 84
  lawsuit against his brothers, 128-130, 282
  marital problems of, 87-88, 281-283
  philanthropies of, 283-284
  pseudonym of, 277, 278
  religion and, 277-278
  Riverside Drive mansion of, 283-284
  romantic affairs of, 279-280, 284, 285
  will of, 285-286
  writings of, 284
  autobiography of, 277-278, 279, 282, 285-286
Guggenheim, William, Jr., 281, 282, 284, 286, 290, 373, 376
  childhood of, 373, 374
  health of, 375
  marriage of, 374
  religion and, 374
  trust fund for, 375

Guggenheim, William III, 32, 284-285, 286, 374-375, 461, 463-465, 526-540
  ancestry of, 529-532
  "automatic writing" of, 527-528, 531, 535, 536
  the book/game of, 533-535
  education of, 532-533
  future plans of, 538-539
  on the Guggenheim family, 539
  inheritance of, 529-530
  jobs held by, 533
  religious mysticism of, 526, 531, 535-536, 538
  See also Butterfly Foundation; Greun Madainn Foundation
Guggenheim, William Douglas, 375, 533, 540
Guggenheim Brothers, 23-27, 129, 130, 461
  Anaconda Copper Corp. purchase of Chuquicamata copper mine, 33, 131-133, 165
  ASARCO and, 130-131
  the Chilean nitrate business and, 165, 176, 193-196
  the Crash (1929) and, 164
  Edmond resigns from, 133, 174
  formation of, 120-121
  Harry resigns from, 133, 305
  Lawson-Johnston and, 464, 466-467, 473-475, 479-480
  the Partners' Room of, 32-33, 160, 466-467
  present-day holdings of, 474-475
  properties owned by (1923), 131
  revitalization of, 464
Guggenheim Exploration Company (Guggenex), 73, 75, 87, 90-91, 99, 120, 251, 253
Guggenheim Fellowships, 30
  See also John Simon Guggenheim Memorial Foundation
Guggenheim Foundations, *see* Daniel, Daniel and Florence, Harry Frank, John Simon, Murry and Leonie, Peggy, Solomon R.
Guggenheim Jeune art gallery, 320-326
Guggenheim mining and smelting empire
  in Africa, 111-113
  in Alaska, 100-108
  in Chile, 117
  in Colorado, 58-61
  controls world's supply of silver, copper, and lead, 117-118
  holdings of (1910), 94
  in Mexico, 66-72
  World War I and, 119-126
  in the Yukon, 113-114
Guggenheim and Pulaski (importers), 54, 56
Guggenheimb, Maran, 41

Haas, Edmund, 145
Halpert, Edith G., 207
Hammond, John Hays, 97-98, 111, 113-114, 115, 167

Harriman, Averell, 82, 219
Harry Frank Guggenheim Foundation, 28, 31, 445-446, 461
 future of, 464, 477-478
 present-day assets of, 444-445
 projects of, 445-446, 477-478
Harry Frank Guggenheim Hall of Minerals and Gems, 478
Hart, Max, 369
Harvard University, 161, 252, 253
Hauser, Gayelord, 502
"Havana Rose" (Crane), 264
Haynes, Denys, 512-513
Hebrew Orphan Asylum, 157
Helion, Davide, 418, 425, 429, 433
Helion, Fabrice, 418, 425, 429, 433
Helion, Jean, 418-419, 422-423, 424
Helion, Nicolas, 412, 413, 418, 423, 425, 429, 432, 433
Hemingway, Ernest, 255, 496
 anti-Semitism and, 349-350, 358-364
 Loeb and, 350, 355, 356, 358-364
"Hemingway's Bitterness" (Loeb), 364
Henderson, Wyn, 320, 324
Herbert, Grace Brown, 87-88, 128
Hesse, Hermann, 22, 500, 502
Hill and Wang, 501
Hilla von Rebay Foundation, 204, 230
Hilton, Judge Henry, 79-80
Hirsch, Olga, *see* Guggenheim, Olga Hirsch
Hiss, Alger, 273
Hofmann, Hans, 343
Hohnsbeen, John, 432, 433
Holden, Edward R., 61
Holmes, Oliver Wendell, 77
Holms, John, 314-317
Honey in the Horn (Davis), 270
Hoover, Herbert, 165, 167, 302, 307
Horgan, Paul, 258, 498, 500-502, 508
Hotchner, A. E., 359, 360
Humphrey, Hubert, 296
Hunt, E. Howard, 265
Huxley, Laura, 509

In Our Time (Hemingway), 359
Institute of Aeronautical Sciences, 169
Institute of Man and Science, 506-507
Intercontinental Rubber Company, 113
International Business Machines Management Training Center, 148
International Steam Pump Company, 129, 239, 240
International Workers of the World (IWW), 125
Isbrandtsen, Jakob, 519
Isherwood, Christopher, 500
Ismay, Bruce, 238
Izvestia, 228

J. W. Seligman & Company, 233
Jackling, Dan, 115-116
Jaffe, Marc, 497
Jarrell, Randall, 500
Jessup, Dr. Philip C., 304
Jet Propulsion Laboratory, Caltech, 170

Jewel, Edward Alden, 207
Jewish Hospital, 85
Jewish Theological Seminary, 157
Jews
 anti-Semitism in Switzerland and, 38-40, 53-54
 artistic and intellectual renaissance of, 12-13
 influence on our civilization, 11-14
 New York City social life (1890s) of, 78-81
 See also Anti-Semitism
John Brown's Body (Benét), 258, 259
John Simon Guggenheim Memorial Foundation, 30, 252-276, 461
 artists, scientists, and scholars accepted as Fellows, 258-265, 275
 artists rejected as Fellows, 265-268
 awards received by Fellows, 258
 compared with other Guggenheim philanthropies, 275
 creation of, 255-257
 criticism of, 268-269
 greatness of concept of, 275-276
 Miller's attack on, 266-267
 net worth of, 272-273, 275
 Simon's and Olga's wills and, 272
 Straus and, 368
 U.S. Congress and, 273-275
Johnson, Philip C., 228
Jong, Erica, 498
Josephine Ford (plane), 160-161
Josephson, Matthew, 353
Josephthal, Edyth Guggenheim, 515
Josephthal, Louis M., 145, 515
Josephthal & Company, 145, 515
Joyce, James, 321

Kahn, Otto, 122
Kandinsky, Wassily, 200, 202, 208, 209, 321-323, 353
Kandinsky, Madame Wassily, 209, 210, 227
Kármám, Theodor von, 161
Kaufmann, Marion, *see* Guggenheim, Marion Kaufmann
Kazin, Alfred, 258, 260
Keith, Marie, 520
Kempner, Sigmund, 406
Kennecott Copper Corporation, 131, 172, 194-195, 220, 221, 257, 373, 467, 468
Kennecott copper mine, 100-108, 117
 development of, 102-106
 labor exploitation at, 120-123
 Morgan and, 101-108
 profits from, 107, 122
 U.S. press on, 104, 107
 value of, 106-107
 World War I and, 120
Kennedy, John F., 46
Kennedy, Patrick, 46
Kennedy, Robert, 274
Kiesler, Frederick, 342
King-Farlow, Barbara Benita Mary, 408
King-Farlow, Denys, 408

King-Farlow, John, 408
Kissinger, Henry, 258
Klee, Paul, 210, 229, 353
Knox, Nettie, 168, 427
Kosinski, Jerzy, 497
Krassner, Lee, 344, 347
Krementz, Jill, 497, 509
Kübler-Ross, Dr. Elisabeth, 532, 538
Kuhn, Loeb & Company, 82, 352, 367
Kupka, Frantisek, 477

L. F. Rothschild & Company, 82, 193
Landon, Alfred M., 284
Lawson-Johnston, Dorothy Hammond, 472, 478
Lawson-Johnston, John Robert, 399, 469-470
Lawson-Johnston, Mary, 479
Lawson-Johnston, Peter O., 27-33, 230, 341, 399, 401, 405, 435, 440, 459, 461, 463, 466-480, 505
  business background of, 468, 471-472
  childhood of, 469-470
  education of, 471
  the foundations' problems and, 475-478
  Guggenheim Brothers and, 464, 466-467, 473-475, 479-480
  Harry's will and, 446, 447, 468-469
  life-style of, 478-479
  as principal heir, 464, 465, 468
  Solomon and, 470
Lawson-Johnston, Peter O., Jr., 478-479
Lawson-Johnston, Tania, 478
Lawson-Johnston, Wendy, 478, 479
Lazarus, Emma, 116
Lee, Ivy, 160, 161
Léger, Fernand, 202, 210, 229, 353
Lehman Brothers, 193, 367
LeMay, General Curtis, 296
Lennep, William Bird van, 295
Lennep, Mrs. William Bird van, *see* Guggenheim, Polly
Leonie (yacht), 173
Leopold II, King, 112
Levi, Carlo, 500, 508
Levinger, Schäfeli, 43
Lewisohn, Adolph, 73
Libby, Willard F., 260
Liberman, Alexander, 525
Lindbergh, Charles, 29, 33, 82, 167, 445
  Daniel and, 163-164
  Harry and, 161, 306, 450, 453
Linus Pauling Institute of Science and Medicine, 261
Lodge, Henry Cabot, 227, 248, 438
Loeb, Albert, 82
Loeb, Barbara, 364, 410
Loeb, Harold, 204, 235, 255, 309, 311, 320, 337, 349-364
  ancestry of, 351
  bookshop of, 352-353
  Broom and, 255, 311, 350-356
  death of, 364
  as family rebel, 355-356
  Hemingway and, 350, 355, 356, 358-364

last years of, 363-364
  writings of, 355-357, 363-364
Loeb, James, 352
Loeb, Marcus, 352
Loeb, Rose Guggenheim, 52, 56, 82, 84, 221
Loeb, Solomon, 82, 352
Logan, John H., 299
Lomask, Milton, 444
Lone Voice Publishing Company, 277, 284
Love, Cornelius Ruxton, 515
Love, Mrs. Cornelius Ruxton (Audrey), 407, 408, 515, 516
Love, Iris Cornelia, 147-148, 459, 461, 463, 465, 511-525
  ancestry of, 514-515
  the archaeological excavations at Knidos, 518-525
  education of, 513, 516-517, 518
  the "Etruscan Warriors" and, 513-514, 518
  honors and awards received by, 524
  inheritance of, 515, 517
  the Knidian Aphrodite and, 511-513, 518
  Peggy on, 524
Love, Noel, 517
Love Game, The, 533-535
Lowell, Amy, 353
Lowell, Robert, 500, 501, 503
Luce, Clare Boothe, 424
Lucky Market Shopping Center, 487, 492
Lundell, Ernest H., Jr., 272
Lyon, Peter, 256, 257, 275

M. Guggenheim's Sons, 90-91, 95
  Benjamin breaks partnership with, 74, 127-128, 234
  dissolved, 120
  founded, 56-57
  William breaks partnership with, 74, 127-128
  See also Guggenheim mining and smelting empire
MacGowan, Kenneth, 486
Machado, Gerardo, 303-306
Mackenzie, Compton, 311
McKinley, Charles, 408
McKinley, Hazel Guggenheim, 128, 234, 235, 239-241, 406-410
  emotional instability of, 407-408
  marriages of, 406, 408
  painting career of, 408-410
  Peggy and, 408-409
  sons' deaths and, 406-408, 410
McKinley Tariff Act (1890), 66
MacManus, John and Adams, 487
McNamara, Hanna, 87
McPherson, Kenneth, 341
Magma copper mill, 115
Malamud, Bernard, 497, 500, 501, 503, 509
Marinetti, Filippo, 508
Marshack, Alexander, 478
Marshall, Margot Love, 512

Martin, Joe, 296
Martin, Thomas S., 255
Massachusetts Institute of Technology, 161
Masters, Edgar Lee, 353
Matisse, Henri, 353
Mauriac, François, 500
Mayo Clinic, 197, 372
Medill, Joseph, 439
Meek, Diane, 28, 441
Menotti, Gian Carlo, 258-260
Messer, Thomas M., 214, 216, 230, 476-477
Meyer, Barbara, *see* Guggenheim, Barbara Meyer
Meyer, Lehman, 48
Meyer, Rachel Weil, 43, 45, 49
Michigan, University of, 161
Miller, Henry, 266-268
    anti-Semitism and, 267-268
Miller, Peggy, 498
Miners' Magazine, 247-248
Minnie mine, 59-60, 90
Miró, Joan, 321
Moe, Henry Allen, 256-266, 269-275
Moholy-Nagy, Laszlo, 200, 207, 229
Mondrian, Piet, 229, 343
Moore, Henry, 321, 424
Moore, Marianne, 258, 353
Moravia, Alberto, 500, 501, 508
Morgan, John Pierpont, 74, 151, 450
    Daniel and, 101-108
Morgan, John Pierpont, Jr., 164
Morgan Guaranty, 121
Morrow, Dwight W., 167, 219, 304
Morton, Caroline, 441
Moses, Robert, 31, 217, 227
Motherwell, Robert, 343, 344, 476
Mount Sinai Hospital, 85, 197, 283, 368, 372
Moveable Feast, A (Hemingway), 359
Moyers, Bill D., 26-27, 440
Mrs. Simon Guggenheim Fund, 271
Muir, Edwin, 314
Mumford, Lewis, 335
"Mural 1943" (Pollock), 345
Murry and Leonie Guggenheim Dental Clinic, 175-176, 195-196
Murry and Leonie Guggenheim Foundation
    disposition of, 197, 372
    Edmond and, 196-197, 372
Museum of Modern Art, 228, 271
"Mysticism of Money, The" (Loeb), 357

Nabokov, Vladimir, 258
NASA Deep Space Network (DSN), 170
Nathanson, Win, 519
Nation, The, 344
National Academy of Arts and Sciences, 258
National Book Awards, 258
National Conservation Commission, 107
National Federation of Women's Institutes, 402
National Institute of Arts and Letters, 272

National Women's Republican Club, 368
Neruda, Pablo, 500, 501
Nevins, Allan, 258
"New Age" (Rebay), 204-205, 208-209
New Masses, 273
New Republic, The, 364
New Worker, 273
New York Botanical Gardens, 157, 172, 196
New York *Daily News*, 439
New York Herald Tribune, 228, 307
New York Hospital, 197
New York Public School Athletic League, 221
New York Review of Books, The, 508
New York Times, The, 27, 32, 153, 167, 176, 196, 206, 207, 214, 220, 272, 298, 362, 406, 408, 502, 504, 509, 514, 523
New York Times Book Review, The, 498
New York University, 159
New Yorker, The, 343, 523
Newell, Elizabeth, *see* Guggenheim, Elizabeth Newell
Newlin, Chauncey, 215
Newsday, 21-27, 31, 439-442, 478
Newton, Sir Charles, 512
Nin, Anaïs, 410
Nipissing silver mine, 114-115
Nixon, Richard M., 26, 274
Nobel Prize, 258, 260, 261, 321
Noble, Joseph V., 514
Noland, Kenneth, 229
Noonday Press, 501

Obre, Mrs. Barbara, *see* Guggenheim, Barbara
Obre, Henry, 400
Ochs, Adolph, 167
O'Connor, Flannery, 500
Octagon Books, 501
O'Keeffe, Georgia, 320
On Native Ground: An Interpretation of Modern Prose Literature (Kazin), 260
Out of This Century (Guggenheim), 347, 431, 432

Paats, Gertrude de, 199
Pacific Tin Consolidated Corporation, 27, 114, 461, 464, 467, 472, 474, 480, 507, 509
Palaces and Prisons (Straus), 507
Palm Beach Life, 208, 215
Papa Hemingway (Hotchner), 359, 360
Papers of Robert H. Goddard, The, 454
Parmeggiani, Tancredi, 422, 423, 425, 427, 429
Partisan Review, 344
Patterson, Alicia, 21, 439-442
Patterson, Joe, 439
Patterson, Robert, 439
Pauling, Linus, 258, 261-262
Peach, Bernard, 268
Peary, Rear Admiral Robert H., 283-284

Peggy Guggenheim Foundation, 241, 430, 435, 436
future of, 461, 477
Pembroke College, 28
Pennsylvania Salt Company, 53
Percy, Walker, 502
Pevsner, Antoine, 321
Philadelphia *Ledger,* 60
Philadelphia Smelting and Refining Company, 61
Phillips Exeter Academy, 252
Picasso, Pablo, 321, 353
Pickert, Raphael, 42
Pinchot, Gifford, 104, 107-108
Platt Amendment, 304, 305
"Plea for the Creative Artist, A" (Menotti), 259-260
Politika, 228
Pollock, Jackson, 331
Peggy and, 343-347, 417-419
Porter, Katherine Anne, 258, 260
Potter, William C., 121, 131-133
Pound, Ezra, 267, 335, 347, 412, 416
Price, Marron, 174
Princeton University, 169, 369
Professors Like Vodka (Loeb), 355
"Protocols of the Elders of Zion," 125
Publishers Weekly, 496, 497, 504, 509
Pulaski, Morris, 54, 56
Pulitzer Prize, 258, 259
Putzel, Howard, 343, 344

Quasimodo, Salvatore, 500, 508

Ray, Gordon, 257, 269, 274
Read, Sir Herbert, 326-327, 424
Rebay, Roland, 215, 230
Rebay von Ehrenwiesen, Baron Franz Hugo, 210, 230
Rebay von Ehrenwiesen, Hilla, 199-222
background of, 202
Bauer and, 207-215
complex nature of, 201-202
Harry and, 223-225
imprisoned as a Nazi spy, 212-214
Irene and, 205-206, 221
last years of, 229-230
the New York art world and, 207-208, 214
nonobjective art and, 201-202
Peggy and, 322-323, 327
Solomon and, 199-221
the Solomon R. Guggenheim Museum and, 224, 228
Wright and, 217
Rhodes, Cecil John, 98, 256
Richter, Gisela M. A., 513
Rickenbacker, Eddie, 158
Rockefeller, David, 450
Rockefeller, John D., 46, 50, 74, 450
Rockefeller, John D., Jr., 115, 123, 248, 450
Rockefeller, John D. III, 450
Rockefeller, Laurance, 450

Rockefeller, Nelson, 450
Rockefeller, William, 73, 74, 234
Rockefeller, Winthrop, 450
Rocketry, *see* Daniel and Florence Guggenheim Aeronautical Laboratories and Jet Propulsion Centers; Daniel and Florence Guggenheim Foundation; Goddard, Robert H.; Guggenheim, Daniel; Guggenheim, Harry Frank
Roger Williams Straus Foundation, 504
Rogers, Henry H., 73, 74
Roosevelt, Franklin D., 213-214
Roosevelt, Theodore, 82, 104
Root, Elihu, 248
Root, Elihu, Jr., 167
Rorimer, James, 513-514, 525
Rosenberg, Helen, 441
Roth, Philip, 498
Rothko, Mark, 343
Rothschild, Cora Guggenheim, 52, 56, 82, 90, 168, 196, 221
Rothschild, Baron Elie de, 476
Rothschild, Irene, 82
Rothschild, Louis F., 82
Rothschild-Hadassah Medical Center, 29
Rudenstine, Angelica Z., 477
Rumney, Ralph, 421, 423
Rumney, Sandro, 423, 425, 429, 433
Russell, Jeanne, 174
Ryan, Thomas Fortune, 112-113, 151

Saarinen, Mrs. Aline B., 204, 214
Samuelson, Paul A., 258
Sands Point Bath and Golf Club, 146
Satterlee, Herbert, 77
Saturday Evening Post, 359
Saturday Review, 508
Saturn V spacecraft, 150
Schiarolli, Francis P., 215
Schiff, Jacob, 102, 103, 107
Schlesinger, Arthur M., Jr., 258
Schoenberg, Arnold, 265, 266
Schwarzenberg, Professor E., 513
Schweizerisches Israelitisches Alterasyl, 91-92, 221
Scott, Tully, 247
Seed Money—The Guggenheim Story (Lomask), 444
Seligman, Florette, *see* Guggenheim, Florette Seligman
Seligman, James, 233, 236, 241
Seligman, Joseph, 79-80, 82, 233
Seligman-Hilton affair, 78-80
Selznick, David O., 485, 486
Sendak, Maurice, 497
Shalit, Gene, 498
Shapiro, Harvey, 498
Sherman Silver Purchase Act, 66
Shirrob (yacht), 483, 489
Shloss, Florence, *see* Guggenheim, Florence Shloss
Short, Mrs. B. B., *see* Guggenheim, Natalie
Showcases (Straus), 442-444, 446, 452, 507

Shrady, Frederick, 508
Silverman, Al, 497
Silvers, Robert, 508
Simon Guggenheim Memorial Collection, 271-272
Simpson, Lesley, 264
Singer, Isaac Bashevis, 498, 500, 501, 503
Sloan-Kettering Institute of Cancer Research, 28
Smith, Cappelen, 193
Soby, James Thrall, 343
Société Internationale Forestière et Minière du Congo (Forminière), 112
Solomon R. Guggenheim Collection of Non-Objective Painting, The, 205
Solomon R. Guggenheim Foundation, 31, 461
    creation of, 205
    funds received from Solomon's will, 221
    present-day problems of, 475-477
Solomon R. Guggenheim Museum, 25, 113, 341
    controversy over, 228-231
    Harry and, 223-227, 444
    impact on America's artistic taste, 228-229, 476
    opening of, 227-228
    Peggy and, 228, 425, 430-431
    plans delayed for, 218, 225
    present-day problems of, 476-477
    Rebay and, 224, 228
    site of, 217
    as the ultimate Guggenheim monument, 231
    Wright and, 217-218, 225-227, 230-231
Solzhenitsyn, Alexander, 500, 502, 503
Sonneborn, Carrie, *see* Guggenheim, Carrie Sonneborn
Sontag, Susan, 497
South Atlantic Quarterly, 268-269
Spiegelberg, William I., 145
Spiegelberg, William I., Jr., 145, 147
Spirit of St. Louis, 161
Stafford, Jean, 500
Stanford University, 161
Stein, Gertrude, 353
Stevens, Wallace, 353
Stevenson, Adlai, 441
Still, Clyfford, 343
Stillmans, James, 234
Straus, Dorothea, 169, 442, 446, 452, 497, 501, 506-510
Straus, Florence Guggenheim, 369
Straus, Gladys Guggenheim, 30, 156, 166, 168, 169, 204, 206, 271, 272, 292, 365-370
    background of, 365-366
    business activities of, 368
    Daniel and Florence Guggenheim Foundation and, 368-370
    marriage of, 366, 367
    Peggy and, 369-370
    philanthropies of, 368-369
Straus, Isidor, 238
Straus, Louise, 336

Straus, Oscar, 23-24, 30, 156
Straus, Oscar II, 369, 440, 461, 506-507, 509
Straus, Oscar III, 461, 480, 507, 509
Straus, Peter, 30
Straus, Roger W., 23, 27, 30, 131, 156, 238, 351, 365, 366
    ASARCO and 365, 368
    background of, 366-367
    John Simon Guggenheim Memorial Foundation and, 368
    philanthropies of, 369
Straus, Roger W., Jr., 22, 156, 267, 369, 370, 444, 459, 461, 465, 496-510
    background of, 499
    education of, 499-500
    family foundations and, 504-505
    Farrar, Straus & Giroux and, 500-504
    authors' loyalty to, 503-504
    life-style of, 496-499, 508-510
    other business activities of, 505
Straus, Roger W. III, 461, 497-498, 501, 507, 509
Straus Minerals, 506, 509
Stravinsky, Vera, 498
Stuart, Andrew Charles Richard, 402
Stuart, Arthur Patrick Avondale, 402, 405
Stuart, Lady Bridget, 402
Stuart, Corin Edmund, 402
Stuart, David, 402
Stuart, Robert, 402
Stuart, Simon Walter Erskine, 402, 405
Stuart, Thomas, 402
Stuart, Tristram, 402
Stucky, Rolf, 521
Studin, Robert Michael, 175
Sullivan, Louis, 216
Sun Also Rises, The (Hemingway), 350, 358-363
Sunwise Turn, The (bookshop), 309, 310, 352
Sweeney, James Johnson, 225-227, 343, 344, 345
Symphony Society of New York, 157
Syracuse University, 161

Tanguy, Yves, 321, 323-325
Tanning, Dorothea, 340-341, 347, 348
Tate, Allen, 263
Tax Reform Act (1969), 274
Teilhard de Chardin, Father, 506
Temple Emanu-El, 81, 83, 370
Tepezala copper mines, 72
Testament (Wright), 216
Thannhauser, Justin K., 438
Thaw, Russell, 174
They Shall Not Have Me (Helion), 418
Thiele, Albert, 215, 219-221, 224, 468, 472
Thomson, Virgil, 258
Thresholds (Straus), 507
Time, 523
Times Mirror Company, 21, 27
Titanic, 128, 238-240, 242, 326
Tocqueville, Alexis de, 243-244
Torrents of Spring, The (Hemingway), 359

Trillora (yacht), 198, 380, 470
Tropic of Cancer (Miller), 266-268
Tropic of Capricorn (Miller), 266, 268
Tumbling Mustard (Loeb), 355
Twysden, Lady Duff, 359, 360
Tzara, Tristan, 334

Ulrich, Johann Caspar, 42
Union Nacionalistas, 305
United Hebrew Charities, 85, 283
United Jewish Appeal, 446
United Jewish Campaign, 157
United Metals Selling Company, 74
Untermeyer, Louis, 263
Utah Copper Corporation, 131

Vail, Clovis, 427, 433
Vail, Julia, 427, 433
Vail, Karole, 427, 433
Vail, Katy, 429
Vail, Laurence, 260, 320, 331, 337, 343
  Peggy and, 309-317, 339, 347
Vail, Mark, 427, 433
Vail, Odile, 311, 312
Vail, Pegeen, 314-316, 325, 331, 343, 347,
  412, 427
  marriages of, 418, 423, 428-429
  memorial to, 429-430
  painting career of, 423-424
  suicide of, 429
Vail, Sindbad, 312, 315-317, 324, 325, 331,
  337, 422, 427-429
Valencia, Gus, 492-493
Van Allen, James, 500
Van Allen, James A., 258
Van de Maele, Albert, 28
Van de Maele, Joan, 27, 28
Venice's Biennale Art Exhibition (1948),
  416
Ventadour, Jacqueline, 422-423
Vidal, Gore, 265, 266
Viereck, Peter, 258
Vogue, 525
Von Braun, Dr. Wernher, 169, 453
Von Fraunhofer, Kiki, 497
Vonnegut, Kurt, Jr., 497, 509
Voyager I and II spacecraft, 170

Wagner, Richard, 86-87
Wagner, Robert, 227
Wahl, Jules Roger, 280
Waldman, Benjamin, 406, 407
Waldman, Milton S., 406, 410
Waldman, Peggy, 320
Waldman, Terence, 406, 407
Wall Street Journal, 97, 101, 107, 128

Ward, Lord Melvill, 145
Warhol, Andy, 426
Warren, Robert Penn, 258
Washburn, Professor Sherwood, 477
Washington, University of, 161
Washington Times, 250
Watson, James D., 258
Watson, Thomas, Jr., 148
Way It Was, The (Loeb), 351, 352, 355,
  358, 360, 363
We (Lindbergh), 161
Weatherford, Shirlee, *see* Guggenheim,
  Shirlee Weatherford
Welty, Eudora, 258
West, Nathanael, 500
Wettach, Fred, 399-400
Wettach, Michael, 400-401, 405
Weyher, Margaret, *see* Guggenheim, Mar-
  garet Weyher
White, Harvey E., 258
Whitney, Cornelius Vanderbilt, 450
Whitney, Gertrude Vanderbilt, 450
Whitney, William, 75, 82
Wiener, Norbert, 258
William Guggenheim (Williams), 284, 286
Williams, William Carlos, 353
Wilson, Carroll Atwood, 256, 257, 275
Wilson, Edmund, 258, 263, 361, 500
Wilson, Woodrow, 121-123
Wolfe, Thomas, 258
Wolfe, Tom, 502, 504, 509
Woolf, Virginia, 353
Woolworth, Norman, 294
World War I
  anti-Semitism and, 121-122
  Bingham Canyon copper mine and, 120
  Chuquicamata copper mine and, 120
  Guggenheim mining and smelting empire
    and, 119-126
  Kennecott copper mine and, 120
Wray, Katie, 513, 516
Wright, Frank Lloyd, 31, 70, 215-217, 438,
  450
  Rebay and, 217
  Solomon and, 216-218, 221
  the Solomon R. Guggenheim Museum
    and, 217-218, 225-227, 230-231
Wright, Mrs. Frank Lloyd, 227

Yale University, 275
Yeatman, Pope, 100
Yeomans, Peggy Angela, 427
Yes I Can (Davis), 400-401
Yngling, Van, 71
Young, Brigham, 115
Yukon Gold Company, 113-114